HAROLD NICOLSON
VOLUME I

HAROLD NICOLSON
VOLUME I

A BIOGRAPHY, 1886–1929

JAMES LEES-MILNE

faber and faber

This edition first published in 2012
by Faber and Faber Ltd
Bloomsbury House, 74–77 Great Russell Street
London WC1B 3DA

Printed by Books on Demand GmbH, Norderstedt

All rights reserved
© Michael Bloch, 1980

The right of James Lees-Milne to be identified
as author of this work has been asserted in accordance
with Section 77 of the Copyright, Designs and Patents Act 1988

This book is sold subject to the condition that it shall not, by way of
trade or otherwise, be lent, resold, hired out or otherwise circulated
without the publisher's prior consent in any form of binding or cover other than
that in which it is published and without a similar condition including this
condition being imposed on the subsequent purchaser

A CIP record for this book is available from the British Library

ISBN 978–0–571–28786–4

To
N.N. and in memory of B.N.

'It is sad, perhaps, that the hopes and energies of a lifetime should be reduced to a few cold lines upon a printed page.'

HAROLD NICOLSON

CONTENTS

1	Childhood and School, 1886–1904	*page* 1
2	Balliol and Cramming, 1904–1907	18
3	Preparations for the Diplomatic Service, 1907–1909	32
4	Foreign Office, Spain and Constantinople, 1910–1912	40
5	Constantinople and Marriage, 1913–1914	59
6	The First World War, 1914–1918	71
7	The Peace Conference, 1919	109
8	Paris Aftermath and the League of Nations, 1919–1920	134
9	London, Foreign Office, 1921–1922	157
10	The Lausanne Conference, 1922–1923	182
11	London Again, 1923–1925	200
12	Journey to Persia, 1925	243
13	Tehran, 1926–1927	264
14	The Bakhtiari and Foreign Office Interval, 1927	303
15	Berlin, 1927–1928	320
16	The End of Diplomacy, 1929	359
Appendix: Notes to Text		391
Index		411

ACKNOWLEDGEMENTS

I wish to record my gratitude to the following authors and publishers from whose books I have quoted extracts in this volume: Anne Olivier Bell (*The Diaries of Virginia Woolf*, Vol. II); Lord Gladwyn (*The Memoirs of*); Sir Rupert Hart-Davis (*Hugh Walpole*); Christopher Isherwood (*Goodbye to Berlin*); Anne Morrow Lindbergh (*Diaries and Letters*); Nigel Nicolson (*Portrait of a Marriage*) and, with Dr. Joanne Trautmann (*The Letters of Virginia Woolf*, Vol. III and Vol. IV); George Painter (*Marcel Proust*, Vol. II); John Phillips (*Violet Trefusis, Letters*); Anne Scott James (*Sissinghurst, The Making of a Garden*). Also to the literary executors and publishers of the following authors and their books: Roy Campbell (*Broken Record* and *Light on a Dark Horse*); Cyril Connolly (*The Condemned Playground – Conversations in Berlin*); Duff Cooper (*Old Men Forget*); Sir Lawrence Jones (*An Edwardian Youth*); Philippe Jullian (*Violet Trefusis, Life*); Sir Robert Bruce Lockhart (*Diaries and Papers*, ed. K. Young, Vol. I and *Retreat from Glory*); Violet Stuart-Wortley (*Life without Theory*); Violet Trefusis (*Don't Look Round*); Dorothy Wellesley (*Far Have I Travelled*); and Denton Welch (*Journals*, ed. Jocelyn Brooke). For the extensive quotations I have made from Harold Nicolson's Despatches I am indebted to *British Documents on the Origins of the War, 1898–1914* (ed. G. P. Gooch and Harold Temperley) and *Documents on British Foreign Policy, 1919–39* (ed. E. L. Woodward and Rohan Butler).

For permission to quote from certain letters written by Harold Nicolson before 1930 I wish to thank Professor Quentin Bell (those to Clive Bell); Mr. Michael Colefax (to Lady Colefax); Sir Rupert Hart-Davis (to himself); Mr. Geddes Hyslop (to Raymond Mortimer); Mr. Stuart Preston (to himself); and Temple University, Philadelphia, USA (to Mr. Michael Sadleir, late of Constable & Co.). Also I thank Mrs. Ralph Partridge for transcribing passages relating to Harold Nicolson from letters written to her by Clive Bell.

It is impossible adequately to thank the many friends who have helped me in different ways. I can only mention by designation or name here: The Librarians of the Script Library, The Written Archives Centre and The Sound Archives Department of the BBC, Mr. Michael Bloch, Lord Carnock, Lord William Cavendish-Bentinck, Lord Clark, the late Sir Charles Clay, Miss Ursula Codrington, Lady Diana Cooper, the

HAROLD NICOLSON

Marquess of Dufferin and Ava, Sir Roger Fulford, Mr. Daniel H Gillman, Lord and Lady Gladwyn, Mr. Benjamin Glazebrook, Sir Rupert Hart-Davis, Hon. David Herbert, Lady Ursula Horne, Mr. John Kenworthy-Browne, Mr. Eardley Knollys, Professor Phillip Kolb, Sir Osbert Lancaster, Mr. Lukin the British Consul at Istamboul, Mr. and Mrs. Martin of Long Barn, Mr. Hugh Montgomery-Massingberd, Sir Philip Magnus-Allcroft, Bt., the late Mr. Raymond Mortimer, the Vicomte de Noailles, Mr. Ian Parsons, Mr. Burnet Pavitt, Mr Stuart Preston, the Assistant Keepers of the Public Records Office, Lieutenant-Colonel D. A. Rowan-Hamilton, Mr Kenneth Rose, Dr. George Rylands, Lord Sackville, Mr. John Sparrow, Mr. Christopher Sykes, Gwendolen Lady St. Levan, Mr. Paul Wallraf, Mrs. Elizabeth Wansbrough, Mr. Peter Westmacott, and of course my wife. I hope I have not through inadvertence omitted to mention other helpers.

Finally, I offer heartfelt thanks to Mr. Nigel Nicolson, Sir Harold's surviving son, without whose invitation this book could not have been begun, and without whose constant encouragement, help, suggested improvements and corrections, it would not have been continued. To him I owe the loan of his father's and mother's letters, his father's unpublished diaries and papers, and practically all the illustrations in the book, as well as permission to quote from Sir Harold Nicolson's letters, books and numerous writings. Before his untimely death his brother Benedict likewise gave me most generous help and put at my disposal every letter his father had written to him. It grieves me to have been deprived of his wise counsel as well as his friendship of more than forty years.

J. L-M.

I

CHILDHOOD AND SCHOOL, 1886–1904

ONE of Harold Nicolson's many endearing traits was to invent occasions brought about by some preposterous and improbable action on his part. It amused him to indulge in daydreams: how he, who was tone-deaf and totally unmusical, brought the audience of Covent Garden Opera House to its feet with acclamation of his singing an aria from Verdi; how he, a butterfingers if ever there was one, made the catch of the century in a Test Match, to receive telegrams of congratulation from the King and Queen and the Prime Minister. In this spirit he enjoyed imagining how his birth was greeted by the 1st Marquess of Dufferin and Ava, Viceroy of India, and his wife Hariot, who was Harold's Aunt Lal, while on a stately progress to Golconda.

> On that very Sunday when my first plaint broke upon the Bactrian air, my uncle was in fact visiting the tomb of Aurungzebe. My aunt has recorded that event in her diary. 'As Dufferin approached it an old man stepped forward and chanted something, the translation of which was, "Aurungzebe, late Emperor of Delhi, I present to you the representative of the present Emperor of Delhi." Then sugar candy and spices were offered to D. and we proceeded on our way.'
>
> They continued their progress to Golconda. Surely, during that journey, some telegram announcing my safe arrival must have been brought to the Viceregal train? I should like to feel that on that Monday morning, at some dusty outpost of the Nizam's dominions, the long white train was jerked to an unexpected standstill; that the local stationmaster, bowing deeply, had advanced towards the detectives who had leapt as a man from every coach; that with a profound salaam he had handed to the first detective a small pink telegram; that the detective in his turn had passed it on to a khitmutgar, who bore upon his scarlet breast a D and a coronet in gold; and that by the hand of the agreeable Captain Balfour, A.D.C. to the Viceroy, the telegram had eventually been passed to my aunt. There she sat in the white and gold saloon with the slatted windows; upon the chintz canopies lay scattered the souvenirs of yesterday's visit to Ellora; she would open the telegram with slow deliberation.
>
> 'Dufferin,' she would have exclaimed, 'Katie has had another dear little boy!'[1]

Alas! no such entry was made in the Vicereine of India's diary.

HAROLD NICOLSON

The unheralded baby born to her youngest sister Catherine[2] on the 21st November 1886 was the third son of Arthur Nicolson, C.M.G., at that date Secretary of the Legation at Tehran, where for the past year he had been acting as Chargé d'Affaires. The child was baptised Harold George in accordance with the rites of the Church of England.

Arthur Nicolson was the surviving son and heir of Admiral Sir Frederick Nicolson, 10th Baronet of Carnock, County Stirling by his first wife, Mary Loch.[3] Sir Frederick having fallen foul of his superiors in the Admiralty through some unspecified error of judgment, retired early from the Navy, and spent the rest of his days in London. A portly, rumbustious, hectoring sailor, he was more fitted for the quarter-deck, of which he had been deprived, than the drawing-room of a small house in Knightsbridge. Arthur, a nervous and delicate child, was terrified of him; and their relations were not improved by the father's second marriage four years after the mother's death, to what his grandson was to describe bluntly as 'a tart'. When she died, after giving birth to two daughters, he married, thirdly, a respectable woman who took to drink. Young Arthur was deeply distressed and ashamed. This stepmother had subsequently to be removed from the house. The humiliating experiences in his home may have been the cause of Arthur's extreme reserve in after life.

On the Admiral's death in 1899 Sir Arthur (he had been made K.C.I.E. in 1888) succeeded as 11th Baronet of Carnock,[4] but inherited little else. In consequence he remained through life a poor man without a country estate, and dependent upon, first his pay, and then a pension from the Foreign Office. In this respect he was exceptional among his colleagues, nearly all of whom, selected from the territorial classes, were men of substance as well as family.

In April 1888 Arthur Nicolson was appointed Consul-General in Budapest. On the journey with his wife and three baby boys across the Russian steppes the last carriage of their train caught fire. The story was so often referred to in the Nicolson family that for years, until his mother pointed out that he was only a year and a half old at the time, Harold believed he vividly remembered every detail of the incident. He certainly remembered the Budapest Consulate in Andrassy Avenue, a little house with a statue of Flora or Pomona in the pediment of the street front, and a terra cotta fountain in the garden. He remembered the station being draped in black, violet and gold hangings in national mourning for the death of Crown Prince Rudolph at Mayerling. He remembered how with white knitted gloves he would brush the first snow from the privet hedges which lined the alleys at the entrance to the public park; and how, beside the benches of the park, in the dark Danubian air which smelled of sulphur springs and yellow leaves, he would pick up and suck the little cardboard

CHILDHOOD AND SCHOOL 1886-1904

holders through which the Hungarians smoked their cigarettes. He remembered the tall, black water-tower at the end of the Avenue, round which the autumn gales howled, bringing cold, fear and sadness to little boys. He remembered the screech and clang of the trams as they rounded the corner; the doleful wail of factory sirens at bed-time, and the interminable winter wind on the great bridge which led to Buda. He remembered too the scarlet devils of St. Nikolaus chasing each other round the cornice of his bedroom, when he lay ill with typhoid.[5]

Fear was the emotion which haunted his otherwise happy childhood. Fear of the unexpected, fear of making a fool of himself, fear of chastisement, and fear, above all, of the dark. In books and articles Harold Nicolson was frequently to relate incidents of his childhood in which he was humiliated by these recurrent, and always irrational dreads. There was the occasion during a summer holiday from Budapest spent at Stübing with Sir Richard and Lady Burton. The explorer played with the Nicolson children,

> thrusting his dark face into theirs, shouting at the youngest baby, 'Hello, little Tehran!' The child yelled; the memory of those questing panther eyes remained with this infant as a thrill of terror and delight.[6]

There was that visit in May 1892 with his mother to the Embassy in Paris, where Lord Dufferin was Ambassador. Harold was terrified that the city was going to be bombarded, because he had been told that such a thing had happened during the Franco-Prussian War. The only person who could console and reassure him was his mother. His desperate endeavours to persuade her to postpone putting down the bedside story-book and blowing out the candle are no less poignant because they have been experienced by other little boys.

> And then the darkness closing round me like red German mattresses pressing me down into my bed. All alone in that sentient darkness except for the smell beside me of an expiring candle; it did not wish me well; above and beyond all that a thin golden crack of light by the doorway. Through which Herr Geverts would creep. He would come in, quite small at first, like a piece of string; but once inside he would swell quickly, and he would creep about the room slowly on all clumsy fours, searching for my bed in the corner, crouching beside the bed quite silently at first, waiting till I should drop off to sleep. None the less, I *knew* it was Herr Geverts, with his whiskers and his steel spectacles – the man who kept the sausage shop at the corner of the Andrássy Ut ...[7]

Yet his brother and sister have affirmed that, although nervous, Harold was a daring and apparently brave little boy, who continually played pranks, and rode his pony 'modestly'.

As a child he was very bright, and very impish. He did not care much for other children. One birthday when asked by his mother what he would most like as a treat, he answered, 'No little friends to tea, please.' He was untidy and grubby. He was frequently smacked for appearing at meals with dirty face and hands. He usually had a ready answer. Once when summoned to his father's study because of a misdemeanour he boldly swung open the door, and, pretending to be one of the footmen, asked, 'Did Sir Arthur ring for coffee?' Sir Arthur was so amused that he forgot to administer punishment.

From Budapest Sir Arthur was transferred towards the end of 1892 as Secretary to the Embassy at Constantinople, where again he was Chargé d'Affaires in 1893 and 1894.

Harold Nicolson was to return years later both to Tehran and Constantinople as a diplomat. Whereas he was little more than a baby in arms when he left Tehran, he was seven when his father moved from Constantinople. He was taken by his father to witness the ceremony of the Selamlik[8] performed by the Sultan Abdul Hamid on a strip of road between the park of Yildiz and the Hamidieh Mosque. Suddenly the gates of the palace were thrown wide open, and a neat little victoria dashed across the square. In the victoria sat the hunched figure of the Sultan, wearing a fez and frock coat. On reaching the Mosque he descended and turned his mask-like face towards the assembled diplomats. They bellowed in response a respectful greeting. After twenty minutes' prayer inside the mosque Abdul Hamid came out and climbed back into the victoria. And now to the shocked surprise of little Harold the Sultan's cabinet ministers, most of whom were middle-aged, and some elderly, portly and decrepit, took hold of a strap attached to the victoria and were obliged to trot beside it in the great heat, panting and sweating.

For a year from 1894 to 1895 Sir Arthur Nicolson was Agent and Consul-General at Sofia. It was in this capital that Harold's love of the macabre got him into trouble. M. Stephan Stambolov, who had as Prime Minister ruled Bulgaria with an iron hand until forced to retire in 1894, was murdered in the street the following year. The assassins had struck him on the head, and in order to protect himself M. Stambolov put up both his hands. His fingers were severed and fell to the pavement. His wife had them picked up and preserved in a large bottle of spirits, which she put in the street window of their house for his sympathisers to venerate. Harold got to hear of this from one of the Legation servants, and begged his father to let him go and look at the fingers. Sir Arthur refused. So

CHILDHOOD AND SCHOOL 1886-1904

having persuaded his mother's maid to take him for a walk he directed her, unsuspecting, to the window of the Stambolovs' house. Before the maid had time to realise what she was gazing at Harold had enjoyed the spectacle of M. Stambolov's eight fingers floating in the bottle 'like little pickled cucumbers.'[9] The lady's maid rushed him back to the Legation where she had hysterics. Harold was immediately sent to bed and soundly scolded for being heartless and disgusting.

The nine years (1895-1904) in which his father was Envoy-Extraordinary and Minister Plenipotentiary in Tangier were the happiest of Harold's childhood and boyhood. He loved Morocco – so he told his wife at the time of their marriage – more than any country in the world. Conditions in Morocco at the turn of the century were archaic. There was no electric light in Tangier. There were no wheeled vehicles, not even a barrow. Rubbish was carried in panniers by donkeys. When asked out to dinner his father rode and his mother was carried in a sedan chair, preceded by a servant bearing a lantern. Harold too when a schoolboy would set out to a party on horseback, the flickering beams of the servant's lantern falling, now upon some iron-studded door in a blank wall, now upon a street fountain spluttering upon coloured tiles, and now upon a rat scuttling from an open sewer. His horse would pick its way cautiously through the mud and garbage. Suddenly a door would open in the silent street, disclosing a small courtyard, with a lamp hanging from a colonnade, its wick smoking angrily across the arches. The lamp was shaped like the lamps used at Pompeii. Years later Harold Nicolson, recalling these evening scenes in Tangier, realised that it was not the glamour of the East which that smoking lamp suggested to him. It was the life of Rome and even Athens which he, as a boy, had been privileged to experience.[10]

Lady Nicolson's constant anxiety lest Harold might do something foolish was not entirely without reason. For one day during a reception at the Legation Harold burst into the drawing-room disguised as a runaway black slave girl, and in a flood of gibberish appealed for protection to the visiting French Minister, 'a most lugubrious person who wore black gloves,' according to Sir Arthur himself, who used to relate the story with much relish.[11]

In going through his father's papers after his death Harold was amazed to discover how worried his parents had been about him as a child. They thought him 'mercurial' and incurably lazy. They did not think him clever, although they found him comical, for he made them laugh. Freddy the eldest son was wild and too easily led; Eric the second was the good boy. There is no doubt that Harold was his mother's favourite. She indulged him, and he became slightly spoilt. He adored her then and ever afterwards, whereas he loved and revered his father.

In 1895 at the age of nearly nine Harold accompanied his elder brothers to a preparatory school, The Grange, Folkestone. Sir Arthur had been told that The Grange boasted a high moral tone. In packing off their youngest son to school in England at such a tender age the Nicolsons aroused some criticism among the local diplomatic body. Sir Arthur assured them that such a course was customary among the English upper classes, for it developed 'character' in the little victim. So in October Harold, with Freddy and Eric, was duly taken from Morocco over to Gibraltar by ferry, and put on a P & O liner for England. It was the first of thirty-six similar journeys he was to make from Morocco to Southampton and back across the Bay of Biscay. For three days the boys suffered acute sea-sickness, and Harold acute home-sickness to boot. As their ship passed through the Straits he could see the lights of his home twinkling from the African coast.

> In the end I reached the bleak unhallowed dormitory of my private school. Never in my subsequent life have I known desolation equal to those grim days ... To assuage my grief I would read in the school library the opening chapters of *Dombey and Son*.[12]

The headmaster, by name Hussey, was a tyrant. He grossly overworked and mercilessly beat the boys. The present Lord Carnock (Eric) has testified that he kept them at their desks from 8 a.m. till 9 p.m. with very short intervals for recreation. While instilling into the boys the necessity for 'high endeavour' Mr. Hussey would kick them if they made a noise. They were under-fed, and the Nicolson boys, accustomed to the Tangier climate, suffered tortures from the cold. They also found school life intensely boring after the pig-sticking, the camp fires and the companionship of bandits in Morocco. But it was the strict regime at which Harold, already a rebel against all established regulations, protested most loudly. On one occasion he and another boy, to whom an uncle had given ten shillings, went to a local tea shop, hid their school caps in their pockets, and gorged. They were detected coming out. They were summoned before the whole school, told they had broken their word of honour, soundly beaten, and shunned as pariahs by the self-righteous for the rest of the term.

One letter written to his mother from The Grange in 1896 survives. It reveals how desperately he was longing for the holidays. Fred and Eric were very kind to him, he protested. So were all the boys, he felt obliged to add.

> So is Hussey. He spanked me for missing a music lesson and said he would cain me next time. On Monday at 12½ he cained me, then next at 2, and he cained me and found out it wasn't my fault he said that next

CHILDHOOD AND SCHOOL 1886-1904

time I ought to be cained he would let me off. There is a boy called Jacks. He is awfully bulled. I try to stop them bullying him ... Your *loving, loving, loving* son Harold.

Little drawings adorn the margins. The letter amply justifies a broadcast Harold gave in 1958 in which he described Hussey's as Dotheboys Hall. What then enraged him was the knowledge that Hussey had left a tidy fortune acquired by his economies at the boys' expense.

The miserable years at Hussey's corresponded with the South African War. Young Harold was rash enough to proclaim himself a pro-Boer – an act of considerable courage – for which he was maltreated in consequence. Alan (A.P.) Herbert, who was a kindly boy, took him aside and advised him to keep his unpopular and unpatriotic views to himself. 'You are a freak,' he said, 'aren't you?'

Another bold and unpopular attitude which, when thirteen years old, Harold adopted was to rejoice at the reprieve of Captain Dreyfus in 1899. It was a prognosis of his consistent pro-Jewish principles, anti-militarism and pacifist tendencies.

Harold certainly hated The Grange, and he had to conquer a deep repugnance before he could bring himself to accept an invitation in 1933, from a successor of Hussey's, to re-visit the school, make a speech and give away prizes. The experience of his four years under Hussey haunted him throughout life. It added fuel to his fears and developed in him a sense of failure which he never entirely cast away. Even after the last war he had nightmares that he was being sent back there. Yet, strange as it may seem in a regimented school existence, he found time and opportunity to read. At the age of ten he won as a Divinity Prize Martin Tupper's *Proverbial Philosophy*. It was scarcely the sort of literature calculated to appeal to a boy, being what the recipient described in later life as full of sententious rubbish. What he read with avidity during the last year of his preparatory school was the works of Henty, H. S. Merriman and *The Idylls of the King*. He was bored by Scott, found Dickens sentimental, and was moved by Swinburne and *A Shropshire Lad*. He had been discouraged by his masters from reading the works of Conan Doyle as worthless literature. This he considered a great mistake peculiar to schoolmasters of his parents' generation, who saw no intermediate stage between *Froggy would a-wooing go* and *The Last Days of Pompeii*. Had he been allowed to soak himself in Sherlock Holmes between the ages of ten and eleven he would have learnt to read more profitably two years sooner than he did. When his own sons were approaching puberty he encouraged them to devour all the shockers they could find. He simply did not believe those authors who made precocious claims to have read and digested all the works of Bishop Berkeley when they were five.

It was a strange little boy who left The Grange, Folkestone, at the end of the winter term of 1899. He was a mixture of fearlessness and fearfulness. He would cause alarm and consternation by jumping along the battlements of Walmer Castle, when his uncle Dufferin was Warden of the Cinque Ports. On the other hand he would be pursued at nights by the terrifying image of Lord Heathfield's statue at Gibraltar rattling a large chain. Bad at lessons and worse at games, refusing to conform to the conventional taboos and patriotisms of the majority, grubby and perky, he was not particularly popular with boys or masters. Being a nervous child he developed tricks which are not conducive to approval in puerile communities. He tended to screw up his eyes in an affected manner. When told not to do this, he dilated them widely whenever he was spoken to.

It was not always possible, or desirable, that for the school holidays the Nicolson boys should go to Morocco. The journey was long, and also expensive. Theirs was a nomad life in that their parents had no settled home of their own. Therefore it came about that they developed great affection for those Irish country houses which belonged to their mother's relations: Killyleagh Castle, Shanganagh Castle, and above all, Clandeboye. It was these houses which gave Harold his main sense of security and background. It was Ireland which he came to regard as home, and where, as he put it, he 'ceased to be a pot-plant for ever being bedded out in alien soil.'[13] He was to give graphic and nostalgic descriptions of these three places in his books, notably *Helen's Tower* and *The Desire to Please*.

Harold would often stay in the school holidays at Shanganagh, County Dublin, a late Georgian baronial castle of his grandmother's.[14] She was a woman of strong character and varied interests. Long before the suffragette movement she championed women's rights and higher education. She endeavoured to break down the narrow social cliques which worked such havoc amongst the provincial Irish Unionists. Harold recorded that she taught him to maintain a state of constant surprise and amazement. Once she took him to a fete or horse-show near Dublin. 'Look!' she exclaimed in sudden excitement. 'Look at that lady over there in the tilbury! And remember that you have seen Mrs. O'Shea.' 'Who is she, Granny?' he asked, perplexed. 'Never mind. Just remember,' she repeated, 'that you have seen Mrs. O'Shea.' And her eyes twinkled. With a sharp ebony stick this matriarchal old lady would rap the floor with indignation if her grandchildren failed to show interest in and wonder at the great events and marvels of the world.

Years later Harold Nicolson re-visited Shanganagh.[15] He went first to the overgrown garden, looked at the Roman statues and then walked down the avenue to the sea. 'Old fears, memories of my childhood,' he wrote to his wife, 'come back to me. My own reminiscences are peopled by terrors. Yet Mummy assures me I was burbling with laughter the whole time. "The gayest of all my children." Yet Shanganagh and its castle turrets and winding staircases, revives old terrors. Strange memory tricks, tactile and even auditive . . . I go up to my old nursery and all that I can recapture is that sense of night-fears.' Always the memory of Shanganagh remained with him as the spirit of old Ireland, irrational, fey, contradictory and conspiratorial. In speculating what would have become of him had he inherited and inhabited it, he assumed that the spell of Ireland would have stolen his wits away.

If the prevailing emotion which darkened Harold Nicolson's life at his preparatory school had been fear, that which stood out in his memories of his public school was boredom. 'It is not that I was ever unhappy at Wellington;' he wrote, 'it is that I was bored there as I have never been bored in all my life.'[16] And the reason was that Wellington boys ceased to have any identity and were dragooned into a corporate system.

Wellington College was one of a number of public schools founded during the nineteenth century. It was different from, say, Cheltenham, Marlborough and Radley, in that it was intended as a memorial to England's greatest soldier, and its purpose was to provide, in the words of its endowment appeal of 1852, 'for the gratuitous, or nearly gratuitous, education of orphan children of indigent and meritorious officers of the Army.' The Prince Consort took a close interest in its foundation and became its first President. It was his wish that Wellington should not become just another Eton or Harrow, dedicated to the classics exclusively, but should impart knowledge of the sciences, modern languages, commerce and even the arts. The Prince was also opposed to excessive corporal punishment and, stranger still, to excessive religious exercise. In 1856 Queen Victoria laid the first foundation stone, and three years later formally opened the school. In the meantime the main central building of scarlet brick and yellow stone dressings had been erected in a style described at the time as 'franco-Flemish with a suggestion of a Louis XV château.' To be more precise the style is suggestive of a mixture of Louis XIII with William and Mary.

When Harold Nicolson was sent to Wellington in January 1900 the exclusive military emphasis of the school had somewhat waned; and the sons of impecunious and not entirely impecunious professional men of all sorts and degrees were accepted. His brother Freddy had already gone there in 1897.

Harold's house, called Stanley, lay to the north of the main block. It is an unsightly Edwardian structure, liberally sprinkled with gables, mansards, bows, bays and crinkly roof-ridges. The windows are of every style, shape and dimension. This unprepossessing building was presided over by the housemaster, the Rev. P. H. Kempthorne, a Fellow of St. John's Cambridge, known to the boys as Kemp. The dormitory to which Nicolson Minor was allotted, faced the drive. The prevailing smell of Stanley was a mixture of cocoa, seed cake and Pears soap.

During the Lent term Queen Victoria paid her last visit to the College, for which she had special affection because of the Prince Consort's part in its foundation. It was the very day on which the Relief of Mafeking was announced. The old Queen drove over from Windsor with Princess Beatrice. The boys were given a whole holiday. In the morning they had rushed about the quadrangles with Union Jacks and streamers cheering Baden Powell. Young Harold had by now either lost or suppressed his pro-Boer sympathies. The Queen on her arrival exchanged her carriage for a wheeled chair, in which she was propelled round the precincts by her Indian servant, the Munshi, in white cotton trousers. The head boy read her a short address. When the time for her departure came the boys accompanied the carriage down Kilometre. Harold caught hold of a mudguard and ran along shouting, 'Hooray! Hooray!' The ancient monarch sat huddled like a round bundle. Her large eyelids blinked behind her gold-rimmed spectacles. The sunshine glinted on the wisps of straw-coloured hair which emerged from under a black bonnet and ribbons. At the College gate the boys stopped running. They watched the carriage bowl along the main road, the coachmen and footmen sitting straight as ramrods above a little parasol of black lace. The boys waved their straw boaters in a last farewell.

Harold's first letter from Wellington to survive is dated the 19th March 1901. He told his parents that he was in a very depressed state. He was good at practically nothing. He was so bad at games that the boys laughed at him. Only at fencing was he making progress. Whenever he got to know other boys they disliked him. 'I am so fearfully sensitive that I mind awfully what people say to me ... Altogether I am a fool,' the letter continued, 'and I'll never get on in the world.' Cooper was the only boy he did get on with. This was R.A. (Reggie) Cooper, a sweet and stimulating character who went into the Diplomatic Service, became a Colonel and won the D.S.O. in the First War. He was one of the few boyhood friends to remain close in Harold's confidence. Amongst the masters only Kempthorne was nice to him, he said, 'and of course Mr. Pollock, but I see so little of him.' As for E. F. Elton, the mathematics master, Harold loathed him. The loathing seems to have been reciprocated. Coming into class late one morning Mr. Elton gave the excuse that he had been kept by the Duke

CHILDHOOD AND SCHOOL 1886-1904

of Connaught. 'Snob!' Harold whispered impertinently. He was overheard, and ordered to stay behind after class. He was beaten viciously by Elton, who was in a fury. Harold always maintained that corporal punishment of boys was legitimate except when administered in public in order to shame the culprit, and except when the beater was angry.

The Mr. Pollock whom Harold saw so little of during his first years was the headmaster, or simply Master, as he was called. The Rev. Bertram Pollock had been appointed Master of Wellington in 1893 at the age of twenty-nine. The civilizing influence he exercised upon the older boys was remarkable. Against the drab, mechanical background of the College he stood out shoulder-high. He was someone apart, above the everyday curriculum, for he brought with him a breath of the exciting world beyond the confines of school life. By the time the boys reached the Upper Sixth their relationship with Pollock expanded quite naturally into close personal friendship. The tall, angular man, with sharp nose and long jaw, with impassive, clean-shaven face and expressive hands, had charm, dignity and grace. To the smaller boys he appeared a distant, theocratic figure, beyond comprehension and contact. To the masters his remote manner was hardly any warmer. He would treat them with an off-hand contempt which was much resented. But to the older boys, provided they were clever, he descended from his lofty pinnacle. He loved to entertain them as equals in the Master's Lodge. A bachelor then, he lived in style, with footmen, silver salvers and sleek Persian cats. His love of literature and the classics was infectious. In school and at the Lodge he taught that Greek and Latin were not just dead languages but the very fabric of the living tradition of western Europe. Harold was to write,

> His method of teaching Latin was wholly personal. When one entered the Upper VI he would present one with a little printed card containing what to his mind were the five or six most beautiful lines in the Latin language ... How carefully would he read to us, how gently would he almost intone, the Sirmio elegy of Catullus.[17]

He became devoted to Dr. Pollock. To him he owed his early love of the classics. Pollock was one of the greatest, as he was one of the earliest influences in his life.

Even so Dr. Pollock was too olympian, too unconcerned to bother with reforming the school curriculum. The arts and music, for instance, were totally neglected. Games remained of paramount importance. The prefectoral system was as rigid as it had been in the mid-nineteenth century. In his Foreword to Bertram Pollock's autobiography (the Master subsequently became Bishop of Norwich) Harold Nicolson wrote:

> So convinced were the authorities [of Wellington] that Satan was lying in wait for any unoccupied little boy, that some precise occupation was devised for every hour and every minute, whether in the form of compulsory games or in that of compulsory lessons . . . All the masters could tell, not only what any boy was doing at any given moment, but also what the same boy would be doing at 3.45 p.m. four weeks ahead. This system may well have produced a machine of the very utmost regularity and precision; but it was certainly not good for the mind.[18]

In spite of these absurd precautions, Satan flourished at Wellington like the green bay tree.

Moreover the house system discouraged boys from knowing boys in other houses for fear of contamination of the good by the bad inmates. Thus in a community of thirty an individual boy was left with no more than ten of his approximate age, with whom he was allowed to consort and make friends. Harold blamed the Wellington system for retarding him mentally and socially. And when he went to Balliol he was conscious of being younger for his age than boys who had come from Eton, Harrow and Winchester.

By September 1903 Harold had already passed Responsions in Latin and Greek. In October he told his parents that he was very worried about the forthcoming exams for Balliol. At the same time he was much looking forward to leaving Wellington. 'Only 72 more days and I will be let out of prison!' On the 15th he wrote to his mother about his viva voce examination at Balliol, and the sarcasm of the three dons who interviewed him. He had had to translate a Horatian ode.

> I am sure they tried to frighten me . . . I took a great swallow, & began in a voice that felt like somebody else's. I began to get dry inside and had to swallow away hard to be able to speak.

He made several mistakes. They laughed. He stammered and got scarlet.

> I saw their upper lips go up in a sarcastic sneer . . . Oh my mummy if you could have seen poor me then, you would have felt sorry for me!

But he passed all right; and told his family not to congratulate him, because that would be beastly bad form. 'It is nice to think I am a commoner of Balliol.'

His letters to his mother and father were easy and affectionate. And they were saucy. To his mother he wrote that he wanted a panama hat for his birthday,

CHILDHOOD AND SCHOOL 1886-1904

but I suppose you would refuse to give me that; it is just like you to refuse to give me something I want & to give me something just as expensive which *you think* I want ... Lord Roberts [a governor of the College] is coming down today – little beast,[19]

a remark which suggests that the suppressed pro-Boer was re-asserting himself. On the 21st November Harold wrote to both parents, 'How awfully generous you are. I feel a brute costing you such an enormous lot.' He was making preparations for a stay in Weimar to learn German, and intending to continue his Iliad and Aeneid-studies there. He must send his books, 217 in all, to Weimar. 'I shall not like saying goodbye to Pollock. He is the most fascinating man I shall ever meet.'

He hoped they would have a nice lot of fast young ladies to flirt with when he came out to Tangier for Christmas. And on the 13th December he wrote,

My dear Family, this is my last letter from Well. Coll. and will be quite historical & figure in my biography when it comes to be written by a devoted wife. I cannot say I am in the least sorry. In work I have succeeded here above my expectations, yet I should not say that I was at the top of the tree. It is so funny to think that it is nearly over and how happy and unhappy I have been ... I shall be sorry to say goodbye to Pollock, Kemp & to Mr. Perkins.[20] They have all done their best for me & I don't think I shall ever forget it. I am beginning to see that brain counts for little but that character counts everything, & it is not a pleasant thought as my character is weak and easily influenced ... In reading through Father's letters I see how clever he is & I wish I could be like him.

The fact that Harold had successfully passed his examinations and been accepted by Balliol, but was still too young to enter the College, shows that in spite of his alleged backwardness in social conduct, Wellington had not done too badly for his education. Christmas of 1903 was spent in Tangier with his parents, with whom he remained until the following February. At the beginning of that month he set out for Weimar for a six months visit.

The Rev. F. E. Freese, although in retirement, was acting as British Chaplain in Weimar. He and his wife inhabited a flat, No. 14a Prellerstrasse, which young Harold found perfectly lovely, with pretty wallpapers. He was given his own bedroom and sitting-room. He was delighted with the Freeses, who were an educated and travelled couple, having recently been in Japan. They had a large circle of acquaintances in Weimar, of whom Harold found the English very dull, and some of the Germans interesting. He described in letters home how awful and common were the English wives, and how coy and flirtatious their daughters. But he was amused by Mrs. Phillips, an American lady, who dressed in the fashions of the last century and wore a crinoline. She was musical, had been a pupil of Liszt, had known Wagner intimately, and had been an *amie* of the present Grand Duke's grandfather, which gave her a certain cachet.

Amongst the Freeses' foreign friends Harold met Max Vogrich, the Hungarian pianist and composer of the opera *Buddah*; and the Belgian architect, Henri Van de Velde, the apostle in theory and practice of functional aesthetics and *pure form*, whom Harold described to his parents as 'the father of modern art in its best sense. He paints his pictures with a penknife.' It is true he attempted through early contact with the Impressionist painters to apply the pointilliste technique to architecture. Van de Velde was bringing about a new style of architectural decoration to Weimar. It was a Germanic version of *art nouveau* then very much in vogue. It was represented by houses in the suburbs, carved under the gables with oversize human faces, their hair neatly parted in the middle and loose locks streaming down in a cataract over the front door.

The Freeses were extremely musical and regularly took their pupil to the opera house, which was practically unchanged since Goethe built it, apart from the addition of some large white statues of Kaiser William II, with dirty faded wreaths of olive and myrtle round their necks. Part of the auditorium was taken up by the Grand Ducal box, in which the occupants (the Grand Duchess looking 'respectable,' the Grand Duke dissipated) kept the electric light on throughout the performance. The opera house was always stiflingly hot and airless: 'The atmosphere was tainted with hot Herr and frowsty Frau.'[21] Harold made friends with a cultivated elderly acquaintance of the Freeses, Herr von Müller, who let him have free use of his box whenever he did not need it himself. Altogether Harold went to the opera twenty-five times when he was in Weimar. Since he always claimed that he positively disliked music, these frequent attendances suggest that the town was poorly provided with other forms of recreation for young people.

At the same time Mr. Freese kept his pupil hard at work. Lessons consisted of learning German, and reading 100 lines of Latin or Greek a day. Freese was such an enthusiastic teacher that Harold enjoyed working with him.

On the 4th April Harold wrote from Weimar a deeply affectionate letter of birthday greetings to his mother.

I do wish I could be at Tangier for it [her birthday] & be able to kiss you myself and tell you how I love you more than anything in the whole world. I can't think what I should do if you died. I think I should kill myself... I wish I could go back and be eight years old again when I had you all to myself & could sit on your knee all day without your feeling tired or other people saying it looked silly. You will have to sit on my knee now, Your loving son, Harold Nicolson.

In July he was given permission by his parents to accompany the Freeses to Switzerland, in order to go on walking excursions with his tutor. They stayed in a pension on Lac Champex, 2,000 feet above a little town called Orsières on the St. Bernard Pass, and ten miles south-west of Martigny, in the Valais. At Champex he met in the pension a youth who was at Oxford. He at once asked Harold what games he was best at.

I shrivelled up at once into my shell [he told his parents], and have not dared come out of it since. I wonder if I shall find incapacity for games coming under the penal code when I return![22]

This worry was forgotten in the long walks he and his companion took in the mountains, laden with cameras. Freese was an accomplished mountaineer. Harold was in his element.

It is a queer experience washing with Pears soap in a glacier pool by the light of the moon at half past two in the morning & 8,000 feet above the sea.

They slept at night in cabins on the mountainside. Harold rather primly disapproved of women sleeping in the neighbouring bunks to his.

In August he and Freese went on a stiff climb up the Grand Combin which nearly ended in disaster. When it was over he wrote an enthusiastic letter, with sketches and diagrams of the route they had taken. The whole party, roped together, had on their return glissaded down the ice. Some were badly hurt. ('If you fuss about this I will not call you Mother any more. It is all over now.')[23] Their guide was very frightened and annoyed Harold by moaning and groaning. 'It is breeding,' he wrote rather portentously, 'that tells more than anything else in this sort of thing.' But they had reached the peak of the Grand Combin on the Savoy frontier. Harold had never felt so well or so proud of himself in his life before.

At Champex he took drawing lessons from a Mr. Lewis, who encouraged him to suppose that he might become quite adept with practice. He had a pretty talent which expressed itself even in these early years in lively sketches in the margin of his letters, a habit he continued and only abandoned in late middle-age. Towards the end of August the party left Lac Champex reluctantly for Weimar. Their luggage having been sent in advance by post horse, they went on foot to Martigny. It was a beautiful day in the grassy valley under the Dent du Midi, with Lac Leman sparkling in the distance. The weather got hotter and hotter, and they were glad when a carriage overtook them and gave them a lift the rest of the way. They stayed the night at Berne and visited the Cathedral, admiring the figures of the Wise and Foolish Virgins carved on either side of the door. 'Very funny the wise ones wearing a priggish & superior smile & the foolish howling like Gwen does.'[24] Gwen, now Lady St. Levan, was Harold's only sister, born ten years after him. She was roughly treated and at the same time greatly beloved by him. In Berne Harold and Mr. Freese threw carrots to the bears in the bear pit. Very early next morning they bathed in the river Aare in ice-cold water flowing at fearful speed. Diving in at one end of a strip they were carried by the current to the grating at the other. After a mammoth breakfast they ran to the station and threw themselves into the train for Weimar.

Harold was not captivated by the Goethe cult in Weimar. He was saturated in Goethe and made to read and see his plays over and over again. He found the sage's major works incredibly dull, being written with an olympian self-satisfaction that was irritating. He would visit the Gartenhaus respectfully, but with the feeling that all the circumambient piety was a trifle exaggerated. It was only years later that his conversion to Goethe came through reading his letters and autobiographical writings, and Eckermann's *Conversations*. Eckermann helped him to understand why Goethe was reverenced by millions. He was a man who knew how to grow old. Of massive culture, he was interested in the unimportant as well as the important things of life. He enjoyed *les faits divers*. Every hour of his old age was planned and occupied to the fullest profit. But these revelations would have little appeal for a seventeen-year-old boy fresh from the bondage of school.

However, it did not escape Harold that the Germans liked to be dragooned. He thought that the citizens of Weimar were treated like children. All the pavements had 'footway' painted on them at short intervals lest someone might walk between the tramlines. Particulars of every citizen were known to the police, down to the number of false teeth he had. In Leipzig the park benches were strictly allocated to children, men or women, and a person was fined if he sat on the wrong one.

When Harold was at Weimar he considered himself grown-up. On looking back he realised that he had been very childish for his age, with not the least idea what he wanted out of life. He was only fairly industri-

CHILDHOOD AND SCHOOL 1886-1904

ous, and little able to concentrate. On the other hand he read voraciously. He was clearly a bright youth, quick to assimilate impressions, and not hesitant in recording them. His letters home show an early amused interest in the foibles of others, with a tendency to mock, even occasionally to disparage, his elders. Already they are buoyant and bubbling with humour. Yet they disclose that Harold craved affection and protection. His love for his mother, which was deep and touching, suggests a certain vulnerability of character, an almost feminine dependence, in spite of his own strong will, upon psychical support in the harsh process of living. As he grew to manhood he realised that his gentle and unintellectual mother, whom he never ceased to love and was in his turn to protect, was unable to provide the particular support he required. He had, like other sons before him, to seek it elsewhere.

At seventeen Harold still looked a mere schoolboy, with his pink and white complexion and merry, twinkling eyes. When an American asked him whether he was thirteen or fourteen he was incensed. But the mistake was pardonable.

On the 29th August Harold left Weimar for England. He spent the afternoon of the 1st September in London, crossed over that night to Ireland, and on the 2nd reached Clandeboye in County Down.

2

BALLIOL AND CRAMMING, 1904–1907

HAROLD NICOLSON was by no means unique among very intelligent boys in setting up on pedestals and venerating older men as heroes. Dr. Pollock, as we have seen, was one superior being endowed with a kind of divine afflatus which he breathed upon the raw schoolboy at Wellington. Another even more splendid hero, seen through Harold's childhood eyes as the quintessence of intellectual and social grace, was undoubtedly his uncle Dufferin[1] who, alas, had been dead nearly two years when his nephew went to stay at Clandeboye in September of 1904. His widow, Aunt Lal, was now living in comparatively straitened circumstances in this large, rather nondescript Georgian house in Northern Ireland, which bore traces, from whatever angle you looked at it, of the Viceroy's alterations, improvements and additions.

Clandeboye was to Harold not only the one country house which meant home to him, but the hallowed shrine of the cultivated, liberal and finally tragic public servant, his uncle – tragic, because at the very end of his honourable life his eldest son was killed fighting the Boers, and because, by unwisely dabbling in business, he became involved in a speculative company which went bust, losing not only the shareholders' money but his own fortune. The love and reverence which Harold bore to Lord Dufferin's memory was never returned by Lady Dufferin. Whereas this correct lady, with her strict code of behaviour, deemed her youngest and ultimately most distinguished nephew a spoilt mother's darling when he was a child, she came to disapprove strongly of what she considered his erratic politics and his loose morals when he was a middle-aged man.

Back in London in October Harold saw his family off for Sir Arthur's last stint of a ten-year-long post in Tangier. Immediately he was faced with the alarming prospect of his first term at Oxford. Having packed, he had his hair cut and unwisely, as it turned out, allowed the barber to give him what was called an alcoholic friction, so that when he arrived at Balliol it was in his own words 'under a cloud of *violette de Parme*. I remained under that cloud for several weeks.'[2] Unaware of the future consequences of this gaffe, Harold hailed a four-wheeler and piling his luggage on the top made for Paddington. He bought a first-class ticket and a paper in which to drown his terrors. As the train neared Oxford he got up, put on and took off his gloves and hat over and over again. The station was

BALLIOL AND CRAMMING 1904-7

crowded with undergraduates. Harold tried hard not to look a freshman. All the hansoms were engaged so he was obliged to share the station bus with a commercial traveller in a white tie, who asked him if he had been 'to this fair city before.' Having discharged the commercial traveller at the Mitre Hotel the bus rumbled on to Balliol. The ostler, in pulling up, exclaimed, 'Balliol, Sir!' which annoyed Harold because the man evidently assumed he did not know his own college. Harold jumped from the bus, hat box in hand, and asked the head porter, Hancock, a smiling, square-built, blue-eyed man, looking like a gamekeeper, and beloved by dons and undergraduates alike, where his rooms were. Lady Carnarvon, mother of his friends Aubrey and Mervyn Herbert, both Balliol men, had kindly suggested Harold's mentioning her name to Hancock, which so delighted the porter that he became all smiles in a moment, and said: 'No. 20 in the Hall Quad. Ground floor, Sir,' while ordering a man to follow with the luggage. Crossing the stridently mid-Victorian Front Quad, Harold walked to the far end of the Garden Quad and after a little searching found round a corner a door with his name painted upon it in white.

In a letter[3] to his family he gave a detailed description of his rooms, with a plan and drawing, showing where every stick of furniture was situated and every picture hung. There was a welcoming fire blazing in the grate of his sitting-room and a kettle sizzling on the hob. A pair of windows faced the Garden Quad. Across the passage was his bedroom. This looked over St. Giles to the Ashmolean. Harold was enchanted with the space, the comfort and the independence betokened. When the new Bulkeley-Johnson block was built in the 1960s his old rooms were done away with.

The first few days were spent finding his feet. Harold was lucky in having as tutor Cyril Bailey,[4] one of the outstanding classical scholars of his generation, and a superb teacher. Bailey's whole life was dedicated to Balliol, and he more than any other don kept alive the Jowett tradition.

When asked if he was going to play games, Harold said he would row. For his first two terms he plied laboriously up and down the river in a tub, fearful of catching crabs. He did not enjoy it. And as for having to row in a race the whole thing was ridiculous torture. In a letter home he described how his behind was made skinless from the effort.

Daily attendance at Chapel was not obligatory, but on Sunday it was correct to be present at one service in Butterfield's dark and dreary building, with its buff-and-red striped surrounds to the translucent 'decorated' windows. Meals were eaten in Alfred Waterhouse's Hall, with high open pine roof, 'Jacobethan' screen and gallery, and a pair of Gothic, stone-hooded fireplaces, the whole smelling of stale mutton-fat. In Hall Harold could have a tolerable cooked breakfast, a bread and cheese luncheon, and a very full dinner costing 1/9d.

In a second letter[5] he told his parents he was getting on splendidly. He was attending sixteen lectures a week, besides doing essays and composition. There was no place in the world like Oxford, except perhaps Tangier, and of course no college like Balliol. But he had to admit that the majority of his colleagues were an odd lot.

> Very few speak without an accent & there are a great many blacks and Rhodes scholars, etc. But the others [meaning no doubt those of his own class and background] are so nice that they make up for all the niggers & atheists in the world.

L. E. Jones,[6] Harold's contemporary, confirmed that his lot shunned all members of the College with wrong accents, like the Blundells scholars. Harold not only took good care not to become intimate with the Rhodes scholars ('One wears a tail coat and missionary shovel hat ... It is said that they keep their money in gold bricks under their beds & that they sleep on their sofas and have their meals in their bedrooms'), but he also kept the female undergraduates at a proper distance. He greatly resented their presence. They had the cheek to behave as though 'they were real members of the 'varsity & not merely hangers-on who bore all the real people by their insolent self-pushing.' They used slang too, speaking of 'leckers' for lectures, and 'Jaggers' for Jesus.

Harold's opinion of the Master, after his first interview, was no less brash and snobbish. He wrote that he was

> an awful old fool & I could kick him. He is like a Scotch Meenister & very dull and stupid. He said, 'Vera glad to see yer Meester Nicolson,' shaking hands like an elephant would.

In fact Edward Caird was a Professor of Moral Philosophy of the highest eminence. He was a strong advocate of education for women (which did not commend him to Harold in those days) and of working-class men. His portrait in Hall shows an open, handsome face with snow-white beard, a great domed forehead and whimsical mouth, a face of innocent strength.

All his life Harold Nicolson was to remain perfectly candid – as he was candid about most of his inclinations, apart from sex – about his snobbishness. He was, like the vast majority of his Victorian contemporaries, an unrepentant snob in so far as his ear was offended by a 'wrong' accent and his eyes by the slightest hint of vulgarity, which to him savoured an uneducated mind. Lack of breeding implied to him uniformity of mental

BALLIOL AND CRAMMING 1904-7

outlook, whereas breeding betokened variety of opinion. He honestly did not believe there was conscious insincerity in his preference for the aristocratic manner and way of life. It was not that he saw greater virtue in a duke than a marquess, or in a marquess than a coal-heaver. But he relished the historic significance of great families and was revolted by the philistinism of the masses. He derived pleasure, and often silent merriment, from the company of the eminent, believing this taste to be endemic in every civilised being. 'I am glad,' he once wrote to his wife, 'that we are well born . . . because it gives one an added sense of belonging.' And if a modern critic should ask testily, 'belonging to what?' the answer is quite simply – the social and intellectual élite, as understood by members of the upper classes until 1939. Yet there were facets of Harold's and Vita's snobbishness difficult to rationalise, even if understandable to their friends. For instance, both parents thought in 1945 it was rather second-rate their son Nigel being a Major and a bearer of the M.B.E. And both of them flushed with embarrassment and shame after 1953, when he was addressed as Sir Harold and she as Lady Nicolson. It was because first their son, and then they themselves were sharing hollow honours – in their opinion – with middle-class officers and city mayors and mayoresses. Had he been Sir Harold, 15th Baronet (which he easily might) that would have been an entirely acceptable difference.

Very soon the censorious freshman was being invited by friends and dons out to 'brekker' – such 'varsity jargon being apparently permissible from the lips of male undergraduates. At one breakfast a paper was read and a discussion ensued about Tolstoy. Harold, for all his bumptiousness, rejoiced in being in the company of people cleverer than himself. Besides it made him feel intellectually humble. Soon he was leading a full social life, going from one prolonged meal to another. He was elected to one of three Balliol societies, namely the Brackenbury, which was recruited from the raffish and sophisticated members of the College. At his first meeting a member moved a vote of censure against a workman who had the indecency to throw a fit outside the College gate. There was much joviality in the debate that ensued.

On the 1st of November he told his parents that he had just lunched with 'a Mr. Urquhart'; and eleven days later that Mr. Urquhart had invited him to two luncheons, brekkers and teas. Which made him suspicious. For what could Mr. Urquhart possibly want out of him? F. F. Urquhart,[7] affectionately known to generations of Balliol men as Sligger (the sleek one) was the Junior Dean. The fact that within little more than a fortnight he had recognised in the new freshman someone worth cultivating, is a tribute to both men. For, with the exception of Sligger Urquhart few of the dons or the undergraduates recognised Harold's latent qualities all the time he was up at Oxford. Sir Charles Clay,[8] who was at Balliol with him, told me that Harold made little impression there, seeming to be a negative character, and a late developer. Sligger however must have found Harold's lack of confidence sympathetic, in that he invited him to meals and kept every single letter Harold wrote to him. Moreover just before his death in 1934 he returned the lot to Harold on condition that he did not destroy them.

What was the secret of this strange, reserved, exclusive, rather cold bachelor, who was a deeply devout Catholic? The type he belonged to is not an uncommon one. He liked, rather than loved – for love presupposes a measure of warmth which Sligger lacked – young men, provided they were nice-looking, well-bred and intellectual. Quite unashamedly he had his favourites. His attentions were never known to have strayed beyond the bounds of cautious companionship. He was essentially an historian with a keen interest in English and French literature, but not a notable academic. He did not contribute to any movement of modern thought. He was not perhaps a true aesthete, preferring the content to the form of works of art. Yet his rooms on the first floor over the back gate to St. Giles, facing the Martyrs Memorial (as it happened, Protestant martyrs), were filled with paintings by Lear. They were also filled with an infinite number of photographs of his friends, over which a large portrait of his beloved mother presided. The favoured undergraduates were permitted to visit his rooms at all hours of the night, and Sligger dropped from his window a key of the back gate to those who would otherwise find themselves locked out of College. Conversations would ensue night after night, year after year, about everything under the sun. Sligger talked to these unfledged undergraduates on absolutely equal terms, without the slightest patronage or censure. Yet he managed to humanise their arrogance, and render their superiority less vulgar.

> He imposed nothing while suggesting everything. He suggested to young men that they would grow out of their affectations and attain to their own realities. He taught them that their failings and even their vices were unimportant and that they must surely possess inside themselves an inner core of energy and righteousness. He inspired confidence in the young.[9]

In short, he hated the fraudulent.

He became for Harold Nicolson the third venerable hero to be set on a pedestal and worshipped. He was not to be the last.

Before his first term was over Harold had even been to breakfast with the most formidable of Balliol's dons, H. W. C. Davis. This reserved and frigid man had a hard, brilliant mind. He was Oxford's leading history tutor, and author of *England under the Normans and Angevins*. With his concise manner of speech he inspired respect. Even the Eton bloods were in awe of him. He was aloof from, not familiar with, the undergraduates. He was referred to (only once to his face, and never again) as 'Fluffy', because of his shock of reddish hair. A drunken undergraduate on being summoned to his room one morning began, 'I say, Fluffy, I'm afraid I made rather a floater last night.' 'If by Fluffy you mean me,' the tutor replied with devastating hauteur, 'my name is Mr. Davis; and if by floater you mean making a beast of yourself, I heartily concur.' Fluffy Davis was, L. E. Jones wrote,[10] 'our frosty weather; his high standards and cold integrity nipped, but braced, us all.'

During his first vacation Harold did not go to Tangier. He spent a few days in Surrey with his mother's brother, Uncle Fred Rowan Hamilton and his wife, Aunt Blanche,[11] and then stayed at the Master's Lodge, Wellington, with Dr. Pollock. The visit was a great success in spite of his host expressing a dislike of Balliol, and calling Balliol men arrogant and conceited.

Already Harold had decided that the Diplomatic Service was to be his ultimate goal. It was why he chose to spend Christmas with strangers at No. 14 rue de Priépus in Paris. He found the family of Pasteur Dumas affable, though bourgeois. Pasteur Dumas was a large fat man with a pointed brown beard and pleasant smile. He repeated his sentences very slowly three times, so that Harold should not fail to understand him. Harold worked every morning, and every afternoon took the metro to the Louvre, systematically doing the rounds of all the galleries. He found the Manets and the ultra-modern school of painting awful. When the museum shut at four o'clock he would be desolate until it was time to go home for the evening meal. He described Paris as a shrieking, hooting mass of whirling motor cars. He watched a man run over in the Place de l'Opéra, with blood bubbling from his nose and mouth. He went to see Sarah Bernhardt in *Phèdre*, and thought her voice marvellous when she was speaking quietly but raucous when she raised it. On New Year's Day of 1905 he lunched with Sligger, who was passing through Paris, and was to see more of him in London on his way back to Oxford.

Yet Harold was lonely. Although he liked the Dumas, their company was heavy. One night, to relieve his boredom, he decided to play a prank on the Dumas' *bonne à tout faire* by pretending to be drunk when she answered the front door. He put his hat on one side of his head and leant crazily against the door. It was opened by Monsieur Dumas, who was profoundly shocked. 'A family like this does make one long to say "Damn!" in the middle of luncheon,' he complained to his mother. How, he asked her, was he to pay the Dumas when he left them? Was he to say, 'Apportez la note, s'il vous plaît'? Or was he to press the money into the Pasteur's hand, and say, 'Keep the change and buy yourself a new frock coat with it,' for his old one was covered with stains? During this visit he began to grow the moustache, brown, short and neatly clipped, which he wore for the rest of his life.

After a short visit to Reggie Cooper, Harold returned to Balliol on the 20th January. He was overjoyed to be back.

Throughout 1905 a repetition of fun and drollery made the highlights of Harold's Balliol terms – bicycling with Hughe Knatchbull-Hugessen[12] to Blenheim, to skate; playing the piano in Sligger's rooms till two in the morning; going to London with Jack Balgonie[13] and Tata Bertie,[14] a son of Lord Abingdon, to see the Earl and the girl, 'which Mother would have called vulgar';[15] driving a tandem; riding in Wytham Park; swimming in summer across the Cherwell in full view of the public; seeing *The Clouds* in the O.U.D.S. – 'It just shows how beautiful men are when dressed as ladies';[16] playing roulette – 'I won 3 pounds; don't be cross Mums darling. I lost it all again'; and driving to the Magdalen Grind in a hired coach, a man in a beaver hat playing tunes from the roof on a long horn. Regrettably, they squirted their fellow travellers with soda water and threw bananas at the bicyclists.

Lady Nicolson, in the face of these undergraduate high jinks, was beginning to fear that her youngest and favourite son was growing away from her. Harold hastened to reassure her.

> My darling Mother [he wrote], Fancy my ever being bored with you – the suggestion is unworthy of you & you must know that I prefer watching your pretty hands do the flowers than going to all the theatres in the world, & that it amuses me more to wait in the dentist's antichamber than to go a tour to the North Pole in a motor.[17]

Emboldened by these words, which were from the heart, he asked his father for a horse. 'I know you are short just now but £10 won't make much difference.'[18]

For the Easter vacation Harold joined his parents at the British Embassy in Madrid, where Sir Arthur was Ambassador from January to October. Two incidents connected with this visit to Spain left indelible impressions upon Harold. One was his attendance at the Repast of the Poor, and the other his meeting with Ronald Firbank.

The Repast of the Poor was held in a long gallery, richly tapestried and carpeted, in the Royal Palace. It was a semi-religious ceremony. Twelve beggars were chosen each year to take part in the archaic charade. After being carefully washed and disinfected the beggars were provided with

BALLIOL AND CRAMMING 1904-7

clean shirts and suits, and ranged on a bench in front of the tiers of boxes in which the diplomatic corps and their wives in diamonds and lace sat watching the proceedings. A roll of distant drums announced the imminent arrival of King Alfonso XIII. The Cardinal Legate made obeisance to a makeshift altar. Acolytes swung silver censers. The Queen Mother entered with a train of ladies, genuflecting to the altar and bowing stiffly to the ambassadors. She was followed by a procession of the Grandees of Spain, who ranged themselves in front of each beggar, 'whose increasing embarrassment and blinking were pitiable to behold.' Then the King entered, a slender youth of eighteen, upright and majestic in blue uniform. Having made his obeisances he approached each beggar in turn. Rapidly the Grandees undid the beggars' boots and bared their white feet. Rapidly the King knelt before each beggar, made a casual movement with water from a silver basin, rapidly flicked a towel over each foot, and as rapidly kissed it. After which, on being handed a silk towel he wiped his own hands. The next stage of the ceremony was to serve the beggars with a meal of eight courses. But the beggars were not allowed to touch the food. Like lightning servants handed the dishes and wine to a line of courtiers who passed them to the King who in turn handed them to the palace servant who whisked them out of the room. The beggars sat open-mouthed and unfed. The whole ceremony passed like clockwork with the utmost speed, deliberately accentuated by the King's dexterity and mischief, until an aged majordomo spilt a bowl of oranges which fell to the floor and rolled to the foot of the altar. This was too much for the gravity of the young King, who burst out laughing. The Queen Mother hid her face behind her fan. Instantly the King recovered his gravity. The token feast was over. Don Alfonso bowed to his mother, bowed to the ambassadors, kissed the Cardinal's ring, genuflected to the altar and briskly left the gallery, to the accompaniment of a second roll of drums. The colourful spectacle of the Repast of the Poor revealed to Harold's eyes that the Spain of the Renaissance, the Spain of Philip II, had survived into the twentieth century.[19]

Ronald Firbank came to Madrid with a letter of introduction to the British Ambassador. He was invited to luncheon. He moved in a sinuous undulating walk. The description given in *Some People*[20] of Lambert Orme's physical appearance has been corroborated by Harold Nicolson as a faithful portrait of Firbank. The moment Ronald Firbank was ushered into the drawing-room, Harold, who was of the same age, was embarrassed, revolted and yet mystified.

> I eyed him with sullen disapproval. He stood for none of the things which I had learnt at Wellington. Clearly he was not my sort.

Harold was to admit later in life that he had a 'Kipling side.' On this occasion his gorge rose within him. He was off-hand and rude to the visitor. Reproved by his mother for churlish behaviour he felt some remorse and invited Firbank to go riding with him. To his intense surprise the effeminate Firbank acquitted himself on horseback with grace and skill. Harold was obliged to readjust his opinion of him. Irritated though he was by his guest's affectations and pretensions to excel at painting, writing and composing music at the precocious age of eighteen, contemptuous of his exotic clothes and velours hat, and annoyed too by the cavalier response to his reluctant proffer of amends, Harold was intrigued. In spite of all his nonsense Firbank succeeded in arousing in him admiration for his genuine interest in literature and the arts, and respect for his seriousness. On the few future occasions when they met Harold's revulsion and respect were revived. These conflicting emotions led him to analyse and revise his puritanical prejudices against artists and poets which had been implanted in him by his ambassadorial upbringing and the highly conventional curriculum of Wellington.

In the summer vacation of 1906 Harold paid his only visit to Sligger Urquhart's famous Chalet des Mélèzes at St. Gervais-les-Bains in the Haute Savoie. Situated above Forclaz on a col overlooking the valley of Chamonix, the Chalet had been built by Sligger's father in 1864. It was the place his son loved best in the world. And consequently it became the place where he delighted to take his pupils and favourite undergraduates on reading parties. The privilege was a highly coveted one. At the Chalet conditions were ascetic, the regimen was strict, the food sparse, and the work strenuous. The work was only relieved by short, sharp walks up the mountain, and sparkling conversations in the twilight after supper. While Sligger was going round the world with Henry Martin in September of that year the Chalet caught fire and was burned to the ground. After the first shock Sligger rebuilt it, but it was not ready for re-occupation for a year or more.

In August Harold went on the first of several visits to Russia. Sir Arthur, having been the British Representative at the Algeciras Conference on Moroccan affairs from January to April, was now Ambassador at St. Petersburg. It was to be his final post abroad, and to last until 1910. In the life of his father[21] Harold described the British Embassy in Petersburg as

> an immense though low-storeyed house, washed in blood red. It stood at the corner of the Troitzky bridge, and the trams would ring their

BALLIOL AND CRAMMING 1904-7

bells wildly as the horses galloped up the incline. The reception rooms were on the top floor, and the staircase (scarlet and white) ran up to them through a series of pile-carpeted landings graced with Empire statues. The bedrooms were in the mezzanine. The saloons above were large and hung with red, blue and yellow damask ... Outside the Neva rushed with twisted waters; beyond, the fortress of St. Peter and St. Paul thrust a slim gold pencil into the sky. The bridge cut the view diagonally; it was decorated with cast-iron eagles painted green, and pylons of polished granite. When the windows were opened, the smell of Russia – that strange smell of leather and fish-oil – would puff into the silken drawing-room as if the scent of blood.

Sir Arthur was immensely impressed by the Czar's Minister of Internal Affairs, P. A. Stolypin, who soon after the Ambassador's arrival succeeded Goremykin as Minister President. He was a frequent guest at Sir Arthur's luncheon table. Tall and black-bearded with cold white hands, Stolypin would explain how, upon the basis of a contented peasantry, the Russian Duma could be reconstituted as a stable parliamentary system. Even Trotsky was to call him a great man. All might have been well with Russia had he not been murdered in 1911. As it was, before this date repeated attempts were made upon his life, because his firm and repressive policy made him detested by all revolutionaries.

On the afternoon of the 25th August 1906 the Socialist Revolutionaries despatched a small band of their number to Stolypin's villa on the Apothecary's Island. They tried to penetrate the house but were stopped by an aide-de-camp in the hall. One of them threw on the marble floor a portfolio packed with bombs. The explosion echoed across to the city and the suburbs beyond. Twenty-five people were killed and thirty wounded. The front of the villa collapsed, burying two of Stolypin's children, who were seriously injured. M. Stolypin, who happened to be in his study on the far side of the villa, escaped unhurt, although hurled to the ground by the blast. The assassins were blown to pieces. On hearing what had happened Sir Arthur told Harold to drive at once with a chasseur to enquire after the Stolypin family, and to offer assistance to his friend. They were allowed to pass through the police cordon. The dust of the explosion was still hanging on the air. The trees surrounding the villa were snapped into fragments. Curtains from bedroom windows were twined around the leafless branches. In the roadway were the shattered remains of a landau and a pair of horses. Stretcher-bearers passed and repassed, and Red Cross motor cars bore the dead and dying to hospital.

It was during this visit to Russia that Lady Nicolson suggested to Harold that he might spend three weeks at Yalta instructing the eighteen-year-old son of her great friend, Princess Youssoupoff, in the ways of Oxford

University, to which the young Prince Félix aspired to go. Young Prince Félix was spoilt and wayward, but extremely handsome. He liked dressing up as a woman in his mother's clothes and wearing her magnificent jewelry. Harold, with his puritanical disapproval of effeminacy (his Kipling side), pursed his lips and declined. In later life he deeply regretted the missed opportunity of making friends with the strikingly good-looking prince. For when he met him after the Revolution he found him charming and keenly interested in the arts. Prince Youssoupoff was above all things a great patriot, who never regretted the Rasputin incident and the grisly part he played in it. Having lost fabulous riches and possessions in Russia he never complained. Rather he claimed to have found his redemption through his sufferings.

With a first-hand experience of violence and carnage in mind Harold returned to Oxford for his third and last year. By now he had left his rooms in College and was sharing lodgings with 'Snatch' Hugessen and 'Crooked' (R.O.W.) Pemberton,[22] a sturdy, ungainly but sympathetic companion, whose distinction was to be President of Balliol's third and most exclusive club, the Dervorguilla. Harold wrote straight off to Sligger, now half way round the world, telling him all the gossip about his friends, and saying how difficult it was to pick up the threads after a three months absence. Of the "freshers", most of whom seemed dull, there were

> [Julian] Grenfell whom I think patronising, [Charles] Lister whom I like, [Ronnie] Knox who frightens me, [V.A.] Barrington-Kennett, with the face of an archangel, & [T.C.] Strachey who bores me. There is a fellow called Jack Horner whom I like very much and who is good looking though Crooked says he is getting 'baned' in college; and I do recognize that he is slightly a 'poseur'. He and Strachey have Puvis de Chavannes and Aubrey Beardsley & the Birth of Venus & that sort of thing in their rooms.[23]

In this short paragraph Harold makes fingernail comments upon some of the freshmen who were to constitute one of Oxford's most famous generation, those pre-1914 young men of exceptional distinction, intelligence, nobility and heroism, the greater number of whom were to die in action in the First World War.

On the 16th January 1907 Harold wrote to Sligger from an address in Paris, 174 rue de la Pompe, which will be familiar to readers of *Some People* as the crammer presided over by Jeanne de Hénaut. He was only there for a few days, prospecting and doubtless being prospected by the alarming lady who ran that establishment for young Englishmen of family intending to enter the Diplomatic Service. He begged Sligger

BALLIOL AND CRAMMING 1904-7

to find out what the subjects for the forthcoming final exams at Oxford were likely to be. By now exams were looming large on his horizon. His English literature, he said, was going all right although Pope filled him with loathing. Within ten days of writing to Sligger Harold went off to Frankfurt.

In the Lent term he met yet another prominent member of the Julian Grenfell-Charlie Lister group, or 'The Corrupt Coterie' as they liked to call themselves in reaction from the preciousness of the 'Souls' of their parents' generation. On the 11th March he told Sligger.

> There is a new person called Shaw-Stuart[24] [sic] appeared, who is most delightful, with a face curiously ugly & unattractive – which destroys your theory of peoples appearances being an index to their character.

Patrick Shaw-Stewart became indeed the very heart and soul of the Corrupt Coterie. He was the most desirable company, also tolerant and affectionate. With all the maddening easy graces of the Etonian, this avowed hedonist was a distinguished scholar, winning Firsts in Mods and Greats.★ No wonder he was beloved by divinities of his own generation like Lady Diana Manners, and even divinities of the older generation like that Queen of the Souls, Lady Desborough. Shaw-Stewart was ambitious to make money and by the age of twenty-five had become a Managing Director of Baring Brothers. He was killed in 1917.

Harold was fascinated but not accepted by the members of the Corrupt Coterie. Their panache appealed to his more timorous nature, but their raffishness and heartiness he could not share. Besides, most of them were two years younger than he was. Furthermore, they were Etonians, of whose precocious man-of-the-worldliness he was curiously envious and, because of his Wellington indoctrination, slightly disapproving.

In the Lent vacation Harold went as a paying guest to Blois. The household of Monsieur Gervais in the rue Maurice Saxe was typical of a French professor's family. Harold would have found it bearable had there not been another English youth in the house, 'with whom,' he wrote to his parents, 'I have to be somewhat cold, or I would speak nothing but English all day.'[25] And there follows a passage which illustrates his already keen power of observation and whimsical style of writing.

> There is the usual linoleum tablecloth with a pink check and a sponge to wipe it after meals; the usual salon which is never used but on grand occasions, with gilt mirrors and a coloured photograph of the 1900 Exhibition; and above all the usual bad rears with its hook and eye lock and its old catalogues of the Magazin du Louvre.

★ *Greats* (i.e. Classics and Philosophy): *Mods* or Classical Honour Moderations (i.e. Classical Languages and Literature).

He deprecated the family being so anti-clerical. He was shocked by the seventeen-year-old daughter of the house saying that Christ was the natural son of a Roman centurion. 'It is absolutely revolting.' He was bored by the Renaissance châteaux of the Loire, 'with their eternal Pompeian mouldings' and the beastly ubiquitous salamander. It was awful that next term was to be his last. He was delighted that Sligger was coming to Blois to spend a day with him.

The last summer term came and went far too quickly, as terms at the university do, because they are so short. Harold did not get a good degree. It was a Third in Greats. To the end of his life he bore the ignominy with shame and remorse. He admitted that he never worked hard enough at Balliol. It was only during his last term he learned that it was essential to take trouble. But he realised that, idle though he had been at Oxford, he was nevertheless learning how to learn through a tentative stage of sensuous and cerebral enquiry. By merely mooching around and reading the backs of Sligger's books he was titillating an elementary taste for literature. What he most bitterly regretted about his university career was that everything nice might come back again, but Oxford never. In a speech to the Master, Fellows and Men of Balliol in November 1930 he admitted that he almost hated Balliol while he was there; that he enjoyed life far more after going down; but that he was happier with his Balliol friends after leaving Oxford than when he first met them. He could not make out what it was that made him love Balliol more as the years went by. Was it that Balliol paid tribute to intelligence? The freemasonry of intellect formed a bond among Balliol men which he had come upon in all parts of the world.

What made Balliol unique in Harold Nicolson's day was, he was convinced, the superior quality of its dons, their careful casualness of instruction; their emphasis on the disgrace of indolence; their horror of intellectual vulgarity and pretension; and the liberalism which they practised. All these principles had immense influence upon Harold's character. In particular the last sowed in his fertile mind a seed which grew to determine his political beliefs and shape his intellectual independence. When in 1953 he was made an Honorary Fellow of Balliol he regarded it as the greatest honour he had won in his life. Cyril Bailey, his old tutor, in writing to congratulate him, said he little thought of this distant association while they sat side by side going through Latin verse together in the first decade of the century. But of course the don to whom he owed more than any other was Sligger Urquhart. Their relationship was the happiest possible between don and undergraduate. From the first Harold treated Sligger with deep respect, affection and intimacy. Sligger in his turn treated Harold with rare understanding of his remarkable qualities, as yet

BALLIOL AND CRAMMING 1904-7

dormant, with gentle irony and with encouragement. Until his death he remained Harold's mentor. In his very last letter of August 1934 he was giving him counsel on the training of the will. He acknowledged touchingly how kindly Harold had always felt towards him. This was as far as he allowed his sentiment to run. On the envelope Harold, who was himself a sentimental man, scribbled in red ink, 'My last letter from dear dear Sligger.' In the brief note accompanying the bundle of Harold's letters, labelled succinctly, 'Nic', which Sligger returned to him, was the sentence: 'They were really excellently written when you were up & when you were working for the F.O.'

In a broadcast delivered in 1951 Harold said: 'Balliol is, I suppose, a rather bleak and certainly an ugly college, but it remains dearer to me than any institution on this earth.'

3

PREPARATIONS FOR THE DIPLOMATIC SERVICE, 1907–1909

FAR from discouraging him Harold's modest university degree spurred him to greater efforts. He knew exactly what he wanted out of life and was determined to achieve it. He would spend the next two years mostly on the continent. He stayed two to three months at a time with different foreign families, in Germany, France and Italy, perfecting his languages and cramming feverishly. But before embarking on this prolonged and intensive course, he went for a short respite to St. Petersburg in August 1907. His father, who in spite of his affection for his youngest son did not have a high opinion of his abilities, was not surprised by his only getting a Third in Greats and certainly did not expect him to pass the Diplomatic Examination. It was therefore a diffident and somewhat abashed youth who found himself the passive resident of an embassy to a vast and inscrutable country in the throes of revolutionary change. Over St. Petersburg brooded a sense of anxiety and oppression. The nerves of the diplomatic corps, in which the British Ambassador was a key figure, were on edge, and it was excusable that men in responsible positions should be alert, wary and apprehensive.

There was much talk in the Chancery, when Harold arrived, of spies and burglars breaking into embassies after dark and stealing secret documents. One night Harold was awakened by the sound of a sharp instrument grazing his bedroom door, which gave on to the archive room. Quietly he crept out of his bedroom, and woke his father and the Resident Secretary, Nevile Henderson, from their slumbers. The Ambassador, a frail figure in a dressing-gown, kept guard at one entrance to the Chancery while the Secretary, armed with a life preserver, stalked his prey from another direction. Sir Arthur, an impatient man with a love of adventure, strayed from his post and stealthily crept in the direction of the Secretary. In the darkness they met head on. Henderson seized Sir Arthur by the throat, shouting, 'Animal, je vous tiens!' and was about to deliver a crushing blow with the life preserver when Harold, fumbling for the electric light switch, turned it on. To his consternation he saw his father struggling in the hands of the Secretary. Much embarrassment was caused by the unwonted behaviour of Nevile Henderson towards his chief whom

THE DIPLOMATIC SERVICE 1907-9

he greatly revered and to whom he was devoted. On further search it was revealed that the Embassy cat had got locked into the archive room.

At the beginning of November Harold was sharing digs at 115 Jermyn Street with Tata Bertie, whose term of duty in Petersburg does not seem to have lasted long. He had been before the Diplomatic Board, of which Sir Charles Hardinge, then Permanent Under-Secretary of State, was in the chair.[1] Hardinge put to Harold questions about Wellington. Harold thought he had not acquitted himself well, and had probably been beaten by Tata Bertie and Jack Leven, which, if that turned out to be the case, would be his conclusive humiliation. In mid-December he was writing to Sligger from 174 rue de la Pompe, Paris, Mlle Jeanne de Hénaut's apartment on the fifth floor, approached by a wheezing and protesting lift. Harold had a top room which looked east and west, and north and south. He had with him Rajah his dog, a bad cold, and a pair of Sandow dumbbells for 'physical arrogance.' The whole apartment could not contain more than three students at the same time. On this occasion the two other English youths were Lord Eustace Percy,[2] extremely intelligent, correct and rather humourless, and Harold Handaside Duncan,[3] the chief contributor to the composite portrait of J. D. Marstock in *Some People*. Jeanne de Hénaut held poor Duncan in utmost contempt. He was obtuse, commonplace and hearty, and his qualities the very antithesis of what she admired in the nimble-witted, intellectual and patrician students she was accustomed to, like 'M. le Baron Kennard[4] qui était d'une élegance, mais d'une élegance...'

Harold Nicolson's description of Jeanne de Hénaut, with her brown hair like a wig, parted in the middle over a square visage, her two dresses of faded gaberdine, her perpetual smoking of hand-rolled cigarettes, her stained fingers, her snobbishness, her beastliness to her slatternly old mother, her love of cats, and her redeeming will-power is a masterpiece of character study. Her system of teaching was based on sheer faith and legend. By keeping before her students the achievements of past pupils she inspired them with fanatical concentration. At the rue de la Pompe these upper-class English youths, living in conditions that were ascetic and squalid, worked with an intensity that amazed them when they recalled it. Duff Cooper, who was also a pupil of Jeanne, confirmed her unique powers in teaching the French language.

> The dominance of her personality was extraordinary [he wrote]. Unruly young men like myself, recalcitrant to discipline, never dared to infringe the unwritten laws of her establishment. Dinner was at seven. After a meagre repast conversation was always continued until nine, she herself doing most of the talking. Then the young men retired to their rooms, like monks to their cells, having been encouraged to work late.[5]

On the 9th March 1908 Harold was writing to Sligger from Frankfurt-am-Main.

> I am working here at this language, and feel more grateful for the Norman Conquest than ever – & more sick of Goethe, & Bismarck, & Maximilian Harden [a Berlin journalist, founder and editor of the weekly *Die Zukunft*, and fearless exposer of court scandals] & Oscar Wilde & other German national heroes, than I have ever been before.

In April he left Frankfurt for Torre Péllice, a large village a few kilometres west of Pinerolo in Piedmont, in order to learn Italian. Torre Péllice was full of educational establishments, both lay and religious. Harold stayed in a college for Protestant pastors, and lived with the director, Professor Falchi. He described his ways as being 'gentlemanly.' Harold's room was like a barn, with odd bits of furniture disposed inconsequently about the boards, as if someone had been playing chess with them. He liked Torre Péllice for its isolated and eerie situation in a valley, shoved as it were into the lower spurs of Monte Viso, which separated Piedmont from France. At the approach of Easter Harold threw his books and good resolutions to the winds. With one suitcase and a volume of Keats he went off to stay with Italian friends called Mazzuchi, in Turin. Signor Mazzuchi was very rich though only three years Harold's senior. He lived in the utmost luxury.

> My bedroom [Harold wrote to his mother[6]] was upholstered in green brocade and had a delightful balcony with a view of all the Alps from Viso to Monte Rosa; on the dressing-table were cut glass bottles of Hippomaea, and there were telephones, armchairs, & reading lamps at every turn; there was also a framed certificate from the Pope to say that Madame Mazzuchi and her near connections had received a special dispensation from all the sins for four calendar years; and as I was not positive whether this gratifying permission extended to her guests, I did not steal the Hippomaea bottles. There was a bathroom next door which made me feel like Poppaea.

He knew that this account of three sybaritic days in a Papist household would scare his Ulster-born mother, with her innate suspicion of luxury and hatred of papistry, out of her wits.

In September Harold was back in the rue de la Pompe, bored stiff. In October he was back in England, and spent one agreeable weekend with Crooked Pemberton at Westgate-on-Sea. He became a member of the St. James's Club, from which address he wrote that he was reading political science at a crammer's, 129 Adelaide Road, Hampstead, commuting there daily. Examination fever was already afflicting him. In December he went to St. Petersburg for a long Christmas recess.

Over Petersburg the skies were leaden. In the streets the dirty snow was blowing about among the tramlines. Mr. Oscar Browning 'of Cantab infamy',[7] as Harold referred to that provocative scholar and over-impressionable lover of young men, was staying at the Embassy and boasting about his friendship with Lord Curzon. There were occasional slap-up luncheons and dinners given by the Nicolsons on the top floor, in the large oval dining-room, hung with rich damask, and overlooking an airless courtyard. There were endless supper parties to which Harold was invited by Russian acquaintances. He was disgusted by the inanity of Petersburg society, the utter fatuity of the *beau monde*, whose clothes flowed in unending streams from Paris and London; of the pretentious talk of the literary ladies; and the anachronistic and reactionary views of the political hosts and hostesses. The evening entertainments seemed interminable. At dawn one stepped out of the heated palaces into a sleigh. A chasseur wearing a cocked hat with feathers tucked a fur rug round one's knees. A coachman in a quilted coat, his beard dripping with icicles, drove one home at spanking speed. The cold was something which Harold had never imagined, and which he intensely disliked. The temperature out of doors was always below zero in winter. One took precautions of course – mufflers, little round seal-skin caps and snow-boots. One rubbed one's nose from time to time to make sure that frostbite was not setting in.

> But always at the back of one's mind there was the glowing certainty that once indoors a radiant warmth would spread through all one's limbs. During the summer months the carts would rattle on the cobbles of the streets, piled high with logs from the surrounding forests. In the courtyards of the houses vast pyramids of logs would be erected until they reached the level of the second storey. In October a man would come to affix the double windows, filling the window ledge between them with a neat layer of cotton-wool. In the walls and flooring of each room were little orifices, known as *bouches de feu*, through which the hot blast of the lower furnace would billow into the rooms.[8]

Harold went to hear Alexander Iswolsky, the Foreign Minister, make a big speech in the Duma. 'I was perched up in the diplomatic loge with all the scents of Paris répandus around me – and below me, the semi-circle of green writing tables.' M. Iswolsky was a dapper little man, dressed in a tight suit from Savile Row. He wore a pearl pin, an eyeglass, white spats and strutted on little lacquer feet. He turned a short neck above a high stiff, white collar, and spoke in a cultured, rasping voice. On this solemn occasion he was distracted by anxiety lest Russia be dragged into war by Austria's intransigent treatment of Serbia, and neither Germany nor Great Britain would lend Russia their support.

For the greater part of each day, the austere silence of the Embassy was broken only by the peal of electric bells in the Chancery and shouts of merriment from the schoolroom. The shouts came from his sister Gwen, now a buxom thirteen-year-old. Just as Harold, the youngest of three boys, had been spoilt by his mother, so Gwen, who was an afterthought and the only girl, was adored by her father. In his eyes she could do no wrong, and the busy Ambassador could never see enough of her.[9] Harold, sensing that his sibling, to whom he was devoted, needed taking down a peg, would tease her mercilessly. Lady St. Levan has recalled how one afternoon he laid her out like a corpse on the Embassy drawing-room floor, and lit candles round her and produced calling cards turned down at the corners, as was customary in Russia when paying respects to a deceased person in the house. He then attached wires to her arms and legs, and telling her that she would be electrocuted if she moved a fraction of an inch, left her. It was only when the Ambassadress came into the room with some guests after luncheon that the prostrate and terrified child was released. Because Harold always mocked himself he could never understand why others minded being ragged by him.

He did not much care for Russia or the Russians. He found the Slav temperament baffling, the Slav values shifting. By his philosophical standards Russians seemed to diminish the value of what he regarded as important things, and to exaggerate the importance of what he termed incidental ones.

After a three months' hard slog at German in Hanover and Wiesbaden, Harold moved to Siena. From the Via Stalloreggi 10 he wrote to Sligger[10] in a very low mood.

> It was a consolation to find something so human [a letter from Sligger] to greet me after so chill a revulsion into medievalism as is a night arrival in Siena. Of course I know it is dreadful but to arrive in, at night, and after a long journey, I fear I prefer the XXth century. You see it is depressing to drive through a street like that of some dead city – & to draw up before a house with gratings like a Moorish prison – and to enter a stone hall like the Escorial – and in one's room to have a tile floor and a picture of Garibaldi in a smoking cap – and one's bed in an alcove with a little mat to stand on – and a candle which gutters like a XVII century one in a brass candlestick.

THE DIPLOMATIC SERVICE 1907-9

And then in a flash all was changed. It was typical of Harold to shift from darkness, where he dwelt so seldom and for such brief intervals, to immediate light. The same letter continued:

> But this morning there was sunshine behind my shutters, and when they were opened two bright warm squares upon my tiles – & on the table coffee and rolls, and those brown roofs and blossoms from the window – and the distant sound of bells and an Omar Khayyam left by some former victim – so that by ten I was myself again.

Besides, the day was enlivened by the arrival of two friends from Balliol, Charles Travis Clay ('less spotty and more Italianate than of yore') and Druce Robert Brandt.[11] The three of them strolled through the city gates and sat on the grass and looked at the great cathedral growing out of the house tops, and at the hills beyond, and caught lizards, and had tea and large cakes; and so back to Harold's barrack-like room which already seemed to have assumed some individuality.

Every morning he walked across the Cathedral square, down some steps, and knocked at a sinister little door of the house of his teacher. Don Orlandi, a delightful old priest, lived in cool rooms smelling of violets and incense, and adorned with one framed photograph of the Martyrs Memorial in Oxford. He wore Balliol socks and did not approve of d'Annunzio, which Harold found rather a relief. And every evening Harold would pass through the red gates into the hush of the country outside. He would read Shelley and Carducci, about whom he was wildly enthusiastic, as about all things Italianate and Tuscan. 'Even the cuckoos here speak with a Tuscan accent.'

By June he was back in Paris under the wing of 'the blatant lady of the North,' Jeanne de Hénaut. This was his last cramming lap and he was resigning himself to the fate which in August would decide the future for him. He was not a little disturbed by the arrival of Eustace Percy, who was so far above him, he imagined, in all subjects, and made him feel thoroughly ashamed of his own shortcomings. Harold always felt a little inferior before Eustace Percy's noble idealism, deep religious convictions, knight-in-shining-armour soul, and high-minded scruples. He begged Sligger for some encouragement in the ordeal so shortly to confront him. 'Say in your letter that I am really a very intelligent young man, only that at Oxford I did not attain to a complete realisation of my own potentialities.'

On the 19th June 1909 he was, by some odd process of the Foreign Office machine, nominated as Attaché. In August he sat for the competitive examination of the Diplomatic Service. He never forgot the nervous anxieties he went through, and when thirty-five years later he had to lecture in the very same room in which he was examined, he recalled the exact spots at which he sat at his desk, and the invigilator sat at his. When the examination was over he rejoined his parents in St. Petersburg for a well-earned holiday, and awaited the result.

Again it was to Sligger that on the 22nd September he announced the joyful news from the British Embassy.

> Et in Olympia ego, my dear Sligger – a 2nd too, which is a real triumph. I have this moment got the telegram ... And what unwonted excitement for this official domicile – my father casting off his ambassadorial dignity and behaving like a schoolboy – and my mother in tears of joy.

Harold had every reason to feel pleased with himself. Whereas Eustace Percy passed in first, and Tata Bertie third, Harold came second. In fact Eustace Percy and Harold Nicolson obtained higher marks than had ever been won by previous candidates. Most gratifying of all was Sir Arthur's jubilation, for he had never for a moment expected his son to pass. He was bowled over by the excitement and surprise.

At last Harold had won his spurs. At the age of twenty-three he was called to his duties as a junior clerk in the Foreign Office in Whitehall. He was master of French and German and had a good smattering of Italian and Spanish. He was to improve the last language two years hence. He was a much-travelled young man, with all the advantages of a cosmopolitan background, but none of the advantages of a settled home. His interests were focused on the career which he had chosen as a child, and from which he had not deviated. He had already developed a lively epistolary style, without as yet having any ambition to write. He was worldly-wise and yet childlike; sensitive and yet bluff; full of fun, with an irrepressible tendency to tease. Without being strictly handsome, he was cherubic, and very lively.

We do not hear much of him during the two remaining months of 1909. Hugh Walpole mentioned meeting 'young Harold Nicolson just down from Oxford' at a dinner party given by Robert Ross at the Reform Club. The other guests were Max Beerbohm, H. G. Wells, Arthur Clutton-Brock and Reginald (Reggie) Turner. Walpole was captivated by their generous and lovable host, who had been the loyal supporter and good angel of Oscar Wilde after his fall.

Harold was launching himself upon London's intellectual world, and

THE DIPLOMATIC SERVICE 1907-9

meeting literary men and women, some of whom were to become his close friends. On the 22nd December he went to Russia for five days' Christmas leave. It was to be his last visit to that disturbed and disturbing country. He was never to return; and the next year Sir Arthur was recalled from his exacting post at St. Petersburg.

4

FOREIGN OFFICE, SPAIN AND CONSTANTINOPLE, 1910–1912

WHEN Harold Nicolson first entered the Foreign Office the junior clerks had practically no clerical assistance. Before 1908 there were no typists in Whitehall, and after that date only a small pool, very few of whom could take down in shorthand. The junior clerks were, it is true, allowed to open envelopes and look out previous papers relevant to the letters which they spread on the desks of their immediate bosses. Even so, all letters and papers of a confidential nature arrived in special green jackets and had to be submitted in that condition after being merely registered by the junior clerks. Most of Harold's time was occupied by subsidiary duties such as indexing, deciphering telegrams and despatching to Cabinet Ministers the pouches in which the Foreign Office papers were contained, and eternally copying and filing. Only gradually were the junior clerks entrusted with more interesting work, such as drafting correspondence for their superiors. In the ministries and embassies overseas, no clerical pool of any kind existed. The Third Secretaries spent their working hours deciphering and registering as well as typing. These humdrum duties left them with little opportunity to learn the language of the country in which they were stationed, or to acquire political knowledge beyond the Chancery walls. And it must be remembered that during their first two years' service they received no salary at all. The work to which Harold first addressed himself at the New Year of 1910 and which occupied him throughout the year was therefore monotonous and unremunerative.

Apart from the Permanent Under-Secretary of State, Sir Charles Hardinge, who was to be replaced by Sir Arthur Nicolson in July, the two dominating personalities of the Foreign Office were Sir Eyre Crowe and William Tyrrell. Crowe[1] was then head of the Western Department, and was to become Assistant Under-Secretary of State in 1912. He was to play an active part in reforming the Foreign Office so as to give junior members increased responsibility. He was the perfect type of British civil servant, industrious, loyal, expert and accurate. Harold had the highest regard for his qualities and grew devoted to him. He accepted Crowe's principles of British policy as the basis of his own. They were that, since Great Britain was a small and overpopulated island, dependent

SPAIN AND CONSTANTINOPLE 1910-12

upon imports from overseas, she was forced to maintain maritime supremacy against all possible enemies; and to prevent coalitions against her, she must identify her policy with the primary interests of the majority of European powers. She must therefore be resolutely opposed to the domination of Europe by any one power.

Tyrrell[2] was at this time Private Secretary to the Foreign Secretary, Sir Edward Grey, whom he endeavoured somewhat officiously to spare all unnecessary worries. In consequence he took upon himself responsibilities which he should have referred to his chief. He was clever and devious, with a remarkable capacity for avoiding diplomatic difficulties. He disliked both Sir Arthur Nicolson and Harold as much as Crowe liked them. He happened to be married to Sligger's sister, Margaret Urquhart. Crowe and Tyrrell had one thing in common, a partial German upbringing. Crowe's mother and wife were German; and Tyrrell had been educated at Bonn University where he took a high degree.

If the nature of the work Harold had to do in the Foreign Office was humble, the hours were not exacting. The world was still at peace. The British Empire was at the height of its prosperity and prestige. The King-Emperor Edward VII was still reigning. Society was in full swing. It was a good moment for a personable young man to embark upon a diplomatic career, if he was well connected, good-looking, clever and amusing. In later life Harold often stated that, in spite of the hypocrisy, cant and wrong values prevailing in Edwardian society, the best thing which the age provided was the country house-party. It gave a young man the opportunity of meeting and getting to know in ideal surroundings distinguished elder statesmen like Balfour, writers like Henry James, and artists like Sargent. Harold's pocket diary for this year mentions little more than strings of names of people met, houses visited – Kirtlington Park, Stratfield Saye ('quite dreadful'), the Vyne – musical comedies attended – the Follies, *The Dollar Princess* three times – skating at Olympia, dancing at Roehampton, and bridge parties. Most of his spare time from society was spent with his school and Oxford cronies, Reggie Cooper, Gerry Villiers, Gerald Tyrrwhitt and Tommy Lascelles, quietly dining at their clubs and gossiping afterwards. The diaries do not vouchsafe much. They are guarded. He makes no mention of the scandal which set all tongues wagging that month, the Sackville Case which was being heard in the High Court. He must have read about it in the newspapers and heard talk of the extraordinary Lady Sackville, who was contesting her brother's and, incidentally, her own claim to legitimacy, in order to retain her husband's and so her right to a title and Knole, one of England's most historic and largest country houses.

The names of two new friends, a woman and a man, crop up repeatedly during the first six months of 1910. For both of them Harold's feelings were romantic. Lady Eileen Wellesley[3] was a sister of his friend Lord Gerald,[4] and daughter of the 4th Duke of Wellington. All that the diary tells us is that he met her at weekends, enjoyed walking with her and exchanging ghost stories. He sat in her studio while she painted and was invited to luncheon at Apsley House. For a short time the couple were unofficially engaged, but it does not seem that they were ever deeply in love.

Harold had met Archie Clark Kerr[5] at the British Embassy in Berlin on his last return journey from St. Petersburg. Clark Kerr was four years older than Harold, a gay, attractive Highlander, unconventional, very entertaining and good company. After seeing Pavlova at the Palace, Harold had supper with Archie at the Carlton. This was on the 3rd May. Next day's succinct entry was 'Frightfully depressed.' On the 6th he lunched with Archie, and in the evening had supper with him, again at the Carlton. Before they had finished eating the waiter approached their table and turned out the lights. 'The King,' he announced quietly, 'is dead.' The following day Archie left for Buenos Aires. Harold's single comment in the diary was 'Blinds down, etc.,' presumably referring to the King's death.

Being the junior clerk of the Foreign Office Harold was delegated by the Lord Chamberlain to bear-lead two representatives of the Haitian Republic at the King's funeral. It was the first diplomatic task assigned to him. He did not enjoy it. 'Take beastly niggers to F.O. and then round by Tower to see London,' he noted on the 19th May. And the next day, 'Pick niggers up at Cecil [Hotel] and take them down to Windsor for funeral. Very hot.' For some reason the Republic's two delegates hated one another and fought with fists for the right-hand seat in the carriage which drove them from the station to their Legation. This was Harold's culminating embarrassment, for he had had difficulty in preventing them bringing to the funeral the largest wreath of all time, made of coloured beads and ribbons, and in restraining one of them from wiping his face with a huge bandana handkerchief on entering the precincts of St. George's Chapel.

In June Harold learned to his sorrow that he was to be transferred from the Western to the Eastern Department. But outside the office there were to be compensations. The 29th of the month was, though he did not realise it at the time, a red-letter day, or rather, the red-letter day of his life. Having lunched at Apsley House where he admired Eileen Wellesley's dress *à la* Kitty Clive, he dined at Mrs. Stanley's house and went on to *The Speckled Band* afterwards. Anne Stanley was the wife of Admiral Victor Stanley, whose uncle the 15th Earl of Derby had married a Sackville-West. It was perhaps through this connection that Mrs. Stanley had

SPAIN AND CONSTANTINOPLE 1910-12

also invited that evening Lord and Lady Sackville and their eighteen-year-old daughter. Harold made no mention of the daughter's presence at the time, although years later he wrote in red ink against the entry, 'This was the first time I met Vita.' Vita remembered it well.

> He arrived late at a small dinner party before a play, very young and alive and charming, and the first remark I ever heard him make was, 'What fun!' when he was asked by his hostess to act as host. Everything was fun to his energy, vitality and buoyancy. I liked his irrepressible brown curls, his laughing eyes, his charming smile, and his boyishness. But we didn't become particular friends. I think he looked on me as more of a child than I actually was.[6]

Probably Harold did not feel at ease in the presence of this beautiful, tall girl, with large melancholy brown eyes and a reticent manner. It was the mother, triumphant after winning her case, whose forthcoming manner captivated him immediately. She took to Harold and invited him to Knole four days later.

He went with an Italian friend, Enrico, the Marchese Visconti Venosta,[7] who had been at Christ Church when Harold was at Balliol. At Knole there was a large luncheon party in the Great Hall, at which Mr. Asquith and Ellen Terry were present. A masque was held afterwards; and it poured with rain. But Harold enjoyed himself hugely, and the next morning walked round the house with his hostess – 'A jolly day.'

On the 19th July he met 'Vita West,' as he called her, at a dinner party; and again the following night at the Strathmores' ball. On the 6th August he paid a second visit to Knole and stayed the night. Next morning he read Lucretius in the rose garden and recorded that Vita West was in bed with influenza. On the 11th he returned to dine and sleep at Knole, and noted that Miss Grosvenor was present. She was Mrs. Algernon Grosvenor's daughter Rosamund, who although four years older than Vita had been an intimate friend since nursery days and was to play a prominent role in the extraordinary tangle of Vita's early love life.

At the end of September Sir Charles Hardinge left the Foreign Office in tears to become Viceroy of India; and his place as Permanent Under-Secretary of State was filled by Sir Arthur Nicolson. Thenceforth Harold was put into the delicate position of a subordinate in his father's office. He went to Knole several more times and the 5th November Vita addressed her first letter to him:

> My dear Mr. Harold, I have been asked to 'ask a man' to dine on Thursday with Mrs. Harold Pearson and go to a dance, so would you like to come?

The ungracious little note was preserved by its recipient, who was already beginning to pay attention to the strange, withdrawn girl reluctantly carrying out those social duties by which her mother set such store, and which meant so little to her.

Harold spent Christmas with his family. On Boxing Day he went to stay with the Sackvilles in the enormous white Villa Malet near Monte Carlo, which they had rented in November for several months. He picked up Archie Clark Kerr in Paris and the two of them took the train for the Riviera. Most of their short visit seems to have been spent in looking for suitable places to play golf. Nevertheless Harold and Vita's friendship developed. She described it as a rather childlike companionship.[8] She was very taken with the exuberance of his youth and the brilliance of his cleverness, which contrasted strikingly with her introverted manner and reservations. Of the two she was at this stage the more interested. He was the best playmate she had ever known. She did not fail to notice that when they spoke French together he once tutoyéed her. Yet when it came for him to say goodbye he did so without any apparent regret. She was rather hurt. They did not correspond or meet until the following September. Meanwhile Vita was left at the Villa Malet with Rosamund Grosvenor, whom Lady Sackville had invited to be with her daughter. It was during the rest of this winter and the spring of 1911 that Rosamund and Vita fell in love and had a passionate affair which, on Vita's part, was purely physical, for Rosamund, although she had a sweet nature, was not a clever girl and soon bored her. Unfortunately her adoption of Sackville expressions, her spaniel-like dependence and her too ready submission to hurt feelings provoked Vita to treat her first casually and then cruelly.

On the 2nd February 1911 Harold Nicolson was appointed Attaché to the British Embassy at Madrid. The Ambassador since 1906 was Sir Maurice de Bunsen, a grandson of Baron de Bunsen, the well-loved Prussian Minister in London from 1841 to 1845, and his English wife. This good-looking, courteous diplomatist of fearless honesty enjoyed the confidence of King Alfonso XIII and Queen Victoria Eugénie. He was highly commended by the Foreign Office for his dignity and discretion in Madrid, where in 1911 and 1912 his unofficial mediation at the invitation of both parties in the dispute between France and Spain over Morocco, was triumphant.

During his brief spell in Madrid Harold renewed his acquaintance with the country which he had first known during his father's ambassadorship. He attended receptions at the royal palace, and was amazed by the tradi-

SPAIN AND CONSTANTINOPLE 1910-12

tional ceremonial still observed by the sovereigns. They would be seated on the great thrones of Aragon and Castille,

> Raised high upon a dais, each step to which was flanked by a golden lion pawing a golden globe, [the King and Queen] would assume an impression of being unaware that there were people around them. They would gaze with vacant eyes upon the clouds that drifted, white upon blue, beyond the great windows, down from Guadarrama towards the south. The grandees of Spain were grouped behind them: the diplomatists, embassy by embassy, were aligned with their backs to the windows: along the avenue thus left in front of the throne, the Ministers, the officers of State and finally the members of the Cortes filed in slow procession, bowing to their sovereigns as they passed. These salutations were not returned. The eyes of Alfonso and Victoria Eugénie continued to gaze with languid inattention at the floating clouds.[9]

This majestic impassivity, this hierophantic inattention, was deliberate and drilled. The moment the procession was over the young King and Queen would descend from their eminence, and with charm and animation do the 'circle', chatting and laughing gaily with their guests.

In June Harold's attachéship was brought to a sudden and ignominious end. He became ill. Years later he confessed to a friend,[10]

> I had (I really blush to state) gonorrhoea. It all came from Spain and the effect of Andalusia and a desire to establish my sex . . .

For five long weeks he underwent treatment. He was obliged to explain the trouble to his father, who in his wisdom took the matter well. He also confided in Sligger Urquhart, who expressed sympathy, adding, 'but as you philosophically say, perhaps the lesson has been valuable.' The only tangible object that Harold brought back from Spain was a worm-eaten effigy of Saint Barbara, which he gave to Vita. It accompanied them everywhere during their married life, even on the expedition into the Bakhtiari mountains of Persia in 1927. Harold never had occasion to return to Spain before the outbreak of the Civil War, and once General Franco was firmly entrenched he made a resolution not to set foot in the country so long as the Falangist régime lasted.[11] The Caudillo outlasted him. But the illness Harold contracted in Spain remained a bitter memory.

While he was recovering in London he resumed his former contacts with the Sackville family. Vita remembered him at Knole in early September 'as rather a pathetic figure wrapped up in an Ulster on a warm summer day, who was able to walk slowly round the garden with me.'[12] On the 12th of that month he was formally transferred back to the

Foreign Office. He soon recovered his strength and spirits. Before the end of the year he was nominated a Third Secretary and passed an examination in International Law. He stayed at Knole for Christmas and again for the New Year. It was then that he fell in love with Vita.

Harold Nicolson's courtship of Vita Sackville-West may appear to the majority of normal human beings so unconventional and strange as hardly to be natural, just as their married life, which as their younger son has shown us proved to be one of the most successful ever known, broke all the accepted rules of orthodox matrimony.[13] But the first thing to bear in mind is that Harold and Vita were not normal people. They were both far more homosexual than heterosexual, a state of affairs in the first two decades of this century that could not be acknowledged or even discussed in the sort of circles into which they were born and in which they moved. They did not even admit to one another what each knew to be his and her proclivity at the time of their courtship, although Vita – not Harold – was tormented by the knowledge of it. We should not however assume that their engagement and marriage were based on deception. Both supposed in January 1912, when he was but twenty-five and she not quite twenty, that their tastes would change in the course of their marriage and the growth of their mutual love. In their case these suppositions did not work out, even though their mutual love waxed stronger and stronger with the years. In fact it was because their marriage became totally divorced from the physical while based upon the same cerebral interests that it endured so as to become one of the idyllic sagas of our century.

When Harold jotted down in his diary under the 1st January 1912 the terse entry, 'See New Year in at Knole in the courtyard. Play golf with Rubens & Lord Sackville. A jolly day,' one wonders how alive he was to the dark undercurrents coursing this way and that within the ancient stone walls of that haunted palace. He certainly was alive to the necessity of quickly making his declaration to the daughter of the house, for on that very morning he learned that he was to be transferred from the Foreign Office to Constantinople as a Third Secretary with a salary of £250 a year and would be leaving England at the end of three weeks.

The Rubens with whom Harold played golf that jolly day was Walter, 'a bit of a bounder and low bred,' and the husband of Olive, also a guest at Knole, who was to become, if she was not already, the mistress of Vita's father, Lionel 3rd Lord Sackville. 'The Rubens lady,' as Vita called her, was tall and good-looking, gentle and affectionate, and probably without

SPAIN AND CONSTANTINOPLE 1910-12

guile. She had a beautiful voice and sang in a concert held at Knole the following day. It was partly on her account that Lord and Lady Sackville's marriage finally broke down in 1919. Already Lord Sackville was much in love with Olive. But if he was tired of his wife he remained devoted to his daughter (his 'Mar'* as he called her) and had little collusive jokes with her behind her mother's back. He had a wry sense of humour, was shrewd, cynical, and yet unashamedly lowbrow. He teased Vita for her love of literature and her liking for intellectual people. 'Of course,' he once wrote to her about some simple friend of his own, 'he is not a friend of Botticelli's, but does that matter? Cimabue himself would be a little out of place in the Paddock.' His pursuits were the time-honoured ones of the English patrician – the Turf, shooting and sailing. He had no illusions about his selfishness and self-indulgence, or the tightrope upon which he and his kind were precariously balancing.

As for Vita's mother, she was without knowing it on the verge of a crisis that was to affect her heart but little, and her purse a good deal. Meanwhile she and Harold had become allies in the household. Whereas he would busily paint the walls of Vita's new sitting-room in the morning, in the afternoon he confided in the mother his love for her daughter. It speaks well for Lady Sackville that she appreciated the young man whose only fortune was birth (a quality she valued), brain, charm and the prospect of a distinguished career; and that at this stage she did not discourage his advances. On the contrary she encouraged them, while warning him that her husband would not think him good enough for their daughter. Harold was only too well aware of it.

When he was back in London, going to his tailor, dining with Gerry Wellesley and Tata Bertie, and philandering with one of his intimates, a young man whom he called 'Uppie', suddenly without warning Sir John Murray Scott died of a heart attack. 'Seery', as he was known to the Sackville family, had for years been Lady Sackville's admirer and beau, and her inseparable companion. It is true her loyalty to him did not match his to her. For only five days before his death – admittedly unexpected – she was complaining bitterly to Vita about his 'bedint'† ways and beastly treatment of her. 'So all the good I have done for our sake, darling, is all undone.'[14] Is it possible that in a moment of exasperation he had threatened to cut her out of his will? Evidently she thought he had. She went on, 'I have simply not got the strength to fight that endless battle, and for a doubtful result ... I feel more *revoltée* than ever & sick to death of him and

* In Sackville parlance Mar meant 'little' and 'vulnerable.' VSW signed most of her letters to HN by this term. It was one of many words and expressions, first used by Lord and Lady Sackville and currently adopted by the Nicolsons.

† 'Bedint,' another Sackville expression, meaning 'common,' 'second-rate,' or 'vulgar.'

his bedint ways.' This was surely the expression of a scheming woman on the verge of defeat, a woman devoid of sincerity. Seery was, in spite of his unpatrician origins, a noble and generous character. The heir to half of Sir Richard Wallace's collection of superb French works of art, he was a a great connoisseur and immensely rich. Vita heard the news of his death while she was staying with her father at Burghley for a hunt ball. They were appalled, for Seery was beloved by them both. They caught the first train to London, and Vita in spite of her sorrow could not help wondering whether she would be allowed to go to the Hatfield ball the following night with Harold. Her fears were unnecessary. She was expecting a declaration from him, half wanting, half dreading it. People had been telling her that he was in love with her,

> which I didn't believe was true, but wished that I could believe it. I wasn't in love with him then – there was Rosamund – but I did like him better than anyone. I hoped that he would propose to me before he went away to Constantinople but felt diffident.[15]

Together Harold and Vita went on the 18th January to stay the night with the Francis Hydes at the Grove, Watford. At the Hatfield ball they danced together and during an interval, sitting in the attic on a guest's hat box, Harold

> asked me to marry him and I said I would. He was very shy and pulled the buttons one by one off his gloves; and I was frightened, and tried to prevent him from coming to the point. He didn't kiss me, but we sat rather bewildered over supper.[16]

Lady Sackville's entry in her diary next day that Vita assured her she had not accepted him, but would think it over, is not borne out by Vita's recollection of the incident. At all events on the 20th, which was the day of Seery's funeral, Harold was invited to Knole for the night to say goodbye. The following morning he walked with Vita, and in the afternoon talked to Lord and Lady Sackville. By now both her parents had misgivings. Vita was still very young, they explained, and probably didn't know her own mind (which was indeed the case, but for reasons unsuspected by them), and Harold was, in their eyes, neither rich nor grand enough for the beautiful and gifted heiress from Knole. Lady Sackville took matters in hand and laid down conditions. These were that no official engagement could be permitted for a year and a half. Vita must feel totally uncommitted. They must not write more than one letter a week to each other, and no terms like 'dearest' or 'darling' might be used. Lady Sackville

SPAIN AND CONSTANTINOPLE 1910-12

added privately in her diary that if the marriage were to come off, Harold 'would like V poor and to love him for himself, but I shall see to all that if I get poor Seery's money.' How often have prospective sons-in-law in the first flush of love not made protestations such as Harold's. And Lady Sackville, in a spontaneous burst of generosity, would stump up if Sir John Murray Scott's will, leaving nearly everything to her, worked out as she fervently hoped. That was still a dubious question.

Harold, having told his mother how matters stood between Vita and himself, said farewell to his parents and on the 24th left for Constantinople via Paris. In the railway carriage he read a letter received by the early post from Vita, beginning, 'My dear Harold', thanking him for the gift of Saint Barbara to be put in the niche of her sitting-room, and ending, 'Yours very sincerely, Vita Sackville-West.' Meanwhile Vita at Knole was confiding to her diary:

> I don't remember ever having been so unhappy. Only today have I begun to understand that I do not love him.[17]

From Paris Harold travelled to Constantinople by the Orient Express. In Sofia he was met at the station by his father's old Legation servant Zacchari, who kissed him on both cheeks. At the Turkish frontier he was met by Custance, the Embassy messenger, who accompanied him on the train to his destination. From the station he was driven in a victoria across the Galata Bridge and up through the winding streets to the British Embassy on the heights of Pera, then, as now, a district separated by water from the ancient city of Stamboul, with its seraglio and mosques. The British Embassy is a majestic building of Sir Charles Barry, and is a mixture of the Reform Club and Bridgewater House, standing within a spacious walled garden shaded by trees.

Harold's first day in Constantinople was spent being introduced to his colleagues in the Chancery. After this initiation he was sent to be interviewed by the Ambassador. Sir Gerard Lowther had been in office since 1908. His ambassadorship coincided with years of tremendous constitutional change in Turkey, revolutions and wars. Although never interested in Turkey's internal problems, Lowther's great endeavour, in which he succeeded fairly well, was to maintain the prestige of the British Empire in the Middle East. During the Balkan Wars he tried manfully to relieve the sufferings of Moslems and Christians alike. But his staff was on the whole inexperienced, and he failed to make use of the Consuls in Turkey who were experienced.

Until 1911 the Ottoman Empire had barely changed since its zenith in the fifteenth century. The Sultan in Constantinople was still recognized as the Caliph of Islam by a large part of the Sunni Moslem world, as far afield as Central Russia and India. The territories over which he ruled in name extended from Albania to the head of the Persian Gulf. The Sultan also retained suzerainty over Egypt. Until 1908 he was an absolute theocrat. In that year the revolutionary Young Turks rose to power. They forced Sultan Abdul Hamid to abdicate. In July 1909 they promulgated a liberal constitution, and set up a new Sultan, Mehmed V, who was to be a constitutional monarch in temporal affairs, although remaining the spiritual head of Islam.

Alarmed by the bloodless success of the Young Turks and fearing lest they might demand the end of the Austro-Hungarian occupation of Bosnia and Herzogovina, authorised by the Treaty of Berlin in 1878, the Emperor Franz Joseph declared these Balkan provinces part of the Dual Monarchy.

In September 1911 occurred the Italo-Turkish War. Of all modern wars of aggression it was perhaps the most dastardly, being wholly unprovoked. Years of pent-up Italian greed and resentment that the African provinces of Tripolitania and Cyrenaica had been ceded to Turkey in 1856 by the European powers boiled over. The eruption was further accentuated by fears of French expansion from Morocco into what Italy regarded as her sphere of interest.

Gradually Italy wore down Turkey's resistance in the African provinces. In spite of strong protests from Vienna she also occupied Rhodes and the twelve islands of the Sporades known as the Dodecanese. The Italians then graciously proceeded to conclude a peace treaty with Turkey at Ouchy. This was in October 1912, ten months after Harold Nicolson had taken up his duties in Constantinople as Third Secretary.

Turkey's humiliation by Italy's reprehensible conduct had a direct consequence in the Balkan Wars. In January 1913 Russia, anticipating the break-up of the Ottoman Empire, and keeping an eye on the Dardanelles began to foment military alliances against Turkey among the Balkan kingdoms. Conditions in Macedonia were to be made the excuse for armed interference. The military advantage was all with the allies, for the Turks could only bring troops overland into Thrace because the Greek Navy was controlling the waters.

The British Embassy in Constantinople was alarmed by the symptoms of disorder in the south-east corner of Europe. Requests for reports of events

SPAIN AND CONSTANTINOPLE 1910-12

and advice how to act flew between Whitehall and Pera. There was little that the British Ambassador could do beyond holding a watching brief. Social life went on among members of the diplomatic corps as though no clouds were on the horizon. The young secretaries accompanied the Ambassador to the golf course, rode with the Counsellor's wife by the Sweet Waters, went to fancy-dress balls and concerts, or merely ambled through the bazaar looking for Persian drawings and carpets. In view of Harold's later contempt for games, it is odd to learn that he constantly played golf, had lessons in squash rackets and dancing, and was even elected secretary of the Polo Club. But he was not entirely wasting his time in frivolities. He took lessons in Turkish and went on various expeditions. In order to extend these excursions he bought himself a small yacht from his friend Nellidoff, the son of the Russian Ambassador, and in May was nearly drowned in a gale in the Sea of Marmara. In fact Harold soon discovered that the current which flowed out from the Black Sea was so strong that there were only occasional days when he could tack against it. His love of sailing dated from these years in Constantinople.

In March he briefly renewed his equivocal acquaintance with Ronald Firbank. The only mention in his diary of the meeting was the laconic sentence, 'Go round and see Firbank who is ridiculous.' But in *Some People* he made a reference to Firbank which suggests that they just failed to meet.[18] Firbank was on his way back to England from Egypt. He left Harold a note saying that he had 'descended' at the Pera Palace Hotel, which was the centre of cosmopolitan life in Constantinople. Firbank announced that he would like to see Harold. So Harold told him to come to the Embassy next morning early and he would take him sailing up the Bosphorus. The day turned out to be ideal for sailing. Harold ordered a suitable picnic luncheon and looked forward to a long expedition, perhaps into the Black Sea. He waited for his guest.

> At 10.0 a man brought me a note in his neat hellenic writing. 'Today is too wonderful,' he wrote, 'it is the most wonderful day that ever happened; it would be too much for me: let us keep today as something marvellous that did not occur.' I dashed furiously round to his hotel, but he had already left with his courier to visit the churches. I scribbled, 'Silly ass' on my card and left it for him. I then sailed up the Bosphorus indignant and alone. When I returned my servant met me with a grin: my sitting-room was banked with Madonna lilies. 'C'est un Monsieur,' he said, 'qui vous a apporté tout ça.' 'Quel monsieur?' 'Un Monsieur qui porte le chapeau de travers.'

Lady Sackville was assiduous in writing Harold affectionate letters which began, 'My dear Boy.' One reveals that the day he left London the

Scott family had decided to dispute Sir John's will, and would be bringing a case against her. She was, as the court ultimately proved, within her rights in claiming the fortune that had been left her, but her attitude was appallingly grasping and selfish. She was unsparing in her hatred of the Scotts. She was furious that the executors of the estate would not allow her to go to Sir John's house in the rue Lafitte in Paris, accompanied by dealers who might make her offers for items of furniture before they were legally hers, items which in any case Seery hoped would go to enrich the collections at Knole.

She showed little understanding of Harold's position as a junior secretary in a post which he had only just taken up. Although his leave was not yet due she urged him to get his father to release him for Easter, so that he might join her and Vita in Paris. Could he not ask Sir Arthur to send urgent telegrams to Sir Gerard Lowther giving fictitious reasons for his return? And, which must have made Harold's blood run cold, she was, she told him, cultivating William Tyrrell on his behalf. Why was this snobbish and ambitious lady so nice to Harold in seeming to favour his suit? It can only be that she found him winning and irresistible. When a year later she changed her mind, she admitted to Vita, 'I wish he was not half so nice.' Certainly Harold, who from the start had no illusions about her, treated her with admirable tact. Never overfamiliar – always addressing her, 'My dear Lady Sackville' – he assiduously humoured, sympathised with, gently flattered and amused her.

It was with eager anticipation that he awaited his weekly allowance of one letter in the bag from Vita. There are regular entries in the diary, 'Hear from V' and 'Hear V.' Vita was much disliking the prospect of the Scott case, was bored by the protracted negotiations with solicitors and wearied by her mother's obsession with her grievances and anxieties. Dutifully but reluctantly she was going from one house-party to another in order to fulfil the undertaking made to her mother that she would spend a full year in society before committing herself to Harold. She complained bitterly of the balls and parties she was obliged to go to. But how anxious was she to commit herself to Harold at the end of the period? After his departure her affair with Rosamund intensified. In her letters to him she referred to Rosamund with affection, but without disclosing what their true relations were. 'Doesn't everyone want *one* subservient person in their life? I've got mine in her. Who is yours? Certainly not me!'

Although terms of endearment had been strictly vetoed, one cannot help feeling that, had she wished, Vita could have contrived to write with more warmth. The tenor of her letters is mocking, casual, and only occasionally loving. On the 21st February she wrote, 'My erratic friend Violet Keppel is coming home in April [she had been in Ceylon], so you will know her. She will amuse you.' Little did she imagine how much. She made no bones about her deep, atavistic love of Knole, which Harold must understand was the really serious rival he had to face. She told him how much she used to hate her Cousin Eddy,[19] the son of her father's younger brother, Charles Sackville-West, because he would inherit Knole and not she. Eddy at the time was ten. Her relations with him were in fact always to remain ambivalent, because he was born a boy and she a girl, because he was indifferent to Knole and she worshipped it.

Harold was very conscious that it was wrong for him to marry an heiress. Vita proudly dismissed such misgivings. 'Harold, I am not rich,' she replied, 'and even if I was it couldn't possibly jar ... It is a good thing that we can always talk about anything without minding, quite brutally. I am glad we fell into that way from the first.'[20]

In April she was allowed a respite from house-parties and the company of eligible young men. She went with Rosamund to stay in a cottage, or *villino*, attached to the Villa Pestellini outside Florence. It was a small ochre-washed house with a Tuscan loggia and guarded by a pair of umbrella pines. The nights were lit for them by fireflies and they were serenaded by frogs. In May Vita was back in England. She was seeing much of Archie Clark Kerr, whom she thought rather bedint for calling her 'my dear,' and whom Lady Sackville had to rebuke for calling her Vita. 'There is so much unnecessary freedom in England in the way boys & girls call each other by their Christian names,' she wrote to Archie, 'and many mothers are banded together to stop it.' Why! even Seery had not been allowed to call her by her Christian name in front of others.

Meanwhile Harold was accompanying Lady Lowther on a picnic to the Sweet Waters at the head of the Golden Horn. They sailed in the Embassy state caique, a slim vessel called *Imogene*, flying a large white ensign and propelled by six oars. At the beginning of June he had to accompany both their Excellencies to the Gulf of Ismid. Lady Sackville continued writing to Harold in coy collusion and warned him that he had better not betray his feelings through his eyes. Then Vita wrote that they could not continue their present ambiguous condition after his next leave; and that Violet Keppel was pressing her to stay in Holland just when Harold would be coming home. Should she go?

In June Reggie Cooper, to Harold's joy, came to join the Embassy staff. At the end of the month the Embassy moved to its summer quarters at Therapia. This was a Greek village tucked in a loop of the European bank of the Bosphorus, where the cool breezes from the Black Sea tempered the oppressive heat of the summer. Harold settled in to his 'awfully jolly room' on the top floor of the secretaries' house. Work seemed to slacken, for his diary concentrated on fishing for red mullet with seine nets in the early mornings, and lolling, reading and bathing during most of the daytime. And on the 31st the arrival of 'Lacretelle' was succinctly noted.

Pierre de Lacretelle was one of the men in Harold's life with whom he was undoubtedly infatuated for a time. There were to be many others with whom he had affairs, and to whom he remained devoted. There were very many more whom he dearly loved, but with whom his relations were absolutely unphysical. Therefore it would be a great mistake to assume, whenever a young man entered Harold's life and evoked admiration either for his looks or his brain, that their relations were not purely platonic. Pierre de Lacretelle, however, was not one of these. The young Frenchman had nearly all the qualities most likely to appeal to Harold's admiration and desires. He was slender, dark, vivacious and highly intelligent. Harold called him 'one of the most brilliant people I have ever known.'[21] And he made him the principal prototype of that composite character, the Marquis de Chaumont in *Some People*. He was well born. He was one of two sons of Amaury de Lacretelle, an agnostic diplomat and his Protestant wife, and was born in Bulgaria when his father was *en poste* at the French Legation. When Pierre arrived in Constantinople as an employee of the Ottoman Bank everyone supposed that he had a brilliant career ahead of him. But he was an unstable character. Opium and gambling were to be his undoing. The brothers had a very rich aunt who undertook to leave all she possessed to them on the one condition, that they agreed to be baptised. Jacques refused. Pierre consented, and thus became sole heir. He turned Catholic and experienced a sort of religious vocation. The aunt after years of apoplectic strokes died in 1925. Pierre thereupon inherited a fortune, several houses and vineyards, and his great-uncle Lamartine's manuscripts. On the strength of this inheritance he went with Jean Cocteau to Monte Carlo. He imagined he had devised an infallible method of winning at the tables. He lost everything. Within a matter of weeks the houses, vineyards and the papers vanished into thin air.[22]

For the rest of his long life Pierre lived in destitution, often in squalor, frequenting the lowest of haunts, for he never attempted to curb his promiscuous homosexuality. From time to time his and Harold's paths crossed – for instance at the Lausanne Conference which Pierre was to cover for the *Journal des Debats*. In the Second World War he suffered atrociously from the Gestapo who, amongst other tortures, broke his leg. But unlike many of his compatriots who suffered less he never complained or spoke of his misfortunes, and emerged from his ordeal with a smile. He helped Harold with his books and articles on French poets and writers, like Constant and Sainte-Beuve, about whom his knowledge was phenomenal. He considered Harold's French so perfect that he might indulge in 'les aisances de la langue', which it would be rash for most foreigners to

SPAIN AND CONSTANTINOPLE 1910-12

attempt. Harold remained loyal and generous to his old friend and would contrive all sorts of methods of giving money to Lacretelle, which he badly needed, without hurting his pride.

But in July 1912 Pierre de Lacretelle was far from the seedy, shifty, broken old man he was to become. He was a handsome, scintillating and romantic youth with whom Harold spent a week tacking up and down the Bosphorus, dawdling on the sun-baked shores of the Black Sea, dallying in a low-ceilinged room in Therapia, and all the while reciting and talking about French poetry, while the water lapped against the walls outside and steamers hooted in the distance. In 1926 the memory of this golden week was brought back to Harold by an encounter in Tehran with the American journalist, Vincent Sheean. After dinner Sheean sang to the assembled party. Suddenly Harold recognised a little tune which Reggie Cooper had composed to some French words. 'Where on earth,' Harold exclaimed, 'did you learn that tune?' Sheean replied, 'Pierre de Lacretelle taught it me when I was staying with him in his château in Burgundy. He told me if ever I met you, to sing it to you.' 'And so,' Harold wrote in his diary, 'Pierre has inherited from an aunt and is rich and lives in a château, and sends spotty-faced Americans to sing to me a song in Asia.'[23]

And now Vita's letters were becoming unaccountably less guarded, more spontaneous and affectionate. She could not marry Harold that autumn, she warned him. Selfish? Yes, but she was only twenty and this was the first year she had really lived, and wanted one more before she settled down with him. Besides, it was what Dada (her father) wanted. 'By the way I am atrociously jealous. So are you ... But you mustn't make fusses about people I speak to more than once because I will always tell you about it.' She was just a little jealous of Eileen Wellesley. Had Harold been hearing from her? She, Vita, had actually had a proposal from a *parti* who didn't even know her! And, she ended, they could be officially engaged now, if he, Harold, liked.

In August Harold left Constantinople for two months' leave. He arrived in London on the 16th. There he found a note from Vita telling him to come to Knole the next day, a Saturday. He was to arrive at eleven, to drive his old car, which they called Green Archie, into the stable courtyard; then walk through the Great Hall and the Ballroom straight to her sitting-room, so as to avoid the house-party. 'Don't be solemnly conducted to the Colonnade.'[24]

Harold paid several short and long visits to Knole during his leave. He played tennis with Vita, motored with her and sat in the Venetian Ambassador's room, where they could be alone, and he kissed her. 'He kissed me! He kissed me! I love him. Io l'amo tanto, tanto ... But I want so much to see R. again,' Vita confided to her diary. She must have seen Rosamund

HAROLD NICOLSON

fairly soon because on the 29th Harold was teaching Rosamund to drive a car. On the 1st September Harold wrote in his diary, 'Things smiling.' In this euphoric state he dashed straight from Knole, where he stayed 'later than I ought,' to London; slept at the Charing Cross Hotel and left next morning for Paris. There he met Pierre de Lacretelle and they stayed at the Astoria together. Pierre introduced him to Cocteau. On the 5th Harold returned to London, leaving immediately for Clandeboye. Back again in London he was soon motoring down to Knole and having talks with Lady Sackville, whom he was invited to call B. M. (*bonne mère*). Unfortunately things were less smiling, for Lady Sackville was now veering away from Harold because there were other more eligible suitors in the offing. 'V is not suited to diplomacy and taking trouble about a lot of bedints. She ought to be a *grande dame*, very rich . . .' was her diary comment.

In spite of B.M.'s waning enthusiasm, which was temporary, Harold seems to have been accepted as a member of the Sackville family, for he was taken to dine with Vita's Uncle Charlie and Aunt Maud,[25] and with the Rubenses. He met Violet Keppel at luncheon, but made no comment about her. He accompanied Lady Lowther, always anxious to improve her mind, to the Post-Impressionist Exhibition where they were conducted round by Roger Fry. On the 8th October he, Vita and Rosamund left together for the continent. On the 11th they separated, he for Venice and Constantinople, the two girls for Florence. 'A dreadful day. Say goodbye at early morning.' Poor Harold, little did he know how many extremely painful partings he and Vita were to endure in their long married life together.

In Constantinople the international situation was extremely tense. It is true that peace between Italy and Turkey was concluded at Ouchy on the 15th. This relieved some of the strain on the Turks. But the Balkan states were on the verge of declaring war, Montenegro actually having done so on the 8th without anyone paying much attention. The united Powers notified the Balkan states that if hostilities broke out there would be no territorial exchanges permitted. This did not prevent Bulgaria, Serbia and Greece declaring war on Turkey on the 17th. The First Balkan War had begun. That day Harold witnessed the ceremony of the Selamlik. From the windows of a pavilion opposite the Hamidieh Mosque near the Yildiz Kiosk he watched the Sultan, enthroned under a canopy in the stern of the State caique, 100 feet long and painted white and gold, fly through the water, manned by twenty-six picked rowers. Salutes were fired from ships and batteries and people took off their hats as the Sultan passed up

SPAIN AND CONSTANTINOPLE 1910-12

the Golden Horn to the Sweet Waters. There he drank tea in a little kiosk under the trees, while the famous Ertogrul baud played sentimental airs, and the diplomatic corps strolled through the flowery meadows.

On the 24th the Turks were defeated at Kumora, and there was panic in the capital. On the 1st November the Bulgarians were rumoured to be approaching. British men of war were sent for, lest the Embassy should have to evacuate hurriedly, and in no time H.M.S. *Weymouth* sailed into the Golden Horn. Immediately the blue-jackets swarmed ashore, their presence bringing confidence to the English residents and the Turks alike. Lady Lowther was busily marshalling Red Cross aid. The secretaries had never been so overworked before, and errors sometimes crept in. In a fit of carelessness Harold awarded the C.M.G. to the Vice-Consul at Hodeidah instead of to the Consul at Basra. An English resident who could type was enlisted to help in the Chancery. Four important despatches were sent to the Secretary of State for India, the Marquess of Crewe. They were returned with a furious note from London. The despatches had begun with the unfortunate spelling, 'My Dorl.'

Harold always enjoyed excitement and movement. For the first time in his career he had to work under pressure within, as it were, the firing line. Out riding by Kiarkhas he heard gunfire in the direction of Buyuk Tchekmedie. The large windows of the houses in Pera shook from the Bulgars' howitzers. Soon there was shooting at Chablia. There was coming and going to and from the front. The Military Attaché returned with better news on the 8th November. But next day cholera broke out among the refugees in the congested camps at San Stefano, on the outskirts of Constantinople, and people were afraid. The day after that, Salonika fell. On the 11th H.M.S. *Hampshire* arrived and the crew disembarked. Towards the end of the month armistice negotiations were well on the way, and by the 28th the sailors had re-embarked, and Harold was dining with the captain on board. The Turks having been brilliantly defeated gave way to the terms of Bulgaria, Serbia and Montenegro. On the 4th December Harold wrote, 'Peace negotiations decided on. How dull!'

Meanwhile Vita and Rosamund were enjoying a second honeymoon in Florence. 'I was never so much in love with Rosamund as during those weeks in Italy,' she wrote in her autobiographical narrative of 1920, not boastfully but in shame. By the end of the year her ardours had not diminished. Nor were the perplexities of the previous summer resolved, for she was driven to distraction by indecision, conflicting loyalties, as well as dismay over her sexual predilections. In her diary of December she wrote in Italian (a language her mother did not understand): 'I talked to her [Rosamund] very frankly about H. I do not think I love him enough to marry him . . . But for a short time I'll let things slide. Perhaps something will happen.' And again on the 18th: 'I cannot, I cannot leave everything for him – at least I don't think I can. He will come back in April, and it makes me shiver.'

And Harold wrote at the end of his 1912 diary: 'A good year – an important year – a satisfactory year.' He at any rate was experiencing no inhibitions like those which tormented Vita. He had absolutely no qualms about the nature of his love for her. It was something primary and steadfast. His casual flings with Archie, Uppie and Lacretelle meant no more to him than a bee's pollination of a foxglove. Nor had he any suspicion as to the meaning of Vita's reservations. In his blunt way he could be imperceptive of the instincts and emotions of others. He did not fathom them because he did not even sense that they existed.

5

CONSTANTINOPLE AND MARRIAGE, 1913–1914

THE peace negotiations in London between the belligerents were not making much progress. On the 23rd January 1913 they were abruptly terminated when news was received of a *coup d'état* in Constantinople. At 3.15 that afternoon the Turkish Army revolted against the practical certainty of the Government's capitulation to the Balkan Powers. Enver Bey, leader of the Young Turks, handsome, low-born and extremely ambitious for fame, and his accomplice, Mahmoud Shevket Pasha, burst into the Cabinet offices and murdered the Minister for War, Nazim Pasha. The assassination caused much excitement in the capital. The following day Harold attended the Selamlik where Enver and Shevket were

> both looking so cocky and not a bit like Lord Midleton would look if he had shot Mr. Haldane with his own hand the afternoon before (and in the body – right low down).[1]

A military Government having been set up by Enver, it immediately denounced the armistice and resumed hostilities against the Powers. But this gesture of bold defiance was of little avail. Turkish troops were everywhere collapsing and fears were again expressed that the enemy troops would try to enter Constantinople. On the 17th April the new Government was obliged to sign an armistice, which was followed by acceptance of the Treaty of London on the 30th May. European Turkey, apart from a strip of land to the west of Constantinople, was partitioned among the Balkan Powers.

All that the party of the Young Turks had achieved was delay in agreeing to peace terms, and rather worse terms than might have been arrived at by Nazim Pasha had he been spared. The usual retribution was the consequence. On the 11th June Mahmoud Shevket Pasha, who had been promoted to Grand Vizier, was in his turn assassinated. Harold wrote to Vita,

> Of course, he means nothing to you, but he was the Cromwell of the Revolution here and the effect of the murder is as though Roberts, Kitchener and Asquith were all murdered on the same day.[2]

The city was thrown into turmoil. A massacre ensued. The Daoud Pasha barracks were in flames. The adjacent wooden houses crackled like holly leaves in a bonfire. From the Embassy in Pera Stamboul looked sinister, drab and squalid under a lowering sky. The twin minarets of Sultan Selim stood out like two black chimneys against the scudding clouds. Fearsome rumours were rife. Martial law was declared, and swift arrests were made. In the middle of these events the Embassy staff learned that Sir Gerard Lowther was retiring and his place would be taken by Sir Louis Mallet.

While Turkish ministers were being assassinated in the streets of Constantinople and the First Balkan War was resuming, Vita was spending the winter at Knole. To relieve her boredom with her parents' way of life she shut herself up in her rooms writing novels, poems and plays. In January *An Eastern Fantasy*, referred to as a Persian play, was performed in the Great Hall at Knole. The prologue was composed by Vita, who took the principal part as the Caliph loved by two dancing girls, appropriately Rosamund Grosvenor and Violet Keppel disguised in yashmaks, veils and flowing drapery. The Persian play was such a success the first time that it was repeated eight days later. 'Think of me,' Vita wrote to Harold, 'as a brown young Caliph lying on a divan, assuming suitable Oriental inscrutability, and really thinking over 1500 miles of country.'[3] If Harold was transferred to Vienna, which he led her to believe he soon might be, would she be allowed to pose as a decadent young Roman Emperor? She supposed not. Anyway, during the performance of the play she mistook Harold's friend, who was also her mother's friend, Oswald, or Ozzie Dickinson, for Walter Rubens's brother, and positively ordered him to swing a censer. Harold, in replying, said he had misgivings whether she would not be bored with the diplomatic life in stodgy Vienna, and assured her that Ozzie was in a way his dearest friend. Ozzie, the brother of Virginia Woolf's intimate companion of early years, Violet Dickinson, was a good deal older than Harold, being of an age between his and Lady Sackville's. He was a cosy, gossipy, 'queer' bachelor with a genuine love of the arts, and a welcome stopgap at luncheon, dinner and house parties. Harold first met him in 1910 in Pavlova's company. Ozzie Dickinson was corresponding with Harold fairly regularly, and ventured to tell him that he could not be sure whether Vita really cared for him, Harold, or indeed for any of her other suitors.

Harold and Vita's letters at this time do not convey the impression that the writers' engagement was secure. Harold's express anxiety. They even tend to carp, for he was the absent one suffering from uncertainty and jealousy of rivals. Vita's were merely lukewarm. He wrote[4] to her sternly

CONSTANTINOPLE AND MARRIAGE 1913-14

about self-control and duty, neither of which was a subject to appeal to her. 'I must be the one who *disposes* in these things,' meaning his career and posts in the Diplomatic Service, a point of view which Vita was driven more and more as the years went by to contest.

When towards the end of February Harold complained in heartrending terms that she did not write – the war made the mails to Turkey erratic, he conceded – did not visit his mother and did not seem to care, Vita retorted, 'Sometimes I think you are really quite happy there with your Gerry and your wars, and I am not by any means all-important, and so again I write you a beastly letter, or I don't write at all.'[5] She was quite wrong about Gerry. But did she know about Pierre de Lacretelle? And if she did, would she have minded?

On the 10th March Vita described without much enthusiasm her twenty-first birthday celebrations at Knole the previous day. Then at the end of the month she accompanied Mrs. Charles Hunter to Spain. This was the doing of Lady Sackville, who was now cautioning her daughter not to be in a hurry to announce her engagement.

Vita's experiences in Spain, her swift romantic passion for this strange, cruel land of her forefathers did something to her, brought about an exaltation that nearly called off her marriage to Harold and surely wrecked her love affair with Rosamund. On the eve of her departure she and Rosamund had spent the night together, when they renewed protestations of eternal love. At all events Rosamund deduced that their love transcended Vita's for Harold, which did not mean all that much. Within a matter of days the friends were at daggers drawn. In a fury Rosamund returned a letter Vita sent her from Madrid in which she wrote that she had fallen 'for a dancer, a divine woman to whom I have completely lost my heart, called Pastora Imperio' and threatened to go on from Madrid to Florence to stay with Violet Trefusis.[6] This letter was a retaliation for one she had received from Rosamund, saying she was having a glorious time with the sailors at Dartmouth where she had gone to stay. In fact Rosamund was engaged to a penniless midshipman called Reggie Raikes, whom she had loved before her affair with Vita even started. Vita's returned letter had ended with a sentence characteristic of the savage Vita of the dual personality: 'Oh, if I could cut you with the nib of my pen as with the blade of a sword, I would do it!' To this outburst Rosamund wrote a spirited letter of remonstrance, telling Vita that Spain was having an evil effect on her. She also communicated what Lady Sackville had just told her, namely that Vita had made up her mind to marry Harold. In which case, what did all her protestations of their last night together before Spain amount to?

Certainly Vita had got herself – and Rosamund – into a proper muddle.

In *Pepita*[7] she gives some indication, a guarded indication, of what that April visit to Spain did to her. To Harold too she wrote from Seville a letter which disturbed him:

> This is the life for me: gipsies, dancing, disreputable artists, bull-fights. Oh Harold, I can't paint to you the state of mind I am in now. I feel I can *never* go back to that humdrum existence,'[8]

by which she meant her engagement to a staid, decent Englishman in the Diplomatic Service. After some further provocative letters of the same sort she wrote him one[9] which upset him very much. She suggested that it might be simpler to break off their engagement altogether. His immediate action was to telegraph asking if he was to take her seriously. Her reply was an unequivocal no.

> No [she wrote] – what you really got was just an ill-tempered storm from a wanderer who felt caged again after weeks of liberty[10]

in Spain, Rome and Paris, which she had visited before turning back to England. She apologised if she had hurt him. The sort of wife he needed was someone 'very gentle, and dependent and clinging' – a sentence containing a sort of gentle backlash. However in her notebook she wrote, 'I loved Harold from that day on . . . but I continued my liaison with Rosamund.' The liaison with Rosamund was in effect doomed after the experience of Spain and Harold's telegram. His ultimatum had brought Vita temporarily to heel.

On the 11th June Vita made up her mind once and for all. In her diary she wrote:

> These days I think so much of Harold that I can't sleep. I so much want him to come home. I have an insane wish to see him again; and I cannot let him out of my life. I shall marry him.

By now they had been unofficially engaged for a year and a half; and Harold was taking the bit between his teeth. He was determined that the situation should not continue. He would insist upon marriage whatever the issue of the Scott case and Lady Sackville's equivocations. He obtained leave to go to England. Just before his departure Gerry Wellesley returned to Constantinople after a month's absence. Gerry, to add to the tragi-comedy that was to develop in their joint lives, was full of excitement. He was engaged to Violet Keppel. Admittedly Harold referred to it in a letter to Vita as Gerry's half-engagement.[11] Yet 'he is tremendously

CONSTANTINOPLE AND MARRIAGE 1913-14

in love.' It was unfair that they would not have to worry about money. He felt sure Vita would be pleased because their marriage would make it so much more agreeable for her, 'to have some sort of outside person in our so nomadic profession.' Vita made no reply to this observation.

While he was en route for home the Second Balkan War broke out. Jealousies among the former Balkan allies opposed to Turkey were the cause. Bulgaria refused to withdraw from Salonika as she was pledged to do under the Treaty of London. On the 30th June she declared war against Serbia and Greece. In July Roumania joined Serbia and Greece, and marched on Sofia. The Turks, profiting from the dissension amongst their victorious enemies, reoccupied Adrianople. This time the Bulgarians were obliged to sue for peace, which was signed at Bucharest on the 10th August.

In an hotel at Avignon Harold opened the English papers and read that the Scott-Sackville case had been going on since the 24th June. It filled him with distress because he foresaw it must bring much discredit to Lady Sackville and publicity to Vita, which she would hate. In London he saw the posters blazing with headlines. He rushed to 34 Hill Street, Lady Sackville's London house, where he found her in tears. He met Vita in the Droghedas' box at the opera, and they and Archie Clark Kerr had supper together at the Carlton. 'What a day!' was his comment.

The following morning Harold went to the Law Courts to hear Lady Sackville, Olive Rubens, Vita and Rosamund all give evidence. Vita's evidence was delivered in a clear, firm voice for which the papers, adopting her affectionately as 'Kidlet', one of her nicknames in the family, gave unstinted praise. On the 7th the case was settled, the judge summing up in the Sackvilles' favour. The jury found that Sir John Scott's bequests to Lady Sackville were not obtained by 'the undue influence' of Lord and Lady Sackville, as the Scott family alleged. B.M. was consequently acquitted. The Rubenses gave a jubilant dinner to celebrate the happy outcome.

After Harold's return to London the news of his engagement to Vita was bandied about. The *Daily Sketch* announced it as a fact.[12] This irritated Lady Sackville, who now did not want Vita to live abroad and be lost to her. So she issued to the press a denial that the engagement was authentic. Authentic or not, it did not prevent Harold constantly visiting Knole. Nor did it prevent Violet Keppel, who was beginning to supplant poor Rosamund in Vita's affections, from writing Vita a cynical letter of congratulation.[13] If, she ended, the engagement was still unofficial the letter would keep until it was official, no matter when or to whom.

Although Lady Sackville's final consent took several weeks to mature, the engagement, before the official announcement in August, was taken by most people for granted. The young couple were invited together to

Lady Cunard's dance at which Chaliapine sang. Vita was introduced to Sir Arthur Nicolson, with whom she was an instant success. Lady Sackville, securely in possession of Seery's fortune, was behaving generously. She undertook to settle £2,500 a year on Vita and motored the couple round England in her Rolls Royce, buying furniture for them in Bath and other country towns.

The friend with whom Harold spent most of his spare time was Archie Clark Kerr. In August Harold motored him in 'Green Archie' to East Anglia. The motor broke down at Hatfield and again at Peterborough where they had to stay the night. They walked about the Cathedral Close, which was misty-pearly like an Oxford quad. 'And Arch was so gentle and nice and understanding. It is in such moments,' he told Vita, 'I realise why I am so fond of him.'[14] And again he told her with candour, 'It is odd the affection I have for him, and he for me for that matter. He is the only one of my friends I am really sentimental about. I am glad you like him too. I wish B.M. did.'[15]

On the 20th Lady Sackville and her new admirer, Mr. William Waldorf Astor, went to Interlaken, taking with them the engaged couple as chaperons. At the end of ten days Harold had to return to the Foreign Office. Vita wrote to him from Interlaken:[16] 'The whole place is littered with coffee cups' (a Sackville expression signifying everyday things which remind the person left behind nostalgically of the departed one). And he wrote to her, equally nostalgically, of the walks, the empty caramel box, their mutual dirty inkpot, and the stained pattern of the carpet, 'all now rushing back into the past like a retreating train.'

Vita and her mother returned to London by way of Paris, where Lady Sackville was having a bust of herself sculptured by Rodin.

On the 3rd September Vita wrote Harold a description of a visit she had been obliged to make by herself to the artist's studio.

> B.M. having worn herself out over sheets for us and bath mats for us to get out on, from the bath which won't exist... B.M. was then too tired to go, and I went alone (terrified), and bearded Rodin, by invitation, of course, in his nice messy atelier which used to be a convent, and which is now very dilapidated and where he is supremely happy. I was shown into his room, and waited there a few minutes – do you know how suggestive a person's room can be, before they come? It was rather dark, and there were huge roughly-hewn lumps of marble, and a chisel left on a chair where he had put it down, and nothing else – and the suggestiveness of it grew on me more and more as I waited, and then he came in, very gentle and vague, and rather a commonplace little French bourgeois with long boots and the légion d'honneur in his buttonhole – rather an unreal little fat man, like a skit on the Académiciens in a funny

CONSTANTINOPLE AND MARRIAGE 1913-14

paper, and the whole thing was a reaction and a come-down from the massive white marbles all round. But not when he talks about them, and points out lines to one with a real sculptor's sweep of his thumb, and he draws his finger lovingly across the marble brow of Mozart, and he and Mozart seem to smile at each other. And he gave me a bronze, signed, a statuette of a man, 'une étude', as he calls it. He has some magnificent things there at his studio; he has two people flying which is supposed to be l'aviation; I admit that it sounds dreadful, but in reality it is beautiful, and rather the same idea as the Florence Mercury (that sounds like a newspaper, but I mean the Gianbologna). And the head of Mozart, which is half strength and half reverie, perfectly marvellous, and then two great clasped hands emerging out of a block of marble, & he says, 'Voyez les doigts entrelacés qui font comme la nef d'une cathédrale – ces mains sont toutes les églises du monde qui se rencontrent.' It is amazing that a man who can have his ideas and execution, can be such a conventional little French Haggite, as in a way he is, and who I am sure fusses about his pardessus and his paletôt and the courant d'air, like the man who wrote, 'Partir c'est mourir un peu,' whose only preoccupation when I met him was whether he had got his feet wet and ought not to prendre un bain de pied.

Which shows one that making Rodin statues and writing Verlaine poetry is a freaky part quite separate from the normal, in a water-tight compartment by itself.

The same day Harold wrote from London: 'I am so happy. The pavements sing at me – and the people smile – and the trees forget to be sooty.' But towards the end of the month he was complaining sadly that she showed few signs of caring for him very much. He hoped that when they were married she would do more than 'like' him. He also detected signs that the Sackvilles considered the Nicolson family inferior to them. They were of course nothing of the sort, only Sir Arthur and his wife were unsophisticated people who did not choose to move in 'society.' Vita's letters were by now only mildly affectionate, slightly mocking and amused. She was amused when Lord Lascelles, who had been pressing her to marry him and took his rebuff well, wrote that Lady Sackville 'has so often told me that Harold Nicolson is not the sort of man she would have chosen for you.' That was like B.M., always running with the hare and hunting with the hounds. And of course Harry Lascelles, heir to the Earldom of Harewood and an immense fortune and estate, was a far greater catch than Harold, with only his brains, his charm, his curly hair, his expressive eyelashes and his upturned nose. Vita remained a little aloof, exclusive, preoccupied and remote. No one, not even Harold, knew for certain what was passing through her mind, least of all her mother.

What with excursions to Fortuny, Reville and Chaumet, where 'finally B.M. buys V a huge chain of diamonds and emeralds,'[17] to the Irish Linen Company for more expensive bath towels, to Harrington Mann's studio for a portrait, unpacking presents at Knole – there were three hundred and eight – with the help of poor Rosamund, which added to her misery, Vita became reconciled to the inevitable wedding. It took place on the 1st October at Knole. A large number of guests were invited, but there was only room for members of the family in the chapel, which was packed with arums and other white flowers from the greenhouses. The Bishop of Rochester performed the ceremony. Walter Rubens presided at the organ, and his wife Olive, 'in a very smart gown of chestnut-red velvet trimmed with skunk,' sang an aria from Gounod's *Redemption*. Lord Sackville gave away his daughter, whose wedding-dress by Reville was of cloth of gold brocade woven in Persian design. From a wreath of myrtle fell an old Irish lace veil of gossamer gold which had been worn by Lady Sackville at the coronation of the Czar. Lord Drogheda's son, Garrett Moore, aged two and a half was a train-bearer. The two bridesmaids were Gwen Nicolson, with her hair up for the first time, and Rosamund Grosvenor who, when the engagement was announced, had written to Vita, 'Don't ask me to visit you. I can't. I am so utterly miserable. I feel that you are going. I simply cannot begin to face it. I am ill with misery.' Harold's eldest brother, Freddy, in the uniform of the 15th Hussars, was best man. Lady Sackville, stricken at the last moment by the onset, according to her own diary, of her period, was too ill to attend the ceremony, and stayed in bed. A band of the West Kent Yeomanry played during the reception.

Lady St. Levan distinctly remembers that there was much tension during the wedding. Vita, torn by her conflicting emotions about Rosamund, Violet and Spanish gipsy dancers, contemptuous of social and religious ceremonial, and indifferent to fine clothes and jewellery, cannot have enjoyed it. On the other hand Harold, whose affairs with men, conducted on a high-spirited, physical and casual level, were quickly forgotten, probably did enjoy it, because he enjoyed most things. Besides, he felt that he had won through. But he made no comments upon his state of mind in his diary.

After the wedding the couple went to Somerset to spend the first three days and nights of their honeymoon at Coker Court, an exquisite manor-house lent them by Dorothy Walker-Heneage, a friend of the Sackvilles. After dinner on their first evening they sat over the fire and Harold talked so long about his uncle Dufferin that Vita began to wonder if he had forgotten he had a wife. On the 4th they left Coker in the morning and Harold noted in his diary, 'I sleep at Cadogan Gardens and V at Hill Street. A regrettable arrangement.' The next day they left London and

CONSTANTINOPLE AND MARRIAGE 1913-14

took the Simplon Express for Florence. There they stayed in the Villino of the Villa Pestellini. Vita was to write in 1920,[18]

> We lived in the little cottage I had shared with Rosamund eighteen months before. This is one of the things I am most ashamed of in my life. It was horrible of me. Besides being disloyal to Rosamund, it was a dreadful 'manque de delicatesse.'

Harold tried to paint watercolours. They went on expeditions. And on the 17th they left, with many regrets, for Brindisi. In a letter to Vita written from Brindisi thirty-nine years later[19] Harold recalled an incident in the train on the way there.

> Oh my darling! How vivid to me was that journey we took thirty-nine years ago! Do you remember the sick woman and the husband who kept on jumping up and giving her sips of medicine? And how when in the autumn dawn we reached, I suppose Bari, and they got out, how you said with your sweet gentle smile, 'I hope you will soon be better.' And she cast back at you a look of utterly resigned despair. There we were, so sweet, so young, so healthy, embarking on what was a long life of love and action and success, and she must have been dead now these almost forty years, and no more than a pinch of dust. Ahimé!

From Brindisi they took a boat to Alexandria. In Cairo they stayed with Lord Kitchener at the British Agency. The visit had been arranged by Lady Sackville in her interfering way, and Vita did not look forward to it at all. Nor did she enjoy it when she got there. She arrived suffering from sunstroke and loss of voice. She did not care for her host, with his bombastic manners and portentous views about Egyptian art. She and Harold scrambled about the pyramids, and went inside them. Ronald Storrs, the Oriental Secretary, conducted them to mosques and entertained them to tea in his rooms, showing them a few of his choice Egyptian treasures. They went from Cairo to Luxor by train, and wandered down the avenue of couchant rams into the forest of columns at the great temple of Karnak. Back again to Cairo, then across the Mediterranean to the Piraeus, whence they sailed through the Sea of Marmora, 'bored and impatient,'[20] to Constantinople, arriving on the 3rd November.

The Nicolsons lost no time in choosing a house for themselves. Harold had already looked at a number before he went on leave in the summer. These they immediately inspected, and within nine days had rented No. 22 Djchanguir, or Cihangir, a district overlooking the Bosphorus and Scutari. Vita described it to a friend as the most attractive house you have ever seen. It is a wooden Turkish house, with a little garden and a pergola of grapes, and a pomegranate tree covered with scarlet fruit, and such a view over the Golden Horn and the sea and S. Sophia. And on the side of a hill, a perfect suntrap.

She instantly set about forming a terraced garden, and this was her first attempt at the art of gardening, at which she was to make herself famous at Long Barn and Sissinghurst in faraway Kent. Harold referred to their first home as 'the little blue house,' but Sir Louis Mallet, the new Ambassador who had arrived during Harold's absence, described it as very large, with broad shuttered windows. In all they employed seven servants, including a twelve-year-old negro boy.

For nearly eight months the young couple – Harold was twenty-seven and Vita twenty-one – led the conventional life of a junior British diplomat and his wife. They were happiest when painting with their own hands the rooms of their house, unpacking the furniture and wine which they had sent from Italy, playing tennis together or turning on the phonograph which she had given him for his birthday. Vita fulfilled the social duties which were expected of her, dinners at the Embassy, exchanges of courtesies with colleagues' wives, unsmilingly and without enjoyment. It was her first experience, and a short one, of diplomacy overseas; and she did not relish it. In her novel, *Challenge*, she described caustically its pettiness, its high opinion of itself, its 'coy platitudes,' and its perpetual and to her mind childish play of the power politics game. Only with a few select friends, who had been Harold's before they became his colleagues, like Reggie Cooper and Gerry Wellesley, did she really feel at ease. To the rest of the British Embassy colony her perfect, if stiff, manners did not betray what she was inwardly feeling. But to Harold she sometimes made it only too clear. When he came home late from work in the Chancery she might ostentatiously go on writing poetry at her table and refuse to turn round and greet him.

It must not be assumed that Vita was bored with Harold. Far from it.

Harold appears to me perfect, so gay, so amusing, so intelligent, so young. I feel that until now I never really knew him,

she recorded in her diary. And when about Christmas time she realised she was going to have a baby she was delighted.

I was pleased [she wrote[21]], but Harold was most pleased. His slightly medical attitude was the only thing that annoyed me, and I tried to counteract it by forbidding him to tell anyone except his own parents and mine.

CONSTANTINOPLE AND MARRIAGE 1913-14

In February 1914 Lord Sackville and Olive Rubens went to stay with them in Constantinople while B.M. was in Rome flirting outrageously with a beau of old days, Baron Bildt, whom she nicknamed Buggy, then Swedish Ambassador at the Quirinal. Rosamund also came to stay, but by now Vita's passion for her was totally extinguished.[22]

Sir Louis Mallet[23] had been Assistant Under-Secretary of State at the Foreign Office and close in the confidence of Sir Edward Grey. He was therefore chosen as a sound and capable diplomat to succeed Sir Gerard Lowther at Constantinople in the autumn of 1913. The post was considered a highly responsible one, the situation in this corner of south-east Europe being fraught with potential dangers. Where so many great powers had conflicting interests, an international explosion might occur at any moment. The Balkan Wars had, in depriving Turkey of practically all the lands under the Sultan's ancient suzerainty, and so bringing to an end the Ottoman Empire, reduced her to a condition of alarming instability.

Immediately after the Balkan Wars were ended Enver Bey, the Minister for War, invited Germany to reorganise the Turkish Army, and help strengthen her defences at Constantinople. His motives were ultimately to recover Turkey's huge territorial losses, and in the process to annoy her mortal enemy, Russia. Germany took every advantage of this invitation. She instantly complied with Enver Bey's request by sending General Liman von Sanders, a soldier of overweening self-importance, to take command of the Turkish forces.

M. Sasonow, the Russian Under-Secretary for Foreign Affairs, was the first to take alarm over von Sanders's assumption of military control of Turkey and his desire that this control should be recognised by the whole diplomatic corps. The unfortunate approach by Turkey to Germany might never have happened had Lowther not been withdrawn and replaced by Mallet. For the new Ambassador had never been to Turkey before and could not speak the language. Still more unfortunately, the highly qualified English Chief Dragoman (the interpreter and adviser on Turkish affairs), G. M. Fitzmaurice, having gone to England on sick leave in 1913, did not return until after August 1914. On the other hand the German Ambassador in Constantinople had a very experienced staff and an active dragoman, who were successful in ingratiating themselves with the susceptible and injured Turks and meeting their demands.

In June the Nicolsons went home, ostensibly on short leave. Vita recorded:[24]

> The correct and adoring young wife of the brilliant young diplomat came back to England in June. I remember a divine voyage by sea from Constantinople to Marseilles, through the Aegean, a second honeymoon. We met Mother in Paris, and both thought that she was going off her head.

Lady Sackville's romance with her beloved Buggy had come to an end, and she was verging on a breakdown.

During the Nicolsons' leave in England the Great War broke out. The Foreign Office had other duties for Harold, and he and Vita did not return to Constantinople. As Lady Sackville put it in her inimitable mixture of French and English, 'Ce sale Kaiser, voilà qu'il a upset le milk.'

6

THE FIRST WORLD WAR, 1914–1918

HAROLD NICOLSON's two and a half years in Constantinople were extremely formative ones. Although merely a Third Secretary he had witnessed at first hand from behind the wings, as it were, the repercussions of the Italian war against Turkey, the alarming threats to East European stability, and further, the likely effects of Russian implication in the general *mêlée* brought about by the Balkan Wars. All these events were assessed and stored away for future guidance when more momentous times might arrive and the shrewd young Embassy clerk should himself become a responsible diplomat. Moreover Harold loved Constantinople, admired the Byzantine beauty of its architecture and surroundings, and appreciated the strategical importance of its setting in the confluence of the Christian and Islamic cultures. Although he was unable to begin his novel, *Sweet Waters*, until long after the war was over, he had forgotten little of the troublesome times and none of the scenery which he described vividly in that underestimated book. Possibly the lapse of eight years enhanced the nostalgia and freshness which so distinguish it. Yet he never had any illusions about the Turkish character.

> For the Turks I had, and have, no sympathy whatsoever [he wrote in *Peacemaking*[1]]. Long residence at Constantinople had convinced me that behind his mask of indolence, the Turk conceals impulses of the most brutal savagery ... The Turks have contributed nothing whatsoever to the progress of humanity: they are a race of Anatolian marauders: I desired only that in the Peace Treaty they should be relegated to Anatolia.

Naturally when Harold and Vita left Constantinople in June they imagined they would be returning, and so left behind all their furniture, pictures, carpets and tapestries. On the outbreak of war these things were stored under the staircase in the Chancery, with the exception of Vita's jewels which were taken to the Dutch Legation. Everything was retrieved intact when the war was over.

When Harold and Vita got back to England they were welcomed by Lord Sackville at Knole. It was to be their home until they found one of their own. Likewise they were given rooms in No. 34 Hill Street by Lady

Sackville when they were in London. Vita was in the seventh month of her pregnancy. By now both husband and wife appeared to be much in love. The attachments and peccadilloes of their engagement period had dissolved like forgotten dreams. When they were apart, which was never for more than a day or two, affectionate little letters passed between them. Harold would address her in those days as '*Karabache*,' meaning in Turkish 'My blackheaded one.'

As her time drew nearer Vita became frightened. She wrote[2] to Harold specifying what she wanted distributed to special friends, like Rosamund, and relations, in the event of her dying in childbirth. She expressed the hope that he would marry again, but begged him not to share with a new wife the expressions they used together. 'We shall have had nearly a year of absolutely unmarred perfect happiness together, and you know I loved you as completely as one person has ever loved another. There hasn't been a single cloud the whole time.'

Towards the end of June 1914 there was a house-party staying at Knole. The guests assembled for breakfast. The morning newspapers were brought in by a footman. They contained headlines announcing the assassination of the Archduke Franz Ferdinand at Sarajevo by a Bosnian fanatic. They were the knell sounding the end of Western civilisation and the life of ease as understood by the privileged in the great country houses of Europe. Yet so unaware were Lord and Lady Sackville's guests of the implications of this Austrian prince's murder that when a Swedish diplomat who was staying remarked in his imperfect English, 'Yermany is certain to yump in now,' the others all thought it frightfully funny, and burst out laughing. They were soon to laugh on the other side of their faces. The immediate consequence of the assassination was that the Foreign Office called in all members of the service who were on leave. Thus by the second half of July Harold was drafted into the Eastern Department, which a few weeks later was fused into the Western Department, where he was to serve throughout the entire war. On the 1st October he was formally transferred from the Diplomatic Service into the Foreign Office.

Harold Nicolson was not one of those who were firmly persuaded that world events progressed according to some unwritten dictate of destiny. Rather he believed that they were brought about by the accidents of human behaviour; that wars were not caused so much by economic or social necessities, as by the follies and idiosyncracies of individuals. Yet when he came to analyse the multitudinous tributaries of causes merging in the great torrent of events which overwhelmed Europe and the world in 1914, he acknowledged that the faulty systems by which the Great Powers had sought to maintain their authority throughout the preceding half-century were mainly responsible for the catastrophe. It is not my purpose

THE FIRST WORLD WAR 1914-18

to recount the history of the Great War in this chapter, except in so far as certain episodes concerned the subject of my biography. But since the consequences of the conflict occupied some of the most fruitful years of his life, when he was endeavouring to help resolve them and bring about a lasting peace – in vain, as things turned out – and then, as an historian, to record them, it seems only pertinent to dwell upon the premiss of his beliefs.

In *Lord Carnock* Harold Nicolson opened Chapter X on the 'Bosnian Crisis' with a paragraph which summarises his general view as to the indirect cause of hostilities in 1914. It runs as follows:

> The War of 1914–1918 was caused by a false conception of international values. In every European State the generations which succeeded each other from 1850 onwards were taught that national egoism was an honourable, and indeed a necessary thing. It was considered 'patriotic' to desire that one's country should be larger, richer, and above all more powerful than any other country. It was not considered patriotic to desire that one's own country should on every occasion set an example of unselfishness, humanity and intelligence. It thus came about that all but a small minority of scientists and intellectuals approached the problem of civilisation in a competitive and not in a co-operative spirit. In organised communities this competitive spirit can be controlled by the authority of law. The European community of nations was not an organised community, and for them the ultimate appeal was not to law but to force.

Harold was equally convinced that the direct cause of the 1914 war was the incorporation in 1908 of Bosnia and Herzegovina within the Dual Monarchy in the face of strong opposition from Serbia, whose western frontiers, adjacent to the two provinces, were extremely vulnerable to Austrian pressure. He frequently stated that this was brought about by the unscrupulous ambition of one man. Count von Aehrenthal was Austria's Foreign Minister. To satisfy his self-esteem Aehrenthal became determined to annex by fair means or foul the two provinces, which by Article 25 of the Treaty of Berlin had been retained under Turkish suzerainty, although actually administered by Austria. He was prepared, even anxious to go to war with Serbia over the issue. But how could he in so doing win the acquiescence of Germany? He carefully devised a little scheme. He invited the German Ambassador in Vienna, Herr von Tschirschsky, to luncheon at a choice restaurant in the Wiener Wald. He ordered quantities of excellent wine, appeared to get very drunk and, much to the embarrassment of the Ambassador, started to rant and rave, shouting, 'My patience with these Serbians is exhausted. I warn you, my dear Tschirschsky, that I am contemplating serious measures, very serious indeed. I shall annex Bosnia and Herzegovina on October 6th next. Just mark my words.' The whole scene had been carefully rehearsed. The German Ambassador reported to his Government that the Austrian Foreign Minister had in his cups made the most outrageous threats which could not possibly be taken seriously. But October 6th 1908 arrived, and Aehrenthal carried out his threat without hindrance. When after the event the German Government feebly protested, von Aehrenthal was able to retort that he had warned their Ambassador face to face.[3]

Thus one man's egregious megalomania led to the assassination a few years later of another, which led to Austria's ultimatum of the 24th July 1914 to Serbia, demanding the abdication of her independence. Germany did absolutely nothing to restrain Austria because it was in her interest that Russian influence in the Balkans should be eradicated. Russia's mobilisation was the penultimate factor that involved the Great Powers in fighting. When the mobilisation was made known to the British Foreign Secretary, Sir Edward Grey, in the middle of the night, he went straight to Buckingham Palace and woke up King George V. The King telegraphed to his first cousin, Czar Nicholas II, to stop it – to no avail. Austria's declaration of war against Serbia, the infringement of the neutrality of Luxembourg and the invasion of Belgium by Germany were the last straws which broke the back of Britain's reluctance to be involved in the conflict.

On the 3rd August Sir Edward Grey, to the depths of his soul a man of peace, delivered his tremendous speech in the House of Commons, in which he gave an eleventh-hour warning to Germany and Austria that the British Empire would fight alongside France unless they immediately withdrew within their frontiers. That evening he returned to his room in the Foreign Office, plunged in pessimism. Darkness was already settling slowly over the trees in St. James's Park. A faint mist was rising from the lake. Grey stood by the window overlooking the autumnal scene of desolation and disaster. He seemed broken, and crushed. It was then that Sir Arthur Nicolson congratulated him on the effects of his speech.

> Wearily Grey walked to the middle of the room. He leant against the standing desk as if in physical pain. He raised his hands above his head and crashed his fists on to the desk. 'I hate war,' he groaned, 'I hate war.'[4]

Harold Nicolson was obliged to spend that night and the following one with the resident clerks in their rooms on the top floor of the Foreign Office building, overlooking the park, on emergency duty. When he had a

THE FIRST WORLD WAR 1914-18

moment to think of his own affairs he worried over Vita, who was about to give birth to their first child. So uncertain until the last were the highest officials in the German Embassy of what was going to happen that Baron Richard von Kühlmann, the Counsellor, asked Harold on the 4th whether he might propose himself to Knole one day, to which Harold replied, 'Of course.'

Harold has recorded in great detail the last few hours of peace in the Foreign Office and the part he was unwittingly called upon to play in them. At dusk all the offices and windows of the building blazed with electric light. Doors were propped open by wastepaper baskets to enable the occupants of rooms to dash from one to another. All preparations were made ready to despatch on the stroke of 11 p.m. (which was midnight in Berlin) telegrams to the Dominions announcing that, because Germany had failed to accept Sir Edward Grey's ultimatum (issued at 2 p.m.) not to invade Belgium, Great Britain had declared war on her. At 9.30 p.m. a thunderbolt fell. A private secretary from No. 10 Downing Street ran hatless and flustered into the Foreign Office. 'Stop!' he shouted, 'Germany has declared war on us!' Hurriedly a letter from Sir Edward Grey to the German Ambassador, Prince Lichnowsky, was re-drafted to read, 'The German Empire having declared war upon Great Britain, I have the honour, etc.' Lancelot Oliphant, Assistant Clerk in the Eastern Department, went round to the German Embassy in Carlton House Terrace, and delivered the letter from the Foreign Secretary, enclosing the Ambassador's passports. He returned at 10.15. At 10.25 an urgent telegram arrived from Ambassador Goschen in Berlin announcing that the Chancellor had just telephoned him that Germany would send no reply to Grey's ultimatum. The recent information that Germany had declared war had been erroneously based on an intercepted wireless message between some German ships. So again all the telegrams to the Dominions had to be changed. Worse still, the letter which Oliphant had delivered to the German Ambassador had somehow to be recovered, and another substituted. A conference was held in the room of the Permanent Secretary. Harold to his surprise was summoned. 'You are the youngest member of the staff,' he was informed. 'You must go and retrieve that document.' Harold's feelings as he walked briskly across the Horse Guards Parade, across the Mall and up the Duke of York's Steps may be imagined. He approached the side-door of the Embassy, since it was late and the lamp over the front door was extinguished. A surly footman answered the side door bell. 'Young man,' said Harold, who was about his age, 'you must rouse the butler immediately. I have an extremely important message to be delivered to His Excellency.' The footman asserted that both His Excellency and the butler had gone to bed. Harold kept his foot in the door, and was insistent that the butler be woken and summoned. After a short interval that functionary appeared,

> opened the door and left young Nicolson in the basement. He was absent for five minutes. On his return he asked Sir Edward Grey's emissary to follow him and walked majestically towards the lift. They rose silently together to the third floor and then proceeded along a pile-carpeted passage. The butler knocked at the door. There was a screen behind the door and behind the screen a brass bedstead on which the Ambassador was reclining in pyjamas. The Foreign Office clerk stated that there had been a slight error in the document previously delivered and that he had come to substitute for it another, and more correct, version. Prince Lichnowsky indicated the writing table in the window, 'You will find it there,' he said. The envelope had been but half-opened, and the passports protruded. It did not appear that the Ambassador had read the communication or opened the letter in which the passports had been enclosed. He must have guessed its significance from the feel of the passports and have cast it on his table in despair. A receipt had to be demanded and signed. The blotting pad was brought across to the bed, and the pen dipped in the ink. While the Ambassador was signing, the sound of shouting came up from the Mall below, and the strains of the Marseillaise. The crowds were streaming back from Buckingham Palace. Prince Lichnowsky turned out the pink lamp beside his bed, and then feeling that he had perhaps been uncivil, he again lighted it. 'Give my best regards,' he said, 'to your father. I shall not in all probability see him before my departure.'[5]

Thirteen years later Harold was to visit Prince Lichnowsky at his home in Czechoslovakia when this enlightened man, who had striven while in London to preserve peace between Germany and England, was in comparative penury and disgrace for having accused his own country of not trying to avoid war, and for allowing his views to be publicly known.[6]

On the 4th August Harold just found time to scribble a note to Vita, 'Such a busy Harold. Such a mémoire-full Harold.'

The day after the declaration of war Harold went down to Knole. During the night Vita's labour-pains began. Harold, while waiting in the dawn outside the wicket at Knole for the doctor to arrive, listened to the troop trains roaring through Sevenoaks station and taking the expeditionary force to France and death in Flanders. On the morning of the 6th Vita gave birth to a son.

The christening of the Nicolsons' eldest son led to the first of many

THE FIRST WORLD WAR 1914-18

subsequent rows with Lady Sackville. She was insistent that the boy's first name should be Lionel, whereas the parents wanted him to be plain Benedict, the name by which he was always to be known. Rosamund Grosvenor, whose influence with Lady Sackville was strong, was called in to arbitrate. She told Vita that she had reasoned with her mother for hours into the night; that B.M. was almost mad, and threatened to ruin Harold's career and withhold Vita's money from her. Rosamund cautioned Vita that she really might wreck her life unless she gave in. Lady Sackville was odious to Harold and insulted him in front of the servants. Finally Harold and Vita capitulated; and Harold wrote his mother-in-law a letter in which he said, 'I don't think you can have the slightest conception what this costs me.' For a time his relations with her were very strained. And when she accused Sir Arthur Nicolson of some quite unfounded charge Harold blew up, and was so rude to her that he felt obliged to apologise. He told Vita he loathed B.M. 'I get hot with shame to think that I have allowed myself to pander to her vanity, to adulate her emptiness, and to abet her insincerity.' He thought she might try to come between them unless they took care. In September he persuaded Vita to leave her tower room and the comforts of Knole for a time and to stay with his parents in Cadogan Gardens, where however he feared she would be bored and '*agacee.*' By December however she was again living under her mother's roof in Hill Street, often going to Knole for long weekends.

In her 1920 *Notebook* Vita wrote, 'We spent the winter [of 1914] in London, and I became quite sociable. I was, in fact, thoroughly tamed.'

For four whole years Harold Nicolson's place in the war was to be the Foreign Office. He chafed at times under the restriction. As early as August 1914 he told Vita that he was uneasy not to be fighting, but consoled himself with the fact that he worked so hard and so late into the night that he felt he was being some use, and was not being a shirker. It irked him when several of his friends in the Diplomatic Service, like Reggie Cooper, Charlie Lister and Gerry Wellesley managed to enlist. The fact is that his outstanding abilities were already recognised by his chiefs in the Department, and they would not let him go. Harold did not of course always agree with them, and already in September he told Vita he no longer felt he was being enough use in the office or earning a reputation for industry, intelligence and reliability. At the same time he gently rebuked her for suggesting that he might leave his duties earlier in the evenings and so come down to Knole for the nights. For the remainder of his life Harold deeply regretted not having shared with his friends the dangers of the front, or discovered whether he would have been a hero or a coward. He had the utmost contempt for cowardice in others, and was himself as morally courageous as could be. At times he feared he was naturally a physical coward, especially during the Second World War when he was occasionally frightened by the bombing. So too was everyone else, but Harold no more showed his fear than did the majority. He admired to an exaggerated extent his brother Freddy, who after all had been a professional soldier in peacetime, for going to France in August 1914. 'It is so how.* Father has brought down Freddy's photograph and has put it on his writing-table – poor little Fred, I can't bear to think of him out there,' he told Vita,⁷ and begged her to write to his mother about him.

Soon after the war began, bad news filtered into the Foreign Office from every quarter. The German armies were advancing on all fronts. Harold was unable to be with Vita as much as he would have liked. He could not help expressing slight jealousy of those friends she was seeing a lot of. It was an emotion which he learned had simply to be subdued if their marriage was to endure. He succeeded in subduing it.

In September of 1914, however, Rosamund was staying with Vita during her convalescence at Knole. Vita was taking a long time to recover from Ben's birth, and when Harold breezed into her room at weekends, full of cheer, while she was still feeling unwell, she occasionally snapped at him. Harold's robust health and irrepressible spirits could lead him to be a trifle insensitive among the ailing or dejected.

To disentangle from the plethora of papers in the Foreign Office what over sixty years ago was the individual contribution of a Third Secretary to the work of his department is well nigh impossible, unless he left some clue in his own diaries or private letters. During the war years of 1914–1918 Harold kept no diary beyond the briefest engagement book in 1918, and he rarely wrote to his wife about office matters because of security reasons and her lack of interest. Therefore the occasional reference in his correspondence to his day-to-day occupation has a certain rare interest. On the 25th February 1915 he told Vita that

> [George] Clerk⁸ had got muddled about the five separate loans we are making to Serbia & he told me to disentangle it – and to go and talk to the Treasury on the subject and they were tiresome and knew more about it than I did & I talked about 'amortisation' & 'note currency' to try to impress them, but they weren't impressed. Then I lunched with Nellidoff at his house ... Then I came back and found a lot of telegrams that had been put on my table in the morning and had got

---

* 'How' used as an adjective, another Sackville-Nicolson expression, meaning pathetic, sad, touching.

buried under Serbian loan papers – and I had to take them into Clerk who was irritable at them not having reached him before – and then I worked on & on & on, till 8.30 – and no Mar at the end.

George Clerk, to become a close friend, was throughout the war head of a new war department of the Foreign Office where he got to know countless foreigners who in normal times would have dealt with undersecretaries. By 1917 Harold found him 'such an angel to work with; so appreciative and encouraging & stimulating. He never snubs one for being uppish, & oh dear I was so uppish today. I suggested peace with Austria against everybody's views, and instead of just turning it down he sends for me and discusses it all.'[9] Clerk was in all respects the typical old-fashioned diplomatist, tall, slender, faultlessly dressed, wearing spats, an eye-glass and a welcoming smile.

In April 1915 Harold was much concerned with the secret Treaty of London, under which Italy came into the war as an ally. In return for joining the Entente Powers Italy was promised by France, Russia, and Great Britain by way of bribe that in the event of victory she would be given various territories on the Dalmatian coast and elsewhere. The Treaty also implied that Albania would be partitioned between Serbia, Italy and Greece, but stated that Fiume should go completely to Croatia, then an independent province. These promises, unwisely made in desperation, were to be the cause of much embarrassment at the Peace Conference of 1919. In the autumn of 1915 Harold's chief concern was the ambivalance of Bulgaria's attitude. Her neutrality and the uncertainty of what she was going to do had hung like a cloud over the Balkans ever since the outbreak of war. Moreover Serbia would not concede Monastir to Bulgaria and so secure her among the Allies. On the Russian armies being driven back by the German troops, Bulgaria was eventually bullied into joining Germany. As a result Serbia was crushed. Greece remained neutral in spite of her King's close relationship with the Hohenzollern family; and, in spite of Venizelos's sympathy with the Allies, was prevented from joining them for fear of Turkey.

In June 1915 the Nicolsons bought the fourteenth-century house which was to be their adored home for fifteen years, where their two sons were brought up, where they entertained hosts of weekend friends on a scale that was lavish compared with that of Sissinghurst, and where they wrote their first books and created their first garden. Long Barn was only two or three miles west of Sevenoaks, and within walking distance of Knole. It was on the outskirts of the small village of Weald, a sprinkling of timber-brick cottages and oast-houses at the foot of Hubbard's Hill, surrounded by hop-gardens and hazel woods. Caxton was said to have been born in the dilapidated little place which, secluded and remote, seemed a part of the hill from which it was dug. Vita gave a fairly faithful picture of Long Barn in a description of the Westmacotts' house in her novel, *Heritage*:[10]

> This house of which I am telling you was nearer to the earth than most; it had, in fact, subsided right down into it, sinking from north to south with the settling of the clay, and the resultant appearance of established comfort was greater than I can describe to you. The irregularity of the building was the more apparent by reason of the oak beams, which should have been horizontal, but which actually sloped at a considerable angle. I found, after I had lived there no more than a couple of days, that one adopted this architectural irregularity into one's scheme of life; the furniture was propped up by blocks of wood on the south side, and I learnt not to drop round objects on to my floor, knowing that if I did so they would roll speedily out of reach. For the same reason, all the children of the house . . . had made their first uncertain steps out in the garden before they climbed the hill or toppled down the incline of their mother's room.

Vita's writing-room on the ground floor was low, with exposed timbering and an ingle-nook. Her bedroom above it had a sloping floor like that of an ancient man-of-war. A sort of dwarf's door led to the boys' bedroom next door. Soon the Nicolsons dismantled a barn fifty yards away and rebuilt it so as to adjoin the cottage at right angles. It was given diamond and square casement windows in the shape of oriels, and the passages were paved with brick, the whole exercise estimated to cost £450. It provided one very long, low room, with a hooded fireplace and beamed ceiling, and a study for Harold at the outer end. The barn, by projecting southwards into the garden, formed a courtyard or enclosure. Then another detached cottage higher up the hill was brought into the complex. It was turned into a separate dwelling for the two boys. All the alterations and additions were designed and planned by Harold and carried out by a small builder in Sevenoaks.

Harold made a plan of the garden, which was to take the place of utter desolation, and dated it June 30–July 1. The garden was to be formal though on a small scale, as though an extension of the house which enclosed part of it. Anne Scott-James[11] has detected in it signs of the future Sissinghurst process of cutting up an area into a series of separate compartments.

> In the course of time [she wrote], they made a box garden, and Harold

THE FIRST WORLD WAR 1914-18

had a plan for a series of 'little colour gardens in rectangles with nuts and trees and things.' There was an apple garden and a nuttery, and at the bottom of the slope a Dutch garden was designed for them in 1925 by their great friend McNed.

This was Edwin Lutyens, Lady Sackville's last attachment, who was devoted to Harold and Vita and became their ally and intermediary when B.M. chose to quarrel with them. When Lutyens paid his first visit to Long Barn he was not enthusiastic. While Vita was showing him round he looked at everything very solemnly through his owl-like spectacles. Finally Vita, bursting with pride, asked, 'Well, and what would you do, McNed?' 'Sell it,' was his immediate reply.

Indeed not all the Nicolsons' friends cared for this rather too neo-olde-worlde residence. Dorothy Wellesley called it 'a damp but attractive house; it consisted of an old ramshackle little building, with a barn stuck on to it at right angles – built on the Wealden clay, yellow above, and blue beneath.'[12] Violet Trefusis damned with even fainter praise: 'Very pretty in its way, but too self-consciously picturesque for my taste. Life in a Tudor cottage is like living *under* furniture instead of above it.'[13] Yet when the house was filled with Vita's rich and colourful furniture and tapestries, and lined with books, and when the garden embowered the house in climbing plants and roses, Long Barn undoubtedly was very pretty and charming. In its way it was comfortable too, because of the number of servants they employed. Leonard Woolf commented upon the aristocratic ménage of Long Barn, the butler, housemaids, silver, opulent furniture and pictures.[14]

Harold who had never had a home and Vita whose beloved Knole was just over the hill and whose loyalty to the Kentish Weald was as passionate as her love for women, soon engrafted their affection upon Long Barn. When he was on his way in the train to the Lausanne Conference in 1922 Harold wrote to her:

> I don't think we could ever leave the cottage; there is not one crack in the wall, or one stain in the carpet, which does not mean something to you and me which it could never mean to strangers; something which has been built and gradually. And with it all a sense of permanence so that as you sit in your room tonight I shall think of you there, I dashing through the Ile de France in a train, and I shall think of the Rodin, and the blue crocodile and the figure of St. Joseph, and *The London Mercury* upon the stool.[15]

It took many months before they were able to sleep in their new house, but they would walk across the fields to it in the summer from Knole when Harold had a night off. It was another seal of their mutual interest and love. Vita was blissfully happy in the contemplation of the absolute independence Long Barn was to give them. She was also pregnant again. She wrote to Harold:

> Every evening when you come back our minds and our hands rush together, and merge, and are happy to be one again instead of two. And everything which is dear and intimate to us is mutually so, and your life is mine, and mine is yours.[16]

And then in the first week of November she gave birth to a baby boy, dead. There is an undated note from her to Harold, written in pencil on the back of a letter of the 12th November 1915 from Marshall & Snelgrove:

> Harold, Mar is sad because she has been thinking of that little white velvet coffin with that little still thing inside. He was going to give you a birthday present next Sunday. Oh darling I feel it is too cruel ... I mind his being dead because he is a person ... It clouds everything and I can't be happy ... Oh Harold darling why did he die? Why, why, why did he? ..

Christmas that year was spent at Knole. When Harold got back to London he wrote:[17]

> It was so beastly having a bag to go to the station with and it got in my way – & wouldn't go under the seat because it was too fat – or on to the rack because it was too broad – & I tried putting it under my knees but that gave me pins and needles & my bedint friend [a train companion] who has found out who I AM – and treats me with cordial deference as is due to the husband of a touf touf court favourite with big black eyes & rows and rows of pearls, my bedint friend said, 'Badly designed things these. The wife gave me one when we got married but I only use the bottles on *our* dressing table.' Fancy if the Mars had an *our* dressing table how they would squabble.

In April 1916 they bought a London house, No. 182 Ebury Street. It stands detached today on the north side of the far west end of this long Pimlico street. In the right-hand part the boy Mozart lived with his father and sister when he visited George III's court in 1764. It is a beautiful and haunted old town house of early-eighteenth-century date. Harold used to refer to 'our two happy homes, Ebury Street rather stern and prim and quiet, and the cottage all untidy and tinkly.'

Ebury Street was too far from the Foreign Office for Harold to lunch there often. So too was his club, the St. James's, in Piccadilly. He usually snatched a meal, when he was able to leave the Office at all, at the R.A.C.

HAROLD NICOLSON

in Pall Mall. From there many of his letters to Vita were written this year. They are mostly short, loving little notes, referring to zeppelin scares or describing how he had to represent his father at Victoria Station to meet Lord Hardinge on his return from India at the end of his Viceroyalty. Harold made a sketch of the ceremony.[18] It included soldiers in uniform, a phalanx of frock-coated and top-hatted officials with solemn faces on the platform, and among them himself, the only person wearing a slouch hat, looking underdressed and insignificant. Lord Hardinge immediately succeeded Harold's father as Permanent Under-Secretary of State at the Foreign Office, for his second term. Sir Arthur Nicolson, wracked by arthritis, frail and bent, was retired and raised to the peerage as Lord Carnock.

It is possible that Harold had again been sounding the Foreign Office about his release for military service, for on the 6th September 1916 he was sent a Certificate of Exemption on the grounds of his important diplomatic duties. In November he compiled a very long memorandum on *The Present Position affecting the Balkans*.[19] He was also put to work on the recruitment of Venizelists in the United States and the supply of stores to the Venezelist forces in Egypt.

In December Archie Clark Kerr was transferred to the Foreign Office after filling various posts abroad.[20] Harold was delighted to have him back. On the 21st he wrote to Vita,

> My own biscuit-coloured Arch appeared – he was just what he used to be years ago – no sulks at all – & not aged – I fear it won't last but it was nice seeing him & cheered me up.

Vita was then at Knole helping her mother to cope with running the enormous house and estate in the absence of Lord Sackville in the army overseas.

The year 1917 opened with the birth in the Ebury Street house of the Nicolson's second surviving son, Nigel. It was an event of great rejoicing after the tragedy of the stillborn son in 1915. 1917 was the first year in which both Vita and Harold in their several ways began making their mark. In the autumn her first book, *Poems of West and East*, was published by the Bodley Head. It launched her as an author who, by the time Harold was to publish his first book, was already established. Harold was always intensely proud of her writings, especially her poetry, because it transcended anything of which he was capable. Excellent prose-writer that he was to become, he was no poet, although a great lover, with a highly selective knowledge, of both English and French verse. Before Vita's first

THE FIRST WORLD WAR 1914-18

volume was out Harold had read it with some perplexity. 'I can't make your poetries out,' he wrote[21] to her. 'They seem to proceed from something that I don't know is you. It is rather a shut out* really, but they are so much better, so much more fluent and forceful,' than her earlier ones.

He, too, was having his successes in the Foreign Office. On the 27th April he wrote:

> I got great kudos out of a parliamentary question, rather unexpectedly. George Clerk, who was lunching at Hill Street, told B.M. Oh dear! oh dear! she was so silly. But I got an up on† her all the same. She is so pretty – and really her silliness is so frank & disarming: and she *is* fond of us.

The tiresome incident over Ben's christening had been forgotten. Harold was beginning to be noticed and appreciated, not merely by the heads of his department but by the Foreign Secretary, Arthur Balfour, and the Under-Secretary of State for Foreign Affairs, Lord Robert Cecil.

> Bob Cecil (who is acting for Balfour who has gone to Paris) sent for me today about the Russian business. You can't think how like he looks to the baby doves in Ben's bathroom.[22]

And two days later Lancelot Oliphant rushed hatless after Harold on the Horse Guards Parade to say that Lord Robert wanted him urgently for help in the debate that day about the Foreign Office. So Harold sat in a little box in the House behind the Speaker, and Cecil said, 'Oh I say, Nicolson, before you go the Chancellor wants to know what to say about America.'

On the 1st August 1917 Pope Benedict XV's Peace Proposals were despatched to the heads of State of all the major Powers. They reached London on the 15th. Even China's views were sought by the Vatican on how to bring hostilities to an end. The Pope's fundamental point was that the moral force of right must be substituted for the material force of arms. There must be reciprocal restitution of occupied territories: for instance, on the part of Germany, complete evacuation of Belgium and France, and restitution by other countries of the German colonies. Also the territorial rights of Armenia, the Balkan States and Poland must be investigated. Harold was at once put on to examine these proposals in detail and present a summary of their content.

His summary of the 23rd was an impressive document, although he misinterpreted Benedict's pleas for peace, which were thoroughly disin-

---

* a 'shut-out,' meaning an exclusion.
† The opposite of a 'down on' – another Sackville expression.

terested, and his motives which were strictly neutral. But, after three years of war, hatred and suspicion among the belligerent powers were too readily directed upon an intermediary. Harold's conclusion was that the Pope's move derived from enemy sources. The opinion of Sir Rennell Rodd, our Ambassador to the Quirinal, and of Baron Sonnino, Italy's Protestant Prime Minister, that the Pope's proposals were insidious and pro-German could not objectively be dismissed. Harold accepted it as correct. Furthermore he found Benedict's reference to freedom of the seas vague. He also criticised his failure to insist upon the Austrians evacuating Serbia, which he saw as a device to leave Germany a loophole for recuperating herself in the east. The Serbian Government was of course infuriated by what it considered the Vatican's partiality towards German Catholics to the prejudice of its own Orthodox subjects. Lord Robert Cecil endorsed George Clerk's view that Harold Nicolson's interpretations were deserving of careful consideration.

For several weeks Harold continued to work on the Pope's Peace Proposals and to draft a reply by His Majesty's Government in concert with President Wilson's reply of the 27th. In the course of his draft Harold ascertained that the Pope had undoubtedly consulted Germany before issuing the Proposals. The Papal Legate in Switzerland admitted to a member of the British Legation that the papal diplomats had experienced much difficulty in inducing the German Government to accept the clause concerning its evacuation of Belgium. This revelation, added to the favourable acceptance of the Proposals by the Central Powers, induced Harold to believe that they were a direct appeal from Germany to the Entente Powers to cease hostilities. Lord Hardinge called the draft a very good one. Lord Robert Cecil expressed his gratitude to Mr. Nicolson for his admirable notes, which were of very real assistance to him. Lord Hardinge 'told Ronnie who told Oliphant who told me that he was much impressed with my work.'[23] The outcome was that Britain never sent a reply to the Pope's Proposals; Count de Salis, our Minister to the Holy See, was told not to lend himself to any further forms of negotiation on these lines; and Harold's reputation within the Foreign Office was much enhanced.

Another preoccupation of Harold Nicolson in this dark year of the war was the task of drafting and re-drafting with a colleague in a dismal basement of the Foreign Office the Balfour Declaration. Far from having been a hasty wartime improvisation, as the document's critics like to represent it today, and an ill-considered expedient, 'devised to placate the Hebraic denizens of Wall Street,'[24] the Balfour Document, although one of brevity and simplicity, entailed protracted consideration. The powerful Jews of the time, whether of London or New York, were mostly anti-Zionist. It was not of the powerful Jews that Mr. Balfour and his assistants were thinking, but of the millions of weak Jews who lived 'not in Kensington Palace Gardens or on Riverside Drive, but at Cracow and Galatz.'[25]

No wonder that when his friend Gerald Wellesley tackled George Clerk on Harold's behalf, suggesting that he might be transferred to Rome, because it was unfair that he should have been kept in England all this long time, he received the astonished reply, 'You don't seriously suggest that I should let Harold go away during the war?' 'Yes,' said Gerry. To which Clerk said, 'But the whole war department would collapse if he went, and besides if *I* let him go (which I never will) Hardinge would never hear of it.'[26] And not only Hardinge. The Secretary of State, Arthur Balfour, was likewise well aware of Harold's usefulness to him. He was constantly summoning Harold to coach him on East European matters which he was to speak about in the House of Commons, and inviting him at short notice to meals. One day he introduced Harold in the House to his brother with the words, 'This is young Nicolson, my staunchest adviser.' No wonder too that a few of Harold's colleagues showed jealousy when the Cabinet had two of his memoranda before them within three days. Oliphant and Clerk were not among those green-eyed ones.

Harold managed to see a number of friends both in London and at Long Barn. There was Henry Drogheda, not very happy with his wife Kathleen, and dear Robbie Ross whom he would call on after dinner. There was of course Archie, with whom he dined and sat in Hyde Park on summer evenings. There was Reggie Cooper on leave and now a Colonel, so modest and so interesting, telling him such wonderful stories about the front, 'a genius in his own little *how* way.' There were Osbert and Sacheverell Sitwell,[27] 'They are two weird people,'[28] he wrote, with whom neither he nor Vita ever clicked satisfactorily. Harold thought they lacked a sense of humour, because they took themselves so desperately seriously. Osbert was the one with whom he got on best and sometimes dined when he was officer on guard at the Tower of London or St. James's Palace. He considered that Osbert impressed his personality so strongly on his generation that the imprint came off on himself. He grew sated with Osbert's recurrent jibes at the public school spirit, Kipling, Hymns Ancient & Modern, and bishops. He regretted that he did not apply his satire to something more up to date and deserving. When Osbert towards the end of his life became ill with Parkinson's Disease and suffered miserably, Harold was much affected and deeply sorry for him.

He also saw a lot of Lutyens, lunching with him or visiting him in his office. He was thrilled with the 'orgy' of his architectural drawings displayed on tables and floor, and intoxicated by his Delhi plans, among the most lovely things he had ever seen; also his war graves and cemetery designs – 'little "pergly" walks of crab apples and irises, with chapels and solemn trees and his great altar.'

In September Vita wrote to Harold that she had never been more in love with him than at present, but she feared the string of intensity might snap, and she wished she could go away by herself for a bit. Did she really wish to be alone? The shadow of Violet Keppel was beginning to hover between Harold and Vita. On the 6th June Harold had written to Vita: 'Damn that little too too – it hates me & misses no opportunity of letting me down.' There is no explanation of what she had explicitly done as yet to menace his happiness. But that Harold did not like her and suspected her as an evil influence, which poor Rosamund had never been, was quite clear.

In fact Violet was like a smouldering, dormant volcano, waiting for the opportune occasion to erupt. She had first declared herself to Vita unavailingly in 1910, and things did not go further than that. The check did not prevent her from writing on the 31st October of that year:

> Je veux faire de la peine à quelqu'un; si tu étais ici je te ferais asseoir; je mettrais mes deux mains sur tes épaules et j'appuyerais . . . je ferais entrer mes ongles dans ta chair, mes mains te crisperaient; je brouerais tes muscles, tes os . . . je voudrais te déchirer, te mutiler, te rendre méconnaissable . . .

The dots are Violet's. Her letters were written in violent, staccato phrases, often without beginning, and without end, in French or English, as she felt inclined, and interspersed with phrases in Italian and Spanish. Abusive, caustic, passionate and terrifying.[29] One derives the impression that during these dormant years Vita was elusive and evasive, except when it suited her to write. Violet did not take this lying down. She rejected with scorn the other's constant pretexts of being too busy. 'Vita, tu me désespères.'

In December 1916 she begged Vita to be allowed to stay in Ebury Street for one night. She said how right Vita was in declaring that one could love the person one fundamentally disliked. She admitted to being wracked with jealousy.[30] The next day she wrote, 'The horrible suspicion is beginning to dawn on me that one can care for two people at the same time in an entirely different way, & that consequently one wishes to part with neither,' heavily underlined.[31] Was she putting words into Vita's mouth?

By August 1917 Violet was scoffing obliquely at Harold. Men claimed that their responsibilities were more important than women's, forsooth, a point of view which Vita readily defended in a letter to Harold. It provoked a reply from him with a self-sketch entitled, 'Piccy of a young man with a curly head deserted by his wife.' Things were moving to a crisis, in spite of the fact that Violet was staying in September at West Coker Court with Dorothy Walker-Heneage, whom she pretended to Vita she loved almost as much as she loved her.

1918 saw the end of the Nicolsons' unalloyed early married bliss, certainly in so far as Harold was concerned. Violet Keppel was the direct cause. The next few years marked the only ruffled phase of the Nicolsons' marriage, which, once the phase was passed through, proceeded on pellucid waters. That the marriage survived was owing to Harold's determination that it should, and to his understanding of, sympathy for and trust in, Vita. The extraordinary mutual confidence and love between the pair which waxed to unprecedented heights during their middle and old age was undoubtedly the outcome of the tempestuous experiences they both went through, for during the course of it both learned that passion was an ephemeral and pitiful disorder which, if treated like a minor ailment, would in due course pass and leave the soul of the afflicted enriched rather than enfeebled. Never again were any of Vita's love affairs a threat to Harold's happiness, even when they caused him worry on account of her worry. Nor were his affairs ever a threat to Vita's happiness.

It is difficult to be certain what were Vita's inmost feelings for Harold between 1913 and 1918. His for her were rock-like. He had his infatuations, emotional and physical, for men. They were by the way. This was an accepted rule with him in the future. It is questionable that he was ever helplessly *in love* with anyone but Vita in his whole life. It is equally questionable whether she was ever *in love* with him, in spite of her protestations during the honeymoon years after the break with Rosamund and before the acceptance of Violet's volcanic advances. There was always a reservation during these first years, a sense that she was caged like a winged bird. She was 'the correct and adoring wife,' dutiful and submissive, of the brilliant young diplomat, contrary to her natural disposition. Her homosexuality was linked with the artist's desire for absolute freedom. She needed complete independence; to be captive to no one. She had to be herself, to develop the poet that she knew was within her struggling to be unleashed. Violet Keppel encouraged these wayward desires. What emerges from Vita's unorthodox story is that her love for and trust in Harold was accentuated by her passions for women. It was not pity that prevented her leaving Harold for Violet. It was certainly not a need for security. She had plenty of that without him or anyone else. It was sheer devotion, coupled with the knowledge that there was no other human being in the world with whom she could share permanent companionship and children, which, un-uxorious and un-maternal though she was, she needed.

In *Portrait of a Marriage* the full account of Vita's homosexuality and her affair with Violet has been told by her son with great sensitivity and delicacy. What does not wholly emerge from the book is the coincidence of the affair with an extremely busy and worrying period of Harold's career. He was working at intense pressure in the Foreign Office at a crucial stage of the war when there were zeppelin raids over London. Harold was more than a mere cog in the Foreign Office machine. He had become a person of consequence at the comparatively early age of thirty-one. By then he had a room in the office to himself. A number of extremely important problems were occupying him. One was Persia. That country was the cause of much anxiety to Britain's stand in the Middle East. In February 1918 Harold prepared a memorandum for the Persia Committee on *The Position and Interests of the Anglo-Persian Oil Company in the Middle East*. He submitted that no agreement should be reached with the Persian Government that did not provide for the secure future of the oil-fields. He feared that Whitehall might be giving way. He followed this memorandum with a second on *Policy in Persia* (22nd February 1918) in which he urged conciliatory treatment of the Persian Government, and strongly deprecated threats or the use of force. Lancelot Oliphant agreed with this argument.

In July Harold was told to write a third memorandum on Persia. He was very depressed that little had been done by the Government in the meantime and considered that the lackadaisical attitude of Lord Curzon, Lord President of the Council and member of the War Cabinet, had been lamentable. Harold's memorandum reiterated that the collapse of the Petrograd Government necessitated an immediate and drastic decision between the policies of conciliation and force. Mr. Balfour read the memorandum and approved it. On the 1st August Harold returned to the attack. He circulated a fourth memorandum to the Eastern Committee. In it he warned that all the odium of the Persian Nationalists would now be turned upon the South Persia Rifles, a large contingent of Persians, 11,000 strong, which had been raised by Sir Percy Sykes with the agreement of the Persian Government towards the end of 1915. The purpose of the Rifles was to prevent the Germans from threatening the flanks of the Mesopotamia Expeditionary Force. Harold in his pursuit of the conciliation policy suggested that we gave nominal command over the Rifles to some Persian notable, while leaving British officers in the contingent during the remainder of the war.

Finally, he submitted a fifth memorandum on the subject of *The United States and Persia*. Its purpose was to allay the misgivings of the American

Government over British behaviour in Persia. Our Government should explain to the Americans that ever since the nineteenth century our policy had been to secure control of the entry to India on her north-west frontiers. We should assure the United States that as soon as the war was over we would help Persia by granting her further concessions and financial assistance towards Nationalist aims, and would welcome American cooperation towards that end. In other words Harold was evolving a new liberal attitude towards mandated Persia which ran counter to the old conservative-imperialistic policy of his Victorian elders in the Foreign Office and Parliament.

In January and February of 1918 he was also hard at work compiling a memorandum on *The Consideration of Future Political and Diplomatic Developments*. The memorandum was printed for and circulated to the War Cabinet in March. Harold's argument was that Germany's position was more favourable than it had been in December 1916, and there was no likelihood of her collapse. The most likely event was her prolongation of the war, and the launching of an attack, not now on the west, but against India. To thwart this aggression the defection of Turkey from the Central Powers should be aimed at. It could be achieved at a high cost, and he specified the means. The passive neutrality of Bulgaria might be obtained by our guaranteeing her Macedonia, allocated to her under the 1912 Treaty at the conclusion of the First Balkan War. The most urgent and effective objective was to secure by political methods Austria's neutrality, she being worn out and the young Emperor Karl pacific. Italy would be bound to support our action. Germany's supplies from defeated Russia, on which she depended, would then be cut off and the Allies would need fewer ships in the Mediterranean. Lord Hardinge was actually quite gushing about the memorandum, telling Harold, 'You know, really it represents a very able view of the situation. I can't think how you managed to concentrate so many ideas in so small a space.'[32] Harold was very flattered. He felt that at last he was becoming an influence, albeit a minor one, in the conduct of the war.

Harold and Vita continued to invite friends to Long Barn in spite of the stringencies of wartime living, the rationing and general deterioration of foodstuffs. For instance, on the 23rd February of this year they had staying Ozzie Dickinson, Lutyens, Hugh Walpole and Maurice Baring. This was only one such weekend parties of distinguished persons. There were many others. Both Harold and Vita were also constant guests at luncheon and dinner parties in London given by well-known hostesses like Mrs. Ronald

Greville, Lady Cunard and Lady Colefax. With most of the London hostesses their relations were merely cordial and formal. Little more. In return for hospitality they rendered the distinction of their presence, which was that of two young notabilities who happened to be man and wife. With the Colefaxes their relations were much more intimate. They reckoned them as close friends. Sibyl was genuinely well read and art-loving. Sir Arthur was a successful barrister with a heart of gold. He was, however, inclined to buttonhole a guest with a relentless grasp from which it was difficult for the victim to release himself. During one of the Colefax dinner parties Harold was separated from Edmund Gosse and Paul Valéry by his host, who pinned him down and began a monologue with, 'Mind you, I've known Bonar Law now for many years; I should say for fourteen, or maybe it is twelve. And mind you . . .' From the other side of the room came from Gosse, 'Je me souviens un jour je suis allé avec mon ami Mallarmé voir Verlaine. Nous nous trouvâmes . . .' Harold was straining to catch the pearls from Gosse's lips. 'And mind you,' went on Sir Arthur, heedless of Harold's inattention, 'Austen, who is a very old friend of mine, is not the man to . . . You agree with me, don't you, Harold, that . . .'[33]

Harold's company in particular was much sought after. He could always be relied upon to enliven a flagging conversation with an amusing anecdote, either at his own expense or that of some figure of the past, for he intensely disliked and despised topical gossip. He would begin with an understatement in a misleadingly hesitant manner, and develop his story with a mounting enthusiasm that held his audience spellbound. As a talker he had few rivals. Yet there was nothing contrived about his conversation which was neither assertive nor competitive. It was the natural overflow of his well-stocked mind, the unavoidable outlet of his high spirits, the release of his enjoyment. 'It is so odd,' he once wrote on his return from what most of his friends would have considered a dull party. 'I enjoyed it. I always enjoy everything. That is dreadful. I must pull myself together and be bored for once.'

In the last half of March 1918 Harold had some leave which he spent at Long Barn, digging and planting, and playing with the babies. Vita was there and he greatly enjoyed it, in spite of the depressing war news and the piercing of the Allies' line at St. Quentin. He returned to the Foreign Office on the 13th April.

On that date his diary discloses that Bear Warre,[34] the architect, and Violet Keppel were staying the weekend at the cottage, as he referred to Long Barn; and on the 22nd, 'Violet still at the cottage.'

Violet Keppel first met Vita Sackville-West when she was eleven and Vita thirteen. Their mothers, Mrs. George Keppel and Lady Sackville were friends. Whereas Vita was a retiring, solemn girl, living an inner life of innocent self-mystification, Violet, although no less precocious, was a pushing, mischievous sprite, and a torment to her elders and betters. A significant bond between the children was the fact that at the first nursery tea they had together they talked of their ancestors. When they parted Violet kissed Vita. It was the pledge of a friendship which quickly ripened into love on Violet's part as the two grew into adolescence and then womanhood. They frequently met in London, at Knole, in Paris and in Italy. Then came Violet's unrequited declaration, Vita's marriage, absorption in Harold and her babies – and the war. Violet had to repress but she never suppressed her desire for her friend. She bided her time. It came in April 1918. She invited herself to Long Barn, went for a weekend and stayed on. Vita related how at first she was bored by the idea of having her. She wanted to write undisturbed, and Violet's restlessness fidgeted her. Her serenity irritated Violet. Suddenly everything changed. They were drawn together. Violet declared how she had always loved Vita. Vita acknowledged her dual nature, and the remainder of the visit liberated, as Vita described it, 'half my personality.' The explosion of this love affair, between the 13th and 22nd April while Harold was in London, is told by Vita at length in her autobiographical confessions, thinly disguised as fiction merely by the alteration of names, and begun in 1920. They were discovered after her death in her tower room at Sissinghurst and first published verbatim by Nigel Nicolson in *Portrait of a Marriage*. There is little doubt that Vita intended them to be published one day in order to help other people who might find themselves in the same predicament as herself.

> I hold the conviction [she wrote[35]] that such connections will to a very large extent cease to be regarded as merely unnatural, and will be understood far better, at least in their *intellectual* if not in their physical aspect.

This was not the case in 1920 when the story would not have found a publisher.

After the thunderbolt of passion had so positively blown Vita off her feet that she, dressed in landgirl's breeches, and pursued by Violet, scampered madly, helter-skelter across the orchards and through the woods of the Weald, she paused for breath and pondered. She decided that she must get right away from Long Barn, with Violet. On the 28th April the two women went off to Cornwall to stay in a cottage at Polperro, called the Cobbles, lent them by Hugh Walpole. It was a whitewashed cottage, built on a cliff overlooking the miniature village and harbour below. It could be approached only on foot and was in those days totally remote, the tranquillity disturbed only by the cries of seagulls and the crashing of waves against the rocks. Harold was left in London immersed in a memorandum on Holland, about which he knew little. He was desperately trying to persuade Mr. Balfour that the Dutch would not resist a German invasion, whereas M. van Swinderen,[36] the Dutch minister in London, assured him that they would. It seems hardly credible that he could have concentrated on this important matter when we consider his unhappiness over Vita's escapade. That very day he wrote no less than five letters to her. They are, like nearly all his subsequent unhappy letters, alternately gently scolding and then forgiving. He could never for long be angry with Vita, and he invariably apologised within a matter of hours for having rebuked her. Thus in one of his letters to her of the 28th April he wrote,

> I get so jealous thinking you are with other people – but I know really you love me best – & that you think of me most. But I get angry when I think of your going away quite gratuitously like that – just for a whim.

He was clearly very hurt. 'But I forgive you,' he wrote in a second, 'and hope you will be velly velly happy with your new companion.' And in a third, 'I suppose that you will now want to go to California with Violet and grow peach-fed hams.' It is accompanied by some amusing sketches of Violet in Mayfair clothes, incongruously enjoying the simple life, shrimping, cooking over an outdoor stove, and having a bath from the pump. But the last letter is one of anguish and abandonment. It describes every minute he has passed through since writing to her three hours ago. The self-pity and pathos are mitigated only by the humour which even at such a time he was able to call upon, and the vividness of the picture of a busy and lonely husband in London on a dismal, dank evening in wartime.

> My own Saint,
> You see what happens is that I talk to Mr. Balfour till 6 p.m., then I come downstairs and draw piccies for my mar; then I work a bit, looking at the clock meanwhile with hope and expectancy that one more day will pass. And then (Oh! solitude, Oh pauvreté) I find it is 7.15 p.m. So I go in and see if there are any more telegrams, but there aren't, and then it is 7.18. Then I lock up slowly and with grace, and by the time I have finished it is 7.22 p.m. Then I go up to see if A.J.B. wants anything more, but it is dark, and his windows stare blank against the wind and rain, and it is 7.32 p.m. So then I get my coat and my hat, and put away the keys, and get my stick with the silver top which you gave me on the fourth anniversary of our so unfortunate wedding, and I go across the Horse Guards Parade. It is getting darker by then, and

THE FIRST WORLD WAR 1914–18

The above is for Violet. It would make a good cover for Vogue.

Goodbye my dearest. This is the third letter today! H.

the Parade is empty except for two middle-aged boys doing bicycle tricks in the rain. I glance at the clock on the Horse Guards and it is 7.40 p.m., and quite inevitably and irremediably it rains. But as I go up the Duke of York's Steps it clears, and although the wind makes me draw my blue coat round me, yet the wet steps reflect the glow of a clearing sky. It is then 7.43 p.m. (Oh Solitude! Oh! pauvreté!) so I go along Pall Mall – and there are two Canadian officers, and an old man hurrying into the Reform Club. And it is 7.47 p.m. Then comes St. James's Street, and it is raining again – and the shops are all shut (Oh solitude! Oh pauvreté) – and with despair in my heart I get to the Ritz. And there in the cloisons under the arcade are Medici prints, and pictures of people who have loved and married in the past – and one of the Doge of Venice – who surely was a successful and companionable man – and by then it is 7.50 p.m.

And thereafter down the dip of Piccadilly (Oh solitude! Oh pauvreté) to where other clubs brighten in welcome to friendly unabandoned bachelors – and up the steps of this deliberate caravanserai – and by the clock in the hall it is 7.58 p.m.

So I wash with such care as I seldom give to the Victorian virtues – and then into the front room where there is a *Sporting and Dramatic* upon the uninspiring pages of which some Chilean attaché has spilt unsweetened coffee. And it is then 8.5 p.m.

But can one (a deserted and suicidal husband) eat alone at 8.5 p.m.? No! So I pick up *The Statist* and read a very brilliant little article upon 'River Drainage and Navigation in Ireland'. And by then it is 8.10.

So by then I go upstairs. And I order soup, and they bring me soup, and I eat it. And by then it is 8.13. And then they bring me a cold dead salmon, with jellified mayonnaise. And again I eat it and it is 8.15. And then they bring me Cabinet pudding. Little standardized cabinet puddings – replete with that combination of individualism and standardisation which has lost us the war. And it is 8.17 p.m.

Then Fleurian comes and sits next to me. And the waitress (who has cold steel pince-nez) brings me croûte à l'Indienne – and I eat it. And Fleurian says, 'Mais! comme on mange mal en temps de guerre,' and I reply, 'Oh solitude! Oh pauvreté!' – and it is 8.22.

And then I push back the table and pay my bill and it is 9/1d – and I come down here to write to you – and it is 8.33 p.m.

Of course I know I eat quick – and that before I was married to you I wasn't married at all – but what is one to do with that great chunk of time between 8.30 and 10.15 (bed time)?

The theatres are shut – and the few buses which sway down the empty Piccadilly are dotted on the top with figures crouching under glistening umbrellas.

And I left my pipe at the office.

Oh solitude! Oh pauvreté!

H.

THE FIRST WORLD WAR 1914-18

The following night Harold dined at Cadogan Gardens with his parents, whom he found old and gloomy, without a single subject upon which they could reach agreement. Moreover there were more reasons than ever to suppose that the Dutch were about to give way. On the 2nd May Vita, having postponed her return by twenty-four hours, was back in Ebury Street, and not very nice to him for the first few days. His diary briefly records, 'Viti rather wanderlust.' In the office he was concentrating upon yet another memorandum – on the United States going to war with Turkey. It was to occupy him well into July.

On the 9th May he was still depressed and wrote to Vita who had gone down to Long Barn, 'I suppose I should be more b.m. [bloody-minded] – but I am b.m. really – only I suppose I am too cultured and fin de siècle to impose my virility,' which was not far from the truth. 'I wish I was more violent and less affectionate.'

To this letter Vita replied in somewhat equivocal terms:

God knows I prefer your gentleness and patience and endurance to the violence you seem to covet. There is nothing, nothing, nothing I would alter in you.[37]

Which was all very fine. But she admitted her wanderlust, attributing it to the spring, the war and the wish to be away from housekeeping and household chores for a bit.

You seem to muddle it up with what you call the desire for 'adventures.' You are wrong. I don't want that sort of adventure, having *you*,

which strikes us as, to say the least, a trifle disingenuous, until we remember that the roots of her affection for him were already so deep as to be ineradicable. She denied that Violet was the cause of her restlessness, without admitting that she was the effect of it.

I don't covet that sort of life, in fact I should loathe it. No, I want to be free with you, that's all, a thing I can't have till the war is done. But in the meantime I feel that Violet and people like that save me from a sort of intellectual stagnation, a bovine complacency, which is the very natural consequence of my present life. I *adore* my present life, but it is, after all, only one side of the medal, and on the other side is all the intellectual stimulus you and I both require ... So don't be jealous of Violet, my darling silly.

The glaring truth is that Vita at that juncture of her life wanted, like most young couples married for five or six years, both sides of the medal. And were it not for the fact that one partner is almost bound to be rendered unhappy, why on earth not? Vita went on to say that she did not care what happened to the war. 'It is all such a fantastically tragic mistake.' To Harold, who was in the centre of the battle to defeat the Germans, this sentiment was more irritating than her denial of desire for adventures. He replied that Violet was irresponsible and demoralising her. To Violet, adventures were daily incidents. Her scale of values was quite different to theirs. The reference to adventures rankled with Harold. In another letter[38] he reverted to this subject.

> Goethe (like Hadji [which was Vita's nickname for Harold, first used by her in 1915], Shakespeare, Leonardo da Vinci, Michelangelo – and unlike the secondary geniuses such as Byron, Christ, Alfieri and de Musset) had no sense of adventure. He had a certain feeling for escapades, but that is a different thing. You see Shakespeare also really was a humdrum, smug old thing, who was more interested in being allowed to put armorial bearings on his note paper, than in discovering America. Incidentally also he had more taste for personalities than for achievements.

Weekend parties at the cottage were resumed and Harold was soon fairly happy again, although he must have sensed that Vita's passion was still simmering under the surface. Meanwhile she launched upon her novel, *Challenge*, which was to be finished in November 1919, but which the Sackville and Keppel families, backed up by Mrs. Belloc Lowndes, whose opinion Vita respected, dissuaded her from publishing. It was, however, published in the United States in 1924, but in this country, with a foreword by Nigel Nicolson, not till 1974. It is not one of Vita's best novels. It was her declaration of defiance against conventional morality, and she wanted it to be read by all her English acquaintances. 'I don't care what you say,' she wrote to Harold who was lukewarm about it, 'it is *damned* good. So there. Now you can think me conceited if you like. I am pleased with it, really pleased.' The characters in the story are easily identifiable. Julian, a rich young Englishman, living in a small republic on the Greek coast incites the offshore islanders of Aphros to revolt, and become their illegal President. He is joined by Eve, his lovely, mercurial cousin. They become lovers until Eve's resentment of Julian's commitment to Aphros leads her to betray him. She wants to have him selfishly for herself, and to hell with everyone and everything else. Julian is of course Vita. Aphros stands for Harold, Eve's rival. Eve was a first-hand portrait of Violet, physically and mentally, a portrait which the subject checked and amended with pride and satisfaction. 'She could not be called beautiful; her mouth was too large and too red. But she was irresistible, malicious, vain and witty. Her eyes were deep-set, slanting slightly upwards.' She was the sort of wild cat animal of the jungle which Vita admired. The novel was dedicated to Violet.

If Harold did not greatly care for *Challenge* he was warm in praise of a poem Vita allowed him to read, pronouncing it a *tour de force*. He admitted to her that he too was contemplating writing a book. 'I have thought out the general lines of my book,' he wrote on 10th June, 'but I shan't tell you.' And then, 'I wonder if you will resent my books. Obviously I must introduce a little savagery into my life; it will be difficult.' Far from resenting, Vita was to take the keenest interest in all Harold's books, jealously defending them against any criticism by other people than herself, jealous of his good name and glorying in his successes as a writer. What book he actually had in mind in 1918 he did not disclose, but it was probably a novel.

In June Vita was sitting to the Scotch artist, William Strang, for her portrait, which had been commissioned by Lady Sackville. At the time she was beginning her life of Aphra Behn, the Caroline poet, which was not published until 1927. Harold went to see the portrait in progress and thought it very successful.

> Darling, I did love the piccy so. It is *absolutely* my little Mar, she's all there – her little straight body – her boyhood of Ralegh manner and above all those sweet gentle eyes . . . It is so young and so grown up. It doesn't date. She is younger than the sham Chippendale chair on which she sits, and the eyelids are a little weary.[39]

It was indeed an excellent likeness as well as a most pleasing picture. Vita is made to sit bolt upright, hand on hip, her long straight torso shown to advantage, her face meditative and imperious like some proud buccaneer's. She is wearing a green jacket, striped and fringed, and a large red hat, by which title the picture is exhibited in the Glasgow Art Gallery today. For apparently Lady Sackville, on a visit to the artist's studio, complained that the mouth was wrong and seizing a brush began to show Strang how it should be altered. Strang was so incensed by this interference that he refused to let her buy the picture. Thus by far the best portrait of Vita, which ought to be hanging among those of her ancestors in the Knole galleries, was lost. Throughout the sittings Violet was present, her eyes fixed upon Vita, adoringly. When the last one was over she wrote to her, 'It was hell leaving you today . . . I am so proud of you, my sweet, I revel in your beauty, your beauty of form and feature. I exult in my surrender.'

In July the lovers went to Cornwall again, this time staying in Polperro village, and visited Hugh Walpole in his cottage.

But Harold was once more plunged in gloom. He was terribly got down by the war and ceaseless work, and could see no sign of the end. Again he was complaining of being in a rut, strongly deprecating as nonsense the Office's pretensions that he was indispensable. He had been previously. Now he was no more than a departmental hack. This, however, was not the opinion of Lord Denman's Committee set up to investigate whether more recruits from the Civil Service should not be enlisted for the fighting.

> Hon. H. G. Nicolson (Age 31, grade 1.) Retained as indispensable. *Reasons.* 'Has dealt with certain subjects from the outbreak of war, and has an intimate knowledge of many difficult and intricate European problems. His technical experience and facility for writing memoranda render him quite invaluable when information on the Balkans and other problems is called for by the War Cabinet at short notice. Mr. Balfour whose opinion was solicited stated that he did not know how Mr. Nicolson could be replaced; that, indeed, he had no hesitation in saying that it would be almost impossible to do so.'

Within a week of Harold's writing to Vita in Cornwall, 'It is a pity that she doesn't love him much. "Je voudrais, si ma vie était encore à faire, qu'une femme très calme habitât chez moi."' Violet on their return was writing to Vita that she felt possessed by her. 'What a perfect life we could have together. How right you were when you said we were made for one another, Mitya.' And on the 14th August,

> Mitya, Mitya, I have never told you the whole truth. You shall have it now: I have loved you all my life, a long time without knowing, 5 years knowing it as irrevocably as I know it now, loved you as my ideal, my inspiration, my perfection.

Harold's attitude was sometimes that of the complaisant but never of the outraged husband. His proposal that Vita should acquire for herself a padlocked cottage in Cornwall so that she might escape there from the 'yoke' and be alone, or take with her whomsoever she wanted, without his ever enquiring who it was; and that, when he was rich enough, he would have one next door on the same terms, was not welcomed as tactful. His attitude was quite unlike that of any known husband in love with a wife who was having a passionate affair with somebody else, let alone a woman. On the 9th September he wrote that he had never loved her so much as during the last few months when she had been slipping away from him. Such a sentiment implied that he never would let her slip away from him irrevocably.

THE FIRST WORLD WAR 1914-18

Violet in her clever way has made you think I'm *schmudel* and unromantic. And oh dear! oh dear! how can an impoverished, middle-aged civil servant cope with so subtle an accusation? You see if I was awfully rich I could have a valet, and an aeroplane and a gardenia tree – and it would be very Byronic – but not being rich or successful, it is just 'poor little Hadji, he's such a darling and *so* patient.' . . . Little one, I wish Violet was dead. She has poisoned one of the most sunny things that ever happened. She is like some fierce orchid, glimmering and stinking in the recesses of life, and throwing cadaverous sweetness on the morning breeze. Darling, she is evil and I am not evil. Oh my darling, what is it that makes you put her above me? It is so difficult to realise. It is so poignant to think of . . .

But, darling, what does it all mean? Darling, what do your odd unconvincing bursts of affection mean? What do your intermittent and (alas) so convincing coldnesses mean? Little one, I am not a fool . . .

This letter is poignant enough. It may be self-pitying. But it is what the Victorians would have called manly, without being mandatory. Harold was never one for ultimatums when there were more subtle means of winning through. His methods were conciliatory, and by conciliatory means he ultimately did win through.

On the same day he wrote to her again:

Don't worry about me worrying about you. I don't really. I get panics – wild panics in the rain under the plane trees when the wet leaves begin to gather round the park railings. But oh my God my love goes out to you like an arrow in the dawn, and I don't care, I don't care, I don't care. Darling can you see when I am dead in purgatory I shall say to Giovanni Malatesta – and Mr. Cross (who married George Eliot), and the curate who was engaged to Jane Austen, and Mrs. Humphry Ward, I shall say, 'But you see, my wife, also, was a very exceptional woman.' And Alfred de Musset will say, 'Je te plains, mon vieux, c'était ainsi avec cette malheureuse et malhonnête George.'

It would be difficult for a decent, honourable and intelligent woman not to be moved by a letter such as this. And Vita was pre-eminently decent, honourable and intelligent.

Towards the end of August the war news suddenly turned from bad to good. By the beginning of September it was as good as could be. In the summer the last German offensive had failed. The attack on Rheims came to nothing and the enemy army had to evacuate the left bank of the Marne under pressure from the French and Americans. On August 20th the British offensive began and three days later the Germans retreated to the Hindenburg Line. The Americans took the St. Mihiel salient, the

French St. Quentin, and the British Cambrai and Le Cateau. Peace was at last within sight.

By the end of September Harold Nicolson was in charge of the department dealing with the Near and Middle East. One day the telephone rang and a colleague in the War Office announced that a telegram had been received from the officer commanding the British forces in the Salonika area. Three Bulgarian emissaries had crossed the lines bearing a white flag. Harold realised that this portended the approach of the end of the war. He rushed to the room of his chief, Sir Eyre Crowe, who denied that it was in sight yet. The Germans would fight until the Allies crossed the Rhine. As it happened they gave up.

Harold was more driven than at any previous period of the war. He was immersed in the complications with the French which had arisen from the British advances in Palestine. He spent the morning of the 27th talking to the C.I.G.S., Sir Henry Wilson; and the afternoon poring over maps with Mr. Balfour and Lord Robert Cecil. On the 28th he completed a memorandum on *The Balkan Situation and Observations*. He reiterated that the ultimate policy of His Majesty's Government was to create a Balkan Federation to constitute an effective barrier to German expansion towards the east. Twice Mr. Balfour asked to be allowed to see and study this paper. By now Harold was concerned with the drafting of the Bulgar Armistice.

Having snatched a short weekend with Ted Lister at Westwood Manor Harold left Hill Street before 7 a.m. on the 1st October on a mission to Rome. Vita scribbled in bed a love letter which she passed to him to be read in the train. She assured him that her infidelities were merely an accident of the imagination, and she loved only him. He answered her from Boulogne. She was such a saint that all the anxieties of the last few months were now swept away.

In Rome he had talks with the Ambassador, Sir Rennell Rodd, and saw his two old friends of Constantinople days, Gerald Wellesley and Gerald Tyrrwhitt. The last had just succeeded to the title of Lord Berners, with £20,000 a year and three English estates. Harold had a high opinion of his talents and versatility as writer, painter and composer of what he called a sort of 'futurist music.' Lord Berners was indeed a brilliant amateur. He did not wish to be an amateur. He wished to be a professional. Yet he was too intelligent not to realise that he was no great writer, painter or composer. He was an extremely gifted and witty man, who told comical stories in a grave, unsmiling manner, which suggested underlying unhappiness. Newt, as he was known to his oldest friends, was at this time Honorary Attaché at the Embassy, and lived in a beautiful *palazzo* in the Via Vansa overlooking the Forum.

THE FIRST WORLD WAR 1914-18

Meanwhile Violet was writing to Vita, pouring scorn on her domesticity and motherliness, as she awaited Harold's return from Rome. 'At dinner you will have the endless furniture decoration conversation, interlarded with scraps of Roman reminiscences and conjugal badinage.'[40] She had confided in Vita when they were in Cornwall together about the man who wanted to marry her, and kept writing to her from the front. He was called Denys Trefusis, a golden-haired, handsome, piratical sort of fellow, sensitive, proud and idealistic. He was a Major in the Royal Horse Guards and had won the M.C. He was madly in love with Violet and while on leave in the summer they had become unofficially engaged. Violet was not in the least in love with him and Vita could have put an end to the romance by raising a finger, had she chosen to do so. Denys became a pawn in the game which Violet and Vita played together, Violet threatening to marry him in order to capture Vita, and Vita encouraging Violet to do so when she felt the pull from Harold was too strong for her. The situation of this charming and good-looking man was intensely humiliating and unenviable. On the very day he went back to the front, Violet wrote to Vita as follows:[41]

> I love Julian [Vita] overwhelmingly, devastatingly, possessively, exorbitantly, submissively, incoherently, insatiably, passionately, despairingly – also coquettishly, flirtatiously and frivolously.

She exhorted her to 'be wicked, be brave, be drunk, be reckless, be dissolute, be despotic, be an anarchist, be anything you like, but for pity's sake be it to the top of your bent.'

On Harold's return from Rome he and Vita were obliged to stay for a time at the Carnocks' house, 53 Cadogan Gardens, while work was being done to their Ebury Street house preparatory to Lord and Lady Gerald Wellesley renting it. Violet wrote to Vita on the 29th, 'Why did you go away to that horrid bedint house? I loathed seeing you in such dowdy surroundings.' It is true No. 53 had a stuffy and decorous air. It was, and is, very ugly. 'I feel those people,' Violet went on about the kind and gentle Carnocks, 'are reclaiming you. That house will suck the colour from your cheeks, it will draw the warmth from your body ... will curb your vagrant gipsy spirit.'

Violet and Vita were hatching plans to go abroad together the moment the war was over, and they were keeping their plans secret.

Harold was ordered by the Foreign Office to hold himself in readiness to be sent to Paris, and in the meantime to co-operate in drawing up peace terms as regards Austria, Italy, the Trentino, Dalmatia, Serbia, Greece,

Roumania, Bulgaria and Turkey. This meant leaving the War Department immediately, and confronting a truly mammoth task. He moved to a green-and-violet dug-out basement in the Foreign Office building. He must have had some inkling of the two women's intentions, for on the 9th November he asked Vita to tell him frankly whether she would prefer not to accompany him to Paris, and go off instead somewhere with Violet. 'I shall be so busy in Paris that I shan't mind *much* – but you would be rather nice there. Perhaps you could combine the two. Talk to B.M. about it. But don't lie to her.' The apparent casualness and indifference of these words indicate a change of tactics from the beseeching to the tough. But the next day his plans were changed. He would not now be going to Paris for some time.

On the morning of the 11th November Harold was in his basement preparing for an eventual peace conference, and studying the problem of the Strumnitza enclave. He required a further map. He went up towards the tower where the map-room was, and on the way called in at the office of the Chief Clerk to order some more tin boxes. He strolled to the window and looked down upon No. 10 Downing Street. It was 10.55 a.m. Suddenly the front door opened. Mr. Lloyd George emerged hatless, his white hair fluttering in the wind. He was shouting a sentence over and over again – 'At eleven o'clock this morning the war will be over.' Soon the whole street was blocked. At first there was no sound. After a pause there was wild cheering. Then silence again. The men bared their heads and sang 'God Save the King.' Lloyd George, looking flushed, pushed himself backwards through a sea of hands, faces and flags, and retreated towards his front door. In a few minutes he re-emerged and approached the little garden gate of No. 10 giving on to the Horse Guards Parade where more crowds were gathering. Two secretaries who were with him urged him to open the gate. He did so, waving his hands for a moment, and withdrew smiling. Harold returned to his dug-out and wrote a note to Vita who was in bed with influenza.

> They have signed – at 8.30 this morning. And I am so busy getting peace terms ready. It is rather fun, though I feel oddly responsible. I feel that what I do is so likely to be accepted – and that the tracing of my pencil in this familiar room and on my own familiar maps may mean the fate of millions of unknown people. I feel almost an impulse – 'God give me the right,' and I feel quite solemn about it.

Violet's mood on this Armistice Day was anything but solemn. She threw herself into the prevailing crowd hysteria. She looted Selfridge's shop for French flags and sat on the roof of a taxi waving at the dense throngs on either side of Regent Street. She greatly regretted that Vita was too ill to join her and witness the unprecedented display of British emotion. How wonderful she thought the British public was, forgetful of her last letter to Vita in which she reviled their smugness, complacency and lack of enthusiasm.

Vita could not make up her mind whether she wanted to go off with Violet, or not. But bullied by Violet and not discouraged by Harold who was up to his eyes compiling a memorandum on the Balkans and interviewing Venizelos, she got their passports and on the 26th left for Paris. An entry in Harold's diary two days before, records, 'A tiresome day explaining to B.M. why Viti is going to France.' Lady Sackville did not however learn the whole truth until her daughter, on her return from France, enlightened her.

For a delirious weekend the two women stayed in an apartment lent them by Edward Knoblock in the Palais Royal. In the daytime Denys Trefusis, who was in Paris, took Violet out to meals. Vita, dressed as a boy, or as 'Julian,' or masquerading as a wounded *poilù* with a bandage round her head, roamed the streets and cafés. She had indulged in transvestism before, in London, even at Knole, changing her clothes in the stables. She and Violet proceeded to Monte Carlo, where Harold addressed his letters to Vita at the Post Restante.

> You are running in my head like some remembered tune [Harold[42] wrote to her]. Little one, God bless you, be happy and enjoy the change, not *in spite* of our separation but *because* of our rediscovered love. And be nice to your poor sick little companion. I don't want other people to be unhappy when I am so glad and secure.

He was under the impression that they would be away only a short time, and was enduring her absence with philosophical patience. He did find it awkward having to explain to Lord Sackville what his daughter's relationship with Violet amounted to, without being too beastly about the latter. 'I fear, darling,' he told Vita, 'that people have really been talking. I noticed last night a certain inquisitiveness on the part of everyone – but it is so easy to explain away.'[43] He exhorted her to avoid talking to her companion about Borgias, gipsies and romance, which would only make her sillier. Answering tiresome questions from Mrs. Keppel and not knowing what lies Violet had told her mother, was a worse predicament. Reggie Cooper, whom he was seeing a good deal of, was a great comfort and gave sound advice, being the only person in whom he confided his matrimonial worries. Harold had been reading Vita's novel, *Heritage*, which was to come out the following year.

I can't write to you what the book has taught me. But I know that you must have suffered terribly, and that only a splendid character like yours could have kept from hating me. Dearest, it is one of the noblest things you have done. I can't find other words. But it makes me love you in a different way again, a sort of spiritual adoration and gratitude.[44]

On the 2nd December he presented a memorandum on *The Present Situation in Roumania*. He stressed the necessity of elaborating some satisfactory frontier between the Roumanians and the Serbians in the Banat.

On this very day Harold had a foretaste of the impending Peace Conference which was to occupy the greater part of the following year and to prove so momentous for the fate of the world. A meeting took place in London between Mr. Lloyd George, representing Great Britain, M. Clemenceau, France, and Baron Sonnino, Italy. Colonel House, the American representative, being ill, absented himself at the last moment. The meeting merely decided that an Inter-Allied Commission be set up to report on the amount the enemy countries could afford to pay in reparations, and that an Inter-Allied Conference should be held in Paris the following month.

Still Vita had not returned from France. Nor had she yet told Harold where she was staying. On the 5th he wrote her one of the very few angry letters of his life.

You really are quite hopeless about such things, and I put it all down to that swine Violet who seems to addle your brain ... You just go mooning on from day to day, with the future in a sort of sloppy fog which you are too lazy to pierce, and quite regardless of the inconveniences you are causing to others. I suppose that sloppy side is one of those which V.K. appreciates and which are dead to me.

She seemed to have forgotten her duties to the children, who were parked at Knole and, as they afterwards attested, quite happy, not because their mother was away, but because they were with their grandparents of whom they were very fond, and their father who now commuted from there to London and back daily. His cross letter was followed next day, typically, by a loving letter.

It gets no better my ache for you. It gets worse. I can't think what I should do if you died ... And then I want you in another way as well, and that makes me restless, and nervy.

THE FIRST WORLD WAR 1914-18

This letter is evidence enough that Harold was still physically in love with Vita. On the 7th he told her that he was going to stay with Victor Cunard[45] in Leicestershire, and wanted her to let Violet know that 'she is not the only string to our bow.' Victor was certainly one of Harold's casual affairs. He was twenty years old, very self-confident, sharp, a little brash, and made no attempt at concealing his homosexual tastes. Harold told Vita he was rather *mal vu* by his family. He hoped he was not going to the dogs. He had felt obliged to give him a severe pi-jaw.

Harold was happy when he was at Knole with the children. He got on well with Lord Sackville, provided he did not bring to Knole what his father-in-law called 'unconventional' friends like Victor Cunard, whom he did not like. When Lady Sackville told her husband that the Nicolsons were on the verge of divorce he wrote Harold a charming letter of sympathy, couched in his usual vague and feckless manner. 'I do hope things will go on all right now. I don't say much about these things but the Mar's happiness is pretty near my heart. But I feel sure you will be able to look after her.' He hoped for the best, and made it clear that he did not want to be bothered. His relations with his own wife were now pretty well on the rocks. And they were bothering him. The couple hardly spoke to one another, and living under the same roof was torment to both. Besides he was longing to instal Olive Rubens permanently at Knole. Lady Sackville was well aware of it. She would make provocative and idiotic remarks, which caused him to make brief, caustic retorts. Harold spent much time bustling between one and the other, trying to give comfort and prevent further scenes. And so his Christmas leave passed at Knole, without Vita. The festivities were sad enough for him without her, and made more so by his having to cable £130 to her, because she and Violet had run out of money and were obliged to move to a cheaper hotel. 'Why did you go off with that little swine? I do hate her so . . . I feel so angry with you tonight, Vita, for liking that little immoral, untruthful, spotty woman more than me.'[46]

He was in London on the 19th to watch from a balcony Sir Douglas Haig, handsome and bedizened with medals, drive in a landau down Whitehall. President Wilson was expected in London on the 27th and announced that he wished to speak with Harold. This meant that Harold had to cut short his Christmas leave. But he was never sent for and his leave was curtailed for nothing. He was back at Knole over the weekend. He had Gerald Berners staying. Gerald was no more agreeable to Lord Sackville than Victor. As for Walter Rubens who was also of the party, he disliked Gerald intensely. He remarked that his looks reminded him of an oyster, and he insulted him about his modernistic music. B.M. on the contrary succumbed predictably to Victor and Gerald's gaiety and flattery, and made intimate friends of them both. She was overheard remarking to Victor, 'No, I never remember the names of books – though I read so much. In fact they call me a blue [pause] stocking.' After she had left Knole and went to live in Brighton Gerald suggested that she painted some of the gasometers which obscured her view black with gold stripes, and one to resemble a paté de foie gras. She was delighted with the first suggestion but was doubtful about the second.

As a grass widower in embarrassed circumstances Harold awaited orders to go to Paris for the Peace Conference, while Lord Sackville incited his wife by coldly calculated insults to leave him in peace. On the last day of the year Harold said goodbye to Knole and the babies. Having embraced B.M. and exhorted her not to talk to Dada incessantly about money, he went up to London and caught the boat train.

7

THE PEACE CONFERENCE, 1919

THE Peace Conference of 1919 was one of the most fateful and tragic in the whole of human history. On its careful deliberations and weighty decisions the future of Europe and indeed the peace of the world depended. The men who conducted it were drawn from the cream of the countries represented. For the most part they were highly intelligent, and even good men. But they were not all wise. Circumstances, as well as their own deficiencies, were against them. The outcome of the Conference was a disaster.

Harold Nicolson at the age of thirty-two was one of many junior advisers on the staff of the British delegation. Healthy and vigorous he was ambitious for advancement in his career. Once the Conference got under way his working hours were strenuous, usually from ten in the morning till one o'clock, with a short break for luncheon, and again from two till eight. Often he was kept at his desk late into the night. He positively enjoyed every minute of his labours. He was directly responsible to his beloved chief, Sir Eyre Crowe in the Central and South-East European Department, which also embraced Asia Minor. The colleague in his department with whom he worked on an equal footing was Allen Leeper,[1] the same age as Harold and like him a Balliol man. Leeper had been born in Australia and was not at the time a regular member of the Foreign Office, but had been drawn from the British Museum and the Ministry of Information. Physically he was tall and thin, with tightly brushed black hair. He was a man of high intelligence and understanding, of the loftiest ideals, and uninhibited in his desire to ascertain the points of view of all the delegates with whom he came into contact. He was a virtuous, deeply religious Anglican, and rather a fusspot. Harold found him the perfect colleague, and became devoted to him. If, as Winston Churchill averred, the competence of the British staff was greater than that of all the other countries represented, and won the admiration of the world, and if, as Sir Maurice Hankey declared, Harold Nicolson was the best Foreign Office man in the Secretariat-General, Crowe's team could hardly have been bettered. Hankey, a small man with a bald bullet head and trim black moustache, was the British Delegation's Secretary, solely responsible for the organisation of an executive staff of 400, plus 200 shorthand typists. His capacities were phenomenal. He remembered every detail, every file, every paper, every date of every event, big and little; and the machinery he set up in the hotels Majestic and Astoria 'hummed with the frictionless efficiency of a British department of state.'[2]

Harold Nicolson's status at the Peace Conference was, to start with, that of a minor executive. But through his remarkable abilities and the opportunities afforded him of meeting and advising innumerable persons of eminence, he soon earned himself a reputation for brilliant diagnosis and sound judgment. He was also a very close watcher of day-to-day events, which he recorded in a diary, ultimately published as the second part of his book, *Peacemaking*, in 1933. Furthermore, throughout this period of great pressure he was distracted by domestic distress and anxiety.

He arrived in Paris with other junior officials on the 3rd January. He at once installed himself in his allotted bedroom in the Majestic Hotel which was comfortable and luxurious. The whole British contingent slept and ate in the Majestic which, for fear of spies, was staffed exclusively by British servants. For the next ten days or so, while the more important officials arrived from England in the van of the actual representatives, Harold lost no time in looking up friends and making contacts with colleagues in other delegations. He dined with Edward (Knobs)[3] Knoblock in his flat in the Palais Royal, among his famous collection of Empire furniture. With Knobs's help Harold found and rented a small flat for himself and Vita, as soon as she would be able to join him. He was longing for her arrival. He had an hour's talk with M. Také Jonescu,[4] leader of the Roumanian Conservative Democrats in the Hotel Meurice. He established friendly relations with his American colleagues, whom he found very intelligent, but regretted their conflicting views on the Balkans. He had a long discussion with Crowe upon the constitution of the League of Nations, and agreed with him that it was unrealistic for the smaller Powers to have equal representation with the greater Powers. Harold felt himself right in the centre of things, had a motor car all to himself, and, after completing his preparatory work, awaited the opening of the Conference with impatience.

The delegates' offices were in the Astoria Hotel, close to the Majestic. Harold's working room was on the fifth floor, which smelt of lysol and iodine, having lately been used as a hospital by the Japanese. He prepared his room which he regretted did not face the Champs Elysées. He found that a lot of Vita's belongings had been delivered to his office. That was all right. But amongst them were 'some infinitely messy things of Violet's – some dead lip-salve tubes, a bit of dirty ribbon, one shoe, the whole thing so grubby and beastly I felt physically sick at their being muddled up with your dear clean possessions.'[5] He had to wash his hands after touching them. In another letter to Vita he could not help referring to your dirty little friend... Damn! Damn! Damn! Violet. How I loathe her. I refuse absolutely to see her, & if you arrive with her I shan't meet you. I don't think I could trust myself to touch her. I feel I should lose my head & spit in her face.[6]

He knew perfectly well too that she must be chaffing Vita about him. A few days later he apologised for this outburst which he admitted was against the rules.

By the 13th the Majestic was fairly flooded with the great. Harold dined alone with Lord Hardinge, who was so flabbergasted when Harold disclosed that his actual net salary amounted to £86 a year that he nearly fell over backwards. He had long talks with Edwin Montagu about the future of Constantinople, with an intelligent young man, Eduard Beneš,[7] about the future of Bohemia, and the next day met the President of the United States, who cross-questioned him about national statistics south of the Brenner Pass. Harold found Woodrow Wilson looking younger than his photographs suggested. His glabrous 'face and broad shoulders are on a larger scale to his body – & he is neat – rather tailor's model.'[8] He did not show his teeth unless he smiled, which was an awful gesture. He had a narrow waist and a Southern drawl.

On the 15th Harold had his second meeting with a man who was to cast a spell upon him. Eleutherios Venizelos[9] made an immediate appeal as hero and child of fortune. His career had been dashing and romantic, in fact Byronic. This fanatical Cretan had played a prominent part in his island's rebellion against the Turks in 1896. He had been a Liberal Member of Parliament and after only eight weeks Prime Minister of Greece. He was a revisionist, a reformer on a stupendous scale and a passionate Hellenist. Besides, he was no philistine, unlike the majority of national leaders. An omnivorous reader, he liked solitude and nature. He was extremely intelligent, gentle and humane. His love and knowledge of the classics was an immediate bond with Harold. Balliol had taught Harold that Aristotle contained the whole of human wisdom, and that Thucydides was the first and finest historian of all time. Throughout his long life Harold never let a day pass without reading for half an hour some passage of Greek or Latin; he never went on a journey, even in the London tube, without carrying a Loeb edition of Euripides in his pocket. Through the classics he came to love Greece with the same blinkered worship as Byron and his contemporaries who fought for Greek independence in the early nineteenth century.

Venizelos, wearing a black silk brimless cap and trim white beard, his bright eyes twinkling through steel-rimmed spectacles, impressed upon Harold that the whole coast of Asia Minor west of the meridian of

Constantinople was Greek in physical and climatic elements. Tentatively Harold pointed out that if Greece obtained all she asked for she might get a frontier impossible to defend. Venizelos assured him that she would have no such difficulty. 'In our days,' he said, 'there will be no more geographical wars.' Every argument that Harold put forward he shot down with the utmost politeness. When under the influence of Venizelos's wizardry Harold told Crowe that Britain's acquisition of Cyprus was a disreputable trick (for the island was wholly Greek and of no use to us), as bad as the Italians taking the Dodecanese islands, Crowe gently snubbed him. The more Harold saw of Venizelos the more he succumbed to his charm. When told to summarise the claims which the old Cretan presented to the Conference he disclosed a pro-Greek bias which did not escape the unfavourable notice of his superiors. Venizelos's claims were, however, so persuasive that the triumvirate of Wilson, Clemenceau and Lloyd George ultimately agreed to Greece's occupation of Smyrna on the 15th May with the help of the Allied Fleet. Even Harold was shocked into writing to Vita:[10]

> It is appalling that these ignorant and irresponsible men should be cutting Asia Minor to bits as if they were dividing a cake. And with no one there except me, who incidentally have nothing to do with Asia Minor. Isn't it terrible the happiness of millions being decided in that way, while for the last two months we were praying and begging the Council to give us time to work out a scheme?

But this was looking ahead.

The first informal meeting of the Peace Conference, still calling itself the Supreme War Council, took place on the 13th January. It consisted of eight persons, that is to say two delegates each of the four Great Powers – France represented by Clemenceau and Pichon; Great Britain by Lloyd George and Balfour; Italy by Orlando and Sonnino; and the United States by Wilson and Lansing. At this meeting it was decided to add two representatives of Japan. Thus the Council of Ten sprang from the Supreme War Council. The British Empire Delegation was a consultative body reinforcing the British plenipotentiaries, and its members were summoned to Paris whenever their expertise was required. The Council of Ten met in secret. The press was not allowed to be present. Harold approved of this decision because it allowed delegates to deliberate spontaneously without being obliged to make set speeches.

Georges Clemenceau was elected President of the Peace Conference. Verging on eighty, he had been a Member of the French National Assembly since 1871. In his youth a politician of the extreme left, he came

THE PEACE CONFERENCE 1919

to represent the intransigence of right-wing opinion. The destroyer of many ministries, he was himself twice Prime Minister of France, from 1906–1909, and again from 1917–1920. He enjoyed the advantage of speaking English, whereas neither President Wilson nor Lloyd George could speak French. He was extremely off-hand with the Council of Ten, usually addressing them like schoolboys and positively delighting in being discourteous and disagreeable to them. Lloyd George observed to Harold, 'You must always realise that Clemenceau is a rude but reasonable man.' Reasonable he may have been to representatives of the Allies, in spite of his boorish manner, but to the Germans, whom he detested, he was unreasonable and vindictive. One example of his unpredictable bad manners was given in a letter from Harold to Vita on the 6th July after the signing of the Peace Treaty:

> We had a terrible meeting at the Council of IV yesterday. Clemenceau arrived in a foul temper, sat down and began: 'Je proteste contre cette assistance non autorisée et trop nombreuse. J'ai convoqué le Concile des Quatre. Je me trouve ici en face d'au moins quinze personnes.' A.J.B. tried to soothe him, and so did Dutasta his son and secretary. Clemenceau flung his ruler with a crash on the table and shouted at Dutasta, 'Mais laissez-moi donc tranquille, vous espèce d'andouille.' A.J.B. was the only person who kept his head. 'But my dear President, I observe that behind you there are three French secretaries and one French expert. Surely I have a similar right to summon my own?' Clemenceau swung round at the wretched French expert, 'Votre nom, Monsieur?' 'Seydoux, M. le Président.' 'Ah, oui, j'ai lu votre rapport. Il était bien mauvais. Il ne jettait aucune lumière sur la chose. Ayant lu ce rapport je ne vous avais jamais convoqué, moi.' 'C'est Monsieur Pichon qui m'a convoqué.' At this Clemenceau swung round at M. Pichon who cowered in his chair like a rabbit. 'Alors,' he bawled at him, 'Alors, M. Pichon, c'est vous le Président de cette Conférence?'
>
> Everybody was acutely uncomfortable, and in the end we were all told to go, and a humiliating little procession headed by Howard Bliss and Hoover, and finishing in Uncle Charlie [Sackville-West] and myself, crept from the room. It was a terrible scene. The old man is a tiger.

His rudeness to Lloyd George on occasions exceeded all bounds of diplomatic procedure. At the Council of Three he said to him, 'You have told me seven lies this morning. This is the eighth.' Whereupon, according to Camille Barrère who was a witness, Lloyd George got up and seized him by the scruff of the neck and they were only separated by President Wilson.[11]

The first plenary session of the Conference was officially opened by the

President of the French Republic, Raymond Poincaré, at the Quai d'Orsay on the 18th January. In his *Peacemaking* diary Harold gives a graphic vignette of the chamber, the delegates taking their seats, the attendants walking from table to table with muffled feet, and President Wilson getting pins and needles and having to pace up and down. In a letter scribbled to Vita[12] Harold – he is rushed off his legs – refers to the room as small but magnificent,

> with armchairs arranged both sides of a huge Régence writing table. At the table sits Clemenceau, and on his right are the Five Great Powers... Then comes Hadji – oh dear, he looks so funny. And then in the middle are secretaries, & an interpreter. This of course is the real Congress where the work is done, but it doesn't look like one as everyone is just sitting about – & they get up and lean against the mantelpiece. The wretched small Powers are brought in and made to state their case. They are set down opposite Clemenceau as if in the dock. It is an odd spectacle. Hadji doesn't say anything except when he's asked – and then he gets pink.

And no wonder he got pink, for whenever he did speak Clemenceau glared at him like an angry, wizened apple. Clemenceau's attitude to the Small Powers was even more arbitrary than to the Great Powers. His method of putting a case was to shout 'Objections?' and, without waiting for a protest, to add in the same breath, 'Adopté!'

Harold Nicolson saw at the start that the Conference was doomed to failure; and as it proceeded his worst fears were confirmed. In the first place he considered the choice of war-scarred Paris for the site of a peace-seeking meeting a psychological mistake. Feelings of hatred against the Germans by the French people were as yet unabated. On one occasion the German delegates to the Conference were stoned by the Parisians. More serious was the immediate revelation that there existed no certainty of purpose among the delegates. Of the five Great Powers it is true that America, Great Britain and France desired above all outcomes peace and security, but often at the expense of the betterment of the lesser Powers. Italy and Japan quite flagrantly desired more power than they had enjoyed before hostilities began. In principle the British and American delegates were at one, at least to start with. But the secret treaties made between the Allies in desperation during the war, before America came in, became the cause of much embarrassment. There was, for example, the Roumanian Treaty of 1916 containing the terms of that country's entry on the side of the Allies; there was also the Treaty of London of 1915 with Italy. Both these treaties were in direct opposition to President Wilson's subsequent Fourteen Points, and to neither of them was he privy.

THE PEACE CONFERENCE 1919

Furthermore, the delegates ought to have been representatives of the peoples of their country at the time, instead of being self-appointed, war-minded leaders who had been in office since 1914. In consequence they were often hampered and censured by current opinion at home. For example, Lloyd George, whose attitude throughout the Conference was temperate and fair towards the enemy, was continuously harassed by the strident Northcliffe press, with its cry, 'Hang the Kaiser', and 'Squeeze the German people till the pips squeak,' a spirit of vindictiveness to which he was bound to pay heed. Wilson's attendance at the Conference was disastrous. He was the only head of state present. Besides, his high-minded principles were thoroughly unpractical at such a time. He implicitly believed that wars were started by handfuls of men in power with evil intentions. Realising that in the Anglo-Saxon democracies 'the people' were overwhelmingly pacific, he assumed that the same democratic reasonableness would, once the militarists had been removed, prevail among all other countries. Harold was to recall how on one occasion, when neutral rights were under discussion, President Wilson raised his long dry face on high and exclaimed, 'Ah, but if there be another war, it will be a League war; and in that war there will be no neutrals.'[13] His touching faith in the League of Nations and his childlike adherence to his Fourteen Points (which he had first outlined to Congress in January 1918), long after they had been proved demonstrably unworkable, might have been modified, had he been accompanied to Paris by other Republican leaders. It was as much Wilson's obstinacy and vanity as the wickedness and self-seeking, as he chose to see it, of his fellow delegates that ultimately brought about the rejection by Congress of his covenent of the League of Nations.

It happened that Germany had capitulated on the basis of Wilson's Fourteen Points which had not been agreed to by the Allies. Hence the disparity in Germany's and the Allies' understanding of the clauses of the Peace Treaty. This vagueness, interpreted by the Germans until 1939 as hypocrisy on the part of the Allies, taught Harold Nicolson that precision was the absolute prerequisite of all good diplomacy, a factor which he never tired of stressing in his books and articles on the subject.

And all the while the spectres of unemployment, famine and Bolshevism were looming over Europe like a black cloud, threatening to burst and overwhelm Germany before the terms of an equitable peace could be arrived at. Across this appalling backcloth of horror an influenza epidemic swept the European stage, taking a heavier toll of life than the war itself.

One of the first things the Council of Ten put its mind to was the setting up of the League of Nations Commission. In the second week of February the draft covenant was presented to the Council, and on the 28th April adopted. The French bitterly opposed the very idea of the covenant as Wilsonian idealistic nonsense, which would merely postpone the peace. They also abused Lloyd George for heeding criticism at home and demobilising too fast. The British press were complaining that he was not demobilising fast enough.

Harold was soon writing to his father about his deep concern over the Council of Ten. It was paying no heed to the memoranda of its staffs; and it was acting in camera, irresponsibly, hurriedly. Towards the end of March he felt desperate. He told Lord Carnock that the Council was completely atrophied by a mass of detail. We were rapidly losing the peace, and Germany would go Bolshevik before the Powers had relieved starvation.

Harold's responsibilities were very considerable. Crowe, who was often absent, relied on him to conduct the Greek Committee. Harold was always conscious of the fallibility of Committee decisions rapidly come to, and of the happiness or unhappiness of thousands dependent on mere lines made on maps. ('Somewhere there must be a definite human desire behind all these lies and lies ... Our views and our decisions must of necessity be empirical.')[14] He told his father that Lloyd George was extremely good to the Foreign Office, and that Crowe was the centre of everything.[15] He extolled Venizelos. At the end of February the Czech Committee was set up, and Harold became its secretary. He admitted to feeling exhausted and unstrung. He actually snapped at a colleague. He only derived comfort from dining with Jules Cambon, that witty, disillusioned but honourable old man.[16] Then at the beginning of March the Council of Ten threw upon the Czech Committee the task of drafting preliminary peace terms as regards Balkan frontiers. No one, Harold grumbled, without experience, could conceive of the difficulty of inducing a Frenchman, an Italian, an American and an Englishman to agree on anything. The detailed work of his committees haunted him day and night. 'Even the puddles in the pavements assume for me the shapes of frontiers, salients, corridors, neutralised channels, demilitarised zones and "becs de canard."'[17] On the 17th March he began to draft the actual terms of the Czech Treaty, the Council of Ten insisting that all reports should be in agreement. 'It is hopeless,' he commented.

His work brought him into close touch with numerous persons of fame who gravitated to Paris from all parts of the world. He met them casually, or at luncheon parties, or at interviews. He had a long talk with Lord Reading about the progress of the Conference. Lunching with Edward Spears he met Ion Bratianu, who as Roumanian Premier brought his country into the war against the Central Powers – 'a bearded woman, forceful humbug, a most unpleasant man. Handsome, and catching his own face in the glass.' He dined with T. E. Lawrence who spoke of his adventures in Arabia. All very vivid and exciting. 'Can't make him out ... His foreground is so different from his background, and he hops from one to the other.' He decided he was a shifty charlatan. Queen Marie of Roumania, Foch and Briand were no more than acquaintances. But when Mark Sykes died[18] suddenly in an hotel Harold lamented the loss of a friend. 'I really mind,' he wrote. It was due to Sykes's endless push and perseverance, enthusiasm and faith that Arab nationalism and Zionism became two of the most successful of the war causes. He overcame all governmental opposition. He was boisterous, witty, untidy, fat, kindly and excitable.

With the two British delegates Harold's relations were that of a junior subaltern to his commanding officers. But unlike his relations with Lord Curzon later on they were neither as distant nor as affectionate. By Balfour Harold was charmed and exasperated alternately. He admired his wisdom, he deplored his somnolence. He marvelled at his good breeding. When dictating one day to Harold's secretary, Balfour treated her like the Queen of Holland. Harold would be asked to dine alone with him.

> I can't tell you [he wrote to Vita[19]] what charm he has. He was so amusing. He said, 'You know when I look round this room and think that the British Delegation all look very intelligent. Of course I don't know them. But then I *do* know you *are* very intelligent.' He told me I could always come straight to him if I felt things were going wrong. Of course I won't, as it would hurt Crowe & Hardinge.

He could be on perfectly easy terms with Balfour, to whom he freely spoke his mind, for instance, on the moral aspect of partitioning Asia Minor.

> I spent most of the afternoon with A.J.B. yesterday. He was infinitely tiresome. I was trying to ginger him up to stopping the P.M.'s madcap carvings. I made a long tirade against the moral turpitude of the P.M.'s plans, and A.J.B. said, 'Yes, that is all very well, but what you say is pure aesthetics!' What it is, is that people like him have got so used to getting what is expedient by dressing it up in a moral dress, that when you want them to condemn a thing as immoral they wish to see why and where it is inexpedient. Anyhow I got my point, but I don't know that he will do much.[20]

And the next day[21] he went on to Vita,

> There is *such* a thunderstorm brewing here against the P.M. It is all about this Asia Minor business, and it is difficult for Hadji to guide his row boat safely in and out of these fierce dreadnoughts. Even A.J.B. is

angry. 'These three all-powerful, all-ignorant men sitting there and partitioning continents with only a child to take notes for them.' I have an uneasy suspicion that by the 'child' he means me. Perhaps he means Hankey. I hope he means Hankey. After all, Hankey is younger by 35 years than A.J.B., which in my case would make him minus three. Yes, my dear, let us assume that it was Hankey.

The three all-powerful, all-ignorant men were of course Clemenceau, Wilson and Lloyd George, who after months of interminable wrangles were alone determining the Peace Treaty, which should have been determined months earlier. But Harold succeeded in rousing Balfour to anger against these cynical settlements. Having achieved his point he deemed it wise to lie low for a bit. He turned his attentions to the proofs of his report on Ruthenian autonomy.

By July Harold had been given by Crowe an absolutely free hand, and Balfour did what he wanted. He got quite alarmed at times at the power he held. 'It is not boasting (I am far beyond that).'

With Lloyd George Harold's relations were less easy-going than with Balfour, but more stimulating. In the first place Harold, with his strong partisan attitude in favour of Venizelos, rejoiced in Lloyd George's loyalty to the Greeks, to whom he was their great hero. They regarded him as their consistent sympathiser and champion. The Prime Minister recognised that Harold shared his Hellenic sympathies and when at the beginning of February the Commission was appointed to settle the Greek business, he chose the Prime Minister of Canada to represent the British Empire and recommended Harold to be secretary. On the other hand Harold was infuriated by Lloyd George's impatient rejection of the carefully prepared reports of the experts, and reliance on his own opinions which often were crassly ignorant. 'He hasn't the faintest idea of what he is talking about, and does infinite harm by vainglorious alarums and excursions.' He recorded an argument he conducted with Lloyd George in May over the Fiume issue. They were sitting round a dining-room table with the Italians, Harold keeping the big maps in place with the aid of forks. The Prime Minister flatly refused to listen to Harold's reasoned arguments against allowing the Italians to extend their zones, and accepted what they wanted. 'But I was saved by the fact that he thought the green bits on my map were Greek populations, whereas they only meant forests. The whole business was heartrending in its frivolity and lack of thought.' Harold did not trust him, and he mistrusted Lloyd George's apparent cult of him. 'I think he feels me just useful, knows I can't refuse to do what he says and realises that if tackled afterwards he can say, "the F.O. expert was consulted."'[22] The British Prime Minister had a maddening habit of

THE PEACE CONFERENCE 1919

always getting his way whether it was the right or the wrong way. Even Clemenceau was aware of this, and when asked by Tardieu why he always gave in to him at the Council of Three, replied, 'Mais, que voulez vous que je fasse entre deux hommes dont un [Lloyd George] se croit Napoléon et l'autre [Wilson] Jesus Christ.'[23]

On the other hand Harold was highly impressed by Lloyd George's wisdom, foresight and compassion in wishing to treat the enemy nations reasonably, and to eschew vindictiveness, an attitude which went contrary to the election manifestos in England. He admired the speed with which he grasped the impending failure of the Peace Conference after two months of abortive wrangling. He applauded the desperate efforts which he made, in the face of bitter misrepresentation both at home and abroad, to render the Versailles Treaty a more sane and workable document.[24] Harold learned from this erratic but brilliant statesman that apparent opportunism in politics is not always irreconcilable with vision – 'that volatility of method is not always indicative of volatility of intention.'

On the 1st April Harold was involved in an unexpected respite from the haggling, the disputes and the apparent stalemate of the peace talks in Paris. At midday he was told that he and Allen Leeper were to accompany General Smuts that afternoon on an important and secret mission to central Europe – Vienna, Belgrade, Bucharest and Budapest. He was not told to which place they would be going first, or for what purpose. Suddenly at four o'clock he was informed by Lord Hardinge that after all Balfour would not allow him to go. However, Smuts, who had a high opinion of Harold's exceptional abilities, insisted that he must accompany him, and Balfour's consent was extracted half an hour before the train left Paris.

Once again Harold's abilities led to his being appointed to a job for which his experiences were inadequate. As evidence that these abilities were generally recognised by his superiors he was this day promoted to Second Secretary. He just had time to scribble a line telling Vita that he might be away for six months for all he knew and no letters from him might reach her. He would keep a sort of daily diary letter to give her on his return.

The Peace Conference had long been distracted by disputes between Hungary and Roumania. The object of the Smuts expedition was to confront in Budapest the leader of the new Bolshevik regime in Hungary, Bela Kun, and see if he would accept temporary military occupation by

Allied troops of the zone between Hungary and Roumania, previous negotiations through the usual diplomatic channels having proved fruitless. The mission consisted of General Smuts, Colonel Heywood of the Military Intelligence, Ralph Butler of the Ministry of Food, Leeper and Nicolson. Also Italian, French and United States liaison officers were in attendance. On the way to Vienna the Austrian landscape presented through the railway carriage windows a deceptively flourishing appearance, although the stations were dismantled and the towns deserted. Vienna was the first halt. The streets there were crowded, but the inhabitants looked pinched, yellow and sad. Harold felt embarrassed by the healthy, well-fed appearance of their small party. 'I feel that my plump pink face is an insult to these wretched people.'[25] And when the head of the Military Mission in Vienna provided them with an expensive meal at Sacher's, Smuts was furious and showed his disapproval of this 'gross error in taste ... His eyes when angry are like steel rods.' The prices in the shops were exorbitant; the buildings unpainted and dilapidated. Smuts at once sent Harold off to the Hungarian Bolshevik representative to arrange for the Mission's safe-conduct to Hungary. The office was in some privately owned palace, and typewriters littered the gilt chairs. Someone there telephoned directly to Bela Kun who said he would be pleased to meet the Mission.

On the morning of the 4th the train sidled into Budapest station. Presently an orderly announced that Bela Kun had arrived. Harold went down the platform to meet him. Kun had only been out of jail a month and his head was still shaven. 'A little man of about 30; puffy white face and loose wet lips ... impression of red hair; shifty suspicious eyes; he has the face of a sulky and uncertain criminal.'[26] He was accompanied by his Foreign Secretary, 'a little oily Jew – fur coat rather moth-eaten – stringy green tie – dirty collar.' While Bela Kun conferred with Smuts through an interpreter, for he spoke only Magyar, and haggled over the terms of an armistice, Harold conversed with the Foreign Minister who in execrable German extolled the prospect of bolshevising Europe, including France and England. Then Bela Kun and the Foreign Secretary withdrew to consider Smuts's proposals. While Harold accompanied them along the platform the engine driver of a suburban train approached Kun in comradely fashion and, enclosing Kun's podgy hand with his black fingers, drew a light from the stump of his cigarette.

The Hungaria Hotel was put at the Mission's disposal by Kun. Although Smuts insisted on all their meals being taken from Army rations – bully beef and beans – in the dining-car of the train from which he would not stir himself, members of the Mission were permitted to visit the town. Harold found it even more depressed than Vienna. He visited the requisi-

THE PEACE CONFERENCE 1919

tioned Hungaria Hotel, at the doors of which Red Guards were posted with fixed bayonets. The foyer had been deliberately filled with people let out of prison for the occasion. They were silent and apprehensive capitalists, made to sit and listen to the strains of a gipsy band as though nothing in the world had changed since 1914. In the streets groups of the Red Guards, preceded by a red flag and followed by a hatstand, slouched in the pouring rain from shop to shop, hanging upon the hatstand such 'voluntary contributions' from the shopkeepers as they could extort.

On the second day Bela Kun, with Garbai the President, surrounded by Red Guards, returned to the railway siding and presented Smuts with a note which they had prepared. The contents of the note made an attempt to do a deal with the Allies that Roumanian troops should withdraw further eastwards before the Hungarian régime would accept peace terms. Smuts read the note carefully twice, found the terms unacceptable, and handed the paper to Harold who shook his head. Smuts said, 'No, gentlemen, I cannot accept.' Bela Kun remained obdurate. Smuts resumed, 'Well, gentlemen, I must bid you goodbye. Mr. Nicolson, you may tell the train driver to start at once.' The whistle blew and the train steamed slowly off. Harold had a last vision of Bela Kun and his associates standing stock-still on the platform, their mouths wide open, in utter bewilderment that the British Mission were not even prepared to argue.[27]

Smuts had rapidly come to the conclusion that Bela Kun was of no importance at all and would be incapable of ratifying any treaty. So he decided to break off negotiations instantly. He did so with absolute firmness, yet courtesy. He spoke to and shook hands with Bela Kun as he would have done to a Duke, and brought his hand to the salute as the train left the platform. As things turned out, by August Kun's Bolshevik régime was at an end. On the way back to Vienna the train stopped at Prague and Smuts had an hour's talk with Thomas Masaryk.

Harold Nicolson's opinion of Smuts at the time of the Peace Conference was of 'a splendid, wide-horizoned man – for whom I have the deepest admiration.' His sense of values raised him above most of the other delegates. They prevented him from condoning the punitive terms of the Peace Treaty. Smuts's opinion of Harold was no less flattering. 'Smuts has been so gushing to me about my help,' he told Vita. 'He wrote Hardinge a letter saying, "my advice and assistance had been invaluable."'[28]

On the 19th April Harold was granted a few days leave over Easter. He crossed the Channel by air, and landed on the cricket pitch at Knole, where white sheets had been spread on the ground to guide the pilot. 'It was too marvellous, darling,' he told Vita, 'a primrose clear evening, and at one moment I could see the Thames, Eastbourne and Boulogne all at the same time. It really was rather like the colour of the wings of a dove.'[29]

Harold's short Easter leave was the first time he had seen Vita this year. Throughout the three busy and hectic months at the Peace Conference he had been without her, eagerly waiting for her to join him. But she remained away with Violet. Although husband and wife had written to each other every day, Harold could not prevent himself telling Vita he felt slightly hurt that she sounded quite so happy.

> I hate all these new friends of yours – they are such a shut out. But *I* have new friends too – et comment! I sit in studios, & chat to models, and am a great dog.[30]

New friends he had made in truth, but actually he was too busy to be as doggy as he would like her to suppose. There was one new friend with whom he became very intimate. This was Comte Jean de Gaigneron, a younger man than Harold, who took him about, introducing him to his friends in the social and intellectual world of Paris – what Harold called 'lancéing' him.

Jean was the younger of two sons of an old Comte de Gaigneron who as a widower married a Gontaut-Biron. His mother was one of ten or twelve children of the French Ambassador to Berlin after the 1870 war. All these children married well. Jean was therefore closely related to the upper set of Talleyrand, Beauvau, Mouchy, etc. He never married. What he most liked was society and, not having much money, he spent his life lunching and dining out. It was an accepted axiom that all the Gontauds were witty (Marcel Proust made use of this legend in referring to 'l'esprit des Guermantes') and Jean made claim to this gift, a claim which many of his contemporaries disputed. For in perpetually trying to make witty remarks he could be tiresome and boring. He had however a certain skill in drawing and painting.[31] Harold made use of Jean de Gaigneron in his composite portrait of the Marquis de Chaumont in *Some People*. A few of that character's adventures were Jean's, also his obsession with quarterings and his war service on Marshal Lyautey's staff in Morocco during the First World War. It was Jean who in the story referred to Lamartine and Chateaubriand as 'ces hobereaux'; and it was he, who on being asked by Proust if he would mind figuring by name in a sketch he was writing in the manner of Saint-Simon, told Harold, 'It moight be jolly well all roight for a foreigner, but moy mother would not loike it.'

Like many other single men unevenly dedicated to society and gossip, Jean de Gaigneron in his old age became embittered and malicious. His small talent for painting was barely recognised. Life passed him by. Nevertheless, he remained attached to Harold's memory and assured

Philippe Jullian that during the Peace Conference he had had an affair with him.[32]

Although 'so faubourg,' Harold told Vita, 'Jean is a nice friend for Hadji as he knows all the clevers.'[33] Indeed it was indirectly through him that Harold met Marcel Proust. Having been introduced by Jean to the Roumanian Princess Soutzo, Harold was invited to dinner by her at the Ritz on the 2nd March. Among the guests was Proust, whom Harold described in his *Peacemaking* diary as 'white, unshaven, grubby, slip-faced. He puts his fur coat on afterwards and sits hunched there in white kid gloves. Two cups of black coffee he has, with chunks of sugar. Yet in his talk there is no affectation. He asks me questions . . .' The story is best continued by George Painter.[34]

> He asked how the English delegation worked.'We generally meet at 10 in the morning,' began Nicolson; but Proust interrupted, 'No, you're going too fast. Begin again. You take the official motor-car. You get out at the Quai d'Orsay, you climb the stairs, you enter the committee-room. What happens then?' Nicolson told all to this 'white, unshaven, grubby' diner, who listened enthralled, exclaiming from time to time: 'But be precise, mon cher Monsieur, don't be in such a hurry!' They met again on the 30th April. 'My dear friend, make an effort, try to be less incomprehensible!' Proust resumed, 'You say an Earl's daughter is called Lady, and his brother Esquire?' 'No, the Honourable.' 'So, when you speak to him, you call him Honourable Sir?' persisted Proust, with a gaze of deep sadness and tortured perplexity. Nicolson suggested that this passion for detail was a sign of the literary temperament. 'Certainly not' exclaimed Proust crossly, and blew a kiss across the table to his favourite Gladys Deacon. Soon, however, they were discussing homosexuality which Nicolson supposed must be 'a matter of glands or nerves.' 'It is a matter of habit,' replied Proust, and when Nicolson demurred he added, still more obscurely: 'No, that was silly of me, what I meant was that it's a matter of delicacy.' Nicolson decided that he was 'not very intelligent on the subject.'

In 1926 Harold was sent by his friend Prince Antoine Bibesco the copy of a letter written by Proust to Bibesco which concerned him. It is true the letter begged the recipient to come to him one Sunday alone, and not to bring Harold Nicolson with him. 'It was really very nice indeed, and gave me that warm, posthumous feeling which Byron experienced when published in America,' he told Clive Bell some years later.[35] The letter ran:

> Antoine, j'ai trouvé Nichsolson [sic] exquis, d'une intelligence. Il a l'air de t'aimer extrêmement. Tout ceci n'est pas pour que tu l'amène car je

serai navré qu'il me vit dans mon liège et mes tricôts brulés. Tout à toi et ma respectueuse admiration à Mademoiselle Asquith,'[36]

to whom the Prince was engaged. Such was the distinction of being mentioned, even with one's name misspelt, in a letter by Marcel Proust. Harold was to meet Proust at least once again, lunching with Jean de Gaigneron.

The friendship with Cocteau was renewed through Jean. After a dinner party Jean and Harold trudged through the snow to Étienne de Beaumont's where Cocteau was reading aloud his latest volume of verse, *Cap de Bon Espérance*. There were present André Gide, Paul Adam and Princess Murat. Harold called the last a perfect darling. She looked like nothing on earth. 'The nearest thing on earth that she looks like is Mrs. Brinton,[37] but a Mrs. Brinton painted like a McEvoy, perfectly glutinous with red paint and ten years younger, and so full of jokes and spirits.' She was an intimate friend of Proust and, unlike Jean de Gaigneron, was proud to figure by name in the novels. After the poetry reading Harold walked away with Cocteau in the snow. 'He is really the wittiest person I have ever met, but otherwise he is rather dreadful. He is *terrible* to look at,' he told Vita.[38] Only at intervals did they meet in after years. Harold retained an amused affection for Cocteau, was half impressed, half shocked by his outrageous opinions, and always read his books with curiosity. 'The intelligence of Jean Cocteau,' he wrote in a review of *The Infernal Machine*[39] 'is like a rainbow springing gaily from the storms of the past, and burying its brilliant head in the storms of the future.' But he grew to consider that he was a self-conscious writer who imposed on his contemporaries the pattern of his curious mind, and depicted regions that lay on the frontiers between illusion and reality.

Harold was under no illusions about Jean de Gaigneron. He found him attractive, friendly, and gay. Gaigneron knew – he made it his business to know – everyone who was worth knowing, and he was proud of his friendship with the brilliant young English diplomatist who spoke French like a native. Their affection for one another was easy and free. Harold was not the least in love with Jean. Besides Jean was hopelessly promiscuous. One day they sat together by the lake in the Bois and Jean poured out all his love affairs. He gets a new set every month, Harold told Vita. 'I am so glad that I only love solidly and singly, but then you think that smug and bourgeois.'[40]

Vita and Violet meanwhile were gallivanting about Monte Carlo. Harold was becoming alarmed lest Violet's engagement to Denys Trefusis might be broken off after all. On the 24th January he wrote sternly vetoing Vita's request to remain in Monte Carlo another three weeks. But a month later she was still there. Harold's weakness was that he could not sustain his annoyance for more than a day, and invariably followed a letter of remonstrance or crossness with one of forgiveness and excuses on Vita's behalf. Then disquieting rumours reached him of Violet's reckless gambling at the Casino and, worse still, of her taking Vita, dressed as Julian, to some charity performance at the Café de Paris, where they were seen dancing together. 'Of course I don't believe it, because, my poor darling, you *can't* dance and never could ... I can't forgive you if you have really done something as vulgar and dangerous as that.'[41] He minded desperately that she had not told him. Vita was able to assure him that the dancing rumour was without foundation.

He was longing for her to join him in Paris. Daily he expected her to turn up. He worried lest, when she did come, she might be bored without Violet while he was at work. He hoped she would bring some pretty clothes because the French women were all so chic. And was her new hair arrangement suitable? By the end of January he was still refusing invitations to dine out in anticipation of her arrival. And why did she not write more regularly? To which Vita replied that it seemed to her indecent to write to him while she was with Violet. 'Oh, do, do, do, do try and see it!'[42] On the 2nd February he woke up feeling so happy that she was at last coming according to plan, and then his happiness was dashed to pieces by receiving letters from her and Violet putting off her return. He felt ill with disappointment, but he conceded with almost superhuman understanding, Violet's suffering was what mattered. 'You see our love is an eternal thing,' he wrote.[43] He had half packed to move from the hotel to their flat. And now he would have to get rid of it. He begged her to pay no heed to gossip. 'Don't let's tell any lies about it. Just say you are staying on & let them draw their own bloody conclusions.' He also beseeched her to fix a date in March for her return and Violet to announce her engagement to Denys. The same day he sent Vita another letter which, for sheer pathos, wrings the heart sixty years after it was written.

> Darling, I am so depressed this evening that I must write to you. Don't think I'm grumbling – but only I feel so miz, dearest, & you *are* the person I write to when I'm miz, aren't you?
>
> Little one – oh my darling – don't think that I shall be permanently miz about it. I am only feeling crushed, & sore, & sad today – because it's Sunday – & I had been packing your things to take round to the flat – and I packed them so tenderly as if they were bits of you my saint – & I was so happy – *so* happy.

And then your letters came – & it was so dark & grim & horrible. I have never been so disappointed in my life. I didn't know it could come on one like that.

But it is childish, of course, and disappointment is after all a very transitory hurt – & nothing compared to poor V's tragic & hopeless position. Little one, don't think I am angry or sad about *you*. I always dissociate these things from you – especially when you tell me frankly what has happened.

But all the sun has gone from Paris – which has become a cold, grey, meaningless city – where there is a Conference going on somewhere – a Conference which meant so much to me yesterday, & today is something detached, unreal and inanimate.

But tomorrow it will be all right again – & when you get this *I* shall be all right again. Only please get a new photograph done of yourself & send it me. I feel you are slipping away, you who are my anchor, my hope, & all my peace.

Dearest, you don't know my devotion to you. What you do can never be wrong.

God bless you, Viti, H.

Luckily Harold was being rushed off his legs at the Conference and somehow managed, with extraordinary self-discipline, to switch off all personal worries when he had to concentrate upon urgent business of the moment.

The worry about the flat, the expenses to be met, the servants to be paid off, were as nothing compared with the greater worry about the children. B.M. was bombarding him with complaints about Ben's horrid nurse who was being unkind to him and ought to be got rid of, and he simply could not deal with that problem from Paris. Nor could he possibly have the babies in Paris. Lord Sackville also wrote to Harold urging him to insist upon Vita's return to Knole for Ben's sake. And Olive Rubens joined in with letters of remonstrance. Since neither of the Sackville grandparents seemed able to cope with the nurse Ben was sent to stay with a friend of his parents, Eve Fleming at Pitt House in Hampstead.

> It is really too bloody having these worries on the top of all I have to go through in the way of work [Harold wrote] . . . Good God, how this Violet business has poisoned our life. I shall always look back on the last 8 months with horror, and they should have been so happy, with peace and work and success.[44]

Receiving no satisfactory reply to these despairing cries he allowed his emotional pendulum, usually so static, to swing, rather shakily it is true, away from Vita.

THE PEACE CONFERENCE 1919

I don't want to write to you at present much, as I don't want to say things which I shall regret. You see I have been quite terribly overworked and all this sorrow and confusion has made me quite unnaturally upset, so I can't trust myself to write ... Day and night there is a voice in my ear, 'She lied to you! She broke her promise to you! She hurts you like this to spare the other!' ... I feel quite different and aged, and all my joy in life and work has left me. What frightens me so, is that I feel now I don't want to see you.⁴⁵

But the next day the pendulum swung abruptly in the opposite direction. Harold wrote her a letter begging her forgiveness. What vexed him now were the cross letters he was receiving from B.M. and the sad ones from Dada, who clearly thought he was behaving weakly; also the untruths he was obliged to tell in excusing her for not coming. Ruby Peto told him that 'all Paris was talking.' Well, let them talk, for he did not mind what people thought about either of them. If it were not for her tender letters he would throw himself into the Seine. 'You see *you* are the anchor and at the same time the storm.' In London too they were certainly all talking. Lady Sackville saw to that, not perhaps out of malice or even mischief, so much as stupidity. She fomented gossip by telling her friends that Violet had bewitched and was demoralising her daughter.

At last the prodigal broke away from her companion in Monte Carlo and returned to England by way of Paris. Between the 15th and 19th March Harold and Vita spent three happy days together, although she stayed separately with friends, the Wedels. Harold noticed that she had lost her light-heartedness. And indeed when she reached Lady Sackville's great, empty, dust-sheeted house at Brighton, which her mother was moving into, Vita felt suicidal. At least she was reunited with the babies, and told Harold what darlings they were, and how much Ben had missed her and how guilty she felt. B.M. was not very nice to her daughter, but Dada on the other hand, whom she saw at Knole, was sympathetic if not understanding. She sat talking to him till three in the morning, 'and I told him more than I ever had, and I love him, but I do not suppose he loves me,' she said to Harold. No one else was very nice to her. Only the Carnocks were exactly the same and made no reference to her prolonged absence.

On the 26th the announcement of Violet's engagement to the luckless Denys appeared in the newspapers, to the amazement of all. Harold was greatly relieved and wrote sympathising with Vita's feelings over the matter, blaming himself for their past troubles, which he believed were now over. He even wrote to Violet, sympathising with her misery, and begging her not to threaten to go off again with Vita, but to be strong and respect Vita's future happiness and responsibilities. His relief was not long-lived. He need hardly have encouraged Vita to keep writing 'kindly and often' to Violet. For on the 29th he felt obliged to refuse to let Vita go off with Violet again. 'There is nothing but leaden sorrow and disease in our life now, and our love which is all that has survived is wild eyed and full of tears.' He was sorry for Denys and thought perhaps Violet ought after all to break off their engagement. He knew, he wrote sadly to Vita, so little about her true feelings, and exhorted her to consult her father as to what was best for her to do.

It is doubtful whether Lord Sackville with the kindest intentions could enlighten her. He was such a straightforward, simple male that a situation such as hers was beyond his comprehension as well as distasteful to his nature. It was something he preferred to disregard. He dearly loved his daughter but did not pretend to comprehend her. He liked to believe that she could and would do nothing which, according to his standards, was dishonourable. He left it at that.

Vita was now bombarded by Violet with letters of intense misery. She beseeched. She reproached. She assured Vita that in the train Denys had promised he would marry her on any terms she specified. Vita would know what that meant. The same day Harold went for a fifteen-mile walk by himself in the Dampierre woods thinking things over and wrestling with his soul.

On the 14th April, while he and Arnold Toynbee were deciding that the Turks should have Anatolia as their own and the Greeks should be given European Turkey only, Violet wrote to Vita, 'Fly, fly, fly, fly with me now.' Harold snatched a moment from Toynbee to write to Vita that he was counting the moments till he saw her at Easter.

In May Vita's novel *Heritage* came out. It is a story of Ruth (Vita), a yeoman farmer's daughter in the Weald of Kent who derives a grim pleasure from ill treatment by her cousin, Rawdon Westmacott, a sort of Heathcliff (Violet), half savage, with the grace of an antelope and the wildness of a hawk. Rawdon's grandmother and Ruth's great-grandmother was a Spanish dancer (Pepita) whose predominating ancestry they share in mixed measure. Mallory, the narrator (Harold), is made to say of Ruth:

> What am I to believe? That she is cursed with a dual nature, the one coarse and unbridled, the other delicate, conventional, practical, motherly, refined? ... And is it, can it be, the result of the separate, antagonistic strains in her blood, the southern and the northern legacy?

Having read the book from cover to cover Harold told Vita, 'It *really* is good. The defects merely a question of organization.' He had no doubt that she would become an important writer. But she must keep her gravity of style and must not try to be funny.

On the 8th May Sir Eric Drummond invited Harold to help organise the Secretariat of the League of Nations.[46] Harold was delighted with the honour and prospect of working for a body which from its inception he supported with enthusiasm. He begged Vita to become League-minded, and to correct him if she saw him becoming too British-minded.

> So when you find me becoming impatient of the Latins you must snub me. It is rather a wrench for me as I like the sturdy, unenlightened, un-intellectual, muzzy British way of looking at things. I fear the Geneva temperament will be rather Hampstead Garden suburb ... But the thing may be *immense* and we must work for it.[17]

He thought he would be posted to Geneva, and might now be put in the Political Intelligence section of the International Secretariat, Eric Drummond, the Secretary General, being absolutely determined to have him. The next month he went to Geneva to look for a house. Lord Hardinge, still Permanent Under-Secretary of State, sent for Harold on his return and asked him why it was his intention to work for the League. He was very displeased because it had been his intention to make him his private secretary. So he put the offer to him there and then. Harold turned it down.

The dramas leading up to Violet's marriage coincided with extreme anxiety on Harold's part over the terms of the Peace Treaty which were nearing completion. He was on the verge of a breakdown. The slightest thing upset him. He was also deeply distressed about the Sackvilles' impending break-up, although he considered that B.M. was reaping the fruits of past selfishness and Dada those of past weakness. Yet he admitted to an inner feeling that a person like B.M., who was capable of making such rows about unreal things, could not feel very deeply about real ones. He suspected incidentally that she was opening his and Vita's letters. He detected a new note of 'wanderlust' in Vita's letters. 'I don't mind "wanderlust" as "wanderlust,"' he wrote to her, 'but I fear it is more than that.' He could not help feeling it was merely lust to wander away from him. He had only seen her for fourteen days out of the past six months. 'So you can't say that marriage is a bond to you, or motherhood a responsibility.'[48]

He was much perturbed by the iniquity of the reparation clauses in the Treaty, which he foresaw were quite impossible to operate. It was some consolation that Maynard Keynes, who was principal representative of the Treasury at the Peace Conference, agreed with him.[49] 'If I were the Germans,' he told Harold, 'I wouldn't sign for a moment.' Harold merely hoped that similar terms would be omitted from the Austrian Treaty. But the sad thing was that the Germans simply had to accept any terms presented within reason. 'I really feel,' he wrote,[50] 'that this bloody bullying peace is the last flicker of the old tradition, and that we young people will build again. I hope so.' It was all the fault of the French, and Lloyd George was endeavouring to alleviate the German terms, although Wilson would not support him. Harold quite rightly wanted Germany brought into the League of Nations. He told his father the terms were punitive, abounding in pin-pricks, or rather dagger-thrusts; and that all the junior members of the Delegation disapproved of them.

On the 30th May Vita wrote that Violet's marriage was to take place in London in a fortnight, and that because she could prevent it merely by raising a finger, she had decided she ought to join him in Paris in order to be out of danger's way. She added in pencil,

> Hadji, my darling, listen; there is about only one thing left in which I unshakenly believe, and that is your essential goodness. Hadji, I cling to you so, you have no idea. I don't know what is going to happen or to become of me, and I simply cling and cling and cling to the thought of *you*.

These words were no mere figure of speech. Vita was gingerly feeling her way along the sharp escarpment between her passion for Violet and her deep love of Harold. Two days later she continued:

> I never ought to have married you or anybody else . . . I am a pig really, and you are the dearest and sweetest and tenderest person in the whole world, and I only hurt you.[51]

No one, she maintained, ought to marry before the age of thirty, for if they did they were being cheated of their youth. And as though to test him, for she still fancied she was not absolutely sure how much he really would mind if she left him, she added cruelly:

> O Hadji, if you knew how it would amuse me to scandalise the whole of London! It's so secure, so fatuous, conventional, so hypocritical, so white-sepulchre, so cynical, so humbugging . . .

These adolescent sentiments were not hers. They were clearly borrowed from Violet.

THE PEACE CONFERENCE 1919

In answering this letter Harold, having told her that he was up till two o'clock that morning desperately trying to persuade the Yugoslavs to accept the Treaty terms, and was worn out in consequence, begged her not to stop the marriage for selfish reasons. He urged her to come over without delay. If she did not, 'it would hurt me so dreadfully that it would kill all that is best in me.'[52] As for her nonsense about wanting to scandalise London, it was 'rotten.'

> You seem to have no will power at all but just to drift and attribute the muddle you have got into to the conventionality of the world. It is as much good as a kitten who has fallen into the river blaming the ground for having been too dry.

And then relenting, 'Poor darling, how hard it is for you to bear.'

Their cat-and-mouse correspondence at this critical period of their married life reveals a terrible indecision and wretchedness on Vita's part, and a firmness of principle and no less wretchedness on Harold's. In actual fact Vita had pledged herself to run off with Violet on the eve of her wedding. Every plan had been made. And it was only Harold's vulnerability and defencelessness which ultimately stopped her.

On the 7th June he wrote that their relations would never again be the same as they were during the first four years of their marriage. She was so hard and indifferent to him – 'a hard fierce woman where there used to be so gentle and so tender a soul.' Her protestations meant nothing. She was breaking his heart, just as Kathleen Drogheda had broken his friend Henry's. It was unkind of her to leave him in suspense whether she was coming over, or not. He knew she was unhappy, but so was he, more so than she realised.

> All I get in reply is, 'Yes, I rely on you, please go on being tender and generous & forgiving and then when I feel better I *may* try to make it up to you. On the other hand I may decide to do the opposite and ruin your life and that of your children. But meanwhile please go on being nice to me about it, as it would all be very unpleasant if you weren't.'[53]

On the 8th Vita wrote that after all she could not come over sooner, for if she did, she would be bound to return and stop the wedding. So she would just come the day before. On the 9th she wrote that Violet

> thinks I will save her from this bloody marriage. How much astonished would you be if I did? I shouldn't be astonished in the least. It would be great fun, anyway.

But she supposed she wouldn't. Instead she supposed she would be a model middle-class wife, darning socks and opening bazaars. To which Harold retorted not angrily, but gently:

> You say it would be 'great fun' to elope with Violet. Why? What 'fun' can there be in doing such a thing, and why does it amuse you to say such cruel things to me? ... Why do you imagine there is nothing between eloping with Violet and cooking my dinner?

The Medusa, he warned her, was turning him into stone too. And in his *Peacemaking* diary[54] Harold, who carefully omitted any word that could possibly be construed as relating to domestic misery, recorded, 'All this fortnight I have been exhausted, hopeless and unhappy ... I see nothing but blackness in the future.' This pessimism was not solely brought about by worry whether the Germans would sign the Treaty or not.

Deeply penitent, Vita wrote to him, 'You don't know your power over me, you don't know it.'[55] It is true Harold did not until she actually crossed the Channel and was met by him at the Gare du Nord. Her terrible conflict had been resolved by Harold's letters which she read to herself over and over again. She told Violet that she was going to betray her. Violet on the morning of her wedding to Denys Trefusis, the 16th June, scribbled a line to Vita from her parents' house in Grosvenor Street, just before leaving for the church: 'You have broken my heart. Goodbye.' Vita was sitting in the gardens at Versailles, watch in hand, visualising the marriage ceremony.

The wedding took place, but trouble and unhappiness for the Trefusises and Nicolsons was by no means over yet. The honeymoon couple passed through Paris where Vita was staying by herself in a small hotel. She went to Violet at the Ritz and physically vented her rage upon her friend for the torment the marriage had caused them both, and the next day she met Violet and Denys. During this embarrassing encounter Violet told her husband that she had meant to run away with Vita and had never cared a jot for him.

On the 24th June General Smuts agreed to the terms of the Peace Treaty under protest and against his conscience; and on the 28th the Germans were obliged to sign. The last entry in Harold's *Peacemaking* diary records the harrowing and humiliating event in detail. He described his drive to Versailles, the arrival at the Château, thickly guarded by troops, the overwhelming presence of generals in uniform, contrasting with his own too

THE PEACE CONFERENCE 1919

civilian clothes and conduct. The Gallerie des Glaces had seats for a thousand participants and witnesses. At the centre of a horseshoe table in the middle of the gallery Clemenceau was sitting, small and yellow. The other delegates, including Lloyd George and Wilson, arrived just before proceedings began. Through a door at the end of the gallery a couple of huissiers in silver chains marched in single file, leading four officers of France, Great Britain, America and Italy. And then 'isolated and pitiable,' came the two German delegates, Dr. Müller and Dr. Bell. They were deathly pale and did not look like representatives of a brutal militarism. They were led to a little table and in stony silence made to sign. In 1928 Chancellor Müller, as he had then become, confided in Harold that he was bathed in a cold sweat caused by agonised endeavour not to let his enemies gloat over the depth of his degradation. Simultaneously from outside came the crash of guns, announcing to the world that the enemy had unequivocally accepted the terms of defeat imposed upon them. After the other delegates had appended their signatures, Clemenceau rasped out, 'La Séance est levée.' Everyone kept his seat while the Germans were marched out of the gallery like prisoners from the dock.

Harold Nicolson was quickly moved to compassion. Whereas most of the allied delegates, mindful of the terrible four years' misery largely brought about by Germany's aggression, were unmoved by her humiliation and plight this June day at Versailles, pity welled in Harold's heart. And not only pity. He was naturally an emotional man, given to sudden changes from indignation to forgiveness. But apprehension gripped his heart as well; and had done so throughout the entire proceedings of the Peace Conference. He had foreseen, as few did – Smuts and Keynes were two other exceptions – terrible consequences to a future generation of the unjust and vindictive terms being imposed upon the vanquished by victorious statesmen who allowed revenge to dictate to reason.

8

PARIS AFTERMATH AND THE LEAGUE OF NATIONS, 1919–1920

AFTER the signing of the Peace Treaty with Germany a tidying up process by the Allies continued in Paris. Much important work remained to be done in connection with drafting and presenting the treaties of peace with Austria and Bulgaria, Hungary and Turkey. Until the end of the year Harold Nicolson remained with the British Delegation. The Supreme Council of the Principal Allied and Associated Powers devolved into the Council of Five, which, since its objective was to control the pacification and remodelling of Europe, soon dropped Japan, becoming a Council of Four – namely France, Great Britain, the United States and Italy. Clemenceau virtually withdrew in order to resume urgent duties as Prime Minister of France. Henceforth he only occasionally presided at important meetings of the Council. President Wilson had gone home to submit the terms of the Peace Treaty to the American Senate which, as everyone knows, refused to ratify them, thus inflicting the first and possibly the most devastating blow the League of Nations ever received. Lloyd George and Balfour left to face up to the reaction of the Government at Westminster, and the Italian Signor Tittoni, the successor of Baron Sonnino, was recalled to Rome. Their places were taken by permanent civil servants, of which the British delegate was Sir Eyre Crowe.

Harold went on a short tour of the battlefields of the front. He watched men filling up the trenches and shell holes. Barbed wire was already being hidden by banks of nettles, and poppies and corn were growing on ground which twelve months previously was the scene of the fiercest fighting. On the 14th July he witnessed the victory parade in Paris. He was seated in the top floor of the Hotel Astoria, looking down upon the Place de l'Etoile and the great Arc de Triomphe. Above the arch, small white clouds chased each other across a sea of blue.

> The vast amphitheatre below me was packed with troops, grandstands, presidential tribunes and the victorious people of France. A massed band played the Chant de Départ with passionate reiteration. The tiny figures on the top of the Arc de Triomphe waved a little flag; the bands stopped suddenly; there was a great hush over Paris, and then, out of the

shadow of the arch and into the diagonal sunlight came Foch and Joffre riding together, their horses stepping delicately upon the pavement. A great roar went up towards us; the flags fluttered in the breeze; distant handkerchiefs waved repeatedly; and the long procession passed. How vividly do I recall the moment when Lord Haig, followed by a glittering staff, passed into that angle of sunlight. The bagpipes swirled. And then followed the flags of all our regiments, erect as a forest of masts, their heavy brocade hanging with embroidered battles – Bussaco Vitoria, Waterloo ... The glories of the past seemed to confound themselves with an assured and powerful future; the world had been made safe for democracy; the cries of happy millions echoed in the summer air.[1]

Work for Harold did not by any means relax. He was secretary to seven committees, of which four sat every day; and every evening he went round to Venizelos, never getting to bed before one o'clock. But he loved it, and the occupation kept him from brooding over his domestic unhappiness. When Crowe was called to London from time to time Harold revelled in the responsibility that devolved upon him and the decisions he had to take. He was made to represent Crowe on all his committees, which he considered the greatest tribute to his trustworthiness. He had his disappointments of course. It distressed him that, whereas he got his way with the Czech Committee, the outcome of which he was relatively indifferent to, he was continuously harassed and thwarted on the Greek Committee, about which he cared very much. He had been let down by the Americans who backed out of all the concessions to Greece which they had previously agreed, so that his work of January and February was in ruins. In July he had to break the news to Venizelos, who was more distressed on Harold's account than his own. He fancied that every country misinterpreted his attitude to their rights and wrongs. On the other hand he had his triumphs. On the 4th August he was sent by Crowe to see Eduard Beneš who was acting Foreign Minister for the newly founded state of Czechoslovakia. This stocky and nervous man, with hideous hands and sly little eyes, reminded Harold of an alert half-back or a spaniel nosing through the bracken. He was an idealist who was inclined to be a bore. 'Votre Beneš,' moaned Clemenceau on one occasion, 'a été d'une longueur – mais d'une longueur!' Beneš's point was that the fate of Teschen was dependent on the attitude adopted by the British delegation. It was hopeless to expect Czechs and Poles to come to an agreement amongst themselves. It must be imposed upon them from outside. Beneš begged Great Britain not to adopt the Polish point of view, but press for a compromise, since he desired an entente with Poland. So Harold recommended, with his customary good sense, that the Poles should keep the greater number of coalfields, and allow the Czechs free access to them, the coal being of vital importance to their economy.[2]

> I've WON all along the line [he told Vita] ... no one except myself and Beneš will know *how* clever, how dishonest, how deeply Machiavellian Harold was.[3]

The diplomatist's was the very opposite to a husband's rôle, he added.

Vita was by now back at Long Barn, still smarting from the shock of Violet's marriage, and Harold dared to hope she was becoming domesticated. But the volcano was not yet extinct. It was temporarily dormant, preparatory to a last eruption. Vita might write to tell him that she now hated London, and had bought twenty acres of land adjoining Long Barn, thus increasing their estate to the immense size of thirty-three. But she was restless, edgy and sensitive to criticism. When Harold told her he had been cross-questioned by Elizabeth Bibesco in Paris about his marriage, and had, while being loyal to Violet, thought it silly to deny the truth to so old a friend of them both, Vita stormed at him. Elizabeth was not a 'kind soul.'[4] On the contrary, she liked having a finger in every pie. She was a swine. Vita would never speak to her again, and if she said a word to outside people she, Vita, would sue her for libel. She also asked Harold not to tell people that he had read her books before they were published, because that would make them suppose he had re-written them. And then her tender side came uppermost, and she wrote, 'Hadji, do you think of me sometimes in the middle of all your work? And of how deeply I love you? And of how happy we shall be when you come back?' She was saddened by B.M.'s troubles, for it was riling for her to know that Olive Rubens had usurped her mother's place at Knole. B.M. was not jealous so much as hurt at her treatment from Lord Sackville. She was also, which was more worrying, suffering from harmless illusions. Her latest stunt was that she had designed the Cenotaph, 'but I do not remind my little Mcned,' she told Vita, referring to the actual architect of that famous memorial, 'and I shall not tell anybody.'

Violet continued to write Vita love letters, reminding her of the beautiful times they had in the past, and the freedom they enjoyed in Polperro. All she now had to live on were memories. Her letters were calculated to make Vita more wretched and unsettled than she might otherwise have been. Harold was understanding and sympathetic.

On the 1st August he attended a simple ceremony which left a lasting impression upon him, and enhanced his love of the traditional, unchanging France of the countryside, so rude and yet so civilised. At the invitation of Jacques-Émile Blanche he went for the day to Offranville, to witness the unveiling of a war memorial which Blanche had painted for the village church. He drove in a gig from Dieppe into country which meant to Blanche what the Weald of Kent meant to Harold and Vita. The sunshine glowed upon the pink brick of the artist's lovely manor house, which reminded Harold of Buckhurst and its walled garden, and the air was heavy with the scent of phlox.

> The sun poured in through the windows, lighting the parquet flooring, lighting the gay chintz, catching some corner of a Sickert or a Conder on the walls. The women of the house were busy round the dining-room preparing the port wine and the biscuits which were to serve as a collation after the ceremony.[5]

Blanche in a top hat and uncustomary town clothes was fussy and apprehensive. Cocteau, who was present, whispered to Harold, 'Ca me donne l'impression à mariage de Jacques Émile avec Blanche.' They walked in procession through the thick dust of the village street towards the church behind a band, choir boys, several curés, wounded villagers and the mayor in deep French mourning. 'The local deputy, who, being anti-clerical in his opinions, smoked cigarettes among the gravestones with a smile of condescending derision on his lips.' And when it was all over the entire company returned to the manor house. While the sun set slantwise across the orchard garden the guests drank port and ate *petits fours*, congratulating their host upon the success of the occasion and expatiating, in the way that only unsophisticated French working people are able to do, upon the merits of his painting.

From Offranville Harold paid a fleeting visit to England and spent two happy days at Long Barn, although he and Vita were not alone. She had warned him in advance that he would find Count Vita Borromeo staying, to which Harold had replied, 'I don't care two pins about Vita Borromeo as long as he doesn't borrow-me-own Vita (Isn't that *awful*?).'[6] Harold left for Paris by air greatly reassured about their future relations. He believed that those two days with Vita had averted a breakdown of their marriage.

On his return to Paris he was instantly plunged into a new job. It was to settle the Italian claims in the Adriatic. At last the Italians were persuaded to abandon their extremely unpopular claim to Fiume. Harold's recommendation that they should be compensated with the Adriatic islands of Lussino and Cherso, which were largely peopled by Italians, was accepted.[7] His next task was the disagreeable one of taking to Venizelos an agreement depriving Greece of Western Thrace, drawn up by the new American delegate, F. L. Polk, Balfour and himself. Harold loathed doing it, for he thought he was letting Venizelos down. Venizelos thought the same, and was enraged. On leaving him Harold went straight to Balfour who agreed that they could not force a settlement on Venizelos. Harold returned to the old statesman with a compromise which was that in Western Thrace Greece should obtain the districts of Xanthe and Gumuljina, and that, with the exception of Adrianople, she should be given the whole of Eastern Thrace. Venizelos, with tears in his eyes, felt bound to accept this adjustment. Harold was then obliged to reconcile his French and American colleagues to this *fait accompli*. Deeply distressed that Venizelos's policy should be thwarted, he showed his feelings before Balfour, who was mildly amused. It led him to wish that A.J.B. were a more violent and less charming man. Crowe's staunch support and pro-Greek policy were the only things which prevented him chucking in his hand at this time.

In August the League of Nations officially requested the Foreign Office to release Harold.

He was entitled to a month's leave from the 1st September to the 1st October. But immediately the Thrace question was settled he was immersed in the Austrian Treaty, involving the tricky settlement of the frontiers of that dismembered empire and the kingdom of the Serbs, Croats and Slovenes. He was now working at the Quai d'Orsay from ten in the morning till eleven at night.

In consequence of this latest responsibility thrust upon him Harold did not get away until a week after his leave was due. Even so Balfour and Tittoni would only spare him two or three days. His abbreviated leave was not wholly joyful. He suffered from toothache and Vita was clearly depressed. 'I would do anything if I could prevent that hard note coming into your dear voice,' he wrote when he left her on the 8th September. 'I know it means you're unhappy.' Having had an interview with Sir Eric Drummond in London, he crossed to France by Le Havre. On the 10th he witnessed the signing of the Austrian Treaty at Saint-Germain-en-Laye. Balfour said to him, 'When I saw you at Saint-Germain yesterday, my head drooped with shame,' at having curtailed his leave. The next day both Balfour and Tittoni left Paris; and d'Annunzio walked into Fiume and annexed it. This was flagrant defiance of the Yugoslavs and a deliberate snub to the Conference. Harold was furious about this act of brigandage, 'out of sheer swank,' by a man whom he considered a buffoon in spite of being a good poet. It totally undid the work on which he had spent hours of discussion with and persuasion of the Italian delegates.

Harold now learned that the League, whose proposed headquarters had already been changed from Geneva to Athens, was after all to be settled in the Swiss city, where Drummond expected him to take up his duties after his next proper leave. After a period of eight months in Geneva he was to return to Paris as liaison officer between the League and the Conference. His salary would be £1,200 a year, tax free, plus subsistence allowance. This would be a great improvement on his present Foreign Office pay which was inadequate. He complained that he was then overdrawn at the bank, whereas he had spent 'nothing' all that year. It is a fact that all his life he was lacking in money sense. He was recklessly generous in entertaining his friends, and never gave a thought to the bill when ordering the best food and wine available. He entirely overlooked this habitual extravagance when at irregular intervals a financial crisis in his affairs obliged him to investigate the cause.

By the end of August Vita, having been badgered by Violet, agreed to go abroad with her again, although she kept postponing departure in fear of a repetition of what happened the last time. Harold, who consented and even helped procure them facilities to visit Greece, where Vita wanted to get copy for her novel, *Challenge*, was however apprehensive. His way of showing his concern was to tell Vita about his own conquests, real or feigned.

> I have got such a funny new friend, a dressmaker, with a large shop in the rue Royale, a charming flat at the Rond Point (where I spent the whole of Saturday night, sleeping on the balcony) and about ten mannequins of surpassing beauty. I am lunching at the shop today. My dressmaker is only 27 ... Mar would like my new friend, I think – very attractive.[8]

He was going to stay with him when and if he came back to Paris from Geneva, instead of going to the Majestic. He hoped she would be a little bit jealous. Four days later he told her that he had again dined with the dressmaker and sat on his balcony overlooking the city under the stars. The dressmaker was no one less than the well-known couturier and collector of Impressionist paintings, Edward Molyneux.

In October Harold was given that part of his leave which had been cut in September; and on the 19th Vita went away with Violet. She left Harold a letter, which she described as 'packed with love.'

> My own darling, my own beloved darling, I scribble this for you to read when I'm gone and you are having your breakfast by yourself ... My own precious love, I only want to say again what I said last night, namely that I love you immutably, sacredly, and rootedly. You are all

the sacred, secret things of my life, my beloved ... and besides that, you're all that I think clean and sweet and good (*really* good, not priggy) and fresh and tout couvert de rosée and like apple blossom.

On the 21st Harold was officially seconded for service with the League of Nations until the 31st May 1920. He promptly moved from Long Barn to London where he was to work in the Political Section of the International Secretariat, installed in Sunderland House, Curzon Street. A few days after Harold was launched on this new job, Balfour was succeeded as Foreign Secretary by Lord Curzon.

Harold had the deepest respect for and belief in the League at the time of his appointment. It was the pernicious theory of the equality of all Powers, whether great or small, that from the first he strongly deprecated. When years later the League failed to prevent a second world war he still denied that the Covenant of the League had never been, as its critics objected, little more than a day dream. On the contrary it remained in his opinion one of the wisest documents ever contrived by civilised man. It was not the Covenant that repeatedly failed. It was the democracies of the world which failed to understand its purpose, its implications and its necessity. Harold brought with him from his experience at the Peace Conference the conviction that the League Secretariat must concentrate on high efficiency. He maintained that hard diamond intelligence was better for the world than all the idealism of the most virtuous of human beings. American idealism, in the person of Woodrow Wilson, had failed. Henceforth the League must be motivated by good sense. All forms of hysteria must be eschewed.

He found time during his first day in Sunderland House to send Vita a reassuring line about her mother's attitude towards her.

> BM is quite recovered and has been an angel to me. She is *not* cross with you, only quite seriously distressed. She has got no down on Miss Mars. Only she says she is inexperienced!![9]

He apologised for breaking down when she left him; but he was happy that she was going to enjoy herself.

On the 23rd October he told Vita that her mother was quite 'loony.' She was writing to all and sundry that her daughter was not really bad, but bewitched by Violet; and that Harold was dying of a broken heart, and was a weak fool. Ozzie Dickinson and Lutyens had each received a letter to this effect. Hazel Lavery had seen another. 'So London is seething with the *potin* and it is very unpleasant.' He sensed everyone gossiping all around him. It was all due to B.M.'s habit of contradicting insinuations that no one had dreamed of making. As for his work it was free and easy.

He was his own master and would be until his boss, Monsieur Mantoux, came; but he liked Mantoux.[10]

On the 25th he wrote to Vita that he had a grievance against her. Why had she told B.M. the most intimate things about themselves?

> It is all right your telling her things about yourself (though I think that very *unwise*), but it is bad luck on me to tell her things about me, which are at once repeated to Ozzie and via him urbi et orbi.

And what was the story of his having 'spurned' her at the Wedels? He couldn't identify it, but B.M. said she had told it to her, saying, 'It was then that Harold *lost* me.' What could she have meant? Lady Sackville was now so unhappy that she cried whenever she spoke of Vita. Her melodramatic behaviour was the very opposite of Lady Carnock's. She remained calm and sweet and when seeing Harold undisguisedly miserable, and knowing, as she must have done, the cause, never once reproached her daughter-in-law; on the contrary she repeatedly told Harold how fortunate he was to have so splendid and distinguished a wife.

Back in Paris he wrote from the Hotel Astoria (and not from Molyneux's flat) to Vita at the Hotel Windsor in Monaco, complaining that she had left Paris after she knew he had arrived there.

> You simply can't have wanted to see me. It hurt me dreadfully . . . What a cruel contemptuous thing it was to do. If you think that you can treat me like V treats D.T. you are wrong. I shan't allow my life to be wrecked. I have done all that a man could to meet you and understand you, and you go out of your way to wound me.[11]

She left him no address, and only a line telling him not to write to her. This was the third time she had given him these cruel slaps in the face, and he winced under them. How Violet would chuckle when she read his letter, which he supposed she would. If Vita did go to Greece he begged her not to be uncivil to his friends, for he counted there, and Venizelos had offered to have her met on arrival. On the same day Vita was scribbling him a line in pencil in the train between Cannes and Monte Carlo about the scenery through the carriage window. She was having endless rows with Violet, she said. If a horrid letter came from him she would not read it. On the 1st November she wrote refuting all his charges. It was true her mother did ask her if Harold was a very passionate person,

> and whether such things played an overwhelming part in our life, and I have answered No. I am sorry to put it crudely. I don't know what she said to Ozzie or McNed.

She was infinitely penitent, and denied that she was hard to him. He was, she reiterated, the best and most sacred and tender thing in her life.

On receipt of this letter Harold's anger evaporated. He forgave her. He assured her that his confidence in her only failed him rarely like the hot water at Knole.

> If I am conventional I have a sort of width of horizon about my conventions, a quite large gesture in obeying them. Whereas V defies them with mean petty little pokes (Oh I forget I mustn't abuse V).[12]

He said he was now arranging for her and Violet to go to Greece on Venizelos's cruiser, leaving Taranto on the 19th November. Therefore he hoped her book would not be too anti-Greek, for that would be embarrassing. And he ventured some advice about *Challenge*, which he referred to as 'V's Little Smuts.'

> I hope you will manage to make the psychological threads clearer ... An underlying symmetry of arrangement gives a greater sense of construction than any of the more obvious devices. I do hope that in the last two pages you will be able to gather up the psychological motives of the whole.[13]

And again he advised that she should give something cosmic to the story so that it concentrated on *Weltwahrheit*, so

> that the same sort of thing would happen inevitably with any human beings endowed with the same elemental forces – whether they live in Whitechapel, Bromley, Java or Montmartre ... It is a question of values and composition like a picture.[14]

And returning to the theme a few days later he said, 'Eve is a devil as she stands, morally. No decent person will have a spark of sympathy for her. She's a bloody little bitch.'[15]

Meanwhile Vita was spending her time in writing her novel and gambling in the Casino at Monte Carlo. The fireworks in the harbour thrilled her and she brought them into the novel when the priest was found drowned and during Julian's conversation with Eve.

Harold's moods veered like a weather-vane at the mercy of whatever breeze, rough or gentle, that blew from Monte Carlo. He was always elated when he got a letter from one of the children, or had good news of them. 'So long as *I* am on the shelf you don't expect me, do you, to be too too too faithful?' Gertie Millar was coming to his birthday party. His letter of the 20th was full of teases. 'Gertie Millar arrives tonight!!!!!' was a refrain interspersed between every paragraph. To which Vita responded a trifle humourlessly, that surely she was old enough to be his mother. As for Eve, she rebutted his strictures; she was not a little swine.[16] She merely had all the faults and weaknesses of femininity carried to the *n*th power, but she was redeemed by her capacity for self-sacrifice, which was likewise a very feminine trait. Julian was an idealist of course. Still it was a bad book, she conceded. Her earlier confidence in it had quite evaporated. 'I might write dozens of quite good books, but I shall never write a great one.'

The expedition to Greece on Venizelos's cruiser had to be cancelled because a plot to assassinate him en route had been unveiled. The would-be assassins knew about the proposal for Vita and Violet to accompany him, and were keeping an eye on their movements. Vita therefore decided to remain in Monaco and glean impressions of an Aegean island from the tamer shores of the South of France.

On the 1st December Harold wrote that he would make a fearful row if she did not join him in Paris within a week. Her absence was putting a great strain on him, not physically, he added without absolute conviction, for he did not want a treat with other people. 'At least I don't want it enough to make it a real grievance. You would love me more if I did.' Two days later he gave reasons why he so badly needed her. He was drinking too much and consorting with the *demi-monde*. Her soothing presence would keep him away from dissipation. To his horror Lady Sackville announced[17] that she was coming to Paris, insisting, 'No, I won't desert little Harold in his hour of need,' but really wanting to see about her Rodin busts and tapestries. She would be in a rage when she learnt that Vita had now gone off from Monaco without leaving an address. Harold beseeched her to return and not leave him with B.M. and her endless harping on the subject. On the 8th he sent a *cri de coeur*. Lady Sackville was with him, threatening to cut Vita out of her life and will. Had Vita, in fact, deserted him? 'I go about with lead in my heart.' If she had gone he would never forgive her, and there must be an absolute separation. All this time Harold was deeply involved in drafting a memorandum for the representatives of the United States, Great Britain and France, in which they unanimously disagreed with the Italian proposal that annexed Fiume should be physically joined to Italy by a thin band of territory running along the coast of Istria. They were also firmly resisting Italy's demand for additional Adriatic islands.

On the 5th December, Vita replied to Harold's scolding and appeals with a counter-offensive which reproached him for not taking her love of Violet seriously:

> I don't think you realise, except in a very tiny degree, what's going on... You have looked on it as more or less transitory and 'wild oats' – your own expression. But surely, darling, you can't think that I have risked – your love, Mama's love, Dada's love and my own reputation – for a whim? (I really don't care a damn about the reputation, but I do care about the rest)... you talk about my being away 'as a holiday'; you write of V as 'Mrs. Denys Trefusis' – don't you realise that that name is a stab to me every time I hear it, every time I see it on an envelope? Yet you write of her as that as a joke.
>
> Then, Oh Hadji, my darling, darling Hadji (you *are* my darling Hadji, because if it wasn't for you, I would go off with Violet) there is another thing. You say you only want to *tromper* me with myself. But that is impossible, darling; there can't be anything of that now – just now, I mean. O Hadji, can't you realise a little? I can't put it into words. It isn't that I don't love you. I do, I do, how much you will never know.[18]

This dulcet letter followed a telegram from Vita in which she had abruptly announced that she did not understand his complaints, and in any case couldn't come. Harold replied to the telegram:

> For the first time you have treated me with quite deliberate cruelty – & with no justification... To make me go through this week in order to keep Violet from her husband... To inflict upon that wretched man a supreme blow & humiliation. That is what I call wicked, and feel so deeply to be wicked that I cannot associate it with you.[19]

He had seldom written to her so outspokenly. Yet he ended with the piteous words, 'Oh come back, come back, darling, come back to me. There is still time.'

The futility of her liaison with Violet was beginning to dawn on Vita. She realised that it was doomed to misery all round. Besides, Violet's irrational jealousy was leading to interminable rows between them. She saw that henceforth it could never be otherwise. Yet the strength of her passion for Violet was still overpowering. At times she felt like some early Christian martyr who was being torn by pincers from all sides. She was worn out by the emotion the affair had engendered. She hardly knew what she was saying, or doing. She wrote[20] to Harold on Hotel Windsor, Monte Carlo, notepaper that he need not be afraid of her running away. That was all over. At the same time the dwindling number of days left with Violet were an agony. Yet they had to part. She took Violet to Cannes to join her husband there. She could only leave her temporarily by promising that she would abandon all and live with her. On the 18th she went to Paris, where she found Harold with an abscess on the knee, having

THE LEAGUE OF NATIONS 1919-20

undergone an operation, and suffering great pain. All her pity was aroused, and she avoided telling him of her promise made to Violet – a promise she did not at that time intend to keep. Harold had been cheered by, and was immensely pleased with, a letter from Lord Curzon notifying him that he was to be awarded the C.M.G. for valuable services rendered to the State at the Peace Conference. Life had its compensations after all. The year ended with the receipt of a solicitous, adoring note from Vita, who was staying at the Hotel Matignon. She had just come from putting him to bed. He was being so brave, and she was so proud of him.

Harold was greatly touched and delighted to receive a proud letter of congratulation from his father on his well-earned New Year honour. He had always, even when a slacker schoolboy slightly below par, felt Lord Carnock's affection. At last he had won his esteem.

Harold was thirty-three, and in spite of his brown moustache, still boyish. His hair, parted high above the right side of his forehead, was thick and curled over the ears. His complexion was milk-and-white; his eyes were bright and very alert, the eyelashes long – 'those absurd eyelashes of yours,' Vita recorded. Although Harold was in middle-age to run to fat, he was now slight in build. All his movements were rapid. Altogether his appearance was winning.

Vita left Paris on the 2nd February 1920, scribbling a note in the train at the Gare du Nord. She sent her love to her mother who had been so kind to her, and was much in her favour. Meanwhile Harold was being maddened by B.M. She was telling everyone she met that she was staying on greatly to her inconvenience, in order that poor Harold should not be left alone. Harold was longing to join Vita and the children at Knole. And she was longing to have him. 'Mind you come Thursday,' she wrote on the 8th. 'Goodbye my precious boy.'

The final stage in the Vita-Violet drama was about to reach its crisis. Harold crossed over to London on the 15th January and on the following day went down to Knole. It was there that Vita announced to him that after all it was her intention to elope with Violet, this time for good. She had already had a dreadful and painful interview with Denys, to whom she had broken the same news. On the 17th she went up to London and had a talk with Harold at Cadogan Gardens, where he had gone to stay with his parents. Vita's diary recalls, 'A perfectly awful day.' All morning she argued with Harold who refused to agree to her leaving with Violet that afternoon. She took him to Grosvenor Street where Violet was staying in her parents' house. Violet was persuaded to 'wait a fortnight, and then, when H has gone, she says she won't. Come back to Knole in a state of collapse.' For the remaining fortnight of Harold's leave not a further word on the subject was mentioned. On the 1st February he returned to Paris, 'without any idea,' his son wrote, 'whether he would ever see his wife again.'[21] She however was taking up her pen and writing.[22] 'Hadji, Hadji, I feel lonely and frightened ... There is so much in my heart, but I don't want to write it because *à quoi bon*.' There then follow passages which are very revealing of her and Harold's different natures, the one passionate and circuitous, the other restrained and straight. The reason, she explained, why she tried to get him to say things such as that he would miss her, was to find weapons with which to fortify herself. It was worth while making herself unhappy in order to keep him happy.

> But when you say things like that you don't miss me in Paris, and that scandal matters, I think, 'Well, if it's only on account of scandal and convenience and above all *because I am his wife* and permanent and legitimate, if it isn't more personal than that, is it worth while my breaking my heart to give him, not positive happiness, but mere negative contentment?' So I fish, and fish, and fish, and sometimes I catch a lovely little silver trout, but never the great salmon that lashes and fights and *convinces* me that it is fighting for its life ... I try to make you fight for myself, but you never will; you just say, 'Darling Mar,' and leave me to invent my own conviction out of your silence ... You are good and sweet and lovable and you are the person I love in the best and simplest way; and there is lots that is neither good nor simple in me, and it is that part which is so tempted.

A more feminine letter could hardly have been composed. For in spite of her abnormally masculine side, Vita's perverse illogicality, and obdurate determination often to ignore what was plain to others, was one of the more perplexing, because unexpected, facets of her make-up. It is almost inconceivable that a sensitive and kind person (which she was at bottom) could have misinterpreted the repeated, harrowing protests and appeals which Harold poured out to her on paper year after year. It is certain, however, that in conversation he did not express strong affection, for he, like her, was curiously shy and reserved when they were together.

In answer to her letter Harold wrote from the Hotel Alexandre, rue Montagne, 'You are wrong in thinking that I look upon you as my 'légitime.' You are not a person with whom one can associate law, order, duty, or any of the conventional ties of life.' He denied saying that he did not miss her in Paris. A soldier in the trenches did not miss his wife; he wanted her all the same. Anyway, if she was going to leave him, she would ruin his life.[23]

THE LEAGUE OF NATIONS 1919-20

A day or two after Harold's return to Paris, Vita and Violet went to Lincoln for Vita to have a look at the fen country. She was writing another novel, *The Dragon in Shallow Waters*, to which she and Harold referred as *Soap* because the first section opens with a brilliant description of soap being manufactured in vats. The setting of the terrible story – one of the best novels she wrote – of two brothers, one blind, the other deaf from birth, and both creatures of almost limitless evil, was the fens near Spalding. The book, in which the influence of Violet is again apparent, was to be dedicated to her. Harold must already have read the first section for in writing to her on the 7th February he cautioned her not to exaggerate the sanctimoniousness of the curate in the story, for he probably had some sense of humour. Although Harold knew that Vita was staying at the Saracen's Head in Lincoln he did not know that she had Violet with her and that they were laying plans for the imminent elopement. He told her he was very busy over the Adriatic and war criminals. Vita wrote to him from Lincoln on the 9th:

> I am not fit to consort and to remain with ordinary, nice, darling people. I hate *myself*... I wish I was dead, or that you hated me & didn't care what became of me.

This was not calculated to make him feel any less apprehensive of what she might be about to do. 'That Fen country,' she added, 'is so strange – all flooded under a blood-red sun. It was marvellous cold, clear weather, and all the floods were out.' The two women then returned to London, saw Denys, 'spurned his pitiful entreaties,' and left for Dover.

The story of the abortive elopement, more comical than tragical when read today, has been told in detail in *Portrait of a Marriage*. Suffice it to say that for some strange reason – which may have been hesitation on Vita's part when positively on the brink of an irreversible action – she allowed Violet to cross the Channel on the evening of the 9th alone. Vita remained behind in the King's Head Hotel, where she wrote to Harold:

> I swear to you by all I hold sacred... that I used every argument, threat and persuasion to make her go back to him [Denys]... I would swear [this] with my last breath.

A second letter from her in Dover announced that Denys had turned up and was accompanying her to France tomorrow to join Violet.

> I will try to make her [go back to Denys], I will, I will, I will; I will only see her in front of Denys, and he shall see that I will try. If she consents and goes with him, I shall come to you.

It didn't quite turn out like that. But she and Denys set sail together the next morning in a howling gale. 'What a ridiculous journey!' she could not help telling her mother. The ill-assorted couple, an aggrieved husband, a very masculine man who had fought gallantly in the war and won decorations, and had gone through innumerable secret adventures in Russia, and his aggressor and rival, a woman who adored her own husband more than anyone else on earth, were crossing the Channel together in one of the worst tempests on record. At Amiens where they joined Violet, Denys once more pleaded with his wife, in vain. He left, and his place was taken by Violet's father, Colonel Keppel, who, having learned about the flight, had also set out in pursuit of the truants. For two days Violet and Vita played box and cox with the Colonel. Meanwhile Harold went to London, where he got in touch with Denys. Lady Sackville was revelling in the situation, and egging the two men to resume the pursuit together. On the 14th Denys somehow managed to get hold of a two-seater aeroplane, and accompanied by Harold, flew to Amiens. Lady Sackville flew to her diary and jotted down her thoughts of those two husbands, each trying to get his wife back. 'Quite like a sensational novel,' she wrote. It certainly was.

After prolonged discussion and argument between the reunited couples, Vita and Violet reluctantly consented to go to Paris with their respective husbands. They stayed at separate hotels. Denys and Violet then drove to Toulon where they stayed with Mrs. Keppel, and Vita followed Harold to England. It was not yet the end of the two women's passionate love, but it was the end of the crisis. Harold had the extreme good sense to realise this. In London the Nicolsons were seen at parties and theatres together as though nothing had happened. And nothing that had happened had destroyed their deep-rooted love for one another. On the 19th Vita left to join Violet at Avignon. Harold even encouraged this expedition. 'I love to think of you going out to the spring-studded country,' he wrote that very day. 'Oh, I want you to be happy, my dear, dear Mar.' He thanked her for her telegram despatched from Dover, 'a bad place to send a telegram from to a neurasthenic husband!' he could not help adding. From Avignon Vita and Violet went to Bordighera to stay with Pat Dansy and a friend. And from there the four of them went to Venice which Violet did not much enjoy. They remained abroad until April, it is true, but their relations were not quite the same as they had been. Vita was submitted to a barrage of reproaches and abuse from Violet and could only restore tranquillity by promising that she was not going to abandon her, although knowing full well that she would. Each realised by now that a further attempt to bolt off and live together for ever and ever was out of the question.

THE LEAGUE OF NATIONS 1919-20

Nigel Nicolson's summary of this episode of his mother's life could not, it seems to me, be fairer, more generous or more true.

> I did not know that Vita could love like this, had loved like this, because she would not speak of it to her son. Now that I know everything, I love her more, as my father did, *because* she was tempted, *because* she was weak. She was a rebel, she was Julian, and though she did not know it, she fought for more than Violet. She fought for the right to love, men and women, rejecting the conventions that marriage demands exclusive love, and that women should love only men, and men only women. For this she was prepared to give up everything Yes, she may have been mad, as she later said, but it was a magnificent folly. She may have been cruel, but it was cruelty on a heroic scale. How can I despise the violence of such passion? How could she regret that the knowledge of it should now reach the ears of a new generation, more compassionate than her own?[24]

As for Harold, apart from his letters to Vita at the time, he did not make any reference in writing to the elopement then or at a later date. I doubt whether he ever made mention of it in conversation with a friend. He always remained firmly reticent, not so much because the memory of it recalled the pain he went through but because he knew the outcome had brought him victory, and he was not the sort of man to vaunt his triumph over another, especially one whom he consistently upheld as his superior in literary talent, or what he would call genius, and, perhaps stranger still, in saintliness of character.

On the 26th February Harold wrote from Sunderland House to his secretary Miss Williams in Paris, asking her to come over and bring with her his papers and books. He had been delegated, on account of the Russian situation, to organise material for a Commission to the Soviet Union. And this was to entail much concentrated work. On the 3rd March another leaf was added to Harold's laurel wreath through a letter from the Foreign Secretary announcing that the King had constituted him a First Secretary, as from the 1st January last. The pleasure in having his diplomatic status enhanced was slightly reduced by Vita's prolonged absence. She was still in Venice in the depths of despair. Violet was being 'horrible' to her. Vita felt that the Grand Canal, in spite of its slime and floating onions, would be preferable to the situation she was in. Harold had some short leave without her. He spent it at Long Barn, working in the garden with B.M. He could not resist complaining to Vita that he too had had a bloody holiday, instead of five blissful days with her, had she only returned when she said she was coming. It was her deplorable muddles that worried him, for he knew this time that she would be returning in due course. The annoying thing was that he had to go to Paris again, and doubtless their boats would cross on the Channel. In fact they did. When Vita got back to Long Barn, the weather was grey and dismal, and when she picked up *The Dragon* she found she could not write.

Harold returned to London, believing he was about to finish with the League. But there was trouble with Venizelos. The old man had indiscreetly thought fit to disclose the terms of the Treaty of Peace which the Allies had at last agreed to impose upon Turkey. The consequence was that more Turkish adherents rallied to the banner of the leader of the Nationalist movement, General Mustafa Kemal, who was to become Turkey's first President, great reformer and moderniser of his country. This anxiety was followed by further difficulties for the League in May with the invasion of Persia by the Bolsheviks. Persia appealed to the League and Sir Eric Drummond insisted upon Harold being involved. It meant that he was unable to join Vita who was now sailing in her father's yacht *Sumerun* off Falmouth. 'Oh damn! Oh damn!' he wrote. 'Anyway it's no good explaining as you ... won't understand it.'[25] Vita was totally unconcerned with international events of the sort. To her they were merely tiresome happenings like bad weather which could be an inconvenience and a bore. At all events Mustafa Kemal in a fury of indignation refused to heed the warnings of the League, and in June joined issue with the Allied forces of occupation. His Army advanced upon the British troops occupying the Ismid area, that tongue of water at the extreme north-east end of the Sea of Marmora. In July Venizelos took upon himself to drive the Turks back to the Ismid line. This defeat of the Turks delighted Lloyd George, while incensing the French and Italians who were anti-Greek. It led to the Treaty of Sèvres in August.

On 15th May, while Vita was sailing with her father off Falmouth, Harold noted in his pocket diary that he had completed 16,000 words of *Paul Verlaine*. He was engaged upon his first book.

He had been fascinated by Verlaine's character for years and, more important still, deeply impressed by his unique place in the modern movement of French poetry. He made a note in his diary of 1910 that he had just read Verlaine's life.[26] That was in April; and in December he read his confessions. During the War he quoted in a letter to Vita[27] the first verse of the poem, *Mon Rêve Familier*, which he thought relevant to her.

> Je fais souvent ce rêve étrange et pénétrant
> D'une femme inconnue, et que j'aime, et qui m'aime,

> Est qui n'est, chaque fois, ni tout à fait la même
> Ni tout à fait une autre, et m'aime et me comprend.

The idea of writing a literary monograph on the poet had long lain in his mind, if only he had the time. And then the Peace Conference drew to its close. One evening in 1919 he descended the staircase of the Hotel Majestic with his friend the novelist and publisher, Michael Sadleir. He told him he would feel rather flat when the Conference was over. He had got so used to being overworked. What should he do with the leisure that would follow? 'You must write a book,' Sadleir told him. The suggestion struck him at the time as highly original. It happened that on the few occasions when he had managed to get a few hours away from the Conference, he had amused himself by visiting the sites which Verlaine frequented.

In January of 1920 Vita wrote to him,

> You *must* write the Life of Verlaine. You would do it so excellently well. I can't imagine anybody who would do it better. You would produce a book which was at the same time picturesque, critical and humorous. Why don't you start on it when you come home this time?

He must, she said, win literary as well as diplomatic honours. And so he would. Vita followed the rapid course of the book with intense sympathy and interest. Harold wrote to her that she had been such an angel to him about the book, and hadn't once laughed about it. 'You are a saint, my Mar.' By July, Constable's, of which Michael Sadleir was a partner, agreed to accept the manuscript on a half-profit basis. Thenceforth, Constable's published nearly every book Harold wrote, down to *The Age of Reason* in 1960. The two men remained on the best of terms, and there exists a copious correspondence, often very entertaining, between them over the years.[28]

Constable's found themselves confronted with a biography of a foreign poet whose morals and manners would strike the average reader of 1920 as highly ambiguous. Actually, although the book gathers fire with the entry of the young Rimbaud, the description of whose vagabond boyhood and disastrous influence upon Verlaine is admirable, Harold shirked facing up to the homosexual relationship of the two poets, showing a fastidiousness excusable perhaps at the time, but not accepted by critics of today, or even of yesterday. In 1944 Edmund Wilson took him severely to task for ignoring the naked truth, in a famous article, *Through the Embassy Window*, in the *New Yorker*.[29]

Harold was back in Paris in the summer, up to his eyes in the preparation of the Treaty of Saint-Germain affecting Austria.

> I went down yesterday to see the ratification of the Austrian Treaty [he wrote on the 17th July]. It was, for me, a strange and rather sad echo of last year's labours. It took place in the Salle de l'Horloge, with a row of empty leather chairs, and a Buhl table for the signatures. There were not more than 25 people in the room, four of whom were photographers. And then old Cambon made a nice kind speech, and the cameras clicked and we all shook hands, and went into the next room for port and macaroons.

In the afternoon he had a meeting of one of his committees. It went very badly. 'I was exceedingly rude. I beat the table, Bang! Bang! Pouf! and at last I pushed back my chair, whirr! Bizz! and said I refused to continue the discussion. So we wait till they come back from Spa on Monday.' He was asserting himself. He was becoming one of the big men himself.

And yet was he? Harold did on one or two occasions beat the table with clenched fists, did almost get angry. But somehow his fists never quite made the noise expected of a man with his strong conviction of the differences between right and wrong, never struck terror in the minds of his auditors. Not overbearing, always ready to listen, usually to understand and often even to adopt his opponents' arguments, he was not made in the mould of an administrator, far less a leader. His methods were rational and persuasive, for he could not raise his voice. They were those of the highly civilised, sensitive, English, ex-public schoolboy, with a strong sense of fair play, not the boy who accepted the shibboleths and hocus-pocus of mass dictation, or the boy who stood up to them defiantly, but the boy who, avoiding the straight fight, fled from the hurly-burly of the playground to the sanctum of his writing-desk. Because of his lack of toughness Harold Nicolson never entirely grew up.

His return to England kept on being postponed. He proposed to bring Jean de Gaigneron with him. Jean would be no trouble, he assured Vita, for he would paint all the time and keep to himself. He wrote on the 19th July, 'Also can you arrange with B.M. for Jean to sleep at Hill Street with me (!!) on Friday night?' Vita was obliged to send a telegram, 'No,' to this proposal because B.M. did not like Jean, who must at all costs, she wrote, bring his paints, so that she could write undisturbed. 'I must finish that beastly book [*The Dragon*] as you can't have all the laurels (damn you, Popsy!).' Seriously, she was rejoicing in his successes.

> I got such a triumphant letter from you today about your treaty; you are brilliant and successful and clever and all that, damn you, and P[aul] V[erlaine] is so good, it's not fair, whereas I am nothing but a muddly failure, damn you again. It will be envy, and not infidelity, that splits up this little ménage.[30]

THE LEAGUE OF NATIONS 1919-20

Harold met the Roderick Joneses in Paris on their honeymoon.

> I met Enid Bagnold. Also Roderick Bagnold. The latter is a nice, clever, gentle, self-confident, in love little man. I liked him. So does Enid Bagnold in spite of your theories. Damn those Amazonian theories of yours! Surely it is less ridiculous to marry and have babies, heaps of babies, than to live on through a translucent virginity. Anyhow she was evidently sensitive about it all. I gave her your message ... I like her very much, but less than I like you my dear dear black gypsy (gypsey? gipsofola? gypsophylla?).[31]

He couldn't help having a dig at Vita's resolute conviction that all women, whether they shared her instincts or not, ought to remain unmarried, and be free from every shackle imposed by tyrant man. She was still the victim of Violet's cajolery and wiles. One day Violet would write that she was about to become Sir Basil Zaharoff's mistress; the next day, that she had fainted at Clemence Dane's dinner-party. The doctor said she was suffering from heart failure. Her mother had turned her out of the house on account of complaints made of her by Denys. And if these things did not melt Vita's heart, she reviled her for having said that their love had become debased and corrupt. Vita, whose love for Violet was by no means extinguished, was merely made wretched. She firmly resisted all pleas either to go off with Violet, or have her to stay, and remained at Long Barn alone. It was in these conditions that on the 23rd July she temporarily threw aside *The Dragon* and began her autobiographical confessions, sitting 'in the margin of a wood and a ripe cornfield, with the faint shadows of grasses and ears of corn falling across my page.' Harold had had to put off his return from Paris for another five days. Could she finish her writing before then? Two days later she got a rather sad little letter from him.

> As a rule he does not allow me to see when he is depressed. His sadness never fails to touch me to the quick. He is the only person of whom I think with consistent tenderness. I can say with truth that I have never, never cherished a harsh thought about him; at the most I have been irritated, but then he has always known it.[32]

On Harold's return they had a house-party at Long Barn. Hugh Walpole was among the guests. It was, he recorded, a very happy occasion.

> We all talked nineteen to the dozen and Vita looked perfectly beautiful in crimson and orange. She is as lovely as she is clever, with just that touch of easiness that gives her complete distinction. Harold too is a very very nice fellow.[33]

Walpole was not the most sensitive of men, and evidently he detected no strain between his host and hostess. Vita's confessions were interrupted by Harold's return, by her going on yet another jaunt with Violet to France in August, and by her resumption of *The Dragon*. The confessions were not finished until March of the following year.

On the 10th August the abortive Treaty of Sèvres (brought about by the Greeks' triumph over Mustafa Kemal) between the Allied and Associated Powers and Turkey, was signed. It prescribed that Constantinople should remain the Turkish capital. The Bosphorus, the Marmora Sea and the Dardanelles were to be an open waterway under international guardianship. Greece was to possess Western and Eastern Thrace up to the lines of Chatalja, the Gallipoli peninsula and the majority of the Aegean islands. She was also to administer Smyrna with its hinterland. Turkey was obliged to submit her armaments to the Allied control; and to enforce safeguards for racial and religious minorities within her boundaries. But the Treaty, into which so much argument and thought had been put, was not ratified. The unexpected death of King Alexander of Greece from the bite of a monkey, the resultant general election, the defeat and flight of Venizelos on board the British yacht *Narcissus*, and the recall of King Constantine, induced the Allies to declare their neutrality in Graeco-Turkish affairs. These reverses in Greece enabled Kemal to recover from his defeat, and so strengthen his position that he made a separate peace with the French. The Treaty of Sèvres was finally superseded by the Treaty of Lausanne.

On the 20th November Harold, now a member of the Central European and Persia Department of the Foreign Office, drew up a memorandum on the Greek situation.[34] He recommended that the British Government should refuse to countenance King Constantine's return; that it should work for his abdication, not by force, but by pressure brought by France and Great Britain on the Greek Government. That Government should be made aware that Greece could no longer be regarded as a friendly country, far less an ally, if the King returned, and would forfeit France's and Great Britain's support. France and Great Britain would withdraw monetary aid and existing trade agreements, and withhold support of Greece's demands for war reparations. Sir Eyre Crowe's comments on this memorandum were that the British Government should not oppose the desires of the Greek nation to restore Constantine, if that was its unanimous decision; and that it was highly undesirable to alienate Greece.

Harold's sympathies with Venizelos's liberal policy were unwavering. For a Foreign Office official they were perhaps too marked. Lord William Cavendish-Bentinck, who was a friend and colleague in the 1920s, is of the opinion that Harold would have made a bad Ambassador in that he was too much given to prejudices and partialities which he never learned to suppress or contain. Harold wrote[35] to Vita from Buck's Club that he had had a good report of Venizelos from one who was close to him. He had behaved superbly throughout his reverses. He showed no trace of humiliation, or bitterness. He showed great courage and optimism.

> In fact just what I should have expected from my hero ... I don't care if you do laugh. He *is* my hero, dear old man in his skull cap and his charming Christ-like smile ... I know you think I'm smug, but I'd chuck everything for what V represents. You see, he is the *winged reason*. He is as sane as any man, and yet his sanity soars. It doesn't flap about like you romantics. It soars. That's what I want to achieve. He and Pollock are the two who have influenced my intelligence, and you are the only one, except Mummy, who has formed my heart.

King Constantine's re-election, which took place, was not recognised by the Allies. On the 20th December Harold presented a further memorandum[36] on the future policy of the British Government towards King Constantine, now he was back on the Greek throne. He acknowledged that this was a turn of events which must be accepted. He began by summarising the attitude of the French, who were jealous of our prestige in Greece. 'Sentimentally they hanker after the prestige which France enjoyed in the East under Louis XIV.' (This was an overstatement.) They sought to enhance their status in Asia Minor (this was true enough). Italy desired a weak Greece. The moment had arrived when Britain had to decide her position. Harold therefore advocated, with the good sense of a man who was not ashamed to change his advice to suit altered circumstances, circumstances which could no longer be reversed, that we now openly supported King Constantine so long as he showed readiness to maintain the Treaty of Sèvres, which after all was greatly to the advantage of Greece and the disadvantage of Turkey.

Sir Eyre Crowe and Lord Curzon minuted this memorandum as 'thoughtful.' They were, however, in favour of adopting a wait-and-see policy. Harold's collaboration with Curzon was as yet in the future. The Foreign Secretary merely knew Nicolson as a very intelligent, rather opinionated and possibly cheeky young man (he was overheard referring to him as 'a clever boy'), who paid too little attention to the customary formalities expected of a junior Foreign Office official. For instance, on coming out of his room in the Foreign Office just before Christmas, whom did he meet in the corridor but young Harold Nicolson, with a pipe in his mouth! Curzon nearly had a fit, and dropped his stick. Harold confided in

Vita that this was the most awful thing to have happened. He drew a sketch of the situation to emphasise what a *faux pas* he had committed. Allen Leeper, who was about to be made Curzon's number-two private secretary ('a bloody job of course,' but the extra pay would enable him to marry) would never have been guilty of such an indiscretion.

9

LONDON, FOREIGN OFFICE, 1921-1922

THE year 1921 opened with Harold Nicolson still working at fairly high pressure in the Central European Department of the Foreign Office. As the fortunes of Greece waxed throughout 1921 so did the pressure increase; as they waned at the beginning of 1922, so did it ease off until the whole Graeco-Turkish settlement was put into the hands of Lord Curzon and referred to the Conference at Lausanne in October 1922. Harold was in England for what was for him a comparatively uninterrupted period. He was able to spend weekends and holidays at Long Barn, where he supervised many improvements, including completion of the new wing, provision of a hard tennis court and an electric-light engine. He saw more of his children than ever before, and he finally retrieved his wife from the shoals and reefs which had beset their marriage and domestic happiness. Vita gradually became more settled and content. Both of them made more friendships, and both became extremely productive in their writings. In 1921 Harold had two books published, and before the year was out was engaged on a third. Vita's novel, *The Dragon in Shallow Waters*, was published in May, and she was composing much poetry.

The fall of Venizelos was regrettable in that it threatened to involve a split between France and Great Britain. The French, gravely suspicious of Greek intentions in the Balkans, favouring the claims of Turkey and resentful of Britain's influence upon Greek internal matters, which they deemed to be flagrant intervention, gave pretty clear warning that as an offset they alone were justified in dealing with Germany. Harold was worried about the whole Greek situation – the likelihood of anarchy in the country and the international implications. He presented a memorandum on the subject on the 8th January,[1] urging several pertinent considerations upon the Secretary of State. They amounted to the necessity of Great Britain taking it upon herself to espouse the cause of Greece against Turkey, even at the risk of grievously offending France. Otherwise it was no use our talking about defending the terms of the Treaty of Sèvres.

Sir Eyre Crowe's minute to this note was that we could hardly enter negotiations single-handed with King Constantine at this stage; and that the question of such positive policy must be discussed at the Conference to be held in Paris in two weeks time. After this Conference Britain might be able to strike out on a line of her own, but he did not think it would be probable. Meanwhile Lord Hardinge, now Ambassador in Paris, was urging Lord Curzon to compromise with the French over the Greek predicament. Harold was told to be ready to attend the Paris Conference at short notice.

The cynical view of the Foreign Office was that we had been outmanoeuvred by Mustafa Kemal and had better admit it. Harold was instructed hurriedly to write a memorandum suggesting compromise with Kemal over Smyrna. The resulting *Memorandum by Mr. Nicolson on the Revision of the Treaty of Sèvres* of the 18th January[2] turned out to advocate the very opposite of compromise. On the contrary it amounted to objections by the author to a revision of the Smyrna chapter in the Treaty. This was an act of courage on Harold's part. His points were that the Greeks were unlikely to agree to abandon Smyrna at French dictation for reasons of prestige and because of their many commitments in the region. King Constantine would be roused to bitter hostility to the Allies and might embark on some extravagant nationalistic crusade. In whatever form a revision was presented to Turkey the Turkish Nationalists would regard it as a justification of their previous claims. The Kemalists would not be satisfied and would make further claims on the Straits and Adrianople. Harold's most vital objection was that this deferment to France would weaken our imperial status, of which Greece was a positive asset. A revision of the Treaty would exacerbate the Greeks, titillate Turkey's further demands, and weaken us in the eyes of France.

Crowe's minute to this memorandum was largely in agreement with Harold, which provoked Harold to remark that, 'I would rather have a look of interest from him than endless panegyrics from others.' Lord Curzon, however, differed from them both. On the 19th he sent for Harold, told him that he, Curzon, would have to modify the Treaty of Sèvres, and instructed him to write yet another memorandum immediately, which he was reluctantly obliged to do until two o'clock the next morning.

On the 20th the Cabinet discussed the forthcoming Conference programme. The outcome of their deliberations was that the British Government would give way to the French for the sake of peace in the Middle East, but not yield to Turkish demands that the Greeks should be turned out of Smyrna.

While Harold was busily preparing for the Paris Conference he began an article on the Civil Service for the press. On the 23rd he crossed the Channel. On the platform was a group of cameramen filming, or as he put it, 'cinemaing' the Prime Minister. The mission reached the Ritz Hotel, Paris, in time for tea. Lord and Lady Curzon, Vansittart, Crowe, Ralph Wigram and Harold all had rooms on the same floor. At 9.30 the

LONDON, FOREIGN OFFICE, 1921-22

following morning Harold was dictating to a secretary his article on the Civil Service.

On the 25th the Conference opened at the Quai d'Orsay. Curzon made a most able exposé of the Graeco-Turkish question; and Lloyd George followed with an eloquent speech on the criminality of buying peace in Turkey at the exclusive expense of Greece. It was agreed that a Conference between the Greeks and Turks should be held in London towards the end of the next month. Harold was satisfied. On the 27th he lunched with Marshal Foch, where Lloyd George, Curzon, Briand and the two Cambon brothers were present. He sat next to the Comte de Fels, the proprietor of the *Écho de Paris*, who asked him for an article and promised to review *Paul Verlaine*. Later in the day he went to see Venizelos in bed in an overheated room in the Majestic, where he received an emotional welcome.

He made an official record of their conversation.[3] Venizelos expressed alarm at the possibility of a drastic revision of the Treaty of Sèvres, but on being assured that the proposal for a Conference between Greece and Turkey came from His Britannic Majesty's Government, was inclined to think that Kemal's conduct would convince the French and Italians of its futility.

On his return to London on the 1st February Harold felt wretched and abandoned because there was no letter from Vita. She had gone off in the middle of January on a final jaunt with Violet. They had wanted to go to Spain. But owing to Harold's undisguised distress Vita had desisted. Instead she joined Violet at Nîmes, and they went on to Hyères. The same procrastinations as during the previous jaunt in Italy took place. Telegrams arrived from Vita saying that she must stay on 'for a bit.' Harold was provoked to write to her that, because she was more selfish than Agrippina in her worst moments, because she was more optimistic than the Virgin Mary at her most light-hearted, and because she was more weak than some polypus floating and undulating in a pond, she refused to look at his side of the question; and she despised 'the squalor of dates.'[4] He went on in a peremptory vein,

> You are to be back in England on Friday February the 25th. On Saturday we shall go down together to the Cottage. So please take some tickets at once. And please also realise that this is definite. I shall be more angry than I have ever been if you do not come back on that date. Don't misunderstand me. I shall really cut adrift if you don't. It is a generous date; it is longer than you promised; but it is a *fixed* date, and you must keep to it.

She had in fact stayed longer in Hyères than she intended to stay in Spain.

He then remonstrated with her extraordinary notion that it was 'indecent' for her to write to him when she was with Violet. 'How grotesque you are, darling!'

By now Vita's feelings for Violet had turned to compassion. Violet fancied herself to be deserted, neglected, unwanted, a failure, and she played upon these states, even threatening to take her own life. Vita felt guilty. She replied to Harold's justifiably scolding letter,

> My own beloved Harold, I am so dreadfully unhappy ... about V being deserted and about my feeling responsible. You see, I *am* responsible. But I only love *you*, with my heart, and you are the person I shall always love ... Wild oats are all very well, but not when they grow as high as a jungle.[5]

Still she did not return. Harold's anger nearly turned to alarm when he received a letter from Denys Trefusis, announcing that he was fed up and had decided to separate from Violet. 'DAMN,' Harold wrote in his diary.[6] He rushed to discuss the matter with Dorothy Wellesley, who was now deep in Vita's confidence. But all Dorothy could dispense was sympathy, and not advice. 'Oh God!' Harold exclaimed bitterly on leaving her, 'je ne suis *pas* consolé.'

After a relaxed weekend at Oxford, where he was entertained by undergraduate friends, Victor Cazalet and Chips Channon, where he met Eddie Marsh and Ivor Novello, where he entertained Vita's cousin Eddy Sackville-West to breakfast, and where he talked to Sligger in Balliol – 'Balliol is subtly changed; more aesthetic and less patrician' – Harold returned to London refreshed in spirit to find that he had been offered by the Serbs the Order of St. Saba. As a member of the Diplomatic Service he was obliged to decline the honour. With his colleague Darcy Osborne he began writing a memorandum for the forthcoming Conference.[7] The authors concluded with suggestions for procedure and stressed the importance of maintaining the fiction that the Greeks were acting as Allies. Crowe told Harold that the Prime Minister was weakening over the Smyrna issue. Harold's comment was that he in any event would fight for its retention by Greece to the last ditch. Curzon, having studied the Memorandum, pronounced himself to be in substantial agreement with it. On the 18th Crowe sent for Harold and turned him on to drafting another Memorandum, how to fit Eastern Rumelia into the Smyrna zone. 'I do this with commendable (and commended) speed and accuracy.'

LONDON, FOREIGN OFFICE, 1921-22

On the 20th he received a loving telegram from Vita at Nîmes that she would be back any day. That cheered him. On the 21st the London Conference opened in Downing Street. Venizelos desperately hoped that at the last moment Lloyd George would manage to admit him to the proceedings, but the official Greek delegates refused to have anything to do with him. He came to see Harold and appeared profoundly dejected. He was still dead against any modification of the Smyrna chapter. He expressed the view that a compromise scheme for Smyrna would give rise to uncertainty and disorder.

When the Turks appeared before the Conference they talked irrelevant generalities, and were soundly snubbed. They were told to go away and come back with more definite proposals. This they did, and to Harold's consternation, demanded everything which they had lost in the war, plus reparations for what they had suffered. The Big Four held a secret meeting at which Harold feared they had decided to send a commission of enquiry to Thrace and Smyrna. 'Oh God! Oh God!' he exclaimed. It really looked as if the Turks would get everything they were asking for. Harold could not understand Lloyd George's apparent volte-face. He felt ashamed and perplexed. Moreover Dimitri Stancioff, the Bulgarian Minister was nagging him for concessions to Bulgaria, complaining that his countrymen were good to the Allies, who did nothing for them, whereas the Turks were enemies and the Allies gave them back territory. Harold sought and for once in a way received no consolation from Crowe. All Crowe did was to put his head in his hands and moan, 'I hate the Balkans.' To crown all Harold received a telegram from Vita that she was not returning the next day. 'Certainly one of the worst days of my life,' he wrote.[8]

After a flying visit to Knole Harold went back to a solitary rented room at No. 9 Bentinck Street. 'Oh God! How unhappy I am. Oh damn life.'[9] Next morning he had to heat his shaving water on a gas ring. He went out to breakfast on weak coffee and a bun at an A.B.C. At the Office he was told by Vansittart of a frightful row made by Winston Churchill with the Prime Minister and Curzon over an interview he, Harold, gave to the head of the Greek delegation, Sicilianos, 'a sly little beast,' whom he had warned that the Greeks had better be conciliatory, for they could be sure the Turks would not be conciliatory.

> So even my own personal position in the office is going wrong now. No home. No affection. No money. No happiness. Oh Viti, Viti, what have you to answer for . . . And I am a harmless, happy creature by nature.[10]

These self-pitying exclamations were hardly fair on Vita. She really could not be blamed for the way the Conference was going, or for a slight indiscretion he might have made in his zeal for the cause of Venizelos.

On the 4th March Harold noted in his diary, 'The wind is changing and blows from Hellas.' The Conference situation was looking up. The Turks at Angora[11] had accepted the commissions imposed upon them subject only to the vaguest conditions; the Greeks at Athens had refused them flatly. Lloyd George in his volatile manner gathered the great ones into the embrasure of a window, and proceeded to defend the interests of Greece. 'One cannot rob a country of its honour,' he said. 'No Government could stand in any country which decided to do that.' Harold attributed the Prime Minister's return to his old love to the fact that the German reparations question was nearing satisfactory settlement. The only fly in his ointment was the receipt of yet another telegram from Vita putting off her return till Monday. 'Probably V realised,' he wrote, bitterly for him, 'that if she came on Saturday we should have Sunday alone together.'

After two more telegrams from Vita, the first announcing that she had missed a train, and the second that she had again deferred her return, she arrived back on the 9th March, looking well. Husband and wife went down to Knole to be with the children, and Harold was content. But before the month was out Vita resumed her autobiographical confessions, 'writing in the midst of great unhappiness . . . It is possible I may never see Violet again . . . it is also possible that she may not choose to live.' Unhappy she undoubtedly was, but reconciled, albeit reluctantly, to marital domesticity.

On the 24th March the Greek Prime Minister Kalogeropoulos, suddenly throwing discretion to the winds, as it were, in defiance of further parleying, ordered from London an offensive against the Turkish Nationalists. The offensive met with failure which did not prevent M. Gounaris, who succeeded him in April, from launching a second in July. Having nearly reached Angora the Greek Army was disastrously defeated in August. King Constantine beat a hasty retreat from Smyrna where he had been hailed as Emperor-designate of the New Byzantium, and Gounaris made for London, where at last in October the Greek Government placed the interests of their country, without any reserve, in the hands of Lord Curzon.

In vain Gounaris tried to persuade Curzon to finance the Greek stalemate in Turkey. All he got was, in the words of Winston Churchill, 'sonorous correctitudes.' Mustafa Kemal cunningly waited a year, keeping the Greek Army in Anatolia, miles from home. Thus, in the opinion of Venizelos and his adherents, including Harold Nicolson, the Allies badly let down the Greeks whom since 1919 they had been encouraging to keep in check the common foe.

After the abrupt break by the Greek Government with the London Conference and its incursions against the Turks, Harold's interests in the

LONDON, FOREIGN OFFICE, 1921-22

Foreign Office were diverted to Albania. On the 4th April 1921 he presented a memorandum advocating that the Albanians should be given a fair start and then be left to work out their future in their own way. On the 27th Aubrey Herbert, who had quixotically thrown in his lot with Albania, told Harold that the Albanians definitely intended offering the crown to the Duke of Atholl. He seemed rather sore about the offer, although he had refused the crown himself. Harold cautioned Herbert that before the Duke made a step in the direction of the Albanian throne he must consult Lord Curzon. Albanian matters and Austrian reparations kept Harold occupied throughout the rest of the summer.

Harold had finished *Paul Verlaine* on the 21st November 1920. He worked very hard to push the book – the only time he did such a thing. He tried unsuccessfully to persuade George Moore to write a preface, and even solicited reviews. On the 10th March 1921 *Paul Verlaine* came out. Naturally very anxious about its reception, Harold dashed that morning to the back door of Knole, where he was staying, to receive the newspapers He was rewarded by an excellent review in the *Morning Post*, which declared the book to contain the best summary of French poetry of the last half of the nineteenth century that had yet appeared. On Sunday week, however, a review in the *Observer* was not favourable, although Harold was oversensitive in calling it 'atrocious and malicious.' At any rate it 'quite does me in. Damn.' The critic had found the tone of his superiority tiresome and his attitude to Verlaine unfair. Harold was sometimes accused of superiority in his writing when all he meant to convey was conviction, just as in conversation he could dismiss with the gesture of someone flicking a horsefly from his sleeve an argument which his quick intelligence at once saw to be erroneous and merely an interruption to the flow of his own disquisition. The *Observer's* animadversions were harsh, and its charge that the biographer disliked his subject was nonsense. On the contrary, Harold sympathised with Verlaine's weaknesses and his three disastrous love affairs which made him into a tragic figure. But he was far enough removed from the Victorian hagiographers not to refrain from censure and gentle mockery when they were deserved. For there was much in Verlaine's story that was squalid as well as comical. H. A. L. Fisher bore this out in a letter congratulating Harold on a brilliant sketch.

> Of all the human beings known to me [he wrote], Verlaine was in his physical aspects the most repulsive, so repulsive that it was a strain to be

in the room with him. The wayward charm and gaiety of his conversation, when he was in the mood, made amends, as if a slug were trying to turn butterfly.[12]

William Rothenstein also wrote warmly congratulating Harold on his splendid portraiture.[13] He had no criticism to make 'of your physical presentiment of Verlaine' as he was when he knew him. He also praised his description of Eugénie Krautz, the jealous and proprietary mistress of Verlaine's old age. She was also 'wonderfully true to life. I can hear her hoarse and 'criarde' voice as she 'engueuléd' Verlaine .. She warned me not to listen to the rival lady or to send her any money in case she claimed any of Verlaine's English earnings. And of course I remember the gold paint – it was in the rue St. Jacques – and the canaries.' Raymond Mortimer on re-reading the book after fifty-five years, found Harold's literary judgment still sound, although his dislike of Verlaine's faults made him seem a little condescending. Mortimer recalled that it was the generalisations about the French character which particularly annoyed Lytton Strachey and caused him to be so rude to Harold when they first met.[14]

On the whole the reviews were encouraging. The *Bookman* paid tribute to the integrity of the book's workmanship and the author's 'fine narrative tact.' Indeed this tact in glossing over what Gosse called Verlaine's tastes 'too delicate to be discussed,' renders the book timorous, however fair and impartial it may be. Gosse's notice was looked forward to by Harold with greater eagerness than that of any other critic. After the book had been out a month, and still there was no review from Gosse, Harold ran into him in the lavatory at the Marlborough Club.[15] He said to him gaily, 'Well, I hear from George Moore that you are going to review my book.' Gosse turned his face away and there was an awkward pause, at the end of which he said rather gruffly, 'Oh, Moore, now do tell me why he has gone to Paris?' Harold deduced either that Gosse, not a young man, was deafened by the rush of roaring waters in that so hygienic place, and only caught the words 'George Moore'; or that he did not intend to review the book at all; or that if he did intend to review it, then in such a manner that it appeared to him better to sever their acquaintance before rather than after the event. He need not have worried. The review did eventually appear in the *Sunday Times*, and Harold was relieved and pleased. 'It was nice of Gosse to temper his anger,' he wrote to Vita, 'with such human charity. It will make all the difference.'[16]

Although the sales were not enormous the Nicolsons' friends and society were praising the book, whether they had read it or not. Harold wrote an amusing letter to Michael Sadleir:[17]

P.V. is, you may be glad to hear, making a certain headway in Mayfair. I lunched the other day with Lady Cunard. P.V. was on the top of a pile of books (Peter Wright's *Supreme War Council*, Lytton Strachey's *Victoria*) on her table. I admit that his position there was due to Smith's (her butler's) expert shuffling before I came into the room. But after all it means something to be shuffled so dexterously by Smith, and in such company! Strachey the ace, Peter Wright the knave, and the Queen. I think it is very satisfactory.

And then today I lunched with Lady Islington. I was rather late; and, as is my wont, I shook hands in boyish comradeship with all my fellow guests, whether I recognized them or not. This is my wont, but I won't do it again. There was one old lady in purple and blue eyes to whom, as befitting her age and dignity, my greeting was particularly boyish, and particularly comradely. She was, I admit, a trifle surprised, but not as surprised as I was when Lady Lavery came in and dropped in front of this old lady a curtsey of practised elegance. I was put next to her at luncheon; it came out that way. Her close kinship to the House of Windsor was evident not only in that cold eye which had so lately fixed me, but in a certain gutteral emphasis of accent. She talked quite nicely about my relations, and then her relations, and about a chase they had given her in Sweden, and about being seasick. And then suddenly she said, 'I hear you have written a book; my onkel liked it verry much.' I was disconcerted by the 'onkel' business. Who could her onkel be? King Edward? But he is dead. The Kaiser? But surely they don't own, like that, to the Kaiser. THE KING? But surely an old woman of such dignity couldn't be the niece of so young, so debonair a man! I suppose it is the Duke of Connaught; rather dull that, after such alternatives. I was a little disconcerted, as I said, by all this. I could not quite muster an answer. I said, 'Oh, that's very nice of him,' and then, recovering myself, I said, 'Oh that's very nice of His –' It was unsafe to go further with this possessive unless I knew what her uncle possessed. ?Majesty? ?Royal Highness? ?Imperial? No, it was safer to stop at 'His'.

It seems highly unlikely that Princess Victoria – for the old lady in purple was she – ever read it, or the Duke of Connaught for that matter.

Between the 23rd and 28th March Harold was at Long Barn, kept there by a bad throat and cold. But these ailments did not prevent him writing 12,000 words of his novel. He was very happy. Vita was with him. She was never to leave him again, that is to say, never with anyone whose influence upon her he deprecated, or made him the least anxious lest her love for him might thereby diminish. Together she and Harold attended Allen Leeper's wedding in London to Janet Hamilton,[18] and, until Long

Barn was ready to receive staying guests, they entertained friends for the day – Eve Fleming and Augustus John, 'like a burly and debauched Christ,' Jack Wodehouse and Margaret Montagu, Victor Cunard and Ronald Balfour, John Drinkwater, 'rather overcome by his own good looks,' Algernon Blackwood, 'shy and attractive with rolling blue eyes,' Clive Bell and the Gerald Wellesleys. Throughout the spring and early summer Dorothy Wellesley was a frequent visitor, often on her own. Her marriage to Gerry was beginning to go wrong. Both Nicolsons were in her confidence, especially Vita, with whom a deep friendship was developing. 'This was one of the great literary friendships of my life,'[19] Lady Gerald was proud to claim of Vita, who dedicated *The Land* to her. She herself was a poet who had earned the commendation of Yeats. She had the face of a Juno, a long straight nose, well-shaped mouth that drooped at the corners, and a firm cleft chin. Her large turquoise eyes were well-like and brimming; and her raised eyebrows gave her a questioning aspect. A friend[20] recalls her cloudless complexion, peaches and cream, and her delicate hands with blue veins like cobwebs along the backs. With advancing years her face became slightly witch-like and her chin too prominent. In the early days her impulsiveness made her lovable. As it turned to unpredictable and totally unreliable behaviour, her eccentricities forfeited her friends' tolerance, and began to madden them. Throughout the twenties, however, Dorothy (Dottie)Wellesley's name features repeatedly in the letters and diaries of Harold and Vita.

At the end of May Harold and Vita sailed down Southampton Water on Lord Sackville's yacht, *Sumerun*, and for a fortnight were at sea or in harbour at Cowes, Weymouth and Dartmouth, Fowey and Falmouth. While Vita rested on her laurels, reading the laudatory reviews of *The Dragon in Shallow Waters*, Harold revised the last chapters of *Sweet Waters* and read the book to Vita, who 'is most sweet about it.' On the 14th June he sent off the manuscript to Michael Sadleir. It was the last day of his leave, and he and Vita were back at Long Barn. 'Dottie comes. Play tennis. Very depressed,' are the succinct entries in his diary. Sadleir wrote accepting *Sweet Waters*, but asking Harold to tone down its modernity, a curious request with which Harold complied, commenting that he was quite right. Three days later Sadleir, giving Harold luncheon at the Garrick Club, made further suggestions of changes, and confessed that he found parts of the story dull.

Early in July he and Vita lunched with Smuts in his little sitting-room overlooking the Thames on the fourth floor of the Savoy Hotel. Smuts was in his best form. No mention was made of Ireland, although the papers were full of rumours that he had gone, or was shortly going there to see de Valera. Talk was of the League of Nations. Smuts blamed

President Wilson for his egoism and vanity. He was surprised to find how quickly the British public had forgiven Germany. He was surprised to find how sincere Mr. Balfour was about the League. He spoke highly of Lord Robert Cecil, regretting only that he was too much Savonarola and too little John Bull. He then spoke of South Africa: the Indian immigration problem: the Victoria Falls: the Temple of Luxor. He spoke about bushmen and pigmies; and how as a field cornet he had once captured two bushmen fighting over a wildebeest they had killed. They were untameable and he had to let them go. He told how they would follow the vultures to find a carcass, running through the scrub with one finger raised to keep the direction. How they would stand on their heads and look like stumps of trees so that one might pass a few feet from them without recognising them.

On the 20th Harold received the first batch of proofs of *Sweet Waters*. Exactly a week later he wrote to Vita,

> I have got the second lot of proofs. Galleys. Well, I won't say what I think about it. You see when one has to turn the page (not verse now, only prose) – one always *hopes* that it will get better on the other side. But with galleys there's no chance of it getting better. One goes down and down the page, and it flops and one flops, and there comes nothing but despair when one turns over. Damn! Darling, you won't leave me, will you? You're all I've got left in the world of galleys and despair.[21]

In September Vita got her first idea of writing a sort of English Georgics. It was inspired by a chance remark of J. C. Squire, who was staying at Long Barn with his wife, to the effect that it was odd how people did not write poems about occupations. The idea lay fallow in her mind for several years before she began composing *The Land*. Harold was kept in his department of the Foreign Office for most of this month, overwhelmed as he put it, with three minor crises – Bulgaria, Burgenland and Albania. But he had time to lunch one day with Elizabeth Bibesco and her mother at the Savoy.[22] Elizabeth was very intimate and confiding, and much improved by her visit to America. There was less snorting and picking, he told Vita. Mrs. Asquith was very polite and acid and ugly. She spoke of her son-in-law Antoine Bibesco. 'What a gentleman he is. None of my family are gentlemen like that; no breeding, you know.'

Vita went abroad on a tour with Gerry and Dottie. Harold was to follow in October when his next leave was due. He accompanied Vita in a taxi bound for Victoria station, but when it halted for a moment in Pall Mall, he jumped out, looking very white, without saying goodbye. Remarking on this in a note which she wrote him in the train Vita expressed surprise that he minded being separated from her, and still loved her so much.

In between drafting, re-drafting and sending off an Albanian formula to the Italian Embassy (it was accepted by the Italian Government) Harold kept turning over in his mind projects for his next book.

> I have no idea what my book is to be about [he wrote to Vita[23] in Dubrovnik], but I shall begin it at Waterloo station on Saturday night. Oh, darling, how lucky we are both of us to write books and to love each other so very much and with such confidence (not in fidelity, darling – don't get that into your head) but confidence in each other's respect and love.

He told her that he had been sprinkled with dewdrops by Lord Curzon for his Albanian drafts. On Monday he had dined at White's with Hartopp, 'my pretty new boy in the Department.' Charles Cradock-Hartopp (he succeeded to a baronetcy in 1929) had served in France during the War. He was then twenty-eight and a First Secretary in the Foreign Office. For the next two years he and Harold were frequently together and he stayed at Long Barn. Vita liked him.

Harold's London clubs were the Marlborough and Buck's. He had resigned from the St. James's. In later years he became a member of the Travellers and the Beefsteak. In September 1921 he found himself involved in an extraordinary discussion at a committee meeting at Buck's (at which meeting the Prince of Wales was elected a member) over Eddie Knoblock having entertained Charlie Chaplin to dinner in the club. The committee had drafted a letter to Knoblock amounting to censure. Harold strongly protested. After much acrimonious discussion it was decided not to send the letter, but to ask Harold to warn Knoblock. The next day he took his friend to luncheon at the Ritz Grill and broke to him as tactfully as he could the disapproval of his fellow members. Eddie Knoblock accepted the rebuke, as though it were deserved, and the matter was quietly dropped.

Harold, having wrestled all September with the problems of the Burgenland, which the Peace Treaty had appropriated from Hungary and unwisely allotted to Austria, was granted three weeks leave. On the 4th October he reached Rome, intending to link up with Vita and the Wellesleys at the Hotel Inghilterra. Vita and Dottie had not yet returned from Dalmatia. But Gerry, who had remained in Italy, met him and took him to Gerald Berners's house. Next day the friends lunched with Mrs. Strong, the Roman archaeologist and writer, who for over thirty years was a venerated authority on all things Roman, and at whose feet no English student with aspirations to becoming an art historian neglected to sit. Talk at her table on this occasion was confined to dalmatics, Early Christian mosaics and Borromini. Harold felt out of his element in her company. He did not care for her. 'At the bottom of that arrogant soul lurks a viper of bad temper. The little tongue flicks out at waiters who give her too large a helping, or at page boys who bungle the swing doors,' he wrote.[24] Another day Berners took Harold, Gerry and Prince Philip of Hesse[25] in his motor, 'with William the Adonis chauffeur on the box,' to Frascati. The Prince and Gerry engaged in a learned discussion about frescoes. At Castel Gandolfo the party lunched above the Lake of Albano off whitebait and wild strawberries soaked in maraschino. They drove home at dusk with Berners's overcoat upon their knees. 'We then went to bed. And at midnight came a rattle at the door & my Viti standing there. My darling Viti.'

Harold, unlike his friend Gerald Wellesley, was not a dedicated or even an informed sightseer. His comments on works of art were often undiscerning. 'We stop at Marina and look at some Domenico frescoes. Are they Domenico? And who was Domenico?' He visited the Pantheon and made no comments. But he admired Bernini's elephant supporting an Egyptian obelisk upon its howdah in the Piazza di Minerva – 'the proporportions of it; the metal work at the top. The mouldings of the base. A perfect bit of art.' On the other hand he was acutely observant of places which took his fancy, especially those with historic or literary association, just as he was of all human idiosyncrasy and caprice.

The friends lunched one day at the Palazzo Barberini with Princess Jane San Faustino, a notorious American socialite whose behaviour was often outrageous.

> A large shuttered room, with a tiled floor. Slowly from the darkness emerges walnut furniture and a painted balustrade upon the ceiling. Eagles and peacocks perch over the big doorways in the centre of the balustrade. Princess Jane is dressed as a widow with a Marie Stuart hat and a white face. She had got drunk at Venice and had fallen down and Ozzie had fallen on the top of her and broken two of her ribs . . . We went into the dining-room – a cool, grey room with a terra cotta wall fountain, two armorial tapestries and a macaw. The arms of the San Faustino, the Bourbon lilies with a bar sinister, sprawled in stucco upon the ceiling, and from their edges hung two lamps in painted metal with a central glass globe. Gerry didn't like the lamps. He told her so. He said he would have preferred wooden chandeliers gilded.[26]

Afterwards they visited Keats's house, and motored down the Via Appia under a tomato-coloured sun. There was a little moon, black silhouettes and the chirping of crickets.

They all, with the happy Prince, motored again to Castel Gandolfo. They lunched under a vine. It dropped pollen upon the table-cloth. They launched paper boats down the cascade, and Siegfried Sassoon, who was with them, threw in his hat from sheer exuberance. It was a holiday of enchantment. After dinner Harold and Vita went to Gerry's room in the hotel and found him talking to Geoffrey Scott, the author of *The Architecture of Humanism*. This was not Vita's first meeting with Scott, whom she had in fact known exactly ten years ago in Rome, when he had a part-time job at the British Embassy, and with whom exactly two years hence she was to have a love affair. Another evening they met him again at dinner. He talked about Baroque architecture, in which he was the first Englishman to revive interest since the eighteenth century, and, pardonably, about Gerry, who was likewise its great partisan. Scott was then engaged on his book, *The Portrait of Zélide*.

Gerry Wellesley was not only an indefatigable sightseer, possessed of boundless vitality and enthusiasm, but he liked to organise, having an unquestioning confidence in his own competence, which was not always justified. Harold recorded in his diary a typical episode at Gerry's expense.

> We all started out to get our wagon lits tickets for Vienna. It was very hot. Gerry took charge. He said that it was no use our going to Cook's office in the Piazza di Spagna as he had a tame friend in the other office near the Termini who would do everything for us. So we took a tram. The tram struck up north for a bit and then East. After a bit Gerry bundled us out into another tram. The second tram struck west for a bit and then south. When it reached the Piazza di Spagna we climbed out. There was a rather ominous silence. Gerry said that in Rome the only way to get along was on one's own feet or in one's own automobile. We agreed, and started climbing the hill on foot. Half an hour later we reached the Termini office. Gerry's friend was away on leave. Vita and Dottie were carefully pushed off to the Baths of Diocletian to stifle their comments.[27]

On the 16th the Nicolsons and Wellesleys arrived in Venice for the day. It was cold and grey, and the Grand Canal looked huddled, untidy and disappointing. Slowly and sedately they went up the Canal in a gondola, arguing about Venetian Gothic. Vita did not admire the Salute, which made Dottie very angry. There was tension. Gerry quizzed St. Mark's like 'a plumber called in to mend the bath. He approves it finally.'[28] Vita thought the Doge's Palace a nice colour. Gerry said it was like a fat German body with coarse lace underclothing, and he pointed to the Salute to show how much better other architects did things. They returned to the station in silence.

From Venice they continued via Vienna to Munich where they stayed in luxury at the Regina Palast Hotel, and were happy again. They went to

LONDON, FOREIGN OFFICE, 1921-22

the picture gallery. Gerry examined every part of every picture as though to ascertain whether they had been darned. Harold did not care for Tiepolo's Adoration. To annoy Dottie he said it differed only in degree from a painting by Brangwyn. Gerry, who was wearing a black tie in semi-mourning because the King of Sweden had died, heard their raised voices two rooms off and was displeased. Vita and Dottie minded being told that they talked too loudly.

By the 24th October Harold was back in London working in the Foreign Office.

In November Harold was chiefly occupied with the problems arising from the Serbian advance into Albania. He crossed to Paris with H. A. L. Fisher, the British delegate to the League of Nations, to attend meetings at the League's office in the rue Vernet. Fisher made a lengthy and reasoned case against the Serbs, which at first they denied. When the Serbs told the Conference they would give way Harold worked out with General Weygand's committee details of the frontier between Serbia and Albania. He really believed that in some slight measure he had helped the League, about which he cared so much.

And now *Sweet Waters* came out.[29] On the whole the reviews were favourable and within two months the novel had sold 3,000 copies. It had a few detractors. Rebecca West in the *New Statesman* complained that the author had obviously read too much and ought to be psychoanalysed, and that the book was too packed with incident. An American reviewer accused him of showing off, and the *Manchester Guardian* found the heroine's occult relations with her dead father far from clear. But a letter of praise from Stephen McKenna cheered him considerably.

Sweet Waters contains vivid descriptions of the Constantinople which Harold knew before roaring overpopulation, wholesale demolition of the capital's old buildings and unrestricted development of shoddy blocks on congested sites ruined it for all time. It was evocative of a lost oriental city from which the country was never far away, a city made shady by large plane trees and sweetened by the scent of crushed thyme and gum cistus; a city in which the frogs were heard croaking at night, and fireflies flitted between the oleanders and the fig trees; a city where the brass bells of the water-carriers, and the sad wistful refrains of the sweet-sellers' flutes were heard at midday; and piles of green and yellow water-melons were sold at every street corner.

The principal characters in *Sweet Waters* are thinly disguised. Harold Nicolson in his self-deprecatory way identified a part of himself with

Angus Field, 'the little over-dressed clerk who looks after the papers' in the British Embassy, who is young, vain, pretentious, unsure of himself, and an inexperienced lover – 'a little sodomitic cad,' he described him in a letter to his publisher;[30] and another part of himself with Tenterden, the cynical, experienced, highly intelligent and masterful Chargé d'Affaires, whom he would have liked to resemble. It is not difficult to detect in the wild, poetic reserved Eirene, hawk-like and straight, the Vita whom he was wooing during his Constantinople days. And in Eirene's mother, social, kittenish, unscrupulous and absurd, there is more than a touch of Lady Sackville. In Edhem Bey, the Paris-educated dandy, only superficially cultured, contemptuous of his countrymen, and ignoble enough to act the spy, Harold has captured one aspect of the Turkish temperament. His macabre end, burnt alive in the ship's boiler as an experiment to see if a live head really exploded with a loud report, endorses Harold's opinion of the Turks' brutality and lack of civilisation.

The slight immaturity of *Sweet Waters* may be explained by the fact that Harold had nurtured the story ever since he was at the Constantinople Embassy as a young man in his twenties before the First War.

In so far as his status at the Foreign Office was concerned, there were no prejudicial repercussions from the publication of *Sweet Waters*. The novel merely enhanced Harold's reputation as an intellectual young diplomat with a gift for writing not vouchsafed to many of his colleagues. It put him on a level with his wife, whose *Dragon in Shallow Waters* provoked the Foreign Secretary, Lord Curzon, to speak of it with passionate enthusiasm. In December Alan Stern drew a caricature of Harold for *John o' London's Weekly* which was frequently reproduced in gossip columns whenever the sitter's name cropped up. It showed a very youthful, spruce and be-piped dandy. It was not a wholly convincing representation.

In December Harold spent one arduous day gardening at Long Barn. When he came in at dusk he had decided what he was going to write next. It was to be a biography of Tennyson. He fetched as many books as he could find on Tennyson from the London Library, and immediately set to work. At the same time Vita was busy on her book, *Knole and the Sackvilles*.

It is not always easy to follow the Nicolsons' domestic movements in London during the 1920s. In January 1922 they were living in Ebury Street. In the ensuing winter months Harold was there throughout the week. In the summer he usually commuted to Long Barn where Vita stayed for months on end, going to London less and less often, although

LONDON, FOREIGN OFFICE, 1921-22

at this period of her life she was not the total country recluse she was to become. Still, she did not share the full social life which Harold enjoyed. A good deal of her time was spent with Dorothy Wellesley, either at Long Barn, or at the Wellesleys' house, Sherfield Court between Basingstoke and Gerry's father's estate, the ducal Stratfield Saye. Sherfield was a moated Georgian house which looked older than it was, being a farmhouse of plaster and timber, with four gables in a row. Gerry built on to one end a single-storey annexe with tall, round-headed windows to serve as library. The house was filled with opulent contents, furniture of lapis lazuli, a flying dolphin bought from an impoverished Russian aristocrat in Rome, and pictures by Caravaggio. Wild flowers grew in profusion on the banks of the moat, and water lilies were planted in the brown waters. The Wellesleys, who were far richer than the Nicolsons, also had a house in Portland Place where, if Vita was away from Long Barn, Harold stayed with Gerry more often than anywhere else. The ties between the husbands and the wives of the two families were close, and the Wellesley and Nicolson children were often together, either at Sherfield or at Long Barn. On the 30th January Vita went to Sherfield for the night and left with Dottie the next day for a tour in Sicily.

While Vita was away Harold contended with a memorandum on Western Thrace. He was at this time at odds with his Foreign Secretary. 'Lord Curzon has quite gone off his head and changes his mind every day,' he wrote. He was not a good Minister. Harold deeply sympathised with Allen Leeper who found Curzon difficult and unpredictable. He tried to reassure his friend that it was he, Leeper, who was silencing the criticisms so frequently being levelled against the Foreign Office, chiefly by Lloyd George. Harold was extremely jealous of the Foreign Office's good name and he resented what he considered its decay and humiliation 'under the present tumid, caddish and disloyal domination of Curzon of Kedleston.'[31] These strong sentiments were aroused by the sharp differences between the High Commissioner for Egypt, Lord Allenby, and the Foreign Secretary over pressure from the former to abolish the protectorate and recognise Egypt as a sovereign state. Harold's sympathies were with Allenby.

> Curzon has come a big cropper over the Egyptian business. Allenby had prepared a series of concessions and had telegraphed from Cairo to Curzon asking him to see them through the Cabinet. C had telegraphed back promising his support, but when the proposals came before the Cabinet there was some slight opposition. C immediately telegraphed to A suggesting a compromise. A replied that he would resign if his proposals were not accepted. C then sent a long telegram with numbered paragraphs pointing out how wrong A had been all along and

how wicked of him it was to suggest resignation. A replied by telegraph that he was coming home and by despatch completely disposing of C's indictment. C suppressed this despatch and A on arrival insisted on it being circulated to the Cabinet. C said it would create a bad impression. A replied, 'Of whom?' C then began to cry. The next day A met the Cabinet and they agreed, not with C but with A. The result is that C (having a perfect case with the Cabinet) has shown them once and for all that he is a coward, and has shown A that he is a shit.[32]

Allenby won the day in this conflict. Harold, however, was not only to modify his strictures, but to understand, appreciate and greatly admire Lord Curzon before the year was out, when he worked in the closest contact with him at the Lausanne Conference.

It is astonishing how Harold Nicolson managed to combine his Foreign Office work, his writing and his social engagements. The year 1922 saw him immersed in all three. He seldom attended a party at which some episode did not contribute to the enrichment of a book or article he was actually writing, or might one day write. On a January evening he dined with Sir Arthur and Lady Colefax. Aldous Huxley was present, rather large, silent and farouche. Harold tried to draw him into the conversation, but failed signally. After the dinner the party went on to Mrs. Robert Mathias's house to hear Edith Sitwell read her poems. The recitation took place in an ordinary London drawing-room with a curtain cutting off the re-entrant end. On the curtain was painted a huge futurist face with a large hole for the mouth. Through the mouth was fixed a megaphone, and through the megaphone came the voice of Edith. Appropriate musical accompaniments were composed and arranged by William Walton. Miss Sitwell recited some twenty poems from *Façade*, with a forced emphasis on the metre. Harold thought the effect good and was rather impressed by the whole show.

In February he attended an evening party at Buckingham Palace to see Princess Mary's wedding presents. She was about to marry Lord Lascelles, who had courted Vita and been cut out by Harold in 1913.

After shaking hands I wander into the Throne Room, where a buffet is arranged down one side. Opposite are the red sofas in tiers, and sitting there, a little shrunken and faded since I last saw her ten years ago, is Ellen Terry. She asks me to get her some iced coffee. I do so, and in return ask her to tell me about Tennyson. She is vague at first and a little muddled in her head. I try leading questions: 'Did he come to the rehearsals or the final performances?' 'No, only the rehearsals. He was very kind. Very vain and very gruff. But so simple. You see, I was just beginning to get tired then of people who were one thing at one moment and one at another. He was always the same. No – not rude. Just vain and simple. Like a child.' I asked her about his reading aloud. She said *The Northern Farmer* was the best. Her face lit up when she remembered it. 'You see,' she said, 'he had the accent already. And he *acted* the thing. Oh, it was very funny,' and she shook her little old head and smiled. I asked her about the other poems. Oh no, she had not heard him recite *Maud*, but *Locksley Hall* – yes, she had heard that. And then she put back her head and began a sort of recitative, humming the metre; and as she went on she remembered Tennyson, how he had done it, and a faint echo of his boom came into her voice and her legs began to work up and down to the rhythm. At which her coffee cup upset on her black jet lap, and I had to mop it up with my handkerchief. When this was done her face was vague again. "Very simple," she murmured, "just like a child. And I reverenced him so. We all reverenced him."'[33]

In March Harold was distressed to be told by Vansittart that the Greeks would fail to raise a loan in London with which to buy munitions and send reinforcements against the Turks. He feared the Turks might launch a devastating attack in a few weeks' time. 'Van's' proposal was to get Yusuf Kemal Bey, the Turkish Nationalist Foreign Minister over from Angora before the Conference, and offer to get the Greeks out of Anatolia at once, on condition that his Government would undertake not to interfere. Vansittart and Harold went at 5.30 to put the idea to Curzon.

He was in bed on the top floor of Carlton House Terrace. As I was taken up in the lift, his valet whispered, 'Very troublesome, sir, his lordship today.' I go into a little room like an 8/- room at the Lord Warden Hotel. Pink and white wallpaper; maple washing stand with cheap wash basin – cornflowers; Pears soap; a thin rather scruffy shaving brush; maple dressing table; half empty bottle of hairwash; a large stained wooden hairbrush; a glass electric light shade above it all; by his bed a red silk and brass reading lamp; on the wall cheap etchings of Belgian cathedrals; photographs of Lady C and the children in cheap blue leather frames; a washing bill on the mantlepiece; an old gladstone bag and a green suitcase in a corner; a brass bed with a pink silk eiderdown, and in it the Marquess in a flowered dressing gown. His spine was hurting him and he winced as he bent over to write. But he agreed with the proposal.[34]

The 9th March, being Vita's thirtieth birthday, Harold gave her a greenhouse and the Encyclopædia Britannica. He told her not to worry about being thirty. Time had no meaning. If she were 'a bullet fired from a rifle into space it wouldn't be your birthday tomorrow at all, it would be Boadicea's birthday, or perhaps Ovid's.'

*   *   *   *   *

HAROLD NICOLSON

The Greek situation brought renewed anxiety and a cause of fresh bother to Harold's department of the Foreign Office. He was hard at work on yet another memorandum about Western Thrace and the Dodecanese, Gounaris having addressed privately to Curzon a desperate appeal for help and an admission of imminent disaster. At the Near East Conference, which met in Paris, proposals for an Armistice and the evacuation of Smyrna were transmitted to the Greek Government at Athens and the two Turkish Governments at Constantinople and Angora. The real Turkish power, which was Kemal Ataturk's at Angora, insisted absolutely on the total withdrawal of the Greeks from Asia Minor, and the severing of all Greek access to the Black Sea.

On Good Friday at Long Barn, having had a final re-read of Tennyson's poems, Harold began writing his book, 'but it does not go well.'[35] Towards the end of April he set off on a Tennyson hunt, first to Cambridge, where he looked at manuscripts in Trinity College library, and then to the White Hart Inn at Lincoln. He visited Somersby Rectory, then little altered, remote and seemingly isolated, where the Tennyson family had lived with the drunken, melancholic father; and, via Alford, to Mabelthorpe where he traced the poet's meanderings along the deserted beach.

On the 2nd May he finished Chapter 2, leaving Chapter 1 to be tackled later. The speed with which he went on writing was prodigious, in spite of interruptions. On the 6th he finished the Cambridge chapter. On the 10th he finished the 1832 chapter. On the 13th Jack and Margaret Wodehouse, Charlie Hartopp and Eddie Marsh came down; and he finished the ten years' silence chapter. He asked Eddie if he would revise the book for him when it reached proof stage. This in due course Eddie did, but was critical of the style which he considered slipshod. 'I suppose it is,' Harold told Vita, apparently unmoved, 'but then I write at such a rattling pace owing to the office. He makes great fun of some of it.'[36] On the 18th Harold finished Chapter 6 on Farringford. On the 19th he was working on the last chapter; and on the 21st he finished the biographical section. On the 22nd he was obliged to go to London for the day because the Foreign Office had got into a muddle over the Treaty of Rapallo. In the evenings at Long Barn Vita read to him and Dottie, who was staying, parts of her Knole book – 'It should be good' – and they played tennis, as many as five sets running. The weather was boiling hot, 86 degrees in the shade. They dined on the terrace and Harold in his turn read to Vita and Dottie extracts from *Tennyson*. On the 25th Vita's *The Heir* was published. Three days later he and Vita sailed with Lord Sackville in the *Sumerun* from Dover to Southampton. It was rough and some of the crew were seasick, but not Harold. From Yarmouth on the Isle of Wight he and Vita walked to

LONDON, FOREIGN OFFICE, 1921-22

Farringford. On the 3rd June, back at Long Barn he wrote out all the bits of Chapter 1 which he had composed on the yacht.

Completion of *Tennyson* was delayed because of pressure of work in the office on the Italian question. In June a delegation from Rome arrived to negotiate an agreement about Italy's claims in the Adriatic. Lloyd George had given the Italians vague promises of an entente. Harold was uneasy over this as it meant, in his opinion, that they would get all they wanted from us and we nothing from them. He expressed his uneasiness in a memorandum which incensed Lloyd George. The Prime Minister complained that the Foreign Office invariably blocked him in whatever he wished to do. Harold attributed his and his colleagues' slights and injuries to there virtually being no Secretary of State to protect them. Curzon was away ill and Balfour who was taking his place, merely smiled blandly and appeared to be amused by 'their' difficulties. As Harold predicted, before the month was out the Italians refused to give up the Dodecanese. This enabled him to insert a clause in the Agreement he was instructed to draft, releasing Great Britain from her obligations under the Treaty of London. In a rage the Italians called off the negotiations and departed for Rome.

While Harold's concentration on *Tennyson* was temporarily distracted by the Italian question, Vita finished *Knole and the Sackvilles* – which he pronounced 'quite excellent' – and began another novel. In the middle of July he was back at Long Barn hard at work on *Tennyson*. By the 1st August he was nearing the end. Putting the book aside he went for a long walk on Ide Hill among the loosestrife, pondering over the finale. Two days later he filled in the part about *In Memoriam* and finished writing at six in the evening. After revising the whole manuscript he sent it to Constable's on the 28th of the month. A week later he received very favourable comments from the publisher's reader. He and Vita then went for a few days yachting with his father-in-law. On his return to the Foreign Office he wrote to Vita:

> Thank you for my nice holiday. We *are* happy together when we're left to each other, aren't we, my darling? I really do feel that it's got established and that only the most terrible of tropic hurricanes could uproot it.[37]

By the beginning of September the Greek situation was very bad indeed. 'Greeks utterly beaten in Anatolia, poor darlings,' Harold noted on the 5th. Indeed Kemal had pushed them once and for all out of Asia Minor, burned Smyrna to the ground and strewn it with Greek corpses. King Constantine fled from his throne and Venizelos was called upon yet again to save his country. Most serious of all, Mustafa Kemal's army was confronting British troops at the Dardanelles. As usual Harold was ordered to prepare memoranda on the attitude of the Balkan States to the Greek crisis, and the dire necessity of preserving the freedom of the Straits. Owing to his close association with Venizelos and the influence he was supposed to exert upon that capricious and compelling leader his opinion was much consulted and heeded by the office. On Sunday the 17th September Leon Melas, Secretary at the Greek Embassy, motored down to Long Barn, having been sent by Venizelos. Harold was authorised to tell him in strict confidence that the Cabinet had decided to hold the Dardanelles by force, with or without French co-operation. He was electrified to read in the papers next day a communiqué disclosing the Cabinet decision which he had imparted to Melas as a great secret the previous afternoon. He found the Foreign Office in consternation over so insane an indiscretion. It transpired that, while Curzon had retired to Hackwood for the weekend, Winston Churchill, Austen Chamberlain and Birkenhead concocted the communiqué which they persuaded the Prime Minister to sign and issue to Reuter's. Harold considered it a disastrous decision, for it would commit the Government to a policy difficult to maintain without loss of face.

He was moved to the Eastern Department to help deal with the crisis that had arisen.

After a meeting[38] in Paris between Curzon and Poincaré at which the two statesmen had an unedifying row, the former making cutting phrases about the French having let Britain down at Chanak by the withdrawal of troops, thus leaving us in sole confrontation with the Turks, and the latter making insulting rejoinders, Curzon left the room in a state of collapse, and wept. Finally it was agreed that General Harington, the G.O.C. at Constantinople, should meet representatives of the Angora Government at Mudania with an ultimatum that Kemal's troops must retire from the neutral zone round the Straits. To everyone's astonishment Kemal agreed to a meeting at Mudania. Hostilities between Britain and Turkey were thereby averted, but the war party in Britain, consisting of Churchill, Birkenhead and Horne, were so disconcerted that they wanted the Cabinet to censure Harington. Curzon however put a stop to that.

On the 29th Curzon sent for Harold who propounded to him his theory that in essence the problem was Anglo-Russian rather than Anglo-Turkish, and that by 'freedom of the Straits' the Foreign Office meant essentially the right of passage of warships through the Straits to the Black Sea. Impressed by the argument Curzon conceded to Harold that he was 'able.'

At first, discussions at Mudania went badly and Harington sent home

LONDON, FOREIGN OFFICE, 1921-22

gloomy telegrams. Kemal was making impossible terms, even threatening to advance further into the neutral zone. Harington resolutely stood firm. Curzon felt obliged to go to Paris. After further hectic discussions Poincaré gave way to Curzon's formula that Allied occupation should fill the gap caused by Greek retirement from the Smyrna area, and that only Turkish gendarmerie should be allowed into the neutral zone. On the 10th the Turks signed the Mudania Armistice, and the crisis was at least temporarily over. Nevertheless they pressed for the forthcoming conference on peace terms to be held at Smyrna. Curzon would have none of this, and insisted that Lausanne in neutral Switzerland should be the venue. On the 14th Harold was told by Oliphant that he was to attend the conference in November. He immediately wrote to Vita suggesting that she should accompany him for the first three weeks.

Relations between the Wellesleys were going from bad to worse. In September Harold, who was staying with Lord Gerald in Portland Place, wrote to Vita:[39]

> Gerry has not spoken yet about the great estrangement. He is quite cheery and happy when he forgets himself, but then he suddenly remembers how injured and abandoned he is & sighs and looks like a boot for a bit. In fact I rather feel that much as he likes my being there he rather resents the fact that my presence takes the edge off the full poignancy of his martyrdom. He felt it so much yesterday that he decided to go today to Sherfield. He took Valerian [his son] with him. They started off after breakfast and walked to the bus - Gerry straight-backed and defiant carrying a grip with their mutual night clothes in it, & Valerian struggling under a large parcel of brocade. So large was the parcel that it protruded beyond Valerian, & its sharp brown paper corner came up against and even *scratched* the shiny blue door which so diversifies the otherwise symmetrical alignment of No. 43. There was a long and rather petulant pause while the handkerchief was got out and the door dabbed to see if it was really serious - & then they started off again to walk to the bus together.

And two days later he wrote again:

> Gerry says he has done no wrong and if Dottie wishes to run away that's her business. I do think Dottie makes a mistake in trying to be at one and the same time the little bit of thistledown *and* the thistle.

Dottie's wish was not to run away with anybody, and only to run away from Gerry. None the less Harold was slightly apprehensive on Vita's behalf.

While Harold was waiting to be sent to Lausanne the Lloyd George Coalition Government was overthrown on the 19th October, and Bonar Law became Conservative Premier. A general election was to follow within a few weeks. On the 22nd Harold recorded in his diary that he was reading Byron's memoirs all day. He was already preparing for his next book.

The last weekend of the month he went to stay with the Asquiths at the Wharf. He had a long talk with Margot on the Sunday morning.

> She shows me her rooms and pictures and books. She talks about Gladstone: he told her that what he was proud of was having conquered his natural stinginess. She told me that when the Asquith Cabinet fell and they were turned out of Downing Street, some of her letters were sent to No. 10 and were forwarded by Lloyd George's secretaries with 'Not known' written across them!! She will not like my book on Tennyson; she says he always spoke nicely about the other poets and was not jealous. She hedged rather when I quoted to her instances of jealousy. She showed me a letter from Lloyd George to Asquith when he had formed his Government in 1916. It began, 'Dear Sir,' and went on, 'The King has called upon me, etc.' and ended with the request that he would not oppose. It was written in holograph and not typed. She also told me lots about Winston's vanity; but she admires and loves him all the same.
>
> Sat next to old Asquith at luncheon. Someone said how odd it was that Lord Midleton was not included in the Cabinet. Mr. A snuffled a bit and then with his strange sucking-in smile said, 'They're afraid of his brains.' He also said that the Kaiser was the only royalty he had met who was of sufficient culture and intelligence to choose as a companion.[40]

During the weekend the Fascists brought off their *coup d'état* in Italy, an incident Harold thought worth mentioning, but without adding any comment. On Monday morning he travelled up to London with Mrs. Asquith in the train from Didcot.

> Regardless of the breathless interest and astonishment of our fellow travellers she embarks on more reminiscences. She had had a letter from Bonar Law. She was cross with Gosse for having abused her book in the *Sunday Times* after writing to her a long letter as to its certainty of immortality. She gave me a copy of that letter . . .
>
> What a strange and curious family [the Asquiths]. Such intelligence and such insensibility! And with it all and all their astonishing exhibitionism and indiscretion they are not in the least vulgar or unkind.

LONDON, FOREIGN OFFICE, 1921-22

They have a sort of dynamic dignity quite different from the statuesque reserve of the consciously dignified. And they will go down, I suppose, to posterity as vain and flippant people.[41]

On the 4th November there was a *coup d'état* at Constantinople, and the Khalif was deposed. Another crisis was precipitated. Curzon made Harold draft late into the night a complete statement of British policy in the Near East for him to send to Poincaré. He also made Harold re-write for the third time a memorandum on *The Freedom of the Straits*.[42] This was a long and careful summary of Britain's assumption of the right to send ships through the Dardanelles and the Bosphorus ever since the mid-nineteenth century. Whereas until 1914 a weak Turkey had looked to Great Britain to protect her from Russian aggression against Constantinople, circumstances had changed. Now Turkey had recovered her strength and was a positive menace to Great Britain and Soviet Russia alike. The memorandum explained the physical difficulty of maintaining the freedom of the Straits, but stressed how the present strength and opposition of Turkey in this regard should be curbed. It also recommended supervision by the League of Nations, with the appointment of a High Commissioner from the United States.

Finally, Harold had to prepare a memorandum on procedure of the forthcoming conference, before packing for Lausanne.

At this juncture of affairs he could look upon the progress and future of his career with justifiable complacency and confidence. The chrysalis period of apprenticeship and drudgery in the Foreign Office was long past. The war had brought him responsibilities, admittedly not onerous, in which he had proved himself. He had drafted documents which members of the Cabinet had studied with care. During the Peace Treaty he had emerged as an individual to whose advice his colleagues, the Foreign Secretary and even the Prime Minister had paid heed. He was now on the threshold of future opportunities in which he would, as adviser to Lord Curzon, become still more influential. He was eager to win further distinctions, higher honours. There was no limit to the posts within the service which he would not fill. His career stretched ahead like a long, straight road ending in a blaze of glory, with no crossroads, divergent paths or obstacles within sight.

On the evening of the 15th November at a party given by Evan Morgan he listened to the General Election results. The Conservatives got in with a large majority.

10

THE LAUSANNE CONFERENCE, 1922–1923

ON the 17th November 1922 Vita called at the Foreign Office in Whitehall at half past twelve. Harold's suggestion that she might accompany him to Lausanne for three weeks had come to nothing. Instead they took what he described as a rather 'choky' farewell of each other. At one o'clock Harold, who was as punctual as his father, got into a taxi and from the little window in the hood watched Vita's silhouette receding against the grey background of the courtyard. It was another of those partings, each of which became more distressing to both of them than the last. At ten past one he arrived, far too early, at Victoria station. He was soon joined on the platform by Sir William Tyrrell, Assistant Under-Secretary of State, and Allen Leeper, Private Secretary to the Secretary of State. A group of eager cameramen and another nonchalant group of detectives gathered. As the hour of two o'clock approached when the Golden Arrow was due to leave for Dover, everyone began to look anxiously at the clock.

> At 1 minute to 2 slowly came a chauffeur with a red box, a footman with a red box, and a masseur with a red box, and 2 porters with six red boxes, and then as if he were carrying himself on a howdah appeared THE MARQUIS, walking at one mile an hour while we waited. Finally he got in and the cameras clicked and the red boxes and green baize things were put in for him to put his leg on, and off we slid past Chislehurst.[1]

In these simple words Harold described in a letter to Vita Lord Curzon's departure for Paris, which furnished his memory for the more picturesque and highly coloured version written in the first paragraph of that inimitable chapter, 'Arketall,' in *Some People*. Harold lunched by himself in the train and read the proofs of *Tennyson*. At Dover Lord Curzon, his aides, secretaries and servants were conducted on board the steamer.

> Again more cameras ... At Calais the same thing. The only difference was that the Marquis's valet was by then dead drunk & kept on dropping a red box. So we had dinner and I had a long talk to the Marquis afterwards. Whenever I spoke the train was quiet, but the moment he began to answer it started to hoot and whistle and clatter. This made him rather cross.

THE LAUSANNE CONFERENCE 1922-23

But when the train condescended to keep quiet their conversation about the Balkans remained genial. On their arrival in Paris at 9.45 they were met by Lord Hardinge, the British Ambassador, and the French Foreign Minister, and driven to the Ritz Hotel.

The next morning, having read the newspapers, Harold was summoned to Lord Curzon's room at 9.30. Lord Curzon read through Harold's memorandum on the procedure of the forthcoming conference, discussing it with him point by point. A luncheon party was given at the Quai d'Orsay, at which Monsieur and Madame Poincaré (a lady with unnaturally auburn hair) received the guests. In addition to the British delegation and Ambassador, were Marshal Foch, General Weygand, Camille Barrère the veteran French Ambassador in Rome, and Maurice Bompard, formerly French Ambassador to Russia and Turkey. After luncheon a five-hour talk about the ensuing conference took place. All the French delegates present were, with the exception of Poincaré, men of the highest calibre or culture. As for Poincaré, whose most favourable commendation by a contemporary was that he was 'un bon petit bourgeois qui veut garder sa pécule,' Curzon simply loathed him. He was unable to forget the scene in Paris the previous September when he took him to task for France's behaviour at Chanak. The French Premier shouted in shrill, irritable tones, and kept tapping his pince-nez against his thumb nail. 'If he does that again,' Curzon mumbled furiously, 'I shall leave the room. I căn't bear that horrid little man. I căn't bear him.' The prospect of having to co-operate with him at Lausanne for goodness knows how many weeks was abhorrent to the Marquis. Poincaré in his turn was enraged with Curzon because the Marquis knew his facts better than he did, and because he was unbending, stiff and patrician. Their relations were no augury of a happy issue out of the Allies' impending conflict with the Turks.

That evening the British party dined together in the Ritz, and Lord Curzon was very gay and affable. After dinner Harold spent two hours composing a telegram for his chief to send to the Foreign Office, which after typing it out several times he had to take round to the Embassy. He did not get to bed till 2.30. He had little sleep that night for the special train to Lausanne left Paris at 8.10 in the morning. Desperately and feverishly he hurled his clothes into a suitcase, the lid of which repeatedly refused to stay shut. On the train, which consisted of three coaches, Poincaré's, Curzon's and then the restaurant, the British delegation worked all day, with a break for a huge luncheon with the French. Harold sat next to Poincaré's private secretary, Hermitte, who had been Secretary-General to President Deschanel. He told Harold that about a week after taking on the job he realised that Deschanel was mad. Hermitte went through agonies of mind lest the President's madness might leak out. But after his attempted suicide from a train Deschanel was shut up in the Château de Rambouillet, where he tried to jump into the fountain. There was only two foot of water in it, and he emerged covered with mud.

After luncheon Harold discussed conference procedure with Laroche, Joint-Director of Political Affairs, and together they drafted a fresh scheme. Harold was reading it to Curzon when the train drew up in Lausanne station. Curzon refused to budge until Harold had finished reading. They then went into the corridor and saw endless pink faces on the platform gazing avidly at the train. They halted there for fifteen minutes, waiting for a reply to a telegram which Poincaré and Curzon had sent Mussolini, inviting him to meet them that evening. At last it came, announcing that Mussolini would receive the two statesmen at Territet. Harold and Allen Leeper and the valet (whose real name was Tippendale) were made to get out while the train carried Monsieur Poincaré and Lord Curzon on to Territet. It was then that Harold and Allen to their acute embarrassment were confronted under a battery of arc lamps by the vast crowd of people expecting to welcome the French Prime Minister and the British Foreign Secretary; then that they saw the inebriated Tippendale raise his bowler hat and advance to be greeted by the Mayor of Lausanne. Having dragged back Tippendale by the shoulders and extricated themselves from a disappointed gathering of Swiss, Harold and Allen established themselves in the Hotel Beau Rivage and dined tranquilly. While awaiting in the lounge the return of their master the glass doors of the hotel swung hastily open at 11.30, and a sulky-looking, unshaven, pompous individual strutted into the foyer, his head swinging from side to side. It was Mussolini who had come back first from the Territet meeting. Shortly afterwards the Marquis arrived, looking magnificent and patrician. They followed him up to his room and talked till one o'clock.

The next morning began with a preliminary conference in Lord Curzon's suite. Poincaré arrived punctually, and they waited. After a quarter of an hour Mussolini burst dramatically into the room, stopped, bowed low and said, 'Messieurs, je vous salue.' Harold watched a slow smile spread over the cold, cruel lips of the Marquis as he took his seat. They went through the memoranda, amended by Harold and Laroche, point by point with Mussolini. Harold had his first opportunity of observing at close quarters this strange individual, whose features 'were still obscured by the dust and fervour of the march on Rome,' for the Fascist revolution was but a mere three weeks old. He had a sallow complexion, yellow hands with prominent black veins, a rather Jewish nose and a high forehead. His mouth was curiously mobile and well shaped, not unlike that of the young Napoleon. He had very small pupils to his eyes, which

THE LAUSANNE CONFERENCE 1922-23

showed the whites all round them both at the top and the bottom. The effect was odd. He made histrionic use of his eyes in that manner which was to be only too often imitated by subsequent dictators and would-be dictators. The impression he made upon Harold was of a second-rate cinema actor. Weygand whispered across to Harold, 'Voilà un homme trop jeune dans un monde trop vieux.' The discussion did not go too badly, and unity was established between the British, French and Italian delegates.

At four o'clock that afternoon the conference was officially opened in the Casino. It was an unusual setting, not conducive to intimacy or easy discussion. There was a small stage for the press, and some chairs for the delegates in the first few rows of stalls. The President of the Swiss Republic entered, preceded by a man robed in red, with a white coat and a cocked hat. The President looked unhappy while he made a speech of welcome. Lord Curzon spoke suitably; and General Ismet Pasha, Turkey's Minister of Foreign Affairs and President of the Turkish delegation, followed with a speech in rather poor taste. After these brief preliminaries the delegates, aides, secretaries and interpreters rose and withdrew. The proper business was postponed till the morrow. The British and French delegates dined together in the hotel.

On the 21st November, which happened to be Harold Nicolson's thirty-sixth birthday (he received a telegram from Vita), Poincaré and Mussolini retired to Paris and Rome respectively. The Lausanne Conference got down to business, and Lord Curzon by the most dexterous manoeuvres, born of long experience of diplomatic conduct, instantly appointed himself Chairman of the Conference, and became the acknowledged leading personality. Indeed his superb handling of the conference was perhaps the culminating achievement of his public life. It was as though he were inspired with an unwonted tact and finesse. By sheer charm of manner, commanding presence and superior astuteness he, with the smile of a docile leopard, mesmerised the delegates into accepting his points of view, and by the mere show of a claw usually frightened the recalcitrant Turks and Russians into abandoning their objections.

It is only fair and right to add that Curzon's task was greatly facilitated by the relations of complete confidence and personal friendship which existed between the technical staffs of the French and British delegations, in spite of the recent differences between the two countries, as illustrated by the consequences of Chanak, and above all by the intransigence of Poincaré.

The importance of the Lausanne Conference lay in the fact that it was the first meeting between ex-enemies of the First World War on terms which were negotiated with and not dictated to the vanquished. The terms reached at the Treaty of Sèvres have already been described. Suffice it to say that the Constantinople Government had been compelled to sign them under duress. But by 1922 the Constantinople Government ceased to have any authority in Turkey outside the narrow areas under occupation by the Allied Powers. The greater part of Turkey was under the effective new Government, of which Mustafa Kemal was undoubted leader in Angora. This Government not only carried on war with the Greeks but was strong enough to repudiate the Treaty of Sèvres. It was therefore in a spirit of rebuff, if not defeat, that the Allied representatives met the Turks at Lausanne in very changed circumstances.

In *Curzon: The Last Phase* Harold Nicolson has given a brilliantly lucid exposition of the proceedings of the Lausanne Conference, which it would be superfluous to paraphrase here. In that book Curzon is made the hero of the conference, and justly accredited with its successful outcome. But the considerable part played behind the scenes in Curzon's interests by the author, who was present throughout, is entirely omitted. Harold Nicolson's activities on the stage itself were by no means inconspicuous. He was one of two British representatives on a Sub-Commission for the Study of Demilitarisation of the Frontiers of Eastern Thrace, of which General Weygand was President; he was a British representative on the Sub-Commission for the Study of Demilitarisation of certain Aegean islands, of which Weygand again was President; and he was a British representative on a Sub-Commission for Prisoners of War and Cemeteries, of which Admiral Guido Chelotti was President. These duties entailed endless meetings in addition to his close and constant attendance on the Foreign Secretary.

Whereas under the Treaty of Sèvres the Greeks had been apportioned Eastern Thrace up to the Chatalja Line, which left the Turks with that truncated peninsula of a few square miles in which Constantinople and the villages of the Bosphorus stood, the Lausanne Conference gave back Eastern Thrace to Turkey, subject to a wide demilitarised zone running from the Black Sea to the Aegean, including the Dardanelles and the Asiatic region behind Chanak. Harold worked tirelessly to bring this about through talks with Duca, the Roumanian Minister for Foreign Affairs and delegate, with Stambolisky the Bulgarian Prime Minister and delegate, and with Venizelos, running from one to another like an eager young labrador in the pursuit of game, and faithfully reporting the result of each excursion to Lord Curzon. At the end of the first day Harold recorded in his diary:

THE LAUSANNE CONFERENCE 1922-23

I get the three Balkans to put up a joint case. Something gained. A meeting after dinner in Curzon's room with Barrère, Bompard, Garroni [the Italian delegate], and Weygand. We go over the West Thrace question and come to agreement. Come back and do proofs of *Tennyson*.[2]

On the 23rd November Harold had to deal with Bulgaria's claim to access to the Aegean, by wringing from her a concession that she would construct a giant port at Dedragatch on Greek territory. To achieve this he had first to win Venizelos's consent to lease Dedragatch to the Bulgars in return for the Allies advancing the Greek frontier of Western Thrace up to the Arda river. A letter to Vita written this day[3] gives some idea how busy he was.

I write to you at odd scrappy moments and in odd scrappy ways – but the instant I get free I *want* to write to you and if I were not continuously interrupted I might sometimes be able to bring it off.

You see what happens is that I get up, and have coffee & honey (yes, I get it here) and the most delicious rolls. And then about 9.00 I go down to see the Marquis and we go through things with Tyrrell and Allen. And at 10 or 10.30 there is the Conference till 1.30, and then after luncheon we begin again; and then about 7.30 I get back and try to have a bath. And then after dinner there is generally a private conference with the French and Italians. In the interstices of this I have to see Greeks, Rumanians, Serbs, Bulgars, Turks, Armenians, Caucasians, Dodecanesians, Italians, Albanians, Egyptians and divers press correspondents. So that I have scarcely time to blow my nose.

It is all far more interesting than the Paris Conference as one has the feeling that it may break down at any moment, & that one never knows what the Turks may or may not do. Curzon is quite magnificent.

That evening Harold discussed with Tyrrell the desirability of sending Sir Gerald Talbot[4] to Athens to try and rescue Prince Andrew of Greece,[5] Gounaris, the ex-Prime Minister, and Baltazzi his Foreign Minister who with five more supporters of King Constantine had been condemned to death by the new military Government under General Plastiras. This Government had invited Venizelos to represent Greece at Lausanne. Curzon instructed the British Minister in Athens to threaten Plastiras that if the executions were carried out Great Britain would break off diplomatic relations with Greece. None the less on the 28th after dinner Tyrrell said to Harold with a gesture of despair, 'They've shot the lot, in a row.' Allen and Harold went to tell Curzon, who was appalled. 'I go to bed quite wretched,' Harold wrote. 'This is the third time the Greeks have let us down, first politically by getting rid of Venizelos;

then militarily by being beaten by the Turks; and now morally by this business.'

In fact Prince Andrew[5] and one or two others were spared through the intervention of the British Foreign Secretary and the superb courage of Gerald Talbot, a large, jovial sailor of the Scarlet Pimpernel fraternity. The initiative of the rescue operation was Harold's. It should have been Sir William Tyrrell's. But at that moment Tyrrell was in one of his periods of alcoholic stupor which rendered him completely incapable of action. When Talbot returned, having successfully completed his mission, Harold was thanked by Lord Curzon in the presence of Tyrrell. Tyrrell, who had never cared for Harold, and had consistently balked Lord Carnock when he was Permanent Under-Secretary, now bore Harold increasing resentment for having witnessed his humiliation.

Harold's third appreciable achievement relates to the freedom of the Straits. He had endless personal discussions with generals and admirals, ministers and delegates of all the Powers on this vexed, but highly important matter. On the 20th December Ismet Pasha accepted Lord Curzon's proposals in principle. They were that the demilitarised zone was to be greatly reduced from what was laid down at Sèvres, and to be closed to both Allied and Turkish forces. The Commission of the Straits was to be retained for conservancy purposes only. The three principal Allied Powers, plus Japan, undertook to resist any violations of the rights and freedom of navigation. Russia did her best to prevent this agreement between Turkey and the Allies, without avail. It was implemented. And it was as much a triumph for Harold as for his master.

There is no doubt that Lord Curzon's success at Lausanne was largely prompted by the assistance he received from the able young First Secretary whom Sir Lancelot Oliphant had detailed to minister to him. Curzon was a sick and irritable man. He was proud and arrogant. He did not brook contradiction. He bullied subordinates who were in any way subservient or afraid of him. But in Harold he met his match. Harold was not afraid of him. Socially he was on an equal footing. His mind was as alert as Curzon's. He was far more active. And above all, like his chief, he had an irrepressible sense of humour. Although infinitely respectful he was vastly amused by the great statesman's idiosyncrasies, and he often showed his amusement. Besides he admired Curzon for his determination to restore Great Britain's diplomatic prestige in Europe.

Harold was fully aware of Lord Curzon's weaknesses. When his master became rattled, or discomposed, he fell into states of despair. Harold sympathised, and knew how to soothe. For instance, on the 4th December the Italian delegation threatened to leave the conference unless Britain gave way to their demands for participation in the mandates over territory

THE LAUSANNE CONFERENCE 1922-23

detached from Turkey. Curzon paced the passage, leaning on a secretary's arm, on the verge of a nervous collapse. 'With all his composure and dignity *we* know that there is somewhere a point where he breaks down and bursts into tears,' Harold wrote. He told Vita, 'Lord C cried on my shoulder because the Italians irritated him (Don't repeat this, my pops)'. Two days later the Italians having climbed down, the Marquis delivered a speech, drafted by Harold and Eric Drummond, which was a resounding success. The Italians and the Turks were deeply impressed.

Lord Curzon was not unnaturally extremely sensitive to criticism, especially when it was unwarranted. Harold recorded a talk he had with him about the attacks which were being made upon him in London behind his back. Lord Birkenhead accused him of withholding from the Cabinet an appeal for assistance made by Gounaris shortly before his execution. The accusation was untrue, as Curzon was able to prove, and he was very angry. He called Lloyd George and Birkenhead 'dirty dogs'. When the Turks would not accept his proposals shortly before Christmas, the Marquis had a nerve-storm and had to be soothed by Weygand and Barrère.

> Curzon in a very curious mood in the morning [Harold wrote on the 22nd December]. Almost hysterical. He had had a conversation the night before with Ismet, Barrère and Garroni. The latter two toady Ismet, calling him 'Excellence' and 'ami et cher collègue,' and this makes Curzon nearly sick with disgust ... he imitated to me the adulatory gesticulations of Garroni. He was half laughing at the imitation and half almost crying at it having all to begin again in half an hour. He is a very odd man. It was like Sarah Bernhardt in Phèdre.

When Ismet went back on his undertakings Curzon was again in despair. He felt he could cope with him if only he were left alone with him, without that wicked Barrère and idiot Garroni.

That evening Harold brought Venizelos to see Curzon and the three of them talked. Harold made a record of the conversation which is printed in the Documents of British Foreign Office Policy.[6] Venizelos stressed the fact that there was a limit beyond which Greece would not follow him in making concessions to Turkey. The influx of refugees into Greece from Turkey would shortly bring about economic collapse. Besides, the Greek army was daily growing stronger, whereas the Turkish army was melting away. Harold warned him that the British Government and people would strongly oppose the resumption of the Graeco-Turkish war. Venizelos assured them that he himself did not want war. Afterwards Curzon said to Harold, 'How impressive that man is!' Harold, in replying that he was very fond of him, had to admit to himself that he was not quite the same man that he had been.

On the 28th the Curzons gave a luncheon party. The Marquis was in excellent form. Harold steered him on to Tennyson. Curzon embarked upon an imitation of the Poet Laureate reciting *Tears, Idle Tears*.

> It is far more effective than any other imitation that I have heard. The slight bur of the r's; the broad o's and a's, and the sudden drop of 'no more' (with the r pronounced as a consonant). He also tells us of Wilde, and of Mr. Monkton Milnes when an old man drunk at a ball at Norfolk House, and sitting in a little alcove all flushed and asleep, with his false teeth fallen out upon his shoulder.[7]

Harold was always captivated by Curzon's sudden relaxation of mood – from indignation to merriment. One day Harold broke it to him that he was drafting a full and not a preliminary treaty, as he had been ordered. It was a daring admission. Curzon gasped. He put his head in his hands in an agony of despair at having to rely upon an inferior who was not only incompetent but also insubordinate. At last he looked up from his despairing posture. 'You have done this?' he shouted. 'You have done it, knowing that it was in direct contradiction of my own decision, in agreement with Monsieur Barrère?' 'I knew that, sir, but in going into it, it seemed the only sensible thing to do the opposite,' said Harold. The Marquis leaned forward in his chair. His eyes glared. 'You thought that, did you? You thought that?' Then he flung himself back. 'Well, I suppose you were right,' he said.

On the last day of the year Lord Curzon left for Paris to discuss with Bonar Law how, as the result of negotiations up to date, the terms with Turkey should be concluded. Harold and Allen Leeper went to see him off at the station. 'Well, sir, the next time you get into this train,' Harold said, 'you will have peace with honour.' 'Ah me, my dear fellow, that will be impossible. Quite impossible . . . Well, of course there is a chance.'

'Poor old man!' Harold recorded, 'It is extraordinary how with all his petulance and difficulty one gets *really* fond of him.'[8]

There were occasions when Harold had free moments to enjoy himself. Pierre de Lacretelle was covering the Conference for the *Journal des Débats*, and they sometimes lunched together. Pierre was as amusing and gossipy as ever, but the youth and romance of him had disappeared. One afternoon Harold and Allen went to Territet where they left a copy of *Knole and the Sackvilles* on Robert Hichens. Another day he lunched alone with Barrère. Barrère told Harold how Verlaine paid him a visit in London in 1872, where Barrère himself was a Communist refugee, and had tried to borrow money from him, assuring him that he was not, as some people said, a pederast. He also told Barrère that when in Egypt in the eighties he heard news of Rimbaud who lived under the name of Monsieur Henri and had great knowledge of the country.[9]

Nor were all Harold's leisure moments spent eating meals with intellectuals or correcting proofs and making an index for *Tennyson*. The moment he and Allen Leeper had seen Curzon's train glide out of Lausanne station on New Year's Eve, they went to Gstaad for some skiing. They dined, danced with the ladies in the hotel, and had a rowdy New Year supper with the troops stationed there.

> Thus ends a happy year [he wrote]. Best year since 1914. Happy year. Think so much of my darling V.

For a month and a half Harold and Vita had been separated. They kept in close touch by correspondence, each writing to the other every day, as they were to continue to do, whenever apart, for the rest of their lives. Neither of them thought that this separation would be a long one, and Harold kept assuring her that the Turks were bound to accept an ultimatum soon and the Conference would be over. He did not describe to her the details of his work, for he knew they would bore her, but related incidents about individuals which he thought might entertain her. They both wrote about the other's books. Harold told her with pride how Curzon produced for him a page, with a picture of Vita, and a review of *Knole* in some paper; that he called her bold, heterogeneous, with a style of gold. 'Goodness!' he said about *The Heir*, 'What a pleasure that story gave me.' Harold was overjoyed to read a glowing review by Garvin in the *Observer*, saying she was a woman of genius, one of the stronger writers of our day, and somebody that mattered.

There was one anxious moment when Harold learned that Violet was going to London.

> She will get hold of you again. She is so utterly unscrupulous ... and you, my darling, are so gullible and weak. Promise, my darling, that you will be careful ... Not that I care in the least how you behave; that's your business. It's simply that I don't want us both to be drawn into that vortex of unhappiness which so nearly overwhelmed us ... that panther sneaking about waiting to pounce upon you.[10]

He had no need to worry. Vita replied.

Darling, darling, *Not for a million pounds would I have anything* to do with V again; I hate her for all the misery she brought upon us; so there. She did ring me up ... and I made Dots stay in the room as a witness, while I told her that nothing would tempt me to see her, and that she was utterly indifferent to me; which is true.[11]

In fact she got in a back-hander a few days later about Clare Sheridan. Harold had told Vita that Clare had turned up at Lausanne and had attached herself to the Italian delegation, much to the embarrassment of the British. She was to be seen dancing the tango in the hotel ballroom with Mario Pansa. That might have been all right had not that high-spirited, old-Harrovian gigolo been Mussolini's private secretary. Clare, beautiful, intelligent, meddlesome and man-mad, was capable of causing mischief. Moreover she had a habit of turning up at conferences and causing harm to her own country's interests by consorting with the representatives of its enemies, or of those who were not its allies. Had she not, at the Mudania Conference, installed herself in a battleship under the protection of the French, who were adopting an attitude towards the Turks opposed to Great Britain's, because she was having an affair with Kemal Ataturk? Lord Curzon, aware of this behaviour, was furious about her presence at Lausanne, and told Harold to try and get rid of her. Vita, who got to hear that Harold was seeing a good deal of her, wrote:

What is Clare Sheridan doing at Lausanne? You aren't going to fall in love with her, are you? I never trust Hadji with women over life-size.[12]

On the 14th December Vita met for the first time the woman who was to have more influence upon her literary standards, and to have more particular effect upon her attitude to people and things, and to arouse in her a more protective love, than any other among the many with whom she had been and was to be intimate – Virginia Woolf. It was at a dinner party given by Clive Bell. He had already entered the Nicolsons' lives, and was at first more of a friend of Vita's than Harold's. They had met him lunching with Lady Sackville in March 1921. Vita began corresponding with him in July of the following year, 1922, because she had come upon his book, *Since Cézanne*, in a Sevenoaks shop and found it 'quite admirable,' and because she and Harold had something (unspecified) to impart, which embodied all his theories. She invited him to stay at Long Barn, which he did one weekend in either July or August. He at once endeared himself to them by his easy, breezy manner, his tremendous enthusiasms and unencumbered intelligence. He was the best introduction to Bloomsbury, of which self-sufficient and restrictive coterie Vita was certainly at this date somewhat in awe. Clive had presumably brought Vita and Virginia together after receiving a letter from Vita in which she said, 'Do tell Mrs. Woolf how thrilled I was by *Jacob's Room*.'[13]

We know the impression Vita made on Virginia from the passage in the latter's diary of the 15th December. Referring to 'the lovely gifted aristocratic Sackville West' she had met the previous night, she wrote:

Not much to my severer taste – florid, moustached, parakeet coloured, with all the supple ease of the aristocracy, but not the wit of the artist. She writes 15 pages a day – has finished another book – publishes with Heinemann's – knows everyone – But could I ever know her?'

Meeting Vita released all Virginia's fantasies about the aristocracy. To Dorothy Wellesley these were a form of inverted snobbery upon which it tickled Virginia to dwell, for, as Dorothy observed, she always asked any member of the upper classes or aristocracy innumerable questions about the manners and customs of these mysterious beings, regardless of the fact that she was perfectly well born herself, and related to several of them. Virginia Woolf went on:

The aristocratic manner is something like the actresses' – no false shyness or modesty; a bead dropped into her plate at dinner – given to Clive – asks for liqueur – has her hand on all the ropes – makes me feel virgin, shy & schoolgirlish. Yet after dinner I rapped out opinions. She is a grenadier; hard; handsome; manly; inclined to double chin.

It was like one wary dog meeting another for the first time, sniffing, snuffling gingerly, hackles erect, and determined not to be generous, keeping the advantage of distance until an overt response became perceptible.

Harold wrote to Vita on the 18th, interested. 'I am glad you met Virginia Woolf. Did she look very mad?' The two ladies were to meet again very soon.

It was quite a flight from Virginia Woolf to Lord Curzon's valet. On Christmas Day Harold told Vita that Tippendale got drunk, went down to the ball room at the Beau Rivage, and danced with the lovely ladies of Lausanne, with the result that he was sacked. In revenge he hid the Marquis's trousers under his bed. The following morning the Marquis appeared in Allen Leeper's room in his dressing-gown and a dreadful state. It was thought the valet had gone off with the indispensable clothing. But they were eventually disinterred in time for their owner to attend the conference. This true incident marked the grand exit of poor Arketall from *Some People*.

* * * * *

Lord Curzon returned from Paris on the 2nd January, exceedingly depressed by the limp, defeatist attitude of Bonar Law. As he put it, 'his feet were positively glacial.' The Prime Minister was in Paris attempting to dissuade Poincaré from occupying the Ruhr and to prevent the Franco-British alliance from disintegrating. He advised his Foreign Secretary to give way to the Turks' demands sooner than press them for further concessions. He believed that in an extremity Turkey was prepared to fight, whereas we had already reduced our forces since the war and could not even rely upon the French for assistance. In fact the Paris Conference on Reparations was on the point of breaking down. Yet the strange thing was that Curzon, usually too readily downcast, pooh-poohed his Prime Minister's pessimism. On the contrary he seemed buoyed to make renewed efforts to obtain from the Turks the outstanding concessions, of which the chief was the Mosul question. It was of paramount importance to Great Britain for strategic reasons that the vilayet of Mosul should not be within the Turkish frontier with Mesopotamia. As it turned out Curzon was completely successful in gaining his point.

It now seemed as if the Conference might be prolonged. Harold therefore telegraphed to Vita on the 3rd, asking her to come out to Lausanne. She replied that she was unable to, which provoked Harold to write to her that he feared gossip from the foolish old Duchess of Wellington about her relations with Dorothy Wellesley. No Wellesley, he warned, would ever admit that another Wellesley was to blame for the rupture of the Gerry and Dottie ménage. They would look about for a scapegoat, and might fix upon her. That evening Harold dined with the Marquis, who confided in him that he believed absolutely in ghosts.[14] Harold found this odd 'in so unspiritual a person.' Curzon also talked about Queen Victoria.

> He tells me that when he was going out to India he was sent for to Balmoral. After dinner they stood in the Tartan Room. His back was bad and Queen Victoria asked him to sit down. He sat beside her on a little hard tartan chair. While he was there a servant came in and handed her a telegram on a salver. She fiddled for her glasses but could not read it. She handed it to him. 'Read it,' she said, 'Mr. Curzon.' He began to read. It was a long telegram from Kitchener announcing the battle of Omdurman. At the bottom of the first page were the words, 'His Royal Highness Prince Christian Victor . . .' Turning over with terror of finding the words, 'was killed this morning,' he was relieved to find the words, 'comported himself as befits a soldier and an officer in your Majesty's Army.'[14]

Lord Curzon prefaced his spirited offensive against the Turks with an emollient for Bonar Law which took the form of warning the Greek

THE LAUSANNE CONFERENCE 1922-23

Government that a renewal of hostilities by them would be universally condemned in England. He sent Harold to show Venizelos a copy of his telegram to the British Minister in Athens. Harold was constantly being made to communicate disagreeable tidings to his old friend. Venizelos assured Harold that his Government would take no such action without the consent of His Britannic Majesty's Government and the French Government. Only an influx of further refugees from Turkish territory into Eastern Thrace might induce the Greek army to renew hostilities on their own initiative, because they knew that the Turkish army was mobilising troops all the time.[15] The first positive show of Curzon's offensive was to set up a Co-ordination Committee, with the object of filtering all the recommendations to the Conference from the several sub-committees in operation. He instructed Harold Nicolson, whom he appointed one of the British representatives on the Co-ordination Committee, to draft certain heads of agreement to serve as a preliminary treaty. This involved Harold in much thought and work. Suddenly Curzon sent for him and was very cross with him for having drafted, not heads of an agreement, but a full treaty. It was a repetition of his fault committed at the end of December. Only this time Curzon did not relent. 'If,' he said, 'we fail to get a Treaty at Lausanne it will be largely your fault.' This distressed Harold so much that he went downstairs at once and telegraphed to Vita, imploring her to come to him. It was a case of the little schoolboy, reprimanded by the headmaster, turning to his mother for consolation. Vita responded to his piteous appeal within a week.

Harold made amends to his chief by lunching with Riza Nur Bey, Ismet Pasha's second-in-command, and persuading him after two hours' argument, to agree to keeping the Orthodox Patriarch at the Phanar* in return for the Patriarch abandoning all his political privileges, this point having been conceded to Harold by 'the dear old man,' Venizelos. Riza Nur, by profession a well-known surgeon, was Minister of Health in the Turkish Government. Unlike Ismet Pasha who, although a foe, was also 'a dear old man,' Riza Nur was oleaginous, ingratiating and deceptive. Harold wrote in his diary:[16]

> I do not like you Riza Nur
> Your table manners are so poor.
>   I do not like you when you pat
>   Me on the back; and when you chat
> About Armenians, I'm quite sure
> I do not like you, Riza Nur.

* The Patriarchal Church in Constantinople was S. Mary Pammakaristos, overlooking the valley of the Phanar.

Nevertheless the next day Ismet Pasha called on Lord Curzon to announce that after all he could not agree to Riza Nur's formula. The Marquis and Ismet 'sat patting each other' until the clock struck eleven, when Ismet agreed to everything the other wanted. The Marquis, having charmed the adversary and having boiled down Harold's draft treaty into a preliminary treaty – 'the result is of course our original treaty' – was very pleased with himself. He sent for Harold and congratulated him on his successful negotiations over the Patriarch.

Vita arrived at Lausanne at six in the morning of the 12th, simultaneously with the first of two ecstatic letters she had written to Harold about Virginia Woolf.

> Tomorrow I dine with my *darling* Mrs. Woolf at Richmond, 'a picnic more than a dinner, as the [Hogarth] press has overflowed both into the dining room and into the larder.' I love Mrs. Woolf with a sick passion. So will you. In fact I don't think I will let you know her. Dots is away at Sherfield so the mouse is playing.

And in the second, oddly enough dated the day of her arrival at Lausanne, she informed him,

> I dined alone with Virginia Woolf last night. Oh dear, how much I love that woman. Mrs. Cameron, her great-aunt, used to say to Tennyson, 'Alfred, I brought my friends to see a lion, but they have only seen a bear.' And she used to cut his hair.[17]

Virginia Woolf was more restrained. She was still feeling her wary way round Vita. Yet on the 23rd she wrote to Violet Dickinson, 'I like Mrs. Nicolson: no nonsense about her.'

Vita stayed at Lausanne nine days. Harold took her to Chillon Castle and they dined twice with the Marquis, who liked her as much as he admired her writing. He told amusing stories of Queen Victoria and John Brown, and also a story of the Queen's ambiguous minute written against the announcement that the missionary, Kitty Smithson, had been captured by Kurds in Persia, 'Why should not Kitty Smithson have her curd?' Harold also took her to some awful dinner parties given by the Japanese and Turks, which must have confirmed her resolution never to lead the life of a minister or ambassador's wife. He read the typescript of her novel, *Grey Wethers*, and urged her to strengthen the end which fell a little flat. He also read aloud to her extracts from his *Tennyson*. Lord William Cavendish-Bentinck remembers seeing husband and wife sitting on the floor of their hotel room, their heads together, Harold's so pink and healthy, and Vita's in the full bloom of her dusky beauty – an unforgettable picture of a young couple blissfully absorbed in each other's creations.

On the evening of the 21st Vita travelled home, leaving Harold in a dark gloom. He almost wished she had never come because her departure was so disturbing. He sent her next day a letter typewritten by himself.[18] and hoped she did not mind, as some people would. It was the first not written in his own neat, orderly hand. Henceforth nearly all his letters to her, and those to his friends which were not dictated, were typewritten by himself. He never learned to use all his fingers, and when he was in a hurry the result was often erratic. His portable typewriter became his indispensable companion which he treated almost as a human being. It (and there was a succession of them) was always referred to by him and his secretaries as 'Tikki'. Hence remarks in his letters like the following: 'Elvira has cleaned Tikki with gin with the result that he runs all groggy and is difficult to control'; and, 'Tikki was so excited when he went to Germany that he made holes in his ribbon.' On this occasion he told Vita that Lord Curzon had decided they could not stay at Lausanne for ever, and the Turks must either accept the British terms, or be damned. Harold's attitude towards the Turks was one of perpetual irritation, at times rising to fury. He was on the War Graves Commission. The Turks announced that they would not surrender the Anzac area where the graves were. They had the impudence to propose digging up our graves and putting all the bodies of our dead in one common cemetery. Harold was so incensed that he could barely write. The Turks were told that we would not leave Gallipoli until the present status of the graves was assured. Lord Curzon made a most moving and effective speech to the Conference on the subject. Harold told Vita:

I shall reply to Ismet Pasha in a single sentence. I shall say this to him. I shall say that I regret that once again the Turkish delegation have missed an opportunity of responding to the elementary principles of humanity and honour.[19]

On the 30th it was learned that the French were about to make a separate peace-treaty with the Turks. The consternation and rage in Lausanne knew no bounds. The British delegation was agreed that Poincaré must be mad. Even the French delegates were aghast. Pierre de Lacretelle fulminated in the *Journal des Débats* against the decision. Curzon remained perfectly calm and presented the Turks with the treaty finalised by the conference. It was a bold and splendid action. 'Britannia has won against the Turks,' Harold wrote, 'against treacherous allies, against rotten public opinion. All due to Curzon. He is a great man, and one day

England will know it.' Poincaré evidently took fright. He climbed down and issued a *démenti*. Harold attributed this treacherous little man's volte-face as much to Pierre's article as to any other influence. Curzon was jubilant. When Riza Nur took Harold aside and asked why the British would not also make a separate treaty with the Turks, Harold replied in his most scathing Foreign Office manner that the British did not do that sort of thing.

On the 4th February after an abortive exchange of notes between the Allies and the Turks Ismet Pasha was summoned to meet the Allies and declare definitely whether or not he accepted the treaty. He came at 5.40 p.m.

> He twists about in his chair, mops his forehead, dabs with his handkerchief and is very nervous. Bompard speaks well. Garroni lamentable. The Marquis unsurpassed. He uses every tone, appeal, cajolery, despair, menace.[20]

All the while the Allies' luggage was being wheeled off to the station, for Curzon was determined not to dally a day longer. Ismet accepted all the terms except those concerning economics and capitulations. They argued. Ismet was obdurate. For once he lost his temper. He stormed at them, 'I shall return to Angora and tell my people that the Conference under the presidency of Lord Curzon desires war.' 'No, no, no,' they shouted back at him. Still Ismet refused to give way. 'Je ne peux pas. Je ne peux pas,' he mumbled. With dignity Lord Curzon, followed by Bompard, Garroni and all the British, French and Italian officials, left the room, and caught the Orient Express for Paris. On arrival in London Curzon, worn out by the strain, took to his bed. Harold joined Vita and the two boys in Ebury Street.

The dramatic departure of the British, French and Italian delegates from Lausanne did not mean the end of the Conference. Rather it was a break. The Turks were told that if they wanted a peaceful settlement it was up to them to take the initiative. At least a convention had been agreed between the Turks and Greeks on the 30th January whereby a compulsory exchange of minorities living on either side of the new frontier between their two countries was brought about. Ismet Pasha on his return to Angora induced the National Assembly to 'vote for peace' subject to some modifications of the terms put forward under Curzon's presidency. These modifications were examined in London by a conference with Curzon (again in the chair), Bompard and Garroni. Harold attended it. A second Conference was opened at Lausanne in April and lasted until July. Sir Horace Rumbold was the British representative. As a result,

THE LAUSANNE CONFERENCE 1922-23

Turkey regained the frontiers in Europe and Asia Minor which she had enjoyed in 1914. No limitations were imposed upon her naval and military forces. And the vexed question of the vilayet of Mosul was referred to the League of Nations. The vilayet was finally apportioned to Iraq.

11

LONDON AGAIN, 1923-1925

BETWEEN returning from Lausanne with Lord Curzon in February 1923 and being posted to Tehran in November 1925 Harold Nicolson remained at the Foreign Office in London, with intermittent brief jaunts abroad. These two and three quarter years coincided with perhaps the most tranquil period Europe has so far enjoyed in the twentieth century. The wounds of the First World War were healing. Mussolini may have been a dim shadow on the horizon, but Hitler was an unknown quantity. Lenin and Stalin were so remote that it was inconceivable to all but the most far-sighted that, in spite of occasional scares like the Zinoviev Letter, their ghastly régimes would ever be a serious menace to free governments in the Western countries. Life in England may not have been as exclusive and luxurious for the upper classes as it had been before the war, but that was no real concern to Harold and Vita. Neither of them ever cared for luxury, however much they accepted privilege. They were still young, in their thirties, abounding in health and vigour. Although not by any means rich – Harold had not a penny of capital – they had affluent backgrounds. They were at the height of their intellectual powers; they were happy together; and they enjoyed life to the full.

Harold at once dived headlong again into the London social whirl of large parties: dinners at the Colefaxes', Lady Curzon's ball at Lansdowne House, and intimate meals with old friends and new acquaintances. He had a very keen eye and a succinct mode of sketching strangers – Ravel, 'a small, wiry, hawk-like man with a grey, unshaven face'; Mary Pickford, 'a little dumpy, cow-faced woman'; and Douglas Fairbanks, 'knotty unshaven and intelligent – a nice man.' Hardly a day passed during the week when he had no engagement for luncheon and dinner, and the weekends were usually spent at Long Barn, gardening, writing and entertaining guests, or at Sherfield with either Gerry or Dottie Wellesley, who played box and cox, or at some grand country house within easy reach of London. In the resumption too of his old intellectual links there was one important addition. That was his introduction to Bloomsbury. It came about through Vita's recent acquaintance with Virginia Woolf and the close friendship, which was by now established, of both of them with Clive Bell.

One Sunday Vita took Harold to Richmond to meet Virginia Woolf.

LONDON AGAIN 1923-25

It was a pouring wet day and he was worried about his father's health which was causing anxiety. Harold registered no impression either of Virginia or her husband, Leonard, on that occasion, but Virginia committed to her diary the acidulous passage:

> We had a surprise visit from the Nicolsons. She is a pronounced Sapphist, & may, thinks Ethel Sands, have an eye on me, old as I am. Nature might have sharpened her faculties. Snob as I am, I trace her passions 500 years back, & they become romantic to me, like old yellow wine. I fancy the tang is gone. Harold is simple downright bluff; wears short black coat and check trousers, wishes to be a writer, but is not I'm told & can believe, adapted by nature.[1]

It is not difficult to interpret the first unsympathetic impression Harold made with his Whitehall clothes, his jaunty manner, his pink face, little moustache, prosaic un-literary looks, and general air of the establishment, which to every true member of Bloomsbury was anathema.

They made the mistake of assessing him by his appearance and background. They imagined he must be what he looked, a typical Foreign Office man of Victorian standards and conventions, a man who was not rebellious. To some extent he always remained un-grown up in that his code of social behaviour was what he had imbibed from his highly respectable parents and schoolmasters. For instance, he did not at once judge whether a stranger was observant, sensitive or affectionate. He judged whether he was 'comme il faut' or 'bedint'. It took him some little time before he scrutinised the stranger through different lenses unclouded by congenital prejudices. Then he would evince an extraordinarily clear view of the stranger's true qualities, and show himself to be a man of abundant understanding and tolerance (understanding and tolerance not being qualities that the code of his upbringing set much store by). In fact Harold was tradition-bound, but not the least convention-bound He was intensely irritated by those conventions for which he could see no practical justification, and he rebelled against them as vociferously as the most non-conforming of the Bloomsburys.

On the 15th March the Nicolsons dined (unchanged) at Gordon Square with, presumably, Clive, for he, Duncan Grant, Lytton Strachey and Virginia Woolf (Harold spelt it Wolf in his diary) were present. Harold's only comment was that Lytton discussed style in a high, intermittent falsetto. But Virginia again had something to say in her diary entry:

> Two nights ago the Nicolsons dined there [46. Gordon Square]. Exposed to electric light eggs show dark patches. I mean we judged

> them both incurably stupid. He is bluff, but oh so obvious; she, Duncan thought, took the cue from him, & had nothing free to say. There was Lytton, supple and subtle as an old leather glove, to emphasise their stiffness. It was a rocky steep evening.[2]

It evidently was. Lytton Strachey was rude to Harold at their first meeting, but whether it was on this occasion I am not sure. Duncan Grant told me that at a party given in Gordon Square Lytton asked him to introduce Harold, and when Grant did so Lytton turned his back on him. Grant was very upset and cross with Lytton for his churlishness. It somehow seems unlikely that such behaviour would have taken place at a small dinner party when, in usual circumstances, guests know beforehand whom they are going to meet, and are anyway introduced to one another by their host on arrival. But Bloomsbury circumstances being seldom usual, the insult may have taken place on the evening of the 15th, which happened to be the date when *Tennyson* came out. Strachey may already have seen the book, or even read what Harold described as the 'wishy washy review' in that day's *Morning Post*. At any rate when Maynard Keynes sent him in April a copy of the book to review for the *Nation and Athenaeum*, Lytton replied, 'I'm sorry to say I can't face Lord Tennyson. Harold N's book is so disgusting and stupid.'[3] Whether Lytton Strachey saw in Harold a rival biographer to himself, or resented what he concluded to be an unworthy imitator, is not made clear in Michael Holroyd's excellent biography. If Virginia Woolf's scrappy letter to Pernel Strachey of the 3rd August is anything to go by, both suggestions are tenable.

> I've been trying to read *Tennyson*, by Harold Nicolson. I threw it onto the floor in disgust. To purify myself I said I will at once write a letter to Pernel . . . Of course he's [HN] due to Lytton . . . What these skilful imitators don't realise is that it is absolutely essential, if you're going to . . .'

and here unfortunately the sentence breaks off.

For his part Harold Nicolson always paid tribute to the detachment, concision, exquisite poise, sustained irony and apparent effortlessness of Lytton Strachey's writing. At the same time he praised his fervent belief in intellectual honesty, and his hatred of the conventional and second-rate. But he tempered this praise with a criticism that he did not solve the relation of biography to science on the one hand and to literature on the other because he worked from a personal thesis. Strachey took one aspect of his multitudinous facts and examined that aspect from a psychological point of view. He enhanced his preconceived prejudices by slanting the materials he used, and discarding those which did not confirm his prejudices. As for

LONDON AGAIN 1923-25

Lytton the man, Harold disliked him intensely. He disapproved of his apparent effeteness and his contempt for what to Harold were serious concerns beyond jest and jibe, like his own Foreign Office, the Mother of Parliaments, the Empire, King and constitution. Harold was not a malicious or malevolent man, but he was wounded by Lytton Strachey's unfriendly attitude towards him from the first. When the Lytton Strachey-Virginia Woolf letters were published he was appalled by their silliness, dirtiness and cattiness. He saw in Strachey a warning of what he must never become himself. 'I shall *not*,' he declared, 'become a flabby old sod like Lytton. I won't, I won't, I won't.'[4]

As for Vita she in her loyal and protective attitude towards Harold always leapt tigress-like to his defence. 'How much I dislike Lytton,' she wrote[5] during his lifetime; and after his death, 'The drooping Lytton must have done its [Bloomsbury's] cause a great deal of harm. I hated Lytton.'[6]

Vita had read *Tennyson* when it was in proof stage, and she was bowled over.

> There are no dry passages [she wrote to him,[7]], usually inevitable in that sort of book; and you seem to have mellowed in a curious sort of way – I mean you are as funny as Lytton Strachey, but in a kindlier way, and also you have more real reverence than he. You are not so merely derisive and destructive. Also I think the actual architecture of the book is excellent – the beginning in gloom, the going on to prosperity, the closing on a note of gloom again. And all the incidental people are so good ... Altogether it is a brilliant piece of work with none of the shallowness of mere brilliance.

This is a very just estimate of what Harold had achieved. There is no doubt that he was influenced by Lytton Strachey in the method of this, his second, literary biography, an impressionistic sketch rather than a full-blooded record of the poet's life. After all, Strachey had brought about a revolution in biographical writing, which Harold was the first to acknowledge. He had been a pioneer, and that does not mean that those who followed in his tracks could not, and did not, advance by different strides and illuminate fresh landscapes on either side of the route. Vita was quite right. Harold, in being less astringent than Lytton, was more poetic. There are no passages in any of Strachey's writings so evocative of the environment as, say, the opening paragraphs of chapter 2 of *Tennyson* on the approach to Somersby Rectory. Nor did Harold ever fall into the temptation to mock his venerable subject. He was amused by his bearishness, his lack of humour and his portentousness. But he sympathised with Tennyson's terrible despair, dubiety and his dread of sex and death. In this book the authentic, wholly mature Harold Nicolson emerges.

A mere six days before *Tennyson* was to appear in the shop windows Harold learnt to his dismay that another book on Tennyson by Hugh I'Anson Fausset had just come out. He need not have worried. It is true that in nearly all the papers both books were reviewed together. But the accolade went to Harold. Nearly every review was flattering. Gosse in the *Sunday Times* pronounced that it was so good there was nothing to contradict in it. The *Spectator* called it beautiful workmanship: French in finish and good taste – whatever that meant. Arthur Waugh, Edward Shanks and Laurence Binyon were loud in praise. Only Sir Herbert Warren and W. F. Rawnsley disliked it. Sir Herbert resented Harold's interpretation of Tennyson as a bear, and intellectually of low calibre; and Rawnsley called it complete and vulgar fiction from beginning to end. But they were older men, who had both known and sat at the feet of the venerated Laureate. Accordingly they resented the slightest aspersions which they considered impertinence and flagrant irreverence. Irreverent or not, Harold Nicolson's *Tennyson* anticipated the present day groping approach to understanding of a great man's character and work. It reversed the Victorian legend of the immaculate bard without reducing his stature. Harold saw him as a tragic martyr to the contemporaries who made him into the pillar of respectability and orthodoxy they wished him to be, and he knew he was not.

Harold was delighted with the reception his book had, and the celebrity it brought him. His friends were impressed, even Gerald Berners, who pretended that Harold had invented some of the Master's poems he quoted; and Sligger Urquhart, who, don-like, could not refrain from picking little holes in what he considered to be a masterpiece by his old pupil:

> But do you know that you talked of a Cambridge 'quadrangle'? Oh Nic, how could you? And the journey to Cambridge, did he *really* go to Lincoln by going to Spilsby first? A curious route.[8]

Harold visited Powys Evans to have a caricature of himself done, a sure sign that he had become a public figure. He looked at Mr. Evans's samples. 'That's very amusing,' he said, 'you've caught Lloyd George's walk exactly – the way he swings his hands.' 'Oh, but that isn't Lloyd George,' said Mr. Evans rather sharply, 'It's Mr. Gordon Selfridge.' In consequence the caricature did not turn out to be a very good one. However successful Harold had become he was very hard up, and rather worried about his finances, a periodical condition which passed as swiftly as it came. So long as he did not cause Vita any embarrassment he did not worry for long. He told her she was an angel about 'the black and haggard poverty' he had

LONDON AGAIN 1923-25

reduced her to. And she didn't even mind. 'A weaker character would just have gone upstairs,' he wrote to her, 'and turned on the gas, and written a little label about "my poor children", and gone (Sackville) West. But not you, my saint.'[9]

So he threw himself wholeheartedly into his book on Byron. For years he had been in love with him. He admitted to himself as much, saying that it was a mistake to be infatuated with a dead person. His Literature Notes of 1908, a year when he was cramming for the Foreign Office examinations, revealed a keen interest in and imparted a new perspective to Byron's poetry. The twenty-two-year-old Harold detected in the first six lines of the first canto of *Don Juan* a sort of dance rhythm, and in the concluding couplet a sort of breakdown of emotion. *Don Juan* was, he observed, the cleverest of all English poems, in that it was addressed to a wide audience, to lovers of verse and those not in the usual sense lovers of verse at all; if Byron did not bring a new idea into the world, he quadrupled the force of existing ones; and Byron's tenderness was no less real because he was perpetually jerking it away.

During the War he wrote to Vita in September 1916 from the St. James's Club, 'Darling, there is a man who has written "Biron", "Byron" on the blotch. Isn't that a background – what was he thinking about?' In August 1922, having just delivered his manuscript of *Tennyson* to Constable's, he wrote in his diary, 'Begin to think about my Byron book.' During the dramatic Turco-Greek crisis in September and October when Harold was extremely busy he had no time to continue thinking about it. But on the 22nd October while tired and resting at Long Barn he read Byron memoirs all day. And on Christmas Eve in Lausanne during a lull in work (Lord Curzon staying over, Harold was obliged to do so likewise) he wrote to Vita that he would start on Byron next day. In January he read and took copious notes from Ethel Mayne's two-volume *Life*, which he found admirable, and in April after influenza was reading Pietro Gamba's Narrative of *Lord Byron's Last Journey to Greece*. He then went to see Lady Lovelace, widow of the 2nd Earl, Byron's grandson, who gave him what she imagined to be unpublished letters of Byron.

On the 2nd May there took place an event, not important in itself, but of interest in view of the great part which it was to play in Harold Nicolson's subsequent life, and the considerable part which he was to play in its development. He heard a wireless broadcast over the air for the first time. Before seven years were out he was to become a master of the broadcasting art in creating an intimate technique of addressing millions of unseen listeners, an art which was entirely personal and original.

In May he first met, while lunching with the Oswald Mosleys, Ramsay MacDonald, the leader of the Labour Party which had not yet enjoyed office. MacDonald, with whom Harold's relations in the next decade were to be very close, created a favourable impression. Harold found him a modest and intelligent man, with his refined face and faint Scotch accent. At their next meeting in the following year he was to modify this opinion, which depreciated as he got to know MacDonald better.

In June Harold made a Byron pilgrimage to Nottinghamshire. Byron's home, Newstead Abbey, was still in private hands. It was the owner, Mrs. Fraser, an old lady, with whom Harold stayed a night.

The following morning he was shown round the Abbey and grounds. Byron's private rooms were still unchanged. Much of his furniture, his two helmets with 'Crede Biron', the family crest, incised on one, his pen and his sabre, his tache case, several swords and claymores and his boxing gloves were exhibited. There was also a little embroidered green coat edged with fur, which he had worn. Harold described his green bedroom, with Turkish floor-rug, brocade chairs, round rosewood table at which he wrote, blue-and-white washing basin, and huge bed with sham bamboo cross-pieces supporting a dome and four gilt coronets over the posts, between which silk hangings were suspended. Next door was a slip of a dressing-room, with Byron's dressing-table, and out of that his page's room. Mrs. Fraser explained that the poet was afraid to sleep alone. As she vividly remarked, 'He always had his boy to sleep with him.' To which a friend staying in the house who accompanied them, a big-game shooter, terribly bored by the whole proceeding and assuming that by 'boy' a son of Byron was implied, asked, 'An ancestor of the present Lord?' at which Mrs. Fraser frowned and made no reply. Mrs. Fraser explained that she had lived at Newstead since she was a child when she knew several people who remembered Byron well, notably an old man on the estate called Potter. When asked for his recollections, Potter would say, 'Yes, his lordship was mostly drunk.' On leaving Newstead Harold went to Hucknall Torkard church where Byron lies buried in the family vault.

On the 29th June he began writing at Long Barn the first few lines of *Byron: The Last Journey*, and by the beginning of July was going ahead at full speed. On the 4th he wrote 10,000 words and by the end of one week had accomplished 40,000 words. By the 26th he had finished his first draft of the book, amounting to 110,000 words. No wonder that when the next day he went to stay at the new house Lady Sackville had acquired in Brighton he took a long walk from Steyning to Amberley. On the 28th he again walked, in pouring rain, on the Downs, his head so full of Byron that he got lost, finishing up at Midhurst where Vita had to fetch him by train. He had covered eighteen miles.

It is now that Geoffrey Scott's name makes frequent appearances in Harold's diary – 'Geoffrey Scott comes' to Long Barn, and, on Harold's return from London, 'G. Scott there.' On the 11th August Vita and Geoffrey went to Cumberland for a week. At the end of the month a political crisis, known as the Corfu Incident, occurred.

The delimitation of the frontier between Greece and Albania, having been left unsettled by the Peace Conference, was belatedly entrusted to an Inter-Allied Conference. The Italian member of that Conference, General Tellini, was unfortunately shot dead at Janina on Greek territory by Albanian brigands. Mussolini sent an ultimatum to the Greek Government, which could in no sense be held responsible for the murder, and without waiting for a reply bombarded and occupied Corfu. The Greek Government at once appealed to the League of Nations. This was the first test of the League's authority. Curzon unhesitatingly agreed that it was essentially a matter for the League's action. The French under Poincaré however espoused the side of Italy. Mussolini said he would abide by a verdict of the Ambassadors' Conference,* still sitting in Paris, but not of the League. Curzon gave way and withdrew the support of Lord Robert Cecil at Geneva. The League was forced to abstain. In Britain's surrender a settlement was imposed upon Greece which, although it entailed the evacuation of Corfu by the Italians was demonstrably unfair. Harold was so closely involved that he was obliged to remain for several days in London, where he stayed either at the Automobile Club or with Gerald Wellesley in Portland Place. He was constantly on the telephone to Curzon at Kedleston and in Paris. He quickly realised that Tyrrell's influence upon Curzon over the affair was disastrous. To begin with Tyrrell encouraged Curzon to support the League because he thought it was the easiest way out of a difficulty. When he discovered it was not a way out, but a way deeper in, he wanted Curzon to back out without saying so. Then Poincaré's betrayal was seized as a golden opportunity for Great Britain to desert the League altogether.

* The Ambassadors' Conference, 1920–1925. With the coming into force of the Versailles Treaty on January 10th, 1920, the Ambassadors' Conference became one of the organs concerned with the execution of the Treaty. It consisted of the representatives of Great Britain, France, Italy and Japan, with the American Ambassador attending as a spectator after 1921.

> I tried in vain [Harold wrote in his diary] to get them to see the issue in wider proportions and to realise that we had a chance of calling the new world into being in order to redress the balance of the old. They would not see it: Tyrrell because he is for an arrangement at any price, and had no intellectual principle or moral stability: Curzon because his inordinate vanity was affected by the Harmsworth press attacks and by a certain jealousy of Lord R. Cecil. The result was that we killed the League and fortified Poincaré. Terribly distressed by this lack of strength and guidance.[10]

Harold was abundantly right and far-seeing. Fewer occasions could have been more favourable or more straightforward for League intervention. The missed opportunity was a tragedy for the League, and the Powers, to whom the matter was referred, consented to a penalty of half a million pounds indemnity by Greece for a crime never proved against her. It was a gross injustice and brought upon the League that lack of respect and deference which was to be its undoing. Having failed at its first test, why should any further questions of international importance ever be referred to it by Great Powers in the future?

When during the Corfu crisis Lord Curzon returned from Paris[11] a posse of Foreign Office subordinates were gathered within the barrier of Victoria station platform to receive him. Beyond the barrier a large crowd had assembled. An urgent message was sent to Harold, who was present, to go at once to the Foreign Secretary in his compartment. Harold rushed forward, ready to receive instructions. Curzon, blandly smiling, said to him, 'I have been reading *Grey Wethers*, a magnificent book. The descriptions of the Downs are as fine as any in the language. Such power! such power! Not a pleasing book of course. But what English!' All the while Tyrrell and others were champing on the platform, eager to learn from the Marquis what Poincaré had said and done.

In September Harold and Vita went to the first night's performance of James Elroy Flecker's *Hassan*. Harold had once met Flecker when they were at Oxford together. Flecker had a marked Levantine appearance. He liked people to come to his rooms in Trinity where he gave them marsala. He was hospitable in his way, and his rooms were known as The Saracen's Head. Harold only visited them once in the company of Alan Lascelles. But according to Francis Birrell, who knew him better, Flecker was snobbish and vicious; and jealous of Rupert Brooke. The performance of *Hassan* was as good as could have been expected. The Nicolsons went afterwards to supper at Goldoni's, a modest restaurant in Rupert Street. The Jack Squires were responsible for the arrangements. There was a long table with a folded cloth as if for The Last Supper, and Windsor chairs. Down the middle of the cloth were six jugs of claret cup with slices of banana

LONDON AGAIN 1923-25

floating on the top. Between the jugs were plates of triangular bread sandwiches, with ham and mustard and cress.

> Squire brings Mrs. Flecker (widow), the Rev. Flecker (father), Mrs. Flecker (mother). Mrs. Flecker (widow) is a Greek, of the intellectual, thin, wizened, toothy type. She is rather nervous; she had not slept the night before; she is obviously upset by this resounding triumph. She had of course expected the Ritz, and photographers, and auratum lilies, and a few well chosen words, and the Crown Prince of Sweden, and Sir James Barrie. She got nothing of the sort; she got her brother-in-law, and her father-in-law, and her mother-in-law, and a ham sandwich, and a glass of banana cup, and little desultory conversation from such inadequates as myself, and a gentleman in the disposals board, and Eddie Marsh. I said idiotic things to her such as, 'You must feel like Mrs. Shelley at the first night of the Cenci.' I saw she was on the verge of bursting into tears; I rushed for Viti to come to the rescue; but Viti was very busy discussing with Gerry his domestic circumstances. I sat there behind tugging at Viti's Chinese jacket and feeling very wretched. The Flecker family returned to the Cotswolds by the 1 a.m. train. Mrs. Flecker remained on, hoping that some sort of apotheosis would happen to break the anti-climax. The claret cup splashed upon the cloth and sprinkled little pink banana discs.[12]

He and Vita motored home to Long Barn, and he, much to her astonishment, burst into tears. Was the cause Mrs. Flecker's disappointment, or Vita's inattention, or Geoffrey Scott's attentions, or a little bit of all three?

This autumn Ben went off for his first term to Summer Fields preparatory school. The parting upset Harold considerably, and only a day or two previously he had walked with him from Long Barn to Knole, talking about his school and endeavouring like so many devoted parents to persuade his elder son that the experience would not be as awful as he knew it would be. And he wrote to Vita a tenth wedding anniversary letter.[13]

> Had I known what joy these years would bring I should have felt less guilty in taking you away from Knole and robbing you of all your other opportunities ... nothing except death (and even that) can come between us or cloud for a moment that serene confidence and love with which we cling to each other.

On the 28th September he left London for Paris where he took the Orient Express, bound for Athens on a second Byron mission.

He went straight to Charlie Hartopp's flat where he was to stay, and had the bath of all baths. Washed and refreshed he walked to the Zappeion Gardens where the statue of Byron glimmered among the palm trees.

> I took off my hat to him and explained why I had come. He was very nice about it. There was a tiresome woman clinging on to him in that maudlin way they had. He was doing his best, poor man, to get away from her. I told him that I knew about it all, and didn't mind, being broad-minded.[14]

Then he and Charlie Hartopp dined together and walked under the vast *stele* of the Temple of Jupiter Ammonca.

The next morning he went to the British Legation, surrounded by dusty trees, and walked up the marble staircase. All the Legation shutters were closed. The porter wore rope-soled slippers which went clip-clop against the marble floor. There was a strong smell of disinfectant. There was an oleograph of Queen Mary. He had a long talk about Byron with Shirley Atchley, Translator and Local Second Secretary, who dwelt in a little hutch on the far side of the hall seated at a long baize table, with files of Greek newspapers kept flat by lumps of marble and lids of tobacco-tins. Atchley was the greatest help. Harold had a talk with the Chargé d'Affaires, Bentinck,[15] about politics. He and Charlie dined with Gladys Stuart Richardson, 'a cheery Lesbian with good teeth.'

At the British School he went through the Abney Hastings papers,[16] which he found interesting. And he motored to Marathon through pine forests nearly the whole way. The road was bright red in colour like the lanes of Devonshire, the pines a vivid light yellowish green, and the few cypresses almost black. Suddenly on turning a corner, he was confronted by a vision of the sea and the mountains of Euboea beyond. Keenly alive to all aspects of nature and profoundly receptive to the classical landscape, Harold decided in a flash of enlightenment that here was by far the most beautiful view he had ever seen in his life. At Sunium, where Byron had carved his name on a column of the Temple of Poseidon, he took photographs and bathed. He went to Patras where he met a descendant of Charles Hancock, the English merchant residing in Cephalonia who cashed Byron's bills. He went by boat to Missolonghi, and was taken round the town by the local schoolmaster. Back in Athens he had further long talks with Atchley, and at the Municipal Ethnographic Museum looked carefully at the bed in which Byron was said to have died. Harold was convinced it could not have been Byron's bed. He left Athens with deep regrets on the 15th, sitting on the deck of the *Celio*, watching Lycabettus and then, last of all, the Parthenon, slide away behind the sparse pine trees of Salamis, and feeling rather depressed and lonely. From Brindisi he set off for Rome in a wagon-lit, reading *The Three Musketeers* and 'aching to see my own darling tomorrow! tomorrow!'[17] On arrival he went straight to the Embassy and met Geoffrey Scott, Vita being at the Villa Medici in

LONDON AGAIN 1923-25

Florence. Having spent the day in Gerald Berners's house, where he found 'the Sitwell brood,' he travelled to Florence with Geoffrey. They reached the Villa Medici together at midnight.

This beautiful villa with balustraded terraces, statues and garden of ancient cypresses had been built by Michelozzo for Cosimo de' Medici and was the favourite residence of Lorenzo the Magnificent. Here it was that Lorenzo passed his leisure hours discussing Platonic philosophy with Politian, Ficino and Landino. It was now the property of Geoffrey Scott's wife, Lady Sybil. Harold stayed there a little over a week. Every morning he sat in the loggia of which the furniture had belonged to William Beckford, amplifying and putting finishing touches to *Byron* in the light of his recent researches and expeditions in Greece. Neighbours came and went – Walter Pinsent the architect; Mrs. Waterfield: Iris Cutting, Lady Sybil's daughter and her fiancé, the Marchese Origo. Geoffrey showed resentment and displeasure at the influx of visitors. They motored to the Villa Montegufoni, a romantic and melancholy palace dominated by a tower like that of the Palazzo Vecchio, which had been bought by Sir George Sitwell; 'a beastly place,' Harold called it. They went to I Tatti, the Berensons' villa and called on Mrs. Ross.

> She is aged 85, has attended Rogers's breakfast parties, and known the Miss Berrys. We found her moving lemon tubs on the terrace. A fierce old thing. She told me stories about Tennyson. She had known the Guiccoli [Teresa, Byron's mistress[18]].

Harold's visit to the Villa Medici coincided with Geoffrey Scott's passionate declaration of love for Vita. Intoxicated by the surroundings, the garden, the orchards of olive trees, the clear Tuscan sky and the moonrise over Florence, Vita responded. It was to be her only affair with a man and it did not last. She was unable to sustain at fever-pitch the fervour of love which Geoffrey poured out and demanded in return. She admired his intellect and was flattered by his genuine admiration of her writing. At the time he was finishing *The Portrait of Zélide*, while she was beginning *The Land*. They exchanged manuscripts; they gave each other advice; they made and accepted criticisms. His were unsparing, but inspiring. Both Lady Sybil and Harold realised what was going on under her roof. She professed not to mind. Geoffrey had been unfaithful so often, and she knew he no longer loved her. She even gave him, in a gesture of renunciation, an un-wedding ring. Harold realised that this gentle and civilised man would never rob him of Vita's enduring affection, and feigned, if he did not feel, pleasure in her transient happiness. Nevertheless the spectacle cannot have been agreeable for him to witness at close quarters, and he was not as indifferent as Lady Sybil seemed to be.

Harold left Florence alone, 'very depressed.'[19] He returned to England by slow stages. In Pisa he visited the Palazzo Lanfranchi where Byron was living at the time of Shelley's death. He had 'a hellish time' at Ventimiglia. He gambled in the casino at Monte Carlo. And when he arrived in London, he said it was 'beastly to be back.'

Having dined with Desmond MacCarthy and gone through his Byron manuscript with him chapter by chapter, Harold took it to Constable's on the 30th November. 'Say goodbye to it without regret.' And he added, 'Now for Pope.' He actually began to read about Pope but found his oversensitive, waspish and brittle character unattractive; nor was he really sympathetic to the eighteenth century. Pope was very soon abandoned.

At the beginning of December came the General Election at which the Unionists were soundly beaten by Labour and the Liberals. Nevertheless Stanley Baldwin held on for another month.

Meanwhile Harold was disturbed by the impending break-up of the Gerald Wellesleys' marriage. Gerry, with whom he dined in Portland Place, hinted that he might not let his desertion by Dottie pass without protest. An extremely proud man, he could be vindictive when he thought himself injured or slighted. Harold knew that there was now no chance whatever of his wife's returning to him. He therefore warned Vita that Gerry would adopt the aggrieved attitude of a husband who has sacrificed everything for his darling children, everything – home, love, possessions, 'my lapis (and it has cost me £6,435. 17. 9d, if you include compound interest)'; and he would solicit and revel in the sympathy of Lady Ribblesdale, Lord Hardinge and every conceivable acquaintance as well as friend. Harold's conviction of how Gerry would react was brought home to him one afternoon in Piccadilly where he watched him being taught to drive his car through traffic. He looked every inch like the Great Duke at Quatre Bras, concentrating on victory over his enemies, come what might. 'I shouted to him but his eyes were fixed in agonised intensity upon a yellow bus.' Vita's response to Harold's warning was that she did not want people to spread rumours that she had anything to do with the break-up of the Wellesley marriage, since it was patently untrue.

Before the year was out Harold received the proofs of *Byron* at which he worked assiduously, and then compiled the index. He was also writing a little article in a miniature book for the library of the Queen's Dolls' House, which he sent off to Ned Lutyens. The Nicolsons were at Knole over the New Year, Dorothy Wellesley and her son, Valerian, staying there too. On New Years Eve Harold had a long confidential talk with

LONDON AGAIN 1923-25

Ben who had been bullied at Summer Fields by another boy. Harold always talked to his sons as if they were grown up, taking their childish problems with deep seriousness, agreeing with them that school days were not the most enjoyable, but endeavouring to assure them that they were a necessary but comparatively brief interlude in a man's life. After dinner, crackers and chess they went out into the Green Court and listened to the Sevenoaks bells saying goodbye to 1923. Harold gave a long synopsis in his diary of the past year's events and achievements.

> I have been well in health and spirits; my piles and constipation better; very happy with my darling Viti and my two boys; not really distressed at the approach of middle age and the consequent extension of my figure and thinning of my hair. Viti also I think has been happy . . . Her literary reputation has increased, and she is now taken very seriously.

As regards his achievements the year had been

> quite memorable. I did myself good at Lausanne and have earned the approval and confidence of Lord Curzon. The Tennyson book has had a great critical success and has more or less given me a settled reputation as a critic. I have not made any very exciting new friends, but I have not lost any old ones.[20]

So Harold, Vita and Dottie, with Lord Sackville and Olive Rubens, saw in the New Year of 1924 under the oriel arch of the Green Court at Knole. 'I decide and resolve,' Harold wrote, 'to be less irresponsible, not to have claret for luncheon, and to suffer fools more gladly. I don't know what Viti decides. Dottie decides a great many fierce Strindberg things.'[21]

On the 15th January Harold witnessed the opening of Parliament in full state. He noted that the crowds cheered the Prince of Wales but did not cheer the King very much; but it may have been because they were overwhelmed by the beauty of his coach. The rest of the day was occupied drafting a letter to the Italian Ambassador, which recapitulated Great Britain's determination to make the cession of African Jubaland to Italy conditional upon that country's surrender of the Dodecanese islands to Greece.

That evening Lord Curzon gave a dinner party to the senior members of the Foreign Office at his house, No. 1 Carlton House Terrace. It was a sort of farewell in that it was common knowledge that Baldwin's interim Government was about to give place to Labour. The party was one of those stiff bachelor affairs when a shy boss means to show gratitude to his subordinates for past loyal services, hard though he and his guests try to make the occasion a resounding success.

> I arrive to find them all standing in a defiant but bewildered row trying to look at their ease. The Marquis comes in limping and genial, & shakes hands. We go into dinner. He puts Ronald McNeill (Under-Secretary of State for Foreign Affairs) on his right and Crowe on his left, and the others just sit as they can. I sit at the end of the long table and see a perspective to right and left of civil service faces. Everyone feels rather shy, and tries to be resolutely at ease; conversation is hushed and stilted; Curzon talks without ceasing to McNeill and pays no attention to Crowe, who in his turn pretends to be deeply interested in a conversation with Vansittart on the modern French novel. The food is bad. I begin to acquire the conviction that the Marquis feels we do not like him, and that Crowe feels that he is being slighted. With coffee comes a certain imminence upon us, a certain feeling that someone, somehow should make a speech. They don't. We go upstairs and move about the drawing-room, making little civil service groups around the pictures. The Marquis, determined to be genial, moves from group to group, and shows them Napoleonic relics. Soon after eleven Crowe leads the way. We file past and say goodnight. A sorry ceremonial.[22]

In the office Harold continued writing drafts for the Marquis on the Italian negotiations while Geoffrey Scott, who had come over from Florence, was staying with Vita at Knole. Harold had long private discussions with Curzon and lunched alone with him and Lady Curzon, who had just returned from America, more radiant than ever. She seemed to imagine that Harold would become Ramsay MacDonald's private secretary, but Harold did not think so. On the 21st the Italian Ambassador came to Lord Curzon and offered to cede four out of the twelve Dodecanese islands to Greece if we recognised the right of Italy to annex the other eight islands from Rhodes to Leros and ceded Jubaland to her at once. Crowe and Harold both advised Curzon not to pursue the matter further, but to leave it to Ramsay MacDonald when his Government took over. He agreed. 'He is rather pathetic sitting there in his big room eating raspberry jam and knowing that he will be out of office in a few hours.'

The very next day Baldwin resigned and MacDonald was called to the Palace where he kissed hands. As well as becoming Prime Minister the Labour leader took over the Foreign Office, making Arthur Ponsonby his Under-Secretary of State. Curzon said his farewells to the staff. He apologised to his secretaries for having been a 'hard tăsk-măster.' On his departure the lift refused to work and he was obliged to walk down-

LONDON AGAIN 1923-25

stairs. MacDonald came to the office, was not recognised, was mistaken for a journalist and conducted to the top floor and asked whom he wished to see. When identified he was escorted by an office-keeper to his room which looked out upon a thick, black fog. This introduction was not auspicious. The private secretaries and Crowe appeared. MacDonald told them that he would see neither papers nor ambassadors. He would leave them to Ponsonby, and Crowe must take orders from Ponsonby. Crowe told MacDonald he could not delegate these duties and, as Secretary of State, he must both see ambassadors and write down afterwards what they said. MacDonald refused to do either. Crowe said he would have to. Then MacDonald went away. No one was pleased. However, MacDonald's minutes turned out to be sensible and definite, although they were apt to be delayed, unlike Lord Curzon's, which were always prompt.

Arthur Ponsonby came to the Office. 'A moth-eaten little man.'[23] He sat in Harold's chair where he used to sit before he had a row with a colleague and was turned out. It must have been rather a triumph for him. But he was friendly and not the least cock-a-hoop. Neville Butler was nominated his private secretary.

Harold was told in the Office that Walford Selby had been appointed MacDonald's private secretary. Although not surprised he was sorry, for he would have liked the job himself. He feared that Crowe and Tyrrell had decided he was not wholly safe and sound, admitting to himself that he was not temperamentally sound. Now what was the meaning of this recurrent, underlying self-depreciation? I believe it to have been Harold's supposition that his sexual tastes were known to his colleagues who, like most normal Englishmen of their generation and upbringing, assumed that homosexuals, however brilliant they might be, were emotionally unstable people not to be relied upon under stress and in crisis. It was the conflict between this supposition and his intellectual self-confidence which sometimes made Harold appear to be arrogant and self-defensive in relations with his colleagues in diplomacy and politics. On this occasion he was told that, since no one better could be found, he was well advised to take over Selby's job of Assistant in the Central Department. Accordingly he moved into Room U, where he had worked on and off for years.

On the 31st January the Nicolsons gave a dinner party at which the name of an additional guest appeared for the first time in Raymond Mortimer.[24] He and Harold had probably met recently in Bloomsbury circles, to which Raymond had become attached as a young and brilliant satellite. After he had worked in hospitals in France during the War he was sent to the Cypher Department of the Foreign Office in 1918. It was then that he remembered Harold Nicolson coming into his department. Harold would sit on a table drinking tea with his subordinates, to whom he talked in a slightly patronising manner which did not make him liked. If the two men failed to take to one another then, they did so in 1924. Raymond also endeared himself to Vita who became devoted to him.

In February Harold's chief occupation in the Office was drafting a letter to Poincaré on Anglo-French relations which for several years, on account of Balkan issues, had been bad. His argument was that both countries should reach agreement about main principles and not squabble over details. The letter, which was accepted by MacDonald and despatched to Poincaré, was published in the press on the 3rd March.

On the 25th *Byron The Last Journey 1823–1824* was published, and there was a silly review in the *Morning Post*. Other reviews quickly followed. The *New Statesman* critic called it 'the best and most entertaining piece of biographical narrative I have read since Lytton Strachey's *Eminent Victorians* and his *Queen Victoria*.' Clive Bell (to whom Harold had written that he would rather be slanged by him than patted by another), in giving it high praise in the *Nation and Athenaeum*, also detected the influence of Lytton Strachey. He agreed with Harold's reasons for Byron's going to Greece, but remonstrated with him – and this was typical of Clive Bell, the champion of every beautiful woman – for disparaging Teresa Guiccioli. St. Loe Strachey in the *Spectator* observed that the book followed Lytton in the literary 'close-up', but had more dash, more hardness than Lytton. No wonder that these odious deductions, not to mention comparisons in Harold's favour, disconcerted Bloomsbury. Virginia Woolf wrote to Lytton Strachey that another of his peculiarities as an author was

> to beget Nicolsons. But the mixture is not appetising to me, for all the praises of Clive and Desmond who have drunk too many glasses of his [HN's] champagne to be trusted. But then Byron seems to me tawdry and melodramatic. And Claire and Trelawny and so on and so on – I conceive them like a cave at some Earl's Court exhibition – a grotto I mean lined with distorting mirrors and plastered with oyster shells.[25]

Gosse, whose opinion Harold, unlike Bloomsbury, valued as sound and objective, was a little guarded in the *Sunday Times*. He remarked that Harold's view of Byron was the negation of romantic idealism. He wished he had been a little less sarcastic, while pronouncing that the book would enhance his reputation. What Harold valued most was a charming letter from Maurice Baring and an affectionate one from Venizelos, to whom the book was dedicated.

LONDON AGAIN 1923-25

The book is perforce the story of a tragedy. Harold demonstrated how Byron's life was a catalogue of false situations. He described the lure of Greece which was too strong for him to resist. The state of turmoil in Greek affairs coincided with Byron's dissatisfaction with his own life in 1823. Before his untimely death, to which disappointments contributed, he was disillusioned by the endless squabbles among the several Greek factions, by the hopeless inconsequence in the Greek character, and by the betrayal of his associates. After fifty-five years Harold Nicolson's *Byron: The Last Journey* holds its own among countless studies of this wayward genius. In spite of some fictional surmise and assumption (as, for instance, what were Byron's thoughts as the *Hercules* slowly sailed away from Leghorn harbour) and a few fanciful passages which are not straightforward biography, the book is still regarded as a reliable, original and brilliant analysis of the poet's character and temperament. It established Harold Nicolson as one of the leading authorities on Byron.

Harold and Vita decided that it would be pleasant to motor to Spain, and they persuaded Dottie to buy a motor for that purpose. She readily assented. They were about to leave when Lord Carnock had a heart attack. It was not the first, but it was a serious one. Only a few months ago he had told Harold he was so proud of his son's achievements at the Lausanne Conference that he could now sing his Nunc Dimittis with a full heart. But he was not to die yet. Again the three friends decided to go to Spain, when Lord Carnock after a bad night had more attacks. So they agreed to chuck Spain altogether. In any case the Prime Minister refused to grant Harold leave because he was about to re-open negotiations with the Italians. He had a long talk with him about Anglo-Italian relations.

> He sits there puffing at a pipe and very down and sad and disillusioned. He waggles his leg with impatience, perplexity or despair, and yet he does not seem to wish to hurry the conversation; but goes slowly, slowly; rather tentative are his remarks and very Scotch in sound. He flares up once at the thought of Mussolini; his eyes give a sudden flash: 'the greatest rascal in the worrrld.'[26]

The Jubaland question had been a source of worry to Curzon, who on the advice of Crowe and Harold had left it for Ramsay MacDonald to settle. Harold had prepared for MacDonald a letter, to be despatched to Mussolini, which while giving him Jubaland was to put him on his honour regarding the Dodecanese, honour in those days being a virtue attributed by British Civil Servants to foreign statesmen, even when they were dictators. Crowe had approved the letter which he took to Chequers on a Saturday in the hopes that the Prime Minister would sign it. But he found MacDonald very sticky about giving away anything to Mussolini. After a long talk the Prime Minister concluded, 'Well, leave me the papers and I will think over it.' The papers came back that morning with a note attached, 'Keep this in front of me.' In consequence no letter went to Mussolini. Yet on the previous Thursday the Prime Minister had announced to the House of Commons that an agreement with Italy was on the verge of conclusion, and Ponsonby followed up the statement with another, saying that His Majesty's Government had decided to separate the Dodecanese from the Jubaland issue, and was awaiting a reply from the Italians. Both statements were in fact untrue. The Italian press not surprisingly exposed the falsehoods. This was the sort of confusion, which to Harold's trained mind and confidence in Foreign Office efficiency, was vexatious. He thought the Labour Ministers very slack in reading papers, and, when they did, in remembering what was in them. They remembered something vaguely and did not bother whether it was from a minute, a draft, or a despatch. They were reluctant to ask for notice of questions in the House, and were thus continually landing themselves in muddles. At the same time Harold liked those he came across very much and wished to do all he could to help them. It was not until the 1st April that the letter was sent to Mussolini. In July the sovereignty of the greater part of the province of Jubaland was transferred by Great Britain to Italy.

The centenary of Byron's death took place on the 19th April. It was a soft, sunny, spring day. Harold went up to London. He attended the ceremony of laying a wreath in Park Lane upon Richard Belt's bronze statue of the poet with his dog, Boatswain, about which statue Trelawny remarked that it did not in the remotest degree resemble Byron either in face or figure. Harold sat near the Achilles statue watching the Greek colony in London, top-hatted and singular, deposit an enormous spray of laurel upon Belt's red granite base. Between him and them flitted the limousines of the wealthy, whom Byron would have hated. Through the purr of Rolls Royces he heard the voice of the Greek Minister extolling the dead hero. Harold attended a Byron luncheon held at the Victoria Hotel, at which Stanley Baldwin took the chair. In the evening he delivered a lecture on Byron at the Bermondsey bookshop, with J. C. Squire in the chair. He spoke without notes for an hour. There were questions, and very intelligent ones, he told Vita:

> which I answered with the tattered remnants of my boyish charm. One old man (he was the milkman) heckled me about Byron's private life: 'If, as Mr. Nicolson admits, Byron was a rotter, why then does he make

out he was a great man?' To which I put on a face something between Christ's and Mrs. Harry MacLaren's and said, 'Byron did not hide his faults like you and I. For myself I feel that he was a better man than I am (slight choke in the voice). Yes, he was a better man; he died more courageously than I could have done. It is not I who would presume to cast a stone (loud applause).[27]

On the 5th May Harold received a doctorate of the University of Athens.

At the end of June and beginning of July Geoffrey Scott stayed at Long Barn while Harold, on leave, was working there at another lecture on Byron, which he delivered in the Central Hall, Westminster. Two days before this lecture Virginia Woolf paid her first visit to Long Barn. She had lunched at Knole alone with Lord Sackville and was fascinated by his solitary figure residing 'in the kernel of a vast nut,' as she put it, in which miles of galleries stretched in all directions and were crammed with chairs that Shakespeare might have sat on, and portraits of bearded and be-ruffed ancestors. Vita, Dottie Wellesley and Geoffrey Scott motored over from Long Barn to fetch her after luncheon. Vita's presence in her ancestral home evoked in Virginia a wondering rumination upon how 'all these ancestors & centuries, & silver & gold, have bred a perfect body. She is stag like, or race horse like, save for the face, which pouts, & has no very sharp brain. But as a body hers is perfection.' Virginia's obsession with the heredity of the patrician mind and body and the aristocrat's lack of inhibitions combined with rigidity of attitude, was unabated. She was conscious of being 'no very intelligent sight-seer beside Geoffrey Scott,' whose suavity and suppleness she did not particularly like. Harold this time she liked better. Watching him 'sitting on the iron bar before the great burning logs, gently butting the tassel from the baldaquin, or whatever it's called' over the fireplace, 'with his forehead,' she found him 'trusty & honest & vigorous. He wore a blue velvet jacket.' She had the odd notion that Geoffrey saw in her a kindred spirit, one who like himself, was excluded from the patrician clique and belonged to the common herd.[28]

Harold must have decided that the time had come to make a will, for he wrote on Knole paper the draft[29] of a very concise testament, in which he appointed Vita his sole executrix and bequeathed to her all monies and personal effects whatsoever, 'in recognition of her affectionate indulgence to me during our married life, and trusting that she will dispose to my nearest relations and more intimate friends such personal effects as she may deem fit.' On the 8th July he and Vita left England for a walking tour in

Austria. At Dobbiaco, a small town across the Austrian border, just in Italy, they bought sticks and a rucksack and went for early morning walks through pine-woods and daphne, looking for wild flowers. One day they walked over twenty-four miles from Pordoi to Carragli. Between the walks Vita composed her short novel, *Seducers in Ecuador*,[30] and Harold worked on another Byron lecture for the *Nation and Athenaeum*.

On their return Harold found a letter from Jack Squire asking him to write a book on Swinburne for the English Men of Letters series. He eagerly accepted the proposition. Meanwhile the Foreign Office was in the throes of the Reparations Conference.

Early in September Harold was put in charge of the Central Department in place of Miles Lampson. He was busily engaged in writing a Minute about disarmament and security. His main argument was that the League must establish a wide system of arbitration, and that this system would become the Public Law of Europe. While recognising that British opinion was unwilling to enter alliances, he maintained that it was essential for this country to co-operate in defence of the new system. Great Britain, like the other Great Power members of the League, must be prepared jointly to impose sanctions against violation of League principles. A regular programme should be drawn up precisely defining when and how financial and economic blockade, or force if needs be, ought to be imposed. Great Britain should contribute naval rather than military strength. Only when the system of arbitration was agreed among the nations, could discussion of international disarmament be inaugurated.

At this stage of Ramsay MacDonald's premiership Harold was wholly loyal to him. Indeed he was secretly more in sympathy with his Government than he had been with Baldwin's. When the unpleasant incident arose of a motor car being given to the Prime Minister and its maintenance endowed by his admirer and friend, a rich biscuit manufacturer, Alexander Grant,[31] who was made a baronet three months after the donation, the right-wing press made ugly capital out of it. Harold, though worried that MacDonald should be so ingenuous, was convinced that his motives were guileless. He was disturbed too that his prestige was damaged with the left wing of the Labour Party. If MacDonald were to go, God alone knew what would happen. Harold did not believe there was another man in the party with an ounce of Ramsay's brain or wisdom. He was called upon to assist at a reception given by the Prime Minister to forty deputies of the Lancashire cotton interests, wishing to protest against the extension of any Franco-German commercial treaty beyond the 10th January next, when the five-year privileges enjoyed by the Alsace products were due to expire. They sat opposite him in a phalanx with red ham faces and orchids in their button holes, the very incarnation of commercial Tory hostility. For an

LONDON AGAIN 1923-25

hour they read to the Prime Minister long statements of objection. MacDonald having listened patiently and courteously, replied to them with great frankness and good sense. Harold's commentary was that it was a very valuable interview from which the Prime Minister emerged with distinct credit.

Three days later General Wauchope, who was head of the Control Commission in Germany, came to see Harold. He warned him that the recent inspections would disclose grave evasions of the Peace Treaty on the part of the former enemy, particularly over Krupp's big gun factory which the Germans were refusing to destroy. Harold noted that in view of the proceedings at Geneva, this situation presented awkward problems.

On the 13th September he did not go down to Long Barn for the weekend because Vita was away spending her first night with Leonard and Virginia Woolf at Monk's House, Rodmell.

Vita was here for Sunday [Virginia wrote in her diary[32]], gliding down the village in her large new blue Austin car, which she manages consummately. She was dressed in a ringed yellow jersey, & large hat, & had a dressing case all full of silver and night gowns wrapped in tissue... I like her being honourable, & she is it; a perfect lady, with all the dash & courage of the aristocracy, & less of its childishness than I expected.

It was then that Vita left *Seducers in Ecuador* for Virginia to read. It won her hostess's approval. 'I rather marvel at her skill, & sensibility; for is she not mother, wife, great lady, hostess, as well as scribbling?' The notion that Vita lived in exotic luxury, in a huge country house, and entertained society people on a scale of Mrs. Hunter or Lady Curzon was of course preposterously far from the truth. Her and Harold's friends were no less intellectual than the Woolfs', and Long Barn, far from being a fine house, was merely an overgrown medieval cottage. Virginia having described Vita as an over-ripe grape in features, and conceding her a manly good sense, concluded,

Oh yes, I like her; could tack her on to my equipage for all time; & suppose if life allowed, this might be a friendship of a sort.

From which we deduce that Vita had at last passed the test as acceptable to, if not necessarily accepted by, Bloomsbury. She was even taken to Charleston

Charleston, the Bell's farm-house, which her presence rendered very grey and shabby. And, 'as for Monk's House, it became a ruined barn, & we pick-nicking in the rubbish heap.' To Harold Virginia sent a copy of her pamphlet, *Mr. Bennett and Mrs. Brown*.

The Nicolsons went away together for two weekend house-parties this autumn. The first was to Hackwood at the invitation of Lord and Lady Curzon. One evening towards the end of September Vita picked Harold up at the Foreign Office, and drove him down to Hampshire. The great grey classical house near Basingstoke was, like Montacute in Somerset, not owned but rented by Lord Curzon. They reached the Hackwood gates after dark. With Vita at the wheel, they raced through them, down the twisting drive, scattering the frightened rabbits with the glare of their headlights. A heavy mist hung over the lakes, and clung to the trees. A butler and posse of footmen greeted them at the front door under the wide portico. Although Lord Curzon's lease of the house was a short one, he had spent a fortune embellishing it, making alterations to rooms, fitting them with rare Flemish tapestries, furnishing them with family portraits and hanging a pair of magnificent silver chandeliers, fashioned to his own design out of various gifts received when he was Viceroy of India, and melted down. Harold remarked on the quantity of red damask and the great number of photograph albums. Promptly at nine o'clock dinner was served. Each man escorted a lady, arm in arm, into the dining-room, and they ate a gargantuan pre-war meal. Harold sat between Mrs. Ambrose Dudley, 'who is God's worst bore and Madame Balzan who is a darling.'[33]

He was able to work at his Swinburne book all the next morning, until luncheon, which was another huge meal. This time he sat between Lady Curzon and Lady Salisbury.

> I like them. We go a walk after and see the macaws & the little birds & the woods & the water garden, & the avenues. The Marquis is in delightful form. Then work again and finish Gosse's book on Byron. Then a huge dinner again and talk after. Bed very late. A pleasant stop. Rex Benson sings coon songs after dinner.[34]

On Monday morning Vita motored back to Long Barn while Harold went to London by train with the rest of the house-party in reserved carriages.

A fortnight later Harold and Vita motored to the Wharf at Sutton Courtenay in Berkshire, to stay the weekend with the Asquiths. The Asquiths' scale of entertaining was far more modest than the Curzons' and thereby more relaxed and stimulating. The only other guest was Count

LONDON AGAIN 1923-25

Constantine Benckendorff[35] who had escaped from the Bolsheviks. 'His experiences have given him a polite and affable look like people put on who don't care for children.'[36] On Sunday they went to Summer Fields, on the Oxford outskirts, where Ben was at school. Harold was delighted that the ten-year-old Ben was so keen on his work, which he had not been at that age. Indeed both parents were much more pleased and interested when Ben's satisfactory reports arrived than they had ever expected to be. Harold thought it was another sign of his middle age in that he was living his life again through his son.

In between these two visits the Labour Government fell. MacDonald returned from the House of Commons crestfallen to Downing Street. A crowd of sympathisers cheered him at his door. Harold's sympathy and even liking for him were much impaired when his father told him that MacDonald had complained to a small audience that on becoming Prime Minister he found the Foreign Office to be lazy, incompetent and ignorant. His loyalty to his Office was affronted for MacDonald's allegations were totally unwarranted. Furthermore all the Foreign Office staff had overreached themselves to help him in his difficult roles of Foreign Secretary and Prime Minister when he was abysmally inexperienced in both. Consequently when, just before the General Election on the 29th October, MacDonald, being highly embarrassed by the Zinoviev Letter, turned on Sir Eyre Crowe and accused him of full responsibility for publishing it – 'What's this I hear about the publication of the Note? Did I not say it was not to be published until I had considered it again?' – Harold flew to the defence of his beloved chief, although he knew Crowe to be partially to blame. The publication of the Zinoviev Letter served to convince the British public that the Labour Government had been discreditably subservient to extremist influences, and undoubtedly helped to defeat it at the polls. Harold listened to the Conservative gains at a party given by Mr. Gordon Selfridge, and was rather disgusted with the jubilation as the results came through. He was also worried lest Lord Curzon might again become Foreign Secretary and make him his private secretary. He even went to Crowe and begged him not to let him be sent to Curzon.

For most of November Harold was alone with Vita at Long Barn. He was blissfully content. Vita was busy composing *The Land*. Harold drank nothing, smoked a lot, helped clear out the wild garden, planted bulbs, and made one expedition to Groombridge to buy azaleas and Irish yews. He began writing *Swinburne*. In one week alone he wrote 20,000 words, and by the last day of the month he had finished chapter 6. On the 1st December the Nicolsons shut up Long Barn for the winter. Nigel, now nearly eight, was deposited at Knole, Harold returned to London, and Vita went to stay for a few days with an old admirer, Walter Berry, in Paris.[37]

Although Vita was to be absent only a matter of days Harold took the parting badly. He wrote to her, as usual, daily. He was bound to see, he said in his first letter, the headline, 'Collision at Sea' on an evening poster. Vita wrote back that Walter Berry had arranged a dinner party for her amusement, to which he had invited Violet Trefusis.

> Oh my God! What am I to do? I can't tell Walter B. I feel sick at the idea. Berners too, how he will enjoy it, the devil. I feel trapped ... Oh Hadji.[38]

The news lashed Harold into a turmoil of anxiety.

> I can't help being worried [he wrote[39]] by your meeting V again. You know I think she has the evil eye and then you are so weak and so easily mesmerized, and all she wants to do is to destroy your happiness. Oh my darling, *do* be careful.

He apologised for sending her a telegram on the subject, hoped she would not be cross, but so dreaded that woman.

> Her very name brings back all the aching unhappiness of those months, the doubt, the mortification and the loneliness. I think she is the only person of whom I am frightened, and have an almost superstitious belief in her capacity for causing destruction and wretchedness.

The dinner party took place, and Vita behaved so distantly and correctly that she provoked a letter from Violet, written in the same old strain of rancorous jealousy of Harold, and complaining of the torture the meeting had occasioned her. 'Please, oh please, don't break me on the wheel again.'[40] It was perhaps as well that on the very next day Vita, hugging several cartons and a roll of tapestry like a travelling rug, was met by Harold at Victoria.

Harold had a drawing done of his head by William Rothenstein. Of all the likenesses taken of him by various artists this in red chalk was the only one that pleased the subject. It depicts him on the verge of middle age, the boyishness gone, but the chubbiness still there, the features a little blurred, but the eyes as alert as ever.

LONDON AGAIN 1923-25

In January 1925 the Nicolsons went again to stay at The Wharf. Harold wrote in his diary[41] a generous analysis of his hostess's character.

> I read Mrs. Asquith's proofs of her new book, *Personalities* – giving accounts of her visits to Egypt, America, Spain and Italy. Atrociously written, carelessly revised, incredibly indiscreet, embarrassingly vain. They give in the aggregate build-up an impression of her real character; her zest and liberalism. It is curious to think how posterity will misunderstand Margot. They will think her a vulgar and disagreeable advertiser. She is nothing of the sort. She is vain of course, but it is no common vanity. She is observant rather than intelligent. Above all, she is brave, affectionate, loyal. Her zest is like champagne. Her generosity of thought and action is like a fresh wind. The love which hangs above her house gives it a spirituality which is different from the ghoulish intellectualism of other circles.. Both V and I feel it is a real privilege to go to the Wharf and come away with added sensitiveness to life.

On the whole Harold did not care for society women. He was irritated by their pretensions and he would not respond to their demands for attention. He resented their claims upon his patience and flattery. He once complained to Vita how Sibyl Colefax – whom, incidentally, he was extremely fond of – kept him waiting for the theatre. 'Can you wonder that I loathe and abhor all women?' Then she would sneeze. 'I loathe women who sneeze,' he added. Vita, surprisingly, agreed in disliking what they both termed women's sillinesses. For instance when her secretary told her that women readers asked for red-backed books in public libraries in order to use the dye for lip-stick, and that nurses in hospitals took the red tulips from patients' vases in order to make rouge, she was revolted. 'How I hate women!' she echoed. There was no such nonsense about Margot Asquith, who amused Harold with her candour and unpremeditated behaviour. She was absolutely no respecter of persons. During this visit she told the Nicolsons about a talk she had had with King George V. She greatly preferred him to King Edward VII, whom she found German and coarse. King George asked her to tea. He said, 'Mrs. Asquith, you are a great specialist in character, what do you say of *me*?' 'Oh, I couldn't, sir.' 'Well, out with it!' 'But you wouldn't like it, Sir.' 'Oh no, go ahead.' 'Well, Sir,' she said, 'you see your great fault is that you don't enjoy yourself.' The King was taken aback, and said quite simply, 'Yes, I know, but you see, I don't like society; I like my wife.' Margot was touched by this reply, but believed that her words may have been heeded. She said she did not like Queen Mary. She thought her hard, stupid and sly. Besides, Queen Mary loathed her children. 'But then Margot's standard of parental affection is a high one,' Harold observed.

Harold was incorrigibly sociable rather than social. He loved select company. He disliked being alone. He may not have cared very much for society women although he liked what they provided. They certainly cared very much for him. He was a great catch at their luncheon and dinner tables. He could always be relied upon to edify and amuse. And a clever hostess knew how to draw him out. She had merely to cast a dexterous fly and retire discreetly from the bank. Like a patient angler she must give him complete freedom of play. He would immediately toy with the subject introduced, turn it over this way and that, tug at it, draw it out, worry it, thrash it and finally dispose of it, hook, line and sinker in coruscating flashes of wit and rhetoric. But he did not like to be interrupted by jejune comments. Unless his fellow guests were as intellectual as himself he did not indulge in repartee. At social functions his conversations were apt to be in monologue. Only with his family and intimate men friends did he enjoy argument. Then he was conversationally in his zenith, at his most outrageous, most mischievous, most funny and most enchanting.

Vita came up to London and they formally re-entered into possession of the Ebury Street house, which was now technically Vita's, Lady Sackville having renounced her interest in it. For the next three years this house was to be their London home, where they and the children came and went.

Venizelos, now in London, called on Harold in the Office. He explained to him the exact condition of Serbo-Greek relations. He was uneasy but not pessimistic. He thought that as long as Bulgaria and Serbia remained enemies, Greece would be fairly safe. But once they came together, he foresaw danger. If however Greece could have ten years of peace, then Greek Macedonia would become wholly absorbed, and Greece's position would be that much stronger. This talk was followed by a meeting in the Office of all senior officials summoned by the Secretary of State, Sir Austen Chamberlain. The purpose was to discuss the future policy of the British Empire. Crowe summed up by stating that imperial isolation was impossible, that Britain must modify the Covenant and Protocol of the League, and come to an understanding with France to protect the Channel ports. The problem that Harold envisaged was whether our foreign policy was a Dominion or a Downing Street one. He was promptly ordered to prepare a Memorandum in the light of the meeting's deliberations. When a month later he got the Memorandum back, with some very laudatory comments by the Secretary of State, instead of being pleased he wrote, 'I always said the man was a fool: I *know* that that memo. is a bad memo.' There was no false modesty in Harold's opinions of his compositions, although, as is the way of authors, he was often mistaken in his self-estimates. He always however had a low opinion of Austen Chamberlain's judgement, and sensed that he did not like him, believing that Tyrrell put Chamberlain against him. Harold's Memorandum was circulated to the King, the Cabinet and the Dominions. On the 2nd March it appeared almost word for word in the papers and caused a stir in this country and overseas.

In spite of the preliminary spurt of composition of the Swinburne book in the previous November, pressure of work in the Office retarded it until the spring of this year. Nevertheless Harold was able to snatch further interviews with persons who had known the poet. One such occasion was recorded at length in his diary under the 24th January.

I go to see Edmund Gosse. There is tea first and a good pink cake, and then Lady Gosse creeps away, and he gives me a little cigar, and we settle down in front of the fire. I say that I have not made up my mind about Swinburne; obviously he is something more than a grotesque – what is he? G says that what it is so difficult to realise was that S was completely un-selfconscious. I said he was so un-selfconscious that he was almost un-conscious, that he had no sense of audience. He agreed thoroughly. He told me the Emerson story, with imitation. He imitated S reciting, the movements of the hands down and upwards, as though he were trying to push himself up and out of a quicksand. I talked of his childhood; nothing new; of Eton; nothing new; of Balliol. G said Nichol [John Nichol, an early friend] *was* a bad influence, but not intentionally so. He was not really sinister. I talked of Howell [Charles Augustus, a later intimate] and Simeon Solomon. G told me that when the latter was arrested for sodomy, Swinburne was horrified. 'But after all,' G had said, 'you must have known about it. Solomon made no secret of his tastes.' 'Oh yes, talked about,' said Swinburne, 'he talked; but I never thought an English gentleman would DO such things.' He admitted that S had a sadistic or masochistic complex, that he was excited by pain. He was not certain whether the Dolmancé orgies were correct in fact! Powell was certainly a debauched and violent man; and in any case S went through vice as a somnambulist. It may have been that he masturbated; he certainly liked being whipped; but all this made but little difference to him. I asked about the Ada Menken story. He told it me as follows. After the scandal aroused by *Poems and Ballads* it dawned upon Rossetti and Howell that it was singularly ridiculous that a man who was hailed by the English speaking world as the greatest voluptuary since Byron should not, in fact, have ever had a woman. They called a council to consider what, in this respect, should be done with and for Algernon. He only liked or noticed strapping women. Now Ada Isaacs Menken was at that time performing at Astley's circus, where she would ride round and round the ring on an old cab-horse with her hair streaming, lolloping round the ring. Here was to be the new Atalanta. They mentioned the lady to S, but he seemed not to hear them; they took S to see the lady herself and appealed to her as a woman of the world to help them out of their difficulty. She was very accommodating; she had read Mr. Swinburne's poems and found them perfectly sweet; all she would ask for this depucilage was the payment of a small fee. They agreed to stump up that fee. They then arranged that she would be brought round after the performance of Mazeppa on Friday evening next. They then told S that the Menken had fallen in love with him through his poems and that she had insisted on an interview. S was *thrilled*. The interview took place. She remained several nights; but after three weeks she appeared suddenly at Rossetti's, plumped down the fee and said, 'I am an honest girl. I took this money for a certain purpose. I have been unable to fulfil that purpose. I have come to return my fee.' Rossetti protested, saying he was sure she had done her level best. But she insisted, and her last words were, 'you see, I can't get Mr. Swinburne to understand that biting isn't enough.' S for his part would always refer to her as 'my mistress.' And he would tell Gosse later how she sat all night on the edge of the bed reading *Infelicia* to him until 'her thighs became as marble.' This, I think, is word for word what Gosse told me.

Gosse, meeting Harold three days later at the Garrick, added that Swinburne's masochism first awoke at Eton where he derived infinite pleasure from being whipped; and that his tutor, realising this, would pour eau de cologne into his wounds.

In February Harold attended an evening party at the Woolfs, which he merely described in his diary as a failure: 'Lytton Strachey and Duncan Grant mooning about helplessly among epicene young men.'[42] The next mention of Lytton Strachey was to be on the 2nd July, when at a late evening party given by George Rylands Harold 'had a foolish tiff there with' him. He gave no details of the tiff. Was it over Gosse, whom the heart of Bloomsbury affected to despise, making their contempt known to the old man and causing him distress? Harold, of course, while being perfectly aware of Gosse's failings, his old-maidishness, prudishness, petulance, defensiveness and amenability to slights, was fond of him. He admired his zest of limitless humanity, his wonderful evocations of the past. When Gosse re-enacted historic incidents his audience heard George Eliot's voice, saw Browning's fat hands patting the air, and felt Swinburne's darting movements. He brought to life the great Victorian dead, for he had known them, and witnessed and recorded their behaviour. He had actually seen with his own eyes Polidori's intimate diary about Byron before it was destroyed. He had seen Lord Houghton drunk, Lord

Tennyson in a growling rage, Browning proposing to a girl young enough to be his granddaughter, and the Carlyles arguing. Withal he had a wonderful gift of imitation. For any younger man Gosse's recollections were a storehouse of literary treasure. But Bloomsbury, in declining to profit from these memories, merely saw in Gosse a self-satisfied old member of the literary establishment, who gloried in social engagements and his knighthood.

Lytton Strachey represented in Harold Nicolson's eyes the kernel of Bloomsbury. But he was personally and physically distasteful to him. Other members of Bloomsbury were not. Harold was devoted to Clive Bell; he acknowledged and admired the genius of Virginia Woolf and Maynard Keynes. He respected Roger Fry without pretending to understand his philosophy of art. He sought and took Leonard Woolf's advice. He venerated Bertrand Russell. He was charmed by Duncan Grant. Many of the younger members on the fringe of the movement became his friends. Through Raymond Mortimer and Eddy Sackville-West he got to know George (Dadie) Rylands, Roger Senhouse, Francis Birrell and Philip Ritchie. He naturally recognised the very distinctive characters and attributes of each individual member of Bloomsbury, giving generous praise to the contribution each made to economics, historical biography, fiction and painting by breaking old moulds and fashioning new ones. But at the same time he did see in the movement certain shared proclivities. Indeed they were vaunted by the group.

Harold could not in fact avoid mildly poking fun at them. The Areopagus of British Culture he called them in *Some People*, where he described a party they gave – was it Dadie Rylands' party of the 2nd July? – in the summer of 1925, which he attended and at which he was humiliated and put in his place. He called them 'a narrow but stimulating lot.'[43] But he disliked their sense of superiority, their exclusiveness and desire to induce feelings of inadequacy in those outside the magic circle of which they were jealous guardians.

There is no doubt that they were guilty of an aggressive moral superiority. Even E. M. Forster, who, if not a member of Bloomsbury counted most of them as his intimate friends, complained that they made him feel small. They belittled other intellectuals whose powers may have been as considerable as their own. And they lacked reverence for everything and everyone but their own principles and persons. Dorothy Wellesley and Ethel Smyth may not have possessed brains of the highest calibre, but the first[44] deprecated the arrogant notion of Bloomsbury that those born into what they called 'Mayfair' (she implied Harold, Vita and herself) were incapable of sincerity from the nature of their upbringing; and the second deplored Bloomsbury's attitude to religion and politics. 'The views of all that Bloomsbury lot,' Ethel snorted, 'are quite childish' on these two subjects. Of religion they had no conception, dismissing any manifestations of mysticism or the established creeds as self-deception or sheer idiocy. 'They think all aristocrats are limited and stupid, and swallow all the humbugging shibboleths of the Labour Party.' Elizabeth Bowen likewise saw a smugness in their virulent godlessness, which not only depressed her, but gave her a feeling of claustrophobia.[45] Keynes alone among the group of friends may have recognised the limitation of their disbeliefs. He once wrote to Lytton Strachey, 'Is it monomania, this colossal moral superiority that we feel?'

By February of this year Geoffrey Scott was back in England and once again a frequent visitor to Long Barn. Harold wrote a review of *The Portrait of Zélide*, which, when he read it in typescript, he had pronounced the last word in biography. 'It is a supreme bit of good work.'[46] The same day he wrote in his diary:

> Think for about three-quarters of an hour that I have got cancer in the left breast, and then for another forty minutes that I have got cancer in the right breast. Decide finally that I have got neither.[47]

Had this imaginary complaint any connection with the return of Geoffrey to Harold's cherished hearth and home? He was addicted all his life to suspicions that he had contracted some dire infection or mortal disease, if not cancer, then pneumonia, consumption, cirrhosis, or diabetes, which turned out to be, as on this occasion, fabrics of the imagination. At one time he was convinced he had caught diphtheria from a friend who had been discharged from hospital four months previously. At another he felt so ill that putting his work aside he motored straight to London to see his doctor. The doctor told him, after an examination, that there was nothing the matter with him. He immediately felt perfectly well again and went back to the country rejoicing. He did suffer repeatedly from very bad colds, even two or three a year, and long before he had his first stroke, he was subject to sudden fainting-fits, without any warning. Otherwise he enjoyed robust health until his sixty-ninth year.

He met at a dinner party at the St. Loe Strachey's – an odd, uneasy, old-fashioned dinner – a young politician, a friend of Archie Clark Kerr, called Robert Boothby,[48] – 'an attractive young man.' There began a friendship of a lifetime, never very intimate but enduring, and based on political interests. Harold was always enlivened by Bob Boothby's com-

LONDON AGAIN 1923-25

pany, and though their views diverged at times, they were to be more often than not allies in the House of Commons in spite of belonging to different parties.

At the beginning of March Harold had his first sitting to Ian Campbell-Gray for a portrait. Campbell-Gray was a new friend, whom Harold described as 'virginal and fierce.' He was also sensitive to criticism, moody and prone to despair. As a landscape artist he was very proficient, and has not yet received the recognition which his poetic compositions deserve. He was to stay a good deal at Long Barn and later in the year became involved in a rather turbulent relationship with Elizabeth Bibesco, about which he confided in Harold. The portrait did not proceed entirely satisfactorily. There were many sittings at which the artist would get angry with himself, fling little bits of charcoal about the room and dash his fingers through his hair. The portrait does not seem to have survived. Harold thought it made him look like a wistful Napoleon, and Vita, who did not care for it, like a butcher.

On the 2nd March Harold lunched for the last time with the Curzons in Carlton House Terrace. It was the day that his Memorandum on security was blazoned in the press. The Cabinet, to his alarm, was about to discuss it, and he appreciated Curzon's tact in making no mention of it. Four days later while staying in Cambridge Curzon was taken dangerously ill. He was rushed to London, underwent a serious bladder operation, and died early in the morning of the 20th. Harold was sitting to Ian Campbell-Gray when he learnt the news. He was profoundly moved by the Marquis's death. He and Vita attended the funeral service in Westminster Abbey. The impression left upon him was of a great crowd in black holding white papers, rows of bald heads in front, the distant vision of a coffin covered with a golden pall, and the sunbeams striking the clerestory as the clouds raced across the March sky. The following day he accompanied a select few to Derbyshire for the interment.

Go up to Kedleston. The 10.25 train from St. Pancras. Two corridor carriages engaged for us and a dining car. Some relations in rusty black. Maud Cunard in a sable tippet. Chips Channon in a blue coat. Ivor Churchill, correct. Scatters Wilson, who has come partly because he is in love with Lady Curzon and partly because it is on the way to the Grand National. Fruity Metcalfe who has come because he is in love with Baba Curzon. They talk racing all the way up. We lunch, soup, fish, chicken. At Derby there is a crowd and several motors. At Kedleston there is another crowd of local people. We enter the hall. There are wreathes against the columns and the coffin on a trestle; dark red velvet with brass nails in panels. We go on to the library where there is a fire and we sit about talking with bated breath. Then the undertaker hurries in. 'You better come now if you want a good place.' So we go into the hall and stand by the coffin. Then the choir files in and the Archbishop of York. Then Lady Curzon, erect, haggard, beautiful, comes and stands by the head of the coffin. *Rock of Ages* by a village choir, and the smell of roses and lilies. An address by the Archbishop, and then with shuffle and shove the undertakers seize the coffin, grasping the brass handles with their shaking black kid-gloves, working their shoulders underneath. It lurches out into the cold March wind and down the stairway. Lady Curzon follows like Antigone. There is a crowd at the little church, and I can't see much. Afterwards I go into the chapel. They have moved one of the malachite slabs and let in the coffin a few feet below. They have sprinkled a handful of silver sand on it. We go back to the house. Baba Curzon and Cimmie Mosley appear. Very upset. Very sweet. Lady C says he has left me some papers. I get back to Derby. And travel for hours talking to Maud Cunard. Then the lights of London and dinner at the Garrick.[49]

Harold was obliged to write an article for the *Spectator* (4.4.25.) about Lord Curzon, in which he described the moving ceremony at Kedleston and Dr. Lang's address in the chapel. He referred to Lord Curzon's passionate emotion, his lavish geniality, his boyishness, unfailing humour, love of old friends, and the simplicity of his religious faith. He showed the article to Lady Curzon who liked it. She gave him touching details of her husband's death: how he prayed hard, repeating over and over again the Lord's Prayer.

Jonathan Cape requested an interview with Harold in which they proposed that he should write Lord Curzon's Life, without making it clear whether the idea emanated from them or Lady Curzon. Harold demurred, and the proposal was put by Benn to Lord Ronaldshay,[50] an ex-Governor of Bengal, who accepted it. A little later he received a letter from Sir Ian Malcolm,[51] one of Curzon's executors, asking him to edit the Marquis's unfinished books on the castles and houses which he either owned or occupied. When Harold visited Carlton House Terrace to look through the papers which had been left to him he found that three of the books were practically in final form, and two in the form of notes. He undertook to edit the one on Bodiam Castle, Sussex, which was published in 1926. On being sent to Persia he was obliged, with little reluctance, to abandon the others.

Evidently the invitation to Harold, and then to Lord Ronaldshay came from the publishers direct, for Lady Curzon sent for Harold and begged him to undertake the Life of her husband. She was displeased with Benn's choice of Lord Ronaldshay, and even proposed to withhold her private letters so that Harold might write something supplementary. He explained to her that this would be too difficult and delicate a task for him When Ronaldshay's first volume eventually came out Harold considered it quite good enough for an official biography, although the author never got thoroughly behind his subject.[52]

At the beginning of April Harold and Vita initiated their elder son into the magic of Italy. At first they stayed at San Vigilio on Lake Como, and from there went to Venice. Ben loved Venice and worked solemnly at an immense diary. His life's dedication to Italian art, from which he never swerved, derived from this visit. Harold found time to continue with *Swinburne*, which he resumed and finished when they got back to Long Barn. Their friend, Lutyens, came to stay in May, and designed for them a new garden on the lower terrace. Harold gave a lecture to the Royal Society of Literature on Swinburne and Baudelaire, which was chaired by John Buchan, and for which Gosse returned a vote of thanks in most laudatory terms. It was this lecture which Edmund Wilson had in mind when he wrote in January 1944 the disobliging article (to which I shall refer in due course) *Through the Embassy Window*, attacking Harold's priggishness and lack of candour. In his lecture Harold stressed that the upbringing and condition of the two poets had a parallel, but that whereas Baudelaire was supremely clever, Swinburne was essentially stupid.

Briefly, the theme of Harold's *Swinburne* was that his subject was a dull poet owing to the narcotic effects of his choice of melody and overemphasis of alliteration. There was lack of co-ordinated meaning in his vague images. There was in fact a lack of a wide basis of experiences. The sources of Swinburne's inspiration were limited. He never acquired new ones after leaving Eton, or at latest Balliol. He had two contrary and conflicting impulses in revolt and submission. Harold's point was that the reader of 1925, who regarded Swinburne as the appendix of an archaic tradition, should bear in mind that his contemporaries in the 1860s had regarded him as the herald of a new, liberated movement. Liberty was then the perpetual cry, the overriding ideal, the primary religion. The success of *Poems and Ballads* had been greeted by serious critics like Ruskin in England and Victor Hugo in France as the final break from the Augustan straightjacket of metre and order, and the dawn of a new freedom in English poetry.

After a holiday of six weeks Harold returned to the Foreign Office to find that Crowe was dying, and Tyrrell had already taken his place as Permanent Under-Secretary. The loss of Eyre Crowe, whom he was to describe in *Lord Carnock* as 'industrious, loyal, expert, accurate, beloved, obedient, courageous,' and his replacement by the one official in the Foreign Office whom Harold held in contempt, was a grievous blow. Indeed Crowe, a man of extreme violence and extreme gentleness, was wholly human. He was acknowledged by Baldwin to be one of the ablest servants of the Crown, and by Vansittart as the greatest public servant of his age. Harold learned from him that, whereas emotional dishonesty could be forgiven for it knew not what it did, intellectual dishonesty could never be forgiven. 'How I adore and respect that man,'[53] he had confided to his diary a mere eight months ago. And now Crowe, 'The Bird,' the curious old figure with his long redingote and borsalino hat, had left the scene and was about to leave the world altogether. The muddle over the Zinoviev Letter had, as Ramsay MacDonald was to admit, killed him.

Harold was sad and bored with his work. He believed for the first time in his life that he was no longer interested in foreign politics. He felt himself out of the swim; he felt that his minutes were being markedly ignored, whereas those of his colleagues were singled out for commendation. He believed that other interests held him more firmly. His situation required thinking over. Yet he suspected that he could not do much better at literature than he was doing at present, were he to give up his profession. If he chucked the Office it would only mean doing a little more writing than what he was doing already, and not necessarily a little better. He decided that he should not abandon his first string merely because it was out of tune. After all he was practically running the Western Department of the Foreign Office. He must wait and see.

The intimate friend who was now most in his confidence, with whom he discussed his personal problems and whom he was constantly meeting, was Raymond Mortimer. Harold's list of engagements was punctuated with, 'Lunch Raymond at the Garrick,' 'On to house warming at Raymond's,' 'On to Eiffel Tower where I meet Raymond,' 'To a play with Raymond and stay with him in Gordon Place.' 'Raymond comes to Long Barn.' Harold had a high regard for his friend's literary judgement. He greatly valued his stylistic criticism because he had the eye of a lynx for grammatical solecisms, errors of syntax and shallow passages. Raymond furthermore never for a moment said what he did not think out of inertia or a desire to please. He was inordinately severe, almost to the extent of relishing his friends' mistakes, whether literary or of any other sort, so much so that in 1942 Harold complained to Vita that Raymond

> is like a spaniel snorting for truffles; the truffles in his case being incompetence on the part of others. Nothing ever seems to him to be right and nobody to have any intelligence. Thus he ignores the really wonderful work done in agriculture and merely delights in a story of a farmer who ploughed up a chalk down ... That is why I hate the *New Statesman* [of which Raymond was literary editor]. I do not believe that anything creative is ever achieved by an attitude of constant suspicion, pessimism and distrust.[54]

LONDON AGAIN 1923-25

His spirit of contradiction was so acute that it drove him at times to accord praise or blame in inverse ratio to commonly held opinion.

Harold's devotion to Raymond did not prevent his teasing him. And in these early days of their friendship it amused Harold to introduce Raymond to his literary friends eminent outside Bloomsbury, of whose fringe Raymond was a bright adornment. 'It is very good for him,' Harold wrote mischievously, 'to get out of his little sterile circle of mutual admiration.' He introduced him to the American poet, Archibald MacLeish. It was not a success. Harold fancied that Raymond felt, if not out of his depth, then out of his element. 'Was it possible that there could be a *bâteau* (however *ivre*) moderner than himself?' Harold wondered; and fancied Raymond answering, 'No, it was not possible; the man was merely a prig; and in any case he would look very foolish, very ponderous, in Gordon Square (Puss, puss, puss).'[55]

The sort of things which Harold knew Bloomsbury affected to despise he, whose horizons were broader than theirs, thoroughly enjoyed. He went to stay at Blenheim Palace. The ex-King of Portugal and Winston Churchill were guests. It was all very grand and pompous; and it was great fun. There was a fête in the afternoon; a ball in the evening. He went for a walk with Professor Lindemann discussing the future of science. A week later he went to stay at Chartwell with the Churchills. The weather was very hot. It was 80 in the shade. Winston was so delighted with his house, which was only fairly nice, that it was a pleasure to witness his enthusiasm. He considered it a paradise on earth, Only the beautiful, sphinx-like Lady Gwendolen (Goonie) Churchill. Harold's friend from Oxford days, the sister of Tata Bertie and now the wife of Winston's younger brother, Jack, was staying, 'and a redheaded Australian journalist called Bracken.[56] A most self-confident and I should think wrong- headed young man.'[57] They motored back to London next day, Winston driving. It was a perilous proceeding. They broke down two or three times on the way.

The summer of 1925 was brimful of delights – dining with Lady Ottoline Morrell and sitting next to Virginia Woolf, whose *Mrs. Dalloway* he was reading in ecstasy, lunching with Lady Ribblesdale, and staying at Sherfield, with, amongst others, Raymond. In truth Harold was by now more in love than he had ever been since his marriage in 1913. He discussed his emotion with Vita, and then wrote to her in somewhat equivocal terms:

> Please realise that it is *not* important – but only important enough to emerge from an emotion to an attitude – and as such implying deception

on my part if concealed. I feel a great load off my chest. I simply loathe to get into a false position with you.[58]

On the contrary the affair was more important to both parties than Harold's words to Vita suggested. The whole thing worried him. He actually expressed the hope that Raymond might care for him less than he cared for Raymond. He did not want to be led into the same predicament that Vita found herself in during her love affair with Violet Trefusis, a predicament from which he had suffered so much. In other words he did not want to lose his head, and his heart, even temporarily, to the extent of causing Vita pain. As though to avoid misunderstanding he warned Raymond against any assumption that he might be tempted to do so. Thus he wrote to him in a round about manner:

It would be too awful if you ever came to resent my ties and my surroundings. You know how much they matter to me and you are an angel of wisdom and tact about it all. You see this sort of thing has never happened to me since I ceased to be irresponsible [although, as he expressed it, 'there have been occasions enough']. I never realised, in my optimistic way, that if it did happen, I should find it difficult to reconcile my desires & my duties. I should like to go away alone with you somewhere for weeks on end. But I can't; and that's the fly in the ointment. But it's a less irksome fly than others might be, and I don't think it need really spoil it all. After all, half a loaf is ever so much better than a whole one.[59]

It is questionable whether Raymond thought so when he made it clear that in Harold he had found the love of a life-time.[60]

Harold certainly did not allow himself to throw his cap over the windmill. He even surprised himself, so he told Raymond, by giving vent to his feelings in his letters to him. Inhibitions made him resentful of these feelings; almost angry with and contemptuous of himself for harbouring them. He was not by nature a very passionate, in spite of being a very lustful man. He was not possessive, although envious of others enjoying the favours that might be denied to him. He managed to keep his emotions under control. Nevertheless Raymond remained 'at the back of everything & everything is conditioned in its importance by reference to you. And, damn it all, what and who are you to have secured so masterful an obsession?'[61]

The obsession, judging by the spate of letters which passed between the two, lasted throughout 1925 and 1926 before settling into a permanent, peaceful and happy affection. And all the while Vita hovered serenely in the background, not disapproving, not minding, but smiling beneficently

LONDON AGAIN 1923-25

upon Raymond. The relationship between the three of them remained unruffled until the end of their days. As Harold wrote to Vita in 1952:

> What a good affectionate friend he is. He is devoted to us. It is a comfort to have such a friendship in one's life. There is a power of sympathy in Tray, not for me, I mean (since I require no sympathy being a happy bumble bee) but for other people less fortunate. The only thing he is unkind about is fraudulence.[62]

Harold was enjoying life so much that he was almost indifferent to the troubles in the diplomatic and political world – the antagonism of China towards the community at Shanghai, the new German objection to the Reparations Pact, and the industrial situation at home which was as black as it could be. What did they matter when Vita had written a really splendid passage on craftsmen in *The Land*? How much more interesting was it discussing with Clive, Virginia and Roger Fry the question whether they were snobbish. The three of them denied that they were either socially or intellectually snobbish. Harold disputed this bold disavowal. They spoke of T. S. Eliot's affected integrity, which Harold again was alone in disputing. He preferred to see in Eliot a tendency to cultural exhibitionism. It was evident in *The Sacred Wood*. When the French Ambassador came to the office begging Harold to take back a Note which he had sent him about inter-Allied debts, and Harold refused, he was indifferent to the whole business and its consequences. He was much more concerned by Elizabeth Bibesco's strange behaviour while staying at Long Barn over the next weekend. She had been in a foul mood and tried to make trouble over Dottie, who was also staying. Poor Vita was ruffled. They were all ruffled, and went to bed feeling that something almost evil had crept into Long Barn. Harold did not believe that Elizabeth was really evil, only so insanely and insatiably egoistic that she liked to destroy relationships. But he feared he had behaved in a detached and timorous manner which was not excusable in a host, and had not been loyal in a husband. The incident – and what it precisely was is not clear – provoked him on his return to London next Monday morning to write Vita a long letter in which he tried candidly to analyse his feelings about her complicated emotional situation at that time.[63]

> My darling, I have been rather worried about the Dottie-Elizabeth business, not because I feel you don't understand, but because I am rather ashamed of myself about it all. I really don't like being mean, and I feel that about that I *was* rather mean.
>
> So let's try and get it all clear:

A (1) *I have a selfish and distinctive dislike of Dottie*:

Because: (a) I am a little jealous because of you. In my foolish moments I think she encourages you to feel and exploit emotional states which would otherwise be controlled. In my wiser moments I regard her as a beneficent safety valve.

(b) I don't like her claustrophobia. I shouldn't like it if it were an eagle-winged and strong pinioned desire for escape. But I should respect it. As it is I regard it as a sparrow-fluttering of egoism – and my dislike is increased by contempt.

(c) I think she is vain and silly. I almost hate her when she tries to be intellectual, since she cannot get her brain round a single impersonal concept. This is increased by (i) intellectual snobbishness on my part at being identified with an intellectual flutter: (ii) jealousy of her poetry – because it is like yours only so much worse. Hence half of my fury when you took me in over her poem (The other half was fury at your tricking me).

(d) I am sore and hurt about Gerry & feel it is her fault. I don't mean I *really* think it her fault, but the Gerry complex tries to get relief by projecting itself on to her.

(2) *I am fond of Dottie*:

(a) Because she is brave and fierce.
(b) Because she is pretty and soft.
(c) Because she is fond of you.
(d) Because one can talk to her about anything.
(e) Because she is rich.

B *I dislike Geoffrey because*

(a) He talks better than I do.
(b) He worries you.
(c) He has got a yellow face & sits up late & is flabby.
(d) Because he is more emotional than I am, and you are impressed by emotion.

C *I am rather a worm with Elizabeth*, because

(a) She sees a lot of people & would be a dangerous enemy.
(b) Laziness on my part.
(c) She is rich and grand.

LONDON AGAIN 1923-25

So you see when my dislike of Dottie, my dislike of Geoffrey, & my wormishness to Elizabeth suddenly fused together, I lost all self-criticism and behaved badly. On the heels of that came my liking for Dottie, & my desire not to make you cross. But although the latter took control for the moment, yet it didn't do so convincingly.

So I felt a shit all day, my sweet.

On the last page he drew a sketch of himself being pursued by the four winged complexes of Dottie, Elizabeth, Geoffrey and Gerry. This letter is, I think, a good example of Harold's determination to be resolutely honest with himself and Vita (a Bloomsbury principle if ever there was one), not to disguise his less estimable sentiments – jealousy and resentment – in regard to her suitors, to subdue that public school monitor's indignation about others not playing the game, and to help Vita sort out another of her recurring muddles.

On the 14th July Harold accompanied Raymond to Paris for two days. Vita wanted to hire for them a private motor, one of her irrational fusses being that French taxi drivers were the most dangerous on earth. But they declined this generous offer. They visited the Exposition des Arts Decoratifs, which they found gay and good, especially some of the Soviet exhibits. Raymond went on to Venice alone and Harold returned to London, very depressed and flat. 'Oh God, you know this is really almost suffering.' he wrote.[64] He was cheered by receiving a letter from Raymond, assuring him that he had never before had a more perfect travelling companion. Harold was 'amazingly unconceited, beautifully thoughtful, never, that I can see, on edge, and I should imagine would never apply to other people severer standards than you observe yourself.'

On the 23rd September Harold was thrown into a quandary. In the office Walford Selby asked him whether he would be willing to go as Counsellor either to Tehran or Peking. Harold's immediate reaction was to refuse both posts for family reasons. He was reluctant to dump the children again at Knole or with Lady Sackville in Brighton. Ben, in particular, who was eleven and a sensitive little boy, needed the constant vigilance of his parents. Vita's journeys backwards and forwards would be more than they could afford. With Lord Carnock and Lady Sackville ill either destination would be too far away. On second thoughts, however, Harold realised that it was always a mistake to turn down a new job in a profession; that the offer meant promotion and in his case a step towards an ambassadorship; and that if Vita only stayed abroad with him in the winter he would not be too lonely without her during the summer. He decided definitely to turn down Peking and to consult Lancelot Oliphant and his father for their views on Tehran.

On his way to the Office next morning he kept turning over the Tehran project gloomily in his mind. He did not want to be selfish about it by considering his career at the expense of Vita's happiness. She would gain nothing by the project, and would lose more than he would. On the other hand he had really reached a turning-point in his career, and if he let slip the opportunity, he would be done for. Besides, of all the foreign posts Tehran would be the one which Vita would dislike least. Oliphant told him flatly that he would be mad to refuse, and advised him to accept at once. He accordingly went down to the Private Secretary's room. Selby was at a committee meeting settling diplomatic appointments. So Harold sent in a colleague to beg him to keep Tehran open for him until Monday. Then he lunched at Cadogan Gardens. His father was loudly persuasive. In the afternoon Selby saw him in the Office, was pleased that he might consent, and indicated that after a year or so it would lead to further promotion. In the evening Harold informed Vita, who was rather dismayed.

He dined with Raymond at Buck's Club and went on to *The Green Hat*. He told him about the Persian project and both were plunged in gloom. Both went to Sherfield for the weekend where they played tennis, bathed and talked a good deal about Persia. A day or two later Raymond wrote, telling Harold how terribly depressed he was at his going away. There was no one whose going he would mind more. Miles Lampson likewise wrote him a letter, saying he was horrified at losing him, who was his mainstay in the Western Department.

As my taxi drives up at the side door of the Office, I see Walford Selby waving at me [Harold wrote][65]. He says that my appointment to Tehran is settled. Go at once and get tickets for Lloyd Triestino for Nov. 4. Dine with Tray and on to *The Offence* with him.

Harold lunched with Lancelot Oliphant and talked about Persia. Oliphant who was six years Harold's senior in age, already a Counsellor and soon to become Assistant Under-Secretary of State, was treated by him as a sort of father confessor. When Harold got to Tehran he would write to him very confidentially about the perplexities of his work, the Persian character (Oliphant had been at the Legation there before the war), his relations with Sir Percy Loraine, the Minister (who was Oliphant's first cousin), and even about the Third Secretary, Gladwyn Jebb's eyelashes – 'Really it is not fair that young men should be so beautiful.' On this occasion Oliphant told Harold he had recommended him to Loraine and gave him a piece of

LONDON AGAIN 1923-25

advice. He must, he warned him, be guided by his head and not by his heart.

Harold had a lot of preparations to make for his journey and long absence in an Asiatic country, like buying leather coats, sun-helmets and a khaki suit at Moss Bros. There were inoculations against typhoid and cholera. Reassurances to Constable's that they might publish his future books. An article to be written – 'On getting stale' – which he had promised his cousin, Ava, for his Eton magazine. Farewell luncheons with the Asquiths (now Lord and Lady Oxford) and the Bibescos; and with Lady Curzon who presented him 'with the dear old Marquis's links, of diamonds and sapphires.' Finally, finishing off at the Office. 'My last day,' he wrote on the 17th, 'in the Central Department after twelve years. Here finishes my career as a civil servant. I have been civil but not servile.'

While Percy Loraine telegraphed to the Secretary of the Foreign Office that no appointment could be more welcome to him, or more completely suitable, 'Warmest thanks,' Virginia in panic was writing, 'My dear Vita, But for how long? For ever? I am filled with envy and despair. Think of seeing Persia – think of never seeing you again.' Vita assured her friend that she merely intended to visit Harold in Persia from time to time, and had no intention of staying there. The remainder of the month was spent by Harold making further farewells, some perfunctory, others painful. Old Gosse gave a special party for him, and was moved. He went to Oxford, and saw Sligger. Then to Summer Fields, where he picked up Ben and took him to Boar's Hill. Ben was distressed at saying goodbye to his father, lent his head against the motor and sobbed, 'I don't like it.'[66] And when Harold left him, wrote a letter, 'My dear Persian Prince, Oh Daddy I thought about you all last night, and I felt what a pity it was for you to go to Persia.' And there was the eight-year-old Nigel who adopted a more stalwart attitude:

> It must feel funny to leave Long Barn for two years, you will forget what it looks like. But it will be lovely to come home to find the new garden blooming with lovely flowers, and your room ... will be arranged by Mummy who will have roses in her hair.

He lunched with his Uncle Freddy Rowan-Hamilton, now an old man of seventy-five, and Aunt Blanche at their home in Surrey. He dined with the Prime Minister. He dined with the Colefaxes, and met Walter de la Mare. He dined at Knole. He dined with Dottie. He spent a last weekend at Long Barn in blazing autumn sunshine. Raymond stayed with them.

On the 3rd November there was last-minute, frenzied shopping with Vita at the Stores. Then he went back to the office for a long farewell to his colleagues. Sir Austen Chamberlain assured him he had no policy in Persia beyond that of Percy Loraine's. Tyrrell was equally uncommunicative. From the Office he went to say goodbye to Aunt Lal Dufferin, Eileen Orde, Geoffrey Scott – and finally, Raymond, who wept. The ghastly round culminated in a family dinner party in Cadogan Gardens. His parents, now the time for departure had arrived, were tearful. These duties done, he went to a supper party at Christabel MacLaren's, where 'all seems very unreal after what I have been through.'[67] And before going to bed he just had time to scrawl a note to Raymond.

> It was almost unendurable saying goodbye to you this evening, and it is a thing I shall never forget . . . Dearest Tray, you are so much to me. You have given me so much. I can't believe that all this will not, in its essence, be durable. Anyway you know that there is someone in the world to whom you are of supreme importance.[68]

Next morning Vita drove him in her blue car, which they called the Kingfisher, to Victoria station, where he registered his heavy luggage to Trieste. After an agonising farewell Harold tore himself away, and boarded the Golden Arrow.

12

JOURNEY TO PERSIA 1925

BEFORE he left on his long journey Harold wrote two letters to Vita which he entrusted to Raymond Mortimer, with instructions that one should be delivered to her only in the event of Lady Sackville, whose health was precarious, being taken ill at the time when Vita was due to join him in Persia. Its content was to urge her not to leave her mother and to excuse her, if obliged to chuck him. The second letter, written in Ebury Street, was to be posted to Vita by Raymond after the 15th November when Harold would be leaving Cairo to cross the deserts, and there was bound to be a gap in the regular flow of their correspondence. He did not want her to feel neglected by him. On the day he left he actually posted her four letters.[1] The first was written on the train to Dover – an anguished love-letter referring to their having wept together in each other's arms that morning; the second on the cross-channel steamer, in which he told her he funked opening his luggage because it would be full of things which reminded him of her, and he was only consoled by the thought of her and Raymond lunching together – 'A perfect dream of a steward has just come for my luggage,' he could not help interpolating. 'Incipit Vita nova. Oh God, it is the old Viti that I prefer.' The third was from Calais, stating that he was delighted to have met on the boat Lionel Smith, a son of the late Master of Balliol, on his way to Iraq where he was Minister of Education; and the fourth in the train to Paris, after he had given way to a flood of weeping, and then turned to read about relativity. He also wrote a loving letter to Raymond, who was much moved by it.

Harold reached Trieste in torrential rain at midnight of the 5th November. He drove to the docks and, boarding the Italian boat for Alexandria, Piroscafo *S.S. Helouan*, went straight to his cabin and slept. Next day in spite of the weather he paced up and down the deck, thinking of his new book. The King of Mesopotamia also walked with great dignity in the opposite direction. 'As I passed him,' Harold told Vita, 'I just, with a slight side-way movement of the hip-joint, indicated that (1) I knew he was a King, (2) I respected his incognito. I am afraid he did not notice me very much.'[2] From Brindisi, the rain still pouring down, the boat crossed the Strait of Otranto. Then the weather cleared, affording a magnificent view of the Albanian mountains above Valona, the great cliffs of limestone glowing in the afternoon sun, the tops wreathed in storm-clouds. It was dark when Corfu was reached. But Harold was up at sunrise to look at the mountains of the Peloponnese against the dawn. By 10 o'clock the ship was opposite Matapan, and Cythera was soon in sight.

While he was contemplating how much Byron would have appreciated the scene before him, a little incident occurred which was to provide him with the subject of his last essay in *Some People*.

> 'Excuse me, sir,' said a gentle voice behind me, 'what is that lovely island?' It was an old lady in a blue veil reading a Tauchnitz Hergesheimer. 'That, madam,' I replied, is the island of Cythera, or Kythera, in modern Greek Cerigo.' 'Oh, indeed!' she said. 'It was the centre,' I explained, 'of the cult of Aphrodite.' She ignored that remark. Looking at me quizzically, but without malice, she said, 'Excuse me, sir, but are you any relation to Sir Ronald Storrs?' I declined that honour. She was evidently sorry ... She looked vaguely at Cythera. 'So that is Cyprus,' she murmured.

This quotation from a letter to Vita of the 9th November coincides practically word for word with the opening lines of *Miriam Codd*. The subsequent story was otherwise wholly imaginary, inspired by the American lady on the boat whom he never saw again.

On reaching Alexandria *S.S. Helouan* was met by a cohort of motor-boats to greet King Feisal on board. One of them brought Harold a letter from Charles Hartopp, now posted to Cairo, who was expecting him to stay. It was handed to him by a handsome and efficient cavass, or mounted messenger, who instantly took him in hand.

He went to call on the High Commissioner at the Residency. This was Sir George Lloyd, to be created that very month Lord Lloyd of Dolobran, whom he had first known in Constantinople before the war. Lloyd had only recently been appointed. A staunch Conservative and unashamed believer in the British imperial mission, he was a man of immense ambition, determination and drive in carrying out improvements for subject races. In spite of Lloyd's affability there was something about him (Jewish, Levantine, Welsh?), he told Vita, which he could not like. Lloyd was in fact one hundred per cent Celtic, without a drop of English blood in his veins.

He was invited to dine at the Residency. It was a formal and chilly meal. The guests were herded together and then lined up in order of precedence. The Lloyds entered the reception-rooms accompanied by a bevy of trimly uniformed aides-de-camps. The guests' names were shouted out as though they were on parade. Harold was allotted to Lady Lloyd, whom he piloted into the dining-room behind her husband, stalking solemnly, in vice-

JOURNEY TO PERSIA 1925

regal isolation. The bowing, the curtseying, the pomp and drinking of the King's health prevented relaxed conversation and enjoyment, in spite of Harold's fondness for Lady Lloyd. It was precisely the proconsular manner of life which he detested. Before the guests dispersed homewards, the High Commissioner invited Harold to accompany him on a visit of inspection. 'I have to go on Thursday to Alexandria,' he said, 'to see the King, and after that I want to visit a model market-village we are constructing at the very edge of the desert, at a place called Burgh El Arab.'[3]

At 7.30 that morning Harold rose, had a cup of tea, dressed in his neatest suit and walked from Hartopp's flat to the Residency. In the street outside a guard of honour and two police cars stood ready. In front of the Residency door were a vast Rolls Royce and a vast Daimler with flags on their mudguards. Scarlet-clad cavasses came, put despatch boxes into the two motor cars, and went. A bell rang. Four policemen on motor bicycles took up their position on either side of the door. The Lloyds stepped briskly into the Rolls Royce. A bugle sounded. The motor bicycles started to splutter, and the cavalcade slid off at a frightful pace, past the guards presenting arms, and through the dense traffic halted by policemen. In the motor the two aides-de-camps made polite conversation with their hands on revolvers. The station yard had been cleared, and a red carpet, edged with ferns and flanked by policemen, led to the platform. The whole Egyptian Cabinet were waiting to conduct the party into a slim, white special train. From the platform a guard of Highlanders climbed into the train after the High Commissioner's party, and stood with fixed bayonets at every doorway. There were four saloons and a dining car. Harold had a saloon to himself, and was served a kipper for breakfast. He spent a happy two hours reading Herodotus, and thinking how much Vita would have enjoyed and been amused by the expedition.

All along the line guards were posted at hundred-yard intervals, with rifles at the salute. Civilians inclined their bodies in respectful salutation as the train passed. At Sidi Gabea station, Alexandria, there were more red carpets and soldiers. Lord Lloyd had a great sense of occasion. There was a political crisis on and he intended to impress King Fuad's subjects with the might and majesty of His Britannic Majesty's representative. At 11 o'clock their Excellencies were driven away at a smart pace for the High Commissioner's audience with King Fuad. Whereupon Harold, a roll of bath towel ('not very viceregal') under one arm, dashed off with R. A. Furness, the Oriental Secretary, a nice, friendly intellectual, to the villa of a Mrs. Borschvedinck, with cool tiled floors and a canary singing in a cage. There they bathed. Harold took care to be back in the train, which had chugged round to the Western Station, by the time the Lloyds returned to their saloon car. At luncheon Lloyd repeated to Harold in high glee what he had said to King Fuad and what King Fuad had replied to him. After luncheon he sent for his secretary and the red boxes, and dictated.

In the early afternoon the train reached Burgh El Arab, which was situated close to the sea-shore, on the fringe of the Libyan desert, littered with the remains of Roman temples and Arab tombs. From the station they drove in a Ford car at snail, or to be precise, camel pace, with an escort of the Egypt Camel Corps beside them, to the model village. It lay behind high walls, with Saracenic battlements and closed balconies projecting over the open desert. An arched gateway led to an enclosure. Delicately the camels stepped from light to shade, their riders sitting hunched upon their saddles, their rifles propped against the pommels. Burgh El Arab contained a market to which the desert folk came to buy their provisions. There were warehouses and store-rooms, and cool whitewashed offices. Over the compound presided the District Commissioner, a strange little man called Colonel Bramley, who had built the court-house and fashioned the whole settlement. After two hours, in which the High Commissioner inspected every corner and peered into every cranny with intense interest and enthusiasm, they returned to Cairo in the viceregal train, dining as they went.

On the 15th Harold left Cairo by train on the first stage of his journey to Baghdad. He crossed the Suez Canal in a ferry, like a Maidenhead houseboat, to El Qantara on the Asiatic bank.

At Lydda he woke up. There then ensued a slow, twisting, panting climb through the bare, rounded Judaean hills, on which a few crocuses were in flower. The train emerged upon a stony plateau with a huddle of buildings, which was Jerusalem. In those days the city occupied no more space than that between Balliol and Magdalen colleges, in Oxford. Jerusalem was by far the least spoilt eastern city Harold had yet seen. He made straight for the house of Ronald Storrs,[4] the Governor of Jerusalem and Judea, for a wash and change. And then to Thomas Cook's office to make arrangements for the completion of his journey. In the 1920s the route from Jerusalem to Tehran was an unpredictable and often hazardous one. There was no direct railway. There were no passenger air-flights. There were no metalled roads, and no buses. Two Australian brothers, by the name of Nairn, operated regular caravans of motor-cars across the deserts as far as Baghdad. The vehicles were ramshackle and untrustworthy, and they were always fully booked ahead. Moreover they were frequently hijacked by bandits, the passengers robbed and their luggage looted. In winter the flimsy bridges were apt to be swept away by floods. After much discussion with Storrs and telegraphing to Cairo there appeared to be no alternative to the Nairn transport. Harold reconciled himself to waiting for a motor and a vacant seat. In the meantime he went

JOURNEY TO PERSIA 1925

sight-seeing. He visited the Holy Sepulchure at dusk. He walked with Ronald Storrs to Bethlehem and back.

He spent the whole of the 19th at the Hotel Allenby trying to board one of the Nairn convoy motors. He failed to persuade a passenger to vacate a seat, trying in vain to exercise his diplomatic privilege (it so happened that he was officially promoted to Counsellor that very day). Instead he watched the convoy leave without him. 'Wretched and furious,' he returned to Ronald Storrs's house. On the next day, having visited the Ecce Homo convent, and seen the pavement on which Pilate sat, he was successful in getting a seat in a car of the second Nairn convoy. He left the 'foul' Hotel Allenby, swung across the Jordan, and drove until midnight to Amman. There Harold opened a birthday letter from Vita which he had received two days before, but would not read until he could do so in the right surroundings. These turned out to be a bell-tent over campbeds of which his was one, all within a barbed wire enclosure. At last he was on the route to Persia.

The convoy started off again at dawn on the 21st, his birthday. The country traversed was a sort of downland, then a waste of shale, then sandy hillocks, a terrible sector of lava, and then mud-flats. Harold was driven nearly mad by the unnecessary delays, the incompetence of the driver and the faulty engine which kept breaking down. At 1 o'clock the next morning they reached Rutba Wells. Here they only stopped for warm drinks and the relief of nature in primitive conditions. On and on they drove through the dark, with a hemisphere of white stars above and a wide arc of the headlights thrown before them. At 10 o'clock they reached Ramadi on the right bank of the Euphrates. After Ramadi the going improved and they made an excellent seventy-mile dash to Falluja, having crossed to the left bank of the river. From there another dash, this time at seventy miles an hour for long stretches across the desert, with mirages popping up ahead. Suddenly a factory chimney soared above a cluster of palms. It was Baghdad. They arrived at 3.30 in the afternoon.

After a wash and a shave at the Hotel Maude Harold called on Gertrude Bell, with whom Vita was to stay on her way to Tehran the following spring and who was to die mysteriously a few months later. She was Oriental Secretary to the High Commissioner in Iraq. In *Passenger to Teheran* Vita gave an account of her house. It was entered by a creaking door in a blank wall by an Arab servant displaying a broad smile. A path, edged with carnations in pots led across a courtyard to a low building at the far end. A white pony lent over a stable door. Dogs rushed from every corner to greet the visitor. The rooms were piled high with English books; the shelves with Babylonian shards. Gertrude Bell, with her long thin nose and enormous vitality, which belied extreme frailty, advanced, eager, enthusiastic and friendly. Harold did not, like Vita, stay the night, and so missed the tame partridge which slept on top of the cupboard in the guest's bedroom. He found the little house hot and stuffy; but his hostess 'adorable', and a rich, generous mine of information about conditions in the Middle East.

That evening he took the train for Khanaqin, the last Iraq town before the Persian frontier was reached. He had a comfortable saloon carriage and bathroom. He arrived at 7 next morning and breakfasted at the station buffet. From Khanaqin onwards his journey across the Persian plains was again to be by road. A small, dilapidated Dodge motor-car, the property of the Eastern Transport Company, met him at the station. The windows were broken and there was little room for his feet. Into this horrid vehicle Harold, the Foreign Office bag and three other passengers were crammed. Their luggage followed behind in lorries. In hideous discomfort they bumped along to the Persian frontier, where was a ramshackle hut and a crazy pole across the road. Almost immediately they had to tackle the dense range of Kermanshah mountains which provides Persia's formidable western barrier. Very slowly the Dodge reached the Peitak Pass. Up and up it struggled along the road made by British troops in 1918 out of the ancient caravan route to the East. To left and right the views of bleak, bare mountains were limitless. The journey was frequently halted by punctures. At last the Dodge came to a straight piece of road, accelerated, and, crash! fell into a trench dug across the road. The driver feared that brigands, warned of their coming, had prepared an ambush. Driver and passengers managed to pull the car out of the trench. There was a tinkling sound. The exhaust pipe fell off. They tied it on with string, and confronted another pass. The steering went wrong. Darkness fell. At Kermanshah in the heart of the Kurd country, at an altitude of 5,600 feet, Harold stayed the night with the Consul and his wife, called Cowan, who were expecting him. They were nice, friendly, provincial people, but their house was bitterly cold.

On the 24th they were to have left at 9 o'clock, but at 10.30 a message came that the driver could not start the Dodge. They did not leave till 2.30, and now the Ottoman Bank Manager of Kermanshah joined the carload. Harold was captivated by the beauty of the country round Hamadan. 'It seizes one by the throat,' he wrote. They covered great plains flat as billiard tables, encircled by mountains a hundred miles in the distance. And over the expanse a pink light, as of sunset, even in blazing noon. The journey was thrilling in prospect and retrospect, but the actual travel was an ordeal. The car seemed to crawl like some tiny insect across the illimitable vastness without appreciably advancing. At Hamadan Harold stayed

JOURNEY TO PERSIA 1925

with the Vice-Consul in a delicious old Persian house with low ceilings, and surrounded by trim poplars.

Next morning he was up at 5, expecting to start at 6. But the car did not turn up till 9.45. In a fury with oriental incompetence and lack of time-sense he walked up and down the streets of Hamadan. That day they had to tackle the Aveh Pass where snow was a hazard. There were also more punctures, which delayed progress. They arrived at Qasvin at 6 o'clock, too late to continue. Harold stayed with the Bank Manager. On the 26th all went well to start with. They left at 9 and drove towards Karej when, crash! – the back springs of the Dodge broke. They were beyond the resource of the driver to mend. There was nothing to be done but walk the four miles to Karej and telephone for another motor. At Karej they waited until a Ford car appeared, bringing some excellent beer and cold partridge from the Legation. Harold and his companions drank and ate these provisions in the courtyard of the inn when suddenly a gholam, a red-coated guard in uniform, came in, saluted and announced that the Minister was outside. Harold ran out of the courtyard to find Sir Percy Loraine[5] sitting in a yellow Legation motor, surrounded by black retrievers, the very picture of an English sportsman equipped for the grouse moors. Harold's luggage was bundled into the yellow car. The last twenty-five miles of his long journey to Tehran were accomplished in style. He watched the sunset turn the bare hills to scarlet while Sir Percy announced that news had just been received of the death of Queen Alexandra.

On arrival at the Legation he was handed seventeen letters from Vita which he read by a fire in his bedroom. He felt happy for the first time since he had left England.

Sir Percy Loraine, 12th Baronet, although only six years older than Harold, might have belonged to a previous generation. Harold called him the best type of 1860 country gentleman. He was slow, sure, and ponderous. And his judgements were usually sound. He was immensely conscious of the dignity of his profession, the superiority of the British way of life to any other, and the British methods of diplomacy. A slight figure of fun in that he looked like a stage ambassador, he became a victim of Harold's sharp wit, which he did not altogether relish. Nevertheless he eventually won his Counsellor's esteem and even affection. Lady Loraine (Louise) was on the other hand void of charm. She was whiny, conceited, bad-mannered and sulky. One day she was agreeable and seemed pleased to see a person, and the next she pretended that he was not there. She had poor health, yellow eyes and a chocolate coloured face. Like all Guthries (she was one through her mother) her laugh was an ugly cackle which shattered with its resonance the favourable opinion she had with infinite trouble endeavoured to establish by a well contrived social manner. She made few friends in Tehran, finding the other officials' wives dull, and all the Persian ladies sticky. Her closest companion was Hilda Arfa, an English dancer from the Diaghilev ballet, married to General Hassan Arfa, who after the Second World War became Persia's Commander-in-Chief. Lady Loraine annoyed Harold, and Vita, by a habit of laughing at what was unusual and different from things and customs to which she had been brought up, such as the elastic-sided boots worn by Prime Minister Ferughi, and the oriental mysticism all Persians implicitly believed and dabbled in. Vita in retrospect dubbed her a 'sour little lemon.'

The Legation staff was enormous. There were soldiers, archivists, interpreters and dragomen; military attachés, oriental secretaries, a doctor, typists and Indian sowars. Godfrey Havard, the Oriental Secretary was a nice reserved man with a French wife. The Military Attaché, Major W. A. K. Fraser, had a nice, simple horsey wife. But the two diplomatic members proper, with whom Harold had to work closely and both of whom he liked immediately were the Second Secretary, Christopher Warner, and the Third Secretary, Gladwyn Jebb. The former, Harold wrote home to Vita on his first day in the Chancery, is 'erudite, slightly uncouth, efficient, rather attractive. The latter of great beauty (half Hugh Thomas and half Lady Curzon) and possessing a gentle charm. Rather shy at first.' Jebb was in those early days of his career indeed painfully shy. He was also very young. Harold, at first a little perplexed by his apparent aloofness, intellectual reserve, and almost virginal standards of honour and uprightness, became extremely fond of him during the two years in which they worked and took their recreation together. After a twelvemonth Harold referred to him as 'so clean and healthy and intelligent, and with it all so broad-minded and amused. This place would indeed be different without him.' Harold respected him. 'I should like Ben to be like Gladwyn,' he said.

Gladwyn Jebb had already been at the Legation a year. When he went there in 1924 Tehran was, he has since written in his memoirs,[6]

> an almost completely medieval town, surrounded by a deep ditch and large mud walls, or ramparts, in which were set a number of lovely gates, with two or four minaret-like towers, covered with blue and yellow tiles,

perhaps modern but in the old Persian tradition. The streets were unpaved, and along the sides ran rivulets of clear water from the melting snow on

JOURNEY TO PERSIA 1925

the Elburz mountains. Within a matter of minutes one could ride from the centre of the town straight into the surrounding country.

> The inside of the town [Lord Gladwyn continues] was like a vast garden... centering round the bazaar,

which was properly roofed in, and not like the bazaar at Baghdad, covered with tin.

> The whole area had a wonderful aromatic smell which seemed to derive basically from pistachio nuts, the Persian nougat, known as *gaz*, charcoal fires, the local flat bread or *nan*, sherbet, recently worked leather, saffron, peaches, hemp and tobacco, which, once smelt, was unforgettable, as indeed, once tasted, is the delicious Persian food.

The real centre of the city was the British Legation, then as now a rectangular Compound surrounded by walls. In a truly spacious garden shaded by immensely tall Persian plane trees with silvery boles, and lawns watered by tanks perpetually filled with rivulets of water, there was, and is, a congeries of dusty red brick buildings, with gloomy round-headed, or Byzantine windows, like Victorian rectories or the precincts of Wormwood Scrubs. The Compound was erected in 1870. The largest and most imposing structure was the Legation residence crouching low over a private garden of weeping willows, oleanders and water-tanks. To the north rose an absurd detached clock-tower of the same dusty brick, the clock having been shipped from Glasgow in 1870. In one of the rectory-like houses Harold had been born when his father was Secretary at the Legation in the 1880s. In another he went to live forty years later. It was situated on the east side of the Compound, a little to the north of the Guard House where the present new entrance is. A few years ago the Fedowsi Avenue was widened so as to encroach upon the Compound. Both Guard House and Harold's house were then demolished.

Robert Byron called the Compound a Victorian lunatic asylum. Another kindlier visitor described it as 'an English public school without the boys.'

The Chancery, Harold told Vita, 'is exactly like all other chanceries, even to the smell of sealing-wax and mail bags.'[7] But his, or as he put it, their house, was a terrible disappointment. He drew a plan indicating its situation. A private garden was non-existent and there was nowhere to sit out of doors without being overlooked by everyone who came in and out of the Compound. As for the inside, it was awkward and bleak. He also drew a plan of the rooms downstairs and up, showing how he proposed to make improvements to Vita's bedroom. His predecessor,

Monson's[8] furniture was so incredibly ugly that he refused to buy more than the absolute essentials. Rather touchingly he assumed that, after her two months' visit in the spring, Vita would come back in the autumn to live with him permanently. He said he knew she would not mind camping in the house during her first visit. 'Oh darling, what a relief that sort of thing is for the Mars. We know exactly what the other can put up with; it is just as though one were making arrangements for oneself.' As for Monson's five servants, they were all so bad that Harold sacked the lot, except the cook, and engaged a sort of valet-butler. He bought Monson's horse, which was an old crock. He was going to ride it to Gulahek with the Loraines that afternoon.

Gulahek, he explained, was the British summer Legation. It was to Tehran what Therapia was to Stamboul, but not so close. It was a village, seven miles from the capital, on the foothills of the Elburz, which formed a steep protective screen to the village on the north. The ground began to rise the moment one left the town-gates, and climbed the dusty track across grey desert relieved by little oases of gardens. Imposing iron gates between white brick piers are the entrance to the Legation garden of superb trees, mostly mature planes, loosely shaven lawns and rushing, clear streams. The residence is far from unattractive. It is in the Georgian colonial style. A colonnade under a pediment is approached by steps rising from the drive on the entrance front. The garden front has a first floor open colonnade, much used by the Minister during the summer months. Below it is a big octagonal tank, or basin of marble lined with old Persian tiles. The grounds are, but for the hum of the main road, fairly quiet, and in summer time the chorus of the nightingales' song reduces the splashing of the waters to silence. Dotted about the grounds and discreetly concealed by trees are the modest, cottage-like dwellings of the Secretaries and servants. It was at Gulahek that Harold passed his happiest days, especially when in the absence of the Minister he became Chargé d'Affaires. Under the odd terms of the presentation of Gulahek to Great Britain in the 1830s by Muhammas Shah, the municipal and judicial administration of the village was put in the hands of the British Legation. Consequently all Gulahekists were exempt from military service in the Persian army.

Harold took up his duties at the Tehran Legation at a very critical moment in Persia's history. To understand the problems with which British diplomats were faced in 1925 it is necessary to know something of the relations between Britain and Persia over the past hundred years. They had been very close, if not always cordial, for Persia's emergence out of

JOURNEY TO PERSIA 1925

total oriental isolation into contact with the western world was chiefly due to Britain. And Britain's interest in Persia had not been wholly objective. Since the early nineteenth century she and Russia had been bitter rivals in the interference with Persian internal affairs. In the minds of successive British Governments dread of Russian expansion towards India through Persia had been constant and real.

In the autumn of 1909 came an upheaval in the Persian constitution. The autocratic Shah Mahommed Ali abdicated in favour of his son, Sultan Ahmed, thus ending the country's long struggle against despotism. Both Great Britain and Russia sympathised with the new regime, and under the Anglo-Russian Convention, which resulted, the latter Power withdrew her troops from Qasvin and Tabriz. The next year the situation changed. The ex-Shah returned from exile, actually crossed Russian territory and marched on Tehran. The capital held out and he was defeated. Russia was made indignant by this abortive move, and became deeply suspicious of Persia's motives. In 1912 she lent herself to a foolish and disgraceful action at the shrine of Iman Reza at Meshed, which was the chief pilgrimage centre in Persia. The Russian Consul-General, after some local disturbance, bombed the tomb, damaging it seriously. This wanton desecration of their country's holiest shrine was never forgiven by the Persians. But Russia's unpopularity with the Persians did not endear the British to them. Far from it. In 1917 the Bolshevik Government published the terms of a secret treaty, called the Constantinople Agreement of March 18th, 1915, in which Britain and Imperial Russia had agreed to incorporate within their respective spheres of influence the south (to us the Persian Gulf and access to our oil-wells being of paramount importance) and the north of Persia. From 1917 onwards therefore Britain was no longer regarded as the disinterested well-wisher but an insidious imperialist Power with an eye to annexing Persian territory. Russian danger on the contrary was regarded as lessened by her pre-occupation with the Revolution. When in August 1919 another Convention, organized by Curzon, was signed between Britain and Persia, by which we made Persia financial and military loans, it was resented. The Majlis, or Persian National Assembly, actually denounced it.

In May 1920 the Bolsheviks, posing as champions of Persian nationalism against the British, bombarded Enzeli on the Caspian Sea, occupied Resht, and were about to march on Tehran. There was panic in the capital, and the Persians were in thorough confusion. Only British threats prevented further Russian encroachments. But now a group of patriots took over the reins in Tehran. By a *coup d'état* in February 1921 a Cossack division seized power from the Government without opposition. Their leader was a senior officer risen from the ranks, and of fairly humble origin, although his father had been a Colonel in the Persian Army. The Colonel died when the son was a mere child. Consequently the son was penniless and deprived of all education other than military. Nevertheless Reza Pahlevi rose to be Commander-in-Chief and Minister for War. Having restored order the first thing he did was to see that his troops received adequate pay. Next he took away all privileges and titles from the nobility; he loosened the Moslem clergy's grip on many phases of public life; and he set about depriving foreign specialists of posts of authority, merely consenting to employ them as technicians. He abrogated the Anglo-Persian Convention made by Lord Curzon. By the autumn of 1923 Reza Khan became Prime Minister. In November Shah Sultan Ahmed left the country of his own accord. In the spring of 1924 Reza Khan attempted to set up a Republic with himself as President, but the project was prevented by the mullahs (holy men, learned in religious law), who were aware that the precedent in Turkey under Ataturk had brought about the abolition of the Caliphate. In the autumn of 1925 Reza Khan deposed the Shah, and was himself elected to the vacant throne by the practically unanimous vote of the Majlis. Britain remained studiedly impartial throughout these operations and Sir Austen Chamberlain strongly affirmed his total disinterestedness, merely announcing that he would observe all previous treaties made with Persia. Reza Khan was suitably impressed by these assurances. Thus after 150 years fell the Qajar dynasty of Persia, and the Peacock Throne was ascended by an upstart, a man of aggressive nationalist intentions, and with no reason to be well disposed to this country. Lord Curzon, when Foreign Secretary, had the vision to recognize that Reza Khan was a man of destiny to be reckoned with. The moment Reza seized power in 1921 the Marquis withdrew, in a somewhat high-handed manner it is true, the British Minister at Tehran, Herman Norman, and replaced him with the man he considered best capable of getting on with the Persian leader. His choice was Percy Loraine.

Lord Curzon was not mistaken. By the time Harold Nicolson arrived in Tehran Loraine had been Minister for four years. He had completely won Reza Khan's confidence, and indeed affection. Reza sent for the British Minister for advice about domestic as well as foreign affairs, and listened even when he did not always accept it. It was extraordinary how neither his ministers nor the prominent Persian dignitaries seemed to resent the English diplomat's influence with their master. On the contrary they respected and liked him. Not for years had a British representative been so popular in Persian official circles.

According to General Hassan Arfa[9] the chief subjects at issue with the British Government in the autumn of 1925 were our demand to use Persian territory for Imperial Airways; a settlement of the sums of money which had been advanced to Persia by us after the war; and our insistence that the Persian Government should compensate Sheikh Khazal of Mohammerah for the property confiscated from him by Reza Khan. The last issue was regarded by the British Government as one of honour, because it was to Sheikh Khazal that in 1916 by a secret agreement we had paid a huge indemnity for the oil-fields in his territory and for his reduction to compliance of the Bakhtiari tribes within his territory. Struggle for a just restitution of the aggrieved Sheikh's rights in money, since his territories could not be restored, was one of the chief worries to concern Harold, while he was Counsellor in Tehran, and even to pursue him after his retirement.

In fact a visit to the Sheikh of Mohammerah was one of the very first duties Harold had to perform after his arrival. He went the rounds of the capital and left cards on those notable Persian personalities with whom he was likely to have diplomatic and social contacts.[10] The Sheikh was one of them. On the 1st December Sir Percy introduced Harold, who told Vita:

> The Sheikh of Mohammerah is a sort of independent feudal despot who tried to fight Reza Khan and got the worst of it. He was brought up here as a sort of honoured prisoner. We are trying to help him out of his mess. His house was all dark and filled with henchmen carrying little lanterns. His beautiful sons on the staircase, ranged in order of precedence, were dressed in purple and gold. He was dressed in black silk and gold at the top of the stairs. We were led into an overheated room and given tea and cakes round an oval table with a flower pot in the middle. He wanted money. He had beautiful hands which he extended. 'I have been used to give; it is painful for me to have to ask,' he said.

Minister and Counsellor then went on to pay a visit to the ex-Governor of Khorassan, Hismet-ed-Douleh. He was sitting on his foot and smoking a pipe with a diamond mouthpiece. He knew all about his guest, and said that he was learned and famous. The next day Sir Percy introduced Harold to the Minister for Foreign Affairs, the head of the Protocol, and his assistant. Harold asked Vita to send him urgently a new top hat and other suitable social adornments, for he soon realised that Loraine did not consider him what he called 'touf touf enough'.

> He is himself rather pomposo, and justifies it by the old bromide, 'But these sort of things mean so much to Orientals.' And of course I loathe going about in grand clothes and with cavasses, and like just pottering in an old suit, or going shooting with Jebb in the old rickety Ford ... Then there is my pipe, poor little thing, which is a great offence.[11]

Harold moved into his house. Until the Office of Works furniture arrived it remained very bare. He feared the furniture might not arrive before Vita. He had a new servant, called Taghi, a Persian who maddened Harold with his stupidity – 'an old dunderhead but such a darling' – and kept the house clinically clean. He was lonely, and dined by himself most evenings, reading Trollope's *Doctor Thorne* and the poems of T. S. Eliot, which fascinated him. There were no tourists or foreign visitors from mid-November to mid-April because the roads from Baghdad were virtually impassable owing to the snow. Everything in the shops was fearfully expensive, and bad. He enjoyed the paperchases on horseback with the staff. From a short distance outside the town gates Tehran was almost invisible. Every house had a garden and no house was more than two storeys high. Consequently one looked across a patch of brown rooftops and green foliage, with a grey veil of lazy smoke from the chimneys. As the sun set, the hills turned first scarlet, then a green lead colour.

He attended the opening of the Constituent Assembly by Reza Khan in the old Royal Theatre, or Circus, called the Takyre Doular, covered by a huge awning on steel supports. Five or six priests dressed in shabby robes lolled at the foot of the platform. Reza was an alarming man, immense, with a prominent nose, grizzled hair and a brutal jowl. He looked what he was, a Cossack trooper, but there was no denying that he had a kingly presence. He was handed a paper. He heaved a tremendous sigh, and, in a tiny voice like a child's, gabbled out a speech. Then he turned to go. The priests crowded round him. He pushed them aside impatiently, and walked quickly out of the Circus.

On the 12th Harold was present at the crucial meeting of the Constituent Assembly, again held in the Circus, to confirm officially that Reza Khan should become Shah. He wrote a long, detailed description of the proceedings to Vita. It is not without comical interest.

> We got there about 3.30 and sat in a sort of box. At least it was called a box but it was really a sort of wine-bin tiled inside. They were discussing whether it mattered that Reza Khan's mother was a Circassian and not a Persian. They got terribly tied up into knots over this discussion and the President kept on ringing his little bell rather aimlessly. Then a funny little man in a black turban and a dressing gown got into the tribune and said it didn't matter what his mother was so long as she was Moslem. They had never thought of that and were so pleased with the idea that they all clapped their hands. Then they got on to the second point which was that of the succession. The Government proposal was that Reza should be succeeded by 'his eldest male descendant'. They got up and said this might mean a nephew. The Government got up and said it couldn't mean a nephew, and embarked on a very frank and

JOURNEY TO PERSIA 1925

horticultural exposition of the mysteries of generation. But a very venerable man then hobbled into the tribune and said that nothing was apt more often to go wrong than the act of fecundation – & he then began to tell a long story about a mule till they told him to sit down. He pushed his turban over his eyes & returned sulkily to his place, still muttering something about a mule. He was succeeded by a spruce gentleman in a black fez & a grey frock-coat. This gentleman was very superior and sarcastic about his fellow members, & ended by proposing that instead of the words 'male descendant' they should insert the word 'boy'. The effect was stupendous. Two thirds of the members rose in their seats. Even the President nodded his appreciation. The point was carried. The final point was at what age the Valiahd, or Crown Prince, should succeed. The Government suggested 20. The gentleman in the grey frock-coat, encouraged by his previous success, suggested 25. By then, he said, one could tell whether the young man was, or was not, going to be insane. He was contradicted by a doctor, who said that of all ages 25 was the worst at which to gauge insanity. It must be either 7, 14, 21 or 28 – but never 25. This puzzled them all terribly and there was a long pause. At last a little man in a skull cap limped up to the tribune, unrolled a whole sheaf of notes, put them down on the green baize in front of him, pushed his glasses up on to his forehead, took a deep breath, and said, – 'I suggest ten.' They were all rather startled by this proposal. There was a respectful silence. But the man in the skull cap did not continue his speech. He merely glared at them, turning himself round in each sector of the semi-circle, repeating the Alexandrine gesture with which he had accompanied his proposal. This was too much for the man in the grey frock-coat. He rose with slow affability in his place. 'I should be glad,' he drawled, 'if the venerable member would explain to the Constituent Assembly his exact reasons for suggesting the age of ten as suitable for the attainment of his majority by the heir to the Imperial Throne of Iran.' The little man in the tribune crossed his arms heroically: he glared round at them circularly from left to right, and then from right to left: then he flicked his glasses on to his nose again, and very slowly began to read his notes. Suddenly he flung them down again, flicked up his glasses, clenched his fist and yelled, 'I *suggest ten.*' At this pandemonium was let loose. Everybody waved their papers, and the President rang his bell with both hands. After about five minutes silence was restored. The President leant forward towards the little man who occupied the tribune. 'The Assembly,' he said, 'would be grateful to the hon. member if he would explain his proposal.' Again the little man went through the business of picking up his notes and flinging them fiercely down again: then he spread his arms wide open like Mr. William Jennings Bryan & said in a voice of great holiness, 'I withdraw my proposal.' They all took this quite naturally & the Government's proposal was then carried unanimously.

This completed the detailed discussion. There remained the main resolution offering the throne to Reza Khan. The Secretary to the Assembly read out the resolution in a low voice & with much discussion with his assistant as to the meaning of some of the words. It took a long time. At one stage the Government photographer came in & they all stopped while they were being photographed. Then some soldiers turned a hose on the awning from outside. This was a good idea because of the dust: only it was then 6 p.m. & quite dark & the water made a noise like a machine gun and descended in a cascade on the heads of the groups of gendarmes who were standing in the far corner. The Constituent Assembly simply loved that part & they laughed & clapped their hands. Then the old Secretary began reading again, but had again to stop because people began shovelling coal on the twenty huge stoves that ran round the building. They took each stove one by one, & made over each stove a noise like an aeroplane ascending. But everybody was quite happy & shouted jokes & went across & talked to each other. And then the reading began again. When it was over three servants advanced in awful solemnity carrying two soup tureens & a silver basin. They then handed the soup tureens round the Assembly & each member threw in a little bit of paper. Then the tureens and the basin were gathered together on the tribune & the Secretary began taking out each bit of paper, glancing at it, & then throwing it into the basin – counting aloud as he did so. There were two hundred and seventy members, & two hundred and sixty-seven votes. There was no contrary vote – only three abstentions. When the President read out the votes everybody stood up including ourselves. There was no applause. They all sat down again, & as we left, the President began to drone out: – 'We must now elect representatives to convey to His Imperial Majesty the King of Kings, Reza Shah Pahlevi, the humble congratulations of this Constituent Assembly on the occasion of . . .'

So that's that.[12]

Throughout this Alice in Wonderland scene one old Qajar Prince, Farman Farma, sat on the presidential steps, holding his head in his hands, gazing at his boots and bemoaning the distressing tides of fortune which had relegated his dynasty to dust and ashes and raised to greatness a phoenix in the shape of a Cossack ranker of no breeding or antecedents.

Harold was settling down for the winter. His social activities were restricted. Lunch with the Frasers, tea with Gladwyn Jebb, dinner and poker with the Loraines. He was buoyed up by the joyful prospect of welcoming Vita in the early spring. He sent her instructions by what routes she was to come, and what clothes she should bring. Everyone in Tehran dressed shabbily. One evening dress would be enough; and no riding-habit was necessary. She would ride astride. A memorable day was when the bag brought her letters, often as many as fourteen at a time. The

JOURNEY TO PERSIA 1925

next day he would feel rather flat after the surfeit. Then unexpectedly two paintings of Long Barn by Ian Campbell-Gray arrived by mail. They delighted him but made him home-sick.

The Sheikh of Mohammerah returned Harold's call, bringing with him one of his beautiful sons. He sighed over the sorrows which afflicted those persons of eminence, including himself, who had defied Reza Khan in vain. He sat for hours at Harold's stove, spitting into it and drinking endless cups of tea, smoking cigarettes and speaking in parables like an Old Testament prophet. And then Harold was taken by Sir Percy to be presented to the new Shah at the Gulistan Palace.

We were shown into a little white room with a huge fire and atrocious Louis XVI furniture. The room gave on to a sort of balcony or loggia and we hadn't been there long before the windows were darkened by an immense figure passing along in front of them. He opened the end window and came in. He was in khaki uniform with a peaked khaki hat, slashed at the corners ... He hadn't shaved very well and glowered out of the corner of his eye at us. He was quite alone. He is about six foot three and inclined to corpulence. He has fat red hands like Gerry's. He has bad teeth, fine eyes and chin, and a determined nose. A clipped greyish moustache. But he looks cross and tired and dirty. Then he sat down. I told him of the interest he aroused in England and how we hoped he would make a good kind Shah. He was pleased by these assertions and relaxed. He gave us cigarettes and cake and tea. Suddenly he took his hat off, disclosing a tiny little shaven head like a Russian cossack. He looked more of a scallywag than ever. But then gradually he began to talk quite calmly about becoming Shah, and his arrangements for his coronation, and how cross everyone was, and how he had felt his collar too tight at the opening ceremony, and how Farman Farma had been photographed sitting on the steps. And then he laughed a sort of non-commissioned officer laugh, and asked me how old I was. He wouldn't believe it when I told him and said evidently I had had no troubles in love or politics. I thought of my darling digging away over there at our mud-pie. Then he laughed a great deal and for the rest of the interview was simple and jolly, and with a certain force and dignity. But I am not so sure about him ... Anyway he was very cordial and told me to come and see him as often as I liked when he was Shah. He adores Percy, and Percy is rather pleased with himself (and with justice) at having backed a winner from the start – and such a winner.[13]

On the 15th Harold laid aside the Memorandum about the Duzdap Railway which he was writing, in order to witness the Shah take the oath in the Majlis. The whole Legation staff went in uniform, furnished with cards to leave afterwards. Reza made rather a floater in forgetting to kiss the Koran. After reading aloud the oath with difficulty (a year ago he could not read at all) he walked away and had to be hauled back. All the guests followed to the Gulistan Palace and Harold nearly fell into a pool when his sword got between his legs. At the Ceremony of the Salaam the next day Reza was resplendent, covered from head to chest in diamonds and emeralds.

Harold was determined to master the Persian language which few of his colleagues succeeded in doing. The very first day after his arrival he engaged a Persian to give him lessons. Each lesson was something of an ordeal, for pride dictated to the teacher, who naturally received payment, that it should be a social occasion. One evening Harold was obliged to dine with his teacher. This meant arriving at 7.30 and sitting in an overheated room for two hours. At 9.30 an enormous spread appeared, consisting of soup, rice in different forms, lamb, turkey, pilaff, creams, melon and, to drink, a liquid yoghout. During and after such gargantuan meals it was the custom among Persians to recite poetry. Harold observed that there was no water closet in his teacher's house, only a tin with some earth in it.

Riding became his favourite recreation, and his favourite companion was Jebb. The moment the bag was got safely off they would mount their horses and ride out of the Compound straight into the country. Sometimes they would take the Legation Ford and motor further distances to shoot snipe, woodcock, gazelle, or ibex. This might entail spending a night, when the weather got warmer, on a camp bed in a deserted palace, of which there were many around Tehran. For nearly all the old villas and palaces were falling to pieces, the beautiful gardens derelict, the fountains smashed, the terraces and summer-houses collapsing. Broken doors swung on hinges and balconies toppled crooked. Harold enjoyed these expeditions, although he was very indifferent with gun and rifle, and rather shy with his companion who was extremely proficient. Altogether he was leading an abstemious and healthy existence and had not felt so well since he first went to Madrid in 1911.

Before Harold left for Persia Vita had begged Clive Bell to correspond with him for he would be lonely. 'He is homesick for friends even now,' she wrote, 'and it will be worse when he gets out there and is really isolated. I *am* a model wife, didn't you know that? It seems to come as a surprise to everybody.'[14] On Christmas Eve Harold was overjoyed to receive, in addition to the daily batch from Vita, several letters from Raymond and one from Clive. Clive was a first-rate letter-writer, amusing, gossipy, a fount of anecdotes, and an inexhaustible purveyor of information on the latest books, reviews, plays and exhibitions. Harold's reply was only the second letter he had addressed to him. Whereas the first had

JOURNEY TO PERSIA 1925

begun, 'My dear Bell', this after eighteen months' interval had advanced to 'My dear Clive'; and on this footing Harold's letters continued at irregular intervals until Clive's death in 1964. They were unlike his letters to anyone else. They were unguarded without being wholly frank; at times facetious, and not always as funny as those to some of his other intimates; self-deprecatory, even arch. It was as though Harold were endeavouring to give better than he got, as though he recognised in Clive the dear, warm, easy-going fellow that he was, and not without his loveable sillinesses, someone with a defter pen than his own. Within a matter of months he was telling Clive that no living person's letters brought him more pleasure; and that he could have no idea to what extent they would be cherished by him as archives. Certainly, apart from Vita and his sons', no other correspondents' letters were so cherished, not even Raymond's.

> My dear Clive [he wrote], No, it was not ambition that made me so dramatically withdraw the foot which I had tentatively placed upon the lowest rung of the giddy Bloomsbury ladder. Had such been my mainspring I should have wished to release it in the hub of Empire.[15]

Harold was still sensitive about his reception by Bloomsbury whom he held in some awe, while inwardly disapproving of their aloofness. He went on to explain that neither Chamberlain nor Tyrrell regarded him with affectionate camaraderie, and had sent him to this remote place to get him out of the way.

> No, Clive, there is such a thing as DUTY. You see, when a man, not by nature very accurate about his sex-life, sees the figure 40 appearing on the horizon, it is not abstinence but absence which is required.[16]

It is not difficult to guess how Virginia and Vanessa would be repelled by such retardatory sentiments. Yet ambition and duty were qualities he set much store by. A year or two later he asked Clive if he was troubled by ambition, and answered for himself with the words, 'I should like as much fame as you have, but only an ounce more.'[17] His opinion of Clive as a writer was certainly high. And as for a sense of duty he confessed to Vita that he was rather smug in having it. He hated the word, but knew that she too had a feeling of duty towards him. Only she always said, 'Poor little Hadji,' which was three words instead of one. His duty to her was to tell her his confessions and not to let her find them out by herself.

> My pipe, I find [he told Clive[18]] has labelled me with my colleagues as 'an original'. The fact that I only brought out 250 visiting cards and not 5,000 has served me the epithet of a 'faiseur de paradoxes'. It does not

make for my popularity. Lord Tennyson wrote a poem once about an alien herd. It was not, perhaps, one of the Laureate's most happy efforts, but the refrain ('pop-gun, pop-gun, popular') was, I have always felt, effective. It is a comfort to me now when I, my pipes and my simplicity (simplex munditiis), are treated with suspicion and hostility.

The Persians on the other hand like me very much indeed. And the Shah, flashing in diamonds and emeralds, gave me a look which (had I been less scrupulous in my sense of values) I should have interpreted as full of meaning. Then I like the country – the great, wide, arid spaces, the sun naked from morning till evening, the smell of caramel and *aubergines farcies*, the smell of petrol and dust. And the women are closely veiled.

The men, on the other hand, are oleaginous and pimpled like the Greeks. It is a strange and stimulating thought that the two civilizations that have gone the whole hog in sodomy should be peopled by males with whom to sleep would be an experience at once glutinous and prickly. Whereas, even in Bloomsbury, even in the glow of [   ]   , no really very convincing bugger-art has been produced. I suppose it is like how (this is the expression which Raymond forbade me, even in correspondence to use) it is how the Swiss can't write or paint or even sculpt mountains; but can, and do, become venereal specialists and waiters.

Oh God, Clive – write again. Patriotism is *not* (really it isn't) enough. Yours ever.

Christmas festivities were practically confined to the Compound and the narrow English circle outside. It is true that Ferughi the Prime Minister held a reception at the Palace on the 23rd to which Sir Percy took his Counsellor. And when Harold's boot-lace came undone in full view of the guests the Minister was shocked. He was shocked again to come upon him in the street walking, yes actually walking, and, worse still, carrying, of all things, a butter-jar. 'But all the same I can't and won't change.' Too old for that,' Harold commented.[19] Taghi made use of the butter-jar for a hideous spray of bamboo as part of his atrocious Christmas decorations for his master. On Christmas Day the sun streamed through his bedroom window. Harold watered Taghi's floral display from his tooth-tumbler; took an ice cold bath in water straight from Mount Demavend; lunched with the doctor's family and pulled crackers, and walked with Gladwyn (they were on Christian name terms now) through the bazaars and beyond to look at some gardens to the north of the town, shuffling feet through the dead plane-tree leaves. It was a very still afternoon, with the sound of falling waters and the scrunch of dead leaves.

On New Year's Eve Harold gave a rather pathetic little party in his sparsely furnished downstairs room to Warner, Jebb and the Vice-

JOURNEY TO PERSIA 1925

Consul in Tehran, J. C. O'Dwyer. They drank each other's health in champagne at midnight to the sound of the absurd clock-tower. 'A heavenly year. Thank God for it.' But was it wholly heavenly? He had made several friends. Harold always made friends wherever he went, but he had no confidants in Tehran with whom he could let his hair down good and proper. He had no loves.

> I am still awaiting [he confided to Clive] 'une de ces aventures géantes qui n'arrivent qu'aux nez recourbé.' I have not as yet nor ever in my life experienced the full force of that apothegm.[20]

That was exposing his soul. He had never been, and was never to be overwhelmed by a *coup de foudre* of love so long as Vita remained his life-line. And then he brushed the allusion aside with an arrested anecdote, typical of his whimsical humour.

> There was the man, of course, who had the top berth in the wagon lit, and who exclaimed with sudden energy, 'Monsieur, permettez-moi de vous le dire, vous avez les épaules magnifiques'. The fact that he was a masseur from Lausanne does not really detract from the romance of that incident.

13

TEHRAN 1926–1927

HAROLD woke up on New Year's Day with a dreadful hangover. 'Although very, very ill, I don't think I am going to die,' he wrote in his diary. The Legation gholams made him a very charming little speech in English, to which he shyly replied. He was always touched by the beautiful manners of the Persians, whether rich or poor, just as he was impressed by their love for their country and their country's poets. Although he considered that no single Persian had a mind above the level of that of an English schoolboy, and their philosophy, or Sufism, was merely an escape into self-indulgent idleness, yet he was irritated in a contrary sense by the sneers and mockery levelled against them by the illiterate English residents. Had not the English been mere savages when Persia was a great Empire? And whereas we might now be superior electricians and industrialists, the Persians remained poets and artists. He never forgot one dawn when, having slept on the balcony of the Gulahek residence he was awakened by a pimply boy singing in cracked falsetto to his sheep. When asked what words he was singing, the boy told him they were from Hafiz. In England Harold had often heard a garage-hand bursting into song, but never from Shakespeare or Milton. Nevertheless, now that he was beginning to read Persian literature, he did not much care for it. He always disliked undue analogy in verse, and the whole of Persian literature was, as far as he could then comprehend, an over-elaboration of metaphor and simile.

Vita was never out of his thoughts. He told her that he did not miss what he called the lobster joys of London, or even his mother whom he loved dearly but who was detached from him. He missed the boys and the garden at Long Barn. As for his love of her, it was mystic. He professed not to be unduly bothered about her and Virginia. 'You are probably very good for each other. I only feel that you have not got *la main heureuse* in dealing with married couples.'[1] He was clearly more bothered than he wanted her to think, and once again could not help letting fall an exclamation, 'Oh dear! what a muddle-puddle you, Dorothy, Geoffrey and the other Rabbit Warren,' – a reference to Dorothy Warren[2] who made a lightning incursion into the lives of Vita and Geoffrey Scott – 'Good thing to go and wash yourself in Ganges.'[3] For Vita had on the 20th January left England for Persia by way of Egypt and Bombay, sending him telegrams

TEHRAN 1926-27

from every stopping-place. Virginia however did not take Vita's departure lightly. 'What's six weeks with Harold to him compared with four months without you to us?'[4] she asked testily. And Clive Bell added fuel to her protests by singing Vita's praises. He 'so raved, with such warmth and emotion, about you, that my heart was touched.' To which Vita, the day after her departure, replied, 'It is incredible how essential to me you have become.'[5]

In fact soon after Harold's departure for Persia Vita's love affair with Virginia began. On the 17th December Virginia had stayed at Long Barn for three nights, and Vita wrote in her diary, 'A peaceful evening.' That very day Harold wrote to Vita that he would not be jealous. As for his feelings for Virginia he would never forget how kind she was to him when he was smarting from Lytton's rudeness. There was no reason why she should have been nice about it except that she saw he was flustered and in real pain. 'So at the bottom of my terror of her glimmers a little white stone of gratitude. Which can only be increased by her loving you.'[6]

On the 18th Vita recorded, 'Talked to her till 3 a.m. Not a peaceful evening.' She did not immediately tell Harold what had happened, and hotly denied to Clive Bell, when challenged, that anything had. On the 19th Leonard joined the two wives at Long Barn.

Vita was understandably preoccupied and Harold feared that she might be withholding things from him. He was hurt to hear from Dorothy Wellesley, and not from Vita herself, that her long poem was to be called *The Land* and not *The Georgics*, just as he was hurt when Vita would not tell him what Virginia's opinion of the poem was. He begged her not to send it to print without letting him read it first. When he did read it he was overcome with admiration. He felt as though he had been bathing in some mountain pool on a hot day. Its dominant impression was power in repose, like a sleepy lion. It was the implicit in it which gave it such immense carrying force. Then its originality was remarkable. Lastly, its mellow atmosphere of love – a Demeter-like pity for men and squirrels and mice – was beautifully pervasive. He found its technical skill and balance perfect. Only in one passage her values broke down, where the dead shepherd was being carried across the Downs. He did not like that a bit, and begged her to alter it.[7] The whole thing was such a great achievement that whether or not it had an immediate success was immaterial. Unquestionably *The Land* is an achievement. It reveals Vita's astonishing knowledge of country ways, nature in all its seasonal aspects, not to mention the traditional agricultural implements, then about to become discarded after thousands of years' use. The poem contains many extremely moving and evocative passages, such as those beginning: 'The country habit has me by the heart,' 'Sometimes in apple country you may see,' and 'Such arid months as only exiles know,' which have since become so familiar as almost to be hackneyed. *The Land* was curiously old-fashioned even for the twenties and some phrases like, 'Poor frightened Wat,' and words like droil, yeavy, ean, lusk and reasty struck contemporary critics as too archaic to be tenable. Vita composed her final invocation to Virgil while she was in Isfahan, and in April sent the manuscript by diplomatic bag to Heinemann, the publishers.

Harold corresponded regularly with Lancelot Oliphant during his first months in Tehran, giving his assessment of Persia's situation and the Shah's standing. Persian nationalism was expressed in the Majlis, which was in his view a collection of ninnies. But so long as the Shah remained in fear of them, that was to the good. When he learned how utterly disorganised they were, and grew confident in his own superior powers he would become a tyrant. And a tyrant who was an uncultivated man was always a serious menace to his country's well-being. Harold spoke in flattering terms of the American Administrator-General of the Persian finances, Dr. A. C. Millspaugh. This man had complete control over the collection and expenditure of the Persian state revenue. Little could be done without his approval. The whole Persian Civil Service was also centralised in his office. Harold further confirmed how Loraine had, through his charm and friendliness, dispelled the hatred of Britain which had prevailed on his arrival.

He was blissfully happy with his colleagues, he told Oliphant in March, and liked Tehran. The only snag was dressing up and having to go to tea parties. Vita hated it too, whereas Lancelot's cousin Percy simply loved it. His only difference with his chief was over questions of protocol which to him seemed totally unimportant. He feared that his loathing of the whole thing distressed Loraine. It certainly did not prevent the Minister making his Counsellor accompany him on formal visitations to other Legations, to members of the Persian Cabinet and the Shah himself. In presenting his letters to the new sovereign Loraine went in what Harold considered a procession of ridiculous coaches. After speeches of fulsome compliments the Shah and the Prime Minister sat down to talk. Reza Shah told Sir Percy that he was playing with the Russians; that he did not like them, but at times had to give way to them in minor matters, whereas in all major matters he could trust the Majlis to refuse surrender. Sir Percy was very pleased with this confidence.

Vita's arrival was preceded by that of an old motor-car which Harold had bought, and his furniture which had come from England. At last the long awaited day of meeting approached. On the 27th February Harold was driven by the Persian chauffeur in the Legation Ford to Kasvin where they spent the night. The snow fell thickly, and it was not until 1.30 two mornings later that they got to Hamadan. The chauffeur was obliged to rouse the proprietor of a café from his slumbers and make him give them rooms. Leaving Hamadan they reached the top of Assadarbad Pass around noon. The front springs of the Ford broke. They reached Kermanshah at 6 o'clock, and Harold stayed with the Cowans, the Consul having just recovered from typhoid. Harold was by now in a terrible state of impatience, anxiety and excitement. At 8 o'clock they began dinner when the noise of approaching cars was heard, and the flash of headlamps seen across the windows. It was the Trans-Desert Mail convoy. Harold leapt to his feet, rushed out, and saw 'my Viti sitting there in a little fur cap with a saluki on her knee.'[8] It was called Zurcha, meaning the yellow one, and had been given her by Gertrude Bell with whom she had stayed in Baghdad. Vita was not very well but nevertheless they started off for Tehran the next morning. They reached the Legation on the 5th, and were both jubilant at being together again.

Vita's desire was to see as much of the country, its people, landscape, wildlife, flowers and gardens as she could during her first short visit. She did not wish to waste her time in paying calls on the dull wives of British officials with whom she had nothing in common, or on pompous social gatherings in the Legation. The occasional Legation party could not be avoided, and when she was obliged to dine at the Persian Foreign Office in honour of the Shah's birthday, she wore her emeralds, looked her most beautiful, sat next to Sir Percy, and was a credit to her husband. But she did not take to Lady Loraine, who did not particularly care for her. She at once took to the intellectual Gladwyn Jebb with whom she talked the same language. Harold told Clive Bell[9] that Vita was an appreciative guest.

> She frightens the Persians out of their lives; she leaves cards obediently on her colleagues, and the Secretary of the Polish Legation, who owns a paper at Cracow and plays Chopin on the battered pianos of the local intelligentsia, says, he will translate, he really will, *Seducers* into Polish.

One of the few friends Vita made in Tehran was Elizabeth Daryush. Harold had already met her at tea with the Baronne Frachon, a temporary French resident and self-appointed leader of the Tehran intelligentsia. He called Mrs. Daryush 'a shy, defensive, little blue-stocking with a pudding face.'[10] She was the daughter of Robert Bridges the Poet Laureate, and when very young had married a Cambridge University graduate, whom Harold described to Clive as a Jew whom she took to be a Persian, and she came to Tehran which she imagined to be like the better bits of Hafiz. She lives in a little house with a tin roof, an apricot tree, and endless books on prosody . . . Her husband is reverting to native ideas. She denies fiercely that she made a mistake. She talks rather poignantly about 'Daddy' and Boars Hill.[11]

Elizabeth was herself a poet, deeply under the technical influence of her father, yet more akin in her doom-laden philosophy to Hardy. Her early verse was disproportionately addicted to syllabic experiments and composed in a sort of private language. While remaining highly fastidious it was to become less pedantic and more and more concentrated and powerful as the years went by. Her theme was the world of nature under seasonal variations and the basic insecurity of human fortunes at its mercy. Vita became interested in her as a fellow poet. She also pitied her relatively unhappy, impecunious and lonely life, neither English among the English, nor Persian among the Persians. She would have tea with her alone while her little husband was seeking a job with the Anglo-Persian Oil Company and dictating terms in rather a high-handed manner to the chairman, Sir John Cadman.

Vita soon learned that the famous Persian garden, if not exactly a figment of the imagination, must be interpreted as an oasis of poplar trees round a pool into which tiny streams leisurely trickled, or a tangle of briars and grey sage, with perhaps a solitary judas tree staining the blue sky with its bloom of magenta blood. The formal, neat Persian garden, packed with flowers like an illumination in a medieval breviary, was no longer to be found, if it had ever existed. But what were described as Persian gardens were good enough for her after the superabundance of floral beds and borders she was accustomed to at home. Expeditions into the Meshed Gap and the foothills of the Elburz led to the discovery of yellow tulips, Iris persica and other indigenous plants. She and Harold would be joined by Gladwyn, tired after his pursuit since dawn after mouflon. A favourite expedition was to Doshan Tapeh, or the Hill of the Hare. It was a slight promontory starting out of the plain, its crest crowned with a cluster of buildings fallen into disrepair like everything in Persia. Here Nasr-ed-Din Shah had kept his wild animals within a walled enclosure and cultivated a garden at the foot of the hill. The views from the broken arcades of the central pavilion were superb.

> As the backbone of the north stretches the whole range of the Elburz; to the south-east the Djarjarud hills split dramatically into what is known as the Meshed gap, where the great road crosses on its way to Meshed and Samarcand; to the south and west lies the open plain, bounded only by the very distant mountains beyond Kasvin.[12]

TEHRAN 1926-27

The walls of the Doshan Tapeh pavilion were still papered with old pages from the *Illustrated London News* of the 1860s, many upside down. This was an odd discovery to make in the heart of Persia and started many a wild surmise as to what mad English recluse had been responsible for the decoration. Fat stucco cupids clung to the ruined walls, or lay fallen upon the dusty floor. Happy evenings were spent listening to Prince Mirza Firooz reading and discussing obscene Persian literature. The Prince, a great territorial magnate, was also a highly cultured man. He told them he would have enjoyed Omar Khayyam more in the original had it not been mistranslated so abominably by the English. He was the only Persian with whom Harold could be natural, with whom, he explained to Vita, 'I feel (si j'ose m'exprimer ainsi) I can touch bottom.'[13] Firooz had an amused and hesitant manner, wore dim pince-nez, had a deep regard for Jean Cocteau and hankered for the Boeuf sur le Toit and Parisian life on the Left Bank.

Lunching with Copley Amory of the American Legation they met the poet Archibald MacLeish,[14] who had come out on the League of Nations Opium Commission. Harold thought him a nice youth who spoke well, somewhat too well, not having the lightness of touch to which they were accustomed. He was very earnest about the essence of poetry and very well informed about the style of various poets. And with it all fluent and oratorical. Harold came to regard him as the most interesting and intelligent of the post-Eliot generation of American poets; and admired him for being determined, unlike others of his compatriots, to remain American.

On the same day Harold recorded, 'Little Tray arrives at 5 p.m. very well and cheerful.' Raymond Mortimer had written begging to be allowed to come out and stay. Harold would have preferred him to postpone his visit until after Vita left him in May, for he wanted to have her to himself. 'Yet it would break his heart if I let him see that . . . I don't want to hurt that poor little Pippin,' he had written.[15] So Raymond was made welcome, and entered into the spirit of the expeditions – to Doshan Tapeh, Kasi-i-Firooz, Protira, Kand and Assadabad. The judas trees were bursting out; the planes were becoming pale green; and the lilac and wistaria were beginning to bloom, in between the snow-storms and the blizzards.

At dawn on the 18th April the three of them set out for Isfahan, taking a servant and a mechanic. Vita narrated the story of their adventures and described the scenery they went through in *Passenger to Teheran*, one of the most poetic of travel books written between the two wars. They passed Qum without stopping and when a hundred miles from the Elburz range noticed that the peak of Demavend towered above its fellow peaks more prominently than it did as seen from Tehran, from which it was a mere fifteen miles away. At Dilijand they all slept in one cavernous room, devoid of furniture but for rows of tea-pots and lamps. They reached Isfahan on the afternoon of the 19th. In her book Vita studiously ignored mentioning the names of her husband and companions, or the people whom they met and who entertained them in the towns they passed through. In fact at Isfahan they joined up with Gladwyn Jebb, Captain Wickham and Sir Percy, who was on a sort of state tour, and stayed with the Consul, by name Bristow. They visited factories and bazaars, as well as the Pavilion of the Forty Columns, the stupendous Masjid-i-Shah and the Madresseh, which inspired Vita to write about it as by far the loveliest building she saw on their tour.

On their return journey they stayed one night at Qum, then famous for blue gazed pottery, in a little house round a courtyard. It was a native household presided over by a grave Persian patriarch with a long, beautifully combed beard and finger-nails carefully stained with fresh henna.

Back in Tehran they were plunged into the Coronation celebrations of Reza Shah. There was a ball at the Italian Legation; a huge ministerial dinner and reception at the Palace; and on the 25th April the Coronation itself.

The only person who took no apparent interest whatever in the Coronation was the Anointed-to-be. He had wanted to become President of a Republic. He had no truck with mullahs, priests, religious ceremonial, oaths and tradition. Barely literate and contemptuous of those who were, he was bored to death by the centuries-old ritual of becoming King of Kings. He shuffled through it because he had to, with a bad grace. But the populace, the Government, and the élite of Persia saw the Coronation with starry eyes. As is the way of things in Persia, preparations had been left till the last minute. The British contingent, accustomed to efficiency and anticipation, were aghast at the belated and makeshift preparations. The Coronation took place in the Gulestan Palace, in an upstairs room, known as the Museum, encumbered with German nineteenth-century candelabra and statues. Until the eleventh hour the columns, the vaulted ceiling, the tiled floor were aswarm with workmen with paint-brushes, dusters and brooms. On the eve of the ceremony Teymourtache, Minister of the Court, a slightly ridiculous personage, a professed lady-killer and socialite, invited Lady Loraine, her mother, Mrs. Stuart-Wortley, and Vita, to make a selection from the vast accumulation of royal treasure of those things most suitable for display. They descended into the Palace vaults. They were flabbergasted by the profusion of the Persian Crown Jewels. Vita described the effect produced upon her.

> The linen bags vomited emeralds and pearls; the green baize vanished, the table became a sea of precious stones. The leather cases opened, displaying jewelled scimitars, daggers encrusted with rubies, buckles carved from a single emerald; ropes of enormous pearls. Then from the inner room came the file of servants again, carrying uniforms sewn with diamonds; a cap with a tall aigrette, secured by a diamond larger than the Koh-i-Nor (known as the Daria-i-Nor, its sister stone); two crowns like great hieratic tiaras, barbaric diadems, composed of pearls of the finest orient.[16]

The ladies plunged their arms up to the elbows in uncut emeralds, and let pearls trickle through their fingers as they watched an artist at work on the new crown he had designed for the morrow.

By 2.30 on the following day the visitors, having walked up the grand staircase and through the principal reception-rooms, decorated with mirror work and encrusted with mosaic from which the sunlight through the windows refracted in a thousand multi-coloured rays, were in their allotted places on a raised dais. A clear passage had been left down the centre of the room leading to the Peacock Throne, from the arms of which hung tassels of emeralds as large as pigeons' eggs. Near the steps of the throne crowded the mullahs, 'dirty, bearded old men in long robes and huge turbans.'[17] When the western diplomats entered with their ladies, allowed by the Shah through the special intervention of Sir Percy Loraine, the mullahs nearly fainted with horror.

Down the aisle the standards of various Persian regiments were borne. Between them walked dignitaries wearing their robes of honour, ecclesiastics of different Churches, the Chaldean Bishop in deep purple, and the hooded archimandrites of the Armenian Church. There were chieftains of great tribes in their richest costumes, sheikhs from Arabistan, khans from Kurdistan, Lurs and Qahgais. But, in accordance with Mahommedan tradition, there was no music because of the presence of the mullahs.

After a good deal of waiting and expectancy there fell a hush. The doors were opened, and a little boy, quite alone, dressed in uniform, marched down the length of the room, saluted the company, and took his place on the lowest step of the throne. He was the Valiahd, His Imperial Highness, the Crown Prince of Persia.[18] Then, escorted by his generals and ministers bearing jewels and regalia, the aigrette in his cap blazing with the diamond known as the Mountain of Light, wearing a blue cloak heavy with pearls, the Shah advanced towards the Peacock Throne. The European women curtsied to the ground; the men inclined themselves low on his passage; the mullahs shambled forward in a rapacious, proprietary wave; the little prince, frightened, possessed himself of a corner of his father's cloak.[19]

The Chief Mullah stepped forward and read an address. The Minister of the Court advanced and handed Reza Shah the crown which he put on his own head. The President of the Council invested him with the jewelled sceptre. The Minister of War, on bended knee, buckled on the diamond-encrusted sword. The Shah read his speech from the throne in a low voice, without a gesture, without enthusiasm, in a manner totally devoid of the theatrical, and with a nonchalance hardly appropriate to the grand occasion. The ceremony rapidly concluded, a salvo of guns from outside rattled the window-panes. The King of Kings rose; his pearl-embroidered cloak was flung back so as to disclose the scintillating jewels with which his tunic was sewn; the light caught the Daria-i-Nor; his sword-hilt flashed; he saluted and stalked sulkily out of the hall.

The following day a Salaam was held in the morning; a military review in the afternoon; and a splendid party at the Palace with fireworks in the evening. Visitors wore their best jewels, and Vita her parure of emeralds. On returning home she discovered that the large emerald pendant was missing. There was consternation. She and Harold drove back to the Palace. They found the Prime Minister on his knees, her emerald in one hand, trying to fit it into the Peacock Throne from which he supposed it must have become dislodged. 'Altesse,' Harold shouted, 'cette émeraude appartient à ma femme!'

The day of Vita's departure drew near. She was to return by way of Russia in the company of General Arfa and his wife Hilda, as far as Moscow. On the 3rd May Harold wrote a letter to Vita, while she was packing in the next room, to be handed to her by the Arfas on her first night at Baku. He wrote her another, which he posted to Brighton, where she would be staying with her mother on arrival in England. On the 4th he and Vita, with Raymond, left at 8 o'clock for Rudbar. Early on the following morning he and Vita parted at Resht. Vita dissolved into tears and Harold was so broken with emotion that he was unable to speak for several hours. When he managed to be alone he sobbed convulsively. While Vita continued to Baku he and Raymond drove back to Tehran in silence. Three days later he wrote to Vita that he was still totally numb and listless, and felt just like a piece of soaked blotting-paper. Raymond, he said, was being a miracle of tact and comfort; and not until the 10th did he become his normal self.

Raymond was appalled by what he considered the gratuitous misery which the Nicolsons were inflicting upon themselves. He thought it was unnecessary and even wrong that two people so devoted should have to submit to repeated, devastating partings which tore their souls to shreds. Rather boldly he took up his pen and wrote to tell Vita so.

> I have never seen anyone so wretched as Harold ... It seems to me imbecile to put yourselves in such a situation, and really makes me rather angry, like every form of unreasonableness ... I think Harold realises as never before what he is giving up, and how entirely his happiness depends on your being there, and it is a general fact, I suppose, that one never appreciates the full value of a thing till one has lost it ... I'd give anything to have a relationship with someone like Harold's with you, and it infuriates me to see it made a cause of suffering instead of happiness. I'm sure anything in the world is dust and ashes when compared with one's feelings for people ... I'm infinitely envious of you both. I am, as I expect you know, a great deal fonder of Harold than he has any idea of my being ... It's suitable that I should be called Tray, for I have a very spaniel-like way of attaching myself to people, which I rather deplore ... Because [Harold] is made wretched by [these partings] himself, he feels in some way that it is all right, which is mysticism and nonsense.[20]

Harold may or may not have seen this letter ultimately; but he would hardly dissent from Raymond's reasons for his self-inflicted martyrdom. In ruminating about his Persian exile a few months later he decided that it was good for him. He was right to have undertaken it. In London he was in danger of becoming a flibbertigibbet. 'I believe in mortification of the flesh,' he wrote. Persia in throwing him back upon himself had given him the opportunity to think. He was slowly evolving a theory of life, of Love as the highest good, guided by intelligence, and not by habituation and prejudice.

In the meantime he was working himself into one of his states about Vita's safety. News came that there was a police revolution in Russia. He was terrified. Vita was bound to get involved in street fighting through sheer unawareness of what was on foot. Then

> Percy came in [to the Chancery] with a face like a boot. I thought that at least someone had written 'cunt' across the virgin page of the Legation Book. He put his hand on my shoulder, 'Look here, old man, I've got something rather bloody for you.' He then produced the Reuter saying a revolution had broken out in Poland,[21]

where Vita had now got to,

Harold was to some extent cheered by the reviews on *Swinburne* which were pouring in by each bag. Most were favourable. A few were downright condemnatory of his unfairness to his subject. But the fervour of the notices of his previous books was on the whole lacking. The *Yorkshire Post* reviewer detected too many mistakes of detail, and like other critics quarrelled with Harold's theme that Swinburne ossified after 1857. The *Spectator* was amused that Harold's prose sometimes fell into the very Swinburnian prosody which the biography deplored, and quoted as examples phrases like 'the salt, sad savour of a tideless sea,' and triple rhyme such as 'white, bright light.' Harold was sensitive to these carpings, and against a perfectly polite notice in The *Saturday Review* by Edward Shanks, scribbled, 'Pig. Beast.' Gosse however in the *Sunday Times* excelled himself in praise:

> And now we receive, from one of the most gifted and responsible of our younger writers, a critical estimate which exceeds in originality all its predecessors – Mr. Nicolson's study of Swinburne is a remarkable contribution to literature.

This was generous in that the book came hot on the heels of Gosse's lively but unbalanced life of the poet. Gosse made a charming and rather touching admission that he, once intoxicated by Swinburne's magic, was now to some extent converted by Harold's objections. He admitted that Algernon was immature and perhaps had suffered from arrested development.

A letter from Clive Bell about the book pleased Harold more than any of the reviews and Gosse's ululations. Clive praised it highly, saying that its disparagement of Swinburne's verse made him feel chilly and grown old, as he was intended to feel. There was nothing wrong with that. But the book showed traces of too hasty composition in parts. One or two adjectives of the 'bright, white light' variety (noticed by the *Spectator*) occurred too often. 'And oh Harold, I can't help regretting – I know I may be old-fashioned – but I can't help regretting that there should be the least suspicion of moral disapprobation.'[22]

Harold replied that he was sorry about the note of moral disapprobation in 'Swinny.' 'How odd of me and unbecoming. I fear (poor Sapphist) that there is a governess in me somewhere.'[23] He was pleased too that Clive was not cross with him for being nice about Gosse.

Later Harold acknowledged that *Swinburne* was a 'half dress book', and he did not want ever to write such another. Perhaps the least approving remark about it came from Raymond. He wrote that Harold's 'book on Swinburne was very painstaking: it was also ungrammatical.'[24]

TEHRAN 1926-27

Social life in Tehran had its intellectual limitations, but also its amusing incidents. The Baronne Franchon was a sort of Madame Verdurin with her pretensions, her local lionising and her desire to extract every iota of romance from the wilder shores of the Orient. Harold was obliged to go alone to a dinner party she had involved him in, for Raymond was indisposed. The party was given

> 'par mon grand ami le Chef Kurd.' We picked her up first at the house, and drove on to the rooms which the Kurdish chief had hired or acquired for the occasion. He was dressed in an apple green sur-coat with a belt stuffed with knives. His hat was draped in a black and white kerchief. He was extremely good looking. Madame Franchon asked if he always dressed like that. He said that he did. His brother (dressed for his part in a grey tweed lounge suit with club tie) said that this was untrue: 'il s'est travesti de cette façon pour faire plaisir à Madame.' The Baron (her husband) was disconcerted by this remark and sought to relieve the situation by addressing some appropriate remarks to the son of our host, a terrified infant of seven or eight. 'Shuma kucheek hastid?' he enquired with a strong French accent. No one understood this question and the silence which followed was painful. 'Mon ami,' said the Baroness, 'tu me fais de la peine quand tu essayes de parler le persan.' The little boy twisted and cracked his finger joints in agony. 'Je ne fais,' said the Baron, 'que lui demander s'il a des frères.' 'Mai voyons, mon ami, *kutchik* veut dire *petit*; le mot pour frère est *pesar*.' 'Baradai,' I murmured, as it were helping her out. 'Baradou,' she corrected. 'Shuma,' began the Baron again, 'baradère hastud?' '*Dareed*, mon ami,' exclaimed the Baroness. Then the lamp went pop. It was one of those lamps which, when going, give a hard white light like an arc-lamp, and when not going make a noise like an owl. It made a noise and the Baron rushed at it. 'Prends garde, mon ami, tu sais que tu as été mordu ce matin par le putail.' (The *putail* was a stoat which Monaco had given her that morning, a disgraceful little animal.) So the Baron retreated back to his chair and the lamp went Whoo! Whoo! and the Kurdish chief, who had been smiling like a young princess at a flower show, smiling to right, smiling to left, shouted, 'Biàr!' suddenly, and a servant, braver than the Baron, came and took the lamp away. 'Shuma', began the Baron when reseated, 'Baradère hasted?' 'Dareed,' snapped Madame Franchon. But meanwhile the little boy had run away.
>
> We then went into dinner. Madame Franchon did not hide her disappointment that it was not on the floor. The conversation languished. Dish after dish appeared, was eaten, was taken away, and was replaced by something even larger. Having exhausted her eulogies of our host's clothes, the Baronne started on the table decoration. Pointing ecstatically at a flower on the cloth she said, 'Il n'est qu'en Perse qu'on sache arranger des fleurs de cette façon. Quel goût exquis que cette rose

enterrée de petales multicolores.' 'Tu te trompes, ma chère,' said the Baron, 'ce n'est que le décor du gigot.' It was in fact the paper frill that had graced the terminal bone of a vast leg of mutton. The Baroness looked up greedily into the eyes of the Kurdish chief. 'Chantez-moi, Excellence, les chansons de Kemarchak.' Which he did in a rather drunken voice. At 10.30 we rose from that too hospitable board.[25]

Harold and Raymond had made friends with an Irish-American journalist who happened to land up in Tehran in the spring. Vincent, or Jimmy Sheean was an attractive mixture of childishness and romanticism, of gentleness and urge for adventure, of idealism and good sense, deep convictions and superficial sentimentality. He was incompetent, vague and unreliable. In his book *In Search of History* (1935) Sheean described the first impression Harold and Raymond made on him. Harold he called a 'witty and irreverent spirit', while his guest was 'clever, dark, inquisitive, interested in everything.' The Legation, he added, was graced also by Jebb, 'whose capacity for forgetting things was a delight to behold.' Sheean and Raymond struck up a warm friendship and in June went off to Shiraz together. But before their departure the three dined with Sir Percy, who was lonely because his wife had gone to England. Harold observed that, much as he adored Louise, Percy became a different person without her perpetual whininess.

The Minister embarked after dinner on an exposition of Persian policy. It was like a beautifully ordered funeral. Now and then there would be a two minutes silence, and then the procession would move on again under triumphal arches. Tray got rather restless and depressed at not being allowed to interrupt. The Minister has a way of pausing for the *mot juste*, and then produces a cliché. 'This policy,' he will say, 'of splendid ... (here he will pause and cogitate. One expects a firework) ... isolation,' he will conclude as if the word were a *trouvaille*. But he was almost gay and we drank champagne.[26]

After a night's camping on the slopes of Mount Demavend with Gladwyn and Raymond Harold had to go to tea with the Shah at Saadebad summer palace, near Pashkolé.

There was a huge long gravel path along the terrace and at the end of it I saw the Shah. But at the beginning of it, out of sheer nervousness, my bootlaces came undone, all four of them. Now why does this always happen when I go to see the Shah? I had known it would happen and had tried on my button boots instead. But three of the buttons had come off, so I put on my Oxford shoes, and had tied the knots as no knots had ever been tied before. On getting out of the motor I glanced at the knots. There they were, firm and tidy. But when they saw that long vista of garden path, a hundred yards of garden path, they got nervous and untied themselves. I knew that the Minister was watching from beside the samovar. It was a trying ordeal.[27]

That was bad enough. Worse was to follow. He thought he would address the Sovereign in his own language. So he ventured to say, 'Hada hafiz i alahazret,' which means, 'Goodbye, Your Majesty.' The salutation passed unremarked by the Shah. Then he went and stood beside the samovar and watched the other guests arriving. One of them was the Minister of War, with rather a startled air. He had been let out of prison for the tea party having been put there for kicking a Dervish in the groin. The Dervish's fault was to tell the Minister that his life was threatened by sorcery, but that on payment of 500 tomans he might get the threat averted. After one strawberry ice the Minister was taken back to jail. 'Oh dear, what a difficult place,' Harold remarked.

Sir Percy Loraine was due to leave Tehran on the 1st July and Harold would be Chargé d'Affaires until October. He was greatly relieved that the Minister's successor would not be Nevile Henderson. He had begged Oliphant not to send Henderson – 'a bloody man.'[28] The Shah when told of Loraine's departure was greatly upset.

It was Harold's task to respond to the Minister's minute of tribute to the loyalty of his Legation staff. So he began and ended with a purple passage about the affection and respect which the staff would all bear him. On reflection Harold decided that *bear* was the animal, crossed it out and put bare. So the words came out, 'The affection and respect we shall all bare you.' It was only when the minute was sent in that he discussed the matter with Raymond, who said *bare* meant naked. Harold said *bear* meant the animal. Raymond said he was wrong. Harold said, 'Not at all. Don't you know the passage in the hymn about the child "she bear"? Now if it had been the child "she bear" the minute would have been even more misleading than it was.' Raymond said *bare* in that sense was an obsolete past tense, and that it could never be in the future tense. 'We shall all bare you' was wrong. 'Oh dear,' Harold wrote to Vita, 'I wish Tray hadn't come to stay with me.'[29]

Raymond Mortimer was, and always has been, a severe critic of the slapdash. He did not consider Harold to be grammarian enough. He deplored his use of the adverb *like* used as a conjunction in, for example, the sentence, 'Perhaps Edhem would break down again like he had broken down last night.' This was a pitfall Harold was constantly tumbling into. He was aware of Raymond's strictures even when they were withheld. In writing to Clive[30] that he had profited immensely from his advice not to flaunt unnecessary adjectives, he admitted to being irked by Raymond's syntactical nagging.

> Raymond has been reading my book on Tennyson. I think he has a destructive mind. He couldn't (damn him) have written the book himself – being a lazy cove, and sits there all comfortable and says little destructive things. Nicely, mind you, and with an affectionate pat on the shoulder. But destructive they are – all about my trying to be funny. I see the spider fingers of Mr. Lytton Strachey stretching their tentacles from Hamspray to Central Asia. Was I – did I – trying, – try, to imitate the Master? Compared to him all my fingers are thumbs. I told him so, and he was rude. I felt, at the time, a drunken and ungainly being.

Nevertheless the Royal Society of Literature thought fit to award Harold the A. C. Benson medal, which gave him pleasure.

On the 7th June the Chancery moved to the comparative cool of Gulahek, with its music of running water, nightingales and frogs. The roses were still at their best, notably one white rose called Gul-i-Shah, looking like clematis montana. Gulahek offered the conditions Harold enjoyed best of all – working, riding, reading, writing and bathing in hot weather. But it seemed to have no point without Vita. He got through the days quickly, contentedly, mechanically, and it was only when someone like Raymond jerked him into being himself and not a machine that he realised how perfunctory his general existence was. Raymond returned from Shiraz, very brown and thin, 'poor little waggy-tail that he is.'[31] He hated Shiraz.

Harold missed the dogs, Henry his spaniel, and Zurcha, whose bad behaviour in the Legation necessitated their being sent back to Tehran until the Minister departed. Henry's final crime was to have eaten a whole tin of caviare. Both Harold and Vita adored dogs and their letters are full of the joys and worries and sadnesses, which their companionship and death brought them. Harold was sure they had a sixth sense, of which humans were devoid, and he noticed how sensitive they were to ridicule. It pained him to see them at circuses dressed in crinolines and carrying parasols in their jaws; and their depression in watching luggage being carried out of the house upset him. He warned Vita that in writing about dogs it was difficult, but essential, to avoid coyness or winsomeness.

When Prime Minister Ferughi's Cabinet, undermined by intrigue, fell on the 6th June, Harold was obliged to put on his top hat and descend to the torrid capital to pay respects to his successor. Mostaufi-al-Mamallek was an old dear, rather like Watts Dunton or George Moore, except that he never wore a collar, only a collar stud. After recording this incident, Harold exclaimed:

> Oh my future biographer! On reading this diary do not say, 'What an empty life! Look rather to my letters to Viti which give a fuller picture of my noble and incessant activities in the cause of life and literature.[32]

On the 28th Loraine paid the Shah his farewell visit. It was not an occasion of exclusive compliments and regards. A good many home truths were delivered by the British Minister. He reproached the Shah for the corruption of the Persian regime. He was disappointed, he said, that he had not succeeded, before leaving, in getting Persia's debt to England paid, or the settlement for the Sheikh of Mohammerah finalised. The Shah expressed crocodilean remorse. Sir Percy then went to make his adieux to Mohammerah. The old Sheikh lay back in his chair and howled like a dog. Sir Percy had to tell him to shut up.

Harold gave a farewell dinner party to Loraine. Thirty-six people were seated at one long table and six little ones in the big durbah tent. Harold was at one end, and Sir Percy at the other of the long table. An orchestra played on the lawn, and there were many Chinese lanterns. Harold made a nice little English public schoolboy speech, and was rather pleased with himself. Sir Percy replied with emotion. When Harold asked Raymond, who had been present, 'Well, how did it go?' expecting praise, Raymond said it made him almost sick, and certainly angry. He hated the Empire-building tenor of Harold's words. He said he was as irritated by Harold as Harold would be irritated if he saw him dressed as a woman in some Paris dancing hall. Harold commented that he would indeed loathe such a spectacle as much as Raymond loathed the Kipling side of him.[33] Raymond wrote to Vita that the speech had sickened him because it was so uncharacteristic of Harold, and yet so sincere. He said it was a pity that when he left there would be no one at Gulahek to tease Harold except Henry.

Raymond was right in remarking that what he called the Empire-building tenor of Harold's speech was sincere. Rather it was Harold's inbred patriotism to which his natural emotionalism sometimes too readily gave rein. This patriotism however was a tenet which his father's example had instilled into him and which Wellington had fostered, a tenet from which only the most radical Victorian intellectuals – and it must be remembered that Harold Nicolson was a Victorian – defiantly reacted. Balliol taught Harold to modify, but never to suppress it. At Oxford he learned, like Samuel Johnson, that patriotism was not to be confused with nationalism or chauvinism. In fact he was just as disgusted by jingoism as Raymond, Bloomsbury and the readers of the *New Statesman*. The only difference between him and them was that he was not ashamed of his pride in British self-assurance, humour, boundless tolerance and that missionary spirit which brought betterment and justice to subject peoples, and sought to impart to them the responsibilities and wisdom of our race. Admittedly he believed that these virtues rendered the British a superior race. On the contrary the pride which he rejected was that of the British intellectuals, like Huxley, Auden, Isherwood and Gerald Heard, who by retreating to America had put the value of their importance to the world above the salvation of their own country. That attitude he condemned as spiritual arrogance.

At 5 o'clock in the morning of the 2nd July Sir Percy left Gulahek for England. The whole staff was assembled under the plane trees, and the mounted escort were champing at their bits. Sir Percy was very sweet and soppy. A great deal of tidy luggage was strapped to the yellow motor. The last handshakes were given, and the motor moved away, the sowars jingling in front and the gholams behind. The slow cavalcade accompanied the departing Minister to the end of the village, whence they returned. Harold detected some increased alacrity in the way the ferrahs saluted him, as he walked into the Legation to take up his charge.

For four months Harold experienced his first spell as a Chargé d'Affaires. He gloried in it. The moment the yellow motor was out of sight he went to his desk and wrote to Lancelot Oliphant, giving his views of the Persian situation. He did not believe in the Shah's good intentions at all. Reza was continually flinging innocent people into prison, and allowing his generals to rob the soldiers. Moreover to be pro-British had become a term of opprobrium, which all Persian politicians were terrified of incurring. He had grave doubts that the Majlis would ratify the debt agreement, or recognise Iraq, or do anything about the tariff. He dreaded a snag over the Sheikh of Mohammerah's retribution. He did not believe the Majlis would reach an agreement with Imperial Airways.

Exactly two hours after Loraine's departure there came serious news. Several divisions of the Persian army had mutinied, had been joined by Russian Turcomans and were marching on Meshed in Khorassan. There were fears of a republic being set up unless the Shah intervened. Harold sent a message in pursuit of Loraine in which he told him he was faced with a problem; either to follow his instinct and report to the Foreign Office in mild terms which would not cause alarm; or send them a telegram indicating that the incident might turn very nasty, and so give them the opportunity of sending Loraine back. In fact Harold chose the latter course. The

Foreign Office did not avail themselves of it; and the situation did not appreciably worsen.

On the 4th Raymond left. Jimmy Sheean was to accompany him as far as Moscow. At 3.30 in the morning Gladwyn drove the travellers and Harold to the aerodrome on the Kasvin road. Raymond was silent and wretched. At the aerodrome he took Harold's arm and his hand was trembling. 'Tray looked a wretched little object in a jumper and a silk scarf and a hat too small for him and a very white and pinched little face.'[34] He climbed into a Junkers machine with Jimmy.

> The sense of severance is even more acute when the departing person actually leaves the earth, becomes a diminishing dot, a dot that gets muddled finally with the spots of one's own livery early-morning vision,

Harold wrote. Devoted though he was to Raymond and stimulated by his intellect, he did not miss him as much as he supposed he might. For company he was perfectly satisfied with Gladwyn, who was besides, a great moral support in his work, and 'old Trott,'[35] one of the Consuls used as an interpreter, whose agreeable and scholarly manner appealed to him. He was revelling in his independence and the exercise of authority. At last he was his own master in so far as a diplomatist ever was that, even in days when distance could be measured in time as well as mileage, and the further a post was from Whitehall the greater a representative's responsibility.

He found the Minister's rooms at Gulahek, now his, delightful – the drawing-room with its tiled floor; the study all green and white; the bedroom, dressing-room and bathroom lavishly equipped; and above all the tiled balcony on which he would sleep at nights when it got really hot, and on which now he had his breakfast, open to the morning breeze. He had his two dogs brought back, Henry adorable with his bloodhound face, and Zurcha silky and good, but nervous. Dressed in a new collar given by Dottie she looked like Mme Balsan. As for Bay Rum, Percy's horse which Harold bought from him, it was a superlative beast. To crown his contentment he received a telegram from the Foreign Office congratulating him on his handling of the Khorassan episode. Meanwhile the position in that province remained obscure. Most of the army was apparently still in revolt, encouraged by the Russians. Tehran troops had been sent to negotiate and the Shah's prestige was badly shaken.

As Chargé d'Affaires he was obliged to entertain people who bored him stiff. He had two English missionary ladies to stay. One was called Miss Eardley ('Oh, not, alack, alas, Eardley Knollys, that hellenic vision with the scented amber curls.') He complained to Vita:

Now how comes it that I, who loathe women in general and virgins in particular, should for three whole weeks have to entertain these *calottes*? How comes it that I who am rendered rather ill by the thought of the Church, who don't like missionaries, and who hate society, should entertain these vestals of the Church Missionary Society? Will you please explain all this to me? . . . I suppose what it is is the white man's burden.[36]

On the 11th July he attended the opening of the Majlis in uniform. It was the hottest day of the year up to date. The diplomatic corps were given ices in an ante-room before being filed like cattle into their boxes. There they stood sweating for twenty minutes until the Shah arrived. He walked in and read his speech sulkily, and walked out again. After this futile ceremony more ices were handed round. Harold was then driven by the Legation chauffeur, with a gholam in attendance, to pay calls. 'It was all very impressive and the guards saluted as they have never saluted before.'

Harold was depressed to receive a letter from Vita saying that her mother's health was deteriorating and she might not after all be able to come out in the autumn. He sent her an understanding reply. In any case he could not face another wrench like the one at Resht. She must of course remain in England for B.M.'s sake. It was consoling that he would have four months' leave early in the next year, after which she might return to Persia with him. A week or so later he confessed to Vita with shame that he had had a horrid half-dream. Iago was whispering in his ear that B.M's health was an excuse and Virginia or someone else was the cause. This ugly suspicion was quickly allayed. As for Virginia, Vita wrote Harold a letter analysing her love and admitting a deadly fear 'of arousing physical feelings in her [Virginia], because of the madness . . . It is fire with which I have no desire to play.' And she ended, 'My darling, you are the one and only person for me in the world; so take that in once and for all, you little dunderhead.'[37]

On the 21st of the month the British Chargé d'Affaires felt obliged to witness the Achowra in Tehran. The Achowra is the feast of the martyrdom of the infant Imams Hassan and Hussein, and one of the main rituals of the Shia schism, which is mainly concentrated in Iran. It is for westerners a terrifying Passion play involving the release of religious hysteria and the shedding of much blood.[38]

We walked into the central court of the Bazaars . . . that great open space into which converge at right angles and under great vaulted gates the three main arteries of the bazaars . . . The western gate gives on to the street along which the trams run and it was by this we entered. We climbed up a little staircase and emerged on the mud roof of one of the shops that fringe the sides of the square.

In the large square below were two dressing stations, with ether and iodine in beer bottles and some lint and bandages in an earthenware basin. A detachment of police was drawn up...

From inside the northern arch we could hear a confused murmur, and at 8 o'clock the front ranks of a procession could be seen forming with wide banners half in black shade, and half in glaring sun. A flute began to play a strange Theocritean elegy like the lament for Adonis. It was answered by a sinister drum. The procession swayed forward into the sun... brass hands on poles, and ostrich feathers like a Roman triumph. In front came a mullah on a horse. The horse was led slowly by a young acolyte and the mullah held both his hands to his mouth while he yodled the call to prayer... Then suddenly the whole movement and colour of the procession altered from sedate slow-moving black to rhythmic, agitated naked forms. A group of butter-coloured torsos and muscular; their palms beating in unison flat upon their breasts. As they came out into the sunlight the flute rose to a more emphatic and more rhythmic wail; the flagellists turned round towards each other making a double circle. The 'Iman Hussein', they shouted, 'is level with the dust.' And at each third word they smacked themselves with flat palms upon their breasts. Smack, smack, smack, above the raucous chanting. And when they turned again their waists and nipples showed flushed against their butter-coloured skin.

... Out they jerked into the sunlight, and with them came the noise of their hissing, 'Hussein,' 'Hassan' 'Hussein' 'Hassan' they hissed like some steam engine, and then the pace quickening to a crescendo, there was a cumulative yell and a hundred swords flashed in the sun. Their bald and shaven heads spurted with blood. They cut their left hands and smeared the blood over their faces. Great gobbets of it splashed upon their white aprons. They swayed jerking and panting past us out under the western gate.

A second procession then emerged from the eastern gate, carrying the symbols of the passion, little boys bearing clumsy models of legs and arms, a tiny model head of the Imam upon a pole, a body on a bier swaying along without a head; a horse led in crimson trappings with arrows suspended from its mane. These again were followed by naked flagellists, and behind them staggered the procession of blood. Their white robes were crimson to the foot – not splashed as previously – but a scarlet wet dabble. Their heads slobbered dripping red in the sun, their swords were running wet. They merely whispered, 'Huss', 'Hass', 'Huss', 'Hass' as they staggered by. Three or four collapsed as they passed us and were taken to the dressing station. Their naked legs stretched out below us were as if stripped of skin, wet and scarlet. The sweet, hot smell of blood came up to us in warm eddies. The flutes died away out into the street. It was all silent again except for the cooing of doves.

Then again a procession. The third procession appeared from the southern gate. Little naked boys screaming in an agony of lament. Biers swaying under green trappings, and then a hundred more bloodstained figures – a nightmare of butchery, their white surgical frocks suggesting a vast hospital that has gone mad and lascivious, a swaying, jerking shambles.

We came down when they had passed, picking our way carefully across the reeking cobbles. Two carts in the courtyard were being laden with unconscious corpses . . .

I do *not* like clergymen.[39]

The following day the village of Gulahek performed its version of the Passion Play in mourning for Hassan and Hussein. More primitive and even more earnest than the celebration in Tehran the performance suggested to Harold a woodcut of the Fortune Theatre in the sixteenth century. An elder stood behind Harold fanning him throughout with a grass flipper. To start with his face was impassive. With the breaking of the participants and spectators into wails, howls, swaying and beating of breasts, the elder could contain himself no longer, and burst into a flood of tears.

With Harold's hatred of organized religions and his contempt for superstitious practices which he believed led people to commit more barbarities than injustices and deprivations of freedom, went a strange, and harmless, addiction to superstitious customs, and a semi-serious belief in auguries. For instance, when depressed or uncertain how to act, he would open the Aeneid or Book of Proverbs at random, and be consoled or guided by the extract his eye lit upon. When the Maltese cross fell off King George V's crown on the arrival of his coffin into Westminster Hall Harold regarded it as 'a most terrible omen.' When an unpleasant thing happened nothing would prevent him from believing that two more unpleasant things would follow. Both Harold and Vita said 'Rabbits!' on the first morning of every month, often inscribing the word at the top of their letters. When his housekeeper once knocked on his door and he unguardedly replied, 'Thank you,' before ejaculating 'Rabbits!', he wrote, 'God will be offended by this oversight and ill luck will pursue us all throughout the month.' He was only reassured when his secretary suggested that the omission no longer mattered because the introduction of myxamatosis meant there were no longer any rabbits to invoke.

Harold's dislike of religions and persons ecclesiastical was by no means minimized by a visitation from the Anglican Bishop In Persia. His lordship came to administer Communion to the Legation staff. At the

Bishop's request Harold ordered Taghi to fetch one wine-glass and a piece of bread. Taghi brought fifteen wine glasses, and champagne, and toast. Henry, having been tied up during the service, yelled throughout. The Bishop preached a sermon which Harold longed to contradict. 'I am glad the Christian religion is on the decline,' he said afterwards.[40] Hard on the heels of the Bishop came the missionaries again. They slept in dormitories in the American College – 'rows and rows of little beds with pos underneath and in each bed a missionary. I wonder whether outraged nature asserts herself,' he asked Vita. They came to dinner at the Legation.

Miss Brighty and Miss Carr sat on either side of me. Miss Brighty, wiping the soup off her moustache, said that Gulahek was like 'fairyland.' Miss Carr felt that 'it was like having dinner in a tent at home.' Mr. Crumps was very cross indeed about something. Then he found Henry and became a different man. I agreed with him that Henry was a real pal. 'A reel pal, that's what he is, Mr. Nicolson, aren't you, old man?' At which Henry in an ecstasy of self-consciousness, lay on his back, opened his hind legs wide and displayed to the ladies what, for his age, is a fine sexual organ. 'Isn't he a dear,' they said.[41]

In spite of the political situation which entailed much work in the Chancery and some worry, Harold's hours were as regular as clockwork. 'My life,' he wrote to Clive, 'is sexless, sinless, simple. Its regularity has about it, and for myself alone, a certain beauty.'[42] He woke at 6 o'clock, and read Greek books till 7, when he had his tea. At 7.10 he shaved, and at 7.20 bathed. At 7.30 he had breakfast, and at 8 wrote his daily letter to Vita. Between 8.30 and 9.30 he wrote his book. From 9.30 to 6 o'clock he worked in the Chancery. From 6 to 7.30 he rode, usually with Gladwyn. From 7.30 to 7.40 he had a hot bath. At 8 he dined, and at 9.30 went to bed. He questioned whether, in spite of the agreeableness, the regular routine was not bad for him, by turning him into a cucumber.

His reading, other than the Greek classics, was the novels of Thomas Hardy, who mystified him. He was determined to go on reading him until he discovered how he got his effects. He thought part of his force came from a curious blend of identification and detachment. He put his figures into a very exact focus in a peripheral zone of outside consciousness. As a result the reader got the maximum feeling of being identified with the characters and also of being able to see them in a setting which they could not see themselves. One aspect of this exclusive vision was Hardy's constant habit of relieving the minute topical Dorset detail by a conveyed sense of the round globe of earth spinning through space.

In most of his letters to Vita he referred to, or sent messages, to his sons.

He was delighted that Ben showed signs of becoming an intellectual and that Nigel was winning prizes. It was surprising and gratifying that both their children should turn out to be so normal. He regularly wrote to the boys himself, at this stage of their youth, in a style half playful, half admonitory. He was well aware that Vita, although she dearly loved their sons, was often at a loss during the holidays how to keep them occupied and out of mischief. So to Nigel Harold wrote:

> I do hope you won't make Mummy nervous by being too wild. Of course men must work and women must weep, but all the same I do hope you will remember that Mummy is a frightful coward and does fuss dreadfully about you. It is a good rule always to ask before you do anything awfully dangerous. Thus if you say, 'Mummy, may I try and walk on the roof of the green-house on my stilts?' she will probably say, 'Of course, darling,' since she is not in any way a narrow-minded woman. And if you say, 'Mummy, may I light a little fire on my bed?' she will again say, 'Certainly, Niggs.' It is only that she likes being asked about these things beforehand.[43]

One August afternoon a Ford motor drove up to the Legation and out of it stepped 'a perfectly charming (yes) and young (yes) and beautiful (yes and no) young man.'[44] His name was Patrick Buchan-Hepburn. He was Honorary Attaché at Constantinople whom a friend had asked Harold to put up. He at once went to bed with fever and a temperature of 104. 'I am a ministering angel to him. Would I be so ministering and so angelic if he were Mr. Cowan,' the Consul at Kermanshah? Buchan-Hepburn became very ill indeed with malaria, and looked like the Severn drawing of Keats on his death-bed. Harold said to himself, 'If you fall in love with this young man it will be ridiculous and awkward. Not for this were you placed by a grateful Government in charge of India's bulwark.' So he decided he had better stay and watch him be sick as a prophylactic. But the wretched invalid begged to be left alone. As he recovered Harold debated whether he were clever or stupid. He decided stupid, 'by our bloody exclusive standards.' Others would probably think differently.

> Haven't slept with Hepburn yet. Don't know whether he would like it [Harold wrote to Vita]. I talk about you to Buchan-Hepburn. Why? Why? I fear he is a rather colourless young man. I think extreme good looks are bad for people. They take the edge off their personality. Hepburn is not ... uneducated, but his mind has got no tang or bite to it.[45]

TEHRAN 1926-27

On Buchan-Hepburn's complete recovery they set out for Polour, a hamlet at the west end of the Haraz Valley below Mount Demavend. Taghi and another servant preceded them two days in advance with six little mules tinkling on a string. Host and guest followed on a pair of mules and descended to the river to fish. Harold shared a tent with 'Bothwell' as he now called Buchan-Hepburn who disclosed that he was descended from Mary Queen of Scott's third husband.

> [He] with firm but kindly tact made it quite clear to me that he wasn't one of that sort. I had already made it quite clear that I was. I think he was a little nervous, Jebb not having arrived, and there being champagne, and only a few camels to appeal to if I lost my head ... I have already read Patrick the parts in this letter which refer to him. He clearly thinks you must be just as odd as me.[46]

Gladwyn soon joined them. The contrast between the two young men was striking, Gladwyn so handsome and real, the other so beautiful and secondrate. Patrick was a perfectly external person with no internal core at all beyond a few odd school-room conventions. 'Of course,' he would say, 'I like some of those clever people, but it's a bad thing to see too much of them.' Worse still, he pronounced the Persian landscape ugly. This was unforgivable heresy to Harold's understanding; to his deep love of Persia's bleak, bare mountains; its crumbling surface; its great sun that so seldom wore clothes; its wide distances and its ruins of a civilisation that had died before that of the west was born. Harold tartly asked him if, then, he thought Surrey was beautiful – surely a comparison beside the point – and the poor young man boldly answered, Yes. The admission did not earn him credit for aesthetic sensibility. Harold thereupon sat on the river bank and read Theocritus.

Harold may have gently laughed at Percy Loraine behind his back, but as soon as he stepped into his shoes he wished, not that he were Minister again, but available for consultation. While believing that Sir Percy had allowed himself to be hoodwinked by the Shah and the Persian character, he realised nonetheless that no one else in Tehran enjoyed the confidence of the Shah or the authority to manage him, which he had. What worried Harold most throughout the summer of 1926 was the growing antiBritish and pro-Russian spirit among the Persians. As for the Government it was in hopeless disarray. All the ministers were terrified of the Shah, and none dared remonstrate with him. There was no question that he was a formidable personage. He had strange searching eyes which it required courage to meet. His manner was very direct and totally devoid of the futile compliments and beating about the bush, common to most Persians. When the Khorassan rebellion first broke out in July the Shah, Harold wrote to Loraine, did absolutely nothing but lose his temper, strike Teymourtache in the face, and complain of the British having a military Attaché at Meshed.

> What fails me – Harold wrote to Loraine, – is that I cannot work up any belief in these people. They seem utterly hopeless in every way – impervious both to gratitude and good sense. The only emotions of which they seem capable are fear and avarice. How, in such a mood of disheartened contempt, can one hope to make anything of this job?[47]

The truth was that the Shah was convinced the Russians wished to get rid of him. He was desperately anxious to buy them off by any means. Prime Minister Moshai and Vissuq-ed-Dowleh, the only two wise heads among his ministers, urged him instead to send the Russians a stern note of warning. But no. The Shah in terror sent Teymourtache, Court Minister and Court buffoon of all people, to Moscow to plead on his master's behalf. Harold was seriously worried. He felt sure the Shah would give way all along the line. 'But what does all this matter to Viti? Who just thinks, Oh Hadji will be shot – and would much rather that Russia occupied the whole of India.'

And so things rested until August. On the 11th of that month the first of a series of despatches, marked 'very urgent', passed between the British Legation in Tehran and the Foreign Secretary in Whitehall. To add to the Chargé d'Affaire's confusion several of them crossed en route. Harold notified Sir Austen Chamberlain that Salar-ed-Dowleh, an exiled Qajar Prince, strong anti-Pahlevist, and Governor of Persian Baluchistan, had advanced to Kwash across the Persian border in the belief that the withdrawal of the frontier garrison from that town signified the collapse of the Persian Government. The advance was a very real threat to British personnel and interests in the Duzdap-Mirjawa railway and to British lives and property in that whole area. The Government of India had proposed that a warning be given to the Persian Government that the British Government reserved the right to take military action. Harold advised that any violation of Persian sovereignty would be deeply resented in Tehran and would be the precedent for similar action by the Russians. It would lead to the matter being raised before the League of Nations. He would prefer that no warning be issued, but that in the last resort unpremeditated and swift action should be taken by the Government of India, only if absolutely necessary.[48]

TEHRAN 1926-27

On the same day Sir Austen Chamberlain sent Harold a despatch ordering him to issue a sort of ultimatum to the Persian Government that they must take action immediately to halt the Governor of Persian Baluchistan's advance, or the Government of India would send in troops.[49] Harold had serious qualms, and telegraphed back to Whitehall that this was a rotten idea. To his dismay he received next day instructions to deliver the ultimatum. He could do nothing but comply. However, instead of formally delivering the ultimatum he motored to Tehran and communicated the message orally to the Foreign Minister in his house. Over cups of tea and puffing at a cigarette Harold made his communication. The Minister smiled and bowed, and talked about the heat. Harold left, wondering if he had understood. On his return to Gulahek he received a further telegram from London telling him to cancel the instructions. It was too late. He telegraphed back:

> Deeply regret misunderstanding . . . I waited nine hours before taking action on the chance that my telegram might lead you to modify instructions. Even then I should not have delivered warning had I not received during the day message from Duzdap saying that rebels were only a few miles from Mirjawa. I therefore did not feel justified in further delaying execution of such explicit instructions . . . The fact that my representations were verbal may diminish bad effects.[50]

The Foreign Office had acted foolishly, and Harold wisely. As it turned out no harm was done, and the Persian Government was suitably alarmed by the threat, without understanding exactly what it amounted to.

Harold confided in Loraine that he had virtually disobeyed Foreign Office instructions; he was commended at a later date for having done so.

It was with distaste and some embarrassment that he had to have two audiences with the Shah at Saadabad. At the first the Shah expressed the belief that it was the British who had sent the Governor of Baluchistan into Persia and raised the Kurds. Harold strongly denied this. At the second the Shah was affable and seemed improved in appearance by his misfortunes. He had lost those puffy, bloated looks which were noticeable when he sat drinking and playing poker all day long. Now he was thin again. Harold almost saw what it was that had won Percy's heart. They sat in a tent in the garden. A gardener watering the paths approached too near. 'Pesar, burro!' the Shah bawled like a sergeant on parade. The man dropped his can and bolted. The Shah continued his slow, soft monologue.

Harold's correspondence with Loraine had aroused in that easy-going pragmatist the notion that Harold was too gloomy, too pessimistic. The charge provoked Harold to give an explanation of his apprehensions. He listed the menacing events in Persia which had taken place since Sir

Percy's departure; and then he specified the polarity in their outlook upon the Persian scene.

> Where I think we see differently is about the Shah. You feel he is something reliable, and solid. I think him infinitely untrustworthy and sly. Again, you believe somewhere in the Persians. I think them the most contemptible race on earth. You believe in good relations as something positive; I only believe in them as something negative, i.e. they won't get us what we want, but they may prevent our being bothered by pinpricks. The Persians have heaps of pins (Gulchek, Capitulations, Gulf) which they could use if they wanted to be nasty. Good relations prevent them from being nasty; but it doesn't make them nice.
>
> Take the Sheikh's business: I had a long talk with Millspaugh and told him of the explicit promise made to you by Vossuq and Mostaufi. He said that they had no right to have made such promises since they knew that they could not be carried out ... He said the Shah would never allow a settlement so long as the Sheikh had a drop of blood left in his veins. Well, I believe this. I believe that the Shah's promises about the Sheikh are all bunkum and that all he is out for is cash.[51]

Indeed the Sheikh of Mohammerah's prospects were no more favourable than before. When Harold paid him a visit he was lying on a mattress, looking like a sea-sick patriarch, and groaning.

Harold Nicolson was by no means a pessimist by nature. On the contrary he was an optimist. So it is ironical that Loraine's opinion that his outlook was gloomy should have been an indirect prelude to the secession from the straight path of Harold's career, his disappointment with his lot, disillusion and ultimate resignation from the service. There is no doubt that Loraine communicated his assessment of Harold's judgement to his superiors in the Foreign Office–Oliphant, arbiter of Middle East matters, Tyrrell who anyway disliked him, and above them both Austen Chamberlain, whose attitude was the least intolerant of the three. It was their adverse prejudice, derived from Loraine, which induced them to misinterpret the tenor of Harold's important Despatch of the 30th September.

The Despatch of the 30th September was written towards the end of Harold's term as Chargé d'Affaires before Loraine's successor, Robert Clive, took over as Minister. Entitled *Between Two Reigns*,[52] the Despatch was a too brilliant summary of the Persian situation and a request for rethinking on the part of the Foreign Office about the basic principles of the present British policy in Persia. It began by referring to the closure by the Shah of the Russian frontier in the previous January, which had already partially ruined the northern provinces of the country. Upon an organism thus weakened Russian propaganda and Russian moneylenders were battening with ease. Those northern provinces were in consequence falling into complete servitude to the Soviet. The Despatch went on to say that there was absolute chaos in Persian administration; the army was subject to sporadic mutiny; the tribes were restless; the people impoverished and oppressed; and the judicature was corrupt. The Foreign Office notwithstanding had placed all Britain's hopes in one man, the Shah, who was proving a broken reed. After discussing the general Persian attitude towards the British and Soviet policies, the Despatch suggested detailed lines that His Majesty's Government might pursue.

Harold's tactical mistake was in beginning with the suggestion that the Foreign Office's Persian policy needed revision, and then continuing that he didn't for one moment advocate a change in the present basic policy in hand. The Despatch was a kind of thinking aloud by an exceptionally prescient man, a warning, a prognosis of future trouble, unless the Foreign Office woke up to the likely consequences of recent events. The interest of the Despatch lies rather in the comments it aroused in Whitehall than in its content.

Sir Lancelot Oliphant's Minute declined to accept the view that the Government's policy needed either re-examination or re-affirmation The representative in Tehran, he said, must contend with difficulties as they arose, which Loraine did with such conspicuous success. The idea of our championing Persia against Russia was grotesque. Loraine had encouraged Persia to live on good terms with Russia. This criticism by Oliphant was a complete misunderstanding of Harold's advocacy. In fine he, Oliphant, suggested that Robert Clive should be told that the Foreign Office would send no reply to a Despatch 'which strikes us here as being unduly alarmist and not entirely logical.' Sir William Tyrrell's Minute was that he was not much impressed by the Despatch. He was puzzled by the author's equivocal attitude to 'good relations'. Here he too was under a misunderstanding, for Harold had not said that good relations led nowhere. What he did say was that, unsupported by positive policy, good relations led nowhere.

Sir Austen Chamberlain's long, hand-written notes on the other hand made good sense. He said, not unjustly, that Nicolson had done his thinking on paper instead of first clearing his own mind and then presenting the Office with the result. As Sir William had pointed out, it was not easy to relate his conclusions to certain passages of his preliminary statement. After some qualifications and amplifications the author's conclusions were generally sound. In any case the Despatch was a serious piece of work, to which a very intelligent man with a fine career before him had given much time and labour. He was shocked that a representative on the spot should be unaware of the purposes and principles of his country's policy. 'If I were Mr. Nicolson I would feel discouraged not to receive a reply.

Oct. 9. 1926

My dear Lancelot,

You see all this Bentinck business turns to be so difficult to explain. It puts me so to speak in a false position. What am I to say tomorrow to Reza shah Pahlavi? What on earth am I to say?

I shall feel rather small I fear after all the times I have told him how good I am, how good you are, how good is Sir Henry Dobbs.

But I don't worry, I am the British lion. I keep on saying it to myself. "You", I say, "are the British

If Mr. Nicolson were a fool I should remove him. As he is certainly not a fool, I infer that, away from daily contact with us, our intentions are not as clear to him as to us. Let us make them clear.'

But he did not make them clear, at least not to Harold. Tyrrell and Oliphant between them saw to it that Harold's Despatch had no acknowledgment, which amounted to a strong, tacit rebuke.

On reading today through this very clever Despatch – clever because it pinpoints salient problems – it is not difficult to understand why it irritated those hidebound Foreign Office pundits. It was a slightly contradictory document, and not entirely logical. It must have struck the recipients as pert, coming from a man still in his thirties. Moreover, it was a reflection to some extent upon his former chief, Sir Percy Loraine. In being pessimistic it demonstrated a state of thinking unwelcome to him and them. Undoubtedly it caused a minor sensation because it called into question the whole Foreign Office policy in the Middle East.

Harold was fully aware that he had caused offence and earned for himself bad marks for insubordination. He told Clive Bell that he also felt frustrated in being prohibited as a civil servant from broadcasting to his countrymen the truth about Persia, 'not in duologue but before an assemblage.' The politician in Harold was already ousting the diplomatist.

By the beginning of October the camels were coming down from the mountains, and the early mornings were heavy with the sound of their grave bells. The mountain folk were returning to the plains. It was time for the Legation to pack up Gulahek till next summer, and move back to Tehran for the winter. Harold dreaded the cold and the long evenings of home-sickness ahead, but if only Vita were with him he would actually prefer being in Persia to England. When the day for leaving Gulahek arrived he managed to avoid the traditional ceremony whereby the elders of the village did homage to the Legation. In Tehran he moved into the Compound residence until the new Minister should arrive.

Harold had by now read Vita's *Passenger to Teheran*, to which he could not give too much praise, except for the title which displeased him. The book surpassed his expectations. It presented a Persia as different from the Persia of other travel books as cameos in a museum shown by Roger Fry were different from cameos looked at by oneself. The beauty of Vita's style amazed him. She never diverged from the same key throughout; and the same colour-tone lent the story continuity. Eddy Sackville-West also sent him his new novel, *The Ruin*. Harold admitted there was something fine about it. But it was too missish; there was too much in it of tea-cups and lumps of sugar.

During the months at Gulahek Harold had been devoting one hour every morning religiously to his own book. This was to become *Some People*. The very day he left England, when writing sorrowfully to Vita in the train he told her, 'I have BEGUN MY NEW BOOK. Mar doesn't know what it is. It's a secret. But it will be very surprising.'[53] He snatched odd moments during the journey to Persia; on the boat from Brindisi; in the hotel in Alexandria; and waiting for the motor convoy in Jerusalem. Once he got to Tehran he dropped the book for the winter. The ambience, the conditions there were all wrong. It is only right to say that he had already written the chapter on Jeanne de Hénaut before he left England, It had been printed by the Hogarth Press as a sort of Christmas card to be sent to friends. Duff Cooper, who like him had learned French under Jeanne's tutelage saw a copy. He was enchanted with it. In June Harold told Vita he was doing more 'Jeanne sort of things.' He had shown one of them to Raymond who said he must re-write it; as it stood it read like A. P. Herbert or A. A. Milne. 'Damn Tray!' Harold exclaimed, 'but I feel he was right.'[54] His friend's discouragement made him put the book aside again for a time. But, left to himself on his verandah at Gulahek, he resumed it. He even wrote one chapter about Vita, which he called *Atalanta in Bloomsbury*, and eventually scrapped at her request. The manuscript has disappeared. In September he wrote to her,

> for practical purposes my head is more efficient than I have ever felt it before... The 'Jeannes' are not serious. They just live in a drawer of my table and are pulled out when I have an off moment... I have practically finished five by now (Jeanne, Arketall, Titi, Atalanta in Bloomsbury, and Malone – the one I am now engaged on.)[55]

He would send them to Constable. 'None of your Hogarths for me,' alluding to the Woolfs' private printing press. They would scorn them. He regarded the whole enterprise as a pot boiler. Besides, without books of reference in Persia, he could only write a novel or an alternative form of semi-fiction.

Encouraged by Gladwyn who had read Arketall in typescript and praised it, Harold in December wrote 4,000 words of Lambert Orme one evening over the fire, while sipping burgundy. He found that quite unconsciously the sketches came to represent himself struggling to know himself and discarding a series of false claims. On the last day of the year he sent the collection off by bag to Constable's, demanding no advance payment. Instead he asked for 15 per cent royalties; American but not colonial rights; page-proofs but not galleys; and above all no blurbs or vulgar advertisements, 'the reason being that I am a little ashamed of the book.'[56] He told Clive Bell that he had written an idiotic book.[57]

Until the new Minister arrived in the first week of November Harold was more lonely than at any other time in Persia. He did not like leaving Gulahek; he dreaded the prospect of living alone once more in his own house, and he had no wish to relinquish his powers to a superior. He was even driven to asking Captain Wickham, the new Assistant Attaché, to share his house with him until Vita came out in the spring. And when Wickham did so he got on Harold's nerves. If only, Harold complained, he would talk about Quetta, which he knew, and not about what he imagined Harold to be interested in. What made English low-brows so stupid was their lack of true curiosity and their disconcertion by the unknown and unexpected. Wickham, Harold opined, was motivated neither by intelligence nor love, but by habituation and prejudice upon prejudice.

Harold was also made unhappy by not being able to share with Vita at home the success of *The Land*. It was being received with rapture in England. The critics hailed her as a poet of first-rate importance. Harold was deeply moved. He wrote to her:

You don't know what *The Land* means to me. I read it incessantly. It has become a real wide undertone to my life. I forget absolutely that it is by you.[58]

He learned passages of it by heart which he quoted out loud on his rides. It was the very stuff of poetry. Coming upon certain lines was as memorable as catching the rarest swallow-wing of thought. If ever there were a work of art about which he felt certain, it was this. It made him pine for Long Barn, and he found himself going for long mental walks in the garden there, thinking of the different sounds his footsteps made on the paths, the lawns and the terrace. *The Land* caused him to turn to reading other contemporary poetry. In modern poetry one must know who the poet was and what was his state of mind at the moment of composition. One needed to be sure that it represented the state of an interesting and not an uninteresting mind. He thought Osbert Sitwell had an uninteresting mind, and he feared that T. S. Eliot had an uninteresting mind also. But as for Valéry, *there* was a mind indeed. His poems were limpid and mad, but with the cool, hard radiance of some crystal polygon, a polygon of a hundred dazzling facets; not a sheet of plain glass. One could not see through his poems, but one could see into them. And as one turned them over in one's mind, fresh shafts and angles of illumination radiated forth, half realised in and out of each other. From one facet Valéry reflected Racine, from another Rimbaud, from another Mallarmé. His was the modern mind. He was the first poet of the age. Harold speculated why the greatest poetry was borne on a wave of gross material success and triumph, instancing the works of Homer, the Augustan Romans, the Elizabethans and the Victorians as the fruits of conquest and national prosperity.

He read Omar Khayyam with his Persian teacher, whom he referred to as the Dab. If only, Harold told him, Edward FitzGerald had had the courage to substitute *he* for *she* in the interrogative *Thou*. The Dab was dreadfully shocked, Harold wrote to Vita:[59]

> He takes the paederastic element as a poetic convention, but when I press him on the subject he says that it is 'mystic' and means 'God'. Now that is all very well but one has to be St. Catherine of Siena or Christina Rossetti to fall physically in love with the Deity, and even the Dab cannot seriously imagine that the tulip-lipped, cypress-waisted moon-faced tapettes of the quatrains are anything better than little bugger-boys from the bazaars ... The actual grave monotony of [FitzGerald's] metre produces a feeling – a tone of seriousness – which throws a certain dignity over these tavern ditties. But they remain tavern ditties all the same.

Having tidied up the Legation and moved away his own belongings Harold on the 5th November set off in the yellow motor to meet the new Minister, his wife and daughter, at Karedj.

Robert Clive (Harry to his friends) had come from being Consul-General in Tangier. He was a member of the Clive family in Herefordshire, being, as the Dictionary of National Biography puts it, a first cousin four times removed from Clive of India. He had white hair and blue eyes. He was faultlessly dressed, a man of great distinction, and totally devoid of vanity or pomposity. In this respect he was a contrast to Sir Percy Loraine. In fact Clive was so modest that he allowed his talents to be overlooked by the Foreign Office, and even endeavoured to disguise them from his colleagues. Nevertheless this did not prevent him being made a K.C.M.G. in the 1927 New Year Honours List. Harold took to him at once, finding him a thoroughly decent man, with no nonsense about him.

After a picnic on the roadside Harold accompanied the Clives in the yellow motor between a convoy of cars to Tehran. Precisely at 3 o'clock, as pre-arranged, they drove through the Bag-i-Shah gate into the Legation Compound. The guard turned smartly out, and the staff which had gathered at the gate, took off their hats. The Minister was affable to everyone. Harold felt ashamed of himself for having resented his arrival and nourished little meannesses which he had never suspected of lurking within him. Clive at once passed on to Harold that the Foreign Office were critical of him for being too pessimistic. Harold confirmed that he was pessimistic over Persia's future, but was able to assure the Minister that he managed to get on well with the Persians in spite of his disbelief in them. Within a few days Clive presented his credentials to the Shah. In reading them he showed signs of nervousness and his coat-tails shook. The Shah, suffering from a bad bout of opium, looked yellow, and was surly and offhand. He just had the grace to assure the new British envoy that he desired to remain on the friendliest terms with Britain and hoped that Prince Teymourtache's recent visit to Moscow had not unduly disturbed the Foreign Office. His purpose had been merely to conclude a commercial treaty with the Soviet over Caspian fisheries. On receiving the Minister's report of his first audience of the Shah,[60] Sir Austen Chamberlain commented, 'Time will show whether the Shah intends to convert his words into deeds.' It was not until the end of the month that the Foreign Secretary made an official reference to Harold's Despatch. He told Clive that it had indicated to him how extremely necessary it was that the Legation in Tehran should be fully aware of the Foreign Office's policy towards Persia. He accordingly transmitted guidance (withheld from Harold) on the relations and maintenance of British interests in Persia. This guidance amounted to some ten paragraphs of pious protestation, in effect repetition of the contents of a Memorandum which Loraine had on his return fired into the Office exhorting it to treat Persia as a friendly power and not to interfere in her internal affairs. In addition, Lancelot Oliphant sent Clive a Memorandum, which was rather more specific. He pointed out that the situation in Persia was becoming thoroughly unsatisfactory, owing to Soviet pressure. He feared the Shah might come up against the Majlis at any moment and be forced to abdicate. Such an event would not help British interests at all. Certainly the Shah's relations with the Majlis could hardly have been worse after he had Modanes, a leading Mullah, shot in the arm, with intent to kill.

It was not long before Robert Clive came round to Harold's opinion, which he agreed was by no means exaggerated, of Reza Shah's total unpredictability. Before the year was out the Shah promised to recognise Iraq. Clive telegraphed that piece of information to the Foreign Office. Hardly had he done so when Reza made conditions that all Persians in Iraq must be afforded capitulatory privileges, which he knew to be impossible. He then went back on his contract over Imperial Airways' route to India, which meant that the Company had to dismantle its landing grounds, already constructed. In other words it was not long before Clive had to reap the harvest of Loraine's credulity and optimism. Clive's five years as Minister in Tehran were to cover a period of increasing Persian nationalism and xenophobia, coupled with British frustration.

At first Harold was not at all sure whether he liked Mrs. Clive. He told Vita[61] he found her affected.

> Now what on earth do we mean when we say 'affected'? Clive Bell, I suppose, is affected, and Raymond, and Virginia, and Vita and Harold. So all one means is that her mechanical habits (whether mental, moral, aesthetic or merely laryngeal) are not the sort of habits I like. One means also that the mechanism is a little too obvious. That certain habits of attitude occur with too regular a precision. Now she has a form of affectation which irritates me particularly ... Thus I say I must be going off to the Chancery. 'Robot!' she says. The catch-words of the day are applied by her to the incidents of daily life, but they are the catch-words of a world I don't like at all, the world that lives in Hans Place, and dines at Princes Restaurant, and has relations in all the counties, and simply revels in the Army & Navy Stores.
>
> Then her meanness is simply terrifying ... Enter Mrs. Clive: 'Daddy, sorry to interrupt you two important people (Oh, yes, I know I'm a bore) but just fancy one has to pay 1 kran 25 for the most rotten little notebook here. Isn't there some rough Government paper on which Mimi can do her lessons?'
> Clive: 'But after all 1 kran 25 is only just sixpence.'
> Mrs. Clive: 'But, my dear man, you should see the notebook. Why, at the Stores one could get something far better for 5d. Of course I sent Mimi back to the shop to return it.'
>
> And then her voice is dreadful. A sort of brave whine, courage struggling against ill-health; a sort of plaintive tolerance, a superior education tolerating a world of fools ('One must have one's sense of humour, etc.')

By the New Year Harold had totally reversed his nasty opinion of Magdalen Clive. Under the affectation he discovered real cleverness. He had grown to love both Clives for their unvarying kindness to members of the staff, high and low, and the infinite trouble they took to make the most humdrum parties, as well as the grandest, enjoyable.

Harold's fortieth birthday was made hateful by his being obliged to have Henry, his spaniel, put down. Henry had developed contagious sores which the vet assured him were incurable. Harold paced his room, wondering what to do, while 'the poor little cause of all this trotted quite happy up and down beside me.' His wretchedness was turned to rage when he discovered that his servant had thrown poor little Henry's body on the dust heap. He made him retrieve and bury it decently. 'A black day,' he recorded, 'and my heart is broken at being 40.'[62]

Vita's relations with Virginia Woolf were reaching a crescendo. Harold, whose antennae concerning Vita's affections were acutely attuned, detected a muted reserve in her last letters to him. He was terrified of a muddle in that quarter. 'It is such a powder magazine,' he cautioned Vita. 'I am far more worried for Virginia and Leonard's sake than for ours.' A lovely paper-chase on Bay Rum drove away those apprehensions momentarily.

> I often think a thing we don't notice is variations in the 'sound tone' of different days. I mean why exactly is a fine autumn morning more *silent* than a fine spring morning? To me this sound tone is as effective as temperature and as variable.[63]

Harold was already beginning to count the days until he saw Vita. He wondered if, after Virginia, he would seem dull to her; if she had become grim and highbrow; would be bored by his chatter and would want to sit up till 2 a.m. nightly discussing the derivation of moral sentiments. He even feared that when they met, he might be shy of her travelling companions, Dorothy Wellesley and Leigh Ashton,[64] just at first. He was already planning how he and she would make their botanising expedition to the Bakhtiari Mountains in the spring. He suggested her writing a sort of 'voyage autour de ma chambre' book about it. She could prepare all the philosophical parts beforehand, and write up the rest from notes taken during the twelve days en route.

As usual Harold weighed the advantages against the disadvantages of the past year. 1926 had been, he concluded, 'a bloody year', because he had been absent from Vita, the boys and Long Barn, and because he was now forty. Until three years ago he prided himself on not appearing middle-aged, and on looking younger than his contemporaries. Nevertheless the unavoidable incursion worried him. He had a good look at himself in the glass, and noticed a change. He had lost a lot of hair during the summer and was now distinctly bald. He was fatter in the face, though no fatter in the body. Yet he quickly put on weight, which he could and did drastically reduced by banting from 12 stone 12 lbs down to 10 stone 11 lbs. On the other hand his health remained good, apart from repeated colds of a semi-influenza type to which he was prone, and occasional fainting-fits. For instance, in the New Year he suddenly, for no apparent reason, fainted before dinner and struck his head against a table. The Legation doctor examined his heart and blood pressure and pronounced that there was nothing the matter with either. Yes, loss of youth was a terrible tragedy, but he thanked God he had made the most of it while it was there. No, he did not regret having come to Tehran. The experience had braced him.

On the 8th January 1927 Harold addressed his last letter to Vita in England, and on the 15th sent one to Moscow, not imagining that it would reach her. In order that they might both know whether any of their letters to and from Persia had gone astray, and, when a whole batch arrived together in what order they should be read, Harold and Vita numbered each on the back of the envelope. His to Moscow was marked No. 247. As the days marched by he became more and more excited. Wickham, the Attaché, was turned out of Harold's house, and Vita's room was got ready. On the 28th Vita and her two companions left London. On the 2nd February they left Moscow, where Vita happened to meet Denys Trefusis. There she received Harold's letter and one from Virginia, who wrote, 'Lord bless me! Think of meeting your paramour's husband. What did he say?'[65] On the 4th Harold set off in his car, staying the night with the Consul at Kasvin. He woke up in a snow-storm, and crept into Resht on the Caspian Sea at 8.30 on the evening of the 5th. Next morning at 10 o'clock he watched the smoke of the steamer crossing from Baku. When it drew into the port at Enzeli he could see Vita leaning over the rails of the steamer, searching for him. Another re-union had taken place. The party went by slow stages to Tehran.

The next six weeks were mostly spent riding, paper-chasing, visiting the bazaars, where Leigh Ashton found a rare Persian pottery blue bird, plant hunting in the foothills, visiting Elizabeth Daryush, that 'poor little lump of suet,' and being entertained by Tehran society. They were also to be the last of Harold's work in Tehran. This work consisted in humiliating endeavours to persuade the Persian Government to rescind its prohibition of the air-routes over Persia to India. The Shah was persistently disagreeable to Sir Robert Clive whenever the subject was broached. In fact after little more than two months of office the Minister wrote to Chamberlain corroborating the pessimism of Harold's contentious Despatch of the previous September. There was, he told the Foreign Secretary, distinct nationalistic feeling in Persia which expressed itself in repeated pin-pricking of His Britannic Majesty's Legation. Not only had the Shah gone back on his word over the Imperial Airways route, but he threatened to abolish capitulations, to re-introduce tariff autonomy, and to reduce the foreign concessions. The chief power of the land lay in the Minister of Court, Teymourtache, who had recently been made a sort of Grand Vizier, with undisputed influence over the Shah. The Majlis was abject to the Shah, whose standing with the army was higher than ever, thus enabling him to defy British advice at every turn. The Minister's situation was unenviable and fraught with difficulties.

The effect of having Vita with him again, and enjoying the companionship of Dorothy Wellesley and Leigh Ashton was to make Harold realise once and for all that his principal interests transcended the Diplomatic Service. He began to question why he should spend the rest of his working life vexing himself over capitulations, frontier boundaries, the tendentious vagaries of oriental despots, and so many hours outside the Chancery in frivolous social duties, while earning a pittance in return. After all, his overriding interest and ambition lay in writing, and he was happiest in the company of other writers and intellectuals.

> Wake up in the morning with conviction that I shall chuck the diplomatic service. I had been fussing and worrying about this problem for months, and then this morning I woke with a calm and certain conviction as if it had come to me from outside. Write to Cadman by bag asking him to give me a job.[66]

That Harold should have asked the chairman of the Anglo-Persian Oil Company to employ him, either in the City of London or in the Persian Gulf, was an astonishing decision. Had Sir John complied, then Harold would have eluded the clutches of the devil to plunge into the deep blue sea. His situation would have been more limited than before. When Cadman replied that he could not offer Harold a job, Harold was nonplussed. Actually one of Cadman's fellow directors had secretly consulted the Foreign Office, and Tyrrell absolutely vetoed the idea. When Vita got to hear of this she attributed to Tyrrell motives of pure hatred, whereas if the truth were known, he thought Harold too valuable to be spared. A year later Harold was glad that Cadman had turned him down.

On the 23rd March Harold and his party left Tehran on the expedition to the Bakhtiari Mountains and the Anglo-Persian Oil Fields in the Gulf. He was not to return. He was handed a touching letter from Sir Robert Clive. Clive had, he wrote, too much English reserve and self-consciousness to give vent to his feelings in words. As their ways were likely to lie apart in the future, he wanted Harold to know how their brief collaboration would remain for him a happy memory. He admitted that at first he was nervous about working with him. 'I imagined you as someone who from the heights of his superior intelligence would inwardly scorn while at best outwardly tolerating my feeble efforts.' He always had misgivings when taking on a new job. But 'Lancelot assured me you were a most devoted and loyal colleague . . . I want to thank you very much. Just that. I shall miss you sadly.'[67]

14

THE BAKHTIARI AND FOREIGN OFFICE INTERVAL, 1927

THE first intimation of a Persian spring was the hooting of owls at night in the Legation garden. This clarion call to restless English residents induced them to make little daily excursions into the country. They would ride to Djoujaroud, watch the first swallows and gather white and scarlet thorn. These early blossoms were the invitation to move further south to the province of Khuzistan. It was Vita's determination to cross the Bakhtiari Mountains in search of wild flowers which prevailed upon her companions. So after a tremendous fuss of tying luggage on to Harold's old Ford, driven by an English chauffeur called Garne, the party went ahead in the Dodge limousine, driven by Vita, with Dorothy Wellesley beside her. In the back sat Harold and Margery Jebb, who had been staying with her brother, Gladwyn. Leigh Ashton had gone off by himself to Shiraz and Isfahan. Garne was accompanied by Bogher, Harold's Persian valet, but not on this occasion by Fakh, his groom, the pair of whom were known collectively as the Sods. Gladwyn and Fraser, the Military Attaché, were up to see the cavalcade off. Old Taghi was so upset that he burst into tears and rushed indoors.

The expedition was fully recorded in Vita's book, *Twelve Days*, published in 1928, and is supplemented by Harold's unpublished diary.

Their drive to Shalamzar was accompanied by a series of misadventures and ludicrous incidents. The cars broke down. First it was the big end of the Ford. 'How I loathe big ends,' Harold was overheard to complain without offering practical assistance or advice. Then Vita drove the Dodge into a rock and smashed the crank-case. At nights they slept in camp-beds all in one room of a deserted villa or village inn. Once a cat jumped on to Dottie's bed. She woke, screaming that a vampire was nibbling at her head.

In the province of Fars they entered the great green plain once occupied by the Sassanian city of Istakh, destroyed during the Arab conquest in the seventh-century A.D. They followed a grass track between the ever-distant mountains, now violet and crowned with snow. At Persepolis they picked up pieces of carved stone, a fragment of fluting, and the tight curls of an Achaemenid beard. Harold in his clumsiness broke a column which had withstood the ravages of 2,000 years. There were unforgettable moments – the discovery of the little red ranunculus sprouting from ruins and lizards of monstrous size darting across the plinths of amber-coloured columns, while overhead black kites wheeled on wings stiff as those on the sculptured reliefs at their feet. And unforgettable scenes – the sudden, unexpected view from the crest of a hill of the plain of Pasargadae and the tomb, like a little white bathing box, of Cyrus, entirely isolated save for the wild asses grazing on the thyme around its base. And unforgettable memories of the senses – the croaking of frogs and clanging of camel-bells; the taste of Shiraz wine like hair-wash, and the smell of burning camel thorn, which was the very breath of Persia. At Isfahan they met Gladwyn Jebb, Lionel Smith and Copley Amory from the American Legation, who had come to join the expedition to the Bakhtiari.

Gladwyn brought with him the proofs of *Some People*, and Harold began to read them. But he was so dejected that he said he could not possibly let the essays appear. 'They read like babbling idiocy,' he protested. 'I shall write no further books.'[1] It was only the remonstrances of Vita that prevented him from destroying the proofs there and then. The travellers stayed the night with a young Persian friend, Assa Dullah. After dinner they sat in a small, dark room, smelling of sandal-wood and spices, and lit by a dim Persian lamp suspended from the ceiling. The moon and planet Venus were visible through the uncurtained window. In these idyllic conditions Dottie recited by heart Tennyson's *Tithonus* until the beautiful almond eyes of their host filled with tears, and he felt impelled to recite in his turn from the poetry of Saadi. The next day Dottie and Margery Jebb left the party for Tehran and Europe, while Gladwyn and Lionel Smith started off ahead for Shalamzar.

Harold and Vita followed the men in another Dodge car hired by Amory. Another Ford adorned with feathers dyed yellow and magenta preceded them with luggage. They passed by pigeon-towers on the roofs of which storks were nesting. They saw white eagles. They lunched in a carpenter's shop. The carpenter carefully spread a carpet over the shavings. They sighted the Bakhtiari Mountains spread open before them like a white screen. From the col above Shalamzar Vita and Harold walked through a wheat field in the sunset. Having rejoined Gladwyn and Copley they were the guests, in his absence, of a Khan in a deserted country house behind a fortified courtyard. They were received by the Khan's steward with great ceremony. The drawing-room was ablaze with occidental mirrors and chandeliers. They dined merrily over Julfa wine and a blazing fire. Here they abandoned the motor-cars.

The next morning they set forth on the actual expedition into the Mountains. Their caravan of pack-mules, saddle-mules, with jangling

BAKHTIARI AND FOREIGN OFFICE 1927

bells affixed to the harness, three servants, including a cook and Harold's Bogher, were gathered in the courtyard. They were furnished with a letter from the Governor of Deh Kurd, which translated ran; 'If you do not show every courtesy and grant every facility to the above-mentioned noble persons, it will be extremely bad for you.'

Next morning at 7.30 Vita and Harold strode ahead on foot. They lost the others; they lost their way. They descended to the sharp gorge of the Karun river, 3,000 ft below them. Footsore and weary they found the caravan at Do-Pulan, and the tents already pitched. They dined avidly off bowls of curdled milk like Devonshire cream, with spoonfuls of apricot jam stirred in. Another day they lunched in a little hut over a fire of ashes and smoke, in the company of a Persian merchant travelling in the opposite direction, who politely unrolled his rugs for them to sit on. Villagers turned up, begging to be treated for various ailments. Again Vita and Harold rashly set off on foot, by themselves, carrying long sticks. In pouring rain they descended another steep gorge. The path was slithery with mud. Harold had on a London flannel suit. Having brought no overcoat, he had been obliged to buy from a peasant a cloak of stiff black felt. As he was too short for it, he looked like a penguin. A terrible despair seized him. He said he loathed the Bakhtiari Mountains and wished he had never come. Vita was an angel of comfort; and the sun came out. They found colchicums and crown imperials in flower, saxifrages and lichens. Then it rained again. More mud.

On the 9th the weather improved. At a bridge they had to cross they were given a reception by representatives of the Tekhani tribe. In a dark tent draped inside with carpets, they were handed little trays of sweets, tea and cigarettes. The reception went on and on. It was impossible to break away because it was considered impolite to be in a hurry. Their host, Ali Khan, called for a brown sacrificial lamb. It was ushered into the tent. It had a brass bowl round its neck to catch the blood. The guests implored that its life be spared. Their request was granted only because Ali Khan was not feeling very well. Lionel Smith took his temperature, and it registered 108°. Finally they got away. While in their tents they were kept awake by a terrible storm of lightning, thunder and snow. They remained in their tents all the next day, waiting for the weather to improve and their clothes to dry before a camp fire. In between sleep, they read the Apocrypha and talked about their favourite cities. They were visited by a giant, 7ft high from the neighbouring village, a dervish carrying a pole with the outstretched brass hand of the Ali, and a blind man chanting an interminable poem about His Majesty Jesus.

They passed Malamir village, a street of mud huts with sloping straw roofs, supported on poles. And then a very unfortunate incident occurred.

They met an extremely handsome dervish on a horse. He was dressed in a flowing robe of sapphire blue, his heavy black curls falling in a cascade upon his shoulders. Politely Vita asked this dazzling apparition if she might photograph him. He was highly flattered. He posed, arranged his robes, and fingered his curls. Stealthily Vita advanced with camera in order to focus. Made suspicious by the stalking movement the horse took fright, reared, bolted and threw the dervish to the ground, trampling him under foot. The dervish's turban fell off. He whimpered, then yelled. His delighted companions roared with laughter. The dervish, more injured in his pride than his bones, was humiliated and displeased. He demanded compensation for three broken fingers. He was handed a toman (the equivalent of one shilling) and was entirely satisfied.

On the plain of Hulagan they watched golden orioles flitting among the myrtle trees, and dug up irises. They found scarlet tulips. They crossed and re-crossed the river Tembi on inadequate stepping-stones; and Vita scolded Harold for wearing shoes with absurdly thin soles, and soaking them in the water. He was clearly not cut out for roughing it on a mountain expedition. On the 14th April, creeping round a corner of Mount Asmari they were confronted by a plume of black smoke from the oil-fields eight miles away, and a smell of sulphur in the air as though from Sheffield or Leeds. Their spirits sank. They dropped down into the plain of Cham Ferakha where they paid their respects to the Dekhani Sarda Zaffer, a splendid patriarchal chieftain with little hawks eyes in a full moon face. He was seated in front of a tent on a very small chair with two young guards behind him, leaning on their rifles. By the light of candles he gave them tea in tumblers, tinned apricots and cigarettes. The Dekhani put Ford cars at their disposal, and had them driven to the oil-fields. Suddenly they were plunged in a world of cement buildings, big and little, and all ignoble, a world of derricks, pipes, boilers, cisterns, tarmac roads, machinery, arc lamps, flares and forests of chimneys belching smoke. They were met by Ronnie Balfour, for whom Harold had found a job in the Anglo-Persian Oil Company. As Legation Counsellor Harold was obliged to feign an interest in the processes of the oil-fields which he did not the least comprehend. After the tranquillity and solitude of the mountains, they were to him a nightmare. And to Vita unadulterated hell. The party drove to Ahwaz, and Abadan, where they stayed in an executive's large bungalow, within a trim little garden of petunias and oleanders. The rooms of the bungalow were decorated, as it might be, by Waring and Gillow, and provided with a gramophone, a billiard table, but not a single book. At Abadan Harold visited a gas-plant and packing-shed, and talked affably with the technical manager and the Consul. In the evening, having said goodbye to Bogher, they embarked on the Company's river steamer for

BAKHTIARI AND FOREIGN OFFICE 1927

Iraq. 'It is then that I leave Persia. We creep slowly up the river to Basra.'

By way of Baghdad (where Harold was able to devote one whole morning to writing an article on Romanticism), Palmyra, Damascus, Baalbek, Alexandria and Marseilles, the Nicolsons reached London on the 5th May. At Victoria they were met by Dorothy Wellesley and Raymond Mortimer. Vita stayed the night with the former in her Mount Street flat, and Harold with the latter in his flat in Gordon Place. In Mount Street Harold was reunited with Ben and Nigel whom he had not seen for a year and a half. 'Ben's nose is bad and his mouth, I fear, always open. Niggs very sweet and grubby,' he commented. He took both boys to dinner at the Criterion and to a movie afterwards. The following morning he saw his parents, and in the evening drove down to Long Barn with Vita and his two sons. He was so impressed by the improvement of the garden, and so excited to be home again that before dinner he was violently sick, and had to be given brandy. The spring days were perfect. 'I have never,' he wrote 'felt so happy in my life. All the weary months of exile are wiped out like a sponge.' The only snag was Lady Sackville's attitude. She was cross and difficult; she refused to let them visit her in Brighton, and then turned up unexpectedly at Long Barn, her nerves all in pieces, a wreck of her former self. 'Poor B.M.' Harold said.

One of the first things Harold did on his return to England was to inform Sir Lancelot Oliphant that he would not go back to Persia. Although he had not told the Foreign Office of this decision before he left Tehran on leave, it had clearly been his intention all along. Certainly Sir Robert Clive in writing his farewell letter did not expect to have his Counsellor back. In fact Harold had practically made up his mind to leave the Diplomatic Service altogether. He wrote in his diary the day before he left Tehran on the Bakhtiari expedition: 'Marks the end of my brilliant career in diplomacy.' And Virginia Woolf, in a letter to Vanessa Bell on the 8th May, must have been repeating what she had learnt from Vita:

> Harold is leaving the Foreign Office. You must admit this is to his credit. He is over 40; has no money of his own; and is throwing up his career just as he's getting to the top. Apparently diplomatic society is so boring that he can't face even becoming an ambassador. Really I think it's a feather in Bloomsbury's cap: a goose feather if you like.

While Vita was with Virginia in Oxford delivering a lecture, Harold went to tea with his old friend, Gosse, who regaled him with anecdotes about nineteenth-century literary celebrities.

He tells me that when a young man Miss Polidori had given him a diary kept by her brother when with Byron in Switzerland. [John William Polidori attached himself to Byron as his physician, and was frequently the butt of his patron's wit.] He read the diary and could only remember that Polidori said B was difficult to manage owing to the volcanic behaviour of his sexual appetite. He would drag the chambermaid into the room, have her, and then kick her out violently. Gosse took no notes from the diary and gave it back to Miss Polidori saying it was a very important paper and should be kept. The old lady thereupon read it for the first time and at once burnt it as being too improper. Gosse also told me many stories of Lord Houghton – of how he always got drunk – of how when he came down to unveil Gray's statue in Pembroke people said, 'Lord Houghton would unveil anything'; of how Lord Houghton at the dinner afterwards got completely drunk, was unable to speak, and had to be pulled down by his shirt-sleeves. Of Gosse's own row with Churton Collins [who attacked the inaccuracy of his Cambridge lectures in the *Quarterly Review* in 1886] and how Tennyson a few weeks later at Aldworth had boomed down the table to him, 'Gosse, do you want to know what I think of Churton Collins? He is a louse upon the locks of literature.' [Collins had offended the Laureate by writing an unfavourable review of *Demeter*]. He tells also of Tennyson's drinking really hard, glass after glass of port, and clay pipe afterwards. Gosse then gives me an unpublished poem by Swinburne. It is a pleasure to hear him talk with so vivid a recollection right back to the 70s.[2]

During this month of May Harold and Vita made the acquaintance of a couple who were to bring them much distress, to repay their hospitality with hostility and to give unwelcome publicity to their sexual predilections. The first mention of Roy and Mary Campbell comes in Harold's diary under the 23rd: 'A South African poet who is staying in the Weald comes to dine with his wife.' Five days later Harold went to tea with the husband in his cottage in the village. He described him as 'an ugly and uncouth creature with fine eyes and brow and immense charm.' Thenceforward there were frequent meetings at Long Barn, where the Nicolsons introduced the Campbells to their friends. Roy who had been born in Durban in 1902 first came to Europe in 1919. A man of ungovernable prejudices, passions and actions, he associated himself with Fascist causes, wrote poetry of a satirical kind in heroic couplets like Pope, and was eventually to die in a motor crash in Portugal. On one occasion Campbell gave Harold the long story of his picaresque and bellicose life. It alerted him to the danger which he saw looming when by August Vita was becoming closely involved with Mary Campbell. In that month the Nicolsons, feeling sorry for the Campbells' poverty offered them free of rent the gardener's cottage at Long Barn. It was a disastrous decision. Roy Campbell went off on prolonged drinking sprees with Augustus John and other bibulous friends, had an affair with Dorothy Warren, and on his return went for his wife with a knife. He would come across to the house in a towering rage against his wife because she dared to remonstrate about his behaviour, and had to be tamed by Vita.

Vita's affair with Mary Campbell was not very serious and did not last long. It was probably induced by her being sorry for her. At any rate Roy Campbell had his revenge by the publication of *The Georgiad* in 1931, in which he portrayed Long Barn and the Nicolsons in the most damaging light, and again in an autobiographical volume, *Broken Record* in 1934.

A hardly less turbulent but far from disruptive, and a wholly innocuous visitor was Ethel Smyth.[3] The composer of *The Wreckers*, now verging on seventy, was practically stone deaf. One Friday evening in early June Harold brought Raymond Mortimer down to Long Barn for the weekend. They found Ethel Smyth already there. She was determined to hear the nightingales for a last time. For hours she sat in the wood, waiting patiently, and straining her ears through her inadequate deaf-aid. At last, as though in answer to her prayer, a bird came, perched just above her expectant head, and sang aria after aria. She was amply rewarded.

During the summer of 1927 countless friends stayed at Long Barn – among them Leigh Ashton, Gladwyn Jebb, Hugh Walpole, Jean de Gaigneron, Dorothy Wellesley, and Vita's cousin Eddy Sackville-West, the transcript of whose novel, *Sinfonia Eroica*, Harold found 'amazingly interesting.'

On the 16th June Vita received the Hawthornden Prize for *The Land* at a ceremony in the Aeolian Hall. Drinkwater, Buchan and Squire were on the platform. Drinkwater made a pompous and dramatic speech, culminating in the announcement of the award.

> V rather shyly advances and receives her cheque. Then a long and foolish speech by Buchan. Then a rather drunk speech by Jack Squire. Then we all break up and chat. Then V and I and Leonard and Virginia go to Gunter's and have ices. Then back to Tavistock Square. Then to dine with Raymond.[4]

From London the Nicolsons went to Oxford, where both parents visited the two boys at Summer Fields, their preparatory school, and Harold saw Sligger Urquhart. They stayed a night with Robert Bridges and his wife at Boars Hill. The atmosphere of the Bridges' sombre and austere household was clearly not to Harold's taste. The Poet Laureate, with his gaunt figure, and handsome, bearded face looked to him like a composite photograph by Mrs. Cameron of George Meredith and Thomas Carlyle. They had cold supper and little to drink. After supper Bridges talked of Paul Valéry, whom he misunderstood, and then they went early to bed.

> The Laureate takes me for a walk in the morning to see his garden and the view of Oxford. He has embarked on a new poem [*The Testament of Beauty*] which is to express the philosophy of his life. It is that the best in one proceeds in the unconscious, the conscious of life being merely mechanical and external. He is writing in a new metre which allows him to say anything and imposes nothing. He is very interested in broadcasting and in his desire to introduce some new symbol to indicate the 'un-trilled r, as in *heart*.' Funny old man.[5]

The mention of Robert Bridges's interest in broadcasting was followed three days later by a note in Harold's diary: 'Buy a wireless receiver.'[6]

On the 23rd June *Some People* was in the bookshops. It had an instantaneous success. Before a month was out Mr. Wilson of Bumpus told the author that the book was booming. It was published simultaneously in America by Houghton Mifflin & Co., and soon received international acclaim, being read by diplomats all over the world. English reviewers, although slightly baffled, were nearly all adulatory. They had never before come upon a collection of essays about individuals purporting to be authentic biography, whereas they clearly were not. Max Beerbohm's *Seven Men* had been the only thing of the sort, and it was admittedly fictional. The *Daily Telegraph* was not sure whether to take Mr. Nicolson seriously. It was apprehensive, even repelled. The *New Statesman* was more discerning and recognised that the author had invented a new autobiographical method as surely as Lytton Strachey had invented a new biographical one. It praised him for wonderfully avoiding the pitfalls of caricature, and so wounding no one. Clive Bell in the *Nation* gave it, not surprisingly, high praise for intelligence and wit. And he ended his review with the words, 'I am not sure that it is the book of a future ambassador.' There of course was the rub.

Lord Birkenhead enjoyed it so much that he felt impelled to write to Sir Austen Chamberlain expressing the hope that it would not prejudice Harold's career in any way. Sir William Tyrrell went up to Harold at a luncheon party of the Colefaxes in order to assure him that he had not found *Some People* indiscreet, which, while it did not prove that he secretly thought it was, indicated that others in the Office did. Sir Percy Loraine was certainly one. He pronounced it 'a cad's book.' This distressed

Harold who wrote him a penitent letter. He admitted to often being a cad, but really hoped that he was not often a shit.

> I expect you are right about my lack of taste, possibly also about my lack of judgment. Moreover my bad habit of ridiculing everybody from myself upwards, may often land me in appearances of disloyalty. But fundamentally I should call myself a loyal and benevolent person. Though I find that few of my friends agree with this pleasing self-portrait. And in any case I *am* affectionate, and I loathe being in disgrace with people whom I sincerely admire and like.[7]

The older diplomats obviously did think it in poor taste, even if not indiscreet, to write flippantly about one's colleagues when one was in the service. Indeed Lord Carnock was of this opinion. Harold had sent his parents an advance copy. The first time that he called at their house after making the gift, his mother met him at the door. 'Don't mention the book to your father,' she warned him. 'He doesn't like it.' A week or so later, however, Lord Carnock who had by then persevered, said to Harold, 'I've been reading your book. It's *so* good.' What is more, Lord Stamfordham told Harold that he had heard King George V shouting with laughter over it in the next room.

It is not difficult to understand how in the ears of 'Pompous Percy' and his generation three out of the nine essays struck a discordant, not to say, an ungentlemanly note. They were Miss Plimsoll, Titty and Miriam Codd. No person of the most high-minded standards could conceivably interpret, in 1927, the remaining six as worse than hilariously funny, unless he took exception to the mockery of Lord Curzon's unfortunate valet. To make a fool of one's governess would of course be an exceedingly insensitive and unkind thing to do. But Miss Plimsoll never existed. As Harold explained to an American friend, Stuart Preston, years later, of the two real governesses he had, when a boy, Miss Corrin and Miss Woods, neither was the least like Miss Plimsoll. If anyone was the prototype of Miss Plimsoll it was an unnamed typist he once had in the Foreign Office. He did, it is true, take some of Miss Plimsoll's archness from the Clives' daughter's governess in Tehran, Miss Palmer-Smith. As for Titty, Harold had remorse about this essay. In the annotated copy of Mr. Preston's *Some People* he wrote:

> I regret this story. It was written about Arthur Hope Vere who died, I think, in 1924. I imagined that he had left no relations behind him and only discovered afterwards that he had a sister who was much incensed by this account.

And if anyone today across the Atlantic should still feel hurt that Harold Nicolson singled out a harmless American lady, whose every remark and action he cruelly pinpointed in *Some People*, they may rest assured that she was wholly imaginary, and only suggested by the single question put to him by a stranger on board the steamship *Helouan* opposite the island of Cythera in November 1925.

Of the remaining characters, not already accounted for, J. D. Marstock was a composite portrait of a man called J. R. Parsons who was at Wellington, and Harold Duncan, who was at Balliol with the author: and Professor Malone was mostly Dr. D. J. Dillon, the eminent philologist, author and journalist, with a touch of Henry Wickham Steed.

Virginia Woolf on receiving an advance copy of *Some People* wrote to Harold a letter of unrestrained approval.[8] The book made her laugh out loud, and at the same time was serious. 'I can't make out how you combine the advantages of fact and fiction as you do.' This point clearly bothered her. She felt jealous. She was also made to feel profoundly and mysteriously shy, she said. But in the *New York Herald Tribune* she reviewed the book, not carpingly, but with reservations.[9] Harold had failed signally to achieve a truthful transmission of personality. *Some People* was not biography, and not fiction, although it was extremely amusing. 'One of the great distinctions,' she wrote, of the new school (meaning Lytton Strachey's), to which Mr. Nisolson belonged, 'is the lack of pose, humbug, solemnity.' Having deftly put him in his place, so to speak, she acknowledged that his subjects showed themselves to the observant eye 'in the tone of a voice, the turn of a head, some little phrase or anecdote picked up in passing.' And then she continued,

> He lies in wait for his own absurdities as artfully as for theirs. Indeed by the end of the book we realise that the figure which has been most completely and most subtly displayed is that of the author ... It is thus, he would seem to say, in the mirrors of our friends that we chiefly live.

Here she had her finger on the essence of *Some People*. It is an autobiographical, not a biographical, or a fictional book. Clive Bell too had observed Harold's capacity to keep himself detached, and yet be the butt of others and of life. Harold himself admitted to Vita that he supposed it was some form of masochism which made him love making of himself a ridiculous and slightly pretentious figure.[10] Certainly this inclination is detectable throughout his letters to Vita, his sons and friends, particularly when illustrated by amusing little sketches, almost always in self-mockery, and even in his articles and broadcasts. It is in fact that quality – never to take oneself too seriously – which distinguishes the patrician from the rest

BAKHTIARI AND FOREIGN OFFICE 1927

of human kind. Nevertheless Harold was irritated that the majority of people misunderstood *Some People*. It was not a mere parody of the gossip column. It was rather a commentary on manners. And when Ben at the age of eighteen told his father that surely the book was meant to be a criticism of life, he was overjoyed by the justness of the remark and his son's intelligence.

The publication of *Some People* brought Harold renown. In after years the author grew sensitive about the book. He almost wished he had never written it. He complained to Vita that it was the one book of his which old ladies, the proletariat and the Earl of Athlone remembered. It was the only book which he had rattled off at great speed, without any preliminary research or forethought. Whereas *King George V* had cost him most labour, *Lord Carnock* was his best book. But the old ladies, the proletariat and Lord Athlone would never realise that! Several times reprinted, and twice re-published; recited by Sixth Form Eton boys at Speeches and dramatised on the radio, *Some People* has always remained deservedly popular. It is a tour de force; a minor masterpiece. When Vladimir Nabokov told Harold that all his life he had been fighting against the influence of *Some People*, like a drug, Harold's only comment was that *Lolita* would never have the same influence on him.

During the summer of 1927 Harold saw a good deal of the Woolfs and their circle. On the 28th June he was one of a party which made an expedition to Richmond, Yorkshire, to witness a total eclipse of the sun. After dinner Leonard and Virginia, Quentin Bell, Saxon Sydney-Turner, Eddy Sackville-West and the Nicolsons took the train from King's Cross sharing a compartment. They sat up all night, reading and talking. He curled up on the seat with his head on Vita's knee. 'She looked like Sappho by Leighton, asleep,' Virginia noted in her diary; 'so we plunged through the midlands.'[11] At three o'clock they got out their sandwiches, and Harold broke a china box. Leonard laughed immoderately. They reached Richmond at 3.30 a.m., and with others boarded a charabanc, which drove them to the top of the moors. The eclipse began at 5.30 and reached totality at 6.30. Alas, clouds obscured the full effect. Nevertheless Harold noticed 'a sudden effect of darkness rushing on one from the west, like some dark wing flashing across the earth. Very impressive.'[12] Virginia 'had very strongly the feeling as the light went out of some vast obeisance; something kneeling down and suddenly raised up when the colours came.'[13] They then returned to London, breakfasting on the train.

Of the Bloomsbury group the one with whom Harold could talk most freely was, after Clive Bell, Leonard Woolf. He admired his sharp intelligence, and his lucid exposition of carefully considered opinions, not all of which he shared. He thought him the sort of man who would be extremely useful in the upper house of Parliament as a senator. He enjoyed discussing mundane and abstract problems with him, and valued his wise guidance. In a talk about imperialism Leonard 'says the question is not whether it is right or wrong, but that it is *practically* impossible. I fear he may be right. But it saddens me as I feel our national genius lies that way and that way only. I do not share Raymond's belief that we could ever be great again in intellectual matters.'[14]

In Montparnasse he stayed with Raymond Mortimer at the Villa Seurat which he had taken. For six days he met several old French friends and made some new acquaintances, including François Mauriac. He went to Auteuil to see the new houses built by Corbusier. They were all made of cement, rose in tiers, and had huge steel casements and windows like those of a shop-front. One of them he considered beautiful, but thought the others spoilt by trivial affectation of detail.

All his life he had been interested in architecture. When a young clerk drudging in the Foreign Office he sometimes wished he were an architect designing Palladian villas for rich and acquiescent clients. As it was, he got no further than designing a few extensions to Long Barn and Sissinghurst. His knowledge of the art was not profound. He dismissed all buildings between 1830 and 1920 except Lutyens's. Yet he admired Corbusier and Erich Mendelsohn as pioneers in the application of modern materials to modern needs, and he saw New York as one of the loveliest cities of the world.

In Paris he engaged a young man, Maurice Couve de Murville, as tutor to his sons in the forthcoming summer holidays. The future French Foreign Minister and Prime Minister proved to be a strangely tied-up and arid tutor. Harold's younger son remembers him as 'a shy youth, brittle as a biscuit, dressed in midsummer tweeds.'[15] When Harold told Réné Massigli years later how young Murville came to Long Barn expecting the grandeur of Chatsworth and the intellectual stimulus of Madame Geoffrin's *salon*, to find that he was expected to teach two schoolboys in a cottage, Massigli said, 'Ah, that explains why Couve is always so anti-British.'[16]

In August Harold was thrown into much confusion by the receipt of a letter from Walford Selby.[17] It informed him that Austen Chamberlain agreed to his not returning to Persia but announced that he must be downgraded from Counsellor to First Secretary; that 'with the best will in the world' they could not find him a place in the Foreign Office, and would he please, therefore, go to Budapest. Harold was extremely hurt. His immediate instinct was to fire in his resignation at once. He had absolutely no ambition, so he protested, to become a Minister or an Ambassador. All he wanted was to be in the Foreign Office. And they would not have him. Vita however, in spite of her hatred of the Foreign Office, was very calm and wise, as well as sympathetic. She strongly cautioned reflection. Accordingly Harold reflected. He decided that it might be foolish after eighteen years service, and because of a temporary setback, to fling himself upon the world without a profession at the age of 41. He had not a shilling beyond what he could earn by writing. 'Of course I know really that it is Willy Tyrrell; he will never forgive me for having seen him in a state of dipsomania at Lausanne.'[18] Crushed and bewildered he retired to his sitting-room. He saw his little Virgil. He picked it out of the shelf. He opened it at random. His eye lit upon line 44 of the seventh book of the Aeneid, and read: 'Major rerum mihi nascitur ordo / Majus opus moveo.'- Greater is the story that opens before me; greater is the task I essay. Had he been unduly superstitious he might have allowed that message to decide him. But he did not. Yet the words had a strangely relevant import. He remained more muddled and distressed than before.

The next morning he was still depressed. He wrote a letter to Selby saying that he thought he was only to be demoted if he remained in the Foreign Office. That he would not be suited to Budapest, because he was too identified with the framing of the existing frontiers at the Peace Treaty to view with necessary detachment the Hungarians' desire to upset them. Besides he could neither dance, sing nor shoot and in that socially conscious capital would be inadequate.

By an odd coincidence he received from his colleague, Owen O'Malley in Pekin, a letter complaining of similar Foreign Office treatment. O'Malley quoted a mutual friend's letter to the effect that both he and Harold were mistrusted because they took an imaginative view of their work. Harold replied to O'Malley[19] that his letter 'came at a remarkably opportune moment, when I felt "in disgrace with fortune and men's eyes", and it has cheered me and encouraged me enormously.' He informed O'Malley that the Tehran Despatch of the 30th September 1926, to which he referred with appreciation, bade fair to be his swan-song. He understood that the Foreign Office deemed it 'impertinent and not in very good taste.' The Office were much annoyed because it contradicted their happy belief that Loraine had achieved the triumph of the 'policy of non-intervention and good relations.' And what did they mean by good relations? 'They mean that the Prefect of Venice should hand Lady Chamberlain a bouquet of rather sniffy chrysanthemums when she arrives at the station. They mean that, in return, Sir A. Chamberlain should present Mussolini with a free hand in Albania.' Already Harold was putting his finger on the weakness of Chamberlain in particular and the British political leaders in general, which was to prove so disastrous in ten years' time.

O'Malley's cheering letter convinced Harold that he was suffering from wounded pride. He walked about the garden all day thinking without resentment of the future. He would not become an embittered failure. 'No, I have Vita and the boys, and that is more than a compensation for anything material. I have my home and my love of nature. I have my friends. I have my energy and my talent for writing.'[20] Raymond Mortimer came down to talk over the problem with him. And then Harold went to Rodmell to see Leonard and Virginia. They walked in the water meadows. Virginia of course urged what she called 'definition.' He must define the situation and not haver. Must make up his mind what he was going to do, and do it without repining. Clive Bell came down to Long Barn and they discussed Harold's future between games of tennis. Lord and Lady Carnock, getting to hear of his desire to leave the Foreign Office, were outraged.

Towards the end of September Harold lunched with Walford Selby who was charming and friendly. He repeated that he did not want to go abroad again, but to remain in the Foreign Office. Selby said that this would be difficult because Tyrrell did not like having people in the Office who, he sensed, were hostile to him. But he promised to do his best for Harold. If he failed, would he consider going to Rome? Harold said he would consider it. On the 14th October he received a letter from Selby, regretting that he could not pull off Rome, but not giving the reason which was that the Ambassador, Sir Ronald Graham, was afraid that Harold might laugh at him. Selby asked if he would go to Berlin instead. Harold commented:

> There are few things which I would dislike more, and it is bad luck on my darling. But I *won't* chuck it if I can possibly help. So I accept, gloomily.

Thus he made up his mind to remain in the Diplomatic Service for a time, at any rate. His disappointment about the post was on Vita's account. Evidently he imagined that because Berlin was, compared to Tehran, close and accessible to England, she would come with him. Virginia Woolf's protest – 'Oh how damned! I'd been hoping for London, unreasonably ... I am so unhappy. Will the people there be an awful bore? Shall you hate it? Does Harold? You won't go for long, will you?'[21] – likewise presupposes that she thought so too.

He went to London to buy clothes for his new appointment. He called on his parents in a foul temper for their having encouraged him to accept the Berlin offer and stay on in the beastly Service, and abused them. When he talked to Oliphant in the Office he found that the pay was to be better than he expected.

Harold's next visit was to Regent's Park to say goodbye to Gosse. He had become very fond of the prickly, prudish old man, now frail and verging on eighty. He was grateful to him for the encouragement and indeed praise of his books, which Gosse had consistently accorded them. Above all he relished his memory which was as fresh as that of a young man's. Harold found him recovering from typhoid and pneumonia, and claiming to feel better than he did before these afflictions. Gosse began talking[22] about his own book, that classic *Father and Son*, and the terrible final disillusionment of his old father, who was a fanatical member of the Plymouth Brethren.

> He told me that the end [of the book] had been slightly 'arranged'. There was no dramatic breach [with Gosse's father], but they continued on terms of mutual politeness till his father's death. The latter, as he grew older, became crazy. He used to sit for hours thinking out what particular honour the Lord would do him when he reached heaven. Would he send an archangel or only an angel to the gate? Perhaps he might step down from his throne, and advance towards him? Perhaps he would come to the gate itself. He brooded like this for years and finally imagined that he had promised 'translation' instead of death. In the end, however, he was inflicted with palsy. He saw that he was going to die. He felt that he had been betrayed. He turned against God, reviling him for treachery. He shouted blasphemies while Gosse and Lady Gosse essayed to hold him down. All night they struggled and at 3 a.m. he died. They dropped to bed with their muscles aching with exhaustion.

Gosse told Harold that in the eighteen-seventies even the free-thinkers were morally earnest, and he well remembered Huxley snubbing him for appreciating the poems of Rossetti and Swinburne on the ground that they were written 'by profligates for purposes of profligacy.'

> He spoke of Froude's *Carlyle*: he felt that Froude hated Carlyle because of his treatment of Mrs. C. He told me that when Browning married he brought his wife to see the Carlyles. There had been a coldness between B[rowning] and C[arlyle] since the latter had been angry at seeing B riding in a fashionable plum-coloured coat: but Browning, who, as Gosse said, was the 'most placable of men', refused to quarrel and so that afternoon he took Elizabeth to Cheyne Walk. The Carlyles were in ('The Carlyles,' remarked Gosse, 'seemed always to have been in'). Mrs. C was in the drawing-room. Browning was sent upstairs to

the Silence Room to see Carlyle. Elizabeth sat talking to Mrs. C. She was overwhelmed by the slush and gush of her passion for B. 'Oh Mrs. Carlyle,' she said, 'how I envy you having been married to your genius all these years.' Mrs. C sniffed. 'Well, as for that,' she said, 'I had for three weeks the pleasure of hope and for fifteen years the pleasures of imagination.' Gosse also told me that the year before Browning died he was sitting with him in the round-about garden at Trinity. B said that the only thing he regretted in life was not having had a regular profession. The lack of that gave him too much time for writing; the temptation was too strong . . . invariably he succumbed [to it], with the result that he wrote too much.

Gosse told Harold he was distressed by Bloomsbury's dislike of him. He said that of the group only Lytton Strachey respected him. Actually Strachey had no respect for him at all and referred to him among his friends as 'Goose Gosse'. 'Poor old man,' Harold commented. He was not to see Gosse again, for he died the following year. From the Gosses' house Harold drove to dine with Clive Bell at 50 Gordon Square, having picked up Raymond on the way. There he met T. S. Eliot for the first time. Eliot was dressed in a white tie and waistcoat, not in the least like Bloomsbury or for that matter like a poet. He looked like a young and successful doctor or lawyer. Harold noticed that his mind did not work quickly. As the years passed he grew to like and respect him.

Ten days before Harold left for Berlin he finished a small book, *The Development of English Biography*. It was published before the year was out by the Hogarth Press as the fourth in their *Lectures on Literature* series. It had required a great deal of reading and had been compiled with extraordinary speed, for the first mention of it in Harold's diary was made on the 7th July. The book, which is an amazingly compendious history of biography from the sixth-century A.D. up to date, opens with a definition of the subject. The author divides biography into two sorts, 'impure' and 'pure'. The first consists of hagiography, a desire to celebrate the dead, to identify an individual with some extraneous theory, or unduly to intrude the writer's personality and predilections. The purposes of 'pure' biography are the reverse of these. They are primarily to reveal as far as possible the absolute truth about the subject. The reader must be made aware of a consciousness of creation in the biographer – 'a conviction that some creative mind has selected and composed' the facts and experiences of the subject's life. It must be a work of intelligence as well as a work of art. In Harold Nicolson's subsequent broadcasts, articles and reviews about biography he re-emphasised the pre-requisite of absolute truth, and elaborated more fully than in the book the need to prevent details of the truth falsifying the ultimate impression of the subject upon the reader's mind.

In *The Development of English Biography* Harold is perplexed by the irreconcilable conflict, as he sees it, between the desire of the biographer to be scientifically accurate and the desire to produce a work of art: in other words the conflict within him of the scholar and the literary purist. He can offer no wholly satisfactory solution to this problem, beyond a sort of compromise. Less convincing is his categorical theme that in times when religious conviction is lax, when men are more interested in material than spiritual pursuit, biographical art flourishes. In the seventeenth and nineteenth centuries on the contrary, when religious fervour led to disputatious, even armed conflict, it declined. He maintains that the seventeenth century in particular was too disturbed for writers to have the leisure or detachment for pure biography. This statement is surely open to dispute, for there were long decades of the seventeenth century which were relatively undisturbed, and many areas of the country where men of letters, unlike their successors during the First and Second World Wars, remained relatively unconcerned by political disagreements and fighting. Another controversial theme that some critics picked upon was Harold's depreciation of Boswell's art as biographer. Harold saw it as a work of the greatest entertainment, indistinguishable from that of the cinematograph, but he denied that it was true biography.

On the whole the reviews were laudatory. Sir Arthur Quiller-Couch considered the book brilliant. And Gosse wrote Harold a letter of warm commendation, affirming that his estimate of the whole trend of English biography was sound. It cannot have escaped Gosse that his *protégé* had derived much from his own contribution on *Biography* in the Encyclopedia Britannica, notably his warnings against theoretical writing, the inclusion of a history of the times with the subject's life, and too pronounced detraction, or sanctification of the subject.

The book had great success in the United States. American reviewers urged Harold Nicolson to cross the Atlantic and lecture to them.

15

BERLIN 1927–1928

ON the evening of the 23rd October 1927 Harold, having bidden Vita an agonised farewell at the entrance to Liverpool Street station, and watched the red rear light of her motor disappear up the incline into the darkness, plunged into the vault-like shed to look for his pullman for Harwich. In the train he read a dear letter she had left with him. The past six months had been the happiest of their married life, she told him. In the pullman he immediately wrote to assure her that, in spite of the pain of parting, he was looking forward to Berlin.

He was met at the Friedrich-Strasse station by Maurice Ingram, the man he was to succeed in the Chancery, and driven to the Hotel Bristol. Within a matter of days he had decided to take over the lease of Ingram's flat, No. 24 Brücken Allee[1] in the Hansa Viertel, a smart residential district in which most of the houses faced the Englischer Garten end of the Tiergarten. It was a quarter of an hour's walk from the Grosse Stern, that circular colonnade sprouting a flamboyant column of Victory over the French in 1870, and half an hour from the Brandenburger Tor. At first Harold was appalled by the flat's ugliness, but became reconciled to it after he had seen others. He found most Berlin flats beastly, with high, gaudy reception-rooms and squalid bedrooms looking on to smelly courts. The reception-rooms had doors of frosted glass. The furniture was usually of bogus French eighteenth-century design, upholstered in red plush. At least No. 24 Brücken Allee was comfortable. After three months Harold managed to get the worst of the landlord's furniture removed and replaced by a consignment from Ebury Street.

Harold at once took to the British Ambassador, Sir Ronald Lindsay.[2] He was a kind, jolly, untidy and welcoming Wykehamist. He had a magnificent physique and dignified bearing. Naturally shy and silent, he was easily roused by a sympathetic interlocutor into animated conversation, when his comments were acute and intelligent. From the start the new First Secretary liked all his colleagues.

After the Locarno treaties of 1925 relations of equality between Germany and her former enemies had been re-established. When Harold arrived in Berlin the country was just recovering from inflation. It seemed determined to forget the past, to concentrate only on the present and to seek compensation for defeat by indulging in every known kind of phy-

BERLIN 1927-28

sical and intellectual stimulus. The dreaded threat of Communism immediately after the Armistice had been averted. Hitler was dismissed as a man who had passed out of history, who displayed cowardice at the time of the Ludendorf *Putsch* in 1923, a man with a comical moustache and a Bohemian accent. President Hindenburg was highly respected and Berlin regarded as a new Paris, the European centre of leading artistic and literary enterprise.

Between Harold's arrival and the departure of Sir Ronald Lindsay in July 1928 despatches between the British Foreign Office and the Embassy were mainly focussed on the linked questions of fixing Germany's reparations liability and bringing to an end the occupation of the Rhineland. Sir Ronald and his Financial Adviser feared that uncertainty about the liability was heightening the chances of a return to inflation. They anticipated a severe depression during the winter of 1928-29 when payment under the Dawes Plan of 1924 was due to reach its maximum. The Commercial Secretary, however, considered that Germany had made immense strides since 1924 and that 'any substantial reduction of her annual reparations payments, the only indebtedness worth mentioning which she has, would give her a most unfair advantage over a heavily burdened country like Great Britain.'[3] Sir Ronald was keen to end the Occupation, until which time relations with Germany must remain uneasy.

In spite of the seeming prosperity of Berlin the great houses remained closed. The Herrenklub had retired into seclusion. The former aristocracy and military had resolved not to receive foreigners but to lead secluded, watchful and suspicious lives. On the other hand the art exhibitions, concerts and operas, as well as the night life flourished; and drew the sophisticated to Berlin from all over Europe and the Americas.

> In the Planetarium one could watch the stars in their slow courses; in the Wellenbad one could battle with the Atlantic seas in the confined space of a swimming bath; at Funkturm one could eat meals perched above the lights of the city; in night clubs and restaurants of the Kurfürstendamm some new device or gadget was invented each week.[4]

To get an idea of the strongly contrasting conditions of life in Berlin during the late 1920s one has merely to read Christopher Isherwood's *Goodbye to Berlin* or look at the paintings and drawings of contemporary artists, Max Beckmann, George Grosz and Otto Dix. The picture they convey of riches and poverty, hope and disillusion, ambition and depravity are disagreeable and frightening. The restaurants, cafés and dives were patronised for the sexual diversions rather than the food and drink they provided. There was the Salomé, run for the benefit of provincial sightseers, very expensive and depressing.

A few stage lesbians and some young men with plucked eyebrows lounging at the bar, uttering occasional raucous guffaws or treble hoots – supposed, apparently, to represent the laughter of the damned. The whole premises are painted gold and inferno-red, crimson plush inches thick, and vast gilded mirrors.[5]

There was the Silhouette, small and intimate, with little boxes as at a theatre, used for amorous retreat while dancing continued on the central floor. There was the Rhezi on Kurfürstendamm where each table was supplied with a telephone and a number on a large card. If you liked the look of a particular diner you rang him or her up and made an assignation. There was the Eldorado, where Harold was initiated into Berlin night life. He noticed a lot of blowsy women in evening dress seated at the bar.

It took some time to realise that they were men and not women. There were a lot of hearty old men in plus fours, and it took some time to realise that they were women and not men. We sat at a table and had beer. I was rather shocked and disgusted; these people danced together.[6]

Harold soon accustomed himself to such spectacles, which however he never grew to relish. In fact a reaction was quietly and dangerously fomenting among the Berliners. The predominant position acquired by the Jews in (left wing) politics, banks, press, theatre, cinema and the entertainment and vice industry was breeding resentment. At Peltzer's restaurant in the Neue Wilhelm-Strasse, which in the Kaiser's day had been the exclusive resort of senior officers and the social élite, every table now was occupied, somewhat too arrogantly by Jews. The writing, with its appalling message, was already on the wall. Few among the foreign visitors discerned it.

'A dreadful sense of the third-rate hangs over Berlin,' Harold wrote before he had been there three weeks, but he could form no opinion as yet about the cause. It would take time. He considered his first nine months in the city to be one of the most stagnant periods of his life. He wrote nothing of importance, and his diplomatic work was only of slight value. What then did he do? He visited museums and exhibitions; he went to the theatre and cinema; he had numerous English friends to stay; he made contacts with countless important people, mostly of course Germans; he consorted with members of the press who provided him with more useful information than any other sources; and he studied and assessed the German character impartially and fairly, thereby accumulating a knowledge of the country and people which was to be of inestimable benefit to him and Parliament when he was in the House of Commons throughout the Second World War.[7]

And how at this time did Harold strike strangers on a first meeting?

Not always favourably. He had a habit of throwing up his head, screwing up his small eyes and talking over their shoulders as though he was depreciating them. Strangers might well decide that this disturbingly intelligent and observant man was a little superior, even patronising. Indeed when he was speaking he could seem brusque and dismissive. Some people imagined too that he was playing a part, trying to impose a personality that was not there while drawing a veil over one that was; that he was anxious to be taken for a masterful, uncompromising person and disguising the fact that he was on the contrary gentle, if not soft, rational and receptive to opinions that were not his. The truth is he was often shy with strangers if he suspected them to be hostile, and this led him to assume a defensive stance that appeared aggressive. When however he found his ease and the new acquaintances sympathetic he dropped his somewhat rebarbative front and became friendly and confidential. His humour and charm quickly disarmed anyone disposed not to like him.

Lali Horstmann,[8] a woman of intelligence and immense fascination, lived in a large house full of art treasures in Tiergartenstrasse, with her husband Freddy. Theirs was the only German household where it was possible to relax and abandon conventional diplomatic attitudes. Lali was possibly the only Jew whom Harold counted among his intimates. Try as he might he could not bring himself to like Jews, although in Berlin he met and made the acquaintance of many. His attitude towards them was irrational. The only valid charges he could bring against them were that they were touchy and insensitive. So they often are, and with some reason. Beyond that his attitude was an old-fashioned prejudice. He found them vulgar. Throughout his life he let fall unconsidered interjections, such as, 'He must be a Jew – oily.' And, 'What liars these Jews are! I do hate them so and wish our boys were not so pro-Semitic.' And once on board ship describing the bathing pool to one of his sons, he wrote, 'I wish I had not this physical aversion from Jews and coloured people ... I think [they] should be forbidden to bathe for they poison the water.' Thus, on first lunching with Emil Ludwig in Berlin, he described him as 'a pretentious little Jew,' while admitting that, although a charlatan, he was a man of interest. Vita's attitude, surprisingly, was less prejudiced than her husband's. It was 'sad for them to look Jewish. It tells against them.' One should be nice to them in consequence. Yet there is no need to stress how revolted Harold was by the Nazi treatment of the Jewish people. To him it was an abomination which no penance, no remorse could ever wipe out.

On the other hand Harold's attitude to Zionism was perfectly rational. Dr. Chaim Weizmann, for whom he had a great admiration, came to see him in November. He said[9] that the Zionist work was easy enough in Galilee, 'but we are breaking our hearts against the rocks of Judaea.'

HAROLD NICOLSON

Harold suggested that Zionism was a sentimental and not an economic problem; that the sentimental idea would be better served by making Jerusalem the intellectual centre of the Jewish race, than by settling a few Galicians in the uplands of Judaea. Weizmann did not, naturally enough, agree. He said that nationality and the soil were one and the same thing; that the universe would be a mere sham unless the foundations of the pyramid rested upon actual earth. Harold respected without accepting this attitude.

Another Jew to become a friend but not an intimate, was Erich Mendelsohn, the pioneer of modern materials and methods of construction in German architecture. Emil Ludwig introduced them. The three men spent an afternoon visiting some of the fantastic buildings put up by Kaiser William II and, by way of contrast, some of the flats and schools put up by Mendelsohn on a system of planes and curves. Harold much admired his new film theatre, with its great, sweeping straight lines, and decoration in mere bands of light. They finished up in Mendelsohn's studio looking at models of houses he was building, including a vast factory in Leningrad.

Harold' private reservation was that Mendelsohn's architecture overstressed the superlative instead of asserting the positive, and was too egotistical – in fact too vulgar, too Jewish.

In December he was taken by a friendly permanent official at the Foreign Office, Ow-Wachendorff, to stay with Prince Karl Maximilian and Princess Lichnowsky at their property, Kuchelna, which was a few kilometres within the Czech border. The Prince was convinced that the frontier had been deliberately shifted by the Delimitation Commission in 1919 out of spite and in retaliation for his advice to the Kaiser before the outbreak of the War, when he was Ambassador in London. Indeed Sir Edward Grey wrote that the British owed Lichnowsky a big debt for having striven to avoid war in August 1914. The visit was a sad one. The two guests travelled by night, sharing a sleeper in all innocence and good fellowship. At Ratisbon they were met by a large motor and servants. Lichnowsky, bent in the body, yellow in the face, and very neurotic, greeted them. To Harold his first words were, 'How is your father?' Harold recalled that the last words he said to him on the 4th August 1914 were, 'Remember me to your father.' He was given a suite of old-fashioned elegance, like one of those at Polesden Lacy. After luncheon they went for a walk. The Prince put on a tweed jacket with a vast vulpine collar. Wachendorff put on a green coat.

> I show[ed] by my swinging gait how young I was, how English, how victorious. We went through the village. The people took off their hats and held them in their hands (I shall try and teach Mr. Hart the gesture when I get home),[10]

Harold wrote to Vita. They passed the hothouses, with chrysanthemums and primulas. Harold's shoes creaked on the crisp snow. Lichnowsky talked about the outbreak of the war.

> Now I find that when people have written a book about a subject they have nothing whatever to say about that subject except what they have put in that book. For a full hour did Lichnowsky talk about those events of 1914.

He talked about Tyrrell, and about Lord Carnock. The latter 'was not our friend, but his manner to me personally was always unexceptional.' Harold longed to ask if he ever opened the envelope or understood the strange meaning of the visit to his bedroom on that fatal night. The Prince sighed deeply. Everything was now lost, his career, his fortune, his castles and his fields. Little did he realise how after his death the Russians would take from his son everything, but everything, that still remained to him then. How well, he said, the English had treated him. Grey had been in tears. Mrs. Asquith was so courageous and generous in coming to see him after war had been declared. Everything in the Embassy had been returned down to the cigarettes in the silver boxes.

Dinner came, with champagne, and footmen in livery. The Prince kept harping on 1914; and how he could have stopped the war had he been in the Wilhelmstrasse. A look of despair crossed the face of the Princess. How often had she not heard the same old wail. Later she talked to Harold about getting old. 'It is nothing,' she said, 'to a man. They can think themselves out of their own flesh; we can't.'

On the 14th December Vita paid her first visit to Berlin. She stayed for five days, and hated it from the start. 'Oh, that filthy, filthy place. How I loathe it,' she exclaimed.[11] Since she and Harold were last together she had been absorbed in collaborating with Virginia Woolf in the preparation of *Orlando*.

There had been adumbrations of *Orlando* in Virginia's diary as far back as the 18th September of the previous year:

> One of these days I shall sketch here, like a grand historical picture, the outline of all my friends ... It might be a way of writing the memoirs of one's own times during people's lifetimes ... The question is how to do it. Vita should be Orlando, a young nobleman.

HAROLD NICOLSON

The idea was germinating in a sort of un-coordinated turmoil. On the 5th October:

> the usual exciting devices enter my mind; a biography beginning in the year 1500 and continuing to the present day, called Orlando: Vita; only with a change about from one sex to another.

The fascination of the hereditary traits of aristocracy and the interchangeable attributes of sex provoked by her first meeting with Vita was now followed by an acute analysis of the experiences derived from their close association. And on the 22nd of the month:

> I am writing Orlando half in a mock style very clear and plain, so that people will understand every word. But the balance between truth and fantasy must be careful. It is based on Vita, Violet Trefusis, Lord Lascelles, Knole, etc.

After Harold's departure for Berlin Vita had been free to indulge in what became for her as well as her friend a compulsive game, on which both of them were hooked. In her daily letters to Harold (there was nothing she did not tell him now) she narrated how they had spent a morning at Knole choosing obscure portraits from which to take bits for Orlando; how Virginia had taken her to be photographed as a Lely; and how she felt wretched draped in an inadequate piece of pink satin with all her clothes slipping off. But Virginia was as happy as a sandboy, and kept diving under the black cloth to look through the camera. Another day Vita was taken to Duncan Grant and Vanessa Bell's studio to be photographed with her head in a frame while Virginia read obituaries from *The Times*, interlarding her own comments which made them laugh so much that they spoilt the photographs. It was all such fun, and provoked her to wish that Harold would become a man of letters, live at home and give up his perverse ideas. Yet she was relieved that he was not feeling too lonely, and that Jimmy Sheean had stayed with him.

> Glad you had Jimmy (No, I don't mean that; honi soit qui mal y pense). Glad you met Noel Coward. Glad you saw night life ... please get compromised and then you'll be removed from Berlin.[12]

She sent him her little book on *Aphra Behn*, the seventeenth-century woman poet. Harold pronounced it 'a ripping book.' She was so clever the way she wove fiction with fact. The effect was very original and intelligent.[13]

Vita's five days in Berlin were spent looking at some horrible flats and deciding for Harold that he had better stick to Brücken Allee; attending a large dinner party at the Embassy; visiting Sans Souci in the snow, and going to the Merchant of Venice, performed in German. He saw her off by the night train on the 19th. They parted in the gloom and steam of the Friedrich-Strasse station, and Harold walked down the steps to the bridge over the Spree in a haze of intense anguish. On the bridge he stood,

> to watch your train go out, but it was all a confusion of lights and water and steam ... and here was I looking into a cold and meaningless river, and there were you in a hot lighted train slipping out into the snow. Oh darling I felt my heart and feet to be of lead. I turned and walked back slowly into the rush and glitter of the Friedrich-Strasse.[14]

Having drunk brandy with Bobby Sharpe, a shy, gentle, child-like American artist – there was nothing in it; she was not to worry – he went home to bed. There he found a letter from her under his pillow.

The arrival of Vita's cousin Eddy Sackville-West to stay was small compensation for her departure, and Harold admitted to having a down on him, which was unjust, for the reason that he was occupying her room. He came, wearing a little short coat and a sombrero, looking like nothing on earth, 'and what remains of my reputation will be gone for ever. Please God may Eddy not get on my nerves.'[15] He took him to the English Club, the Buccaneer, for luncheon. It was not a success. Eddy looked very frail beside all the hearty Englishmen and, when introduced, made a stiff little bow with exquisite courtesy. Thereafter he became rather silent. Afterwards he complained that it was unnecessary of Harold to have taken him to such a place. Harold told him it was good for him to meet different sorts of people.

> He stuck his stick (it is a large knobbly wooden stick such as is carried by very elderly peers in Perthshire) into the snow, jabbing irritably. 'But why? I wish you wouldn't say those sort of things, Harold.' He said it didn't enlarge his mind talking to bank clerks about ballet girls. I said they weren't ballet girls. They were cabaret girls, which was a very different thing.

When invited to walk with the Ambassador on the golf course a few days later Eddy became embarrassed about his sombrero cordovese. So he cut off the bows at the back with nail scissors in the bathroom. 'Then he began to massage his hat, giving it little irregular dabs like the young lady in a hat shop. He kept turning in front of the glass looking over his shoulder at himself, now left, now right. "No," he said finally, "I think I had better wear no hat at all."'[16] In spite of Harold's prayer, Eddy did get on his nerves, badly.

The New Year opened sadly for Vita, and for that matter for Harold. Lord Sackville was taken ill. The King's doctor, Lord Horder, was called down to Knole and pronounced his heart to be in a very weakened state. Vita and Olive Rubens were with him all day and most of the night. Harold in Berlin was hard at work on the Embassy annual report, or he would have crossed over to England sooner. When however he received a telegram on the 19th that Lionel's condition was critical – 'Please come. Don't fly,' – he at once got tickets and left that afternoon. He reached Sevenoaks at 5.30 the following afternoon. On the 27th Horder broke it to them that there was no hope of recovery, and a little after midnight on the 28th Lord Sackville died. 'We go stunned to our beds.'[17]

Harold took everything in hand. He made the funeral arrangements and summoned members of the family. He sent to *The Times*[18] an anonymous appreciation of his father-in-law, whom he had loved. He said he could only have been a product of England. He was a shy, modest, retiring, and humorous man; and more cultivated than he made himself out to be. He loved Knole above all things, and regarded it as his sacred trust, spending nearly all he possessed on its maintenance, and the minimum on himself. Harold referred to his local duties, his sportsmanship and his popularity, adding that his last years were his happiest. This passage did not escape the notice of his widow. Although she may not have known who was the author of the appreciation, B.M. was incensed by the assumption that Lionel had found comfort in her leaving him.

Lord Sackville was certainly a lovable, easy-going but indolent peer whose philosophy is best summarised in one of his pet sayings: 'Never do today what you can possibly put off until tomorrow.' Vita was the first to admit that the aphorism had an unfortunate effect upon her own upbringing. But she was deeply distressed by his death. Now that he was gone she wished she had told him how much she had loved him. It was too late. When Harold tried to convey to his son Ben the real spiritual agony his mother had gone through after Lord Sackville's death he explained that through all the years when they had each other, she had been too shy, and he had been too shy, to demonstrate their deep mutual affection. 'Now I don't want you to make that mistake,' he concluded. Bound up with the loss of her father was also the loss to Vita of Knole. Henceforth it could never be hers. Hitherto it had only been hers by proxy, so to speak. Now it was her Uncle Charlie's, and would afterwards be her cousin Eddy's. Her adoration of the great house was almost mystical. It transcended her love of any human being, even Harold. The first time she went over from Long Barn, to pick up Canute, her father's dog, she had to grit her teeth. She drove into the stable yard. She didn't get out, 'but there was that farm cart with the two horses in it, full of manure. It was hell.' The second time she had to sort out her father's things. That was worse. The rooms were all under dust-sheets. She vowed never to go there again unless she absolutely had to. Uncle Charlie was sensitive and sweet to her. He gave her a key to the garden and his permission to enter whenever she felt inclined. As it turned out she only once availed herself of the privilege within thirty years, and that was in May of 1928.[19]

> I allowed myself a torture treat tonight [she wrote to Harold]: I went up to Knole after dark and wandered about the garden. I have a master key, so could get in without being seen. It was a very queer and poignant experience ... that I should almost have fainted had I met anybody. I had the sensation of having the place so completely to myself that I might have been the only person alive in the world – and not the world of today, mark you, but the world of at least 300 years ago. I might have been the ghost of Lady Anne Clifford ... It may be looney, but there is some sort of umbilical cord that ties me to Knole.

It was a traumatic experience for her. She kept thinking she saw her father at the end of the long grass walks. The next day she had a crashing headache. There was something self-mortifying in her attitude towards this great house of her ancestors, as she admitted.

Harold understood her feelings for Knole. They were bound up with her resentment of changes, which

> are superimposed upon Lionel's memory. They are the little dead leaves which, falling, falling, will gradually efface the imprint of his footsteps. They are the dust of change settling on your childhood ... Knole knows that it belongs to *you* more than to Charlie.[20]

Eddy also acknowledged that he preferred the Knole regime under his uncle to what it became under his American stepmother, whose brashness and brittleness both he and Vita found unsympathetic. He got some good marks from the Nicolsons for these sentiments. The new Lord Sackville did not the least want the responsibility of Knole and the worries it entailed. But for the rest of his life he fulfilled the role of tenant-for-life with an admirable and touching grace. Meanwhile he was distracted by the problem of how to pay the death duties, computed at £230,000. Not until 1946 was he able to transfer the property and responsibilities to the National Trust. Even in 1928 Clive Bell and Roger Fry, while staying at Long Barn, devised a scheme whereby the most important contents of Knole should, at a valuation, become the property of the State, while remaining in their proper place, in part payment of death duties. They proposed raising the question in a letter to *The Times* under the signature of Fry and Ramsay MaDonald, to be followed by a leading article by the editor, Geoffrey Dawson. Needless to say nothing came of it at that time.

The death of Vita's father was followed by an accentuation of the eccentricity and mischief of his widow. Her old age was a tragedy to herself and everyone who had anything to do with her. Her health declined, and she gradually went blind. But her lack of resources, her wilfulness and stupidity led her into behaviour which was inexcusably cruel. It was as though the last fine careless rapture of her spoilt life was to be the torment of her daughter and son-in-law. She feigned terrible umbrage at having been kept away from her husband's deathbed, where she would have been extremely unwelcome. But when informed that Lionel was dying she ordered her maid to telephone to Knole the message that her ladyship had had a very bad day owing to the housemaid making a noise with the carpet sweeper overhead. When he died her resentment at Vita and Olive Rubens's attentions to him boiled over, and she wrote wounding letters to the former. On Lord Sackville's will being opened it was found that B.M. had been made executrix, doubtless many years ago, an arrangement which the indolent testator had omitted to cancel. By a merciful providence she was persuaded to renounce this duty. Nevertheless under the will she benefited from a considerable sum of money, tied up on the Nicolsons, the income from which was hers for her lifetime. The attitude of both the Nicolsons to B.M. was exemplary. Harold counselled Vita, who hardly needed the advice, to treat her mother like a child, with kindness, in spite of her offensive letters. It worried him that she should be so ill and so unhappy. 'I feel no love for B.M. now, and feel no gratitude,' he wrote.[21] 'But I do feel pity. It is a cold, hard pity.' He thought Vita ought before she came out to Berlin again to offer to visit B.M. He did not share the view Dorothy Wellesley had been putting forward, that Vita's right to her own soul precluded attention to whatever disturbed its cultivation. 'I do not take the Dottie view that "you have a right to your own soul." One only realises one's own 'soul' (by which I mean the free development of what is "best" in one's character) by facing difficulties, not by running away from them.' But Lady Sackville was not to be assuaged by any olive branch held out by her daughter. She threatened to withhold the allowance which Vita received from her. Her mounting malevolence culminated in an appalling scene in London in the middle of April.

Vita went to London to give her first broadcast. Before doing so she called by appointment upon her solicitor. She wished to discuss her financial position under her father's will. In the office waiting-room she met, greatly to her surprise, B.M., who had got to hear of her daughter's appointment and came deliberately to accost her. Lady Sackville rose from her chair and screamed at her, 'I wish to see you in Mr. Pemberton's office. Give me your pearls. Twelve of them belong to me. I wish to see how many you have changed, you thief.' She then poured out a flood of abuse like a mad woman, shaking her fist, and screaming, 'Thief and liar!' She shouted that she hated Vita and wished she would die. She then began abusing Lionel. This was too much for Vita. In deadly calm she cut twelve pearls from the necklace she was wearing, handed them to her mother and, without saying a word, stalked out of the office. Lady Sackville straightway ordered the solicitor not to pay Vita's allowance any further and asked to have returned everything she ever gave the Nicolsons, as well as the furniture in the Berlin flat which was hers on loan. She announced that henceforth she was going to ruin Vita and Harold's lives. From this experience Vita, shaking in every limb, went to deliver the broadcast.

Vita wrote that she was deeply sorry for her mother. She feared she was out of her right mind, and suffering from persecution mania. Every time she looked at a present B.M. had given her in the past she felt sad. She was grateful to Harold for backing her up, but did not like the idea of anybody else taking her part against her mother.

Harold was very afraid – and with reason – of what B.M. might do and say, quite apart from the financial damage she was causing them. She might make terrible accusations about them to Austen Chamberlain. Outside people who did not know them might misconstrue the things she put about. Harold told Vita that the furniture which B.M. wanted back was hateful to him, and he would like to get rid of it. At the same time he counselled her to be firm, stick up for her rights and keep all the jewels that B.M. had given her. Vita replied that already B.M. was disseminating dirt about their morals. She strongly advised him to tell Sir Ronald Lindsay what had happened in case rumours should reach him. Harold did not speak to the Ambassador but to Lady Lindsay, who gave excellent and charitable advice how to treat B.M.

After his father-in-law's funeral Harold returned to Berlin in a state of exhaustion. He brought with him for company a little cocker spaniel, another Henry. At the station he was met by Raymond Mortimer, flustered and out of breath, having put a coin into a weighing-machine instead of the platform ticket-machine. Raymond had been travelling in Germany and, seeing the condition Harold was in, readily agreed to stay with him in Brücken Allee. On his recovery Harold resumed a full social life. He met Sinclair Lewis, the American novelist and journalist. Lewis's novel *Main Street*, satirising the dullness of a small mid-western town, had

had an enormous success in 1920. *Babbitt* and *Arrowsmith* were scarcely less popular. Harold described him as

> an odd, red-faced, noisy young man who called me Harold from the start, and wouldn't leave me. He insisted on my going to a bar with him and then he insisted on coming back to dinner with me . . . Lewis talked the whole time, and drank and drank. At 9.30 he remembered that he had got to take his fiancée to a ball, and off he went dragging me with him, as he said he was too tight to dress. He then spoke of Anglo-American relations. What could be done? Were we drifting into war?[22]

During the ensuing weeks he saw much of Sinclair Lewis.

Harold had a new experience in ringing up Vita at Long Barn and speaking to her on the telephone. Each heard every word of the other. Continental telephoning was a novelty which at first amazed and delighted him. But after a few such talks he begged Vita to discontinue it, because it caused him more pain than pleasure. After another short visit from Eddy, who this time was less tiresome, in spite of his finicky egoism, Vita reappeared on the 26th February. She was to stay for just over a month.

In March the Nicolsons made a lightning visit to Copenhagen to deliver a lecture each, Vita on modern English poetry, and Harold on Byron. They came back to Berlin on the 30th just in time for Vita to pack and leave by the night train for England. They had reached an agreement that Harold should no longer see her off at the station since these formal partings were too painful. The next day he lunched with the Stresemanns, where an uncongenial bunch of people were assembled. Dr Gustav Stresemann was from 1923 to 1929 Germany's peace-promoting Foreign Minister, who used most skilful efforts to release his country from the restrictions imposed upon her by the Treaty of Versailles. But his countrymen repaid his endeavours with suspicion, accusing him of submitting to the blandishments of Briand and Chamberlain. By now he was an ill man. The Stresemanns lived in a pretty little 'Villa' on the Wilhelm-Strasse, dating from the reign of Frederick William I, and reserved for the Foreign Minister. Here Stresemann loved to entertain his guests. His wife and sons would be present, and the devotion which they all felt for each other gave to their parties a domestic feeling. There would be Mosel wine, much food and thick cigars. Stresemann would preside with the geniality of a man whose father had been a publican. He would be boisterous, indiscreet, shy and arrogant, gay and gloomy.

> He would speak of art, of which he knew little; of music of which he knew much; and about politics which he approached with subtle rage. His physical appearance was disconcerting. He had a thick neck, a small

bullet head, and eyelids which were fringed with pink. His frame was massive, his shoulders powerful, his whole architecture of the heavy type. Yet he walked delicately; his hands were the hands of a woman; his lips sensitive and extremely mobile.[23]

His wife would watch him with pride and anxiety in her eyes. Harold found it difficult to like her. Frau Stresemann was haggard, ill-dressed, bony, and pretended to be young. She was a vulgar, eager woman. 'Oh yes, Mr. Nicolson,' she said, 'I hear you have great humour. I also have great humour. We must be great friends.'[24] But for her husband Harold had a very high regard. 'What a man he was! He managed to combine the convivial with the authoritative, the humorous with the powerful.'

The same day he had to meet Ethel Smyth at the Friedrich-Strasse station. He arrived late.

There she was sitting on her *how* little trunk. So I took her to her hotel and she dashed up to change her hat as she was off – at 9.30 – to see Bruno Walter. The hat she arrived in was a soft felt sort of business, very crushed indeed. The one she changed into was a tricorne, which made her look more like Frederick the Great than ever.[25]

She was over to arrange a concert of her own music and was pestering with a persistence which only she possessed, impresarios, conductors and anyone she could coerce to provide a hall and an orchestra. Harold had grave doubts from what his German musical friends told him whether she was any good at all. He gave a successful luncheon party for her, on which occasion Ethel wore a ridiculous felt hat with a green feather and a little shooting coat. She had a contract in her pocket and was very pleased with herself. 'God, what a bore that concert will be,' Harold commented.

He spent the long Easter holiday, from Good Friday until the following Tuesday, alone with Henry in the flat. He was very homesick. He detested religious festivals, which entailed public holidays, which entailed no work, and consequent boredom abroad, away from his own home, his library and reference books. So on Good Friday, deciding that he needed money, he sat down and wrote straight off two articles for *Nash's Magazine*, which he had been asked to do, thus earning for himself £200. On the Saturday he wrote a third and, if he had not been interrupted, would have written a fourth. Chips Channon and George Gage[26] had arrived unannounced at the Hotel Adlon and wanted to be taken to cabarets, a thing all his English friends wanted. It bored Harold. 'Don't like other people's vices.' He wrote a long letter[27] to his eleven-year-old son, Nigel:

> Mummy says you are an angel, but have got spots. Now spots come from picking – not just picking blackberries or strawberries, but from picking spots. Also from not taking Eno's Fruit Salts when one is bunged up. Also from eating sweets. I used to have spots something dreadful at your age – and now I have got a complexion of which any schoolgirl should be proud. How did I get that complexion? By Eno's. So next time you see a spot think of me, and say these words: 'My father, although spotty as a youth, has now got a complexion which, though mottled by age and drink, is to all intents and purposes that of a schoolgirl. He knows! 'E knows. Eno's. Then all will be well.

A new excitement entered Harold's life in the person of Ivor Novello, the song-writer (he was the composer of *Keep the Home Fires Burning*), actor and dramatist.[28]

> I like him so much. He is completely unspoilt by his success, and absolutely thrilling about his life. He has contracts which will bring him in £35,000 by November year. He calculates that if his health lasts he should be able to make about £500,000 before he is forty. He is rather appalled by this and very sensible about it; says it makes one feel such a fool to be worth so much money solely because of one's profile. He suffers dreadfully from the worship of flappers. Every day there are two or three of them who wait outside his house just to see him. There were twelve of them at the station to see him off!! All this must be terribly bad for a person, and he is himself terrified of becoming fatuous about it. You can imagine how thrilled I am by so odd a psychological problem.[29]

After the opera they went to a supper party given by the Horstmanns for Lord Birkenhead. Stresemann and Kühlmann were there, and so tight and noisy that Birkenhead seemed quite sober and solemn by comparison.

Two nights later Harold had supper with Novello alone.

> He *fascinates* me. It is an entirely new world, and he is intelligent enough to like talking about it and to give me just the bits I want to know. He *is* so lovely, and friendly ... He is still on good terms with Eddie [Marsh], whom he is really fond of and grateful to. He says that E.M. has never attempted even to stroke his hair. Well, well.[30]

He confessed to Vita that he had a *béguin*[31] for Ivor.

He met Maynard Keynes and his wife Lydia Lopokova, the Russian ballerina. Keynes was just back from his second visit to Russia, where he was very disappointed with the trend of affairs. The country was gradually evolving towards a peasant soviet state; and the fanaticism of the leaders was terrifying. He foresaw a great famine in the country. He told Harold that he had been studying hereditary genius, and discovered that Harold was descended from Boswell, which, in view of Harold's opinion of that biographer, was a two-edged compliment. Harold noticed that Keynes often snubbed the arrogant, but never the humble. He thought him the most compelling personality he had ever come across. Keynes contained a flame of goodness not granted to most men.

Allen and Janet Leeper came to stay. Although Harold had a great regard for Allen's mind and high principles, he found it difficult to keep up with the Leepers' view of life which was based on Holy Communion, or to condone their disapproval of Dorothy Warren. It was a relief when the Leepers' room was taken by Gerald Berners, with his liberalism, his delicious cynicism and sheer fun. He was the most appreciative of guests as well as the most amusing. He was never bored, and he never complained. He liked and was liked by everyone – by Gladwyn Jebb, who was also staying, Lali Horstmann who doted on him, even Dorothy Warren, Ivor Novello, and Miss Scanlan, a middle-aged Australian journalist, who came to interview Harold on the leading men in Germany. The only fly in the ointment was that Gladwyn did not care much for Ivor. Harold suspected that Ivor may have made advances to him. He did, and was imperiously rebuffed.

It was through Gladwyn that Cyril Connolly crept into Harold's circle. Like so many of the very young English intellectuals he found himself washed up in Berlin. He told Gladwyn, who passed it on to Harold, that there were only three English novels written since 1900 that were worth reading, namely *South Wind, Antic Hay* and *Some People*, the last evidently classified in his mind as fiction. Eddy, who was then staying with Vita at Long Barn, sounded a note of warning. Harold should be careful of Cyril. Although very clever he was a sponger and mischief-maker. Harold must not be taken in by his specious charm. But needless to say, Harold was taken in, or rather was bowled over by the intelligence and erudition of this fascinating, monkey-faced youth of twenty-five.

> Cyril came yesterday. Like the young Beethoven with spots; and a good brow; and an unreliable voice. And he flattered your husband. He sat there toying with a fork and my vanity, turning them over together in his stubby little hands. He tells fortunes. Palmistry. But the main point of him is that he thinks *Some People* an important book. IMPORTANT!! And it was just scribbled down as a joke. He was terribly interested in Mr. Peabody, and we had a long talk about him. Mr. Peabody is shaping slowly into a very strange shape indeed. Like an hourglass . . . I really am going to take trouble with that book, and there is a lot of cerebration going on, conscious and unconscious.[32]

The novel was still fermenting. *Public Faces*, not to be published until 1932, had the longest gestation of all Harold's books.

On the 19th May Gladwyn, Gerald and Cyril left the flat, and Harold with joy in his heart went home on leave by way of Paris. He had been re-promoted to Counsellor. Vita met him at Newhaven and drove him to Long Barn, where he made a written note of everything that was out in the garden. His leave lasted a month. Numerous friends came to stay, or came down from London for the day – Margaret Goldsmith who was writing a life of Frederick the Great[33] and was infatuated with Vita, Raymond, Vincent Sheean, the Oswald Mosleys, Ruth Draper and the Sinclair Lewises. Harold wrote an obituary of Edmund Gosse for the *Nation*, and another article for *Nash's Magazine* on learning foreign languages. He gave a broadcast on biography which was published in the *Listener*. It was an amusing and rather flippant talk, but emphasised the prime necessity that his subject must interest the biographer both personally and emotionally. He was greatly cheered by Ben winning a scholarship to Eton. He saw his parents and his sister Gwen St. Aubyn in London. 'Then my darling takes me to Liverpool Street and we say one of those dreadful goodbyes.' The pact the two had made in Berlin had already been forgotten. In driving away from Liverpool Street Vita was so sad thinking of Harold that she got hopelessly lost in the City. He must *not*, she wrote, be acquiescent. He *must* get himself away from that beastly Berlin.

Harold admitted that he was far more homesick in Berlin than he had been in Tehran, although the Persian capital was further from home and the people to be met there were less interesting. But he loved the Persian landscape – my native land he called it – whereas in Berlin the works of God were in short supply. Moreover the only British people in Berlin, discounting visitors, whom he really loved, were the Lindsays and they were leaving for good.

A day after his return to Berlin Harold witnessed the arrival of the three airmen, Köhl, Hünefeld and Fitzmaurice, on the completion of their flight across the Atlantic. That evening the Embassy gave a farewell dinner to the Lindsays, and the new Counsellor had to make a speech.

On the 23rd June Harold had his first meeting with the President of Germany. He told Vita,

> I put on my stiff shirt, my stiff collar, my stiff trousers, my frock coat (what the Americans call a Prince Albert) and a top hat, and went off to tea with Hindenburg. It was a garden party really ... The fountains played, the bands played, the Nuncio in his purple silk trailed across the green grass, the footmen handed round lemonade and ices, old Hindenburg, looking completely four-square, strutted about being polite. He is

terribly old and venerable; a huge warm, square hand clasping one's own; a very dry old hand, but enormous. Well, well, that is the victor of Tannenberg [over the Russians in 1914]. In 1914 Hindenburg was a retired old general of nearly 70, completely unknown outside a narrow circle of brother-officers. By August he became the idol and terror of half the world. For four years he remained a legend. With defeat he retired to a little villa at Hanover where he shot partridges and collected appalling pictures of the Madonna and Child. Suddenly in May 1925 he was elected President of the German Reich. He has a genius for sincerity and loyalty, but for little else. He has the mind of a schoolboy, and never reads books. He triumphed through his integrity.[34]

A few days later Harold and the Lindsays lunched with the President. In the interval between the garden and the luncheon party Vita had advised Harold that Hindenburg, according to an informant, liked people who were natural with him and made simple jokes. She was evidently right, for Harold wrote:

The President is an old darling; he has a trick of raising his eyebrows and laughing like a schoolboy; he talks very simply, almost boyishly, but pretty shrewd; he is wonderful for his age, neither deaf nor blind. I don't wonder that they all worship him. After luncheon we all sat round a table and had coffee. This time I sat next to Hindenburg. He spoke about father, and where I had learned German, and of how when he was a boy there were still many English expressions current at Hanover, and of how he remembered the embassy here before it was an embassy, and of how he had gone up in the first zeppelin, which 'war so empfindlich dass ich eine furchtbare angst gehabt habe.'[35] A splendid old man.

Then the Lindsays left, and Harold was full of regret. At the station to see them off he wore a top hat and talked to the Papal Nuncio.

He is a dear man. He will be pope. Hadji loq (aet. suae 58) . . . 'When I knew the Pope in Berlin in 1928. Quand j'ai connu le Saint Père à Berlin',[36]

he would be saying at dinner parties in 1944. How right he was, for the Papal Nuncio became Pope Pius XII in 1939.

Once again Harold Nicolson was acting as Chargé d'Affaires, from the 1st July to the 9th September, with a break of one week in August. His first duty was to present the Maharaja of Patiala to the President, whom by now he felt he knew. 'Oh that dear old man,' he wrote.[37] The Maharaja was dressed up to the nines with diamonds in his turban, and was rather shy. Hindenburg, who by contrast was very much at ease, was a subfusc old figure in dull grey uniform. He patted Harold paternally on the shoulder, saying, 'Zu jung für einen geschäftsträger.' Harold 'translated glibly with that boyish charm which nowadays appeals only to people who are over forty years older than I am.' The President, completely out of sympathy with the exotic oriental potentate, observed that Patiala was in the north of India, was it not? In the plains, or on the hills? There was a long pause. Were there tigers in Patiala? No, they had all been shot. The President shook with merriment. The Sikhs lived in Punjab, did they not? 'Yes, Herr Reichspresident. I am the spiritual leader of the Sikhs.' The Gurkhas were great soldiers, Harold translated. 'Die Wass?' the President enquired. 'Gurkhas.' 'Gurken? gurken?' murmured Hindenburg. It was then that Harold remembered that *Gurken* meant cucumbers.

The Embassy was hard at work on preparations for the Kellogg Pact, which had first been mooted the previous year, and was to be concluded in August. The objective of the Pact was to allow no questions to arise between Great Britain and the United States, for which a peaceful solution could not be found in talks round a table. The new German Government, elected in May, was much concerned with these developments. On the 4th July Harold Nicolson sent a long Despatch[38] to Sir Austen Chamberlain about the composition of Chancellor Müller's new Government, which he believed had come to stay. Forty-two per cent of the electorate had voted to the left. The Social Democrats were therefore still in power. The bourgeois parties were prudent enough to allow their opponents the odium of resisting Communism. The health of the Foreign Minister, Dr. Stresemann, was precarious. His foreign policy was very precise; his internal policy vague. The Nationalists opposed him because he had been representative of his country at Versailles. Harold had just witnessed the terrible scene when Stresemann, stricken with mortal disease, was greeted with howls of execration as he mounted the tribune of the Reichstag. During his speech the Communists, deriding the status he maintained, shouted, 'Your Chancellor's Palace!' to which he retorted, 'Have any of you seen the Kremlin?' and deflected their jeers to laughter. The Press accorded him a mixed but not unadmiring reception. There was a tendency to rejoice that Germany had got a strong and representative Government. Müller indicated that he would adopt a more positive attitude towards disarmament, and the evacuation of the occupied zones. The Despatch ended with a sentence, typical of Harold Nicolson's nice observance of detail: 'The Soviet Ambassador from the centre of the diplomatic box watched these proceedings with impassive and dyspeptic dignity. He would scrutinise the Communist section through a little opera glass of mother o'pearl.'

During his brief period in charge at the Berlin Embassy Harold learned from first-hand contacts in Munich and elsewhere about the increasing influence of Adolf Hitler and his National Socialists. He was not reassured by the protestations of his German friends that the ex-corporal could never, since the failure of the 1923 *Putsch*, become a serious menace. As all the world now knows, the Nazi votes were at the general election of 1930 to rise from 800,000 to 6,500,000, making Hitler the second greatest power in the State. The one person in Berlin who shared Harold's anxiety over Hitler's gain of supporters was another outsider, the Papal Nuncio Pacelli. Harold went to see him. This wise prelate said, 'It is not given us to foretell the future. But I see danger there; great danger; perhaps a terrible danger.'

Harold was never one to conceal his disquiet from superiors for fear of making himself unpopular. His famous Despatch to the Secretary of State from Tehran, which brought him, if not disgrace, then temporary eclipse, was a signal instance of this openness of opinion. Once again, on the 20th July 1928, he sounded a note of warning to the same Foreign Secretary, Sir Austen Chamberlain about his misgivings.[39] At the same time he said he was thoroughly convinced that so long as the Germans lacked security they would not acquire self-confidence.

His Berlin experiences taught him a lot about the German character, and not least that he did not fully understand it. It taught him that the Germans were self-conscious and diffident; that their lack of national traditions rendered them the least civilised people in Europe. They suffered from the failing of the *nouveaux riches*, a neurosis that made them aggressive towards foreigners whom they met on equal terms. In letters to Clive Bell Harold could write about the German character more expansively and less guardedly than in a despatch to Sir Austen Chamberlain.

> The Germans have every quality except intelligence. Energy, application, memory, selection – they are all here. But what they lack is distinction. They have no sense of quality. There is nothing in Berlin therefore (except perhaps the music of which I know nothing) which is not, at least potentially, better somewhere else. Their stage work is so interesting that one says, 'How I should like to see this in Paris.' Their control of the traffic is so elaborate that one says, 'How I should like to see this in London.' Their films make one yearn for Vienna, their architecture makes one yearn for Passy, for Moscow or for New York; their pictures make one yearn just to go away. Their

food is good; their night life is excessive. But do I care for boys of seventeen dressed up like Ottoline Morrell? No, I DO NOT. And their shops, Clive – well, Sevenoaks is the rue de la Paix in comparison.[40]

Harold Nicolson's conviction that the Germans were wanting in self-confidence did not prevent him from foreseeing eventual German rearmament on a vast scale. The Foreign Office transmitted information that General Groener, who was chief of the *Kriegsamt* during the War, was alleged to be forging unofficial contacts between the Ministry of Defence and the *Stahlhelm*, an association of ex-servicemen, one of several patriotic bodies of a semi-military sort.[41] In actual fact General von Seeckt had been secretly building up the German army and armaments as early as 1922. And Harold knew it. In a further letter to the Foreign Office of the 14th August[42] he confirmed their suspicions about the laxity with which the German Government was regarding the patriotic associations, contrary to the terms of the disarmament treaty. At the moment Germany was sufficiently disarmed to prevent her mobilising an aggressive force before other nations could mobilise their own. But he was sure that no paper undertakings would hamper her if she intended to mobilise. It was true that the clandestine *Grenzschutz* on the Eastern Front could put 50,000 armed men in the field at three days notice. Since it was essential for the Germans to retain possession of the Ruhr a similar association for the western front would doubtless be organised as soon as the second and third zones of the Occupied Territories were evacuated. 'If we are weak on details,' Harold warned, 'we shall find ourselves, before we know where we are, face to face with a fully armed Germany.' He concluded that all we could do meanwhile was to rely on the League of Nations and Germany's pacific elements. Victor Perowne and Charles Howard Smith in the Foreign Office minuted their general agreement with this letter, which was then put aside. Sir Ronald Lindsay stated less cautiously that the French could be depended on to watch these movements more keenly than Great Britain was likely to do.

Harold was instructed by Sir Austen Chamberlain to combine with his French colleague to invite the German Government to join in proposing that the League Assembly should declare Spain re-eligible for membership of the Council.[43] Harold, who was a friend of the French Ambassador's son and daughter-in-law, Roland and Jennie de Margerie, was successful in this mission. He was able to report to Sir Austen that the German Government was in agreement with Great Britain and France in this regard, but questioned the procedure proposed to bring it about.

BERLIN 1927-28

The even tenor of Harold's social life was just slightly jolted by the arrival at the beginning of July of young Lord Poulett to learn German and Daniel Lascelles to join the Embassy staff as First Secretary. Poulett, the 8th Earl of that ancient title, was a very handsome, 'very nice, rather *how* youth who wants to be an engineer but his guardian won't let him. He looks very distinguished but speaks with a bedint accent.'[44] It might have been better for the boy's future if his guardian had allowed him to adopt a useful and honest-to-God profession. As it transpired he achieved nothing but the dissipation and break-up of one of the noblest houses, collections and estates in the west country. But at the age of twenty he was beguiling. Harold was not slow to realise that he needed taking in hand, for on the 12th he noted in his diary, 'Poulett lunches. Give him a talking to.' Dan Lascelles was a different person altogether. He was not good looking, but small and dark, with a sallow complexion and fine eyes. He was silent and solemn. Harold took to him because of his intelligence and sensitivity, and because he was tied up in knots. He was also a romantic, having walked across the plains of Castile and slept under the stars. Harold took the ill-assorted pair of young men to dine in Luna Park and made them watch fireworks and slide down a shoot on a mat.

At the end of July he moved into a rented apartment in Potsdam for the summer.[45] It was not a nice apartment, being poky, underfurnished and rather cold; and to crown everything the po of the landlord was found in the po-stand, still full. At once Harold filled the apartment with guests. Raymond Mortimer arrived from Cologne, followed by Bobby Longden, a man of angelic disposition who was to become Head Master of Wellington College and be killed by a bomb in 1940, and Cyril Connolly.

> Cyril and Tray are very suspicious of each other, and stalk around each other with their hackles up like two poodles.[46]

However awkwardly the visit may have begun it soon turned into a sort of intellectual symposium, in which the shafts of three (for Longden seems not to have taken part) very brilliant minds thrust at each other and clashed together like the foils of nimble fencers. It gave rise to Connolly's *Conversations in Berlin*, a chapter in *The Condemned Playground*.

It was a discussion, as Harold told his wife, about the test of intelligence, which led to writing and happiness. It opened with Cyril pronouncing that he judged a woman's intelligence by whether she had read all through Proust. Harold discounted this as nonsense. He was sure Lady Gosford had done so, and remained a goose for ever after. He judged a person's intelligence by his or her imagination, curiosity and ability to draw quick and original conclusions on any non-technical subject.

Raymond put culture before all other qualities. It was agreed that in writing revision should amount to taking things out of a manuscript, and not putting them in. When they reached happiness, Cyril and Raymond were in agreement that Harold was the happiest and most fortunate of men; and they gave their reasons. Harold was gratified by their assumption, and said he could not remember ever having felt so happy as at that particular moment. Cyril thought that moment was not one of happiness so much as of perfect civilisation. Happiness contained more distress than rapture. Raymond's expression of melancholy and Harold's silence confirmed Cyril's opinion that they, like him, were being forced to refer their greatest happiness to the past.

On the 3rd August Harold had to get up early, put on tails and a top hat, and meet the new ambassador Sir Horace Rumbold at the station. Rumbold came for a week without his wife and family, to present his credentials to the President. 'There is no doubt that I do not like Ambassadors arriving when I am in charge,' Harold observed.

> The train came in and old Rumby bundled out rather embarrassed with an attaché case in one hand and in the other a novel by Mr. Galsworthy ... He is a nice old bumble bee, and I am quite happy with him. But he is not Lindsay, no, no.[47]

Harold gave a dinner party for him. Rumbold asked for a list of the guests with a brief description of each. Against the name of a very rich industrialist, Harold wrote, 'Magnate of Silesia.' Sir Horace was perplexed.

The new Ambassador had not been in Berlin since August 1914 when as Counsellor he had to creep away under escort. As had happened before, Harold was slow to adapt himself to a superior. 'Rumbie is not commode. He is not the sort of person who would like to take Cyril out in a punt.'[48] He certainly was not. Then before many days had passed he was referred to, somewhat patronisingly as 'a dear old thing, old Rumbie'. Vita on the other hand thought he sounded ghastly from the mere fact that he was so eminently *nice*! No, Harold asserted before twelve months had elapsed, the Rumbolds 'really are so perfect of their kind, and there are many far worse kinds.'[49] He belonged to the old-fashioned school of British diplomatist, being sagacious, trustworthy and tolerant. Lady Rumbold was in every respect the perfect Ambassadress, dignified, unassuming and infinitely kind. Harold witnessed an example of her impeccable self-control and breeding. At one of her luncheon parties a guest,

> Frau Weissmann broke a yellow Chinese bowl. She was taking out her little bag (you know those dainty reticules which add such a charm to women's little ways), only it wasn't a little bag; it was a large black bag

heavily bound in steel. The handle of the bag stuck somewhere in her bodice. She tugged. It then sprang into the air, turned several somersaults, and descended rapidly upon a yellow Ming bowl, biting a huge piece out of it. Frau Weissmann turned the colour of one of those purple strawberries. Lady Rumbold said, 'Oh, it was *entirely* my fault; one should not leave such things lying about.'[50]

Harold grew to respect them both, and when he learned in 1941 that Sir Horace had died, he recorded, 'I loved that man.' He paid tribute to him as the perfect diplomatist.[51] As for the Rumbolds they had expressed great alarm at the prospect of having Harold and Vita in Berlin, fearing lest they might pillory them in their books.

A new recruit to Vita's circle appeared in the summer of 1928. Hilda Matheson was in charge of the Talks Department of the B.B.C. She was in reality its first Director though she never enjoyed that title. In the history of the early B.B.C. days she played an important role. She was determined to get every well known writer to broadcast, and she practically succeeded. She insisted on authors reading, naturally, from a carefully prepared script. Her early stars were Vernon Bartlett, Stephen King-Hall, Vita and Harold. She introduced poetry readings, and Vita was so moved by Robert Harris's beautiful rendering of Shelley and Keats that Harold urged her to write and congratulate her. This she did. Hilda Matheson was very efficient, very independent, rather testy and showed slight left wing bias. Owing to her resentment at the Director-General Sir John Reith's policy of caution and his discontinuance of Harold's talks on modern literature – he objected to the mention of James Joyce's *Ulysses* over the air – Hilda threw in her resignation in January 1932.

The consequence of Vita's congratulations in 1928 was that Hilda was invited to stay at Long Barn for the second weekend of July. Vita liked her very much, for she had brains and education. In December Hilda was staying at Long Barn again. Hugh Walpole was also present. Vita called Hilda an angel of unselfishness, and a real friend. She took her and Hugh over to Penns-in-the-Rocks, the little Georgian house and picturesque garden near Groombridge which Dorothy Wellesley had lately bought. Hugh Walpole recorded in his journal that 'they talked all the afternoon in a manner to give any worthy magistrate a fit!'[52] In the evening they also talked before the fire about the forthcoming broadcast discussion which Hilda had arranged between Vita and Hugh on the Modern Woman, which took place two days later. After the broadcast Vita stayed with

Hilda in London. The brief visit provoked from Virginia Woolf the caustic comment: 'And now you're off in the bitter black night with female unknown; fresh, or stale and scented rather, from the arms, to put it euphemistically, of Mary – God! What a succession of flea bites and bug bites the life of a respectable hard working woman is!'[53] and from Harold a familiar cry of slight apprehension: 'Hadji is rather worried about Miss Mathison.'[54] The misspelling of the surname was not meant to be derisive. It was one of Harold's constant foibles to misspell names, even of friends of twenty-five years standing.

Old Lady Sackville's resentment against her daughter was by no means on the decline. Ozzie Dickinson reported to Vita that he had seen her, and believed her to be suffering from softening of the brain, and delusions. She was virulent about Vita. He pressed her for her reasons. She said, 'My dear Ozzie, you do not know the truth. You do not know what her real motive is.' Ozzie said, 'No. B.M., do tell me.' She said, 'It is all a deep-laid plot. She intends to divorce Harold and marry Eddy, and so get Knole. That is why she has worked for Knole all along.'[55] Evidently at the back of her muddled mind she was attributing to her daughter motives not altogether dissimilar from her own in the years gone by. She also told Ozzie Dickinson that Vita had stolen her jewelry and substituted paste.

When Ben and Nigel's summer holidays from school came round at the beginning of August Vita had to cope alone; and she did not relish it. One part of her loved her sons when they were boys; the other was intensely irritated by them. She was not maternal. She wanted to be free to get on with her writing, and the constant interruptions of two boisterous, healthy schoolboys of fourteen and eleven got on her nerves. 'Don't misunderstand me,' she wrote to Harold. 'I like having them here, but I do *not* like having to look after them and everything to do with them. Nor would you.' She was bewildered that they sat around, doing nothing, reading nothing and apparently unable to amuse or edify themselves. She must, she insisted, get someone to look after them.[56] The situation was not improved by the receipt of a lecture[57] from Harold about 'things-we-don't-want-to-do', which he called Acid X. He had his profession which acted like a sponge to mop up his Acid X. It was no good attempting to get rid of Acid X for it would always accumulate. Vita would never succeed in cutting herself off from life and people. There would always be servants, the dogs, or the doves. 'I am sure that when you manage to escape to your desert island, you will have a series of nerve-storms because the wind at sunset will insist on rustling the palms.' As for the boys, if she let them see that they got on her nerves, she would lose their confidence. It would be such a good thing, he added, 'if you could throw a little more eccentricity into your writing and a little less eccentricity into your life. How I wish I could get at the fool who gave you the idea that responsibilities, instead of being the stepping-stones through a marsh, were something to evade and to regard with shame.' By 'your writing' he was referring to her book on the Bakhtiari expedition, *Twelve Days*, which he had just read and liked with reservations. The descriptive passages in it were very good, and he commended the part about the oil fields. He was glad she had cut out some obvious padding, but the book was left too short. It should have been longer. He could not look upon it as a book, but memories of great poignancy, some of them unpleasant.

Vita replied to Harold's lecture, denying that she minded the interruptions of life, but objecting to looking after children for four months in the year. She presumed he thought she ought not to mind just because she was a woman. 'Well, I don't see that that makes any difference,' she retorted.[58]

Vita's calvary was not to last long, for on the 16th August she and the boys joined him at Potsdam to spend the remaining four weeks of the school holidays. Harold took the boys bathing, to cinemas, the Zoo, tennis tournaments, and on expeditions whenever he could get away from his work, and he endeavoured to interest them in their holiday tasks. Nigel has recorded that his father once read the whole of Aeschylus's *Seven against Thebes* because it was his holiday task, and thus Harold could discuss it while it was fresh in his mind too. The boys sensed that whereas their father enjoyed their company, their mother was less at her ease with them. As Nigel has explained, 'Our relationship was one of reaching out with fingertips to grasp what can only be grasped by the whole hand.'[59] While they respected her for never invading their privacy, they understood that she did not expect them to invade hers.

Harold's work this August was pressing. Sir Horace Rumbold, having stayed a week, left Berlin with the Counsellor again in charge. Harold was obliged to look after and entertain the British Delegation to the Inter-Parliamentary Conference. He had to attend a vast banquet in the Marmorsaal, with interminable intervals between the courses when the band played *The Geisha* noisily. He himself had to give a banquet in the Adlon Hotel for fifty-four. He had several interviews with von Schubert, the Secretary of State, who was worried by Britain's naval agreement with France. In the rush of these duties two English tourists turned up. They were Maurice Bowra and John Sparrow, from Oxford. The first was to become Warden of Wadham College, the second Warden of All Souls. John Sparrow, the younger of the two was twenty-two, with Winchester, New College, and a double First in Honour Mods. and Lit. Humaniores recently behind him. Harold brought them out to Potsdam, and at once Sparrow became, what he was always to remain, an intimate

BERLIN 1927-28

friend, almost an adopted member of the Nicolson family. Scholarly and absent-minded, pedantic in delivery, amused, amusing and stimulating, he was sturdy and compact in build, with the good looks of a pugilist. Harold described him soon after their first meeting as always absolutely correct.

> When I say 'correct' I don't mean in a tiresome sense. What I mean is that in every situation he seems to have an absolute poise; due, I think, to a perfect sense of values. It is like a singer whose voice has been beautifully trained. There is a sense of security of conduct. A really charming man ... John is very much of a someone.[60]

The boys, to whom John was nearer in age, became as devoted to him as their parents did. He teased them, as he teased Harold; he sharpened their wits and they respected him as they would an indulgent elder brother with a very mature mind. He had a passion for argument and dialectics, which enchanted his friends and irritated his enemies. It might be said that he trailed his coat advancing reactionary views, seeking as it were by whom he might be devoured. He was inquisitive, and inquisitorial. He would never take yes or no for an answer, any more than he would give a positive or negative reply to a question. Every observation by himself or others needed qualifying. Harold invented an example of the sort of answer you were likely to receive from Sparrow to the simplest interrogative.

> If you said to John, 'Do you like oysters?' he would answer, 'Well now, that's a very interesting question. I do not feel, or even think, that I do. But, mark you, this may be an association which a little consideration could dispel, and so on, and so on.[61]

On the 12th September the Nicolson family, with Knopf, Harold's German chauffeur in attendance, motored from Potsdam to Cologne, by way of Frankfurt and Mainz, where they saw the French and British troops in occupation. They experienced the usual punctures and breakdowns, habitual to motors in the twenties. At Cologne the family had its last evening together, and Harold felt obliged to give Ben a pi-jaw about Eton, where he was going as a new boy. It was made the more necessary by the boy's idiotic schoolmaster having warned him not to make friends with older boys at Eton, 'as they were disgusting.' After dinner father and son took a turn along the quay. Harold did not think Ben understood much of what he was saying, and he loathed saying it. He wrote to Vita next day:

> I explained how when one came to a certain age one had new physical powers and pleasures, and these pleasures if properly controlled were the

best in the world ... Anyway I told him he must work it all out for himself, and that if he got puzzled he could always ask us, as we should always understand. I said that about masturbation he must put it off as long as he possibly could, and then he must only do it on Saturday ... He was very sensible and sweet, and said that he would never worry about those sorts of things as he could always talk to me or you about them.[62]

That evening they parted, Harold taking a train back to Berlin. Vita and the boys went next morning to London, she dreading taking Ben to Eton and leaving him there. On reaching Berlin Harold funked getting out at the Zoo station where he had so happily greeted his family a month previously, and went on to the Friedrich-Strasse. Back at Brücken Allee he was very wretched. He wrote to Vita that he was dispirited about *Peabody* which he had begun revising in the sleeper. 'I fear that novel-writing and office work don't go well together. For a novel you have to absolutely soak in your subject like a mud bath.'[63] He felt passionately that there was a book there somewhere, that it was written, that it had all its shapes and contours, its incidents and its phrases, and that he had only to put out his hand in the right direction and seize it. Vita replied[64] that it was the first time she had heard him admit that his work interfered with his writing. She thoroughly understood and approved his feelings about *Peabody*. She mistrusted too much facility. 'Keep your faith in unconscious cerebration;' she advised him. 'It turns, in the end, to conscious cerebration.'

On the 10th September Sir Horace Rumbold returned, bringing his wife and daughter. Harold's charge of the Embassy was over. He was no longer his own master. Instead of dressing comfortably and colourfully in a lounge suit he was obliged to put on tails when he accompanied the Ambassador to call upon the acting head of the Foreign Office. He found such conventional restrictions a bore. And then there were those desperately sticky dinners at the Embassy when conversation was about careers, and who was to be sent where. This was happening while Vita took Virginia Woolf on a motor tour through Burgundy. Although she wrote to Harold that her life away from him was one long ache, nevertheless she was enjoying the tour immensely. She could talk about life and literature to her heart's content. She felt thoroughly irresponsible and gay. Somewhat ruefully Harold wrote that it was so good for her spirit to be abroad with Virginia, adding a cautionary note: 'She is an important and fragile piece of china to have entrusted to one's hands.'[65] His recreation was reading Eddy's new novel, *Mandrake over the Water-Carrier*, which he found deplorable. It was full of obscure symbolism. It was not even funny. It was a disaster. Dead. The book of a tired invalid, with no passion behind it.

When a person has got comparative command of his medium, when he is obviously quite articulate, then the poverty of his passion and of his vision become devastatingly apparent. When he [Eddy] moved like a young dove fallen from the nest it was all very promising. But now that he can fly from tree to tree one observes that he is only a starling.

This was too severe a stricture on a novel which, while it certainly lacks sparkle and is too much given to arabesques and the occult, has a theme and is written with style. At any rate Eddy, who was staying in Brücken Allee again, was hurt that Harold had failed to grasp the underlying philosophy of *Mandrake*, and told him so. To change the subject Harold discussed with Eddy what they both would have been like if born a hundred years ago. Eddy imagined he would be Earl of Middlesex, which was the courtesy title borne by his ancestor the Duke of Dorset. Of course, he said, he would not be able to be on quite the same terms with his present friends. 'No,' said Harold, 'they would stand up when you came into the room. But perhaps you would like that.' There was a long pause. 'Perhaps,' said Eddy thoughtfully.

On the same evening that Harold was being entertained in a large house in the Wannsee, with a wonderful collection of eighteenth-century pictures, tapestries and furniture – 'appliqués by Gouthière, gouthières by Appliqué' – by Frau Feise, a lady looking like Catherine II and living with a beautiful youth of twenty-three, Vita and Virginia were dining with Ethel Sands and Nan Hudson at Offranville. The two friends had lived since 1920 in the Château d'Auppegard,[66] a lovely little house arranged in faultless taste. Vanessa Bell and Duncan Grant had decorated a loggia with enchanting scenes of idyllic tasks – digging, planting, haymaking, harvesting and so forth. Ethel Sands has left several paintings of the interior of the château, a long facade with pyramid-shaped pavilions beside a church, and rooms inside with splodges of sunlight falling from square window-panes upon English chairs, a round breakfast table, and a cosy white porcelain clock.

After a delicious dinner,

Virginia read us her memoir [Vita wrote[67]] of old Bloomsbury ... I want you to hear it. It is very amusing; and terribly improper; the two old virgins bridled with horrified delight. I wondered whether V was going to shirk any of it; but she didn't shirk a word.

Ethel Sands reported a rumour that B.M. had proposed marriage to Eddy. Virginia too enjoyed a perfect week. She told Harold:[68]

I never laughed so much in my life, or talked so much. It went like a flash – Vita was an angel to me – looked out trains, paid tips, spoke perfect French, indulged me in every humour, was perpetually sweet tempered, endlessly entertaining, looked lovely ... Only I wish she were not so humble. It is perfect nonsense that she should think so lowly of her gifts and works. I can't persuade her that the nimbleness of Raymond, shall we say, the brilliance of Clive, and the incorrigible vanity of Virginia are all qualities we should be better without.

Harold took up with delight Virginia's charge of Vita's diffidence. It certainly was a reversal of her earlier contempt of Vita's writing – her pen of brass. He wrote:[69]

Virginia is quite right about your ridiculous diffidence. It is the same part of you that makes you shy at parties, makes you creep into corners and hide there, and stay put all evening so as not to be seen. But it is absurd your being diffident about your writing since you have such a compelling literary gift.

The week's motor-tour had enabled Vita, so she thought, to understand Virginia through and through. Virginia had a sweet and child-like character, from which her brilliant intellect, totally detached, worked independently. Vita felt profoundly protective towards the frail, the hyper-sensitive person, while she still regarded with awe and even fear the mind, which could not be either controlled, or matched. She believed that hitherto only Leonard and Vanessa understood this duality; now she did too.

At the beginning of October Vita warned Harold that the secret of *Orlando* was already out. People were talking and speculating about the theme of the book. The news made Harold nervous. He already knew that he figured as Marmaduke Bontrop Shelmerdine, Esquire, the young Regency gentleman of rather nebulous personality. He didn't mind if Virginia had made him into a fool, because he knew himself not to be one. But he dreaded what he called a *floater* about Vita, in other words a revelation of her homosexuality to the esoteric public. He could not bear that. He knew that poor old Gosse had been parodied as Nicholas Greene, and Lord Lascelles as the Archduchess Harriet. But Gosse was dead and Lord Lascelles would probably never notice the resemblance. And as for Violet's transmogrification into the unknown Russian skater, Princess Marousha, who cared what Violet might think? However she were depicted she would see flattery in the portrait. The ensuing letters between the Nicolsons are almost exclusively about *Orlando*.

Vita wrote on the 11th that her copy of *Orlando* had come to her from Virginia in a special, lovely binding.[70] She was in ecstasies.

It seems to me more brilliant, more enchanting, more rich and lavish, than anything she has done. It is like a cloak encrusted with jewels and sprinkled with rose petals. I admit I can't see straight about it. Parts of it make me cry, parts of it make me laugh; the whole of it dazzles and bewilders me. I scarcely slept with excitement all night ... It seems to me a book unique in English literature, having everything in it: romance, wit, seriousness, lightness, beauty, imagination, style: with Sir Thomas Browne and Swift for parents. I feel infinitely honoured at having been the peg on which it was hung; and very humble.

The following day,[71] after further fulsome praise of the book, she made a few valid cricitisms of *Orlando*. She thought Virginia had confused the issues in making Orlando marry and have a child. Shelmerdine did not contribute to Orlando's character or problems; and the child contributed nothing. Whereas in reality marriage and motherhood would either have modified or destroyed Orlando as a credible character, in the book they did neither. Again, the more she thought about it, the weaker she thought the end was. What did the wild goose stand for? Fame? Love? Death? Marriage? The symbolism did not come through clearly. Harold had no reservations. His praise was unstinted. He called *Orlando*

a book in which you and Knole are identified for ever, a book which will perpetuate that identity into years when both you and I are dead. This is an intimate secret which the book holds probably for you and me alone. Virginia may not have understood it. But I feel so grateful to her genius for providing what is really a unique consolation ... But what a wonderful book ... The whole thing has a beauty which makes one catch one's breath, like that sunset before Dilijan. It is so far *more* than brilliance. I simply cannot believe that such a book will not survive. The whole world of life has been poured into it, flashing with molten flames.[72]

Vita was delighted with his interpretation of the book and his conviction that it would immortalise the spirit of her Knole. She was touched, rather than surprised by his 'funny mystical side, which he would rather die than admit to. Funny conviction that Knole *knows* ... and likes me; but goes on *being*, just the same.'[73]

They went on corresponding about *Orlando* which had so deeply affected them both. All Harold disliked in it was the photographs which added a note of insistence. That could have been spared. He did not agree a bit with Vita's criticism of Shelmerdine, or think the book tailed off at the end. But he did think the link between poetry and satire was not entirely successful. Harold never modified his opinion that *Orlando* was a great book. In a broadcast in 1931 he called it 'one of the strangest and most brilliant evocations ever composed.'[74]

Early in October Harold was working in the Chancery when a servant opened the door and announced Madame de Landa.[75]

> There in the hall stood Kathleen Drogheda accompanied by a young man of amazing beauty whom I took to be her husband. But he wasn't her husband, he was [Garrett] Moore, who was our page at our wedding. You can't imagine the charm and beauty of that young man. He is like a 10% more attractive Ian [Campbell-Gray]. Very intelligent and self-assured, & smart. Rather embarrassed by Kathleen's . . . indiscretion but evidently fond of her. She herself far too silly for words.[76]

Harold invited them to luncheon the next day. He got Eddy, who was staying, and Francesco Mendelsohn to meet them. Mendelsohn was a rich, spoilt, vague, wild connoisseur of the arts, who lived with his sister Eleanora, a famous actress, in a heavy Jewish house in Grünewald, hung with Rembrandts and El Grecos. He was intensely musical and played the cello. He was infinitely good-natured and devoid of snobbishness. He knew all Berlin society and would unashamedly mix ambassadors, princesses, bar-tenders and milliners at his own parties, treating all his guests exactly the same. He was a frequent companion of Harold at night clubs, where he played the most outrageous practical jokes without causing anybody offence.

Before luncheon Kathleen de Landa announced that she had asked the ex-Crown Prince to pick her up at the flat. Garrett Moore – 'Oh, the charm of that beautiful and insolent young man' – said he did not want to know the Crown Prince.[77] They had hardly begun to eat when the bell of the flat rang. Harold looked through the window and there in front of a scarlet Mercedes was a man in a jumper with his cap turned back to front, and in front of this strange 'Our Boys' figure was Knopf, curtseying. 'He *was* curtseying; no one could have described his pirouettes as a bow.' Harold went downstairs, brought the uninvited guest up, and made him sit on a sofa under the chandelier. Indoors and without his cap the Crown Prince looked like an elderly and bewildered secretary to a provincial golf club. He was very civil, but ill at ease. He had amiable, uncertain blue eyes, a silly mouth, and altogether a silly little face. 'Sir,' screamed Kathleen, 'Your Royal Highness.' Eddy was stiff. Francesco was stiffer, answering in English the questions the Prince put to him in German. He afterwards explained that he did this because he was determined, being a confirmed

Republican, not to call him 'Your Royal Highness', and that 'you' sounded less insulting in English than 'Sie' in German. As for Garrett Moore, he was deliberately rude. 'You mustn't mind my boy's manners, Your Royal Highness,' exclaimed Kathleen, 'He's only shy.' A look of hatred flashed from son to mother.

> At this stage I gave the fallen hope of Germany a glass of port. Bewildered but polite he took it, saying, 'Cheerio!' Eddy sniffed at that. His nose had started to bleed, but it sounded as if he were sneering at fallen monarchy. Francesco was, I must say, extremely dignified.

Vita's sole comment upon this story was, 'Hadji, not fall in love with Moore.'[78]

On the 14th Ramsay MacDonald, accompanied by the Mosleys, arrived in Berlin. He was very nervous about a speech he had to make to the Reichstag. He kept looking at his watch and saying, 'Now the sun of my peace of mind is being eclipsed by the moon of my speech. The rim of the moon has just begun to nip an edge off the circle of the sun.' Harold got a seat among the deputies and listened to the speech, which was only fairly good. The uninspiring delivery was punctuated by too regular emphases; and from time to time the voice assumed the whine of a revivalist preacher. The Mosleys were taken by Frau Stresemann to a round of night clubs. Sir Oswald was shocked by what he saw. The scenes of decadence and depravity suggested to him a nation sunk so deep that it could never rise again. 'Yet within two or three years men in brown shirts were goose-stepping down these same streets around the Kurfürstendamm.'[79]

On the 18th, seen off by Dan Lascelles, Harold went to England for a month's leave. The enjoyment was dispelled by the sudden illness of his father, who, although he had been ailing for some years, seemed quite well on his son's return. By the 4th November it was clear to the family and to Lord Carnock himself that he was dying. He said goodbye to his servants and then to his relations. Harold had a long talk with him. The old man was worried about his wife being left badly off. Harold assured him that his children would look after her. Indeed no filial promise was ever to be more faithfully fulfilled. Lord Carnock told Harold he was glad he had stayed on in the service. He went into a coma and the next day died.

Harold's relations with his father had been consistently respectful, admiring and affectionate, without being intimate. Lord Carnock rejoiced in his younger son's success in what he called his 'own dear old profession,' which to him was the noblest available to an English gentleman. He would have been deeply distressed had he lived another year to witness Harold's long-threatened retirement. Harold rendered his father lasting homage in the biography he wrote. Within a puny frame, bent at the end of his life halfway to the earth by arthritis, Lord Carnock maintained a noble spirit. In the opinion of Lord Vansittart Carnock's chief claim to distinction was the clear vision wherewith he sought to ward off Armageddon before 1914 by consolidating our relations with France and Russia. Even in small matters, he added, he had an annoying habit of being right. But Lord Carnock might not have been very pleased to receive from a very unorthodox member of his 'own dear old profession' the following meed of well-intentioned praise. 'I sometimes think with gratitude,' wrote Guy Burgess from Moscow to Harold in the 1960s,[80] 'that your father invented the Foreign Office jacket, and that superb, useful, and unequalled elsewhere democratic system of Juniors minuting first on anything however important.' It is odd to reflect that owing to the initiative of that most patriotic servant of Crown and State comments of the Soviet-Marxist Guy Burgess remain on Foreign Office documents for the edification of posterity.

Harold returned to Berlin in low spirits, to be greeted at the station by Dan Lascelles with sixty-one letters of condolence. His perplexity about his future was not lessened by the receipt of a heart-rending letter from Vita.[81]

> It's simply sheer misery for me, these perpetual departures of yours; and that's the flat truth. You will never know what it is to me, or how senseless it all seems to one who has neither ambition (of that kind) nor any sense of public duty, but I think it ought to be reserved for those who cannot do anything else, and those who can make lovely books like Hadji should not waste themselves on a lot of humbug and fubsiness ... Oh God, how I hate the Foreign Office, how I hate it with a personal hatred, for all that it makes me suffer. Damn it, damn it, damn it. Vile impersonal juggernaut.

She had not yet got her way; and all that was now needed was a final incentive to push him over the brink. Vita's other indignation at this juncture was over the pronouncement that Radclyffe Hall's *Well of Loneliness* was obscene. She did not think it a good book. That was beside the point; but her sympathy was of course entirely with the author's plea for tolerance and justice for lesbians.

Harold's two sources of consolation were his little dog Henry, who welcomed him with manifestations of joy, and, rather surprisingly, Eddy, who was still staying at Brücken Allee. Eddy had become so companionable that Harold had what he called a momentary 'up on him.'[82] On the other hand he was seriously worried about Eddy's way of life. He went to Försters Restaurant in the Motzstrasse.

> There I found Eddy (rather made up) and Cohen Portheim (also with a touch of rouge on his cheeks) and M. Cornèle Medderup. Yes, that's his name [actually it was Conrad Minderop] ... Eddy I think is rather in love with him. He belongs to one of the best families in Cologne, and he is good-looking in a Byronic way, and dances gracefully. Eddy danced with him at the Silhouette, and the powder from Eddy's cheek came off white on Cornèle Medderup's strong black arm.[83]

Vita begged Harold to give Eddy a talking to about his promiscuity or he would go from bad to worse. This Harold did, and 'poor little Eddy' agreed that promiscuity took the edge off sensibility. Nevertheless poor little Eddy's pettiness got on his nerves again. Harold was intensely irritated by his desire to be famous and to have demands from America for his autograph, and by his pretension and insincerity where the arts were concerned. He accompanied him to the Maillol Collection.

> He is careful not to say from the other end of the room, 'Oh what a lovely Picasso,' fearing that the treacherous Spaniard may be deceiving him, that it may be by somebody else, possibly even by a German. So he is silent at first and strolls about making little irritable noises – 'not much here' sort of noises. Then when he has made sure that Picasso really is written in the corner he says, 'Gets it *every* time.' 'Who gets what, Eddy?' say I. 'Picasso always brings it off.' 'But that isn't Picasso, Eddy, it's Fritz Müller!' Momentary panic on Eddy's part. Reassuring glimpses at *Picasso* – yes, there it is. '*Really*, Harold.'[84]

The Nicolsons' criticism of Eddy Sackville-West may seem excessive and even uncharitable. There is no denying that Vita nourished a sort of prejudice against him since his birth. He had been born a boy and she a girl. He, the heir, was indifferent, even hostile to Knole, which to her was what Bethlehem is to the most pious Christian. Harold necessarily adopted, if unconsciously, this congenital partiality. There can be no doubt that in his early manhood Eddy was finicky, pernickety and often querulous. But it must be remembered that he suffered from chronic bad health. His eccentricities, which got on the nerves of his elders, were more tolerable to his contemporaries. In fact, as he grew older, they became more and more endearing. His friends were then, and were to remain, devoted to him, because he was such good company and so thoroughly himself. Besides, he developed into an extremely intelligent, widely read, highly cultivated, deeply pious and civilized man, and one of the most percipient music and literary critics of his time. Harold and Vita were among the first to acknowledge Eddy's merits as a writer as they emerged from the precious; and on being shown the manuscript of his novel, *Simpson*, in April 1929, both pronounced it admirable, because for the first time the subject seemed to them truly and positively felt.

The misery of Berlin on Bustag (the Lutheran day of Atonement, which fell on the 21st November, his birthday) in the rain, the bells tolling mournfully, ding, dong, ding, from the lugubrious brick churches, and the sound of feet on wet pavements going to service haunted Harold for the rest of his life. German Bustag of 1928 plumbed the depth of his loneliness and homesickness and convinced him that never could he spend another winter out of England without Vita. Yet such was his resilience that a few days later he was writing to her:[85]

> Oh God, how I wish life were twice as long and that the days consisted of 100 hours each!! Every morning I wake up thinking how I want to write a book about Puritanism, and spend a winter in Tahiti, and learn how to fish for salmon, and go a walking tour through Patagonia, and try and get at the secret of Cézanne's landscapes (I am really wild about Cézanne just now), and do nothing for six weeks except visit the Greek islands with my darling and the boys, and build a house in the Lebanon, and visit Australia, South Africa, and America, and do a fuller life of Byron, and Ludwig 11, and through all this to go on being a diplomat, and having Long Barn, and seeing every autumn the wood smoke drift across the dear remembered woods.

And 'go on being a diplomat' indicates how, were it not for Vita, he would probably have remained in the service until the end of his career.

Then Ethel Smyth returned to the Berlin scene. Harold gathered from Frau Louise Wolff,[86] a partner in the foremost musical agency, Wolff and Sachs, who had been arranging her concert, that Ethel was being exacting, conceited and intractable. What a bore it must be to have to produce one's work with the co-operation of several hundred other people. What an appalling fuss of choirs, rehearsals, orchestras, sopranos, all for a thing which, God willing, would only last three and a half hours at the very most. He gave another luncheon party for her. She arrived in a fine to-do. Her tricorne kept on falling over her eyes in her excitement and she screamed (like most deaf people) loud with indignation against the Jewish Republic which Emil Ludwig, who was present, and his friends had established in Germany. Ludwig was rather hurt at this. He retorted that the old gang had done nothing except land Germany into the European War. She said that his beastly Jews had destroyed the old German culture.

He said, 'Not all, not at all.' She said, Yes, they had and ('God, Harold, why do you give me cold sauce with sole? I hate cold sauce with sole), what about the Grand Duke of Weimar? Ludwig said, 'Which Grand Duke?' 'Weimar,' said Ethel triumphantly. Ludwig asked whether she meant the Goethe one. She said, No, she meant the Ethel Smyth one. Ludwig said that that one had been gaga. She said that of course he had been gaga, but at least he had cared for art, and did not think *The Grand Duke of Weimar* a good book merely because it had sold 13,000 copies. Anyway, she had lived in Germany before he, Ludwig, was born – she shouted across the table. 'I tell you, Germans were much happier under their little princes than they are now.'

Ludwig said he did not see why he should be scolded merely because '*The Grand Duke of Weimar*', by which he supposed she was referring to his book, *Napoleon*, had sold 13,000 copies (and if it came to that the number was nearer 130,000). Ethel said, the number of what? She said that she had not read his *Napoleon*, and did not intend to. At which, throwing her head back with a challenging gesture of defiance, the tricorne, wobbling for a minute, fell, not *off*, but right *down* over her face, and for a moment her torrent of invective was stilled.[87]

Shortly before Christmas Ethel Smyth's concert took place at the Philharmonic Hall. In a white-and-scarlet Doctor's gown she conducted the overture to her *Boatswain's Mate*, parts of *The Wreckers* and some of her choruses. The audience were polite but not over-enthusiastic. Harold felt sure the Germans disliked the idea of a woman conducting in the place of Bruno Walter or Furtwängler.

Towards the end of the year a young Attaché arrived at the Berlin Embassy in the person of Christopher Sykes. Although they had met on several previous occasions, Harold's first reference to Sykes was on the 12th December when he and Patrick Balfour[88] dined at Brücken Allee. He took to Sykes at once. 'A nice boy,' he called him. As he got to know him better so he liked him more, finding him bright, original and very entertaining. Christopher Sykes[89] on the other hand, who had been looking forward to meeting the author of *Some People*, whom he understood to have been a close friend of his father, Sir Mark, got a very different impression. He found Harold taciturn and, when he did speak to him, snubbing, patronising and superior. Young Christopher assumed from this attitude that either he had been mistaken, and Harold had a profound dislike of his father, or he disliked him for not being a homosexual. Neither assumption was the least correct. However he wrote to Cyril Connolly telling him that the meeting had been a great disappointment. Cyril in his mischievous manner passed this on to Harold. At least it had the effect of elucidating the mystery. For it transpired that Harold laboured under the misconception that nothing prejudiced a relationship so much as to introduce yourself as a friend of the other's father. When this uncomfortable phase of their relationship was finally dispelled they became friends. Although Christopher had reservations about Harold's character, being irritated by what he considered his unnecessary pose as 'the great personality,' Harold pronounced Christopher to be a real person, and not a shadow of anyone else. He thought him far too gifted for diplomacy, and tried to dissuade him from making it his career.

Vita and the boys came to stay with him over Christmas, and so one of Harold's worst years drew to a close. Lord Sackville had died, and Vita lost her father and her home. Lady Sackville had behaved abominably and caused twelve months of incessant unpleasantness. Lord Carnock had died and Harold had lost in him a counsellor as well as a revered parent. Harold had been away from Long Barn and the boys in a capital which he did not like. He had done little productive work. The only compensation lay in some stimulating new friends, among whom he included the Lindsays, Robert Boothby, John Sparrow, Dan Lascelles and Christopher Sykes.

16

THE END OF DIPLOMACY, 1929

SIR HORACE RUMBOLD'S term as Ambassador in Berlin coincided with the decline and fall of the Weimar Republic. His departure in 1933 took place during the Third Reich under the Chancellorship of Adolf Hitler. There were forebodings of trouble while Sir Horace was settling into the Embassy in 1928. An aggressive speech by Chancellor Müller demanding the immediate evacuation of the Rhineland, which under the Versailles Peace Treaty was to be effected by 1935, caused perturbation among the Allies. The view of the British Foreign Secretary, Sir Austen Chamberlain, was that evacuation was desirable, but should be dependent upon the prior settlement of the reparations question. In January 1929 Sir Horace was slightly worried by further reports of Germany's quasi-military activities in the organization of four more Grenzschutz commandos; and he warned Chamberlain of a secret memorandum which had been circulated to the German party leaders on the desirability of strengthening their armoured cruiser 'A'. This was, to say the least, a tactless directive on the part of Germany just when plans for a Reparations Conference were being put in hand. Yet in April Sir Ronald Lindsay (now in London), maintained, in a Memorandum[1] on the Military Situation in Germany, that so long as Hindenburg remained President the Republic was in no danger, for loyalty to him by the vast majority of moderate Germans was paramount. Apart from a sudden war, danger lay in a coup d'état during some irrelevant crisis, after Hindenburg, who was very old, had been succeeded by a mere 'man in a top hat.' The monarchy, Sir Ronald continued, had few adherents, the Crown Prince and his brothers being held in low esteem; yet the Republic was admittedly not popular, and was only tolerated.

In May Chamberlain transmitted to Rumbold reports which had reached him from our Director of Military Operations and Intelligence of the illegal manufacture of war materials by the Germans, in contravention of the Peace Treaty. The Ambassador was instructed to notify Stresemann of our knowledge of these activities. Next month the Ambassador reiterated to the Foreign Office what Lindsay had already affirmed, that so long as Hindenburg remained, no *Putsch* of any sort was likely, but he foresaw dangers when Hindenburg should die. He put forward the names of possible successors, among whom Hitler's was, of course, not included.

HAROLD NICOLSON

Soon after the New Year of 1929 had been ushered in with a clang of midnight bells and a hiss of fireworks, Berlin was submitted to an invasion – of Bloomsbury. On the 17th January Leonard and Virginia Woolf arrived, to be followed in two days by Vanessa Bell, her son Quentin, and Duncan Grant. Vita and the boys, shortly to return to school in England, were still staying in Brücken Allee; and Eddy was in rooms nearby. They all met for luncheons and dinners, and on the 19th went to a propaganda film, *Sturm über Asien*, which caused such a sensation that Harold referred to it in a despatch to the Foreign Office. In one way and another, if we may judge from a very prickly letter written by Vanessa Bell to Roger Fry,[2] the nerves of the party were frayed, and resentments and misunderstandings ensued. The conglomeration of so many precious intellectuals in Berlin, in January, in the snow and slush, was perhaps asking for trouble.

To begin with, Leonard and Virginia were somewhat at a loose end. They would walk miles to avoid taking a cab, and then go to an hotel restaurant where they had to pay three times more for a meal than if they had gone to a humbler dive where the food was better. Vanessa was clearly irritated that Virginia wanted to be so much with the Nicholsons (as she chose to spell the name), whom she disliked and affected to despise. She considered them an unnecessary importation into her group.

> The human situation here keeps us amused at odd moments [she wrote with some acerbity] ... Vita is miserable here it seems. She hates Berlin & the Germans & I suspect will soon have to face a terrific crisis with Harold. He seems to me to be cut out for the diplomatic world to which he belongs. He reminds me of all the old official world I used to hate so & is really much like them, only perhaps he is nicer & I suppose must have more wits somewhere. Vita hardly ever comes to Berlin & when she does objects to the social duties, so that I suspect in the end he will have to give it up & then he'll be done for. Meanwhile the situation seems to be extremely edgy & is not improved by the Woolves' behaviour,

which amounted to their refusal to go to parties arranged for them. As Clive Bell told Harold, it did not suit the Woolves to travel. They were not at their best abroad; and ought never to stray further from Rodmell than St. Ives. It was the firm conviction of Vanessa that the Nicolsons were stupid. She said that when the film *Sturm über Asien* was over, Vita enraged Leonard by asking him six times whether he thought some soldiers wearing British uniforms and made to flee before Asiatic troops, were really meant to be Englishmen; that both Vita and Harold believed they were not, and yet managed to quarrel with each other about it.

THE END OF DIPLOMACY 1929

> The discussion went on & on, all standing in the melting snow, & the general rage & uneasiness was increased by Eddy who was also of the party, who got into one of his regular old maidish pets, unwilling to stay or go home, flitting about from group to group like a mosquito. He always irritates the Nicholsons [sic], which I quite understand, but at the same time he's so far more intelligent than they are that I can't help sympathising with him.

In fact Eddy wanted to take Duncan off with him to low haunts, and could not shake off Harold, who thought it would be fun to accompany them. Vanessa, always extremely possessive and jealous of Duncan, may have suspected that Harold was trying to get off with him, whereas on the contrary it was Eddy.

Harold was of course blissfully unaware of any under-current. He was perfectly happy in the company of all the group, preferably with one or two at a time. After seeing the boys off at the Friedrich-Strasse station on the 22nd he took Virginia for a long walk in the Tiergarten; and the same night dined with Leonard alone. They discussed the fusion of the Consular with the Diplomatic Service. Harold said he was in favour of it, but the process ought to be gradual. Leonard spoke bitterly of the tortuous and secretive nature of Ramsay MacDonald and the impossibility of working with him.[3]

The cold in Berlin, and indeed all over Europe, was so intense that Harold and Vita went to the Italian riviera for a ten days' search of the sun. They arrived on the 10th February at Rapallo, waking up to see from their hotel windows snow lying on the palm-tree branches. The snow soon melted, but the weather remained so bitter that they retired to bed in the afternoon. Next day they walked to Max Beerbohm's villa, but he was away. Another day they took the train to Sestri Levante and walked across the pass to Moneglia. Yet another day they went to Camogli and looked at a small *castello* which they had heard was for sale and considered buying. Enchanted, they drank vermouth and soda at a little inn, talking to the proprietor about the property.

The jaunt with Vita to the Ligurian coast made Harold more dissatisfied than ever with his lot. His return to Berlin and Vita's departure for home enhanced his discontent. She was aware that he was unhappy, and wrote in contrition for having nagged him to leave diplomacy. But once again she repeated that what distressed her most was the waste of his potentially perfect life. A job in the Foreign Office was, she conceded, perhaps the best solution, since he liked his foreign affairs so much. She was to a large extent influenced by Virginia, who repeatedly let fall disparaging little jibes about ambassadors and diplomats. 'What's to be done with morality in England?' was one of many such pinpricks. 'If Harold would do a man's work there, instead of a flunkey's in Berlin – but hush, hush. "My Harold" isn't that what you'd say?'[4] Still at the back of Virginia's mind was the fear that Vita might cast aside her vaunted independence and, out of her abiding love and sympathy, follow her husband to some outlandish post, and there be lost to her. Harold's indecision was not entirely measured by a genuine desire to leave the Diplomatic Service and yet remain in the Foreign Office. How could he, he asked Vita, make plans so long as there was uncertainty whether her allowance from B.M. would continue, or be cut off? Nevertheless he agreed that, if he were not recalled to the Foreign Office by August, he would send in his resignation.

On the 9th March Harold left Berlin on a carefully prepared lecture-tour on contemporary English literature. In Frankfurt-am-Main he was the guest of Lily Sniltzler, a rich middle-aged widow in the forefront of all local literary and artistic movements.

He lectured at Waldfried, in an overgrown cottage outside Frankfurt which had been built for a rich Jewish merchant, von Weinberg; and was then driven to Cronberg to write his name on the Landgräfin of Hesse. He wanted to visit Friedrichshof 'where the Empress Frederick lived in querulous arrogance for many years,' but that was not possible. Instead he saw the great, sad park, with towering, geometrically planted conifers, throwing thin winter shadows across patches of snow. In Frankfurt he was taken to Goethe's house where the poet was born, where he lived until he was twenty-five, and where he wrote *Werther*. Harold was fascinated by the decent, middle-sized house, with its grand hall and marble floor, wide staircase with fine iron ramp, spacious drawing-rooms with *boiseries* and paintings on the walls, and a lovely little music-room with Chinese wall paper, which confronted an orchard at the rear. Frau von Sniltzler stepped over a bunch of American tourists as if they were a puddle, to lead Harold upstairs. He saw Goethe's own little room, with windows overlooking the leads at the back of the house where cats were playing. The walnut writing-table was spattered with ink. There was a toy theatre. It was all very convincing and peaceful, the epitome of respectable, provincial life.

That night Harold gave a lecture in Frankfurt. It was a great success, 'not so much for what was in it, but because they were surprised to hear a lecture delivered in that conversational form without notes or mumbling. Also they were amused and puzzled by my senile charm. I laid that on thick.'[5]

Nostalgically he strolled about the town, and saw in every Frankfurt bookshop window a picture of himself prominently displayed. In vain he searched for the house in which he had lived in 1907. He experienced just a vague sense of the familiar and would not have been surprised to run into himself, at the age of twenty, coming round a corner.

THE END OF DIPLOMACY 1929

In Cologne he went to see a man whom he described in a letter[6] to Vita as a rather remarkable figure in modern Germany. This was Oberbürgermeister Konrad Adenauer, who after 1945 was to become more remarkable still.[7]

There are some who say that if Parliamentarianism really breaks down at Berlin they will summon Adenauer to establish some form of fascismo. For the moment he rules Cologne with an iron hand, and is responsible for such things as the new Rhine Bridge and the Presse exhibition. There was some sort of fuss going on around his room when I got there, private secretaries dashing about, people opening doors, squinting in, then shutting them again rapidly. I was asked to sit down while bells buzzed and people hurried in and whispered to each other, and then hurried out again. I am to this moment unaware what had happened, but the contrast between the scurrying and whispering outside and the sudden peace of his own large study, was most effective, and the strange Mongol, sitting there with shifty eyes in a yellow face, sitting with his back to the window, talking very slowly and gently, pressing bells very slowly – 'Would you ask Dr. Pietri to come here.' – snapping with icy politeness at the terrified Dr. Pietri when he arrived, possessed all the manner of a dictator. It is not a manner which I like, but it is a manner which once seen is never forgotten...

He was very expansive on the subject of town planning. I told him how impressed I had been by the garden suburbs at Frankfurt, and he was not pleased at this, knowing that his garden suburbs were not up to the same level. He said in the first place that the Frankfurt people had lost a great deal of money by extravagance in garden suburbs, and in the second place that his own aim was not to bring the town into the country but the country into the town. It was at that stage that he summoned the agitated Dr. Pietri and told him to show me all that there was to be seen. Another architect, Dr. Jacobsen, who positively sweated with fear, was also summoned and I then said goodbye to Dr. Adenauer and accompanied the two architects to a large municipal car which took us to the surrounding 'grünen gürtel.'

Harold told Kenneth Rose in 1962 that in order to get rid of him the Oberbürgermeister said testily to the architects, 'Oh, show Herr Nicolson the sewage disposal unit.' Indeed they conducted him to a factory which ground the contents of the dustbins of Cologne into some form of profitable material. Harold was fascinated by the ingenious invention, which he went on to describe in detail in his letter.

He lectured in Cologne to an audience which was appreciative but less intellectual than the Frankfurt one. They stared at him in polite bewilderment. One man who was a Professor of English asked him, 'What part of your country do you come from?' When he replied, 'Kent,' the man said, 'Kent, of course, I should have known from the accent.'

By the time he reached Munich he was suffering from a bad cold on the chest. There he stayed with his Aunt Clementine, his father's sister, who had married in 1885 Herr Ministerial-Rat Bemeelmans, an elderly widower, who enjoyed a humble post in the German Railways. The issue of this inglorious marriage was an only son killed fighting in Flanders in 1914. Aunt Clemmie, now 77, lived alone, poor but extremely proud, at the top of a gaunt block of flats. She hated the Germans, who had shunned her ever since the outbreak of the war. Her sole interests were praying in church and re-kindling memories of the Nicolson family. Harold was tremendously moved by her courage and pitiable state, and was tempted to write a novel around her.

In spite of feeling unwell he had one full and successful day in Munich. He lunched with the publisher Kurt Wolff. He had tea alone with Thomas Mann, the great German novelist, then living in a small modern villa, with a neat garden. Mann's study was lined with books and smelled of narcissus. He was enjoying one of his life's rare phases of optimism. His confidence in Stresemann gave him hope. His country was beginning to recover from inflation and forget its defeat in war. He did not foresee that within a year or two Hitler's daemonic hysteria would assail Germany; that he would be obliged to leave his cosy study, and his Munich home, flee through Switzerland to the United States, there to fulminate against the Nazi system, and in 1938 to trounce Great Britain for losing the chance of preserving peace. On this occasion he remarked how lovely life was, how polite they had been to him at the PEN Club, and how much he admired John Galsworthy. Harold, being snuffly and, as he put it, interested that afternoon in life and death, asked Thomas Mann how long it took him, a fellow writer, to get rid of his colds. Mann said his colds involved three days' preparation, caused three days' suffering, and took three days to disappear.

In the evening Harold lectured to a very intelligent Munich audience which allowed him to treat serious subjects lightly. He sensed that they understood all but the T. S. Eliot poems which he read aloud to them. Aunt Clemmie sat throughout in the front row, blinking like an old owl.

His next stop was Hamburg. He lectured at the Overseas Club to 500 people. His voice gave out. Exhausted, he was precipitated into a refreshment room where he was drawn into discussions. He kept on repeating to himself, 'Don't be rude! Don't be rude!' and *was* rude when a tiresome man enquired whether Proust's soul-tradition was that of Bergson or Plato. He answered that he did not think Proust had a soul.

THE END OF DIPLOMACY 1929

Sir Horace Rumbold was delighted by the success of the lecture tour, which he assured Harold had been extremely valuable.

The Duke and Duchess of York stayed at the Berlin Embassy on their way back from the Crown Prince of Norway's wedding to Princess Martha of Sweden in Oslo. Harold motored them to the Golf Club for luncheon. He found the Duchess delightful, incredibly gay and simple. It was a tragedy that she should be royal. She was clever. She talked to Harold perceptively about *Some People*, whereas the Duke had only read the Arketall story, and got it wrong.

> But she and Cyril Connolly are the only two people who have spoken intelligently about the 'landscape' element in *Some People*. She said, 'You choose your colours so carefully; that bit about the Palace in Madrid was done in grey and chalk-white; the Constantinople bits in blue and green; the desert bits in blue and orange.'[8]

If Harold was over-estimating her intellect, he could not exaggerate her charm. It was overwhelming. The Duke's was less evident.

At the end of March Raymond came to stay in Brücken Allee. As spring returned Berlin began to fill up again with English visitors. Sibyl Colefax had supper alone with Harold in order to pour out the bitterness of her soul and complain how disagreeable people were being about her parties. Somerset Maugham had with him his friend Gerald Haxton - 'not a very nice young man. But I like Maugham. I like his affable cynicism, his petulant friendliness.'[9] The three of them went to the Esplanade to meet Edward Molyneux. Harold was always amused by this dapper little man with the wall eye. He was impressed that someone so successful, so enormously rich and so extravagant should not be spoilt. Molyneux travelled everywhere in state with a valet and private secretary. He had large motorcars which waited outside restaurants all night, if need be. He had orchids in his hotel sitting-room. Yet he was not vulgar; and was one of the strangest characters ever known.

Vita was seriously contemplating buying from Vanessa Bell No. 37 Gordon Square in Bloomsbury for her and Harold to use two of the floors, and let the rest of the house. She was much attracted by the lovely drawing-room which Vanessa and Duncan had decorated. Harold was not so sure that it was a good idea. Would it not be an affirmation that they themselves were Bloomsbury? He knew that they were not. Furthermore they did not aspire to be. The idea did not materialise.

In April Harold renewed a friendship with Robert Bruce Lockhart, diplomat, politician, author and journalist, then representing the *Evening Standard* in Berlin. Their first meeting had been in November 1918 in the

Foreign Office when Harold, a junior colleague, stopped him on the stairs to tell him that his analysis of Soviet personalities in the report of a special mission to Russia was one of the best things he had ever read. For his part, Lockhart was struck by Harold's wandering tie, rather baggy trousers and magnificent head. He recorded that at that time he was the admiration and envy of every young man connected with the Foreign Office.

> Brilliant, self-reliant, clear-headed, he was a glutton for work, and his equanimity, his good temper, and his amazing quickness provided in times of storm a rock behind which even Lord Curzon was not too proud to shelter ... He seemed marked out for a dazzling career.[9]

Now in Berlin Harold was entertaining Lockhart to luncheon to meet Lord Londonderry,[10] a nice man who, in Harold's eyes, looked more like Lord Londonderry than any Lord Londonderry had looked before. When Bruce Lockhart said goodbye a few days later he recorded in his diary that Harold wanted a new foreign policy, a new understanding with America, a balance of power in Europe, a cessation of the Foreign Office trailing behind the Quai d'Orsay, and a new Foreign Minister who did not speak French and would stay at home. Harold told him that Englishmen knew nothing about foreign politics. Their facts were always wrong although their instincts were often right.

Lord Londonderry had hardly left the door of No. 24 Brücken Allee when a young man, with an introduction from Maurice Bowra, called to leave a card. Before he had time to retreat he was invited into the flat. He disclosed that he was feeling ill. Harold took his temperature. It was 104. He had the young man's things fetched from the Adlon, and the young man installed in the flat. It was the Buchan-Hepburn story all over again, except that Sandy Baird – for that was his name – was neither an Apollo nor a respectable youth destined to be a success in the world. He was however not without good looks, charm, and intelligence. Vita when she met him, rather liked him but could not see the good looks for the fleshiness of the face. He was on the other hand a hopelessly weak character, and was to become not the last of those lame ducks on whom Harold was throughout his remaining years to spend money, encouragement and help at considerable cost to his purse, leisure and energy.

Sandy Baird screamed all the first night that he was being murdered. But the next morning his temperature was down to 101. Harold told Vita that he hoped, when he recovered, he would not turn out to be a horrid young man. At present he was too grateful and pathetic for words. 'It would be rather a good story about falling in love with someone at 104, and less in love at 103, and getting to loathe them at 98.[11]' As he got better

THE END OF DIPLOMACY 1929

Sandy got more difficult to manage. He was supposed to be studying for diplomacy, but was perfectly feckless and unable to work. He had been in a Munich family with Quentin Bell. 'He *does* amuse me so. He is an absolute little bum boy, but clever and nice. I shall do him a world of good,' Harold wrote with naive conviction. When Sandy had really recovered he was submitted to a serious talking-to by both Harold and Eddy. He promised to go to a crammer at once. But before this laudable project could be put in hand Harold took him and Mrs. Arthur James, the well known society hostess, to Potsdam. The excursion was a failure. The ideals and idiocies of the Edwardian hostess clashed with those of the carefree youth of the twenties. Sandy Baird observed that he did not like pompous weekend parties. Mrs. James asked, what did he mean by pompous. He said, 'Oh, places where one can't smoke a pipe in the drawing-room.' 'No young man,' thundered Mrs. James, 'would be allowed to smoke a pipe in my drawing-room.' 'Yes,' said Sandy, 'that is what I mean.' When she left Sandy said, 'Well, Harold, you can have that old bitch. And for nothing too.' Sandy, an Old Etonian, and very well read, was thoroughly promiscuous and powdered his face. Harold was perplexed.

He was in a way mystified by the partiality of the younger generation for what he called the lower orders. Possibly because of his fairly starchy, Victorian upbringing he did not relish their company although he undoubtedly had commerce with them in Berlin. Even so these encounters made him uneasy, and their recollection was distasteful to him. They were also associated in his mind with guilt because they lacked all social rapport. He actually admitted to Raymond Mortimer that 'the idea of a gentleman of birth and education sleeping with a guardsman is repugnant to me.'[12] He was only attracted by younger, intellectual men of his own class. Even so he believed that homosexuality should be a jolly vice, and not taken too seriously. Still less should it be boasted about. To be tolerable, he thought it should have a sort of cosmic swing about it, like the swing of tides, the rise of sap, the fermentation of the grape. The moment it became pernickety or cautious he thought it was hell. In other words he could not take homosexual love very seriously. When others took it seriously, he was repelled. Equally, it should not become squalid. 'I think lust is a fine thing, a noble thing,' he once wrote. 'It should not be allowed to get down at heel.'[13] Yet it should never be suppressed. Suppression of lust, he told Raymond Mortimer,[14] meant 'that all the candles are blown out on the Christmas tree and that one's mind will sag also. I fear it is only lust which keep's one's mind buoyant – and if one has to drive that out of one's life one is driving out the impetus of all interest. And if interest goes, brain goes.' Such exclusively physical philosophy would not have appealed to St. Thomas Aquinas. Notwithstanding Harold's ambivalent feelings about homosexuality he was genuinely anxious not to have a bad influence upon young men. That he often had an influence he was well aware. But nothing would fill him with deeper remorse than to be told that he had led any young man astray. He hoped he taught them to be, above all, active, interested, happy, kind, and filled with the zest of experience. It was true he always wanted them to enjoy themselves so much, that he was bad at discouraging them from any experience, even if he knew it might be harmful. Therein, he admitted, lay one of his weaknesses.

All the same Harold was exceedingly curious about the tastes of others, particularly the tastes of his younger friends. One evening he allowed himself to be conducted by a detective around the very lowest haunts of Berlin. At the first place they went to sailors were dancing with each other 'in a manner which even I found pretty stiff.' The next place was the resort of drunken bargees. An old blond (male) of sixty-four wearing a gold locket, and a woman looking like Lady St. John with syphilis followed them with heavy, envious eyes. At the next haunt the detective made an excuse to leave Harold for a moment. Harold on turning round, saw him embracing the barman. 'What a gang!' he exclaimed. 'I was disgusted,' and wanted to get home. And then he let fall a familiar refrain, 'I do not like other people's vices.'[15]

In the middle of April H. G. Wells gave a lecture in the Reichstag. Harold attended but could not hear a word. A dinner was given to Wells afterwards at the Adlon at which Professor Einstein presided. He was a stout little man with a face the colour of a magnolia, with chubby, soft white hands, a deprecatory voice, a shock of iron grey hair and the most bewildered eyes ever seen in an adult. They were childish eyes, kindly, innocent, enraptured, the eyes of a very nice child looking at a conjuring trick. At dinner he told Harold that during the great German inflation he bought a tram ticket, for which he paid 15,000 marks, and was given 4,000 marks change. He complained to the conductor that the right change should have been 4,250 marks. The conductor insisted that he had given the right change. The Professor still protested. The conductor took out a piece of paper and with his pencil proved that the greatest mathematician in history was wrong. Einstein apologised abjectly. He had the laugh too of an enchanting child of five. He made a little speech in homage to Wells which Harold translated. Harold began by saying, 'This is the first thing of his I have ever understood,' which Einstein and the guests considered a funny joke. Two days later Harold dined with Wells and Moura Budberg.

THE END OF DIPLOMACY 1929

Wells sat in the hall of the Eden looking very round and drummy and young. His lady came in later, and meanwhile I tried to do up Wells's link. I failed. When the lady came she did it up at once. It was one of those sorts that have large carbuncles and are attached by a beastly little gold clip that wouldn't clip. We had a good dinner and Wells purred and patted at the Russian lady . . . She is a lovely woman of 41 with that golden-aureole Russian voice. I took them to the Wellenbad, and then to Königin. I then saw that it was safe to say goodnight. Wells, towards the end of the evening, ceased pretending to flirt with the lady and talked intelligently. He spoke of his young life; of the grandfather who had been gardener at Penshurst; of his father who had had very small feet and hands and bowled at cricket; of his mother who lived well over into his success but was always anxious about the insecurity of a writer's profession. One day he showed her a cheque for £6,000 which he had just received from America. She sighed deeply. 'Oh dear,' she sighed, 'how I *wish* you could get something permanent.' He said that on looking back his life seemed a very short one, 'although some things in it seemed a very long way away.' He is a wrong-headed but amusing little man. He believes in the new world very thoroughly, I think. He did not think very much of Lenin as a personality, but realised that he must have been one. What was so funny was that he was embarrassed about going out to pee. We teased him about it, and he admitted that this was one of his conventions.[16]

On the 24th April Harold went to England on leave, travelling via the Hook of Holland with Sandy Baird. He worked hard at the Foreign Office library on his father's papers for the biography of Lord Carnock; and he gave a broadcast on Parents and Children. The talk, a little facetious and contrived, was published in the *Listener*. The moral of it was that children should be encouraged to do something, no matter what, to stop them being bored and boring adults. He was back in Berlin on the 6th May, met at the station by the ever faithful Dan Lascelles. Dan and Christopher Sykes dined, and after dinner a friend of Christopher, David Herbert, the second son of Lord Pembroke, called. 'He is very handsome in a way, and quite nice,'[17] was Harold's first opinion of this twenty-year old boy, whom he was to see much of in ensuing months and become very attached to. Here was another case of Harold meeting a person whose philosophy of life – if David Herbert even had a philosophy beyond wanting to enjoy himself to the full and make everyone else enjoy himself likewise – shocked and intrigued him at the same time. Soon Harold was writing to Vita, 'My word, he is hot stuff, that boy'; and, 'David has a slight tenor voice and knows all the jazz tunes. It is pretty hearing him tinkling away in the back of the car. Oh my God how young that boy is! He is actually twenty, but he seems younger than Ben. He really does believe that it is fun to go to a cabaret and see ladies dancing. And then when he found that it wasn't fun he cried. Such is the descendant of Mr. W. H.!'[18] Again, Harold was afraid of having a bad influence on him, for David obviously saw in Harold a clever man of the world who was able to drink and chaff with schoolboys; he did not understand his hard work side. David 'is inevitably a Wilton-Embassy Club-Eloise Ancaster type of boy. No other background would be possible for him.' He had a sweet character, with a passion for his mother, his home at Wilton, for flowers and animals. He would kiss Harold's virginal old maid so that she bridled with pleasure whenever he came to the flat. Yet he could behave like a cad and, without feeling any remorse, throw mud at somebody's tutor for fun. The fact was that Harold did not understand how a product of the aristocracy and Eton could be content to lead an exclusively frivolous life. Vita was much more worldly-wise. She told Harold that it was no good his trying to influence that sort of person. It was like trying to build a house without bricks. 'They don't *want* to be different from what they are; and after all they are an eternal type which is ornamental if not useful, like birds of paradise. They look nice flying from perch to perch.'[19]

Early in May Harold lunched with the Stresemanns, and was shocked by the decline of the Minister's health.

> He pretends not to be ill. Walks with the old energy and talks as much. But his face has changed; it is small and almost chétif. His eyes look smaller. His mouth looks smaller. He constantly licks his lips with a very white tongue. He has special food. His hand is cold and damp. He is evidently a very sick man. He told me that the Chancellor [Hermann Müller] had spent his time when in bed recently reading *Some People*, and that he had read it twice.[20]

Stresemann was in the last stages of cancer. He had only a few more months to live; and with his departure went the last hopes of the Weimar Republic.

On the 11th May Cyril Connolly, 'rather grubby,' turned up from Paris, and installed himself in Brücken Allee again. He was not an ideal guest. He would stay in bed till luncheon time, and sit talking till 4 in the afternoon, when he would go round the town with Christopher Sykes and David Herbert at their expense, until 4 o'clock the next morning. He was lamentably untidy. He would leave dirty handkerchiefs in the chairs and fountain pens (Harold's) open in books. He had nothing of his own – cigarettes, matches, stamps or soap – whereas although Christopher and David were both chronically in debt, they did not sponge. Harold could not help liking Cyril in spite of his shortcomings, for he was easily amused and interested in everything. Unfortunately he was very thick with Violet Trefusis, and Harold imagined he was disloyal about him when he was with her, for he still believed she wished to avenge herself on him. Altogether he did not trust Cyril a yard; knew he made mischief; was sure he had criminal instincts, and pitied the girl he ultimately married. When Harold got rid of him in the middle of June Cyril, contrary to advice, moved to the Adlon. On leaving Berlin he had the effrontery to ask Harold to pay his hotel bill, and when this was refused, told Harold he was a cad.

But until Cyril proved to be quite intolerable as a guest, he provided much stimulating conversation and merriment. He loved playing the fool. It was one of his endearing characteristics. He, David and Christopher acted charades: Christopher as an Anglo-Indian colonel at the Bohème bar, Cyril as his hideous wife and David as an attractive tart. They gave an initial performance before Harold ensconced in an armchair as the sole audience like Ludwig II of Bavaria, and made him almost sick with laughter. They then repeated the performance before the Rumbolds.

The election of a Labour Government in June encouraged Harold to believe that his friend Sir Oswald Mosley would be sent to the Foreign Office. In which case Sir Oswald might recall him to London. Unfortunately Mosley was made Chancellor of the Duchy of Lancaster. Instead, Arthur Henderson became Foreign Secretary, an appointment little calculated to help. Soon after the new Government was formed Lord Hardinge came to Berlin. One night when the Rumbolds were out Harold dined alone with Hardinge in the Embassy. He never felt wholly at ease with this stiff and palatial personage. He found him sitting very upright in a chair in the drawing-room. They ate solemnly together at a small round table. Hardinge wriggled in his chair as though he were on pins. They talked of the elections. Hardinge spoke about Austen Chamberlain's discomfiture. 'If I may use a vulgar expression,' he said, 'the man has got a swollen head.' He then relaxed, and became more human and friendly. He strongly advised Harold not to enter politics. He said far the wisest thing was for him to stay on in Berlin until called back as Assistant-Under Secretary of State. After that he could do anything or go anywhere he wanted. He implied that he would talk to Ronald Lindsay about Harold's future when he got back to London.

On the 15th June Harold went to England, expecting to have another fortnight's leave. And two days later he and Vita gave a broadcast talk together on Marriage. The frankness of their views caused quite a sensation. Harold started off on this sacred theme with a slightly unorthodox, down to earth synthesis, employing some frivolous analogies. The gist of his argument ran as follows:

> The car of marriage runs on pneumatic tyres. That entails punctures. To avoid punctures one must not only possess a circle of air (let us call it love) encased in a protective and elastic covering (let us call it habit); one must not only drive with care to avoid the glass and the tintacks on the road; one must not only be prepared to face the abrasions of wear, and I fear also, of tear; but one must learn that punctures are inevitable, that they are reparable, and that (if one is cheerful about it all) they are somewhat amusing. I think the secret of a successful marriage is the capacity to treat disasters as if they were incidents and not to magnify incidents into disasters. Marriage is a continuous process and not a static condition. It is a plant and not a piece of furniture. It grows, it changes; it develops. You must tend its growth. Even in the best circumstances it takes 7 to 14 years before the roots have struck. All marriages are pot plants under eight years.
>
> Sex lasts a short time, from three weeks only to three years.[21]

This last statement of fact struck many listeners as unbecoming and, if true, something that ought not to be conceded. Vita in her turn postulated that the necessity for a successful marriage was, not common interests, but a common sense of values. She of course went on to argue against a wife's obligation to sacrifice her career to her husband's, if hers was the more important one of the two. The *Saturday Review* maintained that Vita came out better than Harold in this wireless discussion in that she replied seriously and earnestly to his somewhat wild accusations of women's weaknesses.

Harold's views about marriage never varied. It amazed him that any intelligent couple should suppose that being in love was a satisfactory basis for matrimony. He wrote an article for *Harper's Bazaar* (Oct. 1931) stipulating that marriage should not be allowed, so long as a couple were in love. They ought merely to live together, and if they begat children it should be regarded as anti-social. Presumably he implied that marriage should only be allowed when the couple had fallen out of love. When Rupert Hart-Davis became engaged he was amused to receive a congratulatory letter from Harold which began, 'Yes, you will be very happy for a little time,' and then continued, 'But happiness is not the basis of marriage. The basis of marriage is content.' And he ended with the concession that successful marriages were the best achievements of which homo sapiens was capable.[22]

Hardly had he got down to enjoying his leave at Long Barn when he

THE END OF DIPLOMACY 1929

received a telegram ordering him back to Berlin immediately. The Foreign Office explained that they foresaw difficulties looming at the Reparations Conference, and the Labour Government would not understand why the Ambassador and the Counsellor were both away at the same time. In any case the Germans were surprised that Rumbold had been sent to Geneva to attend an unimportant Red Cross conference at such a moment. Vita was furious, and Harold was vexed at having to chuck receiving a degree at Oxford, attending the Balliol gaudy, having a tooth out, and finishing his book.

Once again he was to be in charge of the Berlin Embassy. He was met on his return by David Herbert and Christopher Sykes who then left Berlin almost at once. Harold, much as he enjoyed their company, was somewhat relieved because they led him into expense and dissipation, and he had a very busy time ahead at the Chancery. He was now staying at the Adlon, in a good room with bathroom on the first floor, overlooking the President's garden. He was glad to have left Brücken Allee which he had come to loathe, and to have sent back to Lady Sackville the furniture which she claimed.

It was a good thing he was back in Berlin because Poincaré was working against Ramsay MacDonald over the Reparations experts' report, and he, Harold, wanted to support the Germans against the French in this issue. During the next six weeks despatches flew between the Chargé dAffaires and the Foreign Secretary, Arthur Henderson. Harold reported that von Schubert told him the Germans wanted to raise at the forthcoming conference the question of the restoration to them of the Saar, in addition to the evacuation of the Rhineland by the French, and the settlement of the Report of Owen Young, the American expert on reparations.[23] The Germans also adhered to the view that London was the most suitable place for the forthcoming conference. The attitude of the Foreign Office to the Saar was that the coal-mines had been ceded absolutely to France; that it had been arranged for a plebiscite to be held in 1935 about the Saar territory; and that in the event of the restoration of that territory Germany would be prepared to buy back the mines from France. In other words the Saar was a closed subject as far as Britain was concerned.[24] In consequence Harold was instructed to inform von Schubert that it was unwise for Germany to raise this particular matter at the conference, lest the French vetoed its discussion. Harold had some sympathy with the Germans, because they believed this would be their last opportunity to enlist Anglo-American cooperation, and the issue would never be settled pacifically with the French alone. Von Schubert failed to see why Great Britain would not understand the importance Germany attached to the Saar.[25]

Fuss about the site for the Reparations Conference continued. The French refused to agree to London. The Belgians refused to agree to the Hague. The Foreign Office telegraphed Harold to persuade the Germans to agree to Brussels. The Germans refused flatly because of the anti-German feeling there. If it were selected Dr. Stresemann would not attend.[26] Harold made excuses for Stresemann on account of his extremely poor health and consequent inability to submit to incivilities. Instead Stresemann suggested the Hague.

At the end of July the Germans were again pressing the inclusion of the Saar question on the agenda. Henderson so far relented as to suggest that, although it could not figure on the agenda, it might be raised informally if an opportune occasion arose.[27] To this suggestion the Germans assented. Harold however felt obliged to warn the Foreign Office that there was a lot of underhand work going on in the Wilhelmstrasse, and he proposed, if the Germans raised any more difficulties, to tell them, unless instructed to the contrary, that the Conference would proceed without them.[28] Harold's proposal was commended. On the 6th August the Conference opened, in spite of the Belgian objections, at the Hague. Next day Harold felt it his duty to warn the Foreign Office of his fears concerning the demilitarized zones. The moment troops were withdrawn, the Germans would start evading demilitarization clauses. Just as every Frenchman felt it his duty to enforce demilitarization, so every German felt it his duty to destroy the Versailles Treaty. He was dubious about Germany's present pacifism lasting.

> I am in no sense being alarmist or pessimistic. I merely do not wish you [he addressed Mr. Orme Sargent] to suppose, from the fact that we have on the whole been reserved on this subject, that we imagine that the new Germany is psychologically different from the old ... It would take but a slight turn of the tide to set the current (of pacifism) swinging in the opposite direction, and carrying with it all the flotsam and jetsam of the very third-rate Social-Democratic politicians. I do not intend to imply that for one second there is any immediate danger or that we need fear anything for, let us say, seven years.[29]

On the 9th he sent a report from Colonel F. W. Gosset, the military expert attached to the Berlin Embassy, showing how the German Government had not fulfilled their demilitarizing agreements, although the German public supposed they had.[30] Orme Sargent replied that Sir Ronald Lindsay, the Permanent Under-secretary of State, was largely in agreement with Harold Nicolson's views. He merely suggested that we and the French would have to rely on the highly organised joint intelligence service informing us of German infractions henceforth. That it would be best to keep the problem of Rhineland demilitarisation in the background for the next few years, 'in the Micawber-like hope that in the interval "something may turn up" to change the present outlook in Germany.' In the meantime Germany was incapable of an aggressive war, and we must hope for progress of general disarmament among the nations.[31] Such were the feeble and short-sighted recommendations of the British Foreign Office four years before Adolf Hitler was swept to power. Harold and Colonel Gosset felt constrained to accept the substance of Sargent's despatch, resting content with the remarkable achievement of having disarmed Germany for ten years at least. Yet Harold believed that Germany would proceed in constructing works ostensibly for *defensive* purposes, making this distinction their excuse if charged. His second point was that since the German public really believed that every clause in the Versailles Treaty had been carried out, it would be wise to publish to the world, before the Rhineland evacuation took place, that Germany had in effect not fulfilled many important items of disarmanent[32]

In spite of heavy pressure of work and responsibility at the Chancery Harold managed to make a good deal of progress on his life of Lord Carnock with the material he had gleaned from the Foreign Office while on leave. He also wrote an article for the *Graphic* on Edwardians. Vita meanwhile was on a walking tour with Hilda Matheson in Savoy. From the Col de Vanoise, where she was listing wild flowers and sleeping in a hut 8,000 ft above sea level, she wrote that

> Hilda is a frightfully good companion, and *so* practical, and produces everything one could possibly want out of a rucksack as a conjurer produces rabbits out of a hat, and is good-tempered and enjoys everything. It is awfully *how* the amount of little gadgets she has brought with her.[33]

Vita therefore was fairly inaccessible just when Harold was badly in need of her advice. For on the 22nd July he received out of the blue a letter dated the 19th, from Bruce Lockhart, beginning,

> When I was in Berlin last April, you hinted that you might not stay on indefinitely in the diplomatic service. I did not take you very seriously, but it may be worth while to put the following before you. Beaverbrook is looking for a man of your ability . . .

Harold instantly quoted in a letter to Vita the content of Bruce Lockhart's proposition that Beaverbook needed someone with his qualifications to edit a column, like *the Londoner's Diary*, in the *Evening Standard*. It would bring him into close touch with politics, he told her, and allow time for his own writing. The pay would be good. He assessed the disadvantages – Beaverbrook's reputation as a disruptive and unscrupulous Tory; Harold's determination not to compromise his radical opinions; the lobbying and the suffering of fools gladly, which would be entailed; and the possible harm to his serious writing. If he accepted he might regret it later. He was consulting Leonard Woolf for his views, and he begged her to telegraph her own. The same day he answered Lockhart's letter. The offer was tempting, he told him, for he was longing to get back to the whirl of real life again. In Berlin he was like 'a stepney wheel of a car that is seldom taken out of the garage.' Nevertheless he must ask some questions, and make some reservations.

> I am by politics and convictions a left-liberal or right-labour. On the other hand I am a pacifist and believe strongly in good relations with America at any sacrifice. On the other hand I am an Imperialist in the modern sense of the term, and I am by no means a passionate free-trader. I could not agree to express opinions which conflicted with these principles ... I should not wish to prejudice my ultimate prospects by association with opinions opposed to my own radical opinions. I put this forward as I do not wish, even at the outset of our discussion, that I should sail under a false flag.[34]

Harold was thrown into an awful confusion by the unexpected proposition. He opened a bible in his bedroom at random and read from *Proverbs* xxv.7. 'Far better it is that it be said unto thee, Come up hither; than that thou shouldest be put lower in the presence of the prince whom thine eyes have seen,' which he interpreted as encouragement to take a leap into the unknown. Vita replied[35] as soon as she received his letter. On the whole she favoured the Beaverbrook job, but he must have more particulars and a week to think them over before committing himself. She did not think Leonard's opinion would be useful because he was so fanatical. Anyway Harold received a letter from Leonard Woolf, recommending acceptance. Leonard did not think that Beaverbrook would leave mud on him, but only a little moth and rust. Harold also got a letter from Virginia, who thought the job would lead to something better, and would give him time to write his books. Why not, and here the true woman was speaking, suggest to Lord Beaverbrook that the column be literary and not political, and be called *Life and Letters*? Vita was amused to learn from the Woolfs that they were flattered and touched to be asked for their advice from

THE END OF DIPLOMACY 1929

Harold. They said to her, 'Are you sure that he didn't consult Raymond? Or Eddy? Or anybody?'[36] Vita assured them that they alone had received his confidence.

Lockhart telephoned from London that the salary Beaverbrook offered was £3,000 a year and that Harold would be allowed to retain full political independence. Harold rather rashly confirmed in writing to Lockhart that these terms were agreeable to him. He also wrote to Vita that Beaverbrook proposed a two-year contract, and did not object to his standing for Parliament as a Labour candidate at the expiration of that term, if he wanted to. Beaverbrook wished him to start work on the 1st October.

Already Harold imagined that he was a Socialist. The notion first dawned on him while he was in Berlin, and the falsity of it did not escape his astute friends, like the young and highly intelligent Christopher Sykes, who was convinced that his Labour proclivities were all talk and affectation. Although Harold was eventually to sit in the House of Commons on the National Labour benches, his allegiance to Labour principles was never total. He was the first to admit as much in later life. If his mind told him to be Labour, his heart avouched that he was Liberal. He regretted that he had not started his political career as a Liberal, and was only put off from so doing by the party's dogmatic acceptance of Free Trade, which, as he told Bruce Lockhart, he could not endorse. In truth Harold Nicolson had not got a firm political mind. He could not view political tenets in black and white. He was too fastidious, too critical and, let it be said, too intellectual to believe blindly in the sanctity of party loyalty. But since his political career did not begin until after his retirement from diplomacy, it will be considered in volume 11 of this work.

Harold was longing, like the schoolboy, who, faced with a momentous decision concerning his future career, rushes to consult his mother, to talk over the Beaverbrook project with Vita. They arranged to meet at Karlsruhe on the morning of the 1st August. Harold got there first. Impatiently he walked around this Bavarian town, and sat on benches in the Zoo. At midday Vita arrived from the Val d'Isère. For four happy days they motored from place to place, walking, and talking about future plans. Harold's decision largely depended upon finance. The salary he was getting in Berlin, plus allowances, amounted to £2,600, more than half of which was exempt from tax. Between them they had roughly £5,000 a year net. Of Vita's income £1,600 came to her under the trust settlement from Lady Sackville. It was this sum which both Harold and Vita were determined to renounce. Harold especially wished to be totally independent of B.M.'s bounty and whims. At Cologne they concocted a letter to Beaverbrook, whose salary offer had been reduced to £2,400, asking for

£4,500 and explaining that Harold could not start work before the New Year. Vita was to deliver the letter by hand on her return to London, and telephone if she heard any news from Lockhart. They decided that if Beaverbrook refused the terms there was nothing for Harold to do but prosecute B.M. and go bust.

He returned to Berlin in a state of anxiety and depression. His poverty was getting him down. He also had a nagging fear that the moment he clinched with Beaverbrook he might be offered the legation at Athens. And what would he do then, having committed himself to leaving the service? Hearing nothing from Beaverbrook, or Vita, he telephoned Bruce Lockhart, who told him that Beaverbrook considered his salary demand £500 too much. It was left that the matter be deferred till September when Harold would be over in London and would have an interview with Beaverbrook. This deferment was a relief. By September he might also know if he had been offered a legation.

Vita was writing that the Woolfs were making Monk's House very comfortable, Leonard having thrown three rooms into one and built himself a lovely room to work in. Clive Bell, in confirming these improvements remarked in a letter that Virginia and Leonard were better pleased with their embellishments and extensions than quite became committed Socialists, to his way of thinking.[37] Duncan and Vanessa were decorating the dining-room at Penns-in-the-Rocks for Dorothy Wellesley, and inserting octagonal mirrors, sunk flush into the walls. Eddy Sackville-West came over to dinner while Vita and the boys were there, wearing Lady Betty Germaine's ring as well as a great black square ring on his middle finger, and a great gold bracelet. He told her that the tapestry was being sold from the Chapel at Knole. She declared she would never go there again. Roger Fry also came to Penns. What a charmer he was, 'but very ill and lame, because his arteries have gone wrong. He asked if he might come back and paint the rocks [in the garden]. "Paint them!" exclaimed Valerian [Wellesley] in horror,' and misunderstanding.[38] Vita was clearly a trifle put out that Harold was relieved by the procrastination of the Beaverbrook business. She suggested that he should tell Lindsay he had been offered another good job which he would only turn down if he were offered a better Foreign Office one.

Vita was worried about some 'love' poems which she had submitted to the Hogarth Press and the Press had accepted. Although they were secretly addressed to Mary Campbell she wished them to be considered purely literary exercises. She did not want people to suppose they were lesbian-inspired. She sent them to Harold for his opinion. On returning them Harold wrote that he did not mind about the possible lesbian undertones, but he did not think them good enough for publication. They were too slight for serious work.

> Their form is not perfect enough for artifice, and their content, if any, is not anything which people will like. If you had got something important to say, then say, and don't care a damn about what people think. But I do feel that to write vers de société without pleasing literary people is a grave mistake.[39]

He begged her to suppress them. Vita was upset. Virginia was furious. 'Damn Harold,' she wrote. 'And why should you attach any importance to the criticism of a diplomat?'[40] They were published before the year was out under the title, *King's Daughter*, and had an immediate success.

In August Vita learned that Geoffrey Scott had died after a brief illness in a New York hospital, far away from all his friends. She was made very sad. 'Oh poor, poor Geoffrey, how lonely he must have felt . . . I wish I could have become friends with him again. I always thought that I should some day. And now he will never be able to edit the Boswell [papers], which I am sure he would have done very well, and so justified himself.'[41] Did she feel remorse? He had been madly in love with her, and she had turned him down for Virginia. In 1927 he was divorced from Lady Sybil, and he never recovered happiness. He hated America. Exactly a year later the Nicolsons received an invitation to his funeral, which struck them as rather macabre. His ashes were brought back from America for burial in the cloisters of New College, Oxford.

Harold's acute depression – the Foreign Office had appointed a man junior to him to be head of a department – was not lessened by the continuance of Lady Sackville's relentless malice. She had written to Eddie Knoblock, who was then in Berlin and a great comfort to Harold, that she had to pay for her husband's debts after his death, which was absolutely untrue. She referred to the Nicolsons as that 'ineffable couple' and to 'the great tragedy of my life.' She had already written to J. C. Chute, Ben's Eton house-master, that his parents did not get on at all well, and the boy had an unhappy home life. Consequently it fell upon her to be kind to him! Now she told her grandsons, aged 15 and 12, that their parents had stolen her silver and her jewels, with which to pay their debts; that she had left Knole on account of Olive Rubens; that Virginia was a wicked woman responsible for the break between her and her daughter, and had been mad three times; and that Vita ought to live in Berlin with Harold. She even asked Ben if he had ever been in love. The boys were highly embarrassed and took against their grandmother accordingly. Vita had a long talk with the boys, who added that B.M. had said it would be better if their mother had been laid in the grave with their grandfather.[42] Ben, white with rage at this remark, had clenched his fists. The boys told Vita it was a horrid experience, and 'We looked at our boots most of the time.' Harold, when told this story, saw red. He wrote to Vita, 'She is not mad, she is just evil.'[43] He feared she might have told them other things which they had not liked to repeat, things they were too young to understand. In fact those communications were to come later.

By the middle of August Christopher Sykes and David Herbert were back in Berlin. Harold was delighted to see them, but made it plain that there must be no more paying for all meals by him. 'David is a golden character, but weak as a kitten.' Harold and Eddie Knoblock went to watch the golden kitten have a life-mask taken by an artist, called Hammann. It was done with wax, not plaster. The wax was cooked like tomato soup in a saucepan and spread on the face with a paint brush. Long straws were stuck up the victim's nostrils. The whole operation lasted longer than an hour, as more and more wax was applied. David's face began to look like some terribly diseased pumpkin. The result was so far successful that Harold submitted himself to the same process, and his mask is preserved at Sissinghurst Castle.

On the 5th September Harold left for home. Before he went he informed his chief about the Beaverbrook proposal. Sir Horace was eminently sensible. He foresaw that the Nicolsons' feelings about B.M. would probably tip the balance in favour of Harold's retiring. He said that being an Ambassador was anyway rather a bore, but that being a Minister was hell. He thought Harold had far better resign, if he really meant to, rather than wait until he was offered 'a bloody post.' He said Lindsay had spoken very highly of him. 'Dear Rumbie – a nice man,' was Harold's comment.

Vita met him at Newhaven and drove him to Long Barn. In London he told Lindsay that he had definitely made up his mind to resign. Lindsay took the news calmly and sympathetically. Then came the interview with Lord Beaverbrook, who offered Harold the original salary of £3,000, the engagement to be for three years, terminable by three months' notice on either side. Harold was to have the right to publish one article a month in a magazine, and to give one broadcast a month. He felt confident that he would be able to supplement his income substantially by this means. He already had a contract to write a series of articles for *Vanity Fair* in New York, which would bring him in £600 and make him financially secure for 1930 at least. Harold reiterated to Beaverbrook that he must not be made to attack anything he approved of, or to defend anything he disapproved of. On these conditions being agreed to, the contract was settled. He left the office and joined Vita who had been waiting in the car during

THE END OF DIPLOMACY 1929

the interview. Harold thereupon wrote to B.M. saying that, if she would pay the arrears of money owed to them up to date, they would release her from all future payments of income. On the 19th a paragraph in the *Evening Standard* announced that Harold Nicolson had resigned from the Diplomatic Service and was about to join the paper's staff. *Truth* was pleased to note that no reputable journalists resented a recruit who had mastered the craft of writing.

The die was cast, the decision made. There was no going back on it now. Even so, having read three consecutive issues of the *Evening Standard* and *Daily Express* Harold had grave misgivings. What had he committed himself to? Could he possibly satisfy the demands for sob-stuff and vulgar sensationalism expected of him? Moreover what he had taken upon himself to do could not possibly be described as public service, in which he implicitly believed, in the sense that, as he wrote to Clive Bell, 'I like doing things that I don't like doing. Masochism? No – a fear, mainly of becoming soft. You will make fun of me about all this, Clive, and I don't care a bit.'[44]

While on leave he and Vita went looking for a flat in London where he would live during the week and she could join him whenever she felt inclined. After a short search they came upon the first floor of No. 4 King's Bench Walk, in the Temple. On the 30th October they heard that they had got it, and the next day, just before Harold left for his last stint at Berlin, they went to look at it with a view to decorating and furnishing. For the past fifty years or so chambers in the Temple, intended for practising members of the law, had become much coveted bachelor residences. Built after the Fire of London in red brick, in the austere, classical style associated with Wren, King's Bench Walk was cloistral, tranquil, mellow and civilized. Harold came to love it, and would say that he was happier there than anywhere else in his whole life. The flat consisted of a small entrance lobby,[45] a good sized living-room, facing Inner Temple Hall and shaded by plane trees, a large and a small bedroom, a bathroom and a kitchenette. The rooms were wainscoted in wide, fielded panels which gave it a warm and cosy atmosphere. Vita with commendable energy and speed took matters in hand, had the living room painted old ivory – it was chocolate before – and consulted Harold by letter on where certain pieces of furniture and pictures should be placed and hung. On the 11th December when the decoration of the rooms was practically finished she wrote to him from King's Bench Walk:

> It is so peaceful here, and every now and then a steamer hoots on the river. I feel as though I had lived in this room for years. It is that kind of room; very very much that kind of room.

It was more than ever the kind of room Vita had in mind when furnished by her with a faded old Persian carpet, a Queen Anne walnut bureau with glazed doors between the windows, a long oak table with bulbous legs against one wall, elegant straight-backed chairs, upholstered armchairs, and fairly crammed with pictures, books and papers. Vita crowned her efforts by importing, as her birthday present to Harold, an oil painting by Duncan Grant. She described it to him as 'the port of Marseilles (with a big sailing ship in it) and a peach-coloured tower that goes wriggling down in reflections in the water. It is the most romantic thing you ever saw, and a lovely colour.'[46] It was hung over the fireplace. All Harold could do in his absence was to join the Inner Temple for £58, which enabled him to park his car outside, to eat in the hall, use the library, have food sent in from the kitchen, and pray in the chapel.

His return to Berlin was more dismal than any previous one. Instead of being met first by Dan or Christopher, then by Knopf and Henry, and driven to his own apartment, there was no one this time at the station. He took a cab, not to the Adlon, which was too expensive, but to a cheap and grim family hotel, the Prinz Albrecht. In his bedroom there was 'a sort of lace cover over a round table, a canopy, a bed with one of those bloody German bolsters.'[47]

The Ambassador having gone to Taormina Harold was for the last time left in charge of the Embassy. His immediate duty was an unenviable one. He had to deliver to Curtius, Stresemann's successor, a Note about disarmament, urging him to instruct the German authorities to open negotiations with the experts for final liquidation of all disarmament questions. His next duty arose out of Philip Snowden, the Chancellor of the Exchequer's refusal to pay back to Germany seized enemy property, which had caused grave offence. Harold considered that our Government had behaved absolutely abominably, and crookedly. Once again he sided with Germany because he believed she had a genuine grievance. Insulting Notes flew from London to the Embassy in Berlin with instructions that they be presented to Curtius. Harold was the neutral, but emollient messenger.

> I am always lucky when in charge. There is always a crisis of some sort, and do I love them so. Absolute meat and drink they are. My heart this morning sings hymns at heaven's gate. It is only at such rare moments that diplomacy ceases to be humdrum, and I love them.[48]

As usual he flourished on over-work. It seemed that he could never have too much to do. And the more occupations that his job thrust upon him the more time he somehow found to devote to his writing. When he was

THE END OF DIPLOMACY 1929

his own master with complete control over his schedule his days were regulated like clockwork. He told Vita in November that every morning he rose early, did his physical jerks, had his bath, drank his coffee and wrote till 9 o'clock in his bedroom. He walked in the Tiergarten till 9.45. He then wrote to her, then filled in his diary and read the papers in the Chancery. Next he worked again at his book, revising early chapters until people began coming and interrupting him. The rest of the day was given over to office work, apart from one hour for luncheon, usually at the Buccaneers Club. After which a further walk in the Tiergarten, and he was ready to work in the office again at 4, until he went to his hotel to change for dinner. If he did not dine out he ate at the hotel and wrote again until he went to bed.

It is time to refer to his book. This was the life of his father, Lord Carnock. Less than a fortnight after the old man's death Harold told Vita that he had bought a huge notebook for his father's biography. He intended the book to be a history of pre-Great War diplomacy, seen through the life of an honourable English gentleman of the finest instincts, culminating in a tragedy, which at first he believed to be impossible, but later saw, with dread, was definitely approaching. His father's career spanned the rise and fall of the German Empire.

As an acting diplomatist Harold was obliged to seek Foreign Office permission to publish such a book. On the 10th December 1928 he had received a formal letter granting permission, with the caveat that he must take care not to offend the Germans. The letter was signed by his friend, Ronald Lindsay, who appended a note from the Librarian, Stephen Gaselee, saying, 'Go ahead, and don't care a damn.'

At first he found research difficult. He had to snatch odd hours of odd days of his leave to consult documents in the Foreign Office library. There were heavy gaps, and he suffered from the disadvantage that none of his father's official correspondence before 1900 was available. But what interested him very much was the discovery that his father's instinctive nineteenth-century pro-German feelings passed through a stage of hating France and Russia, into a stage of wanting to make friends with those two countries, and ending with a hatred of Germany. He hoped to be able to show that it was really the mistakes of the Germans which led to their *Einkreisung*, or encirclement, and not any malignity, or indeed policy on Great Britain's part. His great problem was to demonstrate that his father, although almost incredibly simple, was not in the least stupid. For example with hindsight it might seem stupid in 1928 not to have foreseen in 1893 how dangerous Germany was. But no, Lord Carnock never saw it until 1900.

While Harold acknowledged that on paper the Germans turned out to have been wrong all the time, yet he was certain they were not quite as wicked as they seemed. He therefore got over this unpopular hypothesis by drawing a distinction between the *origin* of the First World War and its *causes*. Regarding the former, Harold maintained that from the years 1900 to 1914 we, compared to the Germans, had a clean sheet, whereas regarding the latter, say from the year 1500 to 1900 our sheet was very black indeed. Our Elizabethans behaved worse than the Kaiser's imperialists. And when the Kaiser's imperialists in the last two decades of the nineteenth century developed predatory instincts in Africa, they met from us 'pained and patronising surprise.' Harold with justice and a good deal of courage blamed Great Britain for the causes and Germany for the origin of the great conflict.

Soon he was worried about the tone he found himself automatically adopting. He feared he was writing with a faint touch of aloofness, in a voice of irony, even of patronage, which verged on what he called parricide, in describing his father's character. For Lord Carnock's early letters were so inordinately 'pi,' so immensely serious, so over-scrupulously concerned with morality. In one he actually wrote to his young wife thanking God that he did not read French fiction, for if one did that sort of thing one quickly became demoralized. At that very moment, so Harold learned, his father was chortling over some extremely risqué French novels. Indeed Lord Hardinge had told him during their tête-à-tête dinner at the Embassy in June that his father when a young man had a series of wild love affairs, one at least with a married woman, before matrimony directed him into a narrow puritanism. Harold believed that his mother had been, in a way, the stronger character of the two. At all costs he wished his book to be as near the truth as possible. Although it was impossible to render his father's charm, at least he could render his integrity.

Then later he was bothered by the question, for whom was he writing the book? Not the expert like Horace Rumbold, not the amateur like Raymond Mortimer, not the ignoramus like Dottie Wellesley. He feared his greatest pitfall would be a change of audience as he advanced.

By August 1929 he declared that he had never enjoyed writing a book more than *Lord Carnock*. By the end of November he underwent every author's recurrent phase of inferiority complex, telling Vita that it was a really bad book, but was meant to show his father's fairness to Germany, and his objection to her humiliation at Versailles. Vita, who had read the typescript, replied that she was overwhelmed by its clarity. Apart from raising one or two minor objections to expressions like 'for his part,' and 'proceed,' which she thought officialese, she gave it unequivocal praise. Early in December Harold sent the book to Gaselee to be censored.

About this time Lady Sackville was making a show of reconciliation. She was suffering from further trouble with her eyes. Harold advised Vita that she ought to visit her mother if B.M. really had cataract in both eyes and wanted to welcome her, but resumption of relations should be on conditions. These were that B.M. must undertake not in future to interfere with her friends, books or movements. She must be told quite frankly not to tell fibs about her or him. They on their side must refuse to take any money from her for their own use, apart from what was due to Vita from the Knole estate.

The month of December was comparatively free from political crises. Sir Horace returned from Taormina on the 12th to take up again his ambassadorial responsibilities. Much of Harold's time was spent at farewell parties given for him by his closest German friends – Francesco Mendelsohn, the Weissmanns, Frau Luber, Ow-Wachendorff (where he had to make a speech), Leopold Plessen and the Erich Mendelsohns. Also tête-à-tête suppers with the Horstmanns, Kurt Wagenseil (who translated some of his books) and Richard Kühlmann. As usual Kühlmann was full of information and confidences about events leading up to the last War in which he played a part.[48] Official luncheons and dinners with gargantuan menus also followed thick and fast. Harold attended a reception specially given for him by Chancellor Hermann and Frau Müller at the Chancellery. In a vast room like a concert hall Frau Müller, apparelled in dove-coloured silk and laughing gaily with gold-tipped fangs, received her guests much at her ease. He was also entertained at the American Embassy. And there were final lectures to be given.

He paid a flying visit to Weimar, without daring to confess to Vita how it happened. At her urgent request he had promised that he would not fly. The promise often caused him inconvenience and he begged a release from it – a passport for suicide, she called it. But she could not bring herself to grant it. It was only in 1936 that she relented to the extent that he might fly in an Imperial Airways machine but never in anything smaller, like a Moth. There were however occasions when no other suitable means of transport being available, Harold was driven to deceive her. On the 11th December he had an engagement to lecture in Frankfurt, but missed the train. He simply had to take an aeroplane, but the weather was so bad the plane came down at Erfurt before it could get to Frankfurt. In consequence he was obliged to chuck the lecture. So he took the opportunity of motoring to Weimar, which was a mere twenty miles away, and renewing old memories of twenty-five years ago.

> What a strange thing the human mind is! I remembered it all vaguely, and in detached views like picture postcards. 'That is the Schloss.' 'That is the Catholic Church.' But I forgot what was round the corner or whether one turned to left or right. I found the house we used to live in. But it awoke no association emotions [beyond] a single recognition. Now memory generally is like a double chord on a piano with several notes blending. This was just like hitting one note with one finger. I suppose therefore that the associative elements in memory die soonest, and that the mere element of recognition remains.[50]

Back in Berlin he lectured to the English section of the University upon German and English psychology. The hall was packed. The Ambassador and his family were present. Everyone was suitably impressed. Afterwards the students gave him a reception.

> There they were, mostly women in pink blouses, sitting at three huge long tables drinking lemonade. In front of them were books called Olde Englysshe part songs, and they sang them loudly. Very odd it was. They sang Bonnie Prince Charlie, the Vicar of Bray and John Peel. Also one in Scotch dialect. Now can you imagine the undergraduates of Balliol or Newnham sitting down in hall and singing Bavarian or Saxon folk songs with complete accuracy of accent and time? God, what funny people.[51]

He went to Schönhausen for luncheon. It was the house where Bismarck was born and spent much of his early married life. It was completely untouched and strongly evocative of the past. Harold travelled by train and was met at a wayside station by a large barouche with two horses and a man in a green Jaeger livery. They drove through a wide, straggling village with tall trees. An untidy entrance led to a high, rambling house, like an overgrown farmhouse. The walls of the rooms were plastered. Old-fashioned chairs were arranged in circles round centre tables. There were paintings of Bismarck, and photographs of Said Pasha and Lord Salisbury. The interior was redolent of 1870. Princess Blücher, frail, dowdy and distinguished, and Gottfried Bismarck, the clever and charming grandson of the great statesman, received him.

After luncheon he was conducted round the house. Then to the church, where he looked at the family pew and the family vault. Everything at Schönhausen was simple and dignified. Next, he was taken for a walk along the high road through ugly, flat country. The impression left on

THE END OF DIPLOMACY 1929

Harold was of the old provincial Germany before the vulgar German Empire came into being. Bismarck's house was like some hard, cold Yorkshire manor, with little isolated groups of trees and the bitter wind howling across the Elbe marshes.

He returned to Berlin in time for a farewell dinner at the Buccaneers Club. There were nearly forty people present, including the British and American Ambassadors. Sir Horace Rumbold made a speech in which he said the Foreign Office ought to have been able to keep Harold, 'had they possessed more imagination,'[52] a remark noted by the press who were present. Harold was deeply touched. He made a very restrained and gulpy speech in reply. There was music afterwards. 'It is quite extraordinary how nice people are to me here. They really are sorry at my going,' he wrote to Vita. And after a large farewell luncheon given him by the Schuberts, 'They have been terribly civil to me . . . I feel such a humbug in a way, as these people really do mind my going, and of course I don't care $1\frac{1}{2}$d for them.'[53]

After a last dinner party at the Embassy he left Berlin on the 19th. His colleagues and several friends gathered on the station platform to see him off. It was a fine departure. Someone – was it Francesco von Mendelsohn, who at a party at the Jockey held on the eve of Harold's last birthday, when midnight struck, put a real live rabbit on his knee? – presented him with a cactus. For Harold had once asked Francesco whether Germans liked cactuses so much because they reminded them of the hideous way they cut their hair, or whether they cut their hair because they so much admired cactuses. As the train sidled out of the station he took out of his satchel the thick leather-covered notebook, which had been his daily companion since 1924, and wrote simply under the date – 'The end of my diplomatic career.'

There were only to be a few more lines inscribed before he closed this notebook for good. About a third of the pages are still left blank. It is not difficult to guess what succinct entries they might have contained had he remained in the service. Another short term as Counsellor overseas perhaps, or even Minister at, as he had suggested, Athens? Next, recall to Whitehall as Assistant Under-Secretary of State for Foreign Affairs, when his old enemy Lord Tyrrell of Avon retired from the diplomatic scene in 1934? And finally the crowning post which his father held – Permanent Under-Secretary of State? Who knows.

As it was, Harold made, for better or for worse, the biggest decision of his life. I have already touched upon the reasons which brought him to it. The principal one was undoubtedly Vita's hostility to diplomacy. She had made it abundantly plain while he was in Persia and Germany (and he did not blame her) that, wherever else he might be posted to, she would not accompany him permanently. At most she would pay him occasional, brief visits. This alone was enough to turn him against his career. As well as the prolonged separations from her, which he found unendurable, there were the inevitable separations from his two sons, now growing up, whom he barely knew. Then his experiences as Chargé d'Affaires had soured whatever delights he used to envisage in the prospects of becoming a Minister or Ambassador. The work had disillusioned him. He had had a taste of the frustration suffered by an intelligent representative abroad who endeavoured to influence the stuffy hierarchy in the Office at home. The fate of his Tehran Despatch was a warning how little support his views would command, and even how little sympathy his efforts would evoke in Whitehall. What Harold would have liked was to be taken back into the Foreign Office. But the hostility of Tyrrell had ruled out that opportunity for an indefinite period. Other motives for his resignation were a desire to earn more money and to write freely, without having to submit articles and books to official vetos. Moreover he was beginning to develop political views which he wished to ventilate, and resented having to bottle up; and he even considered standing for Parliament at a future date.

The extraordinary mistake Harold made in turning to journalism, was to associate himself with Lord Beaverbrook, a man notoriously despotic, capricious, unscrupulous and brash. Harold on the contrary was rational, reliable, steadfast and fastidious. He had nothing whatever in common with Beaverbrook or his shifting policies of popular appeal. Once he had decided to work for the press he ought to have tried to get a job on the *Times, Guardian* or *Morning Post*, where at least he would have consorted with editors and colleagues, whose basic values approximated to his own.

So, at the age of forty-three he threw up a safe and highly respected career, with sure promise of promotion, for the uncertain hurly-burly of journalism. Since he never reached the highest ranks of diplomacy we cannot be sure how successful he would have proved himself. Sir Horace Rumbold foretold for him a great future in the service. Sir Oswald Mosley thought he would have made an excellent ambassador. Harold once admitted that the Bohemian in him would have told against him. By this he meant his dislike of formality in diplomatic conduct and dress. What we do know is that his years of experience made him into one of the leading British authorities on the art of diplomacy,[54] and one of the last of the classical diplomatic theorists.

From having been, first a diplomat and only secondly a writer, he was to become, after a brief and unhappy interlude as professional journalist, first a writer and secondly a politician. Not that he was to think of the roles in that order for, curiously enough, his interest in politics actually transcended his love of literature. Yet by far the greater amount of his

THE END OF DIPLOMACY 1929

writing was done during the next period of his life. Already he had made his reputation as an author of the first class, with seven books, a number of articles, reviews, printed lectures and a few broadcasts to his credit. The felicity of his syntax and the lucidity of his prose were acquired from severe self-training over Foreign Office despatches and memoranda, the most complicated of which he had learned to compose straight off without previous notes or subsequent alterations. They were usually blunt and to the point, often with bright flashes of insight. The extremely individual flavour of his literary style, the perfect balance between the light and the profound, the witty and the serious, was derived from the spontaneity of his abundant letters. His intense curiosity about human beings provides the explanation why his writings, whether the reader agrees with his arguments or not, are never dull.

Harold was met at Liverpool Street station, the lugubrious scene of so many wretched departures, by Vita who drove him straight to No. 4 King's Bench Walk. He was enchanted by what she had done there for him, finding it 'too lovely for words.' He spent the whole of the first day arranging his treasures and books, and revelling in the tranquil atmosphere of the Temple. Clive Bell, Francis Birrell and Raymond came to supper with him. Christmas was spent at Long Barn with Vita and the boys. He delivered to Constable's the finished typescript of *Lord Carnock*, which was to be, in his considered opinion, the best of all his books. New Year's Eve was spent at Penns-in-the-Rocks. Desmond MacCarthy and Ethel Sands were fellow guests. Having sat up to see out 'the end of a bloody year,' and see in the start of a strange unknown one, Harold Nicolson took the train to London to join the staff of the *Evening Standard* on Wednesday, the 1st January 1930.

Appendix

NOTES TO TEXT

Letters to and from Harold Nicolson and Vita Sackville-West from 1912 to 1929 have not hitherto been published, with the exception of a few in Nigel Nicolson's Volume 1 of his father's *Diaries and Letters* (1966) and in *Portrait of a Marriage* (1973). The extracts from Harold Nicolson's diaries before 1930 (excluding the Peace Conference Diaries, published 1933), which are quoted in this book, have not previously been published. Both letters and diaries quoted are the copyright of Nigel Nicolson.

The abbreviations used in the Appendix are:

HN	Harold Nicolson
VSW	Vita Sackville-West
BN	Benedict Nicolson
NN	Nigel Nicolson
VK	Violet Keppel
VW	Virginia Woolf
RM	Raymond Mortimer

Docs. on Brit. For. Pol. *Documents on British Foreign Policy, 1919–1939*, edited by Sir L. Woodward and Rohan Butler

CHAPTER 1   CHILDHOOD AND SCHOOL, 1886–1904

1. *Helen's Tower*, 1936, p. 3.
2. The sisters were daughters of Archibald Rowan Hamilton of Killyleagh Castle, County Down, an Ulster landowner who died in the year of Catherine's birth (1860). Hariot was seventeen years older than Catherine. A third sister, Helen Gwendoline, married 1876 R. M. Stephenson and died in 1886.
3. Daughter of James Loch of Drylaw, M.P., who had been the Duke of Sutherland's factor and instrument of the Highland Clearances from the vast Sutherland estates.
4. His elder brother Frederick, a lieutenant in the Royal Artillery, had been killed fighting in Zululand in 1879.
5. *Spectator*, 10.11.1944.
6. *Lord Carnock*, 1930, p. 79.
7. *Helen's Tower*, p. 29.
8. *Good Behaviour*, 1955, p. 21.
9. *Some People*, 1927, p. 17.
10. *Spectator*, 29.11.1946.
11. James Chandler to NN, 18.4.1977.
12. *Spectator*, 5.3.1948.
13. *The Desire to Please*, 1943, p. 5.
14. Catherine Ann Caldwell, wife of Archibald Rowan Hamilton, HN's maternal grandmother. She inherited Shanganagh Castle, County Dublin, from her mother's father, General Sir George Cockburn, K.C.B.
15. On 7.8.1936 and again on 16.3.1942.
16. *Spectator*, 24.12.1943.
17. Foreword by HN to Bertram Pollock, *A Twentieth Century Bishop: Recollections and Reflections*, 1944.

18. Ibid.
19. HN to Lady Nicolson, 25.10.1903.
20. O. T. Perkins (d. 1939), scholar of New College, Oxford. He took the Upper Sixth form at Wellington. HN in *Some People* described him as 'most exact of Hellenists, most meticulous of scholiasts.'
21. HN to his parents, 18.4.1904.
22. HN to his parents, 24.7.1904.
23. HN to his parents, 14.8.1904.
24. HN to his parents, 21.8.1904.

CHAPTER 2 BALLIOL AND CRAMMING, 1904–1907

1. Frederick Temple Hamilton-Temple Blackwood, 1st Marquess of Dufferin and Ava, 1826–1902.
2. In a speech to the Master, Fellows and Men of Balliol, November 1930.
3. HN to his parents, 14.10.1904.
4. Cyril Bailey, 1871–1957. Balliol scholar 1890.
5. HN to his parents, 23.10.1904.
6. Sir Lawrence Evelyn Jones, 5th Bart. of Cranmer Hall, 1885–1969.
7. F. F. Urquhart, 1868–1934.
8. Sir Charles Clay, 1885–1978, Librarian of the House of Lords.
9. Review by HN in *Daily Telegraph*, 6.11.1936 of *Francis Urquhart* by Cyril Bailey.
10. *An Edwardian Youth*, 1956.
11. Frederick Temple Rowan-Hamilton, b. 1850. He married 1883 Blanche Mary, daughter of Admiral William Fellowes-Gordon. She died 1960, aged 98. They lived at Culverlands, Farnham, Surrey, and were the parents of HN's cousin, Guy.
12. Sir Hughe Montgomery Knatchbull-Hugessen, 1886–1971. Ambassador. HN had a very deep affection for 'Snatch' when they were young men together.
13. John David Leslie Melville, 1886–1913. Lord Balgonie succeeded his father 1906 as 12th Earl of Leven and 11th of Melville. He was an accomplished horseman, and was killed on the hunting field.
14. Hon. Arthur Michael Cosmo Bertie (Tata), D.S.O., M.C., 1886–1957. Attached to British Armistice Commission (Spa) 1918–19. Became the father of the 14th Earl of Lindsey and 9th of Abingdon.
15. HN to his parents, 6.2.1905.
16. HN to his parents, 5.3.1905.
17. HN to Lady Nicolson, 12.2.1905.
18. HN to Sir Arthur Nicolson, 26.2.1905.
19. *People and Things*, 1931, p. 165.
20. In a copy of *Some People* (annotated by HN for Mr. Stuart Preston in 1938), page 55.
21. *Lord Carnock*, p. 204.
22. R. O. W. Pemberton (Crooked), 1885–1960. Clerk in the House of Lords. Inspector for Schools. On 1.3.1960 HN wrote: 'Edward Adam tells me that Crooked Pemberton is dead. Dear Crook! He was an old friend and a nice man. Not stupid.'
23. HN to F. F. Urquhart, 30.10.1906.
24. Patrick Shaw-Stewart, 1888–1917. HN to VSW 10.3.13 refers to 'his sandy coloured cynicism.'
25. HN to his parents, 31.4.1907.

APPENDIX: NOTES TO TEXT

CHAPTER 3 PREPARATIONS FOR THE DIPLOMATIC SERVICE, 1907-1909

1. Charles, 1st Lord Hardinge of Penshurst, K.G., 1858-1944. Viceroy of India 1910-1916, when he succeeded Lord Carnock as Permanent Under-Secretary of State at the Foreign Office, for the second time. Ambassador to Paris 1920-1922.
2. Lord Eustace Percy 1887-1958. Created Lord Percy 1953.
3. H. H. Duncan, b. 1885. Educated at Eton.
4. Sir Coleridge Fitzroy (Roy) Kennard, 1885-1948. Slim, golden-haired and rich. He enjoyed the unusual distinction of being created a Baronet at the age of 5.
5. Duff Cooper – *Old Men Forget*, 1953.
6. HN to Lady Nicolson, 20.4.1908.
7. HN to F. F. Urquhart, 29.12.1908.
8. *Spectator*, 27.2.1947.
9. Even the Czar is said to have complained to the English court that when this child was about Sir Arthur paid too little attention to His Imperial Majesty by listening to what Gwen was saying. Personal information.
10. HN to F. F. Urquhart, 9.4.1909.
11. Druce Robert Brandt, b. 1887. Educated Harrow, and Balliol, 1906-10. He was killed 1915. R. Furze said he was the finest all-rounder he ever knew.

CHAPTER 4 FOREIGN OFFICE, SPAIN AND CONSTANTINOPLE, 1910-1912

1. Sir Eyre Crowe, 1864-1925.
2. Sir William (later Lord) Tyrrell, 1866-1947.
3. Lady Eileen Wellesley, 1887-1952. Married 1916 Captain Cuthbert Julian Orde.
4. Lord Gerald Wellesley, 1885-1972, subsequently 7th Duke of Wellington. After leaving the Diplomatic Service he practised as an architect.
5. Archibald John Clark Kerr, 1st Lord Inverchapel, 1882-1951. Born in Australia, the 5th son of John Kerr Clark of Crossbasket, Hamilton, Lanarkshire. Ambassador at Stockholm and Washington. Married 1929 Maria Teresa Dia Salas daughter of Don Javier Dias Lira of Santiago, Chile. His death came as a great shock to HN. 'Lui mort? Mort mon grand Péché radieux?' In his youth he was much loved by HN.
6. VSW's *Autobiographical Confessions*, henceforth referred to as *Notebook*, begun in 1920.
7. Marchese Visconti Venosta (Enrico), 1885-1945. Gentle and lethargic, luxury-loving and literary, he was attached, at his special request, to the 15th Army Group fighting Germans in the Apennines, and almost immediately was killed in action, aged 60. He figures in *Some People*.
8. VSW – *Notebook*, 1920.
9. *Good Behaviour*, 1955, p. 23.
10. HN to JLM, 8.1.1935.
11. HN held against Spain that she allowed her legionaries in World War II to fight against Russia, and La Linea and Tarifea to be used as enemy observation posts, thus violating the principles of neutrality. The occupation of the Tangier zone was an international outrage which he could neither forgive nor forget. Vita and the author thought HN's attitude to Spain silly.
12. VSW – *Notebook*, 1920.
13. Nigel Nicolson – *Portrait of a Marriage*, 1973.
14. Lady Sackville to VSW, 12.1.1912.
15. VSW – *Notebook*, 1920.
16. Ibid.
17. VSW – Diary, 24.1.1912.

18. HN confirmed that this incident in *Lambert Orme* (*Some People* pp. 67–68) was true of Firbank.
19. Edward Sackville-West, 1901–1965, afterwards 5th Lord Sackville, novelist and music critic.
20. VSW to HN, 24.3.1912.
21. Marginal note (1938) against *The Marquis de Chaumont* in *Some People*.
22. Private source of information.
23. HN Diary, 9.5.1926.
24. VSW to HN, 1.8.1912.
25. She was Maud Cecilia, daughter of Matthew John Bell of Bourne Park, Kent and the mother of Edward Sackville-West. She died 1920. Charles Sackville-West married secondly, Anne Meredith Bigelow of New York.

CHAPTER 5   CONSTANTINOPLE AND MARRIAGE, 1913–1914

1. HN to VSW, 24.1.1913.
2. HN to VSW, 12.6.1913.
3. VSW to HN, 8.1.1913.
4. HN to VSW, 17.2.1913.
5. VSW to HN, 4.3.1913.
6. VSW to Rosamund Grosvenor, 10.4.1913.
7. Vita Sackville-West – *Pepita*, 1936, a biography of her Spanish grandmother.
8. VSW to HN, 17.4.1913.
9. VSW to HN, May 1913. Received by HN on 19th and probably destroyed by him.
10. VSW to HN, 20.5.1913.
11. HN to VSW, 24.6.1913.
12. On 9.7.1913.
13. VT to VSW, 9.7.1913.
14. HN to VSW, 12.8.1913.
15. HN to VSW, 31.7.1913.
16. VSW to HN, 31.8.1913.
17. HN Diary, 11.9.1913.
18. VSW – *Notebook*, 1920.
19. HN to VSW, 25.2.1952.
20. HN Diary, 2.11.1913.
21. VSW – *Notebook*, 1920.
22. Rosamund Grosvenor married in 1924 a soldier, Jack Lynch, and lived in Oxford. She was killed by a flying bomb while in a bus in Aldwych. VSW to HN, 4.7.1944: 'Poor old Rosie has been killed . . . Well, we always teased her about her passion for attending memorial services, and now she is going to have one for herself. It has saddened me rather. That somebody so innocent, so silly, and so harmless should be killed in this idiotic and violent way.'
23. Sir Louis Mallet, 1864–1936.
24. VSW – *Notebook*, 1920.

CHAPTER 6   THE FIRST WORLD WAR, 1914–1918

1. *Peacemaking, 1919*, published 1933, p. 35.
2. VSW to HN, 9.7.1914.
3. HN was told this story by Baron Richard von Kühlmann at a luncheon party in Berlin on 24.3.28 in the presence of Arnold Toynbee, and evidently saw no reason to

APPENDIX: NOTES TO TEXT

dispute it. It left a deep impression on him, and he frequently referred to it in his writings. Kühlmann was however looked upon by several historians as unreliable, and even dishonest. (See Sir Lewis Namier – *The Story of a German Diplomatist* (*Avenues of History*, 1952).

4. *Spectator*, 25.8.1950.
5. *Lord Carnock*, pp. 425–6.
6. Until the last hour Prince Lichnowsky refused to believe that Great Britain and Germany would go to war. He made no preparations for departure, and on leaving the Embassy in London took away nothing but seven canaries, a cat and a dog.
7. HN to VSW, 30.8.1914.
8. Sir George Clerk, 1874–1951, K.C.M.G. 1917.
9. HN to VSW, 22.8.1917.
10. *Heritage*, published 1919.
11. Anne Scott-James – *Sissinghurst, The Making of a Garden*, 1974.
12. Dorothy Wellesley – *Far Have I Travelled*, 1952.
13. Violet Trefusis – *Don't Look Round*, 1952.
14. Leonard Woolf – *Downhill All the Way*, 1967.
15. HN to VSW, 16.11.1922.
16. VSW to HN, 25.6.1915.
17. HN to VSW, 30.12.1915.
18. HN to VSW, 22.4.1916.
19. Dated 18.11.1916.
20. In 1918 he was allowed to enlist as a guardsman in the Scots Guards.
21. HN to VSW, 19.7.1917.
22. HN to VSW, 23.7.1917.
23. HN to VSW, 29.8.1917.
24. *Spectator*, 26.5.1939.
25. Ibid.
26. HN to VSW, 18.10.1917.
27. Colonel C. à 'C. Repington, travelling back to London by train with HN and Sacheverell Sitwell, after a weekend, was amazed to hear the young men discussing, not soldiery, but pictures, Palladio and palaces. *The First World War*, Vol. I. 28.8. 1916.
28. HN to VSW, 17.8.1917.
29. Violet Keppel's letters to VSW from September 1910 to August 1912, kept in a small tin box at Sissinghurst, were not published in Philippe Julian and John Phillips's *Violet Trefusis*, 1976.
30. VK to VSW, 27.12.1916.
31. VK to VSW, 28.12.1916.
32. HN Diary, 13.3.1918.
33. HN Diary, 1.11.1922.
34. Edmond Lancelot Warre, 1877–1961, nicknamed 'Bear' on account of his great size. Architect son of the famous headmaster of Eton, the Rev. Edmund Warre.
35. VSW – *Notebook*, 1920.
36. Jonkheer Dr. R. de Marees van Swinderen, Dutch Minister to London for many years.
37. VSW to HN, 11.5.1918.
38. HN to VSW, 3.6.1918.
39. HN to VSW, 18.6.1918.
40. VK to VSW, 22.10.1918.
41. VK to VSW, 25.10.1918.
42. HN to VSW, 26.11.1918.
43. HN to VSW, 30.11.1918.
44. HN to VSW, 2.12.1918.
45. Victor Cunard was a nephew of Lady Cunard's husband, Sir Bache, 3rd Baronet.
46. HN to VSW, 18.12.1918.

HAROLD NICOLSON

CHAPTER 7 THE PEACE CONFERENCE, 1919

1. Allen Leeper, 1887–1935. Became First Secretary to the Legation in Vienna 1924. Married 1921 Janet Hamilton. He died prematurely of cancer of the liver. HN wrote an article on him in the *Nineteenth Century Review*, Oct. 1935.
2. *Peacemaking*, 1933.
3. Edward Knobclock, 1874–1945. Playwright, and the author of *Kismet*. He was a little, dark, gnome-like man, rather tetchy, but entertaining.
4. Také Jonescu, 1858–1922. Founder of Roumanian Conservative Democratic Party 1908. Delegate at Peace Conference 1919. Prime Minister Dec. 1921–Jan. 1922.
5. HN to VSW, 7.1.1919.
6. HN to VSW, 10.1.1919.
7. Eduard Beneš, 1884–1948. Was Foreign Minister for Czechoslovakia 1918–35, Prime Minister, 1921–2; President, 1935–38 and 1946–48.
8. *Peace Conference Diary*, 13.1.1919.
9. Eleutherios Venizelos, 1864–1936, several times Prime Minister of Greece.
10. HN to VSW (*Peacemaking*, p. 337), 14.5.1919.
11. Told to HN by Camille Barrère, 12.12.1922.
12. HN to VSW, 1.2.1919.
13. *Spectator*, 20.10.1944.
14. *Peace Conference Diary*, 24.2.1919.
15. HN to Lord Carnock, 25.2.1919.
16. Jules Cambon, 1845–1935. Had been French Ambassador in Berlin. His brother Paul, 1843–1924, had been French Ambassador in London, 1898–1921.
17. *Peace Conference Diary*, 5.3.1919.
18. Sir Mark Sykes, 6th Baronet of Sledmere, 1879–1919, M.P. 1911–1919.
19. HN to VSW, 22.1.1919.
20. HN to VSW, 16.5.1919.
21. HN to VSW, 17.5.1919.
22. HN to VSW, 20.5.1919.
23. Ibid.
24. *Spectator*, 6.4.1945.
25. *Peace Conference Diary*, 3.4.1919.
26. ibid. 4.5.1919.
27. ibid. 5.4.1919.
28. HN to VSW, 19.4.1919.
29. HN to VSW, 20.4.1919.
30. HN to VSW, 18.1.1919.
31. Information from two French friends who knew him well.
32. Philippe Jullian – *Violet Trefusis*, 1976.
33. HN to VSW, 17.1.1919.
34. George D. Painter – *Marcel Proust*, Vol. 2. 1965, p. 286.
35. HN to Clive Bell, 17.5.1926.
36. Elizabeth Asquith, daughter of Rt. Hon. H. H. Asquith, Prime Minister, and Margot (Tennant).
37. Mrs. Brinton's first husband was Mr. William James. She had been one of King Edward VII's closest women friends.
38. HN to VSW, 21.1.1919.
39. *Daily Telegraph*, 11.12.1936.
40. HN to VSW, 6.6.1919.
41. *Portrait of a Marriage*, p. 113.
42. VSW to HN, 30.1.1919.
43. HN to VSW, 2.2.1919.

APPENDIX: NOTES TO TEXT

44. HN to VSW, 8.2.1919.
45. HN to VSW, 9.2.1919.
46. The League of Nations came into being when the Covenant was incorporated in the Treaty of Versailles, and Sir Eric Drummond was made the first Secretary-General.
47. HN to VSW, 19.5.1919.
48. HN to VSW, 22.5.1919.
49. J. M. Keynes acted as deputy for the Chancellor of the Exchequer on the Supreme Economic Council, and was a member of the Reparations Commission. He found himself in such vigorous disagreement with the policy of the Commission that he resigned in June and returned to England.
50. HN to VSW, 1.6.1919.
51. VSW to HN, 1.6.1919.
52. HN to VSW, 3.6.1919.
53. HN to VSW, 7.6.1919.
54. *Peace Conference Diary*, 12.6.1919.
55. VSW to HN, 13.6.1919.

CHAPTER 8 PARIS AFTERMATH AND THE LEAGUE OF NATIONS, 1919–1920

1. *Spectator*, 7.7.1946.
2. *Note by HN (4.8.1919) of A Conversation with Dr. Beneš in Paris*, addressed to Sir E. Crowe. *Documents on British Foreign Policy*, 1919–1939. Series I., Vol. VI, No. 83.
3. HN to VSW, 19.7.1919.
4. VSW to HN, 20.7.1919.
5. *Friday Mornings* (1944), 27.11.1942.
6. HN to VSW, 26.7.1919.
7. *Note by HN (6.8.1919) of an Allied Meeting in Paris* – Docs. on Brit. For. Pol., Series 1. Vol. IV.
8. HN to VSW, 15.9.1919.
9. HN to VSW, 21.10.1919.
10. Étienne Mantoux was head of the Political Department of the League.
11. HN to VSW, 29.10.1919.
12. HN to VSW, 5.11.1919.
13. HN to VSW, 8.11.1919.
14. HN to VSW, 16.11.1919.
15. HN to VSW, 19.11.1919.
16. VSW to HN, 26.11.1919.
17. HN to VSW, 7.12.1919.
18. VSW to HN, 5.12.1919. Quoted in *Portrait of a Marriage* with slight variation.
19. HN to VSW, 9.12.1919.
20. VSW to HN, 11.12.1919.
21. *Portrait of a Marriage*, p. 166.
22. VSW to HN, 1.2.1920. Fully quoted in *Portrait of a Marriage*, p. 166–7.
23. HN to VSW, 4.2.1920. Quoted in *Portrait of a Marriage*, p. 168.
24. *Portrait of a Marriage*, p. 173–4.
25. HN to VSW, 15.5.1920.
26. *Verlaine* by Edward Delahaye.
27. HN to VSW, 5.1.1915.
28. The whole correspondence between HN and Constable's, consisting of 428 items, mostly to and from Michael Sadleir from 1920 to 1960, are today the property of Temple University, Philadelphia, U.S.A.
29. I shall refer to this article in Volume 2.
30. VSW to HN, 21.7.1920.

31. HN to VSW, 19.5.1920. Sir Roderick Jones, 1877–1962, Chairman and Managing Director of Reuter's 1920–1941; and Enid Bagnold, writer and playwright, his wife.

32. VSW – *Notebook*, 1920.

33. Quoted from Walpole's diary by Rupert Hart-Davis in *Hugh Walpole*, 1952, p. 195.

34. Docs. on Brit. For. Pol.: First Series, Vol. XII, No. 439.

35. HN to VSW, 29.11.1920.

36. Docs. on Brit. For. Pol.: First Series, Vol. XII. No. 488.

CHAPTER 9   LONDON, FOREIGN OFFICE, 1921–1922

1. Docs on Brit. For. Pol.: First Series, Vol. XVII, No. 7. Dated 8.1.1921.
2. Docs. on Brit. For. Pol.: First Series, Vol. XVII No. 12, Dated 18.1.1921.
3. Docs. on Brit. For. Pol.: First Series, Vol. XVII, No. 24. Dated 27.1.1921.
4. HN to VSW, 8.2.1921.
5. VSW to HN, undated letter.
6. HN Diary, 15.2.1921.
7. Docs. on Brit. For. Pol.: First Series, Vol. XVII. No. 41. Dated 17.2.1921.
8. HN Diary, 25.2.1921.
9. HN Diary, 27.2.1921.
10. HN Diary, 28.2.1921.
11. Later changed to Ankara.
12. H. A. L. Fisher to HN, 10.12.1921.
13. W. Rothenstein to HN, 17.3.1921.
14. Raymond Mortimer to JLM, 13.3.1977.
15. HN to VSW, 11.4.1921.
16. HN to VSW, 18.4.1921.
17. HN to Michael Sadleir, 29.4.1921.
18. Janet, youngest daughter of Vereker M. Hamilton, and a niece of General Sir Ian Hamilton.
19. *Far Have I Travelled*, 1952.
20. Ursula Codrington, who was for a time Dorothy Wellesley's secretary.
21. HN to VSW, 27.8.1921.
22. HN Diary, 9.9.1921.
23. HN to VSW, 20.9.1921.
24. HN Diary, 5.10.1921. Eugénie Strong, 1860–1943, classical archaeologist and historian of art. After her husband's death in 1904 she lived in retirement in the Villa Balbo, Rome.
25. Prince Philip of Hesse, born 1896. Married H.R.H. Princess Mafalda of Savoy in 1925. She met her death in a concentration camp at the end of World War II.
26. HN Diary, 8.10.1921.
27. HN Diary, 10.10.1921.
28. HN Diary, 16.10.1921.
29. On 25.10.1921.
30. HN to Michael Sadleir, 6.8.1921.
31. HN Diary, 2.2.1922.
32. HN Diary, 16.2.1922.
33. HN Diary entry, 23.2.1922. He tells this story with variations, in *Tennyson*, p. 174.
34. HN Diary, 2.3.1922.
35. HN Diary, 14.4.1922.
36. HN to VSW, 29.12.1922.
37. HN to VSW, 14.8.1922.
38. On 21.9.1922.

APPENDIX: NOTES TO TEXT

39. HN to VSW, 13.9.1922.
40. HN Diary, 29.10.1922.
41. HN Diary, 30.10.1922.
42. Docs. on Brit. For. Pol.: First Series, Vol. XVIII. Appendix 1, Dated 15.11.22.

CHAPTER 10. THE LAUSANNE CONFERENCE, 1922–1923

1. HN to VSW, 18.11.1922.
2. HN Diary, 21.11.1922.
3. HN to VSW, 23.11.1922.
4. Commander Sir Gerald Talbot, K.C.V.O., R.N.V.R., M.C., 1881–1945. Naval Attaché to Legation at Athens, 15th June 1918. Appointment terminated 31 May 1920.
5. Father of H.R.H. Prince Philip, Duke of Edinburgh.
6. Docs. on Brit. For. Pol.: First Series. No. 287. E 14403/27/44·, Dated 23.12.1922.
7. HN Diary, 28.12.1922.
8. HN Diary, 31.12.1922.
9. HN Diary, 13.12.1922.
10. HN to VSW, 6.12.1922.
11. VSW to HN, 8.12.1922.
12. VSW to HN, 12.12.1922.
13. VSW to Clive Bell, 10.11.1922.
14. HN Diary, 4.1.1923.
15. Docs. on Brit. For. Pol.: First series, Vol. XVIII., No. 307. E 316/6/44.
16. HN Diary, 6.1. 1923.
17. Julia Margaret Cameron, the great Victorian photographer.
18. HN to VSW, 22.1.1923.
19. HN to VSW, 28.1.1923.
20. HN Diary, 4.2.1923.

CHAPTER 11 LONDON AGAIN, 1923–1925

1. *The Diary of Virginia Woolf, Vol. II. 1920–1924*, edited by Olivier Bell, 1978, 19.2.1923.
2. Ibid. 17.3.1923.
3. Lytton Strachey to J. M. Keynes, 16.4.1922.
4. HN to VSW, 31.12.1926.
5. VSW to HN, 28.6.1929.
6. VSW to HN, 3.8.1938.
7. VSW to HN, 28.11.1922.
8. F. F. Urquhart to HN, 23.3.1923.
9. HN to VSW, 26.4.1923.
10. HN Diary, 4–19.9.1923.
11. On 2nd September 1923.
12. HN Diary, 20.9.1923.
13. HN to VSW, 27.9.1923.
14. HN to VSW, 3.10.1923.
15. This was Charles Henry Bentinck, C.M.G. In 1920 he went to Athens as Counsellor. From 1921 to 1924 he was, on and off, Chargé d'Affaires.
16. Captain Frank Abney Hastings, a Philhellene who bombarded Byron with advice during the Greek campaign, advice which Byron disregarded.
17. HN Diary, 18.10.1923.
18. HN Diary, 27.10.1923.
19. On 28.10.1923.
20. HN Diary, 31.12.1923.

21. HN Diary, 1.1.1924.
22. HN Diary, 15.1.1924.
23. HN Diary, 24.1.1924.
24. Until his death in 1980 for long the doyen of literary critics. At one time literary editor of the *New Statesman* and for years critic of the *Sunday Times*.
25. Virginia Woolf to Lytton Strachey, 24.3.1924.
26. HN Diary, 7.3.1924.
27. HN to VSW, 29.4.1924.
28. VW Diary, 5.7.1924.
29. Dated 5.7.1924.
30. VW Diary, 15.9.1924: 'She left me with a story which really interests me rather. I see my own face in it, it's true. But she has shed the old verbiage, & come to terms with some sort of glimmer of art . . .'
31. Sir Alexander Grant, 1st Baronet (1924). His entry in *Who's Who* of that year refers to him, ungrammatically, as 'realising the importance of an important and happy staff of workers, a first consideration at all their factories is the Comfort and Welfare of workers.'
32. VW Diary, 15.9.1924.
33. HN Diary, 27.9.1924.
34. HN Diary, 28.9.1924.
35. He was the son of the last Russian Imperial Ambassador to Britain.
36. HN Diary, 11.10.1924.
37. George Painter (*Marcel Proust*, Vol. 11, 1965) described him as 'a dignified, white moustached, intelligent and elderly American . . . an expert in international law, an ardent propagandist for the entry of the United States into the war, and President of the American Chamber of Commerce in Paris.'
38. VSW to HN, 3.12.1924.
39. HN to VSW, 4.12.1924.
40. VK to VSW, undated.
41. HN Diary, 6.1.1925.
42. HN Diary, 4.2.1925.
43. HN Diary, 14.7.1925.
44. Dorothy Wellesley – *Far Have I Travelled*.
45. Elizabeth Bowen to Rosamond Lehmann (undated).
46. HN to Michael Sadleir, 21.2.1925.
47. HN Diary, 21.2.1925.
48. Created Lord Boothby 1958. Conservative M.P. 1924–1958.
49. HN Diary, 26.3.1925.
50. The Earl of Ronaldshay, 1876–1961, succeeded 1929 as 2nd Marquess of Zetland.
51. Sir Ian Malcolm, 1866–1944. Private Secretary to A. J. Balfour at the Peace Conference.
52. When Ronaldshay's Vol. 11 came out in September 1928 HN pronounced it excellent.
53. HN Diary, 25.9.1924.
54. HN to VSW, 28.10.1942.
55. HN to VSW, 14.5.26.
56. Brendan, 1st Viscount Bracken, 1901–1958, politician and businessman.
57. HN Diary, 7.6.1925.
58. HN to VSW, 2.7.1925.
59. HN to RM, 27.8.1925.
60. RM to HN, 16.8.1955: 'I have never loved anybody else so profoundly, nor has any other friend been so consistently and patiently and imaginatively affectionate, thoughtful and appreciative. When I have been horrid to you (you have never been horrid to me) it has been from unconscious jealousy (I now perceive) because I knew I could not be so important in your life as you in mine. Odious reason for odious behaviour.'

APPENDIX: NOTES TO TEXT

61. HN to RM, 24.8.1925.
62. HN to VSW, 7.9.1952.
63. HN to VSW, 23.7.1925.
64. HN to RM, 18.8.1925.
65. HN Diary, 1.10.1925.
66. HN Diary, 28.10.1925.
67. HN Diary, 3.11.1925.
68. HN to RM, 3.11.1925.

CHAPTER 12   JOURNEY TO PERSIA, 1925

1. All four letters were written on the 4th Nov. 1925.
2. HN to VSW, 6.11.1925.
3. For journey to Burg El Arab, see *Friday Mornings* (1944), p. 77.
4. Sir Ronald Storrs K.C.M.G. 1881–1955. Governor of Jerusalem and Judaea, 1920–26.
5. Sir Percy Loraine, 12th Bt., 1880–1961. Ambassador. High Commissioner for Egypt, 1929–33. Married Louise Montagu-Stuart-Wortley, 1924.
6. *The Memoirs of Lord Gladwyn*, 1972.
7. HN to VSW, 28.11.1925.
8. Edmund St. John Debonnaire John Monson, b. 1883. Promoted to Counsellor in Tehran, 1923.
9. *Under Five Shahs*, 1965, by Hassan Arfa (born 1895), the son of Prince Arfa-ed-Douleh. Commander-in-Chief 1944–46. Ambassador to Turkey 1958–63. His mother was Russian Orthodox.
10. The card-leaving convention nearly drove HN mad. He wrote to Clive Bell (1.5.1926): 'How I hate that fatuous side of my profession! It is a real torture to me and I hate seeing Vita ... confined to such nonense.'
11. HN to VSW, 24.12.1925.
12. HN to VSW, 12.12.1925.
13. HN to VSW, 14.12.1925.
14. VSW to Clive Bell, 23.11.1925.
15. HN to Clive Bell, 26.12.1925.
16. Ibid.
17. HN to Clive Bell, 16.4.1929.
18. HN to Clive Bell, 26.12.1925.
19. HN to VSW, 24.12.1925.
20. HN to Clive Bell, 29.1.1926.

CHAPTER 13   TEHRAN, 1926–1927

1. HN to VSW, 8.1.1926.
2. VW to VSW, 22.6.1926: 'They say that Dorothy Warren is engaged to Geoffrey Scott. They say she has had every sort of love.' Dorothy Warren ran the Warren Gellery for a time, and married Philip Trotter.
3. HN to VSW, 25.1.1926.
4. VW to VSW, 15.1.1926.
5. VSW to VW, 21.1.1926
6. HN to VSW, 17.12.1926.
7. The passage in *Summer*, pp. 65–6 *The Land*, beginning:-'I remember, I met two shepherds carrying an old man, dead, high on the summer Downs,' and ending, 'I stopped to gaze, since I should gaze no more ... since here was no returning,' etc. Harold evidently thought this trite. Vita did not alter it.

8. HN Diary, 1.3.1926.
9. HN to Clive Bell, 19.3.1926.
10. HN Diary, 3.2.1926.
11. HN to Clive Bell, 1.5.1926.
12. VSW – *Passenger to Teheran*, 1926.
13. HN to VSW, 26.5.1926.
14. Archibald MacLeish, b. 1892. In July HN and Gladwyn Jebb received the following poem from MacLeish:

> *Yussafabad – for G.J. and H.N.*
> And rode
> Out of the sun into all those
> And the low green over us
> Roses
> And one
> Thrush
> And the wall
> And the world's end –
> The garden
> Under the end of the world.
> And we were saying........

15. HN to VSW, 15.11.1925.
16. VSW – *Passenger to Teheran*, 1926, p. 145.
17. Ibid.
18. The future Shah, de-throned in 1979.
19. VSW – *Passenger to Teheran*, p. 149.
20. RM to VSW, 7.5.1926.
21. HN Diary, 14.5.1926.
22. Clive Bell to HN, 21.4.1926.
23. HN to Clive Bell, 17.5.1926.
24. In a review of *Some People*.
25. HN to VSW, 17.5.1926.
26. HN to VSW, 26.5.1926. Quoted, not *in toto*, by Gordon Waterfield in *Professional Diplomat: Sir Percy Loraine*, 1973.
27. HN to VSW, 31.5.1926.
28. HN to Sir L. Oliphant, 18.5.1926.
29. HN to VSW, 4.6.1926.
30. HN to Clive Bell, 17.5.1926.
31. HN to VSW, 16.6.26.
32. HN Diary, 17.6.1926.
33. HN to VSW, 1.7.1926.
34. HN to VSW, 4.7.1926.
35. Alan Charles Trott, in charge of Tehran Vice-Consulate from 31.10.1925, and Acting Oriental Secretary in 1926.
36. HN to VSW, 9.7.1926.
37. VSW to HN, 17.8.1926 (see *Portrait of a Marriage*, pp. 203–4).
38. The majority of Moslems, said to number 145 million, are the Sunni. The Shias, some 15 million, are mainly concentrated in Iran. The sacred sites of the Shia are Rajaf where Ali was buried, and Kerbela, where his son Hussein was murdered and lies in the mosque. The first ten days of the month of Muharrem are devoted to Shia mourning for the deaths of Ali, Hassan and Hussein. The faithful leave the mosques in procession, slashing themselves.
39. HN to VSW, 21.7.1926.
40. HN to VSW, 1.8.1926.
41. HN to VSW, 5.8.1926.
42. HN to Clive Bell, 11.8.1926.
43. HN to NN, 16.7.1926. (Quoted in *Portrait of a Marriage*, 1973.)

APPENDIX: NOTES TO TEXT

44. HN to VSW, 28.2.1926. Patrick Buchan-Hepburn, 1901-74. Gov-Gen The West Indies, 1958-62. Was created Lord Hailes, 1957.
45. HN to VSW, 2.9.1926.
46. HN to VSW, 4.9.1926.
47. HN to Sir Percy Loraine, 17.7.1926.
48. Docs. on Brit. For. Pol.: Series 1a, Vol. II. No. 441, dated 11.8.1926.
49. Docs. on Brit. For. Pol.: Series 1a, Vol. II. No. 442, dated 11.8.1926.
50. Docs. on Brit. For. Pol.: Series 1a. Vol. II. No. 444, dated 13.8.1926.
51. HN to Sir Percy Loraine, 28.8.1926 (partly quoted in *Professional Diplomat: Sir Percy Loraine*).
52. Docs. on Brit. For. Pol.: Series 1a Vol. II. No. 447, dated 30th September 1926.
53. HN to VSW, 4.11.1925.
54. HN to VSW, 26.7.1926.
55. HN to VSW, 11.9.1926.
56. HN to Michael Sadleir, 31.12.1926.
57. HN to Clive Bell, 11.8.1926.
58. HN to VSW, 7.11.1926.
59. HN to VSW, 14.11.1926.
60. Dated 17.11.1926.
61. HN to VSW, 10.11.1926.
62. HN Diary, 21.11.1926.
63. HN to VSW, 4.12.1926.
64. Sir Leigh Ashton. Born 1897. Educated Winchester and Balliol, Oxford. Assistant Keeper, Department of Textiles, Victoria and Albert Museum, 1925-26. Director of Victoria and Albert Museum, 1945-1955.
65. VW to VSW, 7.2.1927.
66. HN Diary, 12.3.1927.
67. Sir R. Clive to HN, 23.3.1927.

CHAPTER 14 THE BAKHTIARI AND FOREIGN OFFICE INTERVAL, 1927

1. HN Diary, 2.4.1927.
2. HN Diary, 18.5.1927.
3. Ethel Smyth, 1858-1944, composer, writer and suffragette. Created D.B.E. in 1922.
4. HN Diary, 16.6.1927.
5. HN Diary, 19.6.1927.
6. HN Diary, 22.6.1927.
7. HN to Sir Percy Loraine, 17.11.1928. (Quoted in *Professional Diplomat*).
8. VW to HN, 15.6.1927.
9. 30 October, 1927.
10. HN to VSW, 30.8.1929.
11. VW Diary, 28.6.1927.
12. HN Diary, 29.6.1927.
13. VW Diary, 30.6.1927.
14. HN to VSW, 17.7.1927.
15. *Portrait of a Marriage*, p. 211.
16. HN Diary, 15.12.1961 (unpublished).
17. Sir Walford Selby to HN, 19.5.27.
18. HN Diary, 20.8.1927.
19. HN to Owen O'Malley, 23.8.1927.
20. HN Diary, 23.8.1927.
21. VW to VSW, 15.10.1927.
22. HN Diary, 20.10.1927.

CHAPTER 15 BERLIN 1927–1928

1. Brücken Allée was badly bombed in World War II and has now totally disappeared. On the site are a number of tower blocks.
2. The Hon. Sir Ronald Lindsay, 1877–1945. A younger son of the 26th Earl of Crawford. He married as his second wife in 1924 Elizabeth Sherman, daughter of Colgate Hoyt, banker of New York. She died 1954.
3. Docs. on Brit. For. Pol.: Series 1a. Preface by M. E. Lambert.
4. *Spectator*, 23.7.1948.
5. C. Isherwood – *Goodbye to Berlin*, 1939.
6. HN to VSW, 3.11.1927.
7. The sort of tasks that engaged HN's energies during the first twelve months of his Berlin post were working out with German legal experts reciprocal exemption from income tax on shipping profits, and dealing with complaints that Britain was imposing severe tariffs on German goods imported, etc., etc.
8. Freddy and Lali Horstmann both suffered atrociously from the hands of the Russians at the end of the war. Lali's account of their experiences, *Nothing for Tears* (1953), with an introduction by HN, is one of the most moving, because least self-pitying, autobiographies.
9. HN to VSW, 27.11.1927.
10. HN to VSW, 2.12.1927.
11. VSW to HN, 8.7.1928.
12. VSW to HN, 7.11.1927.
13. HN to VSW, 6.11.1927.
14. HN to VSW, 19.12.1927.
15. HN to VSW, 23.12.1927.
16. HN to VSW, 28.12.1927.
17. HN Diary, 28.1.1928.
18. The *Times*, 31.1.1928.
19. VSW to HN, 16.5.1928.
20. HN to VSW, 13.10.1928.
21. HN to VSW, 13.2.1928.
22. HN to VSW, 11.2.1928.
23. *Spectator*, 14.1.1944.
24. HN to VSW, 15.11.1927. At a dinner party at the British Embassy Frau Stresemann advised HN to leave diplomacy, as he was clearly unsuited to it. This did not endear her to him (HN Diary, 30.1.1929).
25. HN to VSW, 1.4.1928.
26. Henry (Chips) Channon, 1897–1958, and the 6th Viscount Gage.
27. HN to NN, 10.4.1928.
28. Ivor Novello, 1893–1951, was the son of Dame Clara Novello Davies, and of Welsh birth.
29. HN to VSW, 14.4.1928.
30. HN to VSW, 16.4.1928.
31. A crush on.
32. HN to VSW, 16.5.1928.
33. With an Introduction by HN. Margaret Goldsmith was the wife of Frederick Voigt, German Jew, the author of *Combed Out*, an unforgettable war book. He was a right-wing political writer and journalist, and editor of the *Nineteenth Century and After*, 1938–1946.
34. HN to VSW, 23.6.1928.
35. HN to VSW, 28.6.1928.
36. HN to VSW, 2.7.1928.
37. HN to VSW, 3.7.1928.

APPENDIX: NOTES TO TEXT

38. Docs. on Brit. For. Pol.: Series 1a, Vol. V. Dated 4.7.1928.
39. Docs. on Brit. For. Pol.: Series 1a. Vol. V. No. 99, concerning the Reparations Recovery Act, 1928.
40. HN to Clive Bell, 13.11.1929.
41. Docs. on Brit. For. Pol.: Series 1a, Vol. V. No. 121. Charles Howard Smith to HN., dated 4.8.1928.
42. Docs. on Brit. For. Pol.: Series 1a, Vol. V. No. 131. HN to Charles Howard Smith, 14.8.1928.
43. Docs. on Brit. For. Pol.: Series 1a ,Vol. V. No. 108. Sir A. Chamberlain to HN, 26.7.1928.
44. HN to VSW, 8.7.1928.
45. Manger Strasse, 39, Potsdam.
46. HN to VSW, 26.7.1928.
47. HN to VSW, 3.8.1928.
48. HN to VSW, 7.8.1928.
49. HN to VSW, 5.11.1929.
50. HN to VSW, 11.5.1929.
51. Introduction by HN to Sir Horace Rumbold's *War Crisis in Berlin*, 2nd edition, 1944.
52. Rupert Hart-Davis – *Hugh Walpole*, 1952, p. 301.
53. VW to VSW, 14.12.1928.
54. HN to VSW, 13.12.1928.
55. VSW to HN, 22.7.1928.
56. VSW to HN, 7.8.1928.
57. HN to VSW, 8.8.1928.
58. VSW to HN, 10.8.1928.
59. Introduction by NN to *Diaries and Letters* of HN, Vol. I. p. 17.
60. HN to VSW, 2.9.1929.
61. HN to BN, 6.10.1932.
62. HN to VSW, 14.9.1928.
63. HN to VSW, 15.9.1928.
64. VSW to HN, 18.9.1928.
65. HN to VSW, 26.9.1928.
66. The Château d'Auppegard was looted and occupied during World War II by the Germans who established a launching pad for flying bombs in the garden.
67. VSW to HN, 2.10.1928.
68. VW to HN, 7.10.1928.
69. HN to VSW, 11.10.1928.
70. In December 1928 Virginia Woolf presented Vita with the manuscript of *Orlando*, also in a beautiful binding. Vita described it as 'a sort of brouillon, quite different from the finished version.'
71. VSW to HN, 12.10.1928.
72. HN to VSW, 13.10.1928.
73. VSW to HN, 15.10.1928.
74. HN Talk VII in *The Listener* on Virginia Woolf. 18.11.1931.
75. In 1922 Kathleen obtained a divorce from Henry, the 10th Earl of Drogheda, and married Guillermo de Landa y Escandon. Her son, Garrett, Viscount Moore, is now the 11th Earl of Drogheda.
76. HN to VSW, 6.10.1928.
77. HN to VSW, 8.10.1928.
78. VSW to HN, 11.10.1928.
79. Sir Oswald Mosley – *My Life*, 1968.
80. Guy Burgess to HN, undated.
81. VSW to HN, 16.11.1928.
82. The opposite of a 'down on him'.
83. HN to VSW, 19.11.1928.
84. HN to VSW, 1.12.1928.

85. HN to VSW, 28.11.1928.

86. Frau Wolff presided over Berlin's musical life. In April 1929 she organised the concert which launched Yehudi Menuhin on his distinguished career, a few days short of his thirteenth birthday. When Fritz Busch was unable to conduct at the last minute she persuaded Bruno Walter to take his place. Both Louise Wolff and Sachs, her partner, ended in one of Hitler's death-camps.

87. HN to VSW, 8.12.1928.

88. The Hon. Patrick Balfour, 1904-1976, afterwards 3rd Lord Kinross, author and expert on Turkey.

89. Christopher Sykes to JLM, 18.1.1978.

CHAPTER 16   THE END OF DIPLOMACY, 1929

1. Dated 10.4.1929.
2. Vanessa Bell to Roger Fry, 19.1.1929.
3. HN Diary, 22.1.1929. See also Leonard Woolf, *Beginning Again, 1911-1918*.
4. VW to VSW, 23.2.1929.
5. HN to VSW, 13.3.1929.
6. HN to VSW, 15.3.1929. This letter was published in the German edition of HN's *Diaries and Letters, 1969*.
7. Konrad Adenauer, 1876-1967, became German Chancellor from 1949 (re-elected 1953 and 1957) and his own Foreign Minister from 1951-55. He was the rebuilder of the new Germany after the Second World War.
8. HN to VSW, 8.4.1929.
9. R. H. Bruce Lockhart, *Retreat from Glory*, 1934, pp. 16-17.
10. HN to VSW, 10.4.1929.
11. HN to VSW, 12.4.1929.
12. HN to RM, 5.11.1926.
13. HN to VSW, 3.10.1926.
14. HN to RM, 29.12.1926.
15. HN to VSW, 12.4.1929.
16. HN to VSW, 18.4.1929.
17. HN to VSW, 7.5.1929
18. HN to VSW, 16.5.1929.
19. VSW to HN, 19.5.29.
20. HN to VSW, 8.5.1929.
21. Delivered 17.6.1929.
22. HN to Rupert Hart-Davis, 30.11.1933.
23. Docs. on Brit. For. Pol.: No. 204, Series 1a, Vol. VI., HN to Mr. Arthur Henderson, 27.6.1929.
24. Ibid, No. 208, HN to Mr. Arthur Henderson, 29.6.1929.
25. Ibid, No. 246, HN to Mr. Arthur Henderson, 19.7.1929.
26. Ibid, No. 248, HN to Mr. Arthur Henderson, 20.7.1929.
27. Ibid, No. 278, Mr. Arthur Henderson to HN, 30.7.1929.
28. Ibid, No. 281, HN to Mr. Arthur Henderson, 31.7.1929.
29. Ibid, No. 294, HN to Mr. Orme Sargent, 7.8.1929.
30. Ibid, No. 302, HN to Mr. Henderson, 9.8.1929.
31. Ibid, No. 325, Mr. Orme Sargent to NN, 20.8.1929.
32. Ibid, No. 336, HN to Mr. Orme Sargent, 23.8.1929.
33. VSW to HN, 18.7.1929.
34. HN to Bruce Lockhart, 22.7.1929.
35. VSW to HN, 24.7.1929.
36. VSW to HN, 11.8.1929.
37. Clive Bell to HN, 6.8.1929.
38. VSW to HN, 12.8.1929.

APPENDIX: NOTES TO TEXT

39. HN to VSW, 26.8.1929.
40. VW to VSW, 1.9.1929.
41. VSW to HN, 15.8.1929.
42. VSW to HN, 28.8.1929. What made Lady Sackville's behaviour worse was that she asked the boys not to repeat to their parents what she had told them.
43. HN to VSW, 29.8.1929.
44. HN to Clive Bell, 13.11.1929.
45. Inside the long, wide letter box of the front door hung a key on the end of a string. It was known to all HN's intimate friends who were welcome to enter the flat at any time when he was away.
46. VSW to HN, 18.11.1929.
47. HN to VSW, 2.11.1929.
48. HN to VSW, 22.11.1929.
49. In his (unpublished) Diary, 5.12.1929. HN recorded:

'He tells me (1) that in October 1908 he met Iswolsky [Russian Foreign Minister] at Polesden Lacy [Mrs. Ronald Greville's house near Dorking] and that the latter was so anxious for revenge against Aehrenthal [Austrian Foreign Minister] that he offered Germany anything on this earth – 'a treaty of alliance, anything you like' – if she would abandon Austria to his mercy; (2) that in 1912 Tyrrell worked hand in glove with him, and behind the back of my father, and even Grey; that Konrad von Hoetzendorff [Austria's Chief of Staff] said he wanted war as it was the only thing which could save Austria; (3) that he (Kühlmann) had worked against Metternich [German Ambassador in London preceding Lichnowsky] but not against Lichnowsky. It was the Naval Attaché who had done that; and (4) that the secret of Germany's Fleet Policy was Mahon's *Influence of Sea Power on History*, in which they were all steeped.'

50. HN to VSW, 12.12.1929.
51. HN to VSW, 13.12.1929.
52. HN to VSW, 16.12.1929.
53. HN to VSW, 17.12.1929.
54. Sir Lewis Namier called him 'the most expert and brilliant writer on diplomacy in this country,' 1939.

INDEX

INDEX

Abdul Hamid, Sultan, 4, 50
Achowra (Persian festival), 282-4
Adam, Paul, 124
Adenauer, Konrad, 363
Aehrenthal, Alois, Count von, 73-4
Albania, 79, 163, 167-8, 171, 207
Albert, Prince Consort, 9-10
Alexander, King of Greece, 154
Alexandra, Queen Consort of Edward VII, 249
Alfonso XIII, King of Spain, 25, 44-5
Algeçiras Conference, 1906, 26
Ali Khan, 305
Allenby, Field Marshal Edmund Henry Hynman, 1st Viscount, 173-4
Ambassadors' Conference, 1920-25: 207n
Amory, Copley, 269, 304
Andrew, Prince of Greece, 187-8
Annunzio, Gabriele d', 138
Arfa, Gen. Hassan, 250, 254, 272
Arfa, Hilda, 250, 272
Ashton, Sir Leigh, 299-301, 303, 309
Asquith, Elizabeth *see* Bibesco, Princess Elizabeth
Asquith, Herbert Henry, 1st Earl of Oxford and Asquith, 43, 180, 222, 241
Asquith, Margot (Emma Alice Margaret), Countess of Oxford and Asquith, 167, 180, 222, 225, 325; *Personalities*, 225
Assah Dullah, 304
Astor, William Waldorf, 64
Atchley, Shirley, 210
Athlone, Alexander Augustus Frederick William Alfred George Cambridge, 1st Earl of, 313

Atholl, John George Stewart Murray, 8th Duke of, 163
Auden, W. H., 280
Austria: and World War I, 73-4, 91; Peace Treaty, 134, 138, 151-2, 168; reparations, 163

Bagnold, Enid *see* Jones, Sir Roderick and Lady
Bailey, Cyril, 19, 30
Baird, Sandy, 366-7, 369
Baldwin, Stanley, 1st Earl, 212-13, 218, 234
Balfour, Arthur James, 1st Earl: HN meets, 41; and HN's work at Foreign Office, 85, 87, 90, 94, 100, 102; at Peace Conference, 112-13, 117-18, 134, 137-8; charm, 117; relations with HN, 117-18; leaves Foreign Office, 140; and League of Nations, 167; deputises at Foreign Office, 177
Balfour, Patrick (*later* 3rd Baron Kinross), 357
Balfour, Ronald, 166, 306
Balfour Declaration, 86
Balgonie, Lord *see* Leven, John David Leslie Melville, 12th Earl of
Balkan Wars, 56-7, 59, 63, 69, 71, 91
Balliol College, Oxford, 12, 18-31, 160
Baltazzi, Georgios, 187
Balzan, Madame, 222
Baring, Maurice, 91, 216
Barrère, Camille, 113, 184, 187, 189-91
Barrington-Kennett, V. A., 28
Bartlett, Vernon, 343
Baudelaire, Charles, 233
Beaumont, Etienne de, 124

411

HAROLD NICOLSON

Beaverbrook, William Maxwell Aitken, 1st Baron, 375–8, 380, 388
Beckmann, Max, 321
Beerbohm, Sir Max, 38, 310, 361
Behn, Aphra, 99
Bell, Dr. Johannes, 133
Bell, Clive: HN's friendship with, 166, 192–3, 200–201, 229, 314, 318; on HN's *Byron,* 216; and snobbishness, 237; correspondence with HN, 260–63, 267, 285; praises Vita, 265; praises HN's *Swinburne,* 274; and HN's Despatch on Persia, 293; and HN's *Some People,* 295, 310, 312; manner, 298; discusses HN's career, 316; and Knole, 329; letter from HN on Germany, 339–40; and Woolfs in Berlin, 360; on Woolfs in Monk's House, 378; and HN's *Evening Standard* job, 381; at HN's return home, 389
Bell, Gertrude, 247, 267
Bell, Quentin, 313, 360, 367
Bell, Vanessa, 307, 326, 349–50, 360–61, 365, 378
Bemeelmans, Clementine von (*née* Nicolson; HN's aunt), 364
Benckendorff, Constantine, Count, 223
Benedict XV, Pope, 85–6
Benn (publishers), 232
Bentinck, Charles Henry, 210
Beneš, Eduard, 111, 135–6
Benson, Rex, 222
Berenson, Bernard, 211
Berlin: HN's post in, 316–18, 320; life in, 321–2, 356, 367–8; Vita visits, 325–7
Berlin, Treaty of, 73
Berners, Gerald Hugh Tyrrwhitt-Wilson, 9th Baron ('Newt'), 41, 102, 107, 168–9, 204, 211, 335–6
Berry, Walter, 224
Bertie, Arthur Michael Cosmo (Tata), 24, 33, 38, 47
Bibesco, Prince Antoine, 123, 167
Bibesco, Princess Elizabeth (*née* Asquith), 124, 136, 167, 231, 237–9, 241
Bildt, Baron Carl ('Buggy'), 69–70
Binyon, Laurence, 204
biography: HN's views on, 318–19, 336
Birkenhead, F. E. Smith, 1st Earl of, 178, 189, 310, 334
Birrell, Francis, 208, 229, 389
Bismarck, Gottfried, 386
Bismarck, Prince Otto von, 386
Blackwood, Algernon, 166
Blanche, Jacques-Emile, 136–7
Bliss, Howard, 113
Blois, 29–30
Bloomsbury group, 201, 228–30, 235, 261, 313, 318, 365
Blücher, Princess, 386
Bompard, Maurice, 184, 187, 198
Boothby, Robert John Graham, Baron, 230, 358
Borromeo, Count Vita, 137
Bosnia, 73–4
Boswell, James, 319, 335
Bowen, Elizabeth, 230
Bowra, Sir Maurice, 345
Bracken, Brendan, 1st Viscount, 235
Bradley, Col. (District Commissioner, Egypt), 246
Brandt, Druce Robert, 37
Bratianu, Ion, 116
Briand, Aristide, 117, 159
Bridges, Robert, 267–8, 309–10
Brinton, Evelyn Elizabeth, Mrs, 124
Bristow, Ernest, 270
British Broadcasting Corporation, 343
Browning, Oscar, 35
Browning, Robert, 317–18
Buchan, John (*later* Lord Tweedsmuir), 233, 309
Buchan-Hepburn, Patrick (*later* Lord Hailes), 286–7
Budapest, 120–21
Budberg, Moura, 368
Bulgaria: in Balkan Wars, 56–7, 63; in World War I, 79, 91, 102; Peace Treaty, 134, 161; HN on crisis in,

INDEX

Bulgaria—*contd.*
167; at Lausanne Conference, 187; relations with Serbia, 226
Burgenland, 167–8
Burgess, Guy, 354
Burton, Sir Richard and Lady, 3
Butler, Sir Cyril Kendall, 120
Butler, Neville, 215
Byron, George Gordon, Lord, 180, 205–7, 209–12, 216–19, 308, 332
Byron, Robert, 251

Cadman, Sir John, 268, 301
Caird, Prof. Edward, 20
Cambon, Jules, 116, 152, 159
Cameron, Julia Margaret, 196
Campbell, Mary, 308–9, 378
Campbell, Roy, 308–9
Campbell-Gray, Ian, 231, 352
Cape, Jonathan (publishers), 232
Carlyle, Thomas and Jane Welsh, 317–18
Carnarvon, Elizabeth Catharine, Countess of, 12
Carnock, Arthur Nicolson, 1st Baron (HN's father): genealogy and career, 2, 4, 18, 24, 26–7, 38; and HN's childhood, 4; and HN's Foreign Office examination success, 38; as Permanent Under Secretary at Foreign Office, 40–41, 43; meets Vita, 64; HN's biography of, 73, 313, 354, 369, 375, 383–4; and outbreak of war, 74; Lady Sackville and, 77; retirement and peerage, 83; N's stay with, 103; and HN at Peace Conference, 116; and HN's CMG, 145; health, 201, 217, 239; and HN's posting to Tehran, 240; on HN's *Some People*, 311; and HN's future in Foreign Office, 316; and Lichnowsky, 324–5; death, 353, 358; and Germany, 383–4; wild youth, 384
Carnock, Catherine, Lady (*née* Rowan Hamilton; HN's mother): and HN's birth and childhood, 2–5; HN's love for, 5, 15, 17, 24; in Russia, 27; and Vita's affairs, 141; and HN's position in Foreign Office, 316; character, 384
Carnock, Erskine Arthur ('Eric') Nicolson, 3rd Baron (HN's elder brother), 5–6
Carnock, Frederick Nicolson, 2nd Baron (HN's eldest brother), 5–6, 9, 66, 78
Cavendish-Bentinck, Lord William, 154, 196
Cazalet, Victor, 160
Cecil, Lord Robert (*later* Lord Cecil of Chelwood), 85–6, 102, 167, 207–8
Châlet des Mélèzes (Haute Savoie), 26
Chamberlain, Sir Austen: communiqué on Greek situation, 178; and imperial policy, 226–7; Persian policy, 242, 254, 288–90; relations with HN, 261; on HN's Persia Despatch, 291, 293, 297; on Shah, 297; letter from Clive on Persia, 300; and HN's *Some People*, 310; downgrades HN, 314; weakness with Mussolini, 315–16; and Lady Sackville, 331; and Germany, 338–40, 359; Hardinge criticises, 371
Chanak, 178, 184–5
Channon, (Sir) Henry ('Chips'), 160, 231, 333
Chaplin, (Sir) Charles, 168
Chelotti, Admiral Guido, 186
Christian Victor, Prince, 194
Churchill, Lady Gwendolen ('Goonie'), 235
Churchill, Lord Ivor Spencer-, 231
Churchill, John Strange Spencer-(Jack), 235
Churchill, (Sir) Winston, 109, 161–2, 178, 180, 235
Chute, J. C., 379
Clandeboye (Irish house), 8, 18, 56
Clay, Sir Charles Travis, 22, 37
Clemenceau, Georges, 106, 112–14, 118–19, 133–5
Clerk, Sir George, 78–9, 85–7

Clive, Magdalen, Lady, 296, 298
Clive, Sir Robert (Harry), 290, 296–8, 300–302, 307
Clutton-Brock, Arthur, 38
Cocteau, Jean, 54, 56, 124, 269
Colefax, Sir Arthur, 92, 174, 241
Colefax, Sibyl, Lady, 92, 174, 225, 365
Collins, Churton, 308
Connolly, Cyril, 335–6, 341–2, 357, 365, 370–71
Constable's (publishers), 151, 176, 205, 212, 241, 294, 389
Constantine, King of Greece, 154–5, 157–8, 162, 177, 187
Constantinople, 4, 46, 49–59, 68, 70–71, 171–2, 181
Constantinople Agreement of March 18th, 1915: 253
Cooper, Lady Diana (*née* Manners), 29
Cooper, Duff (*later* 1st Viscount Norwich), 33, 294
Cooper, Col. Reginald A.: friendship with HN, 10, 24, 41, 87, 105; at Constantinople embassy, 53, 68; composes tune, 55; serves in World War I, 77, 87
Corfu Incident, 207–8
Couve de Murville, Maurice Jacques, 314
Cowan, Noel Patrick, 248, 267
Coward, Noel, 326
Cradock-Hartopp, Sir Charles, Bt., 168, 176, 209–10, 244–5
Crewe, Robert Offley Ashburton Crewe-Milnes, Marquess of, 57
Croatia, 79, 138
Crowe, Sir Eyre: at Foreign Office, 40–41, 102; and Peace Conference, 109, 112, 116–18, 134–5, 138; and League of Nations, 110; on Greek settlement, 154–5, 157–8, 160; hates Balkans, 161; at Curzon's farewell party, 214; and Ramsay MacDonald, 215, 223; and Italy, 218; and Zinoviev letter, 223; and imperial policy, 226; death, 233–4

Cunard, Maud Alice (Emerald), Lady, 92, 165, 231–2
Cunard, Victor, 107–8, 166
Curtius, Julius, 382
Curzon, Lady Alexandra ('Baba'), 231–2
Curzon of Kedleston, George Nathaniel, 1st Marquess: lackadaisical attitude on Persia, 90; HN's relations with, 117, 155, 173–4, 181, 188, 190, 195, 213, 366; as Foreign Secretary, 140, 177; and HN's CMG, 145; and Greek settlement, 155, 157–61, 175–6, 178–9; at Paris Conference, 158–9; and Albania, 163, 168; praises Vita's writings, 172, 191, 208; and Egypt, 173–4; and Poincaré, 178, 184; and Near East policy, 181; travels to Lausanne, 182–5; success at Lausanne Conference, 185–90, 194–8; temperament, 188–9; imitates Tennyson, 190; on Clare Sheridan, 192; belief in ghosts, 194; and Corfu Incident, 207–8; farewell party, 213–14; Ns' visit at Hackwood, 223; death, 231; life of, 232; posthumous works, 232; and 1919 Anglo Persian Convention, 253–4
Curzon, Grace, Marchioness, 214, 222, 231–2, 241
Cutting, Iris *see* Origo, Iris, Marchesa
Cyprus, 112
Czechoslovakia, 135–6

Dane, Clemence, 153
Dansy, Pat, 148
Daryush, Elizabeth (*née* Bridges), 267–8, 300
Davis, H. W. C., 22–3
Dawes Plan, 1924, 321
Dawson, Geoffrey, 330
de Bunsen, Sir Maurice, 44
de la Mare, Walter, 241
Denman, Thomas, 3rd Baron, 100
Derby, Edward Henry Stanley, 15th Earl of, 42

INDEX

Desborough, Ethel Anne Priscilla, Lady, 29
Deschanel, Paul, 183-4
de Valera, Eamonn, 166
Dickinson, Oswald (Ozzie), 60, 91, 140-41, 344
Dickinson, Violet, 60, 194
Dillon, D. J., 312
Dix, Otto, 321
Dodecanese islands, 214, 217-18
Draper, Ruth, 336
Dreyfus, Capt. Alfred, 7
Drinkwater, John, 166, 309
Drogheda, Garrett Moore, 11th Earl of, 66, 352-3
Drogheda, Henry Moore, 10th Earl of, 66, 87, 131
Drogheda, Kathleen, Countess of (*later* Madame de Landa), 87, 131, 352-3
Drummond, Sir Eric, 129, 138, 150, 189
Duca, Jon, 186
Dudley, Mrs Ambrose, 222
Dufferin and Ava, Frederick Temple-Hamilton Blackwood, 1st Marquess of (HN's uncle), 1, 8, 18
Dufferin and Ava, Hariot, Marchioness of (HN's Aunt Lal), 1, 18, 242
Dumas, Pasteur, 23-4
Duncan, Harold Handaside, 33, 312
Duzdap Railway, Persia, 259, 288-9

Eardley, Miss (missionary), 281
Edward VII, King, 41-2
Egypt, 173, 243-6
Einstein, Albert, 368
Eliot, T. S., 237, 256, 295, 318, 364
Elizabeth the Queen Mother (*formerly* Duchess of York), 365
Elton, E. F., 10-11
Enver Bey, 59, 69
Eton College, 336, 347-8, 379
Evans, Powys, 204
Evening Standard, 376, 381, 389

Fairbanks, Douglas, 200
Falchi, Professor, 34

Farma, Farman, 258-9
Fausset, Hugh I'Anson, 204
Feise, Frau, 349
Fels, Comte de, 159
Ferughi, Mirza Mohammed Ali Khan, 250, 262, 278
Firbank, Ronald, 24-6, 51
Firooz, Prince Mirza, 269
Fisher, H. A. L., 163, 171
Fitzgerald, Edward, 296
Fitzmaurice, G. M., 69
Fiume, 79, 137-8, 143
Flecker, James Elroy, 208-9
Fleming, Eve, Mrs., 126, 166
Foch, Marshal Ferdinand, 117, 135, 159, 184
Foreign Office: HN passes into, 38, 40-42; pre-1914 procedures and practice, 40; Vita's hostility to, 61-2, 354, 361; HN transferred to, 72; and outbreak of war, 74-6; HN's war duties with, 77-9, 85, 90, 100, 102-4; Archie Clerk Kerr transferred to, 83; pay, 139; HN in Central European and Persian Department, 154-5, 157-8, 160-63, 171, 173, 177-8; HN returns to after Lausanne, 200-201; Bloomsbury on, 201, 203; Raymond Mortimer in, 215; HN takes charge of Central Department, 220, 227; Ramsay MacDonald on laziness of, 223; HN in Western Department, 234; HN bored with, 234, 237; and Persia, 288-9, 291; critical of HN on Persia, 291, 296, 315, 339, 388; HN considers quitting, 293, 301, 307, 316, 362; downgrades HN, 314-15; and German rearmament, 340; orders HN back from Berlin, 373; on German situation, 374-5; HN leaves, 377-9; *see also* individual office holders
Forster, E. M., 229
Frachon, Baronne, 267, 275
France: and Greek settlement, 157-8; and Turkish Treaty, 197; and Ger-

France—*contd.*
    man reparations, 373; *see also* Lausanne Conference
Franco, Gen. Francisco, 45
Franz Ferdinand, Archduke of Austria, 72
Franz Joseph, Emperor of Austria, 50
Fraser, Mrs (of Newstead Abbey), 206
Fraser, Major W. A. K., 250, 258, 303
Freese, Rev. and Mrs F. E., 13–16
Froude, J. A., 317
Fry, Roger, 56, 229, 237, 293, 329–30, 360, 378
Fuad I, King of Egypt, 245–6
Furness, R. A., 245

Gage, Henry Rainald ('George'), 6th Viscount, 333
Gaigneron, Comte Jean de, 122–4, 152, 309
Gamba, Pietro, 205
Garbai, Sandor, 121
Garne (chauffeur), 303
Garroni, Marchese, 187, 189, 198
Garvin, J. L., 191
Gaselee, Stephen, 383, 385
George V, King, 74, 225, 284, 311
George VI, King (*formerly* Duke of York), 365
Germaine, Lady Betty, 378
Germany: military advisers in Turkey, 69; and outbreak of war, 74–5; and Pope's peace proposals, 86; membership of League of Nations, 130; reparations, 162, 237, 321, 359, 373–4; armaments, 221, 340, 359, 374–5, 382; relations with former enemies, 320; HN's Despatch on, 338–40; political situation in, 359, 364, 374–5; HN lectures in, 362–5; seized property, 382; and HN's biography of Lord Carnock, 383–4; *see also* Berlin
Gervais, Monsieur, 29
Gide, André, 124
Goethe, J. W. von, 16, 362

Goldsmith, Margaret, 336
Goschen, Sir Edward, 75
Gosford, Mildred, Countess of, 341
Gosse, Sir Edmund: Victorian reminiscences, 92, 228–9, 317–18; reviews HN's *Verlaine*, 164; reviews Margot Asquith, 180; reviews HN's *Tennyson*, 204; reviews HN's *Byron*, 216; on Swinburne, 227–8; at HN's lecture, 233; despised by Bloomsbury, 228–9; and HN's posting to Persia, 241; reviews HN's *Swinburne*, 274; HN meets on return from Persia, 307–8; anecdotes, 308; HN visits, 317; death, 318; praises HN's *Biography*, 319; HN's obituary of, 336; parodied by Virginia Woolf, 350; *Father and Son*, 317
Gosset, Col. F. W., 374–5
Gounaris, D., 162, 176, 187, 189
Graham, Sir Ronald, Bt., 316
Grange, The (Folkestone prep. school), 6–8
Grant, Sir Alexander, Bt., 220
Grant, Duncan, 201–2, 228–9, 326, 349, 360–61, 378, 382
Greece: in Balkan Wars, 56, 63; neutrality in World War I, 79; HN's love for, 111–12; and peace settlements, 112, 118, 135, 137–8, 154–5, 157–62, 186–7; war with Turkey, 160–62, 175–8, 189, 194–5; and Lausanne Conference, 186–7, 189, 194–5; and Corfu Incident, 207; and Italian settlement, 214; relations with Serbia, 226
Grenfell, Julian, 28
Greville, Mrs Ronald, 92
Grey, Sir Edward (*later* Viscount Grey of Fallodon), 41, 69, 74–5, 324–5
Groener, Lt.-Gen. Wilhelm, 340
Grosvenor, Mrs Algernon, 43
Grosvenor, Rosamund, 43–4, 48, 52–7, 60–63, 66–7, 72
Grosz, George, 321
Guiccioli, Teresa, Countess, 211, 216

INDEX

Gulahek (Persia), 252, 293–5

Hackwood (house), 222
Haig, Field-Marshal Douglas, 1st Earl, 107, 135
Hall, Radclyffe, 354
Hamilton, Catherine Ann (*née* Caldwell; HN's grandmother), 8
Hammann (German artist), 380
Hancock (Balliol head porter), 19
Hancock, Charles, 210
Hankey, Sir Maurice, 109, 118
Hardinge of Penshurst, Charles, 1st Baron: interviews HN, 33; as Permanent Under-Secretary at Foreign Office, 40; 83, 86–7; and HN's draft on Pope's peace proposals, 86; at Peace Conference, 111, 117, 121; invites HN to be private secretary, 129; on Greek settlement, 158; in Paris, 183; visits Berlin, 371; on Lord Carnock, 384
Hardy, Thomas, 285
Harington, Gen. Sir Charles, 178–9
Harris, Robert, 343
Hart-Davis, Sir Rupert, 372
Hartopp, Sir Charles *see* Cradock-Hartopp, Sir Charles
Hastings, Frank Abney, 210
Havard, Godfrey, 250
Hawthornden Prize, 309
Haxton, Gerald, 365
Heard, Gerald, 280
Hénaut, Jeanne de, 28, 33, 37, 294
Henderson, Arthur, 371, 373–4
Henderson, Sir Nevile, 32, 277
Herbert, Sir Alan P., 7
Herbert, Aubrey, 19, 163
Herbert, David, 369–71, 373, 380
Herbert, Mervyn, 19
Hermitte (Poincaré's secretary), 184
Herzegovina, 73–4
Hesse, Philip, Prince of, 169
Heywood, Col. (Military Intelligence), 120
Hichens, Robert, 190
Hindenburg, Field-Marshal Paul von, 321, 336–8, 359
Hismet-ed-Douleh, 255
Hitler, Adolf, 200, 321, 339, 359, 364, 375
Hogarth Press, 294, 318, 378
Holroyd, Michael, 202
Hoover, Herbert, 113
Horder, Thomas Jeeves, 1st Baron, 328
Horne, Sir Robert, 178
Horner, Jack, 28
Horstmann, Freddy, 323, 334, 385
Horstmann, Lali, 323, 335, 385
Houghton, Richard Monckton Milnes, 1st Baron, 308
House, Col. Edward M., 106
Howell, Charles Augustus, 227
Hudson, Nan, 349
Hugo, Victor, 233
Hungary, 119–21, 134, 168
Hunter, Mrs. Charles, 61
Hussey (headmaster of The Grange), 6–7
Huxley, Aldous, 174, 280
Huxley, T. H., 317
Hyde, Francis, 48

Ingram, Maurice, 320
Ireland, 8–9
Isherwood, Christopher, 280, 321
Islington, Anne, Lady, 165
Ismet Pasha, Gen., 185, 188–9, 195–8
Iswolsky, Alexander, 35
Italy: war with Turkey (1911), 50, 56; in World War I, 79, 91; and peace settlement, 137, 143, 177; and Albania, 168; and Lausanne Conference, 185, 188–9; on Dodecanese and Jubaland, 214, 217–18

James, Mrs. Arthur, 367
James, Henry, 41
Japan, 112, 134
Jebb, Gladwyn (*later* 1st Baron Gladwyn): in Tehran, 240, 250–51, 258, 260, 262, 276, 281, 285, 287; and

417

Vita in Persia, 267-8, 270; and HN's *Some People*, 294, 304; on Bakhtiari expedition, 303-4; visits Long Barn, 309; visits Berlin, 335-6
Jebb, Margery, 303-4
Joffre, Marshal Joseph, 135
John, Augustus, 166, 309
Jones, Sir Lawrence Evelyn, Bt., 20, 23
Jones, Sir Roderick and Lady (Enid Bagnold), 153
Jonescu, Také, 110
Jubaland, 214, 217-18
Jullian, Philippe, 123

Kalogeropoulos, Nikolaos, 162
Karl, Emperor of Austria, 91
Kellogg Pact, 338
Kemal (Ataturk), Gen. Mustafa, 150, 154, 158-9, 162, 176-9, 186, 192, 254
Kempthorne, Rev. P. H., 10, 13
Keppel, Col. George, 148
Keppel, Mrs George, 92, 105, 148
Keppel, Violet *see* Trefusis, Violet
Kerr, Archibald John Clark, 1st Lord Inverchapel, 42, 44, 53, 63-4, 83, 87, 230
Keynes, John Maynard, 1st Baron, 130, 133, 202, 229-30, 334-5
Khazal of Mohammerah, Sheikh, 255, 259, 279-80, 290
King-Hall, Stephen, 343
Kinross, John Patrick Balfour, 3rd Baron *see* Balfour, John Patrick
Kitchener, Horatio Herbert, 1st Earl, 67, 194
Knatchbull-Hugessen, Sir Hughe Montgomery, 24, 28
Knoblock, Edward, 105, 110, 168, 379-80
Knole: and Sackville case, 41; HN visits, 43, 46; Vita's love for, 53, 328-9, 344; Vita writes on, 172; Virginia Woolf on, 219; and death of Lord Sackville, 328-9; transferred to National Trust, 329; in Virginia Woolf's *Orlando*, 351
Knopf (chauffeur), 347, 352
Knox, Ronald, Rev., 28
Köhn, Hünefeld and Fitzmaurice (fliers), 336
Krautz, Eugénie, 164
Kühlmann, Baron Richard von, 75, 334, 385
Kun, Bela, 119-21

Lacretelle, Pierre de, 54-6, 58, 61, 190, 197-8
Lampson, Miles, 220, 240
Landa, Kathleen de *see* Drogheda, Kathleen, Countess of
Lansing, Robert, 112
Laroche (French Foreign Office), 184
Lascelles, Sir Alan Frederick ('Tommy'), 41, 208
Lascelles, Sir Daniel William, 341, 353-4, 358, 369
Lascelles, Henry George Charles, Viscount, 65, 174, 326, 350
Lausanne Conference, 81; Lacretelle at, 54; and Greek-Turkish settlement, 154, 157; Treaty of, 154; HN attends, 179, 182-6; opened, 185; importance of, 186; Vita visits, 196
Lavery, Hazel, Lady, 140, 165
Law, Andrew Bonar, 180, 190, 194
Lawrence, T. E., 117
League of Nations: constitution, 110, 115; Wilson's faith in, 115; HN works with, 129, 138-40, 149, 171; German membership of, 130; and US rejection of Peace Treaty, 134; Covenant, 140; Smuts and, 166-7; and Corfu Incident, 207-8; and arbitration, 220; and German rearmament, 340
Le Corbusier (i.e. Charles Edouard Jeanneret-Gris), 314
Leeper, Allen: at Peace Conference, 109; on Smuts mission, 119-20; as Curzon's secretary, 156, 173, 193;

INDEX

Leeper, Allen—*contd.*
marriage, 165; and Lausanne 182, 184, 187, 190; relaxation at Lausanne, 191; visits Berlin, 335

Leeper, Janet (*née* Hamilton), 165, 335

Lenin, V. I., 200

Leven, John David Leslie Melville, 12th Earl of (*formerly* Lord Balgonie), 33

Lewis (drawing teacher), 15

Lewis, Sinclair, 331–2, 336

Lichnowsky, Prince Karl Maximilian, 75–6, 324–5

Liman von Sanders, Gen. Otto K. V., 159

Lindemann, Prof. Frederick Alexander (*later* 1st Viscount Cherwell), 235

Lindsay, Sir Ronald: as Ambassador in Berlin, 320–21; and Lady Sackville, 331; leaves Berlin, 336–7; on German rearmament, 340, 374; friendship with HN, 358; memorandum on German military situation, 359; and HN's career, 371, 378, 380; approves HN's biography of Carnock, 383

Lindsay, Elizabeth S., Lady, 331, 358

Lister, Charles, 28, 77

Lister, E. G. (Ted), 102

Lloyd, George, 1st Baron (of Dolobran), and Lady, 244–6

Lloyd George, David, 1st Earl: and Armistice, 104; and Peace Conference, 106, 112–13, 115–16, 118–19, 130, 134; at signing of Versailles Treaty, 133; and Turks, 150; at Paris Conference, 159, 161–2; and Smyrna, 160; criticises Foreign Office under Curzon, 173; and Italy, 177; Curzon denounces, 189

Lockhart, Robert Bruce, 365–6, 375–8

London: houses in, 82, 103, 172, 226, 381–2, 389

London, Treaty of, 1913: 59, 63

London, Treaty of, 1915: 79, 114

Londonderry, Charles Stewart Henry Vane-Tempest-Stewart, 7th Marquess of, 366

Long Barn (Kent house): Ns' purchase, 79–82; Ns' entertain at, 91, 165–6, 309, 336; Vita purchases land at, 136; extensions to, 153, 157, 314; life at, 172–3

Longden, Bobby, 341

Lopokova, Lydia (Keynes' wife), 334

Loraine, Louise, Lady, 249–50, 267, 270, 276

Loraine, Sir Percy, Bt.: as Ambassador in Tehran, 240–42, 249, 254–5, 259, 262, 266; relations with Shah, 254, 259, 266, 287, 297–8; and Vita in Persia, 267, 270; and Shah's coronation, 271; and Vita's journey home, 273; in wife's absence, 276; leaves Tehran, 277, 279–80; HN consults, 287–90; and HN's Despatch on Persia, 293, 315; memorandum on Persia, 297; on HN's *Some People*, 310

Lovelace, Jane, Countess, 205

Lowndes, Marie Adelaide Belloc-, 98

Lowther, Sir Gerard, 49, 52, 60, 69

Lowther, Dorothy Olga, Lady, 53, 56–7

Luber, Frau, 385

Ludwig, Emil, 323–4, 356–7

Lutyens, Sir Edwin, 81, 87, 91, 140, 212, 233, 314

MacCarthy, Sir Desmond, 212, 216, 389

MacDonald, Ramsay: HN's relations with, 206, 220, 223; as Prime Minister, 214–15, 220–21; and foreign affairs, 215–17; motor car, 220; fall, 223; on Crowe and Zinoviev letter, 223, 234; and Knole, 330; in Berlin, 353; Leonard Woolf on, 361; and German reparations, 373

McKenna, Stephen, 171

MacLaren, Christabel, 242

MacLeish, Archibald, 235, 269

McNeill, Ronald (*later* Lord Cushendun), 214

Madrid, 44-5
Mahmoud Shevket Pasha, 59
Mahommed Ali, Shah, 253
Malcolm, Sir Ian, 232
Mallet, Sir Louis, 60, 68-9
Mann, Harrington, 66
Mann, Thomas, 364
Manners, Lady Diana *see* Cooper, Lady Diana
Mantoux, Etienne, 141
Margerie, Roland and Jennie de, 340
Marie, Queen of Roumania, 117
marriage: N's broadcast on, 372
Marsh, Sir Edward, 160, 176, 209, 334
Martin, Henry, 26
Mary, Queen consort of George V, 225
Mary, Princess (Viscountess Lascelles), 174
Masaryk, Thomas, 121
Massigli, René, 314
Matheson, Hilda, 343-4, 375
Mathias, Mrs. Robert, 174
Maugham, W. Somerset, 365
Mauriac, François, 314
Mayne, Ethel, 205
Mazzuchi family, 34
Mehmed V, Sultan, 50
Melas, Leon, 178
Mendelsohn, Erich, 314, 324, 385
Mendelsohn, Francesco von, 352-3, 385, 387
Menken, Ada Isaacs, 227-8
Metcalfe, Major E. D. ('Fruity'), 231
Midleton, St John Brodrick, 1st Earl of, 180
Millar, Gertie, 142-3
Millspaugh, Dr. A. C., 266, 290
Minderop, Conrad ('Cornèle Medderup'), 355
Modanes (Mullah), 297
Mohammed Reza Shah Pahlavi, Valiadh, 271-2
Mohammerah, Sheikh Khazal of *see* Khazal of Mohammerah, Sheikh
Molyneux, Edward, 139, 365

Monson, Edmund St John Debonnaire John, 252
Montagu, Edwin, 111
Montagu, Margaret (*later* Countess of Kimberley), 166, 176
Montenegro, 56-7
Moore, Garrett, Viscount *see* Drogheda, Garrett Moore, 11th Earl of
Moore, George, 163-4
Morgan, Evan, 181
Morocco, 5
Morrell, Lady Ottoline, 235
Mortimer, Raymond: on HN's *Verlaine*, 164; relations with HN, 215-16, 229, 234-7, 239, 307, 309, 314, 336; intellectual rigour, 234; and HN's departure for Persia, 240-44; corresponds with HN, 260-1; criticisms of HN's style, 262, 277-8, 294; visits Persia, 269, 272, 276; and N's separations, 273; on HN's *Swinburne*, 274; criticises HN's imperialism, 279; leaves Persia, 281; manner, 298; on intellectual greatness, 314; and HN's position at Foreign Office, 316; visits Germany, 331, 341, 365; values and ideals, 342; and HN's views on homosexuality, 367; and HN's *Evening Standard* offer, 377; at HN's return home, 389
Moshai (Persian Prime Minister), 288
Mosley, Lady Cynthia (Cimmie), 232
Mosley, Sir Oswald, Bt., 206, 336, 353, 371, 388
Mostaufi-al-Mamallek, 278, 290
Mosul, vilayet of, 199
Mudania, 178-9, 192
Müller, Dr. Hermann, 133, 338, 359, 370, 385
Murat, Princess, 124
Mussolini, Benito, 184-5, 200, 207, 217-18, 315

Nabokov, Vladimir, 313
Nairn brothers, 246-7
Nash's Magazine, 333, 336

INDEX

Nasr-ed-Din, Shah, 268
Nazim Pasha, 59
Nellidoff (Russian friend), 41, 78
New Statesman, 234
Newstead Abbey, 206
Nichol, John, 227
Nicholas II, Czar of Russia, 74
Nicolson, Sir Arthur *see* Carnock, A. Nicolson, 1st Baron
Nicolson, Benedict (HN's elder son): born, 76-77; name, 77, 85; and mother's absence, 126-7; at school, 209, 213, 223, 309; first visit to Italy, 233; character, 239; and HN in Persia, 241, 307; and death of Lord Sackville, 328; at Eton, 336, 347-8, 379; and mother, 344-5, 348; visits Germany, 345, 347, 358, 360; HN lectures about Eton, 347-8; and Lady Sackville, 379-80
Nicolson, Catherine, Lady *see* Carnock, Catherine, Lady
Nicolson, 'Eric' *see* Carnock, Erskine Arthur, 3rd Baron
Nicolson, Sir Frederick, Bt. (HN's grandfather), 2
Nicolson, Frederick (HN's brother) *see* Carnock, F. Nicolson, 2nd Baron
Nicolson, Gwen (HN's sister) Mrs. St. Aubyn, *see* St. Levan, Gwen, Lady
Nicolson, Sir Harold George: birth, 1-2; earliest memories, 2-4; love for mother, 5, 15, 17, 24; at prep school, 6-8; reading, 7, 17, 285; at Wellington, 9-13, 26; at Balliol, 12-13, 18-31; in Weimar, 13-14, 16, 385-6; drawing, 15-16; snobbishness, 20-21; appearance, 24, 38, 145, 299; at Paris crammer, 28-9; degree, 30; language studies and travels, 32-8; clubs, 34, 82, 164, 168; passes Foreign Office examination, 38; early relations with Vita, 43-5; as Attaché in Madrid, 44-5; contracts gonorrhoea, 45; in Constantinople, 46, 49-53, 56-7, 59; courtship and engagement, 46, 48-9, 52-3, 55-6, 60-64; sexual proclivities, 46, 54, 58, 215, 367-8; and Lady Sackville, 47, 51-2, 56, 77, 85, 129, 307, 330, 379; and Lacretelle, 54-6, 58, 61, 190; wedding, 66-7; Foreign Office service during War, 72, 74-7, 87, 90, 94, 102-4; and outbreak of war, 75-6; and Pope's peace proposals, 85-6; helps draft Balfour Declaration, 86; and Violet Trefusis, 88-9, 94, 98, 100-101, 104, 106-7, 110-11, 124-8, 141, 145-6, 224; marriage relationship, 89, 94, 97, 100-101, 106-7, 125-7, 129-32, 136, 141-6, 149-50, 157, 159, 209, 320; conversation, 92; writing, 99, 151, 163, 165, 176-7; 'indispensable' to Foreign Office, 100; and Victor Cunard, 107; at Peace Conference, 106, 108-18, 122, 126, 129-30, 134-8, 151; salary, 111, 139; regularly reads classics, 111, 245, 285; on Smuts mission to Central Europe, 119-21; and Gaigneron, 122-4, 152; and League of Nations, 129; and Versailles Treaty, 133; work with League of Nations, 138-40, 149, 171; finances, 139, 200, 204, 377; and Molyneux, 139; relations with sons, 142, 157, 209, 213, 223, 241, 285, 307, 345; awarded CMG, 145; and Vita's elopement, 148-9; character, 152; at Paris Conference, 158-61; offered Serbian honour, 160; Stern's caricature of, 172; at Lausanne Conference, 179, 183-9; drafts Near East policy statement, 181; typing, 197; social life, 200-201, 225-6; sensibilities, 201; and Bloomsbury, 201-2; and broadcasting, 205-6, 343, 352, 369, 371; and Geoffrey Scott, 211; self-depreciation, 215, 312; university doctorate, 219; makes will, 219; Rothenstein drawing of, 224; memorandum on security, 226-7, 231; hypochondria, 230; Campbell-Gray portrait

421

Nicolson, Sir Harold George—*contd.*
of, 231; lectures, 233, 332, 362–5, 386; and Raymond Mortimer, 235–7, 239, 269, 272–3, 277–8, 281, 307, 365; at Tehran embassy, 239–44, 247; learns Persian, 260, 264, 296; wins RSL's Benson medal, 278; pet dogs, 278, 281, 298, 331, 354; patriotism, 279–80; as Chargé d'Affaires in Tehran, 280–82, 285, 287–90, 295; superstition, 284; and Buchan-Hepburn, 287; Loraine's assessment of, 290; Despatch on Persia, 290–91, 293, 297, 300, 315, 339, 388; contemplates leaving Foreign Office, 293, 301, 307, 316, 354, 362; reads modern poetry, 295; health, 300; returns from Persia, 307; on architecture, 314, 324; downgraded by Foreign Office, 314–16; Berlin post, 316–18, 320; manner, 323; attitude to Jews, 323–4, 356–7; and Ivor Novello, 334–5; regains rank as Counsellor, 336; as Chargé d'Affaires in Berlin, 337–8, 348, 382, 388; Despatches on Germany, 338–40; in Virginia Woolf's *Orlando*, 350; and father's death, 353–4, 358; lecture tour in Germany, 362–5; Lockhart on, 366; and Sandy Baird, 366–7, 369; views on marriage, 371–2; returns from Berlin, 372–3; offered post on *Evening Standard*, 376–7, 380; socialism, 376–7; as MP, 377; life mask, 380; joins *Evening Standard*, 381, 389; flying, 385; lectures in Berlin, 386; quits Berlin and Diplomatic Service, 387–9

WORKS: *The Age of Reason*, 151; *Byron: the Last Journey*, 206, 212, 216–17; *Curzon: the Last Phase*, 186; *The Desire to Please*, 8; *The Development of English Biography*, 318–19; *Helen's Tower*, 8; *King George V*, 313; *Lord Carnock*, 73, 313, 354, 369, 375, 383–5, 389; *Paul Verlaine*, 150–51, 163–5; *Peabody*, 348; *Peacemaking*, 71, 110, 114, 123, 132; *Public Faces*, 336; *Some People*, 33, 51, 54, 122, 182, 193, 229, 244, 294, 304, 310–13, 335, 365; *Sweet Waters*, 71, 166–7, 171–2; *Swinburne*, 220, 223, 233, 274; *Tennyson*, 172, 176–7, 180, 187, 191, 196, 202–5, 213

Nicolson, Mary, Lady (*née* Loch; HN's grandmother), 2

Nicolson, Nigel (HN's younger son): as wartime Major, 21; born, 83; foreword to Vita's *Challenge*, 98; at Knole, 224; and HN's posting to Persia, 241; HN writes to, on Vita, 286; and HN's return from Persia, 307; at school, 309; tutored by Couve de Murville, 314; spots, 333–4; and mother, 344; visits Germany, 345, 347, 358, 360; and Lady Sackville, 379–80; *Portrait of a Marriage*, 90, 93, 147, 149

Norman, Herman, 254
Novello, Ivor, 160, 334–5

O'Dwyer, J. C., 263
Offranville, 136–7
Oliphant, Sir Lancelot: with HN at Foreign Office, 75, 85–7, 90; and HN at Lausanne, 179, 188; and HN's Tehran posting, 240, 266, 280, 302; and Loraine's report on HN, 290; and HN's Despatch on Persia, 291, 293; Persian memorandum to Clive, 297; and HN's return from Persia, 307; and HN's Berlin posting, 317
O'Malley, Owen, 315–16
Omar Khayyam, 296
Orde, Eileen *see* Wellesley, Lady Eileen
Origo, Marchese A., 211
Origo, Dame (Marchesa) Iris (*née* Cutting), 211
Orlandi, Don, 37
Orlando, V. E. M., 112
Osborne, (Sir) Darcy, 160
O'Shea, Katharine, 8

INDEX

Ottoman Empire, 50, 69; *see also* Turkey
Ouchy, Treaty of, 1911, 50, 56
Oxford, 12-13, 18-31

Painter, George D., 123
Pansa, Mario, 192
Paris, 23, 28-9
Paris Conference, 1921: 158-60, 194
Parsons, J. R., 312
Patiala, Maharaja of, 338
Peace Conference, 1919: and Treaty of London promises, 79; HN attends, 106, 108-18, 122, 126, 129-30, 134-6; terms and outcome, 109, 114-15, 121, 129-30, 132-3; composition of, 112; HN describes, 114; ends, 151
Pearson, Mrs. Harold, 43
Pemberton, R. O. W., 28, 34
Percy, Lord Eustace, 33, 37-8
Perkins, O. T., 13
Perowne, Victor, 340
Persia: HN's memoranda on, 90-91; Bolsheviks invade, 150; British relations with, 252-5, 280, 287-90, 297-8, 300; Constituent Assembly meeting described, 256-8; Vita visits, 258, 264-70, 300-301, 303-5; HN on situation in, 266, 280, 287, 297; crown jewels, 271; and Russia, 288-9, 290-91, 297; HN's Despatch on, 290-91, 293, 297, 300, 315, 339, 388; increasing nationalism in, 297-8, 300; HN leaves, 307
Peto, Ruby, 127
Phillips, Mrs. (of Weimar), 14
Pichon, Stephen, 112-13
Pickford, Mary, 200
Pinsent, Walter, 211
Pius XII (Eugenio Pacelli), Pope, 337, 339
Plastiras, Gen. Nikolaos, 187
Plessen, Leopold, 385
Poincaré, Raymond: opens Peace Conference, 114; relations with Curzon, 178, 183; and Turkish settlement, 178-9; and Curzon's Near East policy, 181; qualities, 183; and Lausanne Conference, 183-5, 197-8; and occupation of Ruhr, 194; and Turkish Treaty, 197-8; and League of Nations, 207-8; and Anglo-French relations, 215; and German reparations, 373
Poland, 135
Polidori, Miss, 308
Polidori, John William, 308
Polk, F. L., 137
Pollock, Rev. Bertram (*later* Bishop of Norwich), 10-11, 13, 18, 23, 155
Ponsonby, Sir Arthur (*later* 1st Baron), 214-15, 218
Pope, Alexander, 212
Portheim, Cohen, 355
Poulett, George Amias Fitzwarrine, 8th Earl, 341
Preston, Stuart, 311
Proust, Marcel, 122-4, 364

Quiller-Couch, Sir Arthur, 319

Raikes, Reggie, 61
Rawnsley, W. F., 204
Ravel, Maurice, 200
Reading, Rufus Daniel Isaacs, 1st Marquess of, 116
Reith, Sir John (*later* 1st Baron), 343
Reparations Conference, 373-4
Reza Pahlavi, Shah: on throne, 254-9; HN meets, 259, 262, 276-7, 289; rule, 266, 280, 287-8, 301; coronation, 270-72; and Loraine's departure, 279; at functions, 282; and Russia, 288; and Baluchi advance, 289; HN on, 289-91; receives Clive, 297; unpredictability, 297, 300
Rhineland, 321, 359, 373, 375
Ribblesdale, Ava, Lady, 235
Richardson, Gladys Stuart, 210
Rimbaud, Arthur, 191
Ritchie, Philip, 229

423

Riza Nur Bey, 195–6, 198
Roberts of Kandahar, Field-Marshal Frederick Sleigh, 1st Earl, 13
Rodd, Sir Rennell, Bt. (*later* 1st Lord Rennell), 86, 102
Rodin, Auguste, 64–5
Ronaldshay, Lawrence John Lumley Dundas, Earl of (*later* Marquess of Zetland), 232–3
Rose, Kenneth, 363
Ross, Mrs., 211
Ross, Robert, 38, 87
Rossetti, Dante Gabriel, 227–8, 317
Rothenstein, Sir William, 164, 224
Roumania, 63, 106, 114, 119–20
Rowan Hamilton, Blanche, 23, 241
Rowan Hamilton, Frederick Temple, 23, 241
Royal Society of Literature, 278
Rubens, Olive: and Lord Sackville, 46–7, 63, 107, 136, 213; at Vita's wedding, 66; visits Ns in Constantinople, 69; and Vita's absence from children, 126; and death of Lord Sackville, 328, 330; Lady Sackville on, 379
Rubens, Walter, 46, 56, 66, 107
Ruhr, 340
Rumbold, Etheldred, Lady, 342–3
Rumbold, Sir Horace, Bt.: at 2nd Lausanne Conference, 198; as Ambassador in Berlin, 342–3, 354, 348, 359; and HN's lecture tour, 365; and HN's Beaverbrook job, 380; holiday, 382, 385; speech at HN's departure, 387; and HN's career, 388
Ruskin, John, 233
Russell, Bertrand, 229
Russia: Carnock in, 26–7, 38; HN on, 35–6; 1914 mobilisation, 74; in World War I, 91; 1920 Commission to, 149; and Turkey, 181; and Lausanne Conference, 185, 188; and Persia, 253, 266, 287–8, 290–91, 297; Keynes on, 334–5
Rylands, George (Dadie), 228–9

Saar, 373–4
Sackville, Edward, 5th Baron (*formerly* Sackville-West): and Knole, 53, 328–9; HN entertains, 160; HN's friendship with, 229, 309, 313, 353–4, 378; in Berlin, 327, 332, 352–5, 360–61; on Cyril Connolly, 335; character, 355–6; and HN's *Evening Standard* offer, 377; *Mandrake over the Water-Carrier*, 348–9; *The Ruin*, 293; *Simpson*, 356; *Sinfonia Eroica*, 309
Sackville, Lionel, 3rd Baron (Vita's father), 43; and Olive Rubens, 46–7, 63, 107, 136, 213; and Vita's engagement, 48–9; visits Ns in Constantinople, 69; war service, 83; and Vita-Violet Trefusis relationship, 105, 126–8; relations with HN, 107, 126; marriage relations, 107–8, 136; Virginia Woolf on, 219; illness and death, 328–31, 358
Sackville, Victoria, Lady (*née* Sackville-West; Vita's mother): 1910 court case, 41; HN meets, 43; marriage relations, 47, 107–8, 136; relations with HN, 47, 51–2, 56, 77, 85, 129, 307, 330, 379; and Vita's engagement, 48–9, 56, 61, 63–5; and Scott case, 52, 62–3; trip to Interlaken, 64; misses Vita's wedding, 66; and Bildt, 69–70; and Benedict's name, 77, 85; and Lutyens, 81; and Strang portrait of Vita, 99; and Vita's relations with Violet Trefusis, 105, 127, 140–41; trip to Paris, 143, 145; and Vita's elopement, 148; in HN's writing, 172; health, 239, 243, 282; and HN's return from Persia, 307; and Lord Sackville's death, 328, 330; malicious behaviour, 330–31, 344, 358, 379; furniture in Berlin, 373; and grandsons, 379–80; eye trouble, 385; attempts at reconciliation, 385
Sackville-West, Charles (*later* 4th Baron Sackville), 53, 56, 113, 328–9

INDEX

Sackville-West, Maud Cecilia (*née* Bell; wife of above), 56

Sackville-West, Victoria (Vita; Lady Nicolson): snobbishness, 21; HN meets, 43–5; and Rosamund Grosvenor, 44, 48, 52–3, 55–7, 61–2, 66–7, 72; courtship and engagement, 46, 48–9, 52–3, 55–6, 60–64; sexual proclivities, 46, 57–8, 89–90, 93; relations with father, 47; and Violet Trefusis, 52–3, 63, 88–90, 92–3, 97–105, 122, 124–5, 130–32, 136, 139–45, 147, 153–4, 159–60, 192, 224; and Knole, 53, 60, 328–9, 351; trip to Spain, 61–2; and Scott case, 63; marriage settlement, 64, 377; wedding, 66–7; first gardening in Constantinople, 68; pregnancies, 68, 72, 75, 82; birth of sons, 76–7, 83; marriage relationship, 89, 94, 97, 101, 106–7, 125–7, 129–32, 136, 141–6, 149–50, 157, 159, 162, 209, 320; Strang portrait of, 99; transvestism, 105, 125; neglects children, 106, 126; elopement with Violet, 147–9; confessions, 153–4, 162; poetry, 157, 309; and Geoffrey Scott, 170, 206, 211, 264, 379; meets Virginia Woolf, 192–3; praises Virginia, 196; relations with Virginia, 221–2, 264–5, 350, 361; and Walter Berry, 224; and Dorothy Wellesley, 237–8; and HN's posting to Persia, 239–43, 251–2; visits Persia, 258, 264–70; love affair with Virginia, 265–6, 299; and Shah's coronation, 270–72; HN writes on in *Atalanta*, 294; second trip to Persia, 300–301, 303–5; and Mary Campbell, 308–9; receives Hawthornden Prize, 309; visits Berlin, 325–7, 360; and Virginia's *Orlando*, 325–6; and father's death, 328–9; difficulties with mother, 330–31, 344, 358, 377, 379; lectures, 332; broadcasts, 343, 371; and Hilda Matheson, 343–4, 375; relation with sons, 344–5, 348; tours France with Virginia, 348–50; diffidence, 350; hostility to Foreign Office, 354, 356, 387–8; and HN's *Evening Standard* offer, 376–8; love poems to Mary Campbell, 378–9; furnishes King's Bench Walk flat, 381–2, 389

WORKS: *Aphra Behn*, 326; *Challenge*, 68, 98–9, 139, 142–3; *The Dragon in Shallow Waters*, 147, 150, 152–4, 157, 166, 172; *Grey Wethers*, 196, 208; *The Heir*, 176, 191; *Heritage*, 80, 105, 128; *King's Daughter*, 379; *Knole and the Sackvilles*, 172, 176–7, 190–91; *The Land*, 166–7, 211, 223, 265–6, 295, 309; *Passenger to Teheran*, 247, 269, 293; *Pepita*, 62; *Poems of East and West*, 83; *Seducers in Ecuador*, 220–21, 267; *Twelve Days*, 303, 345

Sadleir, Michael, 151, 164, 166

St. James's Club, London, 34, 82, 168, 205

St. Levan, Gwen, Lady (*née* Nicolson; HN's sister), 16, 36, 66, 336

St Petersburg (Leningrad), 26–7, 32, 35, 38

Salar-ed-Dowleh, 288

Salis, John Francis Charles, Count de, 86

Salisbury, Cicely Alice, Marchioness of, 222

Sands, Ethel, 201, 349, 389

San Faustino, Princess Jane, 169

Sarda Zaffer, Dekhani, 306

Sargent, John Singer, 41

Sargent, Orme, 374

Sasonow, Sergei, 69

Sassoon, Siegfried, 170

Scanlon, Miss (Australian journalist), 335

Schubert, Carl von, 373–4, 387

Scott, Geoffrey: relations with Vita, 170, 207, 209–11, 214, 219, 230, 238–9, 264; HN's attitude to, 238–9; and HN's departure for Persia, 242; death, 379; *The Portrait of Zélide*, 211, 230

425

Scott, Sir John Murray ('Seery'), 47-8, 51-3, 62-3
Scott, Lady Sybil, 211
Scott-James, Anne, 80
Seeckt, Gen. Hans von, 340
Selby, Walford, 215, 239-40, 314-16
Selfridge, Gordon, 172, 223
Senhouse, Roger, 229
Serbia: in Balkan Wars, 56-7, 63; and World War I, 73-4, 78-9, 86; and Peace settlement, 138; offers honour to HN, 160; advance into Albania, 171; relations with Greece, 226
Sèvres, Treaty of, 154-9, 186, 188
Shah, Muhammas, 252
Shanks, Edward, 204, 274
Sharpe, Bobby, 327
Shaw-Stewart, Patrick, 29
Sheean, Vincent (Jimmy), 55, 276, 281, 326, 336
Sheridan, Clare Consuela, 192
Sicilianos (Greek delegate), 161
Sissinghurst, 314
Sitwell, Dame Edith, 174
Sitwell, Sir George, Bt., 211
Sitwell, Sir Osbert, Bt., 87, 295
Sitwell, Sir Sacheverell, Bt., 87
Slovenia, 138
Smith, Charles Howard, 340
Smith, Lionel, 243, 304-5
Smithson, Kitty, 196
Smuts, Field-Marshal Jan Christian, 119-21, 132-3, 166
Smyrna, 112, 154, 158, 160-61, 176-7, 179
Smyth, Dame Ethel, 229-30, 309, 333, 356-7
Sniltzler, Lily, 362
Snowden, Philip, 1st Viscount, 382
Sofia, 4
Solomon, Simeon, 227
Sonnino, Baron Giorgio Sidney, 86, 106, 112
South African War, 7, 10
Soutzo, Princess of Roumania, 123
Spain, 24-5, 61-2; *see also* Madrid

Sparrow, John, 345, 347, 358
Spears, Edward, 116
Squire, J. C., 167, 208-9, 218, 220, 309
Stalin, Josef V., 200
Stambolisky, Alexander, 186
Stambolov, Stephan, 4-5
Stamfordham, Arthur John Bigge, 1st Baron, 311
Stancioff, Dimitri, 161
Stanley, Anne, 42
Stanley, Admiral Victor, 42
Steed, Henry Wickham, 312
Stern, Alan, 172
Stolypin, P. A., 27
Storrs, Sir Ronald, 67, 246-7
Strachey, Lytton: relations with HN, 165, 201-3, 228, 265; biographical method, 203, 310, 312; and HN's *Byron*, 216; and Bloomsbury, 229-30; HN criticises, 278; and Gosse, 318
Strachey, Pernel, 202
Strachey, St. Loe, 230
Strachey, T. C., 28
Strang, William, 99
Stresemann, Dr. Gustav (and Frau), 332-4, 338, 353, 364, 370, 374
Strong, Eugénie, 168
Stuart-Wortley, Mrs. Edward, 270
Sturm über Asien (film), 360-61
Sultan Ahmed, Shah, 253-4
Swinburne, Algernon Charles, 220, 227-8, 233, 274, 308, 317
Sydney-Turner, Saxon, 313
Sykes, Christopher, 357-8, 369-71, 373, 377, 380
Sykes, Sir Mark, Bt., 117, 357
Sykes, Sir Percy, 90

Taghi (Persian servant), 256, 262, 285, 287, 303
Talbot, Sir Gerald, 187-8
Tangier, 5, 13
Tardieu, André, 119
Tehran: HN's birth and childhood in,

INDEX

Tehran—*contd.*
2–4, 251; HN's diplomatic post in, 239–41, 249–51; described, 250–51, 256; *see also* Persia

Tellini, Gen., 207

Tennyson, Alfred, Lord, 172, 174–7, 180, 196, 203, 308

Terry, Ellen, 43, 174

Teschen, 135

Teymourtache, Mehrpour, 270, 288, 297, 301

Tippendale (Curzon's valet), 184, 193, 311

Tittoni, Tommaso, 134, 138

Toynbee, Arnold, 128

Trefusis, Denys, 103, 124–9, 132, 144, 147–8, 160, 300

Trefusis, Violet (*née* Keppel): relations with Vita, 52–3, 61, 63, 88–90, 92–3, 97–105, 122, 124–5, 130–32, 136, 139–47, 153–4, 159–60, 192, 224; HN meets, 56; in Knole play, 60; and Gerald Wellesley, 62; on Long Barn, 81; HN's attitude to, 88–9, 94, 98, 101, 104, 106–7, 110–11, 124–8, 145–6, 191, 224; in Vita's *Challenge*, 98–9; marriage to Denys, 103, 124–5, 127–31, 136, 144, 147; and Armistice Day, 104–5; elopement with Vita, 147–9; and Virginia Woolf's *Orlando*, 326, 350; and Cyril Connolly, 370

Trotsky, Leon, 27

Trott, Alan Charles, 281

Tschirschsky und Bögendorff, Heinrich Leonhard von, 73

Turkey: 1911 war with Italy, 50, 56; in Balkan Wars, 56–7, 59, 63, 69; coups and assassinations in, 59–60; German military advisers in, 69; HN on, 71; and World War I, 73, 91, 97; Peace Treaty, 134, 150, 154–5, 157–9, 186; at Paris Conference, 161–2; war with Greece, 160–62, 175–8, 186, 189, 195; and Mudania Armistice, 178–9; as threat, 181; and Lausanne Conference, 185–6, 188–9, 191, 194–9; and war graves, 197; French treaty with, 197; agreement reached, 198–9

Tyrrell, Margaret, Lady (*née* Urquhart), 41

Tyrrell, Sir William (*later* 1st Baron Tyrrell of Avon): at Foreign Office, 40–41; Lady Sackville and, 52; at Lausanne Conference, 182, 187–8, 315; incapacitated, 188; influence on Curzon, 207–8; relations with HN, 215, 227, 233, 315–16, 388; as Permanent Under-Secretary, 233; and HN in Persia, 242, 261, 290–91, 293; and HN's application to Cadman, 301; on HN's *Some People*, 310; and Lichnowsky, 325; retires, 387

Tyrrwhitt, Gerald *see* Berners, G. H. Tyrrwhitt-Wilson, 9th Baron

United States of America, 90–91, 97, 101

Urquhart, Francis F. ('Sligger'): and HN at Oxford, 21–4, 26, 28–31; correspondence with, 33–4, 36–8, 45; HN revisits, 160, 241, 309; on HN's *Tennyson*, 204

Valéry, Paul, 92, 295–6, 310

Van de Velde, Henri, 14

Van Swinderen, Dr. R. de Marees, 94

Vansittart, Robert Gilbert, 1st Baron, 158, 161, 175, 214, 234, 354

Venizelos, Eleutherios: sympathy with Allies, 79; at Peace Conference, 111–12, 116, 118, 135, 137–8, 150; and Vita's trip to Greece, 141, 143; fall from power, 154, 157; HN praises, 155; and Paris Conference on Greek settlement, 161–2; recalled after Smyrna massacre, 177; and Lausanne Conference, 186–7, 189, 195; and HN's *Byron*, 216; and Serbo-Greek relations, 226

Venosta, Enrico, Marchese Visconti, 43

Vere, Arthur Hope, 311

Verlaine, Paul, 150–52, 163–4, 190–91

427

Versailles Treaty, 119, 132-3, 359, 374; *see also* Peace Conference
Victoria, Queen, 10, 194, 196
Victoria, Princess, 165
Victoria Eugénie, Queen of Spain, 44-5
Vissuq-ed-Dowleh, 288
Vogrich, Max, 14
Vossuq (Persian Minister), 290

Wachendorff, Ow-, 324, 385
Wagenseil, Kurt, 385
Walker-Heneage, Dorothy, 66, 89
Walpole, Hugh, 38, 91, 93, 99, 153-4, 309, 343
Walter, Bruno, 333, 357
Warner, Christopher, 250, 262
Warre, Edmond Lancelot ('Bear'), 92
Warren, Dorothy (*later* Trotter), 264, 309, 335
Warren, Sir Herbert, 204
Waterfield, Mrs., 211
Wauchope, Maj.-Gen. Arthur Grenfell, 221
Waugh, Arthur, 204
Wedel, M. and Mme, 127, 141
Weimar, 13-14, 16, 385-6
Weissmann, Frau, 342-3, 385
Weizmann, Chaim, 323-4
Wellesley, Dorothy Violet (*later* Duchess of Wellington): and Long Barn, 81, 166, 309; HN's friendship with, 160, 166, 200, 213, 219, 299; marriage difficulties, 166, 179, 194, 212, 238-9; relations with Vita, 166, 173, 176, 194, 238, 264, 299, 307; N's tour with, 167-71; and Virginia Woolf, 193; and Bloomsbury Group, 229; HN on, 237-9; visits Persia, 301, 303-4; and Lady Sackville, 330; at Penns-in-the-Rocks, 343, 378
Wellesley, Lady Eileen (*later* Orde), 42, 55, 242
Wellesley, Lord Gerald (*later* 7th Duke of Wellington): HN's friendship with, 42, 47, 200, 207, 238-9; and Violet Trefusis, 62; in Constantinople, 62, 68; serves in World War I, 77; and HN's wartime Foreign Office service, 87; rents Ebury Street house, 103; N's entertain, 166; marriage difficulties, 166, 179, 194, 212, 238-9; N's tour with, 167-71; homes, 173
Wellesley, Valerian (Gerald's son; *later* 8th Duke of Wellington), 179
Wellington College, 9-13, 26
Wells, H. G., 38, 368-9
West, Dame Rebecca, 171
Weygand, Gen. Maxime, 171, 184-7, 189
Wickham, Capt. J., 270, 295, 300
Wilhelm, German Crown Prince, 353, 359
Williams, Miss (HN's secretary), 149
Wilson, Sir Matthew, Bt. ('Scatters'), 231
Wilson, Edmund, 151, 233
Wilson, Field-Marshal Sir Henry Hughes, 102
Wilson, Woodrow, 86, 107, 111-16, 118-19, 130, 133-4, 140, 167,
Wodehouse, Jack (*later* 3rd Earl of Kimberley), 166, 176
Wodehouse, Margaret, Countess of Kimberley *see* Montagu, Margaret
Wolff, Kurt, 364
Wolff, Frau Louise, 356
Woolf, Leonard: on Long Barn, 81; Vita visits, 221; HN admires, 229; and wife's relationship with Vita, 265, 299; at Vita's Hawthornden Prize ceremony, 309; friendship with HN, 313-14, 316; understanding of wife, 350; visits Berlin, 360-61; and HN's *Evening Standard* offer, 376; in Monk's House, 378
Woolf, Virginia: and Violet Dickinson, 60; Vita meets and praises, 192-3, 196, 200; on N's, 201; on HN's *Tennyson*, 202; on HN's *Byron*, 216; visits Long Barn, 219; Vita visits, 221; relations with Vita, 221-2,

INDEX

Woolf, Virginia—*contd.*
  264–5, 350; HN admires, 229, 235; and snobbishness, 237; and HN's post in Persia, 241; love affair with Vita, 265, 299; on HN's career, 307, 316, 360–61; at Vita's Hawthornden Prize ceremony, 309; praises HN's *Some People*, 312; sees eclipse of sun, 313; on Hilda Matheson, 344; tours France with Vita, 348–50; on Vita's diffidence, 350; visits Berlin, 360–61; and HN's *Evening Standard* offer, 376; in Monk's House, 378; rejects HN's criticism of Vita's poems, 379; *Mrs Dalloway*, 235; *Orlando*, 325–6, 350–51

York, Duke and Duchess of *see* Elizabeth the Queen Mother; George VI, King

Young, Owen, 373

Youssoupoff, Prince Felix, 27–8

Youssoupoff, Prince Felix Soumarokoff (father of above), 27

Yusuf Kemal Bey, 175

Zaharoff, Sir Basil, 153

Zinoviev letter, 200, 213, 234